HISTORY IN DISPUTE

ADVISORY BOARD

HISTORY IN DISPUTE

Volume **4**

World War II

Edited by **Dennis Showalter**

A MANLY, INC. BOOK

ST. JAMES PRESS

AN IMPRINT OF THE GALE GROUP

DETROIT • NEW YORK • SAN FRANCISCO
LONDON • BOSTON • WOODBRIDGE, CT

HISTORY IN DISPUTE

 ## Volume 4 ▪ World War II, 1939–1943

Matthew J. Bruccoli and Richard Layman, *Editorial directors.*

Karen L. Rood, *Senior editor.*

Anthony J. Scotti Jr., James F. Tidd Jr., *In-house editors.*

Philip B. Dematteis, *Production manager.*

Kathy Lawler Merlette, *Office manager.* Ann M. Cheschi, Tenesha S. Lee, Bridget R. Schmitt, *Administrative support.* Angi Pleasant, Kathy Weston, *Accounting.*

Phyllis A. Avant, *Copyediting supervisor.* Thom Harman, *Senior copyeditor.* Brenda Carol Blanton, James Denton, Worthy B. Evans, Melissa D. Hinton, William Tobias Mathes, Jennifer S. Reid, *Copyediting staff.* Ronald D. Aiken II, Rebecca Mayo, Michelle L. Whitney, Jennie Williamson, *Freelance copyeditors.*

Margo Dowling, *Editorial associate.* Alex Snead, Cory McNair, *Indexing specialists.*

Janet E. Hill, *Layout and graphics supervisor.* Karla Corley Brown, Zoe R. Cook, *Layout and graphics.*

Charles Mims, Scott Nemzek, Alison Smith, Paul Talbot, *Photography editors.* Joseph M. Bruccoli, Zoe R. Cook, *Digital photographic copy work.*

Cory McNair, *SGML supervisor.* Tim Bedford, Linda Drake, Frank Graham, Alex Snead, *SGML staff.*

Marie L. Parker, *Systems manager.*

Kathleen M. Flanagan, *Typesetting supervisor.* Kimberly Kelly, Mark J. McEwan, Patricia Flanagan Salisbury, *Typesetting staff.* Delores Plastow, *Freelance typesetter.*

Linda Holderfield, *Librarian, Thomas Cooper Library of the University of South Carolina.* Virginia Weathers, *Reference-department head.* Marilee Birchfield, Stefanie Buck, Stefanie DuBose, Rebecca Feind, Karen Joseph, Donna Lehman, Charlene Loope, Anthony McKissick, Jean Rhyne, Kwamine Simpson, *Reference librarians.* Caroline Taylor, *Circulation-department head.* David Haggard, *Acquisitions-searching supervisor.*

Copyright ©2000
St. James Press
27500 Drake Road
Farmington Hills, MI 48331

ISBN 1-55862-410-4

St. James Press is an imprint of The Gale Group.

Printed in the United States of America

10 9 8 7 6 5 4 3 2

CONTENTS

CONTENTS

CONTENTS

CONTENTS

CONTENTS

CONTENTS

CONTENTS

PREFACE

World War II had its origins in a toxic blend of unfinished business and new traumas. The Great War of 1914–1918 had left Europe exhausted but unsatisfied. France and Britain were almost as suspicious of each other as of their former enemy. Germany emerged with a festering sense of grievance at being made to bear the moral and financial responsibility for what its people saw as a defensive conflict. In the east and south, a network of middle-sized "successor states" to the Habsburg Empire sought to establish legitimacy and gain advantages over their neighbors. Italy, which in 1914 had been the least of the great powers, hoped for relative gain at the expense of others' weaknesses.

Added to this situation were the psychological traumas generated by the squandering of prewar Europe's moral capital in the trenches, and by the climate of violence generated in all the combatants during four years of near-total war. In addition, there were the economic dislocations accompanying newly drawn frontiers and the diminished capacities of industries and agricultures strained to their limits and beyond. Not only men but also animals had been sacrificed in pursuit of a victory that in the end eluded all the war's participants; even manure to replenish exhausted farms was in short supply.

Frustration bred contempt: there was the dangerous rhetoric that blamed current miseries on ethnic minorities, malevolent foreigners, or greedy capitalists; there was the ideology of total war that asserted survival, let alone victory, and demanded total militarization even in times of a peace that was only war's continuation by other means; there was the mutual mistrust that permeated every state and every society in Europe, leading people to regard themselves as the victims of neighbors who had somehow gained an unfair advantage; and there were the politicians and the ideo-

logues who synergized and concretized amorphous grievances into programs of revenge.

It began with Benito Mussolini, whose Fascist doctrines sought to mobilize Italians behind a program of militarization and imperialism. In Germany the Weimar Republic, unable either to conciliate or to suppress widespread domestic opposition, faded then collapsed under the pressure of the National Socialist movement, whose dynamic leader Adolf Hitler declared that if he were given ten years in power, no one would recognize Germany. It took twelve years, but he kept that promise.

The rise—and the appeal—of Fascism in its various forms was facilitated by the survival of the Soviet Union as a state with the avowed aim of extending the Communist revolution to capitalist Europe, whose self-confidence was further shaken by the Great Depression. Beginning in 1929, its progress—in contrast to the U.S. experience—was just slow enough to give governments and citizens alike a full chance to perceive their fate. Fascism, with its combination of economic corporatism and public activism, seemed to offer a "middle way" between Bolshevism and entropy. As much to the point, "Europe" as a concept and an entity had already been shaken to its foundations by the Great War, by the self-exclusion of Russia, and by the refusal of the United States to participate in a "new European order" in any but the most limited contexts. To exclude Italy and Germany as well was to reduce Europe to an Atlantic fringe—a fringe whose principal members, France and Britain, were simultaneously facing challenges to their global positions from Japanese, Chinese, and colonial variants of nationalism.

It was scarcely remarkable, then, that the Western powers did everything in their power to encourage Hitler and Mussolini to participate in the conventional paradigms of international relations. Left to his own devices, the

Italian dictator might have played the game of appeasement within its recognized rules. He was, however, increasingly seduced to the dark side by the successes of Hitler, as driven by ideology as either Vladimir Lenin or Joseph Stalin—and even less willing than the Soviet leaders to make even temporary, cosmetic compromises with his enemies. A badly structured rearmament campaign that strained German resources to a literal breaking point gave Hitler a practical incentive for "flight forward"—increasing his demands and his pressures with the aim of provoking while he was still at the height of his powers. The military occupation of the Rhineland in 1936 was followed that same year by overt intervention in the Spanish Civil War. In the spring of 1938 a jubilant Austria was brought "home to the Reich." Three months later, Hitler demanded cession of the Czechoslovakian borderlands inhabited by the "Sudeten German" minority. France and Britain, unwilling to risk war with their own resources, unwilling as well to trust either Italy or the U.S.S.R., brokered a final concession—one that British prime minister Neville Chamberlain declared meant "peace for our time."

In March 1939 Hitler occupied Prague and declared a "protectorate" over a Rump Czech Republic that, whatever else might be said about it, was in no way ethnically German. To all but the most optimistic, war had become inevitable. France and Britain, still mistrustful of Soviet intentions and Soviet capacities, instead guaranteed the territorial integrity of Poland and increased their rearmament programs. Germany in turn sought a thieves' alliance with a U.S.S.R. that was by then fully convinced that the differences among the capitalist powers were no more than cosmetic. Italy, still digesting its 1938 conquest of Abyssinia, and Japan, which since 1937 was increasingly bogged down in an unwinnable war on the Chinese mainland, perceived windows of opportunity opening for states audacious enough to jump through them. No one ever accused either Mussolini or the militarists controlling Japan of fearing risk.

The conclusion on August 1939 of the German–Soviet Nonaggression Pact set a match to long-accumulating tinder. For Hitler—and for the generals who supported his aggressive imperialism—the pact was a golden opportunity to avert the two-front war of attrition that had brought about Germany's defeat a quarter-century earlier. On 1 September, the German army rolled into and over Poland, whose determined initial resistance could not stop the armored spearheads that took full advantage of an unexpectedly dry summer in a country with few paved roads. As the Polish army began recovering from the initial shock, Soviet troops crossed its eastern border. *Rotarmisten* shook hands with the Panzer crews as the extermination squads of their respective governments went to work on "subversive elements": anyone, Gentile or Jew, who might pose an objective threat to the new orders.

As Poland died, France and Britain marked time. Their armies had neither the doctrine nor the spirit for offensive operations, even against the weak screen of second-line troops that was all Hitler could spare for the western front. Their governments had as yet no coherent war aims beyond avoiding bloodbaths like those of 1914–1918. As one of the century's hardest winters set in, the allies went to ground. The German army digested its experiences and corrected its mistakes while Hitler fumed over his generals' lack of offensive spirit. The U.S.S.R., seeking to secure its northern flank, provoked a war with Finland that highlighted the drastic shortcomings of the Red Army, whose command echelons had been bled white by repeated purges.

The "phony war," the *Sitzkrieg*, came to a brutal end in the spring of 1940. In February Hitler, influenced by his admirals' demands for a coastline long enough to provide some operational flexibility, launched an invasion of Denmark and Norway. Allied response was limited and ineffective. Outnumbered, at the far end of a long supply line, the *Wehrmacht* (German Army) nevertheless bested the British at their own historic game of power projection—albeit at the cost of most of the ships originally expected to take advantage of the Norwegian bases. Scandinavia, however, became a strategic backwater when, on June 10, Nazi Germany launched an all-out offensive through Holland, Belgium, and northern France.

The Allied high command, expecting a repeat of the Schlieffen Plan of 1914, rushed every available man, gun, and tank into Belgium. The weight of the German attack, however, was further south, through an Ardennes Forest considered impassable by large motorized forces. Brushing aside weak screens of cavalry and cyclists, the Germans fought their way across the Meuse against second-line French troops whose tactics and commanders, rather than their courage, failed them at crucial points. As German tanks swung west and thrust deeply into the Allied rear, French commander Maurice Gamelin, asked where were his strategic reserves, replied laconically *"aucune"* ("there are none"). British and

French troops already facing strong German forces to their front did the best they could to cut off the German spearheads. It was not enough. By June the British Expeditionary Force and most of a French army group were cut off without hope of relief, withdrawing toward the English Channel and hoping for a miracle.

The miracle—often overlooked—was that the Alliance held. Winston Churchill, who succeeded a thoroughly discredited Chamberlain, sent what remained of British ground troops to France to help restore the line. The Royal Air Force fought the *Luftwaffe* (German Air Force) to a stalemate in the skies over beaches where jetties improvised from now-useless vehicles carried British and French soldiers, in a ratio of one for one, to the waiting ships of the Royal Navy, undeterred by brutal losses. None of this was enough for the increasingly despairing French government. It sufficed, however, for the last French units in the Dunkirk pocket, who held to the end to give the last of the BEF a chance to get home and fight again.

It remains a point of dispute whether Hitler held the Panzer divisions back from Dunkirk as a goodwill gesture to Britain out of a hope to conciliate, or whether it seemed an unnecessary risk to send tanks across broken ground against fixed defenses. There is no doubt that the armor generals were far more comfortable with the conditions they faced when they turned against France in June. Within days a new government, headed by Great War hero marshal Phillippe Pétain, was suing for peace while it still had some negotiating room. Britain's refusal to follow suit arguably owed as much to Churchill's belief in imminent U.S. intervention as to any military or moral factors. In any case Britain's defiance confronted the Wehrmacht with a situation in which naval weakness made air supremacy a prerequisite for a successful invasion. Through the summer and early fall of 1940 the outnumbered Royal Air Force stood off the Luftwaffe, which was handicapped by short-range aircraft, and by leadership unable to pursue a consistent strategy. At the end the German invasion force stood down, leaving to the U-boats the task of bringing Britain to reason.

Hitler in the meantime had increasingly focused on the Soviet Union as his next objective. In a strategic context, destroying Russia would deprive Britain of its "continental sword." Ideologically, the U.S.S.R. was both the home of Bolshevism and the source of the "living space" needed to make the dream of Greater Germany a reality. Operationally, the Wehrmacht was convinced it had developed a

way of war that negated traditional Russian advantages of numbers, space, and resources. "Blitzkrieg" may have been a term invented by Western journalists rather than Wehrmacht theorists; nevertheless, by the fall of 1940 German generals were arrogantly confident in the synergy of speed and shock that had taken them through half the capitals of Europe.

Planning the invasion of Russia, however, absorbed only part of Hitler's attention. His long-range goal of global domination could be achieved only by war with the United States. In the fall of 1940 he began working to secure bases in North Africa to sustain future operations in the Atlantic. He promptly ran afoul of the ambitions and interests of his Mediterranean clients—Vichy France, Falangist Spain and its wily Caudillo Francisco Franco, and Mussolini's Italy. The latter state had pursued its Mediterranean objectives independently, by a quickly stalemated invasion of Greece and an attack toward the Suez Canal that met with a series of disasters at the hands of a far smaller, far more effective British opponent. Even after the French navy surrendered, the Italian navy, built at tremendous cost and effort proved no match for the Royal Navy's Mediterranean Fleet and its pugnacious commander, Admiral Sir Arthur Cunningham. The Regia Aeronautica's pilots were as skilled and courageous as any, but their obsolescent aircraft could achieve no more than temporary, local successes.

By the spring of 1941 it was clear to Hitler that pulling Mussolini's chestnuts from the fire was a necessary prelude to securing the southern strategic flank of the campaign that would end the European phase of the war once and for all. Armor-tipped German armies overran Greece and Yugoslavia. An airborne assault captured the island of Crete, inflicting near-crippling losses on the Royal Navy, once again standing in to take off the survivors of a land disaster. In addition, General Erwin Rommel, with an Afrika Korps improvised from the Reich's military leftovers, began giving the British in North Africa an eighteen-month lesson in mobile warfare.

Given the imbalance between resources and successes in the first months of Germany's Mediterranean campaign, it has been frequently questioned whether Nazi Germany missed an opportunity by not increasing its commitment to that theater. Even a small proportion of the tanks lost in Russia, it is argued, could have opened Rommel's way to the Caucasus, to Persia and its oil fields, perhaps to India itself. Critics respond that the United States, by this time a belligerent in all but name, would have sustained Britain in the war no matter what losses a declining empire might suffer. The issue remains one of the most provocative counterfactuals in the historiography of World War II. It was rendered contrary to fact, however, by Hitler's determination to pursue the Russian option as quickly as possible. On 22 June 1941, the Wehrmacht, supported by a mixed bag of more or less reluctant client states, crossed the borders of the Soviet Union, which was still digesting the geographic fruits of its earlier agreement with Hitler.

For two months, as Panzer spearheads sliced deep into Russia and the infantry ground up isolated Russian units, the Germans won a string of tactical/operational victories unprecedented in military history. But the Red Army and the U.S.S.R. refused to crack. As the Germans drove deeper into Russia, their losses mounted. Hitler and his generals could not agree on either objectives or time frames. At the front and behind the lines, Nazi ideology bore fruit in atrocities and massacres, with Wehrmacht participation more the rule than the exception. Nor was the Reich able even to exploit its conquests effectively. The material cornucopias so confidently expected before the war began turned out to be mere trickles of resources and manufactured goods. Slave labor, on the other hand, was a flourishing commodity—one that further alienated the civilians on whom production depended.

Well before the invasion of Russia the Nazis had begun implementing the "Final Solution" of the "Jewish question" that was at the center of their racially-based ideology. What has been called a "twisted road to Auschwitz" becomes a bit straighter once it is understood that the Nazis believed that Jews were literal parasites. In other words, isolating them from their "host communities" of more or less unsuspecting gentiles was itself a final solution. Left to their own resources and devices, the Jews could reasonably be expected to die off with only minor assistance.

Isolation, impractical in Germany even during the war, could be implemented more openly and comprehensively in Poland, which was viewed in any case as a test bed for Nazi racial principles. Ghettoization began in the fall of 1939, steadily increasing the concentration of Jews in particular areas of large cities. Deportation was added in 1940, as the first of hundreds of trainloads of Jews from Germany, Austria, and the conquered states of Western Europe began arriving in Poland. The Nazi cover story, to the victims and their neighbors alike, was that the Jews were being deported for forced labor. Jews were indeed put on work gangs and used as factory slaves. But despite steadily reduced rations, steadily worsened environments, and steadily increased oppression, the Jews stubbornly refused to die en masse.

That stubbornness led Heinrich Himmler and the SS to employ more direct methods in Russia. *Einsatzgruppen,* "Action Squads," of killers followed the armies into the Soviet Union. With help from the Wehrmacht, and from local gentiles, they accounted for more than a million and a half Jews, gypsies, and slavs, most between June and December of 1941. The psychological strain of direct mass murder, however, led to a movement in favor of establishing an organized structure of genocide. Sometime in the autumn of 1941, Himmler, with Hitler's approval, began establishing facilities for mass killing by poison gas. On 20 January 1942, the Wannsee Conference accepted the proposal for the "complete solution of Europe's Jewish question"—ultimately involving the murder of around eleven million people.

Deportations from the ghettoes to the killing centers began in early 1942. By year's end most of the Jews in eastern Europe were dead. The years 1943 and 1944 witnessed the roundup and extermination of those overlooked, usually because they were employed producing goods for the Wehrmacht, and Jews deported from western and southern Europe. Beginning in July 1944, the advance of the Red Army led Himmler to authorize the dismantling of an execution machine that had been outstandingly successful in performing its task.

The exact number of Jews and other "enemies of the Reich" killed in the camp system and its offshoots has never been determined. Perhaps the most noteworthy feature of the operation is the relatively limited direct impact it had on the Nazi war effort. The Holocaust was accomplished with the spare change of a total war.

As the Germans struggled to cope with success, the Soviet Union, having transplanted much of its industrial plant beyond the Ural Mountains, caught its second wind. Autumn mud slowed German tanks; winter snow immobilized them. By December 1941 the Wehrmacht had reached the outskirts of Moscow. It would get no farther, as Russian counterattacks stabilized the front and constrained Hitler and his generals to wait till next year.

The Russo-German War was also the harbinger of direct U.S. involvement. Even before 1939, President Franklin Roosevelt understood the danger to both American interests and American principles posed by Germany in Europe and Japan in the Far East. He understood as well the many-faceted impulse to isolationism and neutrality that made assertive diplomacy a political impossibility—particularly for a president seeking an unprecedented third term. Taking advantage of a China lobby that, however small, was nevertheless more influential than the supporters of France or Britain, Roosevelt put increasing pressure on Japan to modify its policies and behavior in China. He used the outbreak of war in Europe to initiate a peacetime mobilization, while simultaneously insisting that its aims went no further than defending the Eastern Hemisphere. After the fall of France he obtained congressional and public support for a policy of "lend-lease," by which Britain, whose foreign exchange was exhausted, could "borrow" equipment from the United States on the promise of returning it after the war. He conducted discussions with Churchill—discussions sufficiently specific that the two statesmen were able to agree on a strategy of "Germany first."

Critics and admirers alike have described Roosevelt's policies as "two steps forward, one back." This judgment is excessively Machiavellian. In the war's first two years, neither Germany nor Japan behaved in any way Washington might interpret as conciliatory. Instead, the Battle of the Atlantic brought the war to the Atlantic coast, as convoy after convoy of British and Allied merchantmen fought their way past the U-boats to sustain Britain's lifeline. By the summer of 1941 the U.S. Navy was engaged in what amounted to an undeclared war with a *Kriegsmarine* (German Navy) increasingly insistent that Hitler allow retaliation. On the other side of the world, Japan, whose multiple atrocities had by now guaranteed the failure of its China policy, received a bloody nose from the Red Army in September 1939 in a border skirmish in Manchuria. The conquest of South Asia, with its populations restive under Western rule and its rich supplies of raw materials, was an alternative to revising Japan's entire approach to foreign relations. The German victories in 1940 seemed to offer a chance that would never recur—even if the price was conflict with the United States whose naval construction programs would in any case within a few years give it unchallengeable superiority over the Imperial Japanese Navy. By the summer of 1941 at the latest, Japan's U.S. diplomacy was an exercise in smoke and mirrors, camouflage for the "jump off the roof" that would decide the empire's destiny.

The strike at Pearl Harbor on 7 December 1941 was only one element of an operational plan that within six months gave Japan control of the western Pacific at almost no cost. The abject surrender to inferior numbers of the British garrison of Singapore epitomized the Rising Sun's achievement. Hitler for his part enthusiastically declared war against America on 11 December. He was confident that Japan would distract a decadent country ruled by a paralytic long enough for the "real" war in Eurasia to be ended, after which the United States alone, facing two warrior cultures, was likely to seek negotiations.

The Japanese armed forces never intended to wage total war against the United States. Their strategy was rather that of "barrier and javelin": establish a perimeter, supported by the full strength of the Combined Fleet, and allow the Americans to exhaust themselves against it. The process was not expected to take long for a nation of businessmen, without a sense of honor or an ethic of sacrifice. The problem was where to establish the barrier. As Japanese ground troops struggled through the jungles of New Guinea, America began pouring resources into Australia. The navy's high command, already disturbed at the prospect of confronting an entire new generation of U.S. warships, forced battle with the Pacific Fleet by attacking the island of Midway, widely regarded by the Americans as a springboard to the Hawaiian Islands.

The outcome—four carriers sunk and the cream of the navy's pilots lost—owed something to an excessively complex Japanese plan. It owed something to U.S. codebreakers' ability to read Japan's mail. It owed something to luck: an air strike commander spotting and following the wake of a single ship to a fleet whose carriers had been turned to floating bombs in order to rearm aircraft more quickly. In the final analysis, however, Midway was the victory of a U.S. Navy that had learned the lessons of Pearl Harbor and gone beyond them—in six months. In 1942, the United States, determined on vengeance took the war to its enemy, invading the south Pacific island of Guadalcanal with its counterpart of samurai: the U.S. Marine Corps.

On 19 December 1941, Hitler assumed supreme command of the Wehrmacht. Many key commanders were relieved or reassigned. In their places stood new men, hard men convinced that will power and fighting power would end the war in the next campaign—particularly after Soviet offensives in the early spring were repelled with relative ease. The Fuhrer Directive of 3 April 1942, provided for the concentration of all available resources in southern Russia. Their mission was to destroy the enemy in that sector and secure the oil fields of the Caucasus and the mountain passes to the Middle East. On 28 June the great offensive began, with armored columns rolling across the steppe under an air umbrella providing safety and support for the men on the ground. This time, however, the Russians fell back rather than stay in place to be overrun. Then Hitler changed the plan, making the city of Stalingrad, on the left of the German axis of advance, the principal objective. Forces already stretched dangerously thin were further divided, then committed to the kind of close urban combat that nullified German skills in war maneuvers. As Hitler's obsession with its capture increased, Stalingrad became at once magnet and mousetrap, drawing in forces from other sectors, leaving them vulnerable to the hammer blow Stalin and his generals were preparing. On 19 November, the Russians struck—not Stalingrad itself, but the open steppe on the city's flanks. Defenses largely manned by poorly equipped German client forces crumbled. Within a week the Germans in Stalingrad were surrounded. Not a single general had the moral courage to defy Hitler's order to hold the city at all costs. On 2 February 1943, 200,000 survivors surren-

dered to the Red Army that had learned its lessons and was preparing to become the teacher.

During 1942 another learning curve had been demonstrated in the Mediterranean. On land, British forces had been able to do no more than keep the field against Rommel in a series of wide-open seesaw battles that highlighted British shortcomings in mobile warfare. At sea and in the air, however, the story was reversed as Britain increasingly challenged, then reversed, de facto Axis control of the Mediterranean. In the process as well, Italy's remaining material and moral resources were steadily eroded. The tide definitively turned in August, when a physically exhausted Rommel launched his final attack against the British Eighth Army which was finally balancing its material superiority with operational skill. Checked and stalemated by Sir Claude Auchinleck, the Afrika Korps was hammered into defeat at El Alamein by a new commander, one who understood the capacities and the limitations of his forces better than any of his predecessors. Sir Bernard Law Montgomery would be heard from again.

—DENNIS SHOWALTER, COLORADO COLLEGE

PREFACE

CHRONOLOGY

1939

1 SEPTEMBER: The Germans launch Operation White (Fall Weiss) and cross the Polish frontier. (*See* **Appeasement, Blitzkrieg, German Conquests, Hitler: War Leader, Hitler's Aggression, Hitler's Foreign Policy,** and **Wehrmacht**)

3 SEPTEMBER: France and Great Britain declare war against Germany. (*See* **Appeasement** and **Wehrmacht**)

5 SEPTEMBER: The United States proclaims its neutrality regarding the conflict in Poland.

19 SEPTEMBER: The Soviet army joins up with German troops at Brest-Litovsk. The first British troops land in France. (*See* **Hitler's Foreign Policy**)

27 SEPTEMBER: Warsaw surrenders to Germans.(*See* **Blitzkrieg** and **Hitler's Aggression**)

30 SEPTEMBER: A Polish government in exile is set up in Paris. The German pocket-battleship *Admiral Graf Spee* sinks the British steamship Clement.

27 OCTOBER: Belgium proclaims its neutrality.

1 NOVEMBER: The Free City of Danzig and the Polish Corridor are officially annexed to the Reich, together with the frontier territories ceded to Poland in 1919 under the Treaty of Versailles. (*See* **Blitzkrieg, German Conquests, Hitler's Foreign Policy,** and **Versailles**)

7 NOVEMBER: Queen Wilhelmina of the Netherlands and Leopold III of Belgium issue an appeal for peace, offering themselves as mediators.

17 NOVEMBER: The Supreme Allied Council meets in Paris.

28 NOVEMBER: The Soviet government renounces the nonaggression treaty they entered into with Finland in 1932. (*See* **Stalin**)

30 NOVEMBER: The Soviet army invades Finland. (*See* **Stalin**)

22 DECEMBER: The Soviet army is defeated in its first battle with Finland.(*See* **Stalin**)

24 DECEMBER: Pope Pius XII makes a Christmas Eve appeal for peace. (*See* **Nazism and Religion**)

30 DECEMBER: Adolf Hitler gives a New Year message to the German people: "The Jewish-capitalistic world will not survive the twentieth century." (*See* **Hitler: War Leader**)

1940

12 FEBRUARY: The Dominican Republic announces a contract to resettle one hundred thousand European refugees.

16 FEBRUARY: The British destroyer *Cossack* attacks the German ship *Altmark*, liberating some three hundred English prisoners. Norway protests the attack, which violated Norwegian territorial waters.

21 FEBRUARY: In the small Polish village of Auschwitz, construction begins on a German concentration camp. (*See* **Holocaust: Complicity** and **Holocaust: Theories**)

1 MARCH: Italian laws restricting the professional practices of Jews go into effect. (*See* **Fascism** and **Nazism and Religion**)

12 MARCH: Defeated in the Soviet-Finnish war, the Finns sign a treaty ceding the Karelian Isthmus and the Rybachi Peninsula in return for their continued independence.

18 MARCH: At a meeting on the Italian side of the Brenner Pass, Benito Mussolini informs Hitler that Italy will enter the war against Britain and France. (*See* **Fascism** and **Hitler's Foreign Policy**)

19 MARCH: The U.S. ambassador to Canada, James Cromwell, declares in an official

address that Hitler is bent on the destruction of American social and economic order.

20 MARCH: French premier Edouard Daladier resigns; the next day Paul Reynaud forms a new cabinet and creates a war council in expectation of a German invasion. (*See* **Fall of France** and **Vichy France**)

9 APRIL: Germany invades Denmark and Norway. Belgium refuses to allow the British to move their troops through the Low Countries. (*See* **German Conquests, Hitler: War Leader,** and **Hitler's Aggression**)

10 MAY: Germany invades Belgium and Holland, beginning its *Blitzkrieg* (lightning war) through the Low Countries into France. Neville Chamberlain resigns as British prime minister and is succeeded by Winston Churchill. (*See* **Blitzkrieg, Churchill, Fall of France, Hitler: War Leader, Hitler's Aggression,** and **Vichy France**)

14 MAY: The Dutch army surrenders to Germany. Authorities report that 100,000 Dutch troops, more than one-fourth of their army, have been killed in the fighting. The official capitulation papers are signed the next morning. (*See* **Blitzkrieg** and **German Conquests**)

17–18 MAY: German troops take Brussels and Antwerp in Belgium. (*See* **Blitzkrieg** and **German Conquests**)

20 MAY: The German army takes Amiens, France. (*See* **Blitzkrieg** and **Fall of France**)

27 MAY: The British begin to evacuate Dunkirk, France. By 4 June their flotilla of warships, private yachts, and fishing boats has removed nearly 350,000 troops. They leave 2,000 guns, 60,000 trucks, 76,000 tons of ammunition, and 600,000 tins of fuel in France. England is left practically disarmed by the defeat, but in the house of Commons on 4 June Churchill declares, "We shall defend our island whatever the cost may be, we shall fight on the beaches, we shall fight on the landing ground, we shall fight in the fields and in the streets . . . we shall never surrender." (*See* **Churchill** and **Fall of France**)

28 MAY: King Leopold III of Belgium surrenders his country to the Germans. (*See* **Blitzkrieg** and **German Conquests**)

7 JUNE: King Haakon VII and his Norwegian government go into exile in London.

10 JUNE: Italy declares war on Britain and France. The next day its planes bomb British bases on Malta and in Aden, while the British hit Italian air bases in Libya and Italian East Africa. (*See* **Fascism, Montgomery,** and **Rommel**)

12 JUNE: The heaviest single Japanese bombing attack on Chungking, China, kills 1,500 people and leaves 150,000 homeless. Between 18 May and 14 August, Japanese planes drop 2,500 tons of bombs on the city, killing more than 2,000 civilians and injuring nearly 3,500. (*See* **Japanese Way of War** and **U.S. Asia Policy**)

14 JUNE: The German army enters Paris; Hitler orders a three-day celebration of the victory. The French government relocates to Bordeaux. The Soviet Union occupies the small Baltic nation of Lithuania; two days later it takes over neighboring Estonia and Latvia, demanding that all three countries put themselves under Soviet protection. (*See* **Fall of France** and **Stalin**)

17 JUNE: French premier Reynaud resigns and is replaced by World War I hero Marshal Philippe Pétain, who calls for surrender to the Germans. (*See* **Fall of France** and **Vichy France**)

18 JUNE: German planes raid the east coast of England. In a radio broadcast from London, General Charles de Gaulle of France calls on his countrymen to rally behind him as he continues to oppose Germany from exile. (*See* **Luftwaffe**)

22 JUNE: The French government signs an armistice with the Nazis at the same site in the Compiegne Forest where Germany surrendered to the Allies in World War I. Germany occupies three-fifths of France, leaving the southern portion as a so-called Free Zone. De Gaulle announces the formation of the French National Committee in London to continue fighting alongside the British Empire. (*See* **Vichy France**)

24 JUNE: France and Italy sign an armistice. (*See* **Vichy France**)

26 JUNE: Turkey declares itself a nonbelligerent.

30 JUNE: The Germans occupy the Channel Islands. (*See* **German Conquests**)

2 JULY: The French government establishes itself at Vichy. On 10 July it abolishes the Third Republic and adopts a new constitution creating an authoritarian government and investing full power in the chief of the French State, Pétain. (*See* **Fall of France** and **Vichy France**)

6 JULY: Hitler makes peace overtures to Britain.

10 JULY: The Battle of Britain begins. (*See* Bombing of Civilians, Churchill, and Luftwaffe)

16 JULY: Hitler issues Directive 16, ordering the invasion of Great Britain. During the Battle of Britain, which lasts from early August to November, the British lose 827 aircraft, but they shoot down 2, 409 German planes. (See **Churchill** and **Luftwaffe**)

21 JULY: The Soviet Union annexes Latvia, Lithuania, and Estonia. (See **Stalin**)

25 JULY: The United States places severe restrictions on the export of scrap metal, petroleum, and petroleum products, and it bans the export of aviation fuel and lubricating oil outside of the Western Hemisphere; the measure is aimed chiefly at Japan, which relies heavily on American oil. (*See* **U.S. Asia Policy**)

6 AUGUST: Germany orders the expulsion of all Jews from Krakow, Poland. (See **Holocaust: Complicity** and **Holocaust: Theories**)

17 AUGUST: Germany announces a total naval blockade of the British Isles.

24 AUGUST: The first German bombing of London occurs. (See **Blitzkrieg** and **Luftwaffe**)

25 AUGUST: The RAF bombs Berlin, an event Luftwaffe head Hermann Goring had assured Hitler could never happen. (See **Churchill** and **Luftwaffe**)

7–15 SEPTEMBER: The London Blitz, a massive bombardment of London, occurs.

12 SEPTEMBER: Italian troops invade Egypt from Libya. (*See* **Fascism**)

16 SEPTEMBER: The United States adopts a peacetime draft.

22 SEPTEMBER: Vichy France accedes to a Japanese ultimatum demanding bases in northern Indochina near the Chinese border. (See **Japanese Way of War** and **Vichy France**)

25 SEPTEMBER: After meeting heavy resistance from Vichy French forces, British and Free French Forces led by General de Gaulle abandon an invasion of Dakar, in French West Africa.

27 SEPTEMBER: Germany, Italy, and Japan sign the Tripartite Pact in Berlin, committing themselves to providing each other with military assistance in case of attack by any nation not already at war against them. (*See* **Hitler's Foreign Policy** and **Japanese Way of War**)

2 OCTOBER: All Jews in occupied France are required to register with police. (See **Holocaust: Complicity** and **Vichy France**)

7 OCTOBER: German troops move into Romania. (See **German Conquests** and **Wehrmacht**)

12 OCTOBER: Hitler postpones Operation Sealion, a German invasion of Britain, until spring 1941. (*See* **Hitler: War Leader**)

18 OCTOBER: Vichy France bars Jews from positions in government, the teaching profession, the armed forces, the press, movies, and radio. On 30 October, Pétain announces a policy of collaboration with Germany.

28 OCTOBER: Italian troops invade Greece.

5 NOVEMBER: Franklin D. Roosevelt is elected president for a third term.

11 NOVEMBER: British fighter planes cripple much of the Italian fleet in an engagement at Taranto.

14 NOVEMBER: The English automotive center of Coventry is carpet-bombed by 449 German aircraft. The attack creates a firestorm that kills more than 550 people and destroys the city's fourteenth-century cathedral. (See **Luftwaffe**)

20 NOVEMBER: Hungary joins the Axis.

23–24 NOVEMBER: Romania and Slovakia sign the Tripartite Pact with the Axis.

24 NOVEMBER: Slovakia joins the Axis.

9–11 DECEMBER: The British crush the Italians at Sidi Barrani, Egypt, wiping out four divisions and taking more than twenty thousand prisoners. (See **Montgomery**)

17 DECEMBER: In North Africa the British take Sidi Omar and Sollum from the Italians. (See **Montgomery**)

29 DECEMBER: The Germans drop incendiary bombs on the center of London, causing the worst damage to the city since the fire of 1666. (See **Churchill**)

1941

22 JANUARY: Tobruk, Libya, falls to British and Free French forces. (See **Montgomery**)

6 FEBRUARY: British forces capture Bengasi, in eastern Libya. (*See* **Montgomery**)

10 FEBRUARY: Great Britain breaks off diplomatic relations with Romania because German troops have deployed there.

12 FEBRUARY: General Erwin Rommel arrives in Tripoli to take command of German and Italian forces in Libya. (See **Rommel**)

24 FEBRUARY: The German army counterattack under Rommel begins in North Africa. (*See* **Rommel**)

1 MARCH: Bulgaria joins the Axis.

3 MARCH: The Soviet Union denounces Bulgaria for allying itself with the Axis powers.

11 MARCH: The United States adopts lend-lease legislation. (*See* **Lend Lease**)

25 MARCH: Yugoslavia joins the Axis; anti-Nazi riots erupt in Belgrade, and on 27 March the pro-Axis government is overthrown in a military coup.

28–29 MARCH: The British navy destroys much of the remaining Italian fleet off Cape Matapan, Greece.

3 APRIL: Italian and German troops force the British to evacuate Bengasi, Libya. (*See* **Montgomery**)

4 APRIL: The German army invades the Balkan Peninsula. (*See* **German Conquests**)

6–8 APRIL: German, Italian, and Bulgarian troops invade Greece and Yugoslavia.

13 APRIL: The Soviet Union and Japan sign a Neutrality pact. (*See* **Japanese Way of War** and **Stalin**)

17 APRIL: The Yugoslavian army surrenders to the Axis.

19 APRIL: The British land troops in Iraq to protect oil fields after the Baghdad government has displayed an increasingly pro-Axis bias. Military exchanges between the British and Iraqis follow.

24 APRIL: The evacuation of Greece begins.

27 APRIL: German forces occupy Athens.

9 MAY: The RAF conducts devastating air raids on Hamburg and Bremen.

10 MAY: Rudolf Hess, Hitler's personal deputy, parachutes into Scotland.

10–11 MAY: Nazi bombers blitz London, damaging the House of Commons, Westminster Abbey, and Big Ben.

20 MAY: The Germans launch an invasion of Crete, completing their conquest of the island on 1 June. (*See* **German Conquests** and **Wehrmacht**)

21 MAY: The U.S. ship *Robin Moor* is torpedoed and sunk by a German U-boat off the coast of Brazil.

24 MAY: The British battle cruiser Hood is sunk by the 35,000-ton German battleship Bismarck between Greenland and Iceland.

27 MAY: The British navy sinks the Bismarck off the French coast.

31 MAY: British forces enter Baghdad and the Iraqi government agrees to an armistice.

8 JUNE: British and Free French troops invade Syria, taking Damascus on 21 June.

18 JUNE: Germany and Turkey sign a ten-year friendship treaty. (*See* **Hitler's Foreign Policy**)

22 JUNE: Germany and Italy declare war on the Soviet Union as Germany launches a massive attack on three fronts. Turkey declares its neutrality. Britain assures the Soviet Union of aid, as does the United States, as President Roosevelt declares on 25 June that the neutrality act does not apply to the Soviet Union. (*See* **Hitler's Foreign Policy, Lend Lease,** and **Stalin**)

26 JUNE: Finland joins the Axis attack on the Soviet Union; German troops are already within fifty miles of Minsk, which falls to them on 30 June.

27 JUNE: Hungary declares war on the Soviet Union.

3 JULY: Soviet premier Joseph Stalin announces a "scorched earth" defense; two days later German mechanized troops reach the Dnieper River, three hundred miles from Moscow. (*See* **Eastern Front, German Army and Atrocities, Second Front, Stalin,** and **Wehrmacht**)

7 JULY: The United States occupies Iceland with naval and marine forces; the Icelandic parliament approves the occupation on 10 July. (*See* Eastern Front and **Second Front**)

8 JULY: The Nazi advance into Russia stalls. An estimated 9 million men are engaged in the war between Germany and Russia. (*See* **Eastern Front** and **Second Front**)

25 JULY: The United States and Great Britain freeze all Japanese assets; Japan retaliates the next day by freezing American and British assets. (*See* **U.S. Asia Policy**)

1 AUGUST: President Roosevelt places an embargo on the export of all motor fuel oils outside the western hemisphere except to the British Empire.

19 AUGUST: German troops lay siege to Odessa. (*See* **Eastern Front** and **Second Front**)

4 SEPTEMBER: German U-boats attack the U.S. destroyer Greer en route to Iceland; the Greer counterattacks with depth charges.

5 SEPTEMBER: German artillery begins shelling Leningrad. (*See* **Eastern Front** and **Second Front**)

11 SEPTEMBER: President Roosevelt authorizes American ships to protect themselves by shooting first if they feel threatened by Axis warships; the next day Berlin announces that it will take appropriate countermeasures.

CHRONOLOGY

18 SEPTEMBER: Stalin orders the conscription of all Soviet workers between the ages of sixteen and fifty for after-hours military training. (*See* **Eastern Front, Second Front,** and **Stalin**)

21 SEPTEMBER: German troops enter Kiev and reach the Sea of Azov, cutting off the Crimea. (*See* **Eastern Front** and **Second Front**)

2 OCTOBER: German offensive against Moscow begins. (*See* **Eastern Front, Second Front,** and **Stalin**)

16 OCTOBER: Axis troops capture Odessa. In Japan premier Konoye resigns. On 18 October Lieutenant General Tojo Hideki forms a new cabinet, making himself premier, minister of war, and home minister. (*See* **Japanese Way of War**)

19 OCTOBER: The Germans lay siege to Moscow. (*See* **Eastern Front** and **Second Front**)

6 NOVEMBER: The United States announces $1 billion in lend-lease aid to the Soviet Union. (*See* **Lend Lease**)

17 NOVEMBER: Special envoy Kurusu Saburo delivers Japanese premier Tojo's ultimatum to President Roosevelt. Tojo demands American withdrawal from China and the lifting of the U.S. economic embargo in return for peace in the Pacific. (*See* **Japanese Way of War** and **U.S. Asia Policy**)

18 NOVEMBER: Britain begins an invasion of Libya that drives Rommel's forces back to the point at which he began his invasion of Egypt. (*See* **Rommel**)

30 NOVEMBER: In an inflammatory speech, Japanese premier Tojo declares that Anglo-American exploitation of Asia must be purged. (*See* **Japanese Way of War**)

6 DECEMBER: The Soviet Army begins a counteroffensive along the Moscow front. (*See* **Eastern Front, Second Front,** and **Stalin**)

7 DECEMBER: In a surprise attack, Japanese planes bomb U.S. naval and air bases at Pearl Harbor, Hawaii, destroying two battleships and four other capital vessels. Japanese air forces simultaneously attack U.S. bases in the Philippines, Guam, and Wake Island and British bases in Hong Kong and Singapore, while also invading Malaya and Thailand by air and sea. A Japanese declaration of war on the United States is delivered after the attack. (*See* **Japanese Way of War**)

8 DECEMBER: The United States, Great Britain, the Free French government, and the Dutch government in exile in London declare war on Japan, as do Canada, Costa Rica, Honduras, San Salvador, Guatemala, Haiti, and the Dominican Republic. Thailand capitulates to the Japanese.

11 DECEMBER: Germany and Italy declare war on the United States; the U.S. Congress unanimously responds by declaring war on Germany and Italy–as do Cuba, Costa Rica, Nicaragua, Guatemala, and the Dominican Republic; Mexico severs relations with both nations.

13 DECEMBER: Japanese forces take Guam.

14 DECEMBER: Turkey and Ireland declare neutrality in the U.S./Japanese war.

22 DECEMBER: Prime Minister Churchill and other British officials visit Washington, D.C., to establish a combined American-British military command for the war. (*See* **Churchill** and **Eisenhower**)

23 DECEMBER: Japanese forces complete their invasion of Wake Island. (*See* **Japanese Way of War**)

1942

1 JANUARY: In Washington, D.C., twenty-six Allied nations, including the United States, Great Britain, the Soviet Union, and China, sign a pact agreeing not to make separate peace with Germany.

2 JANUARY: The Japanese take Manila.

17 JANUARY: The Japanese invade Burma.

20 JANUARY: Leading Nazi officials meet in Wannsee, near Berlin, to plan a "final solution" to the "Jewish problem."

21 JANUARY: In North Africa, Rommel begins a counteroffensive that drives the British back into Egypt within two weeks. (*See* **Montgomery** and **Rommel**)

26 JANUARY: The first U.S. troops arrive on British soil.

15 FEBRUARY: Japan occupies Singapore and Malaya.

28 FEBRUARY: Invasion of Java begins.

3 MARCH: The RAF bombs the Renault works outside of Paris, destroying the factory, which had been manufacturing tanks and aircraft engines for the Germans.

9 APRIL: U.S. troops on Bataan surrender.

18 APRIL: "Doolittle's Raiders," a squadron of U.S. Army Air Corps bombers led by Brigadier General James H. Doolittle, raid Tokyo and other Japanese cities.

4–9 MAY: American and Japanese naval forces trade blows in the Coral Sea.

6 MAY: U.S. forces surrender the Philippines to the Japanese.

26 MAY: Great Britain and the Soviet Union sign a twenty-year alliance. Rommel begins a

new offensive in the western Sahara. (*See* **Churchill** and **Stalin**)

27 MAY: Reinhard Heydrich, second in command of the Gestapo, is shot in Czechoslovakia; he dies on 3 June. In retaliation the Nazis kill thousands of Czechs, including everyone in the town of Lidice. (*See* **German Army and Atrocities**)

30 MAY: More than one thousand Allied bombers level Cologne, the major railway center of western Germany.

3 JUNE: Japanese aircraft attack a U.S. naval base in the Aleutian Islands. A few days later they land troops on Attu and Kiska, in the western Aleutians.

4–6 JUNE: The United States cripples the Japanese fleet at the battle of Midway.

21 JUNE: Rommel captures Tobruk. (*See* **Rommel**)

25 JUNE: Major General Dwight D. Eisenhower is appointed commander in chief of Allied military forces. (*See* **Eisenhower**)

28 JUNE: Germans launch an offensive toward the Volga and the Caucasus.

1–9 JULY: Rommel's troops attack El Alamein, attempting to reach and gain control of the Suez Canal, but they are turned back by British forces. (*See* **Montgomery** and **Rommel**)

16–17 JULY: During the *Rafle du Vel' d'Hiver* (Roundup of the Winter Velodrome) more than twelve thousand Jews are arrested and held in a Paris sports arena for deportation to Germany and the occupied countries of eastern Europe. (*See* **Holocaust: Complicity** and **Vichy France**)

26–29 JULY: The Allies conduct one of their most successful bombing raids on Hamburg.

7 AUGUST: The United States lands troops on Guadalcanal, where the Japanese have been building an airstrip since early July; on 12–15 November, American naval forces score a costly victory in a major sea battle for control of this strategically important island in the Solomon Islands, but the Japanese fight on until February 1943. (*See* **Conventional War** and **Japanese Way of War**)

25 AUGUST: German troops reach the outskirts of Stalingrad.

14 SEPTEMBER: The German siege of Stalingrad begins. (*See* **Eastern Front** and **Second Front**)

5 OCTOBER: Prof. Gilbert Murray helps to found Oxfam to help relieve starvation in occupied Europe.

23–26 OCTOBER: The British Eighth Army, under the leadership of Lt. Gen. Bernard L. Montgomery, defeats Rommel's forces at El Alamein. (*See* **Montgomery** and **Rommel**)

8 NOVEMBER: Allied troops under General Dwight D. Eisenhower land in French North Africa to support the British offensive in Egypt. The United States and Vichy France break off diplomatic relations. In a speech in Munich, Hitler announces, incorrectly, that Stalingrad is "firmly in German hands." (*See* **Eisenhower** and **Vichy France**)

9–11 NOVEMBER: German troops re-occupy the so-called Free Zone of France.

19–22 NOVEMBER: A Soviet offensive lifts the siege of Stalingrad, but heavy fighting in the area continues until February 1943. (*See* **Eastern Front**)

20 NOVEMBER: Marines land on Tarawa.

1943

14-27 JANUARY: Churchill and Roosevelt confer with the joint chiefs of staff at Casablanca and demand unconditional surrender by the Axis powers. (*See* **Churchill**)

22 JANUARY: American and Australian forces overrun the last pockets of Japanese troops in New Guinea.

23 JANUARY: The British Eighth Army takes Tripoli.

31 JANUARY: On the outskirts of Stalingrad, the Germans under General Friedrich Paulus capitulate. Stalin announces the capture of more than 45,000 prisoners, including thirteen generals, and the deaths of 146,700 Germans. The remaining German troops in the area, including eight more generals, surrender on 2 February. (*See* **Eastern Front** and **Second Front**)

9 FEBRUARY: The last Japanese forces retreat from Guadalcanal. (*See* **Japanese Way of War**)

20 FEBRUARY: At the Kasserine Pass in Tunisia, Allied troops are forced to retreat by Rommel's Afrika Korps. On 25 February, Allied troops retake the pass. (*See* **Rommel**)

2-4 MARCH: The Japanese are defeated by the United States in the battle of the Bismarck Sea, losing a convoy of 22 ships and more than 50 aircraft.

20 APRIL: The Nazis massacre Jews in the Warsaw ghetto. (*See* **Holocaust: Complicity** and **Holocaust: Theories**)

7-9 MAY: After the Allies take Tunis and Bizerte, the German forces in Tunisia surrender unconditionally.

13 MAY: Axis powers surrender in North Africa.

CHRONOLOGY

24 MAY: German U-boats are withdrawn from the North Atlantic, conceding Allied victory.

3 JUNE: French generals de Gaulle and Henri Giraud form the French Committee of National Liberation (CFLN) to coordinate the French war effort.

5 JULY: Germans troops attack at Kursk.

10 JULY: The Allies invade Sicily, overcoming the last remaining forces on the island at Messina on 17 August. (*See* **Italian Campaign**)

19 JULY: Allied forces bomb Rome for the first time. (*See* **Italian Campaign**)

25 JULY: Mussolini resigns. Italian king Victor Emmanuel III asks Marshal Pietro Badoglio to form a new government. (*See* **Italian Campaign**)

1 AUGUST: The Japanese grant independence to Burma, which declares war on the United States and Great Britain. (*See* **Japanese Way of War**)

14–24 AUGUST: Allied representatives meet in Quebec to plan a war strategy.

23 AUGUST: Soviet troops retake Kharkov.

3 SEPTEMBER: The Allies invade Italy. (*See* **Italian Campaign**)

8 SEPTEMBER: Eisenhower announces the unconditional surrender of Italy to the Allies. Stalin permits the reopening of many Soviet churches. (*See* **Eisenhower** and **Stalin**)

9 SEPTEMBER: Allied troops land near Salerno, Italy. (*See* **Italian Campaign**)

10 SEPTEMBER: Germany announces the occupation of Rome and northern Italy.

12 SEPTEMBER: German commandos led by Capt. Otto Skorzeny rescue Mussolini from house arrest in San Grasso and take him to northern Italy, where he forms a new fascist government. (*See* **Fascism** and **Italian Campaign**)

30 SEPTEMBER: The Allies occupy Naples. (*See* **Italian Campaign**)

13 OCTOBER: The Italian government led by Badoglio declares war on Germany. (*See* **Italian Campaign**)

19–30 OCTOBER: The Allies confer in Moscow and agree that Germany will be stripped of all territory acquired since 1938.

1 NOVEMBER: American forces land at Bougainville in the Solomon Islands.

6 NOVEMBER: The Russians retake Kiev.

19 NOVEMBER: Sir Oswald Mosley, a British Fascist leader imprisoned since May 1940 as a security risk, is released on grounds of failing health.

22–26 NOVEMBER: Churchill, Roosevelt, and Chinese Nationalist leader Chiang Kai-shek meet at Cairo to plan a postwar Asian policy. (*See* **Churchill**)

28 NOVEMBER – 1 DECEMBER: Stalin, Churchill, and Roosevelt meet in Teheran to discuss war strategy and plan the structure of the postwar world. (*See* **Churchill** and **Stalin**)

AIRCRAFT CARRIERS

What role did the aircraft carrier play in World War II?

Viewpoint: Aircraft carriers were decisive naval weapons in World War II, especially in defeating Japan in the Pacific and protecting convoys across the Atlantic.

Viewpoint: The aircraft carrier was only one of several weapons in the Allied arsenal. It was relatively unimportant in the European theater and less important in the Pacific than codebreaking and the island-hopping policy.

Generally regarded as an auxiliary weapon, albeit an important one, before World War II, the aircraft carrier by 1945 had emerged as the backbone of a modern surface fleet. Three navies, the U.S., British, and Japanese, had taken the lead in carrier development after 1918; during the war they remained the only ones to deploy carrier air power. For the United States and Japan, the carrier developed as an offensive weapon, with its air component built around attack aircraft. In both navies, as well, carrier task forces operated independently of those built around capital ships. The Royal Navy's carriers were more closely linked to surface forces. Their aircraft were intended to provide fire control and fighter protection and, since they were increasingly expected to operate in range of land-based air forces, the newer ones had armored flight decks.

The Pacific War demonstrated both the striking power and the vulnerability of carriers. If not opposed by their own kind, carrier aircraft could discover and cripple any surface operations with impunity. At the same time, with their burdens of aviation fuel and high explosives, carriers were floating bombs—boxers with heavy punches and glass jaws. As a consequence both sides tended to reorganize their fleets so as to provide maximum protection to the flight decks. The result was a synergistic process, with surface ships increasingly restricted in their scope of operation while the carriers did most of the work.

Carriers proved vital as well in antisubmarine operations and in supporting amphibious landings. Both the United States and Britain turned out a large number of "escort carriers," based on merchant ship designs. Slow and unglamorous compared to their fleet counterparts, the escort carriers were arguably even more important—not least because they were expendable enough to be risked. By the last six months of the war American carriers, in particular, were becoming increasingly defensive, embarking larger components of fighters at the expense of strike aircraft and absorbing more and more surface ships in their screens. This shift was an immediate consequence of the success, psychological as well as operational, of the Japanese kamikazes. It foreshadowed, however, a postwar evolution of the carrier battle group into a force that arguably exists more for self-protection than for attack.

Viewpoint:
Aircraft carriers were decisive naval weapons in World War II, especially in defeating Japan in the Pacific and protecting convoys across the Atlantic.

At the outset of World War II, most naval strategists believed that the battleship would remain queen of the seas. Battleships constituted the main striking force of the navies of Great Britain, the United States, Japan, France, and Italy. Even Germany, better known today for its use of the U-boat *(Unterseeboot,* or submarine), had developed a "Z-plan" to build ten battleships and three pocket battleships but only four carriers. Nevertheless, it was not battleships that proved decisive on the high seas in World War II. Rather, newer weapons such as submarines, and in particular aircraft carriers, proved more effective and deadly than the big-gunned warships of the past.

In the period between the two world wars, three countries—Japan, the United States, and Great Britain—formed the vanguard of naval powers developing carrier aviation doctrine, tactics, and technology. In the 1920s American general William A. (Billy) Mitchell's sinking of the German prize ship *Ostfriesland* by air attacks encouraged future U.S. naval admirals such as Ernest J. King, William A. Moffett, Chester W. Nimitz, William V. Pratt, and John H. Tower to pursue carrier aviation. The Washington Naval Conference of 1921 directly aided these efforts. At this conference, the United States and Great Britain agreed to limit construction of capital ships and imposed these limitations upon a resentful Japan. Left with two surplus cruiser hulls destined for the scrap heap, the United States smartly converted these to aircraft carriers (*Saratoga* and *Lexington*). The Imperial Japanese Navy (IJN) was also quick to recognize the offensive potential of carriers, building ten by 1941. Nevertheless, throughout the 1930s carriers remained subservient to battleships, as most admirals believed that carrier aircraft were useful primarily for scouting and for spotting the fall of shells fired by battleships.

Why did the world's foremost naval powers continue to invest enormous resources in battleships? Battleships were a tried and tested technology with a highly developed doctrine and supporting industrial infrastructure. They also reinforced traditional and highly esteemed naval skills such as gunnery and ship handling

at close quarters. The Nelsonian tradition of skilled seamanship, of closing with the enemy, of exhibiting bravery under fire, still prevailed in the world's navies. With so much invested in battleships, naval officers were reluctant to embrace new and largely untried technologies.

Aircraft carriers, on the other hand, were an untried technology. Carriers themselves were not fighting ships-of-the-line; they were thin-skinned (except for British carriers that had armored flight decks) and relied primarily on speed and their aircraft for defense. To deploy carriers properly, naval officers had to learn entirely new and untraditional skills such as airmanship. Furthermore, until the late 1930s carrier aircraft (often biplanes) remained primitive. Their light bomb loads lacked the destructive power of a battleship's main guns, and their radius of action was limited. As a new generation of fast monoplanes with greater range and increased carrying capacity became available after 1936, carriers showed more promise. Nevertheless, they represented a risky investment in material, training, and unproved equipment and tactics at a time when the Great Depression constrained most countries' military spending.

Carriers began to show high return on investment early in World War II when torpedo planes from the British carrier *Illustrious* heavily damaged three of Italy's battleships at Taranto in November 1940. Further revealing the vulnerability of unprotected capital ships to air attacks was the Japanese attack on the U.S. Pacific Fleet at Pearl Harbor, followed by Japan's sinking of the Royal Navy's new battleship *Prince of Wales* and the battle-cruiser *Repulse* in December 1941. The Battle of Coral Sea in May 1942 was a harbinger of fleet battles to come, as the U.S. and Japanese fleets never made visual contact, relying on their aircraft to strike at each other.

The turning point of the war in the Pacific came at Midway in June 1942 and hinged on the abilities of American and Japanese carriers. Planned as a battleship fight by Admiral Isoroku Yamamoto, the battle instead became a duel between Japanese and American carrier aviation. Fortunately for the United States, the IJN split its forces and gave them conflicting missions of striking Midway Island and the American navy. Indecisiveness on the part of Admiral Chuichi Nagumo left his carriers highly vulnerable to attack. As Nagumo dithered between arming planes for land versus sea attacks, American dive-bombers caught his three carriers unprotected, their decks crowded with aircraft, fuel lines, bombs, and torpedoes. In five minutes all three were mortally wounded, with a fourth soon joining its

comrades at the bottom of the ocean. With a decisive victory in hand, Admiral Raymond A. Spruance wisely decided to retire. His decision denied the IJN the chance to bring the superior guns of its large battleships to bear on the U.S. fleet.

In sinking four Japanese carriers, U.S. carrier aircraft proved decisive at Midway. After Midway, the U.S. Navy canceled orders for five sixty-thousand-ton battleships and built five hundred thousand tons of aircraft carriers instead. President Franklin D. Roosevelt supported the reorganization of the navy to replace battleship admirals in command of fleets and task forces with admirals having carrier experience. Carriers now formed the nucleus of task forces, with battleships demoted to defensive roles and to providing shore bombardment in support of amphibious operations. In the vast spaces of the Pacific, carrier air groups, with their superior range and striking power, became the U.S. Navy's principal strike arm to project power and to wrest control of the seas from the IJN.

Equal in carrier strength to Japan until after Midway, the United States quickly outproduced its rival in the Pacific. From 1942 to 1945 the United States launched seventeen fleet carriers, ten medium carriers, and eighty-six escort carriers. Japan, by comparison, launched only six fleet carriers, two of which the U.S. Navy sank on their maiden voyage. More critical to Japan than lost carriers were dead aircrews. The IJN discovered that it could not train replacement pilots quickly enough. Rushed into combat with inadequate training and inferior aircraft, Japanese pilots suffered high losses. During the "Great Marianas Turkey Shoot" in June 1944, the Japanese lost 243 planes and three carriers while shooting down only 29 American planes.

With the deployment of *Essex*-class fleet carriers and the continued improvement of logistics and resupply at sea via the fleet-train concept, the U.S. Navy seized control of the Pacific in 1944. Fast at thirty-two knots and capable of carrying ninety-one aircraft, the *Essex*-class carriers pummeled the IJN as well as garrisons and land-based bombers stationed on Japanese-held islands. Using carrier aircraft, the U.S. Navy prevented the Japanese from resupplying or reinforcing these garrisons, thereby enabling the Army and Marines to mask and bypass several heavily fortified

The U.S.S. *Bon Homme Richard,* renamed the *Yorktown* after the aircraft carrier that was sunk in 1942

(U.S. Naval Historical Center)

Japanese installations. Due to fanatical Japanese resistance, U.S. soldiers and Marines sustained high casualties in assaulting Japanese fortifications on Tarawa, Saipan, Iwo Jima, and elsewhere. That these casualties were kept within bearable limits testified to the effectiveness of the firepower brought to bear by carrier aircraft in support of U.S. ground troops.

Carriers, indispensable to Allied victory in the Pacific, were also important in other theaters. In the Mediterranean, fleet carriers proved essential in supplying Malta with aircraft during the Italo-German blitz against that island. The linchpin of Britain's position in the Mediterranean, Malta's successful reprovisioning enabled Britain to disrupt General Erwin Rommel's logistics and supply lines, leaving him with insufficient fuel and supplies to take Egypt. Due to tighter geographical constraints in the Mediterranean compared to the vastness of the Pacific, however, and given the ready availability of airfields on land, carriers proved less vital in this theater.

In the Atlantic, however, carriers were essential to Allied victory. Well into 1943, German U-boats, operating in concentrated "wolfpacks," launched devastating attacks on Allied merchant shipping. U.S. escort carriers helped turn the tide. Carrying as few as sixteen aircraft, escort carriers provided essential air cover to convoys, forcing U-boats to submerge and flee else risk destruction. By May 1943 these aircraft helped drive up German losses of U-boats to unsustainable levels, forcing Admiral Karl Dönitz and the *Kriegsmarine* (German navy) to withdraw U-boats from the Atlantic. Without this victory, U-boats may have sent tens of thousands of U.S. troops, and untold thousands of tons of supplies, to the ocean floor during the Allied buildup for the cross-Channel invasion of France. D-Day succeeded because the Allies had enough men and supplies to secure beachheads at Normandy and to push inland. In helping to protect Atlantic supply lines from the depredations of German wolf packs, escort carriers contributed significantly to D-Day's success and Germany's defeat.

By war's end aircraft carriers had become the capital ship of choice of the major powers. Only with carriers could naval powers successfully contest with an enemy for sea control, and then exercise that control by projecting power in strategic air raids or in tactical strikes in support of amphibious operations. A new naval paradigm was born which by the 1960s and 1970s hardened into dogma. Naval strategists continue to debate how long carriers will remain decisive weapons in gaining and exercising command of the sea. The misplaced faith in battleships shared by the world's navies at the outset of World War II, however, provides a salutary reminder that navies must guard against neglecting new technology even when it undermines established doctrine, tactics, and traditions.

–WILLIAM J. ASTORE, U.S. AIR FORCE ACADEMY, COLORADO

Viewpoint:
The aircraft carrier was only one of several weapons in the Allied arsenal. It was relatively unimportant in the European theater and less important in the Pacific than codebreaking and the island-hopping policy.

Aircraft carriers, like many other weapons systems that were either developed or that came of age during World War II, were of value in the Allies' war effort against the Axis Powers. However, the war was neither won nor lost because of them, and they were not alone decisive in either the Atlantic or the Pacific theaters.

World War II witnessed the first extensive use of aircraft carriers in combat. Yet, in considering whether aircraft carriers were decisive, one should first recall that the war began as a ground war. Germany attacked Poland by land on 1 September 1939, supported by strong air forces but only the most minimal of naval forces. Germany followed this opening act with its Ardennes offensive against the Allies in May 1940. Of the nations immediately involved in the fighting in the fall of 1939 and the spring of 1940, only England and France possessed aircraft carriers. France's lone aircraft carrier was employed as an aircraft transport. England possessed six aircraft carriers, with a further six modern fleet carriers being built, but they would not be available until late 1940 at the earliest. In any event, the existing aircraft carriers played only an auxiliary role, and were often mishandled. A U-boat (*Unterseeboot*, or submarine) torpedoed and sank HMS *Courageous* on 17 September 1939, and the German battleships *Scharnhorst* and *Gneisenau* sank HMS *Glorious* on 8 June 1940 while it was ineffectually supporting British operations in Norway. Another U-boat torpedoed HMS *Ark Royal* in the Mediterranean where it subsequently foundered and sank on 14 November 1941 due to poor damage control design. The German Navy possessed no aircraft carriers, and although it had laid the keels for two such vessels, they were never completed.

THE BATTLE OF THE CORAL SEA (1942)

An eyewitness on the USS Yorktown *described the action as follows.*

The Coral Sea fighting was just beginning. On May 5 the *Yorktown* joined forces with the carrier *Lexington,* and on the afternoon of the 7th came the ominous news: "Two Jap carriers in immediate area." They were less than 130 miles away. Together the *Yorktown* and the *Lexington* launched their planes and together attacked a Jap carrier. Back on the *Yorktown,* as in other battles, the ship's crew waited for news. To them was relayed the *Lexington's* historic "Scratch one flat top," and cheers rolled out across the water.

Later at dusk the planes started coming back, swung into their landing circle around the carrier. Suddenly one of them began firing at the plane in front. Three Jap Zeros by mistake had got into the *Yorktown's* landing circle. Immediately anti-aircraft, tracer bullets, machine guns opened up in a steady stream. All the U.S. planes ducked into the clouds and the Japs winged off toward their own ship. One or two of them may have been shot down.

A few minutes later the *Yorktown's* planes again began coming in, but two of them had disappeared. The last heard of them, they radioed they were circling the ship. Unfortunately, they were not circling the *Yorktown.* Fellow pilots thought they might have made the same mistake the Japs had made . . . landing on an enemy carrier. . . .

At 8:30 in the morning came the announcement, "Two Jap carriers sighted." Before 10 a.m. the attacks were launched from both the *Lexington* and *Yorktown.* On the way to the Jap carriers, the fliers passed Jap bombers en route to attack the U.S. ships. The planes paid no attention to each other but continued on their way. . . .

Over the loudspeaker came the calm announcement, "Large groups of enemy planes approaching ship 30 miles distant." Then later, "Air department take over. Gunnery department take over." The ship's engines began to hum faster and faster. The ship began to zigzag in tight turns. "Stand by for torpedo attack on port bow." Everybody at Repair 4 braced himself.

Suddenly the anti-aircraft let loose, a crashing crescendo. "Stand by for torpedo attack on starboard beam." "Stand by for torpedo attack on port quarter." The ship heeled from side to side, dodging the torpedoes. . . .

"Boom". . . a near miss. "Boom." "Boom." The deck in the galley compartment jumped three feet. The ship lurched sideways. Another bomb and another. The engines kept on roaring, the ship dodging, the AA firing. The men's stomachs drew up in knots. Suddenly there was a terrific bang in the adjoining compartment, the door flew open and a bloody sailor staggered in.

His face and hands were burned, one leg dangled. "We've been hit," he said. "I'm blind. They've been blasted to hell." From the next compartment rolled black smoke. The *Yorktown* had received a direct hit.

Said the battle telephone, "The *Lexington* is hit badly." But the battle was over.

Source: *Gordon Carroll, ed.,* History in the Writing *(New York: Duell, Sloan & Pearce, 1945), pp. 182–185.*

Instead, the German navy made its strongest contribution to the war effort with the U-boat campaign against the Allied sea lines of communication. Beginning in September 1939, this strategy significantly threatened England, especially after the defeat of France left England isolated and opened French Atlantic ports to the U-boats.

Indeed, Germany nearly won the "European" War in the fall of 1941. In arguably the single most significant theater of the war, the Eastern front, aircraft carriers played absolutely no part. Russia managed to fight Germany for almost four years, and it contributed an army of more than 6 million men that tied down more than 3 million Germans. How long it would have taken the United States, the United Kingdom, and the Commonwealth to defeat Germany without Russian manpower thrown into the equation is problematic. That Russian manpower saved the United States from having to raise an army of more than two hundred divisions of its own is denied by few. This situation freed the United States to concentrate the manpower thus saved in manufacturing as the "Arsenal of Democracy." Even after the failure of Barbarossa (the code name for the invasion of Russia) and the coincident entry of the United States into the war in December 1941, Germany managed to hold the Allies at bay for nearly three and one-half years after it was clear it had no chance to win the war.

The United States entered the war with seven aircraft carriers. Before the war the United States began a building program that resulted in the construction of 177 aircraft carriers of all types and sizes. This total included 14 being built but not completed in time for service in the war, and 60 "escort" carriers built for England and designed for use as aircraft transports and in convoy escort. Indeed, the majority of those built by and for the United States were also "escorts." While Britain never matched this prodigious rate, it, too, built a number of useful light and escort carriers.

An area of operations where the Allies employed significant numbers of aircraft carriers was in the war at sea in the Atlantic. Early, if minor, successes by escort carriers converted from merchant hulls, such as HMS *Audacity*, pointed to the potential for these ships in embarking small numbers of fighters to cover convoys from *Luftwaffe* (German Air Force) interference. *Audacity*, for example, carried only six aircraft. The possibility that a few torpedo or scout aircraft could also be embarked to attack U-boats was considered premature, and adjustments were made to air complements accordingly. Escort carriers did not become available in appreciable numbers, however, until late 1942 to mid 1943 as American industrial capacity kicked in and delivered these ships in large numbers. The war in the Atlantic had not been won by the spring of 1943, but the tide had certainly turned against the German *Kriegsmarine* and their U-boats. The U.S. Tenth Fleet used Signals Intelligence to route convoys to England and then to reroute them around concentrations of U-boats, the famous "wolfpacks." American, British, and Commonwealth operational forces employed improved World War I innovations such as sonar and new technology such as radar to locate U-boats both below and on the surface of the water. Despite the German employment of the wolfpacks, the convoys and their escorts were gaining the upper hand in the Atlantic well before hunter-killer groups based around escort carriers made their appearance in any appreciable numbers. The arrival of the hunter-killer groups did not turn the tide, but it did seal the fate of the U-boats.

Japan began the war with eight fleet and light carriers in the Pacific, while the United States had four there, and Britain had none. Japanese aircraft carriers certainly featured prominently in the first ten months of the war in the Pacific, spectacularly so in the attack at Pearl Harbor, then in the ill-fated thrust to Port Moresby at the Battle of the Coral Sea, and finally in the disastrous Japanese defeat at Midway. However, Japan might well have managed with fewer aircraft carriers than it had in 1942. For example, instead of the aerial attack of Pearl Harbor it might have conducted a bombardment with its battle fleet similar to the British fleet's attack on the French squadron at Mers-el-Kebir in Algeria. On 3 July 1940, in a mere sixteen minutes of bombardment by two battleships and one battle cruiser, supported by two cruisers, eleven destroyers, and a few air strikes by the aircraft carrier HMS *Ark Royal*, the British did serious damage to the French vessels. The battleships *Dunkerque* and *Provence* and the destroyer *Mogador* were disabled, while the French battleship *Bretagne* was hit, rolled over, and sank in two minutes with the loss of 977 crewmen.

If the Japanese battle fleet had crossed the northern Pacific and attacked Pearl Harbor in a similar manner on the morning of 7 December, it could have been covered by a few aircraft carriers launching large numbers of new Zero fighters to counter American land-based air power. The resultant destruction may well have equaled the losses inflicted on the U.S. Fleet in the actual attack, and probably would have destroyed the all-important support facilities ashore, especially the fuel oil tank farm. The Japanese may have lost a battleship or two to American land-based aircraft if the Zeros were not completely successful. The results would have been worth it, however, especially if Pearl Harbor had been denied as a base for a long period in the critical early stages of the war USS *Yorktown* could not have been repaired in time for Midway, for example, following such a strike.

Without the vital information provided by the intelligence community's code breakers the American aircraft carriers would not even have been at Coral Sea or at Midway. If the code breakers had not discovered the Japanese intent to attack Midway, the American aircraft carriers would likely have only reacted too late to the attack and may have been intercepted and sunk by the Japanese submarine screen, or the main fleet, as Admiral Isoroku Yamamoto had intended. Instead they passed through the screen's interception line early and turned the tables on the Japanese, sinking four of the six aircraft carriers that had attacked Pearl harbor six months before.

Despite heavy losses of their own in 1942, the Americans still had two aircraft carriers in the Pacific, and one small carrier in the Atlantic. In late 1942 the American building program began to deliver the first of the new light and fleet carriers. Some of these ships provided the first mobile airfields that permitted Admiral Chester Nimitz to leapfrog over Japanese garrisons in the Central Pacific, and so speed his march toward Japan. However, Nimitz, beginning with only a few carriers, could have carried on with just a few after that. He could have attacked and gained the first base, and then created a large air base for land-based aircraft. From there, he could have then slogged his way across the Central Pacific, island chain by island chain. It would have taken more time, but the Americans could probably have attacked across the Central Pacific without large numbers of fleet carriers. The Japanese used an "air bridge" to support and supply their island bases. The Americans could have "walked back" along that same bridge to Japan.

Certainly, General Douglas MacArthur's drive to the Philippines in the Southwest Pacific was accomplished almost entirely with land-based air support. In fact he got along relatively well without aircraft carriers, except in the Philippines campaign, just as aircraft carriers had played only a relatively minor role in Nimitz's first campaign at Guadalcanal in 1942. Once the initial Guadalcanal landings were covered, the aircraft carriers had withdrawn to refuel and only seriously returned once during the battle of Santa Cruz where USS *Wasp* was lost. They were absent for example from the engagements between August and November around Savo Island, and land-based aircraft filled the gap continually. Even at Leyte Gulf in the Philippines in late 1944 the large American fleet carriers played no role, as they were off chasing the chimera of the Japanese Combined Fleet. Only a handful of escort carriers played any role at Leyte, and while it was significant, it is doubtful that the United States would have lost the war if the escorts had not been in Leyte Gulf that day. It is undeniable that it would have taken the Americans a great deal longer to defeat Japan without going across the Central Pacific. It probably would have entailed their seizing Formosa after the Philippines as a base for land-based bombers and attendant fighter cover for later landings such as those planned for Okinawa in the spring of 1945. However, that the Americans would overwhelm Japan with their industrial might was never seriously in doubt.

General Hideki Tojo felt the aircraft carrier was but one component of the American victory in the Pacific. As a second component he pointed to the American strategy of leap-frogging and neutralizing major Japanese bases, such as Truk. This success was of course facilitated by the aircraft carriers, but could have been accomplished, if more slowly, without large numbers of them. However, Tojo's third component of the American victory was the destruction of the Japanese merchant fleet by the American submarines. It is arguable that in the Pacific the truly decisive role was played by the American use of unrestricted submarine warfare against the Japanese sea lines of communication. The American submarines began a blockade of Japanese access to Southeast Asian resources that was all but slammed shut by the American occupation of the Philippine airfields in 1945. Some carrier proponents note the success of the American carriers in attacking the Japanese home islands at the end of the war. However, care should be taken to note that this success occurred after the Japanese air forces had been decimated by the attrition of three years of war, by the B-29 strategic bombing campaign, and after they were starved of resources by the submarine campaign. Japanese officials contended after the war that Japan was indeed starving and the blockade would have forced them to surrender by November, without the atomic bomb or invasion.

Aircraft carriers, like the other components of the land-sea-air team, were of considerable value in the Allies' war effort against the Axis Powers. However, they were not, in and of themselves, singularly decisive in the war effort, and the war was neither won nor lost because of them alone.

—DUANE C. YOUNG, DE MONTFORT UNIVERSITY

References

James H. Belote and William M. Belote, *Titans of the Seas: The Development and Operations of Japanese and American Carrier Task Forces During World War II* (New York: Harper & Row, 1975);

Walter J. Boyne, *Clash of Titans: World War II at Sea* (New York: Simon & Schuster, 1995);

David Brown, *Carrier Operations in World War II: The Pacific Navies, Dec. 1941–Feb. 1943* (Annapolis, Md.: Naval Institute Press, 1974);

Paul S. Dull, *A Battle History of the Imperial Japanese Navy 1941–1945* (Annapolis, Md.: Naval Institute Press, 1978);

Tom Hone, "Carriers," in *The Oxford Companion to World War II,* edited by I. C. B. Dear (Oxford: Oxford University Press, 1995), pp. 192–198;

Edwin P. Hoyt, *Carrier Wars: Naval Aviation from World War II to the Persian Gulf* (New York: McGraw-Hill, 1989);

Hoyt, *How They Won the War in the Pacific: Nimitz and His Admirals* (New York: Weybright & Talley, 1970);

Hoyt, *MacArthur's Navy: The Seventh Fleet and the Battle for the Philippines* (Annapolis, Md.: Naval Institute Press, 1983);

John Keegan, *The Price of Admiralty: The Evolution of Naval Warfare* (New York: Viking, 1988);

David M. Kennedy, "Victory at Sea," *Atlantic Monthly*, 283 (March 1999): 51–76;

Donald Macintyre, *Aircraft Carrier: The Majestic Weapon* (New York: Ballantine, 1968);

Nathan Miller, *War at Sea: A Naval History of World War II* (New York: Scribners, 1995);

Samuel Eliot Morison, *The Two-Ocean War: A Short History of the United States Navy in the Second World War* (Boston: Little, Brown, 1963);

Mark P. Parillo, *The Japanese Merchant Marine in World War II* (Annapolis, Md.: Naval Institute Press, 1993);

E. B. Potter and Chester W. Nimitz, eds., *Triumph in the Pacific: The Navy's Struggle against Japan* (Englewood Cliffs, N.J.: Prentice-Hall, 1963);

Clark G. Reynolds, *The Fast Carriers: The Forging of an Air Navy* (Huntingdon, N.Y.: Robert E. Krieger, 1978);

Ronald H. Spector, *Eagle Against the Sun: The American War with Japan* (New York: Free Press, 1985);

Geoffrey Till, "Adopting the Aircraft Carrier: The British, American, and Japanese Case Studies," in *Military Innovation in the Interwar Period,* edited by Williamson Murray and Allan Millett (Cambridge & New York: Cambridge University Press, 1996), pp. 191–226;

William T. Y'Blood, *Hunter Killer: U.S. Escort Carriers in the Battle of the Atlantic* (New York: Orion Books, 1989);

Y'Blood, *The Little Giants: U.S. Escort Carriers Against Japan* (Annapolis, Md.: Naval Institute Press, 1987).

AIRCRAFT CARRIERS

Did American soldiers in World War II have a strong sense of fighting for a cause?

Viewpoint: Yes, while American soldiers, sailors, and airmen fought for a wide variety of reasons, one primary motivation was a strong sense of fighting for a worthwhile cause.

Viewpoint: No, during World War II Americans often enlisted in the military for patriotic reasons, but once they entered combat they fought for the survival of themselves and their comrades.

The motivation of American soldiers during World War II was a mystery to their enemies and their generals alike. The issue was complicated by a GI culture that strenuously denied overt idealism, instead emphasizing that what they did was a job—the only way to get home. The point has been explained in the context of a Great Depression–era mentality that made a job something more than forty hours a week of time lost for life. Nevertheless, idealism has generally been discounted as an element of American performance.

S. L. A. Marshall is the most familiar student of the GIs' war to assert the primacy of comradeship and small-unit cohesion. According to his model, soldiers fought because they did not wish to let down their buddies or, more fundamentally, be considered cowardly or incompetent by the "primary group" that was the focus of their emotional identity in an impersonal army fighting an impersonal war. "Belonging" was also a survival mechanism. An individual without connections in a squad or platoon was subject to be given high-risk jobs while thrown on his own emotional resources—an often fatal combination.

In those contexts a personnel system based on individual replacements and a force structure that restricted regular rotation of units out of the line were major negative factors in combat motivation. On the other side of the equation, American soldiers responded well to competence. Effective leadership, efficient fire support, regular deliveries of hot food and mail—such things could compensate for cohesion disrupted by heavy casualties. Perhaps as well, idealism entered the mix through the back door. When asked by Stephen E. Ambrose why, in the brutal winter of 1944, more soldiers did not accept a military prison as an alternative to the line, he was told: "no man would choose disgrace." That is not a shame-based attitude. It is an affirmation of an honor that does not depend on glory.

**Viewpoint:
Yes, while American soldiers, sailors, and airmen fought for a wide variety of reasons, one primary motivation was a strong sense of fighting for a worthwhile cause.**

Scholars often avoid focusing on single, monolithic explanations for complex issues—and with good reason. Much recent scholarship concerning the motivations of American fighting men in World War II, however, has overemphasized the "buddy theory" of combat motivation and almost completely forgotten that genuine patriotism remained a significant factor supporting the American soldiers' resilience. While one cannot deny that extensive research into unit cohesion and the psychological aspects of combat has provided useful insights into the behavior of American fighting men, this focus on a single aspect of combat motivation needs a corrective. American soldiers, sailors, and airmen possessed a strong belief in their cause that provided considerable strength to their determination to fight. In short, America's servicemen were motivated by many factors, one of which was sincere patriotism, and this element was as pervasive as any of the psychological explanations that are currently in vogue in the historic community.

It is important to look at this issue with balance. Research and scholarship have made a good case that soldiers (for brevity, all fighting men—soldiers, sailors and airmen—will be referred to as soldiers), once in combat, often have a strong sense of fighting for their buddies. This case, however, has been overstated. The essential point is not to disprove that soldiers felt a strong obligation to their comrades, but to show that these men also had a powerful desire to fight for the American cause. In the end, these reasons were reinforcing and not mutually exclusive.

There are many ways to approach this discussion, but it is useful to look at four general questions. First, what is the "buddy theory" that dominates current scholarship and the evidence used to support it? Second, what are the differences between the soldiers' initial motivations to enlist and the reasons for his continued willingness to engage in combat, as well as differences between the major types of soldiers—combat and support? Third, a comparison of the American soldier's view of the war with other national views raises the entire issue of ideology in warfare and posits the question—do the majority of combat soldiers divorce themselves from the basic causes of their struggle for the sake of seeking personal survival and approval of their fellow soldiers? Finally, is there substantial, but often overlooked, evidence that patriotism is a strong factor in the soldiers' desire to fight?

An examination of the buddy or "cohesion" argument of soldier motivation reveals that the underlying argument has some validity but is often grossly oversimplified. Perhaps the most well-known study of soldier motivations for fighting was S. L. A. Marshall's *Men Against Fire: The Problem of Battle Command in Future War* (1947). Basing his argument on postbattle interviews, Marshall emphasized that few soldiers actually engaged in combat and hinted that fighting men were more interested in survival than supporting a noble cause. Another work

published shortly after World War II, Samuel A. Stouffer's psychological examination of the American soldier, *The American Soldier: Combat and Its Aftermath* (1949), is similarly both valuable and misused. Like Marshall, Stouffer focuses on the elements of superior unit cohesion, and minimizes the role of soldier patriotism as a motivating factor. Gerald F. Linderman, in *The World Within War: America's Combat Experience in World War II* (1997) provides a more recent view of soldier motivation that looks at a greater base of evidence but does not stray far from Souffer's conclusions. Other recent scholarship on the American army in World War II, to include works by Stephen E. Ambrose and Peter R. Mansoor, does much to correct the denigration of the American soldiers' fighting performance, but their work still tends to focus almost exclusively on the benefits of unit cohesion and training.

All of these above works are excellent contributions to the literature of World War II, but they can potentially lead to a mistaken impression of soldier motivation. One weak area is a failure to look at the full view and nuance of these authors' arguments. For example, Ambrose and Mansoor demonstrate that the American soldier displayed superb toughness in combat, and that training and organizational structures made American units surprisingly effective. Both authors do not specifically address the motivation of the soldiers, however, and their focus on other issues could lead one to conclude that American soldiers were blank slates whose effectiveness was solely dependent on training, comradeship, and lower-level unit leadership. Perhaps even worse interpretations could be drawn from Marshall, Stouffer, and Linderman's works. One problem with these efforts is the multiple views and interpretations given to the buddy theory of soldier motivation. The following questions illustrate the myriad of issues that are included in their writings. Did soldiers fight for the approval of their comrades? Was it for the positive praise of friends or to avoid their condemnation? Did they fight for some abstract concept of proving their manhood? Did they fight for hatred of an enemy who wanted to kill them, or perhaps even the more "noble" cause of destroying an unjust enemy? Did soldiers fight for mere survival, regardless of supposed peer pressure from their fellow soldiers? Did soldiers fight out of grim devotion to duty or simply a passive acceptance of their fate? Did they fight because small-unit leaders built a true sense of identity in their group? In short, the idea of "fighting for one's buddy" is a complex concept. More importantly, answers to the above questions do not exclude the possibility that American soldiers fought for the nation's cause. For example, Linderman presents a powerful argument that the American sol-

U.S. troops on Okinawa in May 1945

(U.S. Marine Corps)

dier often felt alienated from his home front. A possible interpretation is that soldiers lost all connection with the reasons for the war; perhaps they even felt their nation had betrayed them. A closer look at Linderman's evidence, however, reveals that soldiers often grew to resent, or at least feel separated from, the people living the "easy life" at home. Perhaps these soldiers never doubted their cause but resented those at home who did not contribute as strongly to the war effort.

Another potential problem with the scholarship of the buddy theory is the evidence used to support the case. Marshall's work is probably the most infamous example of problems with evidence; he has been accused of fabricating statistics. Regardless of this accusation, the nature of Marshall's evidence raises some questions because he only interviewed a limited number of Marines in the Pacific theater. Similarly, Stouffer's work focuses on a relatively small sample of American soldiers in Italy. Linderman shows more breadth in his evidence, but from a statistical perspective, his selection of letters, memoirs, and interviews is not definitive. In all honesty, these efforts, especially Linderman's work, deserve credit for making use of limited available evidence, and it would be intellectually dishonest to denigrate their efforts. Nonetheless, it is always difficult to generalize the motivations of large groups of people, and despite the best efforts of many historians, their evidence gives snapshots of individual opinions, but is not statistically conclusive.

A second perspective on the motivation of America's soldiers concerns the differences between their initial reasons for enlistment and later attitudes of veteran soldiers in combat, as well as variations between soldiers in different branches. A vast majority of the scholarship on soldier morale is focused on the narrow perspective of infantry combat in the front lines—a worthwhile objective, but limited in its scope. Few writers examine the reasons for the initial enlistment of American fighting men, and few works address the motivations of the majority of America's armed forces that were not frontline ground troops. Initially, the overwhelming majority of American fighting men enlisted for patriotic reasons. Especially after the Japanese attack on Pearl Harbor, enlistment offices were filled with recruits who believed in the American cause. Although the United States instituted a draft prior to Pearl Harbor, the Army Air Corps and navy relied almost exclusively on volunteers, and even the army's draftees displayed a willingness to serve and a general belief in the correctness of the nation's cause. Perhaps after prolonged contact with the enemy, servicemen showed a greater cynicism towards authority, but there is almost no evidence that they abandoned their underlying belief in the cause. In addition,

AMERICAN TROOPS

a significant number of support soldiers who were essential to the war effort were not conditioned by combat conditions. What motivated the millions of troops who worked in logistics and administrative duties, and did not actually participate in combat? These soldiers did not face the dangers of the infantryman at the front, but they made a major contribution to the Allied victory, and no one has argued that they were motivated by the need for peer approval or survival. In sum, the majority of American soldiers initially enlisted for patriotic reasons, those that did not see combat probably continued to serve in belief of the nation's cause, and many soldiers in the front lines who felt a great kinship with their fellows did not necessarily abandon their initial motivations even as they lost their innocence.

For another view of the American soldier's motivation one can look at literature concerning other nations' soldiers in World War II. For example, Omer Bartov's recent scholarship on the German army, *Hitler's Army: Soldiers, Nazis, and War in the Third Reich* (1991), while controversial, has certainly punctured the myth that German soldiers were completely divorced from the Nazi cause. However, current work on the Japanese fighting man has reflected greater complexity beyond the caricature of mindless followers of the emperor. In both cases, the Axis soldier suffered in combat, fought for his survival, and often found comfort in the support of his comrades as did their American counterparts. Yet, these soldiers also retained their belief in their country's cause. The common element of these studies is that ideology played a strong part in the common soldiers' motivation. Interestingly, unlike the large number of historians willing to posit the "patriotic" motives of soldiers outside of America, few scholars seem willing to claim that America's soldiers had similar motivations. In any case, the complex mix of motivations behind the efforts of German and Japanese soldiers, as well as other nations, indicates that most fighting men maintained a firm belief in their nation's cause. It is only logical that America's soldiers would not be the sole exception.

Finally, there is substantial evidence that American soldiers believed firmly in the righteousness of their cause. Letters, diaries, and interviews with veterans contain many references to a belief in America's war effort. This evidence is not reflected in a blind belief that was sometimes portrayed in contemporary propaganda. Instead, much of this attitude is revealed in a determination to carry through to victory. Also, there is a certain amount of hatred against the Axis powers, who were considered an evil enemy that needed to be crushed, particularly in the Pacific war. This attitude does not support the idea of fighting for one's buddy, and in fact, is much more closely connected to a belief in fighting for the Allied cause against an evil opponent. The tremendous bulk of evidence from American soldiers that expresses a longing to return home to loved ones also indicates a continued connection to life at home, as much as a desire to fight for comrades at the front. Prose, poetry, movies, and music from World War II were strongly patriotic and should not be dismissed as mere wartime propaganda. Modern Americans, in an environment of cynicism, may have come to expect the bitterness of the Korea of *M*A*S*H* (1970), the Vietnam of *Platoon* (1986), or even World War I's spawned antiwar works, such as Erich Maria Remarque's *All Quiet on the Western Front* (1929) and Humphrey S. Cobb's *Paths of Glory* (1935). For a war of such enormous magnitude, World War II has produced relatively little antiwar, cynical material: one noted exception is Joseph Heller's *Catch-22* (1961). It seems that many soldiers believed in the correctness of America's cause, and despite the harsh realities and immediate demands of combat, most soldiers retained this belief.

The motivations of America's soldiers in World War II were varied and complex, but they never eschewed a belief in their nation's cause. There has been much good work that focuses on the psychology of frontline soldiers and makes a strong case that in the midst of combat these men leaned heavily on fellow GIs in their unit. However, these arguments should not obscure the fact patriotism—a belief in America's cause—was also a crucial factor in many ways. Most soldiers initially enlisted for patriotic motives; a large majority of soldiers were never deferred from this belief; support soldiers were never shaped by combat experience; and even hardened veterans at the front did not necessarily abandon a faith in their nation. A balanced view of this issue reveals that a genuine belief in the nation's cause was a powerful motivation for America's troops throughout the war.

–CURTIS S. KING, LEAVENWORTH, KANSAS

**Viewpoint:
No, during World War II Americans often enlisted in the military for patriotic reasons, but once they entered combat they fought for the survival of themselves and their comrades.**

Over the course of World War II the United States fielded a total force of 16.3 million persons, of which fewer than one million took part in extended combat. The U.S. Army alone fielded a force of roughly 8,250,000 men. The ranks of the fighting men in World War II primarily consisted of America's citizen soldiers, sailors, and airmen. The vast majority had been born between 1915 and 1925 and had endured the rigors of the Great Depression. Most entered combat between 1943 and 1945. From Europe to the Mediterranean, from the Pacific to Burma, fighting men comprised roughly 10 percent of the field force. They came as liberators, not conquerors, and were only too happy to return to their homes as soon as the war was over. Infantrymen, constituting 14 percent of American troops overseas, suffered approximately 70 percent of the casualties. This imbalance invites the question: "Why do men fight?"

In his brilliant exposé of combat motivation during the American Civil War, *For Cause and Comrades: Why Men Fought in the Civil War* (1997), historian James M. McPherson opined that Civil War soldiers fought for cause and country even more than they fought for comrades; the motivation was just the opposite for GIs in World War II. Recent evidence, including wartime diaries, journals, and correspondence, suggests that the American GI was equally motivated for cause and country, but as historian Stephen E. Ambrose indicates in *Citizen Soldiers: The U.S. Army from the Normandy Beaches to the Bulge to the Surrender of Germany, June 7, 1944– May 7, 1945* (1997), the difference between Billy Yank and Johnny Reb and their twentieth-century counterparts was only that of expression. Heirs of their fathers' legacy in World War I and products of the Great Depression, the American GI found patriotic words hollow and tended to emphasize the comradeship that formed among combat soldiers sharing a common fate in the greatest war of the century.

Americans who contemplated World War II without the experience of battle viewed the conflict as essentially a struggle between the forces of good and evil, between fascism and democracy. To the men fighting in the front lines, however, battle assumed a far more frightful and dangerous dimension. To willingly risk one's life by charging into a machine gun or leading a platoon against an entrenched enemy on an exposed beach is so unnatural an act that it defies human comprehension. Yet, that singular act of courage was repeated on countless battlefields in World War II. Even Audie Murphy, America's most decorated soldier of the war, could not explain it. As recorded in Gerald F. Linderman's *The World Within War: America's Combat Experience in World War II* (1997), in approaching France's Mediterranean shoreline, Murphy pondered that "little men, myself included, who are pitted

"ALL RIGHT, POUR IT ON"

WITH THE 5TH ARMY ON ANZIO BEACH HEAD, ITALY (Delayed)—A young American artillery observer, finding himself surrounded by German infantry in today's fluid fighting southeast of Carroceto (Aprilla), performed the highest act of heroism possible for a field artilleryman. He ordered a barrage put down on his own position—a farmhouse which was being overrun by enemy troops.

In a steady, quiet voice, this twenty-four-year-old lieutenant, a former Mid-West school teacher, gave by telephone the co-ordinates of the yellow concrete farmhouse from which he had observed and reported a German advance. At the other end of the wire Captain Harry C. Lane, of Tulsa, Oklahoma, protested, but the voice said firmly: "What difference does it make? Go ahead and shoot."

A moment later shells from twenty howitzers crashed down upon the farmhouse and surrounding area. The telephone went dead.

It was assumed that the lieutenant either was killed by the barrage or was taken prisoner by the Germans, who, despite heavy losses, remained in control of the area. He had been warned at dawn by Major Franklin T. Gardner, of Tulsa, that the Allied outpost line probably could not withstand another attack. He was told that when the infantry retired to new defensive positions he should fall back with them.

But the lieutenant had won the Silver Star in December by staying after infantry had fled. In that action near Venafro, he called for fire on his own position. The barrage killed scores of Germans and broke up their counter-attacks. The lieutenant came out uninjured, and possibly he figured today that he could do it again.

So, when the Germans began their infiltration tactics the lieutenant kept lowering the range of Allied guns until the heavy howitzer shells were bursting a few hundred yards in front of the farmhouse. His protecting screen of infantry began to retreat and the lieutenant sent his own men back with them. They took the radio, leaving him alone with a telephone.

For thirty minutes the lieutenant continued to adjust two fire missions—on the Germans approaching the farmhouse and on another enemy group just beyond. Then the Germans closed in. The lieutenant adjusted the fire first to the right of the farmhouse, then to the left. He told Captain Lane that he was burning his codes. Then he said: "All right, pour it on."

Source: New York Herald Tribune, *20 February 1944.*

AMERICAN TROOPS

against a riddle that is as vast and indifferent as the blue sky above us."

While it is difficult to achieve consensus among World War II veterans, several possible explanations emerge from the men and women now more willing to address their combat experiences. Captain Joseph Dawson, the commander of the first rifle company to penetrate German lines above Omaha Beach during the Normandy invasion on 6 June 1944, attributed his enlistment in the army in May 1941 to the perception that his country and his freedom were in peril from a force bent on destroying American society. Len Lomell, the Ranger who personally destroyed the German battery of 155 mm guns at Pointe du Hoc on D-Day, joined the Rangers for the adventure and excitement that such a unit promised. Many others simply went to war because they were drafted, caught up in the maelstrom of a war that confounded their human expectations.

Few realized what they were getting into when they entered military life. Military service functioned solely as an intermission in their lives. War could hardly be expected to be an extension of domestic life. Once in combat the GI found that war severed the traditional bonds of family and security. By December 1944 casualties were so excessive in the European Theater of Operations there existed a shortfall of three hundred thousand riflemen. Ambrose estimates that nearly one half of the three million men who served in the army in Europe came onto the Continent as replacements. Of these men roughly one half became casualties within their first three days on the front line.

Whether or not the individual rifleman or commander would measure up to the trial of combat was also a powerful motivating force. In the breakout across France and Belgium, Dawson tempered his resolution to meet the final tests with the realization that he was growing awfully weary and must not falter. George Wilson, a company commander of F Company, Twenty-second Infantry, recorded in *If You Survive* (1987) that he eventually reached his breaking point in the Hurtgen Forest. Wilson had seen so many others falter, he realized he too was on "the black edges." Still the vast majority of leaders continued on, leading their men until casualties had taken a personal toll. In *The Men of Company K: The Autobiography of a World War II Rifle Company* (1985), a collection of the thoughts of a group of combat soldiers, Harold P. Leinbaugh, a lieutenant in Company K, 333rd Infantry Regiment, 84th Division, freely admits that "We had questions about ourselves that could be answered only in combat." Morton Eustis, recently assigned to an armored division, expresses how worried he was "not whether I'm

killed, wounded or taken prisoner . . . but how well I acquit myself when I come up against the real thing."

In reflecting on his own role in the war in *Not in Vain: A Rifleman Remembers World War II* (1992), rifleman Leon C. Standifer made a revealing distinction between going to war and going into combat. Not surprisingly, his motivations between war and actual combat differed as well. Most American GIs went to war for their country and local communities, but as they got closer to actual combat, that community became less the United States and more First Squad, Easy Company, Second Battalion. While God, Roosevelt, and Country were important, Standifer attacked a machine gun at Le Hirgoat for the approval of his squad. He wanted them to know that he was reliable because within a few minutes he might be badly wounded and need their help; if one of his team members were wounded, then Standifer willingly would risk his life to come to his aid.

What held the men of World War II together once they entered combat was unit cohesion. In the Pacific, Marine Eugene B. Sledge stated emphatically, in *With the Old Breed, at Peleliu and Okinawa* (1981), that "Company K . . . was home; it was 'my' company. I belonged to it and nowhere else." William Manchester agreed in *Goodbye, Darkness: A Memoir of the Pacific War* (1980): "Men . . . do not fight for flag or country, for the Marine Corps or glory or any other abstraction. They fight for one another." War correspondent Ernie Pyle also noted the sacred circle of comradeship among soldiers in the front lines. In describing the fighting in Italy during the winter of 1944, Pyle wrote, "There is a sense of fidelity to each other in a little corps of men who have endured so long, and whose hope in the end can be so small." Major Dick Winters, the central figure in Ambrose's *Band of Brothers: E Company, 506th Regiment, 101st Airborne Division: From Normandy to Hitler's Eagle's Nest* (1992) added a particular distinction concerning the role of officers in Easy Company, 506th PIR, 101st Airborne Division: "I may have been the commander, but I was not a member of the family. The family belonged to the men; I was a mere caretaker." Even at unit reunions the original members of the Easy Company family sit together at a separate table.

The American GI fought in World War II because there was a job to do and there was simply no one else to do it. They were motivated by patriotism and community, but God and country faded the closer the GI approached the forward edge of the battle area. A popular wartime adage was that patriotism died five miles from the front. Then the soldier's or sailor's communal attachment to his comrade at arms assumed a far more important role. In actual combat, the American GI fought primarily for personal survival and for the survival of his comrades.

–COLE C. KINGSEED, U.S.
MILITARY ACADEMY, WEST POINT

References

Stephen E. Ambrose, *Band of Brothers: E Company, 506th Regiment, 101st Airborne Division: From Normandy to Hitler's Eagle's Nest* (New York: Simon & Schuster, 1992);

Ambrose, *Citizen Soldiers: The U.S. Army from the Normandy Beaches to the Bulge to the Surrender of Germany, June 7, 1944–May 7, 1945* (New York: Simon & Schuster, 1997);

Ambrose, *D-Day: June 6, 1944: The Climatic Battle of World War II* (New York: Simon & Schuster, 1994);

Omer Bartov, *Hitler's Army: Soldiers, Nazis, and War in the Third Reich* (New York: Oxford University Press, 1991);

Joseph T. Dawson, Personal Papers, Robert McCormick Research Center, 1st Infantry Division Museum, Cantigny, Illinois;

Michael D. Doubler, *Closing with the Enemy: How GIs Fought the War in Europe* (Lawrence: University Press of Kansas, 1994);

John W. Dower, *War without Mercy: Race and Power in the Pacific War* (New York: Pantheon, 1986);

Paul Fussell, *Doing Battle: The Making of a Skeptic* (Boston: Little, Brown, 1996);

Meirion and Susie Harries, *Soldiers of the Sun: The Rise and Fall of the Imperial Japanese Army* (New York: Random House, 1991);

Samuel Lynn Hynes, *Flights of Passage: Reflections of a World War II Aviator* (New York:

F. C. Beil / Annapolis: Naval Institute Press, 1988);

Harold P. Leinbaugh and John D. Campbell, *The Men of Company K: The Autobiography of a World War II Rifle Company* (New York: Morrow, 1985);

Gerald F. Linderman, *The World Within War: America's Combat Experience in World War II* (New York: Free Press, 1997);

William Manchester, *Goodbye, Darkness: A Memoir of the Pacific War* (Boston: Little, Brown, 1980);

S. L. A. Marshall, *Men Against Fire: The Problem of Battle Command in Future War* (New York: Morrow, 1947);

Peter R. Mansoor, *The GI Offensive in Europe: The Triumph of American Infantry Divisions, 1941–1945* (Lawrence: University Press of Kansas, 1999);

John C. McManus, *The Deadly Brotherhood: The American Combat Soldier in World War II* (Novato, Ca.: Presidio, 1998);

James M. McPherson, *For Cause and Comrades: Why Men Fought in the Civil War* (New York: Oxford University Press, 1997);

Audie Murphy, *To Hell and Back* (New York: Holt, 1949);

Eugene B. Sledge, *With the Old Breed, at Peleliu and Okinawa* (Novato, Cal.: Presidio, 1981);

Leon C. Standifer, *Not in Vain: A Rifleman Remembers World War II* (Baton Rouge: Louisiana State University Press, 1992);

Samuel A. Stouffer, and others, *The American Soldier: Combat and Its Aftermath* (Princeton: Princeton University Press, 1949);

James Tobin, *Ernie Pyle's War: America's Eyewitness to World War II* (New York: Free Press, 1997);

George Wilson, *If You Survive* (New York: Ivy Books, 1987).

AMERICAN TROOPS

APPEASEMENT

Was appeasement the right policy for Great Britain and the other Western powers to follow in the 1930s?

Viewpoint: Yes, appeasement was the right policy because it was based on traditional perceptions of foreign interests and a rational assessment of military means and political will.

Viewpoint: No, appeasement of the Axis powers led directly to World War II, and it was unnecessary because Germany did not yet have the military strength to oppose France and England.

Appeasement is the name given to the French and British policies during the 1930s intended to avert war by making concessions to Germany, Japan, and Italy on matters generally to be of substantial, if not vital, interest to the powers making the concessions. Usually used in a pejorative sense, appeasement nevertheless had roots both in traditional diplomatic practice and in the particular diplomatic circumstances of 1930s Europe.

Sometimes described by its defenders as a tactic used to buy time for rearmament, appeasement is more accurately understood as an end in itself. Appeasement, indeed, might be called one of the essential elements of effective diplomacy at any time and place: few successful negotiations have been based on pushing every disputed issue to the limit. Interwar appeasement reflected as well the Western powers' strong commitment to maintaining peace after the experience of 1914–1919. It reflected a sense, present in France as well as Britain, that the Versailles Treaty (1919) had either been too harsh initially or had become unenforceable. Finally, appeasement incorporated a consciousness that was understood just as "Europe" seemed to be shrinking. The U.S.S.R. was at best a marginal participant. The "successor states" of eastern and southern Europe were poor substitutes for Austria-Hungary. If Italy and Germany were also to be considered beyond the pale, what remained except an Atlantic fringe?

However well reasoned and well intentioned appeasement may have been, its premises were denied by the mixture of ideology and opportunism that drove Germany in particular to use every gain as a springboard for fresh demands. France and Britain accepted the reoccupation of the Rhineland and the conquest of Abyssinia. They tolerated German and Italian intervention in the Spanish Civil War. They acceded to Adolf Hitler's annexation of Austria. Appeasement's climax came at Munich in 1938, where conceding the dismemberment of Czechoslovakia was described by British premier Neville Chamberlain as securing "peace for our time." The Nazi occupation of Prague in March 1939 showed instead that appeasement had bought peace for only six months.

**Viewpoint:
Yes, appeasement was the right policy because it was based on traditional perceptions of foreign interests and a rational assessment of military means and political will.**

Standing up to tyranny is a course that, in principle, anyone would wish statesmen to pursue. How to define and execute this policy is more problematic. Anyone considering this question should reflect on the record that governments of the late twentieth century have made in this regard. The application of force may have punished the rulers of Iraq and Yugoslavia for aggressions against their neighbors and their own citizens, but the persistence of these regimes shows the limitations of that approach. These states were relatively weak. When it came to relations with the Soviet Union, anticommunist alliances to "contain" bolshevism were formed regularly. Yet, these alliances did nothing to prevent Soviet forces from crushing dissident movements in Hungary (1956) and Czechoslovakia (1968); nor did they dissuade the Soviet government from developing thermonuclear weapons and ballistic missiles necessary for their delivery. In addition to living under this threat, the U.S. intervention in Vietnam caused sharp political divisions at home and produced results to its national interest that are still a matter of debate. These points should be kept in mind when considering British prime minister Neville Chamberlain's appeasement of Adolf Hitler's Nazi Germany.

To Chamberlain, who came into office in 1937, appeasement meant maintaining European international stability by means of redressing the grievances of those states that could challenge that stability. He faced a dramatically altered international situation. Hitler's coming to power in 1933 had negated previous efforts to satisfy German complaints about the financial and territorial settlement forced upon it by the Versailles treaty (1919). Hitler challenged the Versailles settlement with bold initiatives: withdrawing from the League of Nations (1933), canceling war debt payments (1933), beginning a program of public rearmament (1935), and moving troops into the demilitarized German Rhineland (1936). The success of these measures not only demonstrated the unwillingness of France and Britain to coordinate a determined opposition to Hitler, they also undermined further efforts to revise the Versailles treaty by such means as collective security and negotiation through the League of Nations. In effect, Hitler took the initiative in foreign policy away from the French

and British. In 1937 he had made international politics radically unstable. Chamberlain inherited, therefore, a European scene at once more dangerous and complex than had any of his predecessors.

Chamberlain also inherited two aspects of policymaking that had driven British foreign affairs for more than two hundred and fifty years. The first of these was a determination to avoid entangling Continental alliances. Behind this determination lay the theory that traditional rivalries among the Continental states formed a balance of power, allowing Britain to choose sides when necessary and intervene to preserve the balance. Intervention was based on a clear and direct threat to British interests, the main one being an invasion of the territory of Belgium, "a dagger pointed at the heart of London." Because Hitler's initiatives at first lay in central and eastern Europe (Austria, Czechoslovakia, and Poland), they posed no such clear and direct threat. Lacking a clear case for intervention, the best alternative, according to this perspective, was negotiation.

It was also true that the assumption that the European states formed a balance of power was itself a fiction. By 1937 attempts by France and the Soviet Union to cooperate over the security of eastern Europe had fallen apart. Chamberlain, moreover, had no wish to ally with the Soviet regime of Joseph Stalin. Chamberlain also thought, with good reason, that the French would no longer take up the initiative against Hitler. Looking further afield, the possibility of an alliance with the United States was unlikely. During the 1930s the U.S. Congress had been busy passing laws and resolutions against involvement in European affairs. If a balance of power was the means to achieve Continental stability, British diplomacy would have to construct it out of the flimsiest of materials.

Such a policy also required a British military strategy based on deterrence. In the context of the 1930s this meant building up a land army and a bomber force, the theory being that these provided the main offensive threats. These goals, however, could not be attained. By December of 1937 the realization set in that building a strategic bomber force was too expensive, could not match German aircraft production, nor cover enough essential targets in Germany. Instead, British military planning shifted to a strategy of defense, relying on fighter aircraft and naval strength to survive the onslaught of Germany's war machine. By 1938 the Chamberlain government was committed to the position that, if negotiation failed and war came anyway, Britain would survive the first phase and use its financial reserves to build up the capacity to endure over the long haul.

APPEASEMENT

To these considerations of foreign and military policy should be added the need to gain the approval of Parliament. Since late in the seventeenth century kings and statesmen had chafed at the unwillingness of Parliament to spend on military preparedness. During the 1930s the same was true in France and the United States. The national mood in Britain was strongly against an active military policy. Lacking the clear case of an attack on British vital interests, the best appeal for a strategy of collective security and deterrence was a propaganda campaign painting Hitler as a dangerous radical bent on aggressive war and sensible only to the counter-threat of force. Such appeals, however accurate they may have been, made no rational sense and their effect on parliamentary opinion was at best uncertain. There is no point making threats that cannot be backed up and therefore cannot persuade.

Appeasement rested upon both a traditional perspective on foreign interests and a rational assessment of military means and political will. Its critics often condemn it more in terms of its rhetorical supports than in terms of its rationale. The image of Chamberlain waving a piece of paper, after the Munich settlement, proclaiming "peace in our time," and referring to Czechoslovakia as a land "far away," inhabited by "a people of whom we know nothing" has been used to portray him as a painfully naive fool, his folly bordering on criminal negligence. A fairer assessment would see these phrases as examples of a politician assuring everyone that all would be for the best, a common enough aspect of democratic politics. In retrospect Chamberlain's folly came after German troops occupied Poland (September 1939). By giving an unconditional guarantee of Polish sovereignty, Chamberlain created a clear cause for war, one now acceptable to parliamentary opinion. He did not, however, negotiate to enlist the aid of the Soviet Union, the vital ingredient in the guarantee's credibility. If war came, this failure assured that it would begin on the least favorable terms.

This failure indeed is the principal criticism of appeasement: Britain squandered opportunities to provide a credible deterrent to German aggression. Anyone subscribing to this argument should, however, consider the following. Granted, a credible network of alliances might have ensured a cheaper and quicker victory over Hitler, had war come. On the other hand, what would have been the prospect if this network only deterred Hitler? What of a European scene stabilized around armed camps? Would a Europe divided among democrats, fascists, and communists, and possessing jet aircraft, nuclear weapons, and ballistic missiles, be more inviting than that one that emerged after 1945? By contrast, appeasement, the redressing of grievances by

negotiation, was consistent with British traditions, military and political realities, and created the circumstances in which war was a clear and acceptable alternative. Anyone wishing to place understanding over sympathy should recognize that it was a policy right for Britain.

—ROBERT MCJIMSEY, COLORADO COLLEGE

Viewpoint:
No, appeasement of the Axis powers led directly to World War II, and it was unnecessary because Germany did not yet have the military strength to oppose France and England.

Appeasement of the Axis powers in the 1930s was a failed policy and perhaps hastened World War II, a conflict it was meant to avoid. The term *appeasement* was never actually defined clearly in the 1930s and may have meant subtly different things to the politicians who either espoused or criticized it at the time. The term is now generally conceded to mean, however, the policy of attempting to accommodate and conciliate the dictators in Germany and Italy for their perceived grievances stemming from the treatment their countries received under the Versailles Treaty (1919).

Following World War I, the League of Nations was established to ensure peace in the world. The League's ability to keep the peace was, however, damaged from the start by the United States, the world's strongest democracy, which turned isolationist and refused to join the League, while Great Britain refocused its attention on its empire and commonwealth. That left a severely weakened France the dominant power in postwar Europe. France increasingly demonstrated its lack of faith in the Covenant of the League as a guarantee of its survival, and turned its attention to building up a new collection of allies along Germany's eastern borders—to simultaneously surround the Germans and isolate the Soviet Union. As long as Germany remained economically and militarily weak this policy allowed France to pose as the dominant Continental diplomatic power. When Germany began to recoup its power and, along with Fascist Italy, defied the League in the 1930s, France's inability to contain a resurgent Germany, as well as its own military and internal political divisions and weaknesses, became evident.

Britain by late 1931 was ruled by a coalition "National Government,"—consisting of the Conservatives, and parts of the Liberal and Labour parties—formed to deal with the world financial crisis. It was maintained right up through the start of World War II in 1939 for the various political reasons of its constituents, even after the Conservatives won the general election in the autumn of 1931, winning a massive 479 out of 615 seats in the House of Commons. Almost from the beginning, the government under Ramsey MacDonald and then Stanley Baldwin pursued a foreign policy of appeasement. At the time, few in Britain viewed appeasement as a sign of weakness. Winston Churchill, then out of government and relegated to the Conservative back benches in the House of Commons, was a notable exception.

It was, at least early on, not at all necessary to appease Adolf Hitler. A more forceful stance would have made him back down. The will on the part of Britons generally—and their leading politicians especially—was, however, totally lacking. By 1931 Britain's vengeful mood of 1919 had shifted to one of guilt for the excesses done to punish Germany. That sentiment, coupled with a loathing and fear of a repeat of the "Butcher's Bill" of World War I, drove British politicians to the mistaken belief that "righting" the wrongs of Versailles would ameliorate the situation and restore calm. Perhaps if appeasement had been tried from the beginning with the fledgling Weimar Republic, as was the case with Germany and the Marshall Plan (1948) after World War II, it might have succeeded. To believe that such a policy would assuage dictators, however, let alone dictators of a sort that Hitler and Benito Mussolini proved to be, was sheer folly.

During his first two years in power Hitler paid lip service to peace while hurriedly commencing to rearm Germany. In March 1935 he felt strong enough to abrogate the disarmament clauses of the Versailles treaty. In 1936 he reoccupied the Rhineland in defiance of the treaties of Versailles and Locarno (1925). The Germans could not as yet have resisted any British and French military response, but Britain did nothing and France, which mobilized 150,000 troops behind the Maginot Line, would do nothing more without British support. Hitler later confessed that if the French army had advanced into the Rhineland in response to his actions, the Germans would have had to withdraw as they were incapable of mounting real resistance. Where armed defiance, or even a short if bloody riposte, would have set him back on his heels and might have even led at that early date to his political downfall, the feeble reaction only encouraged Hitler. Instead, shortly afterward Germany and Italy formed the Rome-Berlin Axis, and in 1937 Italy followed Germany and withdrew from the League of Nations.

Neville Chamberlain and Adolf Hitler at the Munich Conference in 1938

(World Wide Press)

When Hitler reoccupied the Rhineland, he announced he had no other territorial demands. He was lying. By early 1938 both the German army and the *Luftwaffe* (Air Force) were becoming powerful forces. Hitler then felt strong enough to try uniting all German-speaking peoples under one *Reich* (Empire) and the first step was to annex Austria in the *Anschluss* (Union) in March 1938. When the *Wehrmacht* (German Army) occupied the country, the Western democratic powers did not intervene to help the Austrians. Indeed, the British ambassador to Berlin inferred that Britain would permit it if it were done peaceably!

Building on this success, Hitler turned to the annexation of the Sudetenland, the western border of Czechoslovakia, populated mainly by Germans and not coincidentally the site of the well-fortified Czech border defenses. Hitler reminded British prime minister Neville Chamberlain that the Versailles principle of self-determination should apply equally to the Sudeten Germans. Moreover, Hitler falsely charged the Czechs with mistreatment of the German minority. Britain and France consistently ignored both the Czech government's record and its statesmen during the crisis, the last major international issue decided only by the European powers. On 29 September 1938, Chamberlain flew to Munich, Germany, to meet with Hitler, Mussolini, and French prime minister Edouard Daladier. Chamberlain persuaded Daladier that sacrificing Czechoslovakia would save the peace of Europe, and so the French abandoned their ally to its fate. All of Hitler's demands were accepted and Chamberlain returned to London infamously proclaiming he had secured "peace in our time." Millions of fear-crazed Europeans thought war was averted. The more insightful awaited the next crisis. Churchill solemnly warned his fellow countrymen not to "suppose that this is the end. This is only the beginning of the reckoning."

Deprived of its military defenses, the rump of the Czech State soon fell foul of Hitler. In March 1939 German troops crossed the Czech border and occupied Bohemia/Moravia. Slovakia was made an "independent" client state. In April, Italy occupied Albania, and the two dictators then forged a military alliance, the "Pact of Steel." With the destruction of Czechoslovakia, however, the Western powers could no longer ignore the fact that Hitler's promises were worthless or that his territorial ambitions were probably limitless. Desperately, Britain and France began to prepare for military resistance. They sought negotiations with the Soviet Union, whose earlier efforts to form an anti-Axis coalition they had rebuffed. The French government also initiated emergency powers to speed measures for national defense. In Britain, the appeasement policy was ended and for the first time in its history Parliament authorized a peacetime draft, but these maneuvers were too late.

Apologists for Chamberlain's actions have argued that appeasement made good sense in principle but was just a bad choice for dealing with Germany, and Chamberlain could not have been expected to know it. Yet, it was Chamberlain's job as prime minister to have known better. He was wholly unsuited by his political career for the post of prime minister in the turbulent late 1930s. A businessman, Chamberlain had risen through the Conservative Party apparatus as Lord Mayor of Birmingham in 1915, Director of National Service in 1916, and was elected to Parliament in 1918. In 1923 he joined the government as Chancellor of the Exchequer (Treasury Secretary) and then became Minister of Health in 1924. In 1930 he assumed the role of Conservative Party Chairman, a powerful post in which he applied his business skills to rebuilding the party infrastructure. Following his reelection to Parliament in 1931 he was again appointed Chancellor of the Exchequer in the new national government, a post at which he was quite successful. In his tenure at Party Central Office, however, he had in essence created his own "machine." For example, many of the men who stood in the 1935 general election personally knew him and as a result were not unsympathetic to his views. Arguably, this ultimately secured for him in 1937 the top post as prime minister. Throughout his career Chamberlain sought to apply "business sense" and a spirit of compromise to his dealings. It should come as no surprise that he sought to do the same as prime minister. Unfortunately for Britain and Europe, he sought to do this with Hitler, foolishly believing he could be reasonable and fair-minded. Chamberlain took over the direction of foreign policy in a vain attempt to explore every means to reach an accommodation with the Axis dictators, and often did so while at odds with his own Foreign Office and Defense chiefs. Indeed, he managed to foment a crisis with his foreign secretary, Anthony Eden, over moving too fast to secure a deal with Mussolini at the time of the Anschluss, and the result was Eden's resignation in February 1938.

Chamberlain should have known he had to rely on three things for any war with Germany: Soviet military intervention, renewed British military strength, and French support. He knew from his defense attachés, however, that Russian military force was suspect as early as 1936. That is, at the time of the reoccupation of the Rhineland, and before Stalin's purges of the military, the Soviets had not the capacity to launch successful offensive operations across Poland or through Romania to aid the Czechs or anyone else against Germany. Soviet marshal Mikhail Tukhachevsky had admitted this privately to the U.S. ambassador in Moscow. Chamberlain could do little about the Soviets, but he did have the power to affect the other two variables. He was loath as late as the end of 1937, however, to contemplate either greatly increased military spending, except on the air force, or closer military collaboration with France. Thus Chamberlain was personally responsible for several of the decisions that boxed him into appeasing rather than standing up to the dictators.

Indeed, appeasement was a denial of reality and was well in keeping with British thinking in the interwar period. Just after World War I the cabinet had imposed on the defense staff the so-called Ten Year Rule that stated "that at any given date there will be no major war for ten years." This assumption was not dangerous in 1918, and basing defense spending upon it immediately after the war was not imprudent. This premise was maintained for more than a decade and defense spending suffered accordingly. Not until 1932 did the cabinet direct the chiefs of staff to dispense with the assumption. Only in October 1933 did the Chiefs submit their first annual review that was not based upon it. By this measure, and without massive exertions at a time of worldwide economic dislocation, Britain could not expect to be prepared to fight in a major war before 1939 and perhaps not even then.

Understanding this constraint on British military policy, some have argued that appeasement was pursued because Britain needed to rearm. In other words, Chamberlain was merely buying time for British rearmament. Aside from the threat from then nonexistent German submarines that the Royal Navy had later to take into serious consideration, however, the first real threat Germany posed was that of an aerial bombardment of British cities. Following the theories of the Italian air force strategist Emilio Douhet, these would be on a grand scale, probably with poison gas bombs, as depicted graphically in the prewar movie *The Shape of Things to Come* (1938), starring Raymond Massey. In the early 1930s no nation possessed fighters capable of matching the speed or range of the bombers of the day. At the time the British had tried a policy of détente with the Germans, backed by an offensive bomber force of the type Douhet

envisioned. Indeed, Prime Minister Stanley Baldwin had admitted in March 1933 that he was frightened of the thought of German aerial bombardment.

The Royal Air Force, however, was never really at the mercy of the Luftwaffe in 1933, 1936, 1938, or for that matter in 1939. First of all, Germany never possessed the long-range bombers that such a strategy entailed to counter the British because initially they had no air force to speak of as a result of the Versailles treaty. When they did commence development, Hitler required the Luftwaffe to eschew any such theory as Douhet's in favor of developing medium and short-range bombers, including dive bombers (such as the famous Ju-87 *Stuka*), to provide direct support to the army's mobile forces over the battlefield. As such, only after overrunning Belgium and France in 1940 and moving the force of medium bombers practically to the English Channel did Germany possess the means to mount a serious bomber attack on Britain. In contrast, Britain possessed the kind of bombers, albeit in small numbers, to reach Germany from its own airfields. Secondly, in 1936 Britain adopted a new strategy of defense based on a fighter air force. This defense was possible as Britain began the development of two fighters, Spitfire and Hurricane, that possessed the speed and altitude to overmatch any German bombers, in service or on the drawing board. Practically simultaneously, Britain developed radar, which was a massive breakthrough for the defender, as it meant smaller numbers of fighters could now protect any number of cities by being vectored onto an approaching bomber force. Thus, when Britain in 1936 failed to stand up to Hitler's reoccupation of the Rhineland there was no practical threat of German aerial attack upon it. Again in 1938 the threat was far less than feared, and Britain now possessed in limited numbers (the first two Hurricane squadrons and first radar stations were already fielded) the means to defeat that threat anyway.

Hitler believed the West was too weak morally to stand up to Germany. He expected to win much of his program through bluff and bluster with only a meager show of force. Thus a clear example of German weakness was shown when he instructed his generals to be prepared to withdraw if it looked as if France would react militarily over the Rhineland. Indeed, the one time the British and French stood up to a dictator clearly demonstrated how such a policy could succeed. Shortly before Chamberlain forced Eden's resignation, Eden had succeeded at the Nyon Conference in late summer of 1937 in gaining British and French accession to naval action in the Mediterranean against "pirate" (Italian) submarines preying on British, French, and Russian merchant ships bound for Republican Spain. Faced with the threat, the submarines stopped their attacks. Had such forceful action been taken against Hitler in 1936 in the Rhineland, or even over Anschluss, the Czech crisis might well never have materialized. War might finally have come anyway, perhaps in 1942, and unless Hitler was eliminated it was probably inevitable. As Churchill foresaw, however, with a policy of appeasement, it came sooner than later.

–DUANE C. YOUNG, DE MONTFORT UNIVERSITY

References

R. J. Q. Adams, *British Politics and Foreign Policy in the Age of Appeasement, 1935–39* (Basingstoke, U.K.: Macmillan, 1992);

Peter Bell, *Chamberlain, Germany and Japan, 1933–4* (Houndmills, Basingstoke & Hampshire, U.K.: Macmillan, 1996; New York: St. Martin's Press, 1996);

John Charmley, *Chamberlain and the Lost Peace* (London: Hodder & Stoughton, 1989);

Winston S. Churchill, *Blood, Sweat, and Tears* (New York: Putnam, 1941);

Churchill, *The Gathering Storm* (London: Cassell, 1948);

R. H. Haigh and P. W. Turner, *British Politics and Society 1918-1938: The Effect on Appeasement* (Sheffield, U.K.: Sheffield City Polytechnic, Department of Political Studies, 1979);

Donald N. Lammers, *Explaining Munich: The Search for Motive in British Policy* (Stanford, Cal.: The Hoover Institute on War, Revolution and Peace, Stanford University, 1966);

Keith Middlemas, *The Strategy of Appeasement: The British Government and Germany, 1937-39* (Chicago: Quadrangle, 1972);

R. A. C. Parker, *Chamberlain and Appeasement: British Policy and the Coming of the Second World War* (Houndmills, Basingstoke & Hampshire, U.K.: Macmillan, 1993; New York: St. Martin's Press, 1993);

P. A. Reynolds, *British Foreign Policy in the Inter-War Years* (London & New York: Longmans, Green, 1954);

William R. Rock, *Appeasement on Trial: British Foreign Policy and its Crisis, 1938-1939* (Hamden, Conn.: Archon, 1966);

R. W. Seton-Watson, *Britain and the Dictators: A Survey of Post-War British Policy* (Cambridge: Cambridge University Press, 1938; New York: Macmillan, 1938);

Neville Thompson, *The Anti-Appeasers: Conservative Opposition to Appeasement in the 30s* (Oxford: Clarendon Press, 1971);

Wesley Wark, "Appeasement Revisited," *International History Review,* 17 (1995): 545–562;

Donald Cameron Watt, *How War Came: The Immediate Origins of the Second World War, 1938-1939* (London: Heinemann; New York: Pantheon, 1989);

Robert J. Young, *France and the Origins of the Second World War* (Houndmills, Basingstoke, U.K.: Macmillan, 1996; New York: St. Martin's Press, 1996).

APPEASEMENT

BLITZKRIEG

Was Blitzkrieg a successful strategy?

Viewpoint: Yes, Blitzkrieg worked so well that armies have used it successfully throughout the second half of the twentieth century.

Viewpoint: No, the early successes of Blitzkrieg during World War II were less the result of German martial acumen than of their opponents' incompetence or unpreparedness.

Blitzkrieg (Lightning War) is the conventional name for a body of doctrine, allegedly developed in Germany after World War I, based on using vehicles powered by the internal combustion engine and radio communications to prevent the repetition of the trench deadlock of 1914–1918. Large formations moving on tracks and wheels—supported from the air and controlled by radio—were projected as first rupturing the front, then so disorganizing the rear that countermeasures became counterproductive. Tested against Poland in 1939, Blitzkrieg crushed the armies of western Europe in the summer of 1940, then a year later took the *Wehrmacht* (German Army) to the gates of Moscow.

In fact, the term "Blitzkrieg" was never part of the title of a German official manual or handbook. It was widely used in the Wehrmacht—but regarded as a loan word, borrowed from the English and Americans. Between the world wars, tanks, trucks, and aircraft were understood in Germany not as components of a military revolution, but as multipliers facilitating traditional German operational objectives: outflanking an enemy, threatening his lines of communication, forcing him to fight on unfavorable terms, and as quickly as possible.

What the Germans were good at was exploiting opportunities—and in that context they benefited significantly from "obliging enemies" who made of their own volition not merely mistakes but the kind of mistakes suiting German purposes. It was not, for example, German doctrine that led France to send a half-dozen of its best mobile divisions lunging into Holland in June 1940. Nor did German doctrine prevent the French divisions holding the Sedan sector in the winter of 1939–1940 from improving the state of their training and positions. What its victims called "lightning war" was in fact good, old-fashioned professionalism. It was easier—and perhaps more comfortable—for the Wehrmacht's opponents to mistake the trappings for the essence. Being victimized by a paradigm shift may be embarrassing. It is, however, less embarrassing than being outgeneraled and outfought.

Viewpoint:
Yes, Blitzkrieg worked so well that armies have used it successfully throughout the second half of the twentieth century.

No one can be sure of the origins of the term *Blitzkrieg* (Lightning War). It appeared on a few occasions in German professional literature in the late 1930s in the context of describing a "short war" strategy. The term was popularized by British newspapers in 1939 to describe the German attack upon Poland—a rapid, motorized advance combining the shock effect of air strikes with the power and speed of massed armored formations that ran roughshod over an army with a World War I style of warfare. The Germans soon picked up the word; appreciated it for its image of speed, fire, and destruction. German propagandists, along with Western journalists, began to use the term routinely in 1940 to describe the German style of warfare without any attempt to ascribe a clear meaning to the term. In short order, Blitzkrieg became one of the most famous terms to come out of World War II and it remains in common use—still without an agreed-upon meaning.

Along with confusion about the meaning of the word, many myths grew up about blitzkrieg in the early days of World War II. Indeed, some of the myths have taken hold so strongly that they persist in military and popular literature. One of the first great blitzkrieg myths originated in 1940 when the defeat of the French Army was attributed to the superiority of German armored forces. The campaign was one of the most dramatic and decisive victories in the history of modern warfare; Western journalists and military leaders sought an explanation. The immediate analysis of the blitzkrieg was that the French Army, which had put its resources into the Maginot Line, was simply overwhelmed by the masses of German tanks that poured through Northern France. It was an explanation that satisfied the admirers of France—who could then blame the failure of the French Army on German numerical superiority. It also supported the military critics of France in Britain and America who demanded armored divisions for their armies in order to match the German threat.

In fact, the British and French armies in 1940 had as many armored and motorized divisions as the Germans, and the French possessed more and better tanks than their enemy. Later analysis of the 1940 campaign showed that the British and French were not defeated by German superiority in numbers or quality of equipment

but rather by superior German leadership, training, and doctrine.

Perhaps the greatest myth about blitzkrieg is that it represented the essence of the grand strategy of the Third Reich. From 1939 to 1941 it appeared that Germany had chosen each moment carefully—striking quickly and decisively at weak and unprepared countries before they could properly organize, equip, and defend themselves. First Poland, then Denmark and Norway, and finally France and the Low Countries collapsed with a speed that was astounding to the generation that had seen the bloodbath of World War I and remembered the months-long campaigns to occupy a few square miles of ground on the Western Front. All of the German casualties from the early victories of 1939 to 1940 did not add up to the typical losses of one World War I campaign. Only in the air battle over Britain did the Germans fail in their offensive onslaught.

The Germans repeated their success in 1941. The *Wehrmacht* (German Army) quickly overran Greece and Yugoslavia; the Germans overcame British forces on Crete by the new tactic of airborne assault; and Erwin Rommel's Afrika Corps drove British forces out of Libya. The blitzkrieg strategy hit full stride when Adolf Hitler invaded Russia in June 1941. Germany might seemed unstoppable as whole Russian armies were surrounded and forced to surrender. British and American military leaders expected Russia to collapse in six weeks. Then, seemingly by a miracle, the Russians found the strength to stop the Germans at Leningrad and Moscow and to hold off collapse as winter arrived. With the failure to overcome Russia in 1941 and America's entry into the war, German blitzkrieg strategy halted and the nature of the war changed into one of grinding attrition on every front. Germany had not prepared for such a war and was eventually overcome by Allied superiority of men and matériel.

During World War II it seemed plausible that Hitler and the Wehrmacht had developed a strategy of lightning war, in which the first step was the rapid conquest of the European heartland, with a plan to later strike out toward the Middle East and America in a program of world conquest. Hitler and his propagandists fueled such perceptions by telling the German people in 1939–1941 that the war was progressing according to Hitler's grand plan and that every step had been the product of the Führer's genius. Even the most perceptive of the Allied leaders, Winston Churchill, credited the German blitzkrieg of Norway in April–May 1940 to careful long-term planning and preparation.

One view of blitzkrieg is that Hitler and the Nazi leadership insisted upon a short war

BLITZKRIEG

strategy in order to minimize the disruption of the German economy. One of the great lessons of World War I was the vulnerability of civilian morale when Germany had been subjected to years of rationing and hardship. In 1918 civilian morale had collapsed and, with it, the war effort. Thus, Hitler planned to keep the campaigns short in order to avoid total militarization of the economy and to keep up production of consumer goods. This appeared to work. When the war bogged down in Russia in 1941, however, the German economy had been only partially mobilized for war and was unable to catch up with the Allied nations in producing the ships, planes, tanks, and trucks required for a long war.

The reality of the Nazis' so-called blitzkrieg strategy is much more mundane. If grand strategy consists of a plan and process in which national objectives are set and the means of attaining them are identified and outlined, then Nazi Germany can be said to have had no grand strategy worthy of the name. Before the war, apart from plans to fight obvious enemies such as the Poles, Czechs, and French, the General Staff and senior leaders of the Wehrmacht were given little strategic or political guidance by Hitler. He was the heart and soul of Nazi ideology, and Germany's strategic vision flowed directly from him to the armed forces. Hitler's strategic worldview included a variety of vague geopolitical concepts and beliefs about German racial dominance. Hitler's goals included eliminating Jewish influence from Europe (later eliminating the Jews themselves), overthrowing Bolshevism, placing Germans as masters over Slavic lands, creating a European federation controlled by Germany, and even expanding German influence to the Americas and to Germany's former colonies.

Hitler's worldview, however, was scarcely something that could be translated into any coherent strategic guidance for the government and armed forces. Indeed, Hitler's racially oriented outlook caused Germany to make some disastrous strategic mistakes even before the start of the war. For example, through the 1930s Hitler believed that Britain would become Germany's natural ally because of the racial affinity of the Germans and British. Hitler ignored the obvious facts that Britain would never accept German domination of Europe and that the British were repelled by Nazi ideology. Hitler was so optimistic about gaining an alliance with Britain that he ignored British reactions to German rearmament and the reoccupation of the Rhineland. It was only in April 1938 that Hitler directed the General Staff to include Britain on the list of possible enemies in case of war. Thus, the German armed forces had less than one and a half years to collect intelligence and develop plans for fighting one of the leading world powers. This lack of intelligence and prior planning greatly hindered the Germans when it came to actually executing an aerial offensive against Britain in 1940.

Despite Churchill's description of the German invasion of Denmark and Norway in 1940 as a carefully planned operation, the German attack upon Scandinavia was actually thrown together in short order to secure the strategically vital ore port of Narvik in Norway before the British could occupy it. Although Hitler had some grand dreams of incorporating the Nordic nations as partners in the Third Reich, the Wehrmacht only started planning for a possible move into Scandinavia in December 1939. The Germans decided to move on Norway only in February 1940 when a British destroyer entered Norwegian waters to apprehend the German supply ship *Altmark* and free British prisoners on that ship. With the strategic requirement that a campaign in the north had to be concluded before the planned attack upon France in May, the Wehrmacht High Command had only a few

weeks, with limited intelligence and little prior planning, to put together a major operation to seize Norway. The invasion of Denmark was included in the plan because the Germans needed the airfields in northern Denmark to stage Luftwaffe aircraft into Norway. Meanwhile, the Wehrmacht's grand plan for the invasion of France and the Low Countries was decided upon only a few weeks before the actual attack on 10 May 1940.

Other notable blitzkrieg operations were characteristic of a spirit of improvisation and opportunism rather than any long-term strategic vision. Hitler had some vague ambitions in the Mideast before the war, but the Germans found themselves invading Greece and Yugoslavia in April 1941 because Germany's ally, Italy, was losing to the Greeks and needed German support. The German troop commitment to North Africa originated with no strategic objective other than keeping the Italians from folding in that theater. Finally came the invasion of Russia, the grandest blitzkrieg operation of them all. Hitler, without consulting his generals or senior Nazi leaders, simply decided that the time was right to attack Russia. Until 1941, German soldiers, tactics, and air units had proven to be notably superior to their opponents on the battlefield. In 1941 the German strategy for Russia consisted of throwing large armies and air forces into Russia in the expectation that Russian forces would be defeated in a few weeks and Germany could proceed to occupy and exploit territory all the way to the Urals. The Wehrmacht had little intelligence on the Russian army; the logistical planning and preparation for the grand offensive was appallingly inept. There was no coherent plan on how Russia would be occupied, what political arrangements would follow the invasion, or what the Germans might do if the Soviet government simply retreated to the Urals and continued fighting. Hitler, the Nazi leadership, and the military high command were simply infected with the idea that Hitler's vision would not fail and that the Führer would know what to do when the time came. Relying on superior soldiers and tactics worked well as a strategy for a few weeks, but when Moscow did not fall in October and the Germans were stopped by the weather, poor logistics, and fresh Russian forces, there was no strategy left—only the option to keep fighting. From that point of the war on, German strategy consisted of little more than trying to counter the increasingly powerful offensives by the Russians and Western Allies.

The idea that the Germans adopted a blitzkrieg strategy in order to reduce the required sacrifices of the population has been refuted by recent examinations of the war economy of the Third Reich. R. J. Overy in *War and Economy in the Third Reich* (1994) has argued convincingly that, rather than holding back the military share of the economy prior to 1941, the Germans had moved full bore into a war economy by 1939. The relatively low production rates of airplanes and tanks that plagued the Wehrmacht in the early stages of the war were not intentionally planned as part of a blitzkrieg economy but were the result of a lack of competent and coherent direction in the German armaments industry. The directors of the Nazi economy at the start of the war—Hermann Göring, as leader of the four-year plan, or Ernst Udet, chief of aircraft production—were simply not competent war planners or economic directors. German armaments production and efficiency improved dramatically after 1941, not because of any decision to move from a blitzkrieg economy to a full war economy, but rather because of the efforts of the new armaments minister Albert Speer and others who corrected some of the appalling inefficiencies of the Nazi economic system.

If blitzkrieg cannot be described as a grand strategy, then what was it? It was essentially an operational/tactical doctrine that emphasized maneuver warfare with combined arms. The German way of war in 1939 evolved out of the World War I experience. In the 1920s the commander of the German Army, Colonel General Hans von Seeckt, led the General Staff in analyzing the lessons of world war and concluded that while firepower had been the predominant element from 1914 to 1918, in future wars maneuver would be the most important element. In the 1920s and 1930s, German Army doctrine emphasized maneuver warfare, while the Allied victors of 1918 based their doctrine on the notion that firepower would remain the dominant element of warfare.

The concept of maneuver warfare fit the German tradition. The wars of 1866 and 1870 had been won by outmaneuvering the enemy, surrounding his forces, and annihilating his armies. The central concept of German war fighting prior to World War I was the Schlieffen Plan, a strategy for the envelopment and destruction of the French Army. On the Eastern front in World War I, the Germans had conducted maneuver campaigns that succeeded in destroying whole Russian armies. Maneuver warfare emphasized speed, a fluid style of tactics, and decentralized decision making. These things had long been emphasized in German officer education. It required no grand leap to apply the potential of the internal combustion engine to the concepts of

Helmuth Karl Bernhard Moltke and Alfred von Schlieffen. The major innovation of the interwar period was to emphasize the effective employment of all arms (infantry, motorized troops, artillery, flak, tanks, and so on) and coordination of air and ground forces. For twenty years the German Army emphasized maneuver warfare and trained with combined arms for joint air-ground operations while the British, French, and American armies remained stuck in the 1918 paradigm of the slow offensive supported by massive artillery firepower.

Germany's primary opponents from 1939 to 1941—France, Britain, and Russia—had large, modern, well-equipped armies and air forces. Professional soldiers of those countries, however, were generally unprepared to fight a war of maneuver. Superior doctrine, training and leadership gave the Germans victory in the first years of the war. Yet, maneuver warfare was not a purely Germanic concept. The Allied powers copied German tactics to create armies of their own that could apply maneuver warfare against the Wehrmacht. The Allied offensive across France in July–August 1944 or the Russian 1944 summer offensive can be described as blitzkrieg just as much as the German campaign of 1940. Maneuver warfare, as developed by the Germans is still the basis for conventional tactics and operations in many successful armies from the Israelis in 1956 and 1967 and the American-led coalition in the Persian Gulf in 1991.

–JAMES S. CORUM, U.S. AIR FORCE SCHOOL
OF ADVANCED AIRPOWER STUDIES

Viewpoint:
No, the early successes of Blitzkrieg during World War II were less the result of German martial acumen than of their opponents' incompetence or unpreparedness.

On 1 September 1939, Germany attacked Poland. Within twenty days Poland's capital city, Warsaw, surrendered. In the early spring of 1940, Germany attacked and won another quick victory against Norway. While the western allies of Great Britain and France prepared their forces for a replay of World War I, German leaders conducted after-action reviews of their own operations. In adjusting their plans and shifting forces they refined the methods of what was becoming known to the world as *Blitzkrieg* (lightning war)

The attack for which the world waited started on 10 May 1940. Along the Franco-German border the French waited in their massive prepared positions, collectively known as the Maginot Line. Attacking north of this line, into the Netherlands and through the Ardennes forest of Belgium, the Germans hoped to drive a wedge between the forces of France and Britain. To accomplish this goal they had concentrated all ten of their Panzer divisions along a single axis.

Finding themselves increasingly isolated from the rest of the Allies, the Dutch surrendered after only five days. Belgium lasted slightly longer; they maintained their defenses until 28 May. The worst would fall on France. Three days after beginning their attack German forces were working to cross the Meuse river. Within six days elements of Germany's armored component had broken free and were driving hard for the coast. On the tenth day the German army arrived on the coast of the English Channel. It was a tenuous position, but apparently the chaos prevalent in the Allied rear areas prevented them from realizing this and making a coherent counter. The main armies of England and France were separated.

After strengthening their positions, reorganizing, and replenishing, the Germans continued their attacks. Pressing the British in the north, they forced them to abandon France and evacuate from Dunkirk (28 May to 4 June 1940). The Germans subsequently enveloped the Maginot Line from the rear. France ultimately surrendered. The Germans had defeated what many considered the greatest land power in Europe in little more than six weeks.

These German successes in the first half of World War II are often ascribed to their ability to wage Blitzkrieg upon their enemies. The problem is that ever since the Germans accomplished their rapid victories over the Polish, Norwegians, Dutch, Belgians, French and others, nobody has quite been able to agree on why they won. Some focus upon the idea that the Germans perfected a new method of warfare; others contend that their actions constituted a "Revolution in Military Affairs." Over time the term used to describe the German method of warfare has mutated.

The short version of the history of the idea of blitzkrieg might run something like this: After World War I, Germany and the Allies lay exhausted from the struggle. The Allies had, in the closing years of the war, developed a partial technological solution to the stalemate of the Western Front in the tank, but it had never really come into its own before the armistice. In the same time frame the Germans opted for a doctrinal solution. They focused upon increased small-unit leadership, initiative, and infiltration tactics. Following the war the British, wartime leaders in the development of armor, conducted experimentation in the concept of armored warfare. Lack of funds and the traditional preference of the British for naval over land forces saw these experiments wither on the vine. British military theorists, notably J. F. C. Fuller and B. H. Liddell Hart, developed ideas of mobile warfare centered upon the technology of the tank and the internal combustion engine. By the 1930s, however, all that remained were their theories. The Germans picked up where the British left off. They experimented and created the material to support the concepts. When theory and material were tied together and unleashed against the rest of Europe beginning in 1939 the result became known to the world as blitzkrieg.

The first recorders and interpreters of the German method of "lightning war" were correspondents. Sportswriter turned military analyst S. L. A. Marshall was probably the first widely read author on the subject. His book, titled naturally enough *Blitzkrieg: Its History, Strategy, Economics and the Challenge to America* (1940), appeared within months of the Fall of France in 1940. In that book, as well as his follow-on work, *War on Wheels* (1943), Marshall identified the German victories as the cumulative result of a decision to mechanize and to develop the integrated use of motorized power which confused and rattled the opponents. For all intents and purposes this became the popular starting point for later analysis of Blitzkrieg.

What was Blitzkrieg? Was it merely a descriptive term used to cover the events as they happened, or was it a deliberate doctrinal creation of the German General Staff developed to avoid the pain of a long, drawn-out battle in which the limited material resources of Germany would inevitably be exhausted? Did the German victories against the Allies stem from their own prowess, or were they a function of the material and doctrinal unreadiness of their opponents? In short, did the Germans win because they were that good, or because their opponents were that bad?

In the period immediately following the outbreak of the war in Europe the Germans were seen as supermen with superweapons. While many people marveled at the speed with which they rolled over Poland, it was not until the blitz across France that near panic appeared in the United States. Reports coming from France claimed that massive German armored formations were responsible for the crushing defeat of the French army and the humiliating evacuation required of the British at Dunkirk (28 May to 4 June 1940). Marshall's *Blitzkrieg*, while slightly more balanced than the initial wire reports, still gave the Germans great credit.

LIGHTNING WAR

WITH THE GERMAN ARMIES IN POLAND, September 11—Having hurled against Poland their mighty military machine, the Germans are today crushing Poland like a soft-boiled egg.

After having broken through the shell of Polish border defenses, the Germans found inside, in comparison with their own forces, little more than a soft yolk, and they have penetrated that in many directions without really determined general resistance by the Polish Army.

That is the explanation of the apparent Polish military collapse in so short a time as it was gathered on a tour of the Polish battlefields . . . in the wake of the German army, and sometimes, in the backwash of a day's battle while scattered Polish troops and snipers were still taking potshots at motor vehicles on the theory that they must be German. . . .

Even a casual glance at the battlefields, snarled by trenches, barbed-wire entanglements, shell holes, blown-up roads and bridges and shelled and gutted towns, indicates that the Poles made determined resistance at the border. But even these border defenses seem weak, and beyond them there is nothing. . . .

Again God has been with the bigger battalions, for the beautiful, dry weather, while converting Polish roads into choking dust clouds on the passage of motor vehicles, has kept them from turning into mud as would be normal at this time of year; this has permitted the German motorized divisions to display the speed they have.

But the Germans have proceeded not only with might and speed, but with method, and this bids fair to be the first war to be decided not by infantry, "the queen of all arms," but by fast motorized divisions and, especially, by the air force.

The first effort of the Germans was concentrated on defeating the hostile air fleet, which they did not so much by air battle but by consistent bombing of airfields and destruction of the enemy's ground organization. Having accomplished this, they had obtained domination of the air, which in turn enabled them, first to move their own vast transports ahead without danger from the air and, second, to bomb the Poles' communications to smithereens, thereby reducing their mobility to a minimum. . . .

With control of the air, the Germans moved forward not infantry but their tanks, armored cars and motorized artillery, which smashed any Polish resistance in the back. This is easy to understand when one has seen the methods of open warfare attempted by the Poles and an almost amateurish attempt at digging earthworks for machine-gun nests.

To German and neutral experts the Poles seem to have clung to eighteenth-century war methods, which, in view of modern firing volume and weight, are not only odd but also futile. This does not mean that the Poles have not put up a brave fight. They have, and the Germans themselves freely admit it.

As a purely military matter, the German army is the height of efficiency. It moves like clockwork, without hurry and apparently almost in a leisurely manner. Yet that army moves with inexorable exactitude. The roads into Poland are jammed but not choked with heavy vans and motor trucks carrying food and munitions, while the Poles have to depend mainly on their smashed railroads or on horse carts. Bombed bridges are soon passable for the Germans and they move forward quickly. Communications lines follow them almost automatically.

Poland may not be lost yet and may be even able to offer further resistance by withdrawing into the eastern swamp. But as long as the present disparity between the military resources and her will to fight exists she faces terrible odds.

Source: The New York Times, 11 September 1939.

BLITZKRIEG

Following American entrance into the war the popular image of the Germans was naturally downgraded. The enemy was well equipped, but according to propaganda they were now merely dogmatic, fanatical, and misguided humans who could be beaten. Following the war the German reputation, now separated from the Nazi ideology, began another climb. This resurrection of reputation was aided in no small part by a man who could not easily be considered unbiased. British military theorist B. H. Liddell Hart was originally one of the most vocal advocates of the theories of armored warfare. Unfortunately for his reputation, in the period immediately preceding World War II, his views had shifted. Observing the dismal results of armored usage in the Spanish Civil War, and the apparently formidable fortifications on the Franco-German border, Liddell Hart downplayed the potential of the tank in his published analyses. Thus, when the Germans attacked and won their major victories at the outset of the war, Liddell Hart's reputation suffered accordingly.

After World War II, Liddell Hart conducted a series of interviews with former German leaders. Their "revelations" appeared in the book *The Other Side of the Hill: Germany's Generals, Their Rise and Fall, With Their Own Account of Military Events, 1939–1945* (1948, published in the United States as *The German Generals Talk*). In it the generals revealed that they actually owed much of their success to an external source, which, surprising nobody, was the early "visionary" writings of Liddell Hart. Despite this obvious conflict of interest this improved reputation of German armor remained the general interpretation for some time to come. In American historical circles interest waned somewhat as events elsewhere attracted attention.

The United States entered a period of limited wars in Asia across terrain in which "lighting war" was not only generally unfeasible, it was inappropriate. First Korea and then Vietnam focused the attention of the military and many military historians alike. As they shifted their attention away from the inter-German border and toward problems of limited wars, so too did many military historians find interests in other times. This had an inadvertent effect on the quality of historic interpretation and analysis about the events of 1939 to 1941, the heyday of the Blitz.

This is partially because of a phenomena almost unique to military history. Unlike many other fields of the social sciences, military history is intensely studied not only by academicians but also by the practitioners. The idea that the Germans perfected a form of lightning war that might serve as a model for modern warfare played no small part in this ebb and flow of interest. Just as political historians around the world tie themselves to their various national departments of state, and as gender historians find their fortunes tied to the political actions of various women's movements, so too do military historians find that their attentions are sometimes directed by present-day events. Thus, when the U.S. Army looks for a way to "fight outnumbered and win," it seeks lessons from history. The sometimes unfortunate result is that the attention thus focused is not always entirely unbiased.

It was not until the United States started to withdraw from Southeast Asia that the Army and historians once again turned toward Europe in any meaningful way. In the 1970s and early 1980s the threat of the Soviet Union and the Warsaw Pact loomed ever larger in the eyes of a military that was reaching its own nadir. In the wake of the withdrawal from Vietnam, the U.S. Army also had the painful transition to an "all-volunteer" force to negotiate. As the size of the armed forces decreased, the threat of the Soviets remained constant, and in some eyes increased. The Cold War remained, regardless of the Americans' true abilities. Poised just across the inter-German border were the forces of the Soviet Union and Warsaw Pact. This led American doctrinaires and analysts to search for a solution to the intractable question of how to fight outnumbered and win. The military turned to historical analysis and found the Germans all over again.

Suddenly there was new interest in understanding how the Germans fought in World War II. The Germans were now allies in the North Atlantic Treaty Organization (NATO). It was possible, in a way that it had not been before, to examine their military actions separated from the horrors of the political regime that had started World War II and committed the atrocities of the Holocaust. Military leaders and historians alike began to focus upon the Wehrmacht in a search for lessons that might prove useful to the situation NATO faced. In both the offense and the defense the Germans were apparently formidable—why had that been the case?

Initial assessments by men such as Trevor DuPuy and Martin Van Crevald suggested that the Germans were, at the tactical level, no less than 120 percent as effective as their Allied opponents throughout the war. These and other related examinations determined that German abilities derived from a distinct staff system, a tradition of decentralized control known as *auftragstaktik,* and coordinated combined-arms actions. These elements alone, however, did not explain the success of the Blitz in 1939–1940.

Some of the focus thus shifted away from the Germans and onto those they defeated, most notably the huge military forces of France. Military historian and U.S. Army officer Robert Doughty wrote one of the most often cited works, *The Seeds of Disaster: The Development of French Army Doctrine, 1919–1939* (1985), about the French military system between the two world wars. This one book, more than any other, struck chords among modern Army leaders frustrated with inadequate resources and the inconsistent military policy of a democratic republic. For many the parallels were frightening.

Prior to *The Seeds of Disaster* the German victories were ascribed to German prowess. The notable exception, though rarely read outside of academic circles, was French historian Marc Bloch's *L'Etrange defaite* (1940), translated and published as *Strange Defeat: A Statement of Evidence Written in 1940* (1949). Bloch, a founder of the French *Annales* school of history, served as an officer in World War I and was again mobilized in World War II. His firsthand account and analysis, written soon after the events from inside occupied France, is particularly damning of the French regular officer corps and the tempo of the French Army. If he had written a second more-detailed analysis, his would likely have been the last word on the issue. However, there would never be a follow-up. Bloch joined the French resistance, and in June 1944 the Germans caught this historian-turned-soldier-turned resistance leader and executed him.

For many people, without access to Bloch's "Statement of Evidence" the French role in their own defeat focused upon the military and political folly that had created the Maginot Line of fortifications. For years military pundits pointed toward the massive French fortifications as an example of poor military planning and a lack of foresight. Doughty and those that followed his lead turned that line of reasoning on its head. The French lost not so much because they relied upon the Maginot Line. They lost because of their doctrine. The irony here was that, within narrowly defined margins, the Maginot Line had worked as intended. It was French doctrine and force structure in their field army that lost the Battle of France—not necessarily German prowess against the odds.

Both England and France generally neglected their armed forces in the period immediately following World War I. Although Britain conducted some limited experiments with mechanization, these had fairly well fallen by the wayside by 1930. The French, digesting what they felt were the real lessons of the war, refined the doctrine that they had developed in the second half of that war. The concept that "artillery conquers, infantry occupies," dominated French military thought. As infantry-artillery coordination became paramount, the system of the "methodi-cal battle" developed ever-greater refinements. Warfare was less art and more science in the French vision. Bringing the weight of their massive artillery to bear upon the enemy became the overarching concern for French doctrine and force structure.

Within this doctrine there was little room for freewheeling armored forces moving across the battlefield. Armor, it was decided, was best utilized in direct support of the infantry. Accordingly, French force structure divided their tanks in penny-packets among their infantry formations. The French system was well thought out, consistent with the lessons of history (at least recent history), and matched the French military and political systems. Large numbers of highly trained regular-armored forces capable of independent action were not needed. The system of the methodical battle could be supported with a large, less-well-trained, conscript force.

This system of methodical battle was not equipped to deal with rapid penetrations. Faced with a deep attack by German armor, and an upset to their preplanned schedules, the French could not react with the same speed. Neither their forces nor their doctrine equipped them for operations at the tempo the Germans pushed upon them. Although in the final few months prior to the German attack the French created some limited independent armored forces, these were too little and too late to stem the tide.

The French also suffered from mechanical issues in their combat equipment. French tanks, although well designed for protection, were woefully inadequate for warfare involving maneuver against other tanks. Only one French tank in five had a radio, while all German tanks had them, and some of the best French tanks (as measured by armor and firepower) had room for only one man in the all-important turret position. While this use of men may not prove decisive against static or slow-moving infantry, in a tank versus tank engagement it was a fatal flaw.

Historians following Doughty's lead discovered other flaws in the French system and its application. As the Germans were attacking one portion of the French plan, known as the Breda Variant, the French diverted a significant portion of their limited mobile forces to support the Dutch and keep their twenty-eight divisions in the fight. The speed with which the Dutch collapsed, however, resulted in these French forces being diverted without any real effect.

As these problems and issues came to light, there was a reevaluation: for a new generation of historians and military thinkers alike, the torch of German military prowess dimmed. The collapse of the French, and like them the Polish, Dutch, Belgians, Norwegians, the British Expeditionary Force, and others was just as much the fault of the recipients' incompetence as it was of German abilities.

Adding to this trend some scholars began questioning the origins of the term Blitzkrieg. It appears that at no point prior to the war had the Germans used the term to specifically describe any one doctrine. The word *blitz* (lightning) was used, but generically so, to describe a "fast" anything. A fast attack at the tactical level could be described by several words modified by the prefix blitz. When the Germans used the specific term Blitzkrieg before World War II they were merely referring to a "fast war" and not some overarching operational and strategic concept. Even in the writings of some of Germany's most forward-looking theorists of the interwar period, the term is broadly used to explain a concept of wars that are completed rapidly, not some explicit method used to achieve that objective.

In the end, according to this line of reasoning, it was not the Germans that won so much as it was the French and British that lost. Blitzkrieg, it turned out, was not a deliberate creation of the German General Staff. Despite the interpretations put forward in *The German Generals Talk*, there was no deliberate plan for the blitz. In fact, it appears that the Germans were nearly as surprised by the speed of their success as the Allies were horrified. It was the German ability, or more accurately, the ability of a few specific Germans, to capitalize upon the success that they saw which created the rapid victory.

–ROBERT L. BATEMAN III

References

Larry H. Addington, *The Blitzkrieg Era and the German General Staff, 1865–1941* (New Brunswick, N.J.: Rutgers University Press, 1971);

Robert M. Citino, *The Evolution of Blitzkrieg Tactics: Germany Defends Itself Against Poland, 1918–1933* (New York: Greenwood Press, 1987);

James S. Corum, *The Roots of Blitzkrieg: Hans von Seeckt and the German Military Reform* (Lawrence: University Press of Kansas, 1992);

Robert Allan Doughty, *The Seeds of Disaster: The Development of French Army Doctrine, 1919–1939* (Hamden, Conn.: Archon Press, 1985);

Karl-Heinz Frieser, *Blitzkrieg-Legende: Der Westfeldzug 1940* (Munich: R. Oldenbourg, 1995);

Heinz Guderian, *Achtung-Panzer!: Die Entwicklung der Panzerwaffe, ihre Kampfstaktik und ihre operativen Moglichkeiten* (Stuttgart: Union Deutsche Verlagsgesellschaft, 1937); translated by Christopher Duffy as *Achtung-Panzer!: The Development of Armoured Forces, Their Tactics and Operational Potential* (London: Arms & Armor, 1992);

Alistair Horne, *To Lose a Battle: France 1940* (Boston: Little, Brown, 1969);

Eugenia C. Kiesling, *Arming Against Hitler: France and the Limits of Military Planning* (Lawrence: University Press of Kansas, 1996);

B. H. Liddell Hart, *The Other Side of the Hill: Germany's Generals, Their Rise and Fall, With Their Own Account of Military Events, 1939–1945* (London: Cassell, 1948); published in the United States as *The German Generals Talk* (New York: Morrow, 1948);

S. L. A. Marshall, *Blitzkrieg: Its History, Strategy, Economics and the Challenge to America* (New York: Morrow, 1940);

Ferdinand O. Miksche, *Attack, A Study of Blitzkrieg Tactics* (New York: Random House, 1942);

R. J. Overy, *War and Economy in the Third Reich* (Oxford: Clarendon Press; New York: Oxford University Press, 1994);

Bryan Perrett, *A History of Blitzkrieg* (London: Robert Hale; New York: Stein & Day, 1983);

Norman Rich, *Hitler's War Aims* (New York: Norton, 1973);

Albert Speer, *Erinnerungen* (Berlin: Propyläen-Verlag, 1969); translated as *Inside the Third Reich*, by Richard and Clara Winston (New York: Macmillan, 1970);

Jehuda L. Wallach, *The Dogma of the Battle of Annihilation: The Theories of Clausewitz and Schlieffen and Their Impact on the German Conduct of Two World Wars* (Westport, Conn.: Greenwood Press, 1986);

Gerhard Weinberg, *A World at Arms: A Global History of World War II* (Cambridge, U.K. and New York: Cambridge University Press, 1994).

BLITZKRIEG

Could the Catholic Church have been more effective in opposing the policies of the Nazi State?

Viewpoint: Yes, the Catholic Church compromised its integrity and its claim as guardian of moral law by not taking a firm stand against Nazi policies.

Viewpoint: No, there was little that the Catholic Church could have done to oppose the Nazi menace without endangering even more people.

The Catholic Church understood National Socialism no better than most other Western institutions. Initial and successful efforts to negotiate a Concordat with the Third Reich to safeguard Catholic rights followed what had in the past half-century become standard practice for the Roman Curia. Despite Adolf Hitler's subsequent anti-Catholic campaign within Germany, the Church continued to appeal to reason and conscience—neither particularly marked Nazi characteristics. By the outbreak of war in 1939, German Catholicism had been reduced to the status of a private association whose behaviors were even more constrained as the war progressed.

The Nazi conquest of other Catholic countries, notably Poland, placed the official Church squarely on the horns of a dilemma. To denounce Nazi persecution of Polish Catholics, to say nothing of Jews, was meaningless unless accompanied by a credible threat of sanctions, up to interdict and collective excommunication. Should these fail, the Church had no further recourse save individual martyrdom. That kind of courage was not lacking, from Pope Pius XII downward through the hierarchy. Nor was the Church committed to the principle that a Nazi-dominated Europe was preferable to a Soviet hegemony. Instead, it heard prelates from occupied lands insisting that Vatican intervention would only make things worse. It feared to put to the test the allegiance of German Catholics, and it underestimated the Nazis' determination to eliminate Europe's Jews in preparation for a more comprehensive ethnic cleansing. Evil in that measure challenged the moral compass of the Pope himself—until it was too late to do anything for Hitler's victims except to pray for their souls.

Viewpoint:
Yes, the Catholic Church compromised its integrity and its claim as guardian of moral law by not taking a firm stand against Nazi policies.

When World War II broke out in 1939, the relations between the German Evangelical church, which was divided into the anti-Nazi Confessing Church and the pro-Nazi German Christian movement, and the National Socialist state had already been shaped during the six preceding years by limited cooperation, regular harassment, and acts of outright persecution. This pattern continued throughout the war years. The Catholic Church of Germany, even though united, also faced difficult times in its dealings with the National Socialist government. Its standing was distinguished from the

Evangelical church, however, since there was a German episcopate and the international papacy. Churchmen, many laymen, and leaders of the Nazi party recognized that antagonisms between the Nazi state and the churches could not be overcome. *Reichsleiter* (German leader) Martin Bormann asserted in 1941: "National Socialist and Christian concepts cannot be reconciled." His position found wide support among the party, but the official party policy during the duration of the war, according to Adolf Hitler's directive, was not to provoke the churches into an open conflict even when some of the public speeches and private interventions of leading clergy became an ever-greater irritant to the Nazi government. Hitler insisted that he would take revenge and settle accounts with the churches once victory had been won.

Given Hitler's attitude and the inclination of Nazi authorities to treat most of the higher clergy with some consideration as long as the war lasted, could the churches have been more assertive, and perhaps more successful, in averting Nazi atrocities and genocide? By examining the reaction of church leaders and authorities in two areas—euthanasia and racial policies—it is possible to gain some estimate of what was done by the churches to alter the Nazi regime's measures and what might have been done had there been more courage, and especially moral will, to act against Nazi policies.

The euthanasia program in the Third Reich was inspired by the National Socialist view that "the weak must be eliminated." Early Nazi efforts at euthanasia affected mentally ill and deformed children, selected as "unworthy of life." In October 1939, Hitler signed a decree, backdated to September 1, the outbreak of the war, that authorized specified doctors to grant a "mercy death" to those who were found to be incurably ill. This measure was never turned into law. A division of Hitler's chancellery supervised its implementation. Before long, church offices received reports that elderly, feebleminded, epileptic, and other patients had been taken from various sanatoria, hospitals, and asylums. Soon after such a transfer, relatives were notified that their loved ones had died of appendicitis, pneumonia, strokes, or other sudden illnesses. To prevent spreading infectious diseases, relatives were informed, immediate cremations had to be done, and they were handed an urn with ashes upon request. Even though these actions were carried out in secret, a fair number of families throughout Germany received such unexpected death notices, causing alarm.

Both Protestant and Catholic churches initiated protests of these unlawful killings. The earliest protests came from the Protestant side when in June 1940, Pastor Gerhard Braune, director of the Hoffnungstal institutions near Berlin, complained to the Reich chancellery and the ministry of justice and also sent a memorandum to Field Marshal Hermann Göring. These efforts soon led to Braune's arrest and temporary imprisonment. A fellow pastor, Fritz von Bodelschwingh, who headed the well-known Bethel institutions that cared for epileptics, similarly engaged in protest efforts in 1940 and 1941. More pointed was a sharp letter of criticism by Bishop Theofil Wurm of Württemberg, asserting that euthanasia measures were contrary to all Christian principles, which he addressed to Minister of the Interior Wilhelm Frick in August 1940. When Wurm received no reply he sent another letter in September. Since his letter was being widely distributed, Wurm emerged as one of the foremost spokesmen of the Protestant churches. Also in August 1940 the presiding bishop, Cardinal Adolf Bertram of Breslau, on behalf of the episcopate addressed written protests against euthanasia to the head of the Reich chancellery and to the minister of justice. In November, Cardinal Michael von Faulhaber of Munich also protested the killing of innocent people to the minister of justice and demanded an answer to Bertram's earlier letter. Finally, Bishop Clemens August, Graf von Galen of Münster, in several homilies delivered in July and early August 1941, denounced euthanasia from the pulpit. Copies of his sermon of 3 August were widely distributed and aroused public concern. Even though several Nazi officials proposed that the bishop be hanged for committing treason, Galen escaped the death sentence because Hitler and Joseph Goebbels worried about morale among civilians and soldiers and did not want to make a martyr of Galen.

Several weeks after Galen's August sermon, Hitler suspended the euthanasia program on 24 August 1941, after thousands had been killed. Even though the program was not revived, individual and group killings by injection and starvation diets continued, as did the mercy deaths for children with birth defects. There is no doubt that the protest actions of church leaders against the killing of innocent people helped solidify German public opinion, which Hitler did not dare to violate even though he stood at the height of his military power.

While Protestant and Catholic church leaders had been outspoken in protesting euthanasia, they were silent when Jews were

persecuted during the 1930s and did not raise their voices in protest even when the Nazis unleashed the first pogrom against German Jews during *Kristallnacht* (Night of Broken Glass) on 9 November 1938. Anti-Semitism was highly prevalent among hierarchy and laity alike, which made it easy to rationalize antipathy to Jews on religious and social grounds. A distinction was made, however, between "Jews" and (baptized) "Jewish Christians." It resulted in efforts to provide some protection for the latter before deportations began but to leave the former to fend for themselves. The Nazi definition of "Jew" was based solely on racial criteria and disregarded religious conversions, and thus only a few Jewish Christians escaped deportation.

More serious than the church leaders' concern for non-Aryan members before deportation, was the question of what was happening to Jews after they had been transported "East" starting in February 1940 and getting fully under way in October 1941. After the Nazi attack on Soviet Russia in June 1941, soldiers who returned from the eastern front, against orders from their superiors, were telling gruesome stories of the shooting of Jewish civilians in occupied Russia, which were carried out by *Einsatzgruppen* (special action commandos). By the end of 1941 there were even some sporadic reports coming back to Germany that deported German Jews had been shot by

detachments of such killing commandos near Riga and Minsk. Late in 1941 the first death camp began operations in Chelmno near Lodz; Auschwitz and three additional killing centers were opened for mass gassing in 1942. News of extermination camps were beginning to reach Germany in 1942, and by the end of the year the Catholic bishops had fairly accurate information on what was happening to Jews in eastern Europe.

Still the principal concern of the German Catholic bishops remained the fate of Jews married to Aryans rather than all Jews. In 1942 the Nazi government was contemplating an ordinance that would have required the dissolution of racially mixed marriages. Jewish partners of such dissolved unions were to be subject to deportation. In November 1942, Bertram, in the name of episcopate, sent letters of protest to the ministers of justice, interior, and ecclesiastical affairs, arguing that many thousands of Catholic marriages would be affected, which according to Catholic doctrine were indissoluble. Wurm and several Protestant leaders also addressed protests to Nazi ministries. Speaking louder than the exhortations of the church elites were most likely the action of many hundreds of Berlin women married to Jews, who staged a week-long peaceful protest demonstration in the Rosenstrasse in February and early March 1943, after their husbands had been rounded

Pope Pius XII on the morning of 19 July 1943 after Rome had been bombed for the first time by the Allies

(Attualita Giordani)

CATHOLIC CHURCH

up for deportation. Goebbels and the Nazi authorities decided to shrink from the use of brutal force and released two thousand imprisoned Jews. Also, the compulsory divorce legislation was never enacted.

What was notable about Wurm's protests to the authorities in 1943 was their broad inclusiveness. In his letters to several of the ministries he called not only for cessation of agitation against Christianity and the church but specifically for an end to "all the measures through which members of other nations and races, without trial by civil and military courts, are put to death simply because they happen to belong to another nation or race." In a letter to the head of the Reich chancellery, Hans Heinrich Lammers, on 20 December 1943, he explicitly stated that because of religious and ethical convictions, "I must, in agreement with the opinion of all positive Christian circles in Germany, declare that we Christians consider this extermination policy directed against the Jews as a great and disastrous injustice committed by Germany. Killing without justification because of war and without trial is against God's command, even if the government orders it, and as every deliberate violation of God's commandment is avenged, so will this be sooner or later."

Even though two other Protestant bishops, Hans Meiser of Bavaria and August Marahrens of Hanover, who were in contact with Wurm and had at other times spoken out against Nazi policies, were urged to protest against the persecution of Jews, they remained silent. In France, the Netherlands, and Hungary, Reformed or Calvinist church leaders protested against anti-Jewish measures and also carried out rescue actions of Jews.

The stance of the German Catholic hierarchy was also disappointing when it came to speaking out against the deportation of Jews. This passivity was quite in contrast to the Dutch, Belgian, and French bishops' efforts to protest and thwart the removal of Jews from their own countries. These bishops used the pulpit to denounce the deportations, and some of them actively participated in rescue efforts together with priests and members of the monastic clergy in order to save Jewish lives. Their work, no doubt, was made easier because they were acting against an oppressive foreign occupier, whereas German bishops would have had to oppose their own legitimate government. A pastoral letter of the German bishops read from pulpits in August and September 1943 was the closest to a joint protest made by the Catholic hierarchy. It was largely couched in commentaries on individual commandments. The comment on the Fifth Commandment, "Thou shall not kill," asserted that the killing of innocents, mentally ill and others, even if done for the common good was wrong as was the killing of "peoples of alien race and descent." There was no clear mention of "Jew" or "non-Ayran" in this or other Catholic pronouncements. Guenter Lewy's conclusion several decades ago in *The Catholic Church and Nazi Germany* (1964) continues to be valid today: "Unlike the case of the extermination of Germans in the euthanasia program, where the episcopate did not mince words and succeeded in putting a stop to the killings, the bishops here played it safe. The effect of their public protests on the Final Solution consequently was nil. These very general statements neither changed the policies of the government nor inspired any change in the behavior of German Catholics."

No discussion of the churches' stance on Nazi atrocities and genocide is complete without a brief consideration of the Pope's attitude. The election of Cardinal Eugenio Pacelli to the papal chair in 1939 as Pius XII had much to do with the policies of the Vatican during the war. The new Holy Father appeared to harbor pro-German sentiments, was not a fighter, and used diplomacy rather than denunciation of Hitler's policies in the conduct of papal affairs. Despite pleas from the French hierarchy to denounce the discriminatory legislation against Jews that the Vichy government enacted in 1941, the Vatican did not raise any formal objections. Similarly, when reports of the extermination of Jews in Polish death factories became more and more prevalent in 1942, papal silence was said to be the result of the need to maintain the absolute neutrality of the Vatican in the worldwide conflict. There was also the concern that loud protest would exacerbate the condition of Catholics in Nazi-controlled areas and provoke harsh retaliation by the Nazis. In addition, most of the Catholic leaders looked upon Bolshevism as a greater threat than Nazism. Whatever public pronouncements the pontiff made, as in his lengthy Christmas message broadcast over the Vatican radio in 1942, he repeatedly called for a more humane conduct of hostilities without any direct indictment of those that committed atrocities. Papal diplomatic interventions, though not yet fully known, were more active and direct.

Representations of the papal nuncio in Slovakia in 1942 halted deportations of Jews until 1944; similarly, when the nuncios in Hungary and Rumania were threatened by the Pope with public denunciation of the mass murders, they were able to stop deportations, albeit only temporarily. When Italian Jews

EASTER MESSAGE

In his 1941 Easter message, Pope Pius XII addressed the plight of the world.

In the lamentable spectacle of human conflict which We are now witnessing We acknowledge the valor and loyalty of all those who with a deep sense of duty are fighting for the defense and prosperity of their homeland. We recognize, too, the prodigious and, in itself, efficacious development made in industrial and technical fields, nor do We overlook the many generous and praiseworthy gestures of magnanimity which have been made towards the enemy; but while We acknowledge, We feel obliged nonetheless to state that the ruthless struggle has at times assumed forms which can be described only as atrocious. May all belligerents, who also have human hearts moulded by mothers' love, show some feeling of charity for the sufferings of civilian populations, for defenseless women and children, for the sick and aged, all of whom are often exposed to greater and more widespread perils of war than those faced by soldiers at the front!

We beseech the belligerent powers to abstain until the very end from the use of still more homicidal instruments of warfare; for the introduction of such weapons inevitably results in their retaliatory use, often with greater violence by the enemy. If already We must lament the fact that the limits of legitimate warfare have been repeatedly exceeded, would not the more widespread use of increasingly barbarous offensive weapons soon transform war into unspeakable horror?. . .

However, under the vigilant Providence of God and armed only with prayer, exhortation and consolation, We shall persevere in

Our battle for peace in behalf of suffering humanity. May the blessings and comforts of Heaven descend on all victims of this war: upon you who are prisoners and upon your families from whom you are separated and who are anxious about you; and upon you refugees and dispossessed who have lost your homes and land, your life's support. We share with you your anguish and suffering. If it is not allowed Us as We would honestly desire—to take upon Ourselves the burden of your sorrows, may Our paternal and cordial sympathy serve as the balm which will temper the bitterness of your misfortune with today's greeting of the Alleluia, the hymn of Christ's triumph over earthly martyrdom, the blossom of the olive tree of Gethsemane flourishing in the precious hope of resurrection and of the new and eternal life in which there will be neither sorrows nor struggles. In this vale of tears there is no lasting city (Hebrews 13: 14), no eternal homeland.

Contemplation of a war that is so cruel in all its aspects and the thought of the suffering children of the Church inspires in the heart of the Common Father and forms upon Our lips words of comfort and encouragement for the pastors and faithful of those places where the Church, the Spouse of Christ, is suffering most; where fidelity to her, the public profession of her doctrines, the conscientious and practical observance of her laws, moral resistance to atheism and to de-Christianizing influences deliberately favored or tolerated, are being openly or insidiously opposed and daily in various ways made increasingly difficult.

Source: *World War II Resources Web Page.*

---

were to be deported from Rome in the fall of 1943, Pius XII did not speak out publicly, but approved the hiding of Jews in monasteries and houses of religious orders in Rome, including some in the Vatican itself.

It is impossible to say what effect a forceful papal denunciation of the Nazi murders of Jews would have had on Hitler's policies, but it is doubtful it would have halted the fury of extermination that the Führer and his criminal henchmen had unleashed. It is more likely, as Lewy points out, that some prospective vic-

tims of extermination might have been warned by public protests or denunciations coming from the Vatican and induced to escape. Also, many more Christians might have been encouraged to help and hide Jews. By not taking a decisive public stand against such egregious crimes against humanity, the head of the Church and the Church itself compromised their integrity and claim to be the guardian of the moral law. Apart from some individual acts of both Catholic and Protestant leaders of publicly praying for the Jews and providing assistance in hiding them to prevent deportation, the churches' record of averting atrocities and genocide marks a disappointing failure.

–GEORGE P. BLUM, UNIVERSITY
OF THE PACIFIC

Viewpoint:
No, there was little that the Catholic Church could have done to oppose the Nazi menace without endangering even more people.

A drawback intrinsic to a work conceptualized like *History in Dispute* is a residue of perspectives that do not find ready voices. This viewpoint is arguably chief among them. Even as an intellectual exercise it is difficult to make a case that the Christian churches did what was in their power as institutions to stand against the crimes of the Third Reich. The only convincing evidence to the contrary would be witness borne by at least the leaders of Christianity. Had such witness been ultimately that of the confessors and martyrs of the Church's early centuries, when bishops walked at the head of those directly confronting civil authority, this type of essay would be easier to write. Its absence, however, cannot be dismissed as a consequence of two millennia of soft living or of bureaucratized accommodation to secular power. Individual moral—or for that matter physical—cowardice was not a dominant characteristic at the top levels of either the Roman Catholic or the German Protestant churches. It is possible, without casuistry or apologetics, to explain their behavior in other terms.

The German Protestant churches had been engaged in a virtual death grapple for the allegiance of their communicants almost since the Nazi seizure of power. This *Kirchenkampf* (Church Struggle) was the product in good part of evangelical misjudgment of Adolf Hitler's intentions. That misjudgment in turn reflected the deep nationalism of Germany's Protestant congregations. It was as well a response to Hitler's apparent desire to assist in bringing about a long-sought institutional unity that Protestant leaders regarded necessary to balance the power of organized Catholicism. Individual clergymen saw the true nature of the Nazi regime—and acted on their understanding—while the institutional church was slower to follow. The result was, simply put, that German Protestantism exhausted itself in maintaining itself, well before the persecution of the Jews became homicidal, much less genocidal. The Protestants had no cards left to play.

That situation may be described as a consequence of a state church, a phenomenon dating to Martin Luther (1483–1546). It is more accurately considered, however, in light of the sixty-forty balance between Catholicism and Protestantism that had existed in Germany since the Catholic Reformation. Even at full strength and speaking with a united voice, Germany's Evangelicals were "fighting above their weight" in a contest with a modern totalitarian state whose leadership was indifferent alike to persuasion and condemnation, understanding only force of a kind no local institution with a moral, as opposed to a physical, base was able to apply. It represents no denigration of its individual confessors to describe German Protestantism as roadkill in terms of its institutional capacities for challenging Nazi atrocities as they came to stage center after 1940.

The Catholic Church was another paradigm and another story. It was, by contrast to the Protestants, an institution with universal pretensions and a universal perspective. It possessed power bases outside of Germany and millions of adherents completely beyond the grasp of Hitler's Reich. Above all, in the Papacy the Catholic Church had a single moral voice—one, moreover, it was not historically reluctant to use. Institutional Catholicism's relative silence has been a corresponding target for attack. It has been ascribed to the character—or lack of it—of Pope Pius XII. Critics depict a principled supporter of authoritarianism who was correspondingly suspicious of Hitler's democratic opponents. They describe a man whose concept of the Papacy was predicated on its universality and, as a result, refused to condemn publicly any individualized atrocity, whether it involved the murder of priests or of Jews.

Pius has been more harshly attacked as a cynic, concerned with the power and wealth of the Church, unwilling to take even limited personal or institutional risks for the sake of justice—particularly when Jews were involved. Hitler, for example, entertained plans to seize the person of the Pope, and almost certainly would have done so had Pius taken any clear public action against genocide—collective or specific excommunication, for example. Popes had been martyred before, however, and for lesser reasons. Nor was martyrdom the only alternative. A papacy in exile would have had a moral weight denied to one undergoing at Nazi hands a second "Vatican captivity" such as that following Italian unification in 1871.

One might say that if the negative image of Pius is accepted even in part, then the Catholic Church can legitimately be considered to have done all it could against the Third Reich. Should the supreme Pontiff be morally wanting, then private, individual, secret charity—like that exercised more than once by Pius himself—was the most that might be expected. In that same context attention is frequently called to institutional Catholicism's history of anti-Semitism, to an anticommunism that purportedly generated a certain empathy for Hitler's war on Russia, and to a distrust of democracy, particularly its American version. Such matrices as well offer little scope for heroic institutional intervention on behalf of oppressed "others."

Anti-Catholicism, however, has long and legitimately been described as the anti-Semitism of intellectuals. The story has another side. Defenders of the Pope and the Church describe limited options and weak positions on specific issues. They concede misjudgment of National Socialism's true nature but correctly assert that the Church was not alone in that error. They stress the physical risks to German Catholics that would have accompanied any root-and-branch Papal denunciation of Nazism. They highlight Pius's ultimate decision—which he repeatedly affirmed—that overt, public condemnation of Jewish persecution would be counterproductive for the victims themselves. This was a mistake certainly, a culpable mistake perhaps. "Papal infallibility," however, has never been interpreted to mean a pope cannot err grievously in political matters.

These kinds of moral and intellectual hairs can be split indefinitely. Further disclosures from various Vatican archives will keep the question alive well into the twenty-first century. A better way of evaluating the issue of institutional Christianity's performance in the face of Nazi crimes is to step backward a thousand years. The appropriate relationship of church to state had been a central issue of Western civilization for at least that long. Arguments against theocracy had been central to political, religious, and social debate—central indeed to the rise of modern secular society since the Enlightenment. By the last quarter of the nineteenth century the case seemed closed. The churches were expected to eschew interfering in the affairs of this world and concentrate on those of the hereafter. Their adjustment to that situation should not be especially surprising. The real irony emerged when the very same forces of liberalism and secularization that had been loudest in their demands that Christian churches end their involvement in mundane matters suddenly became righteously indignant at the consequences of their long-sought success. A watchdog whose teeth have been pulled can scarcely be expected to bite—even in the best of causes. In confronting the Nazi challenge, Europe and the West may not have had the Christianity they deserved. They did have the Christianity they wanted.

—DENNIS SHOWALTER,
COLORADO COLLEGE

References

Victoria Barnett, *For the Soul of the People: Protestant Protest Against Hitler* (New York: Oxford University Press, 1992);

John S. Conway, *The Nazi Persecution of the Churches, 1933–1945* (London: Weidenfeld & Nicolson, 1968);

Donald J. Dietrich, *Catholic Citizens in the Third Reich: Psycho-Social Principles and Moral Reasoning* (New Brunswick, N.J.: Transaction Books, 1988);

Ernst Christian Helmreich, *The German Churches Under Hitler: Background, Struggle, and Epilogue* (Detroit: Wayne State University Press, 1979);

Guenter Lewy, *The Catholic Church and Nazi Germany* (New York: McGraw-Hill, 1964);

Franklin H. Littell and Hubert G. Locke, eds., *The German Church Struggle and the Holocaust* (Detroit: Wayne State University Press, 1974);

Peter Matheson, ed. *The Third Reich and the Christian Churches* (Edinburgh, Scotland: T. & T. Clark; Grand Rapids, Mich.: Eerdmans, 1981);

Nathan Stoltzfus, *Resistance of the Heart: Intermarriage and the Rosenstrasse Protest in Nazi Germany* (New York: Norton, 1996);

Gordon C. Zahn, *German Catholics and Hitler's Wars: A Study in Social Control* (New York: Sheed & Ward, 1962).

CATHOLIC CHURCH

CHURCHILL

Was Winston Churchill a great war leader?

Viewpoint: Yes, Winston Churchill's strategy of attacking the Germans on the periphery and delaying a main European invasion enabled Britain to survive World War II.

Viewpoint: No, Churchill's vision of grand strategy, which emphasized peripheral operations, lacked the practical and economic foundations needed for it to succeed.

Winston Churchill's status as a war leader was a matter of both style and substance. He personified Britain's determination to fight to the finish. His fundamental decency, his moral condemnation of Nazism, and his support of democracy overshadowed his equally profound commitment to preserving the British Empire, as well as a set of domestic social values that were increasingly outdated and unpopular.

At policy levels Churchill was able to sustain a wartime coalition cabinet incorporating both Conservative and Labor members, whose personalities as well as their politics seldom meshed smoothly. He simplified the decision-making process, concentrating it around his own person. Not the least of his achievements was sustaining—perhaps even creating—a "special relationship" with the United States and Franklin D. Roosevelt.

At strategic levels Churchill's primary achievement was the postponement of a cross-Channel invasion in favor of a series of smaller-scale Mediterranean operations that served as preliminaries, providing experience for a main event that could be done only once. His second success was maintaining Britain's place as an equal partner with the United States in 1944–1945, despite the steep relative decline in Britain's contribution to the final campaigns. Operationally, he maddened his service chiefs by what they considered inappropriate meddling in details and excessive support for sideshows. He never quite understood the logistical and administrative demands of modern war—particularly in regions such as the Middle and Far East, which had almost no infrastructure in place. Even Churchill's uniformed critics, however, recognized the importance of his insight, energy, and willpower in what was Imperial Britain's last and greatest achievement: the crushing of the Axis.

Prime Minister Winston Churchill in the streets of London, 10 September 1940

(Hilton)

Viewpoint:
Yes, Winston Churchill's strategy of attacking the Germans on the periphery and delaying a main European invasion enabled Britain to survive World War II.

In most men their virtues often become their vices. While this peculiarity of the human psyche is normally more or less harmless, in those possessing great power, such as Winston Churchill, it can affect the course of history and the lives of millions.

It is hard to contest Churchill's nomination as a primary candidate for Man of the Century, Savior of the West, and the epitome of the English bulldog spirit. He was all of these epithets and more. He was the last great orator. Listening to his "We will fight them on the beaches" speech can still make anyone not hopelessly enervated by cynicism want to grab a rifle and head for a bunker. For England in the early war years, Churchill's speeches were of more use than another army corps.

Man of the Century though Churchill may be, he was certainly a man of the nineteenth century. He had a view of war as one of individual manly action, such as his own participation in the last great cavalry charge against the Mahdi in the Sudan at the Battle of Omdurman (1898) or his epic escape from captivity during the South African (Boer) War (1899–1902), when he spent over a month behind Boer lines. Churchill could never understand the need for logistics demanded by modern war. He seemed, at times, to believe all that was necessary was for the infantry to fill their haversacks with hardtack and their pouches with cartridges and march forward with bayonets fixed. Yet, conversely, Churchill was extremely reluctant to force any decisive battle.

That ambivalence is most evident in his Mediterranean strategy of 1942 and 1943. Churchill wanted to protect the Suez Canal and the route to India as well as protect Middle East oil fields. India became more important than the oil fields, however, after the Japanese pushed south into Burma. As a true nineteenth-century imperialist, Churchill later summed up his attitude by saying, "I am not here to oversee the dissolution of the Empire."

That Churchill was pugnacious cannot be questioned. He wanted to fight the Germans and fight them hard. His most difficult adversary in 1942, after German general Erwin Rommel, who was rampaging through the deserts of North Africa, was General George C. Marshall, Chief of Staff of the United States Army.

CHURCHILL

Marshall wanted to fight as badly as did Churchill. What he did not want was American troops to be used as reinforcements for British forces, especially at a time when there seemed to be a regularly scheduled airline run to Cairo, dropping off a new commander and picking up a disgraced one. Furthermore, Marshall did not want his troops dissipated over many little battlefronts that he loosely defined as anything Mediterranean. Marshall feared any one of Churchill's targets in that region could easily become a suction pump for men and matériel.

Marshall presented an alternate plan, calling for a direct cross-Channel invasion in 1942 (code-named Sledgehammer) to open a beachhead for a main attack in 1943 (code-named Roundup). This plan scared Churchill and the rest of his General Staff almost witless. They considered Sledgehammer suicidal, which it probably was, although Marshall maintained it was possible until the day he died. Churchill successfully convinced Roosevelt of the basic unsoundness of Sledgehammer/Roundup. That left a big question: what to do with the expanding Anglo-American forces in the final months of 1942? Three problems immediately presented themselves to Churchill: how to check the Germans at Suez; how to relieve the pressure on Russia as he had promised; and how to keep the Americans from siphoning off resources to fight the Japanese, who were proving to be more formidable than imagined when the Europe First policy was formulated.

The best option, Churchill finally convinced Roosevelt, was Operation Torch, a landing in North Africa. It was the only time Roosevelt overruled Marshall. Success led in 1943 to the invasion of Sicily and then, inexorably, to Italy—complete with the bloodbath at Anzio (1944) and the whole costly trail up the ridges along the spine of the Italian boot.

Marshall, like Cassandra, saw his predictions and fears come true. Allied energies, men, and equipment, especially of the British Army, were dissipated on minor fronts. Thousands of casualties were suffered for no good strategic purpose. The date for the invasion of France (code-named Overlord) was delayed until 1944. The British army lost some of its best units and by D-Day was scraping the bottom of the manpower barrel. The real cost of the Mediterranean strategy was borne by the Russians, who got no relief from any of the Allied battles. The Germans did not have to shift forces from the eastern front; on the contrary, they were able to strip the west of some of its best units as reinforcements.

Even after the fiasco of Anzio, and after being forced to agree to the date of 1 May 1944 for Overlord, Churchill continued to lobby for continuance of the Mediterranean campaign with not bulldog but pit-bull tenacity. Churchill's immediate concern was that the landing in Normandy would bog down on the beaches, as had been the case at Gallipoli (1915–1916) in World War I. His larger fear was that Montgomery's army, the last reserve of Britain and the empire, would be destroyed in the process of conquering Germany. The second anxiety at least had merit. Almost from the beginning of the campaign, front-line British units had to be broken up to replace casualties in other formations. But on V-E-Day, Great Britain stood—just barely—as a full military partner in the Grand Alliance. Winston Churchill's strategic vision was clouded by his memories of World War I, by his determination to preserve the empire, and by his distrust of the high-stake, high-risk policies of his American allies. He nevertheless played masterfully a hand with few trump cards, and correspondingly merits recognition as a great war leader.

–JOHN WHEATLEY, BROOKLYN
CENTER, MINNESOTA

Viewpoint:
No, Churchill's vision of grand strategy, which emphasized peripheral operations, lacked the practical and economic foundations needed for it to succeed.

More than any one person, Winston Churchill was the guiding force behind Great Britain's conduct of World War II. Between 1940 and 1945 Churchill held the posts of prime minister and minister of defense and ruled over a coalition government as a national leader standing above partisan politics. His stirring speeches, as well as energetic and defiant public presence—the British bulldog spirit—created a "halo-effect" of sympathy for his vision of British grand strategy, a vision limited by Churchill's particular notions of Britain's military traditions. These notions offered quick-fix solutions to military problems that could be resolved only over a longer term. In the arena of grand strategy Churchill's stewardship of British interests most clearly displayed these limitations.

Grand strategy involves the weaving together of a nation's war aims, material resources, diplomatic commitments, and long-term interests into a military plan of action. In outline, the definition and execution of Britain's grand strategy during World War II was clear enough. War aims

CHURCHILL ON NAZI AGGRESSION

Winston Churchill ranks as one of the greatest British orators. In this speech to Parliament on 13 May 1940, the prime minister prepared his people for the long road ahead.

On Friday evening last I received from His Majesty the mission to form a new administration. It was the evident will of Parliament and the nation that this should be conceived on the broadest possible basis and that it should include all parties. I have already completed the most important part of this task.

A war cabinet has been formed of five members, representing, with the Labour, Opposition, and Liberals, the unity of the nation. It was necessary that this should be done in one single day on account of the extreme urgency and rigor of events. Other key positions were filled yesterday. I am submitting a further list to the king tonight. I hope to complete the appointment of principal ministers during tomorrow.

The appointment of other ministers usually takes a little longer. I trust when Parliament meets again this part of my task will be completed and that the administration will be complete in all respects. I considered it in the public interest to suggest to the Speaker that the House should be summoned today. At the end of today's proceedings, the adjournment of the House will be proposed until May 21 with provision for earlier meeting if need be. Business for that will be notified to MPs at the earliest opportunity.

I now invite the House by a resolution to record its approval of the steps taken and declare its confidence in the new government.

The resolution:

"That this House welcomes the formation of a government representing the united and inflexible resolve of the nation to prosecute the war with Germany to a victorious conclusion."

To form an administration of this scale and complexity is a serious undertaking in itself. But we are in the preliminary phase of one of the greatest battles in history. We are in action at many other points—in Norway and in Holland—and we have to be prepared in the Mediterranean. The air battle is continuing, and many preparations have to be made here at home.

In this crisis I think I may be pardoned if I do not address the House at any length today, and I hope that any of my friends and colleagues or former colleagues who are affected by the political reconstruction will make all allowances for any lack of ceremony with which it has been necessary to act.

I say to the House as I said to ministers who have joined this government, I have nothing to offer but blood, toil, tears, and sweat. We have before us an ordeal of the most grievous kind. We have before us many, many months of struggle and suffering.

You ask, what is our policy? I say it is to wage war by land, sea, and air. War with all our might and with all the strength God has given us, and to wage war against a monstrous tyranny never surpassed in the dark and lamentable catalogue of human crime. That is our policy.

You ask, what is our aim? I can answer in one word. It is victory. Victory at all costs—Victory in spite of all terrors—Victory, however long and hard the road may be, for without victory there is no survival.

Let that be realized. No survival for the British Empire, no survival for all that the British Empire has stood for, no survival for the urge, the impulse of the ages, that mankind shall move forward toward his goal.

I take up my task in buoyancy and hope. I feel sure that our cause will not be suffered to fail among men. I feel entitled at this juncture, at this time, to claim the aid of all and to say, "Come then, let us go forward together with our united strength."

Source: *Winston Churchill, "Blood Sweat and Tears," The History Place: Great Speeches, Web Page.*

focused upon the defeat and unconditional surrender of Germany and Japan. The utilization of material resources meant total mobilization—war to the last guinea—and ultimately dependence upon the prodigious capacity of American industry. Diplomatic commitments entailed an as-close-as-possible relationship with the United States and ongoing support of the Soviet Union. Long-term interests included the maintenance of British imperial connections, its global commercial and financial interests, and its position in international affairs as a great power. At the operational level the formulation and execution of British grand strategy took place in the European theater and concerned in particular the relationship between British and American planners. At issue were both considerations of where the war would be waged and of the military doctrine governing its conduct.

Churchill's approach to these matters was expansive. He believed in offensive measures, striking the enemy whenever possible. By 1943, as plans for attacking Adolf Hitler's continental empire were taking shape, he envisioned operations in northern Norway, northern Europe, and at various points in the Mediterranean, the latter extending to offering inducements to draw Turkey into the war. The Mediterranean strategy had the advantage of securing British commercial interests along its trade routes. It also offered the possibility of decisive and relatively cheap operations that, in turn, would comfort allies and hasten the end of the war. Although Churchill accepted that the northern European front would require a massive buildup, his arguments implied that the other areas could utilize somewhat smaller contingents and emphasize well-timed amphibious landings and quick exploitation of the element of surprise. In effect, these measures imaged the classical British strategy—used since the late seventeenth century—of striking at a continental enemy from the periphery, encircling its forces, and dispersing their concentration by opening a series of small fronts. It also played to Churchill's own enthusiasm for combined operations. This strategy fit a military doctrine known as *maneuver*.

By contrast, American planners, principally U.S. Army Chief of Staff George C. Marshall and Supreme Allied Commander Dwight D. Eisenhower, continually pressed for a doctrine of attrition. Attrition favored the application of superior force at carefully selected sites and the persistent buildup of overwhelming resources. It was an expensive strategy, dependent upon the amassing of huge resources and attacking along a broad front. By its emphasis on the concentration of troops and supplies, attrition competed with maneuver operations for these resources. In late 1943 and early 1944 the issue was the number of

landing craft needed to conduct operations in Italy and northern Europe (Operation Overlord) and a supportive landing in southern France (code-named Anvil). Both Eisenhower and Marshall were skeptical of Churchill's maneuver operations, and with good reason. In January 1944, Eisenhower allowed himself to be persuaded to divert landing craft to an operation (Shingle) designed to break the deadlock in Italy by an assault south of German lines at Anzio. Despite the provision of a sizeable force of ships, landing craft, and troops, the beachhead assault bogged down and the entire Italian campaign turned into a hard slog, more costly to the Allies than to their German counterparts. The vision of quick, cheap, and decisive victory evaporated.

Churchill and his military advisors had counted on the success of Shingle to validate their Mediterranean strategy and prepare the way for additional operations in the Adriatic, the Balkans, and into Greece and Turkey. They also envisioned that its success would delay Overlord and keep the planning initiative in British hands. Shingle's failure left the British with Overlord and the weak claim that Shingle had, after all, tied down German troops in Italy, thereby diverting them from the western front. Now the extra resources Churchill had committed to Shingle had gone for naught, and the British had to throw in with the Americans, with attrition, and with Overlord. Churchill's grand strategy had to give way to American ideas simply because it could not deliver on its promises.

It was clear that only American resources could sustain Overlord and attrition. By 1944, Britain had reached the limit of its productive capacity but was dependent upon the United States for between 40 and 50 percent of its munitions. At the same time, American industrial production was continuing to grow. For Britain to remain a viable partner in the alliance required both an early ending to the war and one in which British forces played a significant role. Such an opportunity presented itself early in 1945. The defeat of the German counteroffensive of December–February 1944–1945 (Battle of the Bulge) opened the prospect of a quick breakthrough on the northern flank of German resistance and a drive toward Berlin, a swift and decisive knockout blow. This prospect included the hope that British forces and a British commander would be prominent in the operations. Such a strategy would insure victory while Britain still had a major role to play and would contribute greatly to support for a British presence at the peace table. It would also place as much of Germany as possible under Anglo-American control.

This fresh emphasis on northern Europe revealed a persistent weakness in Churchill's strategic thinking, his willingness to press the offensive across most of the map of western and southern

Europe. Until January 1945, when plans for the assault on Germany took final form, he had argued that the Italian front be kept strong. Doing this would hold open opportunities to exert influence in Austria and Yugoslavia, should German resistance in Italy collapse. At a meeting in Malta, the British and American joint staffs decided that pressing the offensive in northern Europe would require the diversion of British and Canadian divisions from Italy. This decision ended hopes for decisive action on the Italian front. While it increased the British presence in the northern campaign, it also failed to place the command structure under either British control or influence. Eisenhower, at the urging of Marshall, kept the command structure divided among Montgomery and the American generals Omar Bradley and George S. Patton. This division also supported a strategy of advance along a broad front, not the dramatic thrust against Berlin the British had hoped for. The American commanders had had enough. In particular, Marshall persuaded Eisenhower to resist further efforts of the British commanders and Churchill himself to influence the endgame of the war. The Americans would finish the war based on their understanding of the needs of men and material rather than in terms of Churchill's desire to use their forces to redraw an idealized version of postwar Europe.

That Churchill was a leader of vision, determination, and energy there can be no doubt. In the early war years his desire to strike the enemy quickly and hard over a broad front had the merit of engaging the American allies in the European conflict as soon as possible and later of showing support for Russia, which was suffering greatly in its eastern European campaigns.

All the same, his emphasis on maneuver warfare, featuring combined operations striking along Europe's periphery, could inflict only marginal damage upon German forces. The American emphasis on attrition placed great strains on British industry, but at least the United States had the capacity to support it. The Americans also forced choices based on the allocation of men and material, choices placing Churchill's ideas under the tests of feasibility. These tests revealed the British prime minister to be a better promoter of morale and more skillful diplomat than he was a strategic planner.

–ROBERT MCJIMSEY, COLORADO COLLEGE

References

John Charmely, *Churchill, The End of Glory: A Political Biography* (London: Hodder & Stoughton, 1995);

Martin Gilbert, *Road to Victory: Winston S. Churchill, 1941–1945* (London: Heinemann, 1986);

Michael Howard, *The Mediterranean Strategy in the Second World War* (London: Weidenfeld & Nicolson; New York: Praeger, 1968);

Ronald Lewin, *Churchill as Warlord* (London: Batsford, 1972);

David Reynolds, Warren F. Kimball, and A. O. Chubarian, *Allies at War: the Soviet, American, and British Experience, 1939–1945* (New York: St. Martin's Press, 1994).

CHURCHILL

CONVENTIONAL WAR

Were the demands of conventional front-line combat approaching the practical limits of human endurance by 1945?

Viewpoint: Yes, the front-line combat soldier reached the limits of his endurance in World War II; he was denied the periods of rest experienced by soldiers in earlier wars, and he had to cope with the severe psychological demands of modern warfare—demands that most soldiers could endure for only about six months.

Viewpoint: No, despite the grueling conditions of front-line combat in World War II, victors and vanquished alike found ways of coping that allowed them to continue fighting effectively right up to the end of the war.

The exponential increase in the destructiveness of conventional war between 1939 and 1945 was the product of several factors. The first was the development of weapons systems. Infantry rifles and automatic weapons, for example, had far higher rates of fire and were far more reliable than their World War I predecessors. Improved fire-control systems made artillery a precision killing tool as well as an instrument of mass destruction. Tanks and aircraft, both marginal in World War I, became direct participants on the battlefield, capable of engaging particular targets down to individual foxholes and bunkers. By 1945, firepower was on its way to asserting almost the same superiority over mobility that had produced the gridlock of 1914–1918. From Iwo Jima to Berlin, individual movement, particularly unprotected movement, was becoming a near-suicidal risk.

At the same time, the "battle space" of conventional war was increasing. By 1945 aircraft could comprehensively negate the concept of "rear echelon" up to a hundred miles behind a fighting line and increase the hazards at five times that range—as German armored reserves discovered on their way to the D-Day (6 June 1944) landing sites. On the human end of the spectrum, guerrillas complemented aircraft in making life away from the front random, risky, and uncomfortable.

Geography also enhanced the demands of war on combatants. As late as World War I, large-scale fighting was sustainable only in regions with developed infrastructures, and corresponding possibilities to escape stress, if only for brief periods. World War II was fought in the world's remote spaces. "Liberty" for the sailors of the U.S. Pacific fleet meant pickup softball games on a bleak island. "Furlough" on the Russian front meant days in slow-moving trains, with partisan ambush a frequent possibility. In addition, not everyone was fortunate enough to enjoy such amenities. For most of the war, an American tanker or infantryman had only one way home: the "million-dollar wound."

Global war also meant increased space-to-force ratios. Compared to earlier conflicts, fewer men were available for a given number of miles. In

World War I, formations could count on being rotated out of the line on a regular basis. A quarter-century later, such large-scale reliefs became the exception rather than the rule. It was a small wonder that U.S. Army psychiatrists calculated the number of combat days a man could expect to endure and still remain functional at around 120. By 1945 that figure was probably generous for any of the combatants—even the Japanese.

Viewpoint:
Yes, the front-line combat soldier reached the limits of his endurance in World War II; he was denied the periods of rest experienced by soldiers in earlier wars, and he had to cope with the severe psychological demands of modern warfare—demands that most soldiers could endure for only about six months.

Saving Private Ryan (1998) set a new standard for the movie re-creation of combat. One combat veteran of the Big Red One (First Infantry Division) and a survivor of Omaha Beach, who watched the movie unflinchingly, commented that, "They finally got the sounds right, bullets hitting bodies. But the smell, a movie will never give you the smell of fear, bodies blown apart and death." For those who have never experienced combat, especially individuals who teach history, the best they can hope to do is provide a forum for veterans to tell their stories to the students. When meeting a combat veteran, it is like looking through a darkened glass into a forbidden land. Often, when they speak, their eyes become unfocused, seeing things others can never imagine. At such moments these old men tend to look at each other, and the rest of the people in the room disappear . . . for only one who has been there can truly understand. Like Lazarus, they have been to the land of the dead and returned but have forever left something behind in that other world.

The combat experience of World War II, for a wide variety of reasons, was unlike anything experienced before or since. Soldiers in World War I, especially on the western front, indeed transcended the limits of endurance, but the full fury, the stretching to the limit of human capacity—both physiologically and psychologically—did not fully hit until 1941. The technology of the industrial revolution is perhaps the main factor at play in this evolution of warfare, especially in the realm of logistical support.

One Civil War historian, after watching *Saving Private Ryan*, compared the assault on Omaha Beach to Pickett's charge at Gettysburg (3 July 1863). Both involved mass formations of men, out in the open and charging into a wall of fire, who were striving to take the high ground. Both actions produced thousands of casualties in a fairly compact area. Regiments from Virginia, both in 1863 and 1944, were not just decimated (which actually means only a 10 percent loss) but instead were annihilated.

There is, however, a profound difference between the two assaults. The horror of Pickett's Charge was compressed into but one short afternoon, three hours of combat, and less than forty-five minutes for the actual charge. After that attack most of the Confederate and Union troops involved would not see combat again for ten months. Those who survived the assault of 6 June 1944, however, woke up the following morning to another day of combat, and another, and another. The Omaha Beach veteran quoted above was wounded on the third day, sent back to England, and within four weeks was back at the front yet again, catching his fifth and final wound in the closing days of the campaign in Czechoslovakia, hundreds of miles from where he started.

Modern technology and logistics made this rapid return to battle possible. The two armies that met at Gettysburg carried with them enough ammunition for not much more than four days of sustained combat. After that, one or the other would have to fall back on a base of supply and take weeks, if not months, to prepare for another onslaught. This logistics restraint, as much as anything else, was the driving factor behind General Robert E. Lee's desire to seek a sharp battle of decision after the inconclusive results from the first two days at Gettysburg. In 1944 a glut of supplies flooded to all fronts. The amount of firepower expended at Gettysburg could now be hurled out within a matter of minutes, with a thousand times that amount readily at hand, day after day, on battle fronts around the world.

Wounds that were debilitating, if not fatal, in 1863 would, thanks to the technology of modern medicine, be considered minor in 1944, thus allowing an experienced veteran to be quickly returned to action where he could again face death. Preventive medicine and the modern science of health and public sanitation also made the creation of mass armies truly possible for the first time. Camp diseases of the American Civil War (1861–1865) such as typhoid, smallpox, and dysentery were things of the past, except in extreme situations. Modern diets, vitamins, and

American infantrymen at rest following the landings at Normandy, 6 June 1944

(Robert Hunt Library)

a scientific approach to physical training created soldiers primed for the exertions of combat. Environments where mass warfare would have been impossible only fifty years earlier, such as the jungles of New Guinea and the frozen tundra of Finland, now became blood-soaked battlefields as a result of special diets, equipment, and medication. Even the supposed physical limits of the individual soldier could, at least temporarily, be transcended. Drugs were readily available to ward off sleep, pump a soldier up, keep him going, ease his pain, and even still the agony of dying.

The one factor, however, that could not permanently be changed was the psychological limits of the human mind. That point was reached and exceeded because of the demands of modern war. The wars of Julius Caesar (58–50 B.C.), Sun-tzu (fourth century B.C.), Napoleon Bonaparte (1785–1815), and Lee were contained by the limits of logistics and available technology. The U.S. Civil War could be defined as a war that was on the cusp of the Industrial Revolution (1750–1900). The siege of Petersburg (June 1864–3 April 1865) clearly demonstrated this new style of warfare with its fifty miles of siege lines, but the "depth" of the experience had yet to be realized.

Combat regiments of the Civil War were considered veteran after but two or three days in action. A regiment that had seen a dozen days of battle was considered well seasoned. Rare was the man of that conflict who could claim to have spent thirty days under fire. Granted, the rate of losses was tragically high, but these horrific losses were compacted into a few short days of terror, usually with long periods in between to recover. Even then the stress was clearly evident when, by 1864, both sides found it increasingly difficult to motivate troops to go into a direct assault.

The experience of combat troops on all sides during World War II, and particularly on the German side, was one of profound "depth," with depth meaning that the zone of danger was no longer the range of a rifle shot, but extended clear back to the very homes many were defending. In terms of time, the depth of combat extended not just across a few days or even months but continued unabated for years. A soldier, home on leave after a year in Russia, could be just as cruelly maimed by an aerial bomb at home as by a mortar round on the front line. More than one German combat veteran said he was more frightened at home during an air raid than by anything he had experienced at the front, since a bombing raid was so random in its killing and the sounds impossible to sort out.

Logistical support and modern technology allowed the rapid deployment of troops to far-distant fronts such as Stalingrad, Burma, and Guadalcanal. Once there, however, the laws of supply and demand firmly took hold in regard to the lives of the men sent to these distant hell holes. It had taken a supreme effort to move that soldier or marine across two thousand miles of steppe or ten thousand miles of ocean. Once there he was far too valuable to remove unless no longer useful, for example, if either crippled or dead. Even the removal of the wounded was carefully studied for maximum economic effect. How far back behind the lines should the man be taken was a mathematical formula based upon amount of treatment required, rations consumed, gas expended, and whether he could be recycled again for combat. When he did recover he would be pumped with vitamins, medications, and concentrated rations, burdened with ammunition, and sent to kill others who like him had been well trained, supplied, and shipped.

Throughout the war all armies, but particularly the German and American forces, conducted in-depth studies of combat troops, if for no other reason than to maximize their usage. Both sides came to basically the same conclusion. There was a fairly precise correlation between the number of days in combat and the chances of being killed or wounded. Men in their first two weeks of combat were particularly vulnerable, especially if they were with other men who were not experienced. Sounds had to be learned: which was a shell screaming overhead but winging its way harmlessly to the rear, or a mortar round, whispering in to land only feet away? When was it time to duck, stand up, run, or lay still? What were the subtle indications that the ground one was about to step on was mined, and where were the likely spots that a sniper might be lurking? Who were the officers to be avoided, or in fact encouraged to stick their heads up; and who were the officers that had that "lucky aura" that seemed to protect the men around them?

Once these basic survival skills were mastered, the odds of surviving shifted in favor of the veteran. He knew what he could and could not do and how to beat the odds. Even then, the odds were ultimately against him. More than one combat survivor has spoken about the horror of sitting in a foxhole under a German or Russian artillery barrage, knowing that it was all a matter of luck whether the next one coming in would turn them into a pulpy spray or kill the hysterically screaming recruit in the hole a dozen yards away.

Physiologically there is an ultimate limit to what anyone can withstand, and modern combat quickly pushes to that limit and beyond. There is no time to recover, no time to escape. Even when sent back behind the lines for a brief "R&R"

(rest and relaxation) the knowledge always lingered that in a matter of days it would end and that the front still awaited their return.

The German and American studies both concluded that for nearly everyone the limit was reached after approximately six months of actual combat. After surviving the first few weeks the odds indeed shifted, but no matter how skillful or lucky, there was still the random shell, hidden sniper, booby-trap (even the name, booby-trap, implies that it is a killer of fools, but many a savvy veteran hit them as well), or strafing plane that suddenly pounced out of the smoke-filled sky. By the end of four months something began to break inside a veteran. There was an ultimate weariness that one can glimpse in the drawings of cartoonist Bill Mauldin—a numbness to the horror and to one's own fate.

The rate of losses, at this stage, inevitably curved back up again. Reaction times are off; one too many adrenaline rushes leave one numbed. The statistics showed that after six months a veteran's number was up, and he knew it. The demands of modern war, however, rarely gave him a way out. American combat pilots were perhaps the only group given that option with a set limit on missions. The demands for experienced pilots to train new ones and the sheer number eventually trained was the primary reason this luxury was allowed. British pilots would be cycled out of the system for four to six months, but they knew that in the end they would have to go back. German, Japanese, and Russian pilots flew until they died, and nearly all the old hands did.

Some might argue that superior training and ideological motivation transcended this finite limit of human endurance. That belief could only come from the one society that ultimately did not have to face the full brutality of the conflict on its home soil. The Japanese "banzai" charges were not so much acts of heroic resistance as they were a frenzied explosion for soldiers who believed there was no alternative left. Many Japanese soldiers, driven to the final extreme of stress, chose instead to clutch a grenade and pull the pin, a final act of madness in an insane war. It should be remembered as well that in the last weeks of the conflict, in the Philippines and on Okinawa, thousands of Japanese troops did begin to surrender, a remarkable act of desperation when one considers all that they had been taught about the treatment they would receive as prisoners.

On the infamous Russian front the limit of endurance was clearly demonstrated by both sides. At Stalingrad more than ten thousand Soviet soldiers were summarily executed, and tens of thousands more sent to near certain death in penal battalions, for failure to "do their

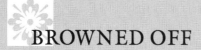

BROWNED OFF

Joe Desloge Jr., an American ambulance driver in Italy who was attached to the British Eighth Army, recalled wartime fatigue.

"Browned off" was the Tommies term for a chap who was so completely demoralized that he just didn't care anymore. He had seen too much and just wanted to chuck it all and check out of the war, out of life if necessary. Well, by the time we'd slogged through several hundred miles of Italian countryside, I had it. Here I was, all of twenty years old, stuck in a beat-up old truck, hauling mangled men I didn't even know back and forth over impassible roads, while my whole youth slipped away in this interminable war. So one day, when I was once again waiting in the middle of a field in the middle of some Italian nowhere, I just lost it. Things had quieted down after the advance, and the Tommies were hunkered down because the Jerries reportedly had left a sniper behind to make life a little irritating for us. We didn't know he was there, but somebody somewhere, high up in the all-knowing command, said he was there, so therefore he must be there. "Keep your head down," we were told.

Well, I didn't give a damn anymore, so I just walked around fully upright. So what if I "copped a packet?" My absence would make no difference at all in the grand scheme of things. Besides, if I survived I'd be sent to a hospital and then please, dear God! home. Well I walked around as cocky as you please and nothing happened; and pretty soon the Tommies began walking around too. Later, they found parts of a Jerry sniper's rifle scattered about and gave me the telescopic sight, which is now in my attic. The sniper, it turned out, had surrendered rather than die for Der Faderland. Maybe he was browned off too.

Source: Joseph Desloge Jr., Passport to Manhood *(St. Louis: St. Louis Humanities Forum, 1995).*

who was "legitimately" hurt and who was trying to avoid continued front line service.

German troops by the hundreds of thousands broke down and risked the near certain death of Soviet captivity or simply left the ranks. The roads of German retreat in the final months of the war were festooned with bodies hanging from lamp posts, bearing the sign "coward." A saner world would have called these victims heroes for trying to escape the madness.

The Omaha Beach veteran quoted in the first paragraph of this essay was eighteen when he scrambled out of a landing craft, the water around him flayed by shells and pink with blood. He earned five Purple Hearts and a Silver Star. When he spoke of that time his words were soft, drifting, whispering about the smell those not there could never imagine. His eyes, however, said it all. He had seen that dark land a horrific vision the post-Vietnam generation has been spared.

–WILLIAM R. FORSTCHEN, MONTREAT COLLEGE

Viewpoint:
No, despite the grueling conditions of front-line combat in World War II, victors and vanquished alike found ways of coping that allowed them to continue fighting effectively right up to the end of the war.

War exacts a terrible physical and psychological price from those who participate in it. This fact is nowhere more true than among those at the tip of the spear in ground combat. They face the physical burdens of exposure to the elements, disease, hunger and thirst, being weighted down with the impedimenta of war, and the deliberate attempts of a hostile adversary to maim or kill them. They also face the psychological burdens of fear, loneliness, and constant uncertainty. These forces remorselessly combine to grind down both the body and the spirit. Lord Moran, Winston Churchill's personal physician during World War II, served as a regimental surgeon in the previous war. Observing closely the effects of front-line combat, he said in *The Anatomy of Courage* (1945), "Men wear out in war like clothes." Given this constant attrition, one would expect that by 1945, after three to five years of fighting, the armies of World War II would have been at the breaking point. Strangely, however, this assumption was not the case. The victorious American and British armies at the end of the war were clearly capable of con-

duty." Given the fact that members of the *Narodny Kommissariat Vnutrennikh Del* (NKVD, People's Commissariat for Internal Affairs) stood with machine guns poised, behind front-line soldiers, is a clear enough indicator that the Soviet high command knew it was pushing its personnel beyond the limit. Yet, even with that threat, men by the hundreds of thousands broke down, refused to continue, and therefore died. Tens of thousands more shot themselves, stuck a hand out of a trench in order to get hit, or even arranged pacts with comrades to shoot them. This maiming became such common practice that victims of hand and foot wounds were subjected to special interrogation to try and sort out tinuing to fight and surely would have done so had it been required. Even more astounding, the conquered German army continued to offer significant resistance until its ultimate defeat.

Why was this so? It happened because each national army found a mechanism that provided the human incentive, through some combination of motivation and coercion, and the sustenance of life, through logistical support, that gave desperate men the will and capability to continue fighting. These institutional props were abetted by the propensity of soldiers to cling to their compatriots, a phenomenon psychologists refer to as "primary group cohesion." To these factors was added the grim logic of the situation. For the victors, the logic was that the only way to end the war was to kill as many German or Japanese soldiers as quickly as possible. For the vanquished, the logic was somewhat different: survival in a doomed cause. A brief survey of selected American, British, and German experiences illustrates these themes.

The experience of Company K, 333rd Infantry Regiment of the 84th Infantry Division, is indicative of the American combat experience in Europe. After having halted the German onslaught along the northern shoulder of the Battle of the Bulge (16 December 1944–16 January 1945), the 84th Infantry Division, along with other elements of the VII and XVIII (Airborne) Corps under the First U.S. Army, was ordered to attack and seize the Belgian town of Houffalize. On the morning of 13 January 1945, the first sergeant of Company K made the following entry in the unit's official log: "Co.[Company] moved by truck and foot at 0400 to Petites Tuilles, Belgium and jumped off in attack at 1015. Majority of men exhausted and scarcely fit for combat." Despite this condition, the company successfully attacked to capture an intermediate objective that allowed other members of the division to seize Houffalize, thus effecting the linkup between the First and Third American armies. This capture earned the weary riflemen a respite of seven days out of the line. They were then trucked north to join the Ninth Army. From 23 February to 5 March 1945, they attacked from the Roer River to the Rhine. During this offensive, they captured the town of Hardt, Germany, losing a quarter of their strength in just six hours. Despite these casualties, they kept going. Ultimately, they crossed the Rhine and drove to the Elbe in three weeks of headlong advances as the German Reich collapsed. As one reads the account of their combat experience, one has to ask what kept them going. The answer that emerges is a complex web of psychological and material forces. Among the former are strong-group cohesion reinforced by a positive dislike of those not sharing their dis-

comforts and a grim realization that they were in the war for the duration. The latter included enough food to keep them marching forward and an abundance of ammunition and supporting arms with which to keep killing Germans.

The British experience of front-line combat in World War II has been captured in a remarkable memoir, *Quartered Safe out Here: A Recollection of the War in Burma* (1992), by George MacDonald Fraser. Fraser, who served as a private in the Border Regiment, specifically rejects the argument that the World War II combat experience represented some sort of "unacceptable reality." The reality of the war, he says, was not only acceptable; it was accepted, particularly by those engaged in the grim business of carrying it out. Fraser's narrative begins in early 1945, shortly after British forces had crossed the Irrawaddy River. Although the fighting was desperate at times and the Japanese put up stiff resistance, there was no hint in his account that either he or his section mates could not and would not continue to advance. In fact, after the battles of Meiktila (March 1945) and Pyawbwe (April 1945), two Burmese cities whose capture opened the road to Rangoon, Fraser describes in detail how intensely one of his section mates voiced his desire to make sure it would be their division, rather than another, that captured the Burmese capital, "the ultimate prize of a long and dreadful war."

What was it that kept the men fighting besides this desire to bring the war to conclusion? Fraser cites several factors. First was the feeling of mutual dependence developed among members of his ten-man section. Second was a sense of loyalty to the larger unit, the regiment. In addition, in a rarity for the recollections of private soldiers, he also praised the quiet, matter-of-fact, confidence-building leadership of the 14th Army commander, General Sir William Joseph Slim. Here, one gets insight into another factor as well. Slim was not only a morale-building genius, he was also a logistical genius; and he saw how the two fields were interrelated. One of the secrets of the 14th Army's success against the Japanese was Slim's ability to convince front-line troops that if they got cut off by the Japanese, they would still be resupplied by the ubiquitous C-47 cargo planes. As promised, when it happened, they were. The final testimony to the combat capability of the 14th Army in the spring of 1945 was its over three-hundred-mile advance from Meiktila to the outskirts of Rangoon in just thirty-six days.

German combat experience of 1945 was similar in many respects to that of the men of Company K and Fraser's section, though it had somewhat different nuances. It is reflected in the gripping account of Guy Sajer, an Alsatian drafted into the *Wehrmacht* (German army) after the fall of France. Sajer, in early 1945, was caught up in a desperate rearguard action to defend the Lithuanian port of Memel from an advancing Soviet army. Having fought their way across Russia and back again, Sajer and his compatriots appeared to be near the physical and psychological limits of their endurance; but their actions indicated they still possessed a critical reserve. They held together as an effective fighting force and delayed the Soviets long enough for thousands of German civilians to be evacuated to East Prussia. In fact, the German resistance on the northern side of the Soviet drive to the west was so effective that it caused the Red Army to halt its Vistula-Oder operation and conduct several subsidiary attacks designed to clear their flanks for the final push to Berlin.

What kept Sajer and his comrades fighting? First, an intensely personal camaraderie that developed among them. It is no exaggeration to say that Sajer, and his compatriots, Hals, Wiener, and "the veteran," really did become a band of brothers, willing to risk their lives for one another in the certain knowledge that these risks would be reciprocated. Their incredibly intense and periodically reinforced combat training, a staple of the German military system, deliberately fostered this cohesion. Furthermore, the German combat doctrine known as *Auftragstaktik* (mission-type orders) encouraged the development of battlefield initiative down to the level of the lowest private. The military cultural forces that kept these men fighting were reinforced by a steady stream of National Socialist propaganda, a draconian policy of executing those who deserted their posts, and the ferociousness of a Soviet army bent on revenging acts of German barbarism. In the defense of Memel, one must add material factors as well to understand the German soldier's motivation. German soldiers were well fed and abundantly supplied with ammunition; additionally, naval gunfire support from German warships in the Baltic prevented Russian tanks from concentrating for a concerted offensive. Thus, the German experience reveals a good deal of commonality with that of the Americans and British, but also the particularities of the National Socialist regime and the dynamic of being on the losing side.

In his masterful *Commander in Chief: Franklin Delano Roosevelt, His Lieutenants, and Their War*

(1987) Eric Larrabee observed that "Strategy includes the working out of its consequences. The ranks of martial authority from multiple star to modest chevron correspond to an ordering of reality in which plans produce orders, orders produce actions, and actions produce isolated episodes of swirling fury where the issue hangs or falls on the skill and fortitude of individual human beings, under conditions of indescribable repulsiveness and stress." One of the sad conclusions about the human condition to emerge from an analysis of the fighting experience of 1945 is that even in the repulsive conditions that Larrabee so aptly cites, the motivational and coercive powers of the state; its ability to provide the physical sustenance of combat; and the tendency of men in battle to bind together in small, tightly-knit groups can keep people killing each other for much longer than one would ordinarily expect.

–HAROLD R. WINTON, MONTGOMERY, ALABAMA

References

John Ellis, *On the Front Lines: The Experience of War Through the Eyes of the Allied Soldiers in World War II* (New York: Wiley, 1990);

George Feifer, *Tennozan: The Battle of Okinawa and the Atomic Bomb* (New York: Ticknor & Fields, 1992);

George MacDonald Fraser, *Quartered Safe out Here: A Recollection of the War in Burma* (London: Harvill, 1992);

Eric Larrabee, *Commander in Chief: Franklin Delano Roosevelt, His Lieutenants, and Their War* (New York: Harper & Row, 1987);

Harold P. Leinbaugh and John D. Campbell, *The Men of Company K: The Autobiography of a World War II Rifle Company* (New York: Morrow, 1985);

Lord Moran, *The Anatomy of Courage* (London: Constable, 1945);

Guy Sajer, *Soldat oublié: recit* (Paris: Robert Laffont, 1967); translated as *The Forgotten Soldier: The Classic WWII Autobiography* (Washington, D.C.: Brassey's, 1990).

CONVENTIONAL WAR

Was the failure of German armed forces in the East inevitable?

Viewpoint: Yes, the Germans were not organizationally or doctrinally prepared for the scale of warfare called for on the Eastern Front.

Viewpoint: No, failure in the East was not inevitable, but deteriorating morale, harsh weather conditions, and economic limitations helped to defeat the Wehrmacht in Russia.

Germany's defeat on its Eastern Front continues to generate controversy. Did the Reich miss opportunities to end the war on its own terms in the steppes of Russia? Or did Russian resources and Russian weather, Nazi Germany's structural and ideological nature, or specific errors in planning and shortcomings in execution, doom Operation Barbarossa before it began?

The question must be addressed in a German context because it was Germany that initiated hostilities. Whatever Joseph Stalin may have intended in the long run, he had no immediate intention of sending the Red Army westward in the summer of 1941. The spectrum of approach is further narrowed because German planners were well aware of the objective military potential of the Soviet Union. They were also convinced that their way of war made that potential irrelevant—speed and shock would paralyze the Soviet system, then force it to implode. All that was needed, in Adolf Hitler's words, was "to kick the door down."

This scenario was not an entirely unrealistic. Earlier German victories had been based on maintaining the initiative, staying inside their opponent's decision-action loops. To stand still in the summer of 1941 was to invite the emergence of just the kind of mass, attritional war Germany had little chance of winning. Such a "use it or lose it" situation offered little margin for fog or friction. At the most basic level, German military intelligence significantly underestimated the forces available to the U.S.S.R. That in turn led to harder fighting of longer duration than expected. German losses in personnel and equipment rapidly exceeded replacement capacities. These losses meant taking ever-greater risks to maintain the momentum that was at the heart of German strategy. It had the predictable result of conflict at high policy and command levels over which risks made the best sense, since the margin of error had shrunk to near zero. By December 1941, Barbarossa was gridlocked by negative synergy: the elements that had generated its initial successes were now proving counterproductive. Paradigm shifts, however, were not among the strong points of National Socialism, or of the *Wehrmacht* (German Army) high command.

**Viewpoint:
Yes, the Germans were not
organizationally or doctrinally
prepared for the scale of warfare
called for on the Eastern Front.**

Germany attacked Russia on 22 June 1941. The final German operational plan, code-named Barbarossa, dictated a massive attack across a broad front. In this attack the Germans pushed forward along three divergent axes across the Ukraine and into Russia proper. Adolf Hitler attacked, firmly convinced that all that was required was "one solid kick and the whole rotten structure will come tumbling down." Despite recurrent and well-founded fears within the German military high command over the dangers of a two-front war, Hitler committed Germany to an all-out struggle for *Lebensraum* (living space) to the east. Six months later German forces were at the gates of Moscow, but they did not enter. Just as there were three axes of the German advance, there are as many views as to exactly why the Germans failed.

Generally speaking, most historians agree that in order for the Germans to win against Russia, their window of opportunity was open only from the start of the invasion until the onset of winter. Most also agree that Hitler's capture of Moscow may well have toppled the Soviets from power; warfare might have continued for some time after that point, but an eventual negotiated settlement on German terms would likely have ultimately resulted. Debate among historians and military theorists alike therefore centers upon the question of how these conditions might have been met or the specifics of why they were not.

One school of thought broadly contends that the Germans were, more or less, doomed. According to advocates of this position several complimentary factors contributed to their failure. The year 1941 saw one of the harshest winters on record. "General Winter" is historically the Russian's most able commander. Coupled with the effects of weather, adherents of this school of thought, was the massive economic potential of the Russians. This group contends that the sheer mass of manpower available to the Russians could not be overcome. Even as the Germans moved eastward, the Soviet system mobilized manpower reserves that poured in, providing a seemingly limitless pool of replacements. Finally, the German army sat at the end of an overextended and dangerously exposed logistics pipeline. Partisan warfare fueled by patriotic fervor, or merely hatred of the Germans exacerbated by their policies toward the "inhu-

man" Slavic peoples, created a "front behind the front," which further eroded the German war machine.

In contrast to this position is the idea that the Germans were organizationally and doctrinally incapable of succeeding in an offensive war across the distances involved on the Russian front. The famous *Blitzkrieg* (lighting war) of the German war machine could overwhelm the Poles, crush the Norwegians, and humiliate the French, but these were theaters of war quite different from the steppes of Russia. Various decisions made by the Germans in the allocation of national assets dictated that the effective range of the "blitz" was but a few hundred miles, not the eight hundred miles needed to achieve a capture of Moscow. Further, although the Germans had gone through a deliberate and thorough review of their Polish campaign, doctrinally focused historians note that the Germans did not continue this process after the fall of France in 1940. Rather, it appears that they rested upon their laurels and believed their own press releases about the invincibility of the armed forces of Nazi Germany. The "blitz" as it was represented in the popular imagination in 1940–1941 was in reality largely a product of the Nazi media machine.

Finally, some historians suggest that the Germans could have won were it not for a few crucial decisions. It is argued that there were actually several ways to beat the Russians, that the combination of the Soviet system and Russian people was not invincible. This line of reasoning attaches blame to several different sources: either it was the meddling of Hitler in operational planning or the recalcitrant independent streak evident in some German army leaders. This reasoning is rich, if counterfactual, historical terrain. It is all the more attractive to some for the very reason that none of the assertions can be absolutely proved or disproved, given the evidence that now exists.

Russia is a vast nation. In manpower, matériel, and raw resources the potential for the Soviet Union to create a military force for offensive action is staggering. If forced to wage a defensive war the Russians have recourse to two assets, the immense space of their territory and the inevitable onslaught of the brutal Russian winter. The combined effects of these elements have defeated all those who have attacked Russia since the days of Czar Peter the Great.

On 1 January 1941 the Russian armed forces numbered 4,207,000 men, 81 percent of whom were in the ground forces. While this number is indeed large, Soviet manpower is perhaps most eloquently illustrated by the number of soldiers the Soviets lost as prisoners to the initial German onslaught, manpower that they effectively wrote off and still managed stop the Nazis outside of Moscow. Prisoner figures are some of the only reliable numbers available from the beginning of the conflict; for various reasons the numbers of Soviets killed and wounded are difficult to accurately estimate. Between 22 June and 12 August the Russians lost some 390,700 men as prisoners west of their defensive line along the Dnieper river. Before the end of 1941 the Russians lost a total of 2,258,535 prisoners. Add to this staggering total the number of casualties they suffered in this same time frame, and one begins to comprehend the scale of warfare that the Soviets proved capable of waging. By way of comparison, the entire U.S. Army in 1939 stood at fewer than 150,000 soldiers, while the U.S. Army of 1999 is less than 480,000. Against such strength as the Russians presented, even at the outset, it is amazing that the Germans succeeded as much as they did.

It was not just in manpower that the Soviets dwarfed their opponents. On 22 June 1941 the Red Army had, in front of just one of the German axis of attack (that of German Army Group Center), an estimated 4,278 tanks. Even this large number was far below the strength that they should have had in place, an estimated 6,748 tanks of all types. Contemporary Western intelligence estimates and historians' analyses suggest a total armored force in excess of 22,000 tanks of all types. Accepting the fact that the majority of these tanks were antiquated, they still represent an incredible concentration of force. As any infantry soldier equipped with only small arms will relate, when their bullets are bouncing off the steel plate of a tank and its treads are about to roll over their head, they really do not feel that the tank is "outdated."

These tanks, antiquated and modern alike, were made by an industrial base with an enormous potential. The Russian war industry, or more accurately the industry that the Soviets reallocated toward war-matériel production, also spelled defeat for the Germans. Although the overall production of war matériel was relatively low prior to the German invasion, in the second half of 1941 the Russians accomplished something of a dual miracle. Not only did they physically remove huge portions of their industrial base from the western portion of the Soviet Union to safer areas around and behind north and east Moscow, they also managed to outproduce the fixed facilities of the Germans. From June through December 1941 the Soviets produced 4,177 tanks. Through 1942 they manufactured 24,700 tanks compared to the German total of 9,300 for the same period. This trend would only accelerate as the war progressed. Supplemented by logistically important vehicles such as trucks and locomotives provided by the United States through the Lend Lease program, the Soviets amassed the support materially critical to success in modern mobile warfare. By 1945 the Soviets had an estimated 665,000 vehicles in service, more than half of which were built in the United States. Over the course of the entire war the United States sent Russia some 427,000 trucks.

A military adage states that while amateurs talk tactics, professionals talk logistics. Logistics wins wars. Support of this kind is crucial when operating in the open steppes of Russia. For the Germans there was only one major artery along which supplies could reliably flow from their start point to Moscow. Military forces operating in either direction had to account for and adapt to the poor infrastructure of the Soviet Union. Over the more than eight hundred miles of mostly open terrain the Germans intended to cross, the minimum straight line distance between the German start point and the Russian capital, there was little to support life, let alone concentrated military forces, upon the exposed expanses of the steppe. Exacerbating this issue was the requirement that forced the Germans to attack along three divergent axes in the first place. The sheer size of Soviet forces, combined with the available space over which they might maneuver, dictated that the Germans could not penetrate in a single penetration in depth. "Ignoring your flanks" may have been a viable concept when facing France's two hundred miles, but not across the entire length of the road to Moscow.

Finally, there is no denying the power of the Russian winter. In 1941 it arrived early and developed into one of the worst in memory. Winter warfare is one of the most miserable experiences man may inflict upon himself. In temperatures so extreme that engine blocks freeze when not in use, human life is exposed and fragile. The Germans, by failing to complete their operational or strategic goals prior to the onset of the Russian winter, were doomed to defeat.

Although they attacked with a total of 3.3 million men in the combat and supporting units, the Germans had only seventeen true Panzer (Armored) divisions and eleven motorized divisions committed to the offensive. The majority of the remainder of the 154 German divisions dedicated to Barbarossa were infantry. This fact alone is not reason enough to suggest failure, but when one conducts a detailed analysis of the equipment available to those armored, mechanized, and "traditional" infantry divisions, it is discovered that the Germans were ill prepared to conduct Barbarossa in the manner they believed they could. Their weakness stemmed from three foundations: a lack of a true doctrine of deep attack, a lack of sufficient appreciation for the logistic issues involved in a deep attack, and a general dearth of material support in all combat arms.

Despite the persistent search for hard evidence to the contrary, it now appears that the Germans never truly developed a single coherent document that advocated the concept known to history as Blitzkrieg. In fact, prior to the invasion of Poland in 1939 the term itself, although used periodically in various German professional military journals, did not have any doctrinally accepted definition. Its usage suggests that the term was used generically to describe a short war, not specifically as a description of the technique to be used to achieve that objective. Only after the success of the Polish invasion did the word come into widespread usage. Thereafter, both in Allied and especially in the Nazi controlled German media, Blitzkrieg came to describe events that had already happened, as though they were a part of a predefined plan in accordance with an inspired doctrine that the Wehrmacht developed before the war.

However, no such coherent doctrine ever existed. The doctrinal adjustments that were made by the Germans based upon their analysis of their own operations in the early part of the war did not fully envision the concept of an attack of the depth needed in operations against Russia. Blitzkrieg, as practiced by the Germans in the Low Countries and against France, used penetrating attacks and massed combat power but only to an operational depth of a few hundred miles. Their organizations were not structured to support sustained attacks, either in manpower or material support, any further than this.

There is no way to ignore the issue of logistics as it relates to the German ability to wage offensive warfare. Certainly, despite the fact that the German high command did not approve the creation of the first three Panzer Divisions prior to 1936, they recognized the importance of wheeled and tracked support vehicles. In simple terms, tanks win battles, but it is the trucks of the logistics elements that win campaigns and wars. Unfortunately for the Germans, it was in many ways a choice of one or the other. The Nazi regime, painfully aware of the civil unrest that had played such a large role in the collapse of the German war effort at the end of World War I, did not convert its national economy to a full war-production footing any earlier than 1942–1943. Thus, for the Wehrmacht, it became a choice between tanks or trucks. Perhaps their ultimate choice was the result of a cultural myopia. Alternately, it may have been the influence of the preponderance of former combat-arms officers at the upper end of the German command structure that chose tanks over trucks. In either case the end result of decisions made in this regard was that during Barbarossa, only those few Panzer and mechanized divisions were fully supported by internal-combustion-driven logistics. The rest of the *Heer* (German Army) marched on foot and was supported in the main by horse-drawn guns and wagons, thus limiting the practical range of any single German attack. It was, therefore, not possible for Barbarossa to penetrate all the way to Moscow in a single thrust. The force structure of the German army limited each successive attack to a depth of roughly two hundred miles.

Finally, while the majority of the German armored formations were admittedly more advanced than most of the Russians, the Germans only managed to amass a total of 3,582 armored vehicles of all types at the outset of the attack. (Remember that the total Soviet armored force numbered some 22,000, while those opposing German Army Group Center alone numbered 4,278.) This fact again points out prewar industrial and political limitations of the Germans and their effect upon the conduct of the war.

In the end it is difficult to escape the idea that the German attack of 1941 was doomed to failure. Although there are a host of explanations, one stands out beyond the others; the German military of 1941 was not designed to accomplish the Herculean task set before it. This doctrine had not changed to reflect the scale of warfare on the Eastern Front. Blitzkrieg was designed to defeat nations the size of France and Poland. Doctrine drives force structure, and as a result the German army did not develop the type of robust logistics needed to support deep attacks. Without this structure the Germans were forced into an operational plan that resembled four successive "mini-blitzkriegs" (although each was, on its own, the size of the original Blitz against Poland) with a short pause between each for resupply, consolidation, and reorganization. Operations, in turn, slowed to the point where it was nearly impossible to take Moscow before the Russians could collect themselves and build their own combat powers to defend the city. If Moscow was the key to the defeat of the Soviet Union, then the Germans failed because they were looking too far beyond the simple solution and instead were trying to break open a combination lock.

–ROBERT L. BATEMAN III,
U.S. MILITARY ACADEMY, WEST POINT

EASTERN FRONT

**Viewpoint:
No, failure in the East was not inevitable, but deteriorating morale, harsh weather conditions, and economic limitations helped to defeat the Wehrmacht in Russia.**

No historical outcome is inevitable. Germany's failure to defeat the Soviet Union resulted from the inability of the *Wehrmacht* (German Army), and to a lesser extent the *Luftwaffe* (Air Force), to win three interrelated "battles": the battle of morale, the battle versus nature, and the battle of supply. These battles demonstrated serious structural weaknesses in the German military's *Blitzkrieg* (lighting war) doctrines. The Wehrmacht, designed to win short wars close to Germany, was ill-suited to win a war against Russia, but its defeat was not inevitable.

Of these three battles, Germany should have been well poised to win in the case of morale. In June 1941 the euphoric German army stood as conquerors of western Poland, Czechoslovakia, France, Norway, the Low Countries, the Balkans, Greece, and Crete. Historians talk of a "victory disease" that infected the German military, but in the spring of 1941 the Wehrmacht looked anything but diseased. With remarkably light casualties, it had enforced its will over any part of continental Europe that it coveted. It had driven England into constant invasion panics and had moved into North Africa. It stood in a strong position to capitalize on these successes by invading Russia.

The Red Army, on the other hand, stood in shambles. In the 1930s, Joseph Stalin's Great Purges had removed thousands of officers of presumed political unreliability, regardless of their military attributes. In all, Stalin removed 36,671 officers, including 403 of Russia's 706 brigade commanders, three of five marshals, all eleven deputy defense commissioners, and sixty of sixty-seven corps commanders. Only 15 percent of these officers ever returned to service. Most were executed. These purges continued up to the eve of the German invasion. The Great Purges thus wiped out an entire generation of Russian military and intelligence leaders. Those who remained had to command in an atmosphere of constant fear and suspicion.

Furthermore, interwar changes to Soviet society produced enormous dislocations. Between 1929 and 1939 the U.S.S.R. went from being 18 percent urban to 33 percent urban. As many as fifteen million peasants were moved, many of them forcibly, to achieve this change. Millions more starved as a result of Stalin's agri-cultural policies. Yet this very group, the peasantry, filled the ranks of the Red Army. Almost half of them were ethnically non-Russian. Most felt a great deal of bitterness toward Stalin's regime for the dislocation and starvation that collective agriculture caused. The loyalty of both the officers and the soldiers was therefore suspect.

Lastly, in great contrast to Germany, Russia's recent military experiences had been disastrous. In November 1939, Russia invaded Finland, which the Nazi-Soviet Pact earlier that year had placed in the Soviet sphere of influence. The Red Army committed one million men against a 175,000-man Finnish army. By the end of March 1940, Finland had surrendered, but the Russians lost 200,000 men to Finland's 25,000. The debacle further isolated Russia (seen as a possible German ally after the Nazi-Soviet Pact) from potential allies such as Britain and the United States and went a long way toward convincing the German high command that a quick victory against the Soviet Union was likely.

Yet, the surprise German invasion of Russia motivated military and civilian, Russian and non-Russian, to incredible levels of sacrifice and activity. The barbarity of the German threat to their homeland rallied the Soviet people in a way that few could have predicted. An outside invasion created a level of internal unity that no Stalinist policy could achieve. Nazi ideology grouped all Slavs together as subhuman, thereby complicating attempts to exploit the internal divisions of Soviet society. German atrocities alienated non-Russians and made their cooperation with the invading Wehrmacht increasingly unlikely.

Early losses of men, land, and resources only served to strengthen Soviet will. Women and men too old for service dug tank ditches, served in anti-aircraft gun crews, and worked long hours in Soviet factories to keep supplies flowing to the fronts. To be sure, the Stalinist system brutally punished those who did not do their part, but there can be no denying the high level of motivation inside the Soviet Union. Stalin encouraged Soviet morale by taking the immensely important step of reopening Russian Orthodox churches, though not mosques or synagogues, in September 1943.

For German soldiers, nourished on exaggerated dreams of quick victory and propaganda that dehumanized their Slavic enemies, the invasion proved to be a tremendous disillusion. Even their rapid early movements east produced few concrete results. The Russian steppes seemed endless and the supply of Russian soldiers inexhaustible. Winter brought frigid temperatures, snow, and frostbite; spring brought the infamous

Russian mud. One German soldier wrote to his family in July 1942, "This war has ripped my joy away from me." German morale never completely collapsed, but the heady days of 1941 gave way to a darker, more pessimistic mood that contrasted sharply with the increasing confidence of the Red Army.

"General Winter and Colonel Mud," according to a familiar cliché, won the war for Russia. While this statement is surely an exaggeration, one can confidently say that the Soviets fought a more successful war against the brutal climate and harsh conditions of Russia than did Germany. Counting on a quick victory and expecting to be in control of Russian cities and resources before winter, the Germans made inadequate preparations for severe weather. Their soldiers lacked warm clothing and boots; their equipment lacked winter oils and antifreeze. Wehrmacht units were sometimes as far as two thousand miles away from German supply bases. As a result, many units had to virtually fend for themselves in the barren steppes. The Soviets also denied the Germans factories and housing. Whatever they could not dismantle and move east they destroyed.

Russian soldiers faced the same natural conditions, of course, but were better prepared to meet them. Some Russian units, like the Siberians who helped to break the siege of Moscow, were specially equipped and trained for winter warfare. The Red Army also benefited from its proximity to supply centers and a mostly sympathetic civilian population. Furthermore, many Russian soldiers had learned to deal with severe weather from a young age and knew how to cope with snow, rain, and mud.

The third "battle" that the Russians won was the battle of supply. Here Britain and the United States, though still suspicious of Stalin and the Soviets, played a critical role. Hitler's invasion of Russia made the Soviet Union an overnight ally in the war against Nazism despite long-standing tensions between Stalin and the West. Winston Churchill acknowledged both his deep dislike of the Soviet system and his new support for the Red Army thus, "I will unsay no word that I have spoken about [communism]. But all this fades away before the spectacle which is now unfolding." The Americans, too, offered support by extending the Lend Lease program to the Soviet Union in September 1941. American Lend-Lease aid provided the Russians with fifteen million pairs of boots, four million tons of food (much of it in the form of Spam), and thirty-four million uniforms. This aid allowed the Russians to clothe and feed their men and to focus their own industry on the production of artillery, tanks, and Katyusha rockets.

Soviet industry responded to the challenge. Despite the invasion, the Soviets were able to keep their industry operating by moving it east of the Ural Mountains. More than 2,500 factories, 80 percent of the total Soviet industrial base, were uprooted and reassembled hundreds, in some cases thousands, of miles east. Soviet authorities cajoled, coerced, and convinced a largely female civilian-labor force to work long, hard hours to keep factories operating. Failure to report to work was treated as military desertion. As a result, much to Germany's surprise, the Russians were able to vastly increase their production of military hardware and even outproduce Germany in several key areas just a year after the invasion. In 1941, for example, the Russians built 8,200 combat aircraft. In 1943, after two years of German occupation, they had more than tripled production to 29,900 combat aircraft.

Germany, on the other hand, was never able to match Soviet levels of production. Their principal allies, Italy and Japan, were less industrialized than Germany and thus unable to provide the kind of economic assistance that Britain and the United States provided to Russia. Furthermore, the Nazis resisted putting the German economy on a full military scale until 1944. Hitler wanted to keep the civilian standard of living as high as possible to avoid the morale problems that he believed led to German collapse in 1918. Many German units therefore depended heavily upon hardware captured from their enemies, dramatically complicating supply problems. The Germans used 151 types of truck; the Russians used two.

The centralized Russian war-planning system allowed for a greater degree of control over the quality and quantity of military-hardware production. Germany did not even begin to develop a rational system until Albert Speer became armaments minister in 1943. Unlike Russia, where more than half of all industrial workers were women, Germany never called women to work in large numbers; Nazi ideology, which stressed women in traditional roles (notably motherhood), forbade it. Instead, the Nazis used laborers drafted from occupied territories and concentration-camp victims. The Nazis used more than seven million slave laborers during the war; these workers had a life expectancy of just four months, yet at one point they comprised 25 percent of the German labor force. Lastly, German production had to be divided between the Russian, Norwegian, North African (until 1943), Italian, Balkan, and French fronts.

Hitler's invasion of Russia in June 1941 seemed at the time to have a high probability of success. The Germans counted on it, the British feared it, and the Americans expected it. The Wehrmacht was battle-tested, confident, and

DEATH IN THE SNOW

In the following account, Dr. Heinrich Haape describes a German battalion's determined stand against overwhelming odds northwest of Moscow in December 1941.

The casualty register made depressing reading that night. There had never been so many names to enter. 14th December was a black day for the 3rd Battalion. 182 casualties, dead, wounded or frostbitten; in one afternoon we had lost more men than in the whole of the Russian campaign up to that point. But the "suicide battalion" had held out for many valuable hours against the Siberian hordes.

It was nearly midnight before I finished and was able to get back to the battle-post. . . .

By 3 A.M. all seriously wounded men had been evacuated to the rear areas. The panje wagons had kept up a constant shuttle service and the drivers . . . had worked heroically through the unbearably cold night. Towards dawn I was awakened from a light sleep by Müller, who said: "There are cries from the wood in front of us. They sound like cries for help. . . ."

Cautiously, with guns at the ready, we crunched through the snow towards the wood. It might be a trap. The cries became louder and more pleading. "For God's sake help me, someone! Where is everyone? For God's sake come and help me."

At the fringe of the wood we saw a figure staggering towards us, his arms outstretched. He did not seem to see us. We called out to him: "What's the matter?"

"Aaah!" he screamed. "Come and help me. I can't see. They've gouged out my eyes."

In a few strides we were at his side and shone a torch on his face. Where his eyes had been were only two bloody holes; bits of flesh hung on his cheekbones and the blood had streamed down his face and frozen there. . . .

He was an artilleryman—one of four men who had gone out to lay telephone wires to an observation point beyond our positions.

"We weren't expecting to see any Russians," he said, "then suddenly several shots and the other three dropped in the snow. I ran back the way we had come—straight into the arms of the Russians. They grabbed hold of me and dragged me along . . . I shouted for help and one of them told me to keep quiet . . . he spoke broken German . . . but I kept on calling for help. Then they said something to each other and threw me to the ground. One of them came at me with a knife...there was a terrific flash of light, a sharp pain and then the same with my other eye . . . then total darkness. The man who had hissed at me in broken German grabbed my arm and whispered into my ear: 'There. Go straight forward, to your brothers, the other German dogs, and tell them we'll destroy them all. We'll cut out their eyes and send what's left to Siberia—that will be Stalin's revenge. Now get going.' And he gave me a push and I heard them run away through the snow. . . ."

Then the Russians, determined to seize that vital escape road from Kalinin, attacked again just as dawn broke. Our soldiers grabbed their machine-guns from the warm ovens and fired into the waves of Red troops that poured out of the wood. The attack petered out in the snow in front of our hastily-prepared positions. And as they retreated, our artillery and mortars let them have it.

No sooner had they disappeared than our men were out among the dead Russians, stripping them of their fur caps, fleece-lined jackets and those magnificent felt boots. There were about sixty pairs of boots for distribution and preference was given to men with light frost-bite. In that way they could be kept battle-worthy. . . .

We left Krasnova and toiled back across the frozen Volga leaving the bodies of one hundred and twenty of our comrades on the battlefield. Close on a hundred and fifty others had been wiped from the battalion's strength by wounds or frost-bite.

Sixty-four Iron Crosses had been won in the battalion's suicide stand and the German radio devoted a special programme to the little battalion that had withstood the onslaught of four Siberian divisions so that half an army could escape. . . .

Source: *Heinrich Haape,* Moscow Tram Stop: A Doctor's Experiences with the German Spearhead in Russia *(London: Collins, 1957), pp. 226–229.*

eager. The Russians were internally divided, demoralized from the Finland fiasco, and poorly equipped. Nevertheless, few at the time saw how poorly positioned the German system was to deal with a war against not only the Red Army but against the unforgiving nature of Russia itself. This positioning, not historical inevitability, led Germany to defeat on the eastern front.

–MICHAEL S. NEIBERG, U. S. AIR FORCE ACADEMY, COLORADO

References

Omer Bartov, *The Eastern Front, 1941–45: German Troops and the Barbarisation of Warfare* (Basingstoke, U.K.: Macmillan in association with St. Anthony's College, Oxford, 1985);

Bartov, *Hitler's Army: Soldiers, Nazis, and War in the Third Reich* (New York: Oxford University Press, 1992);

Antony Beevor, *Stalingrad* (London: Viking, 1998);

George E. Blau, *The German Campaign in Russia: Planning and Operations, 1940-1942* (Washington, D.C.: Department of the Army, 1955);

Horst Boog, and others, *Angriff auf die Sowjetunion* (Stuttgart: Deutsche Verlags-Anstalt, 1983), translated by Dean S. Mac-Murray and others as *The Attack on the Soviet Union,* volume 4 of *Germany and the Second World War* (Oxford: Clarendon Press; New York: Oxford University Press, 1998);

Alan Clark, *Barbarossa: The Russian-German Conflict, 1941–45* (New York: Morrow, 1965);

John Erickson, *The Road to Stalingrad* (London: Weidenfeld & Nicolson, 1975);

Joachim C. Fest, *Gesicht des Dritten Reiches: Profile einer totalitateren Herrschaft* (Munich: Piper, 1963), translated by Michael Bullock as *The Face of the Third Reich: Portraits of the Nazi Leadership* (London: Weidenfeld & Nicolson, 1970);

Stephen G. Fritz, *Frontsoldaten: The German Soldier in World War II* (Lexington: University of Kentucky Press, 1995);

Bryan I. Fugate, *Operation Barbarossa, Strategy and Tactics on the Eastern Front, 1941* (Novato, Calif.: Presidio Press, 1984);

David M. Glantz and Jonathan M. House, *When Titans Clashed: How the Red Army Stopped Hitler* (Lawrence: University Press of Kansas, 1995);

Frederick Kagan, "The Evacuation of Soviet Industry in the Wake of 'Barbarossa': A Key to the Soviet Victory," *Journal of Slavic Military Studies,* 8 (June 1995): 387–414;

Rolf-Dieter Müller and Gerd R. Ueberschär, *Hitler's War in the East, 1941-1945: A Critical Reassessment,* translation of texts by Bruce D. Little (Providence, R.I.: Berghahn Books, 1997);

R. H. S. Stolfi, *Hitler's Panzers East* (Norman: University of Oklahoma Press, 1991).

EASTERN FRONT

EISENHOWER

Was Dwight D. Eisenhower an effective military leader?

Viewpoint: Yes, Eisenhower was an effective military leader who brilliantly led the Allied Expeditionary Force to crush the Wehrmacht in western Europe.

Viewpoint: No, at best Eisenhower was an effective coordinator of Allied resources; he remained too removed from actual battle to be called a leader.

Dwight D. Eisenhower was a master of the political aspects of coalition warfare. From the entry of the United States into World War II, he distinguished himself by his ability to cooperate with the British, both in strategic planning and in developing structures for joint commands. When in May 1942 Chief of Staff George C. Marshall sent Eisenhower to London as spokesman for an early cross-Channel invasion, the British supported him for command of the invasion of North Africa that was the eventual outcome of the negotiations.

In the Mediterranean campaigns, and later as commander-designate of Operation Overlord, Eisenhower succeeded in establishing both institutional and personal cooperation among armies, navies, and air forces with greatly different mentalities and long records of internal rivalries. He was able to keep Britain's most distinguished and difficult soldier, Field Marshal Bernard Montgomery, a functioning member of the Allied team until the end of the war; he was able to drive in harness a team of senior U.S. officers whose opinions of their own talents were often higher than combat would sustain.

Eisenhower's success as a coalition commander, matched by few and surpassed by none, merits on its face inclusion in the ranks of great captains. His critics nonetheless argue that as a general, Eisenhower's record was mediocre. He learned his craft on the job—often with no help from subordinates—and his performance steadily improved. From start to finish, however, he remained cautious, preferring to hedge his bets whenever possible. During the D day campaign he pursued a broad-front strategy, taking advantage of local opportunities such as the Normandy breakout, but never sought to push success. Arguments that his caution dissipated chances to end the war in 1944, or capture Berlin and Vienna before the Russians, or a half-dozen other alleged failures of omission, have the advantage of hindsight. Eisenhower had both a clear understanding of his own capabilities and a solid sense of what the forces under his command could do—and what they could do well. He had the wisdom to "play within himself," and to recognize that modern war seldom rewards the spectacular. In May 1945 Eisenhower stood as master of the field in the Western Alliance.

Viewpoint:
Yes, Eisenhower was an effective military leader who brilliantly led the Allied Expeditionary Force to crush the Wehrmacht in western Europe.

General of the Army Dwight D. "Ike" Eisenhower emerged from World War II in resplendent glory. As Supreme Commander of the Allied Expeditionary Force, Eisenhower directed the vast array of Western armies that landed on D-Day (6 June 1944) and in the ensuing campaigns crushed the *Wehrmacht* (German Army) in the west. By Eisenhower's own account on the day of the surrender, there were more than three million Americans serving under his direct command. Combined forces led by Eisenhower on V-E Day (8 May 1945) exceeded four million combatants. He was by any standard one of the most successful coalition commanders in history.

Successful leadership in modern warfare is based on two fundamental principles: knowing what to do and knowing how to do it. A commander can learn the first tenet by schooling and experience. Comprehending the second principle is what marks a successful commander. The twenty-six years of Eisenhower's career prior to World War II witnessed the development of a highly adept professional officer. By taking advantage of the opportunities for formal military education, by learning the complexities and efficient operations of multi-echelon staffs and by studying under the tutelage of the army's most forward-looking officers, Eisenhower developed the techniques that prepared him for the awesome task confronting him. From 8 November 1942 until the ultimate defeat of Nazi Germany, Eisenhower commanded the most effective military coalition in history. He had no precedents on which to base his decisions. He faced innumerable obstacles, including the organization of a truly joint and combined allied staff.

During the war, Eisenhower's subordinate commanders were often critical of his method of command. Omar Bradley considered him a political general of rare and valuable gifts, but unable to manage a battlefield. George S. Patton repeatedly criticized his boss for "timidity and the inability or unwillingness to command [Field Marshal Bernard] Montgomery." Sir Arthur Bryant, in *Turn of the Tide, 1939–1943: A History of the War Years Based on the Diaries of Field-Marshal Lord Alanbrooke, Chief of the Imperial General Staff* (1957), noted that British commanders were equally critical, attempting to push Eisenhower "into the stratosphere and rarefied atmo-

sphere of a supreme commander" in order for Montgomery actually to manage the battlefield. In spite of this dissension, Eisenhower succeeded because he demonstrated that he not only knew what had to be done, but how to accomplish it.

The path to the top was not always easy. Like most successful commanders, Eisenhower matured in the job. Available primary sources clearly indicate that as theater commander in North Africa, the Mediterranean, and Europe, Eisenhower concentrated his personal attention on two basic concerns. One was the creation of an allied command structure and organization, and the other was the planning and execution of broad strategies to defeat the Axis forces in Europe. Additionally, the central theme of his wartime correspondence to George C. Marshall revolved around his education as a combat commander. Eisenhower was much less sure of himself in 1942 than in 1944, when his letters brimmed with confidence in his ability to manage the battlefield. In the interim Eisenhower greatly improved his comprehension of the tactical, operational, and strategic levels of war, as well as their accompanying political implications.

As the Allied commander of the invasion of Northwest Africa (Operation Torch), Eisenhower fumbled badly in the political arena when he consummated the infamous "Darlan deal" without prior consultation with the Army chief of staff. Despite initial operational success, his forces were locked in stalemate in Tunisia in mid-February 1943 when Erwin Rommel counterattacked and delivered a crushing defeat at Kasserine Pass. Despite personal misgivings, Eisenhower promptly relieved the American commander of II Corps and took a more active role in directing operations, but the overall performance of the American army in North Africa and Eisenhower in particular, was less than satisfactory and did nothing to mollify the British perception that the Americans were amateur soldiers and could not hold their weight against the more experienced German army. The campaign did achieve two noteworthy effects—it hardened Eisenhower as a commander and gave the green American troops battle experience that they exploited in the next operation.

In Sicily the American Seventh Army, now commanded by Patton, achieved far more spectacular success, but Eisenhower continued to direct operations from an African command post, seemingly comfortable in commanding coalition forces through British air, land, and sea subordinate commanders. If a word characterized his operational style in the Mediterranean, it was "cautious." He remained strangely distant from the planning process and in the execution phase failed to intervene directly when the situa-

tion warranted. Consequently, the coordination between Montgomery's and Patton's forces throughout the campaign was haphazard at best. As a result, the majority of the German army escaped across the straits of Messina to live and fight on the Italian mainland. Though the American army came of age during the Sicilian campaign, the same could not be said of Eisenhower.

During Operation Overlord, the invasion of northwest Europe, Eisenhower emerged as a superb coalition commander. Prior to D day he made several crucial decisions that ensured the success of the amphibious invasion. Upon his initial review of the Overlord plan, following his designation as supreme commander, Eisenhower directed that the beachhead be expanded and more forces allocated for the initial invasion. Next, his insistence that strategic-air assets be diverted from attacking oil and petroleum cen-

ters in Germany to the destruction of France's transportation network successfully isolated the lodgment area and prevented timely reinforcements from engaging the invasion force. Third, Eisenhower's judicious employment of the British sixth and American eighty-second and 101st Airborne Divisions, against the strong advice of Air Chief Trafford Leigh-Mallory, sealed the lodgment area and allowed the Allies to establish and then expand the bridgehead. Finally, he made the decision that he, and he alone, could make—the decision to launch the invasion. In the process, according to historian Stephen E. Ambrose, he fixed his place in history.

During the ensuing campaign in Normandy, Eisenhower refused to become decisively engaged in the ground battle, again preferring to direct operations through Montgomery, his ground-forces commander. Unwilling to issue

Supreme Allied Commander General Dwight D. Eisenhower talking to American paratroopers before D-Day

(Photograph by Robert Hunt)

EISENHOWER

decisive orders to Montgomery, Eisenhower flitted away valuable time as allied casualties mounted in the fighting through the Norman *bocage* (French farmland crisscrossed with hedges). Only by late July when German forces were stretched thin did the forces under Eisenhower achieve the necessary breakout. The failure to close the Falaise-Argentan pocket and quite possibly end the war during the summer of 1944 was the result of Eisenhower's indecisive command style, but on 1 September 1944 Eisenhower assumed command of all operations. That decision created a predictable rift within the Allied command structure, most notably with Montgomery and the British Chief of the Imperial General Staff, Field Marshal Lord Alanbrooke. Nevertheless, Eisenhower remained fixed that with the German army in full retreat, the time had arrived that he should not only command, but also control the pace of the Allied advance across France and Belgium.

His decision to advance on Germany along a broad front, against Montgomery's preferred single thrust, remains debatable, but the broad advance ensured that the Germans were unable to establish a coherent defense prior to the time that Allied patrols approached the German border. Logistical constraints, not enemy action, finally halted the Allied drive west of the Rhine. If Eisenhower was to be faulted for Allied operations in the autumn of 1944, it lay in his failure to comprehend the necessity of opening the port of Antwerp in a timely manner, which represented the only real chance of ending the war in 1944. Though Antwerp fell under the jurisdiction of Montgomery, the ultimate responsibility lay with Eisenhower as supreme commander, and he missed a golden opportunity because he issued indecisive orders and vacillated between his principal subordinate commanders over logistical priorities.

When the Germans finally launched their counterattack in the Ardennes on 16 December 1944, Eisenhower first recognized the offensive was greater than a local thrust and initially realized the enemy attack now presented the Allies with an unparalleled opportunity to destroy the bulk of the Wehrmacht west of the Rhine. Immediately allocating American forces north of the Bulge to Montgomery's command, Eisenhower ignored national parochial prejudices that American forces serve only under American commanders, and he supervised the eventual destruction of the enemy within the ever-shrinking pocket. The Battle of the Bulge produced the heaviest American casualties of the European war, but in the process, the Allies destroyed Adolf Hitler's remaining operational reserves in the West.

Simultaneously, personal relations with Montgomery continued to deteriorate. When Montgomery again questioned Eisenhower's ability to direct the land battle, the supreme commander had enough. Writing to Montgomery, Eisenhower regretted the development of such an "unbridgeable gulf of conviction between us that we would have to present our differences to the Combined Chiefs of Staff." Whereas Eisenhower appeared initially reluctant to relieve Major General Lloyd Fredendall in the wake of the Kasserine debacle, he was on the verge of relieving Great Britain's senior field commander if Allied solidarity was now in jeopardy. Faced with his own dismissal, Montgomery backed down and assured Eisenhower that henceforth the supreme commander could rely on him and "all under Montgomery's command would go all out 100%" to implement Eisenhower's strategy. If Eisenhower exerted his authority more ruthlessly by 1945 than he had in 1942, it was because the exigencies of war dictated more drastic measures.

By March the Western Allies crossed the Rhine and within two months destroyed the bulk of Germany's remaining forces. Though Eisenhower's decision not to drive on Berlin was harshly criticized by Winston Churchill and Montgomery at the time, the decision was not controversial to Eisenhower, who remained fully cognizant of the postwar boundaries as determined at Yalta (4–11 February 1945). At the same time he fully understood that American forces in the European theater would likely be transferred to the Pacific to bring the Japanese war to a successful conclusion. Unless otherwise directed by President Harry S Truman or Marshall, Eisenhower was not content to allow American soldiers to die for what he termed strictly political reasons. Moreover, the possibility that Hitler might be preparing the Alpine Redoubt dictated the dispersion of Allied forces toward Bavaria. By May the war in Europe was over. In the final analysis, the true measure of a field commander's success is ultimate victory on the battlefield. Eisenhower was no exception. Command experience in war reflected his prewar service under Generals Fox Conner, John J. Pershing, Douglas MacArthur and Marshall. Enjoying Marshall's full support, Eisenhower succeeded in defeating the Axis forces in Europe by clearly defining a command organization based on unity of command and by carefully selecting skilled commanders and staff personnel capable of executing his broad plans and objectives.

How does Eisenhower rate in the pantheon of military heroes? Eisenhower made far more correct decisions than he made poor ones. Though he never possessed a commander's intuition of the battlefield, he matured in command from the cautious days in Tunisia to the final capitulation of Germany at Reims. His greatest strength lay in his complete dedication to Allied unity. He understood far better than Bradley, Patton, and even Montgomery, that the final victory was to be an Allied victory, not a national triumph. Best evidenced by his broad-front advance, Eisenhower intended that no single general or national army was going to win the war alone. He clearly understood how important the war was to the British. How else might one explain his approval to allow Montgomery to launch the ill-fated Market-Garden in September 1944, an obvious effort to restore British morale after the fast-paced American advance in the aftermath of Bradley's Operation Cobra the preceding July. In March 1945 he intentionally withheld permission from Jacob Devers's sixth Army Group to cross the Rhine when U.S. and French forces could easily have done so until Montgomery launched Operation Varsity, in order that Great Britain could take pride in Montgomery's success. In short, Eisenhower was the most successful coalition commander and, within eleven months of launching the cross-Channel attack he was able to cable the Combined Chiefs of Staff: "The mission of this Allied force was fulfilled at 0241 local time, May 7, 1945."

–COLE C. KINGSEED, U.S.
MILITARY ACADEMY, WEST POINT

Viewpoint:
No, at best Eisenhower was an effective coordinator of Allied resources; he remained too removed from actual battle to be called a leader.

From the early years of World War II, Dwight D. Eisenhower's fitness to lead Allied soldiers became a controversial issue, and it remains so. Nationalism, service pride, and individual egos have influenced the international debate on Eisenhower's effectiveness as the strategic commander of Allied forces. When the war started in Europe in September 1939, Eisenhower was a lieutenant colonel with considerable staff and administrative experience, but little experience in leading soldiers and commanding tactical units. By 1944, as Commander of the Allied Expeditionary Forces, Eisenhower commanded and directed all Allied air, sea, and land forces in the Normandy invasion. He then planned and directed the northwest Europe theater strategy until the end of the war in May 1945. Eisenhower's rise from lieutenant colonel to general was nothing less than amazing. He achieved senior rank without commanding major tactical or operational units, and without service in combat. The question is: was Eisenhower an effective strategic commander, despite his lack of command experience at tactical and operational levels?

When Eisenhower was given command of the landings in North Africa in 1942, he had neither the experience nor the knowledge in operational and tactical doctrine to command such an operation. During the campaign Eisenhower's lack of experience was consistently obvious. As recorded by Martin Blumenson and James L. Stokesbury in *Masters of the Art of Command* (1975), the British Chief of the Imperial General Staff, Field Marshal Lord Alanbrooke, wrote that Eisenhower

> had neither the tactical nor strategical experience required for such a task. By bringing Alexander over from the Middle East and appointing him as Deputy to Eisenhower, we were. . . . flattering and pleasing the Americans in so far as we were placing our senior and experienced commander to function under their commander who had no war experience.

The British, with the approval of U.S. Army Chief of Staff George C. Marshall, responded by putting in place a command structure that in essence elevated Eisenhower to the status of supreme commander and effectively removed him from the battlefield and the conduct of operations while retaining for Americans the top position. The British assumed the positions of deputy for ground, sea, and air, and essentially took over the conduct of operations in the Mediterranean theater. These operations were primarily a function of British strategic thinking. As recorded in Norman Gelb's *Ike and Monty* (1994), Alanbrooke concluded: "The main impression I gathered was that Eisenhower was no real director of thought, plans, energy or direction. Just a coordinator, a good mixer, a champion of inter-Allied co-operation, and in those respects few can hold the candle to him. But is that enough?"

Some American commanders formed the same impression. In reference to the Sicily campaign Omar N. Bradley wrote, with Clay Blair in *A General's Life: An Autobiography* (1983):

The Combined Chiefs named Ike commander in chief for the Sicily operation. But Ike had no direct command responsibility for planning and executing the operation. The Combined Chiefs delegated this responsibility to Ike's deputies for ground, air and sea. . . . Ike had become in his own description, "chairman of the board," presiding over a committee of three to run the war.

The situation remained unchanged in the campaign for the invasion of Europe. The British again managed to retain all the top-level operational command positions: Montgomery as ground commander, Admiral Sir Bertram H. Ramsay as commander-in-chief of naval forces, and Air Marshal Trafford Leigh-Mallory as commander-in-chief of air forces. As a result, Eisenhower never had the opportunity to mature as a tactical and operational commander in war. He never personally led a combat unit of any size in battle. He was not a traditional American military commander in the vein of George Washington, Ulysses S. Grant, William Tecumseh Sherman, John J. Pershing, or Douglas MacArthur. His lack of combat experience precluded him from obtaining the respect automatically given to those who have served in battle. The words of Montgomery—"nice chap, no general"—, Alanbrooke, and other British generals were blunt and often unkind in their appraisal of Eisenhower's abilities as a general. Certain American generals and admirals were also critical of Eisenhower's leadership. George S. Patton was probably the most critical of Eisenhower, and in his diary accused him of one of the worst sins an American commander could be charged with: failing to look after the welfare of his soldiers:

> The U.S. Troops get wholly separated and all chance of being in at the kill [the conclusion of the North African campaign] and getting some natural credit is lost. Bradley and I explained this to Ike and he said he would stop it. He has done nothing. He is completely sold out to the British. . . . Ike must go. He is a typical case of a beggar on horseback—could not stand prosperity.

Patton believed that Eisenhower was "too weak in character to be worthy" of his loyal subordinate commanders. In his diary in January 1945, Patton wrote: "It is too bad that the highest levels of command. . . . have no personal knowledge of war. . . ." Bradley, too, held a low assessment of Eisenhower's knowledge and understanding of the art of war, writing in his memoir that "Ike sent me my first official letter as II Corps commander. It was very long, patronizing in tone, and it contained some specific tactical suggestions which were dangerously ill-conceived and proof to me (if further proof were needed) that Ike had little grasp of sound battlefield tactics."

During the war Eisenhower increasingly developed a British outlook. This is not surprising given the fact that all his operational commanders throughout the war were British. At the strategic level this meant that major campaigns tended to be a function of British strategic thinking. In 1942 and 1943 the British were the senior partners in the British American alliance, and dominated Allied planning. The campaigns in North Africa, Sicily, and Italy were primarily a function of British strategic and operational thinking. Under these conditions the American practice of war through Eisenhower was subordinate to the British strategy. In 1944 and 1945, as American resources dominated the British American war effort, Eisenhower took a more active role in operations. The result was a sequence of serious mistakes.

After the war Admiral John Leslie Hall, commander of Task Force "0," which landed the First Infantry Division at Omaha Beach, wrote, as recorded by Susan H. Godson in *Viking of Assault: Admiral John Lesslie Hall, Jr., and Amphibious Warfare* (1982), Eisenhower "was one of the most overrated men in military history." Eisenhower's knowledge of tactical and operational doctrine was undeveloped. In particular, he did not grasp the complexities of amphibious operations. This lack of understanding precluded him from accurately assessing the merits of Montgomery's invasion plan. The following statement made by Eisenhower and recorded in Jeter A. Isely and Philip A. Crowl's *The U.S. Marines and Amphibious War: Its Theory, and Its Practice in the Pacific* (1951) reflects Eisenhower's inability to appreciate the complexity of amphibious landings:

> "You know an amphibious landing is not a particularly difficult thing," he said, "but it's a touchy and delicate thing, and anything can go wrong. In some ways, from the land fellow's viewpoint, it is one of the simplest operations. You put your men in boats and as long as you get well-trained crews to take the boats in, it is the simplest deployment in the world—the men can go nowhere else except to the beach."

This statement is clearly the view of the uninitiated. It is indicative of two things: Eisenhower was not tactically and operationally sophisticated in amphibious operations, nor did he talk to or listen to his American operational and tactical commanders. Admirals Hall and Henry K. Hewitt, as well as Generals Patton, Leonard T. Gerow, and Clarence R. Huebner, were more or less left with the impression that the supreme commander did not care to hear what they had to say. They were unable to present their views and too

EISENHOWER DECLARES VICTORY

On 8 May 1945 General Dwight D. Eisenhower issued the following message to his troops:

The crusade on which we embarked in the early summer of 1944 has reached its glorious conclusion. It is my especial privilege, in the name of all nations represented in this theatre of war, to commend each of you for the valiant performance of duty.

Though these words are feeble, they come from the bottom of a heart overflowing with pride in your loyal service and admiration for you as warriors. Your accomplishments at sea, in the air, on the ground and in the field of supply have astonished the world.

Even before the final week of the conflict you had put 5,000,000 of the enemy permanently out of the war. You have taken in stride military tasks so difficult as to be classed by many doubters as impossible. You have confused, defeated and destroyed your savagely fighting foe. On the road to victory you have endured every discomfort and privation and have surmounted every obstacle that ingenuity and desperation could throw in your path. You did not pause until our front was firmly joined up with the great Red Army coming from the east and other Allied forces coming from the south.

Full victory in Europe has been attained. Working and fighting together in single and indestructible partnership you have achieved a perfection in the unification of air, ground and naval power that will stand as a model in our time.

The route you have traveled through hundreds of miles is marked by the graves of former comrades. From them have been exacted the ultimate sacrifice. The blood of many nations–American, British, Canadian, French, Polish and others–has helped to gain the victory. Each of the fallen died as a member of a team to which you belong, bound together by a common love of liberty and a refusal to submit to enslavement. No monument of stone, no memorial of whatever magnitude could so well express our respect and veneration for their sacrifice as would the perpetuation of the spirit of comradeship in which they died.

As we celebrate victory in Europe let us remind ourselves that our common problems of the immediate and distant future can be best solved in the same conceptions of cooperation and devotion to the cause of human freedom as have made this Expeditionary Force such a mighty engine of righteous destruction. Let us have no part in the profitless quarrels in which other men will inevitably engage as to what country and what service won the European war.

Every man and every woman of every nation here represented has served according to his or her ability and efforts and each has contributed to the outcome. This we shall remember and in doing so we shall be revering each honored grave and be sending comfort to the loved ones of comrades who could not live to see this day.

"General Eisenhower's Victory Order of the Day, and His Proclamation on Germany's Defeat," The New York Times, *8 May 1945.*

---

often went into battle with plans they knew were defective. Hewitt wrote in an unpublished manuscript, "The Navy in the European Theater of Operations," that:

With the exception of certain officers temporarily detailed to planning committees, there were no naval officers, either British or American on the Supreme Commander's Staff. Admiral Cunningham felt that the General [Eisenhower] should look to him for naval advice, and that there should be no naval officer on the staff to exert a direct influence on the Supreme Commander's decisions.

Hewitt was two levels of command below Eisenhower and rarely saw the supreme commander. Eisenhower made little effort to see his subordinate naval commanders or seek their advice. He permitted himself to be separated from the nuts and bolts of operational and tactical planning. As a consequence, when he took charge of planning the Normandy invasion he was a novice in the conduct of amphibious warfare. He had to rely heavily on the experience and knowledge of Montgomery and other senior British operational commanders.

A further example of Eisenhower's incapacity to make decisions regarding the combat employment of American soldiers was his directive to maximize the loading of landing craft in order to secure sufficient craft to conduct Operation Anvil, the proposed amphibious assault on southern France that was originally to be conducted in conjunction with the Normandy invasion. Because of a shortage in landing craft the plan was reviewed. The British believed Anvil could and should be canceled, not only for this reason but also because the landing site was too far away to act as diversion to draw German forces away from Normandy. Eisenhower, in an effort to maintain the operation, had his staff develop a loading plan for landing craft that maximized the capacity of the vessels, but destroyed tactical organizations and flexibility. Montgomery initially opposed the new loading plan on the grounds that it would "compromise tactical flexibility, introduce added complications, bring additional hazards into the operations, and thus generally endanger success." Eventually Montgomery, however, perhaps for the sake of Allied cooperation, backed away from his initial response and accepted the proposal. Perhaps in this case Montgomery was the better judge. The new organization disrupted unit integrity, and thereby diminished combat power. In the army there is an old common-sense saying, "Train the way you fight." Huebner and the staff of the First Infantry Division believed that this common-sense principle was violated at considerable cost in the invasion at Normandy.

Eisenhower did not exert the type of influence traditionally expected of American military leaders because he did not have the authority to select his subordinate commanders. Those decisions, rightly or wrongly, were made by political leaders—Franklin D. Roosevelt and Winston Churchill. His primary objective also was to maintain the coalition. Furthermore, he adopted in part the British doctrine of war. Finally, he lacked the tactical and operational experience to assess and make decisions on the basic principles and doctrinal considerations upon which the plan was based. It may also have been that his inexperience caused a lack of confidence, producing a tendency to defer to the supposed superior knowledge of others. Eisenhower procured, allocated, and managed resources; coordinated the use of assets; generated consensus; and informed superiors and political leaders. He placated, cajoled, appeased, compromised, and occasionally dictated. There were those rare occasions when Eisenhower stood his ground and was immovable. Two such occasions arose in the Normandy campaign: one over command of the strategic air forces of both nations, and another over Operation Dragoon, the invasion of southern France. British and American air commanders believed the quickest way to end the war was through the strategic-bombing campaign. They opposed the commanded structure and bombing plans proposed by the Supreme Commander. Eisenhower, however, was successful in gaining some level of control over Allied air power. Eisenhower also fought to maintain the amphibious landings in the south of France. The landing was postponed, but ultimately took place bringing ashore another Allied army and French forces. In both cases Eisenhower knew he had the support of Marshall. Eisenhower did not lead or command in the traditional sense, nor did he formulate a strategic vision for winning the war. Eisenhower was an effective coordinator—not an effective military commander.

– ADRIAN LEWIS, UNIVERSITY OF NORTH TEXAS

References

Stephen E. Ambrose, *Eisenhower,* volume 1: *Soldier, General of the Army, President-Elect, 1890–1952* (New York: Simon & Schuster, 1983);

Ambrose, "Eisenhower's Generalship," *Parameters,* 20 (June 1990): 2–12;

Ambrose, *The Supreme Commander: The War Years of General Dwight D. Eisenhower* (Garden City, N.Y.: Doubleday, 1970);

Larry I. Bland and Sharon R. Ritenour, eds., *The Papers of George Catlett Marshall,* 4 volumes (Baltimore: Johns Hopkins University Press, 1981–1996);

Martin Blumenson, "Eisenhower Then and Now: Fireside Reflections," *Parameters,* 21 (Summer 1991): 22–34;

Blumenson, *The Patton Papers,* 2 volumes (Boston: Houghton Mifflin, 1972–1974);

Blumenson and James L. Stokesbury, *Masters of the Art of Command* (Boston: Houghton Mifflin, 1975);

Omar N. Bradley and Clay Blair, *A General's Life: An Autobiography* (New York: Simon & Schuster, 1983);

Sir Arthur Bryant, *Turn of the Tide, 1939–1943: A History of the War Years Based on the Diaries of Field-Marshal Lord Alanbrooke, Chief of the Imperial General Staff* (New York: Doubleday, 1957);

EISENHOWER

Harry C. Butcher, *My Three Years with Eisenhower: The Personal Diary of Captain Harry C. Butcher, USNR, Naval Aide to General Eisenhower, 1942 to 1945* (Garden City, N.Y.: Simon & Schuster, 1946);

Alfred D. Chandler Jr., and others, eds., *The Papers of Dwight David Eisenhower: The War Years,* volumes 1–5 (Baltimore: Johns Hopkins University Press, 1970);

Ed Cray, *General of the Army: George C. Marshall, Soldier and Statesman* (New York: Norton, 1990);

David Eisenhower, *Eisenhower at War, 1943–1945* (New York: Random House, 1986);

Dwight D. Eisenhower, *Crusade in Europe* (Garden City, N.Y.: Doubleday, 1948);

Eisenhower, *Dear General: Eisenhower's Wartime Letters to Marshall,* edited by Joseph Patrick Hobbs (Baltimore: Johns Hopkins UniversityPress, 1971);

Eisenhower, *The Eisenhower Diaries,* edited by Robert H. Ferrell (New York: Norton, 1981);

Norman Gelb, *Ike and Monty: Generals at War* (New York: Morrow, 1994);

Susan H. Godson, *Viking of Assault: Admiral John Lesslie Hall, Jr., and Amphibious Warfare* (Washington, D.C.: University Press of America, 1982);

Jeter A. Isely and Philip A. Crowl, *The U.S. Marines and Amphibious War: Its Theory, and Its Practice in the Pacific* (Princeton: Princeton University Press, 1951)

Cole C. Kingseed, "Education of a Combat Commander," *Military Review,* 65 (December 1985): 12–19;

Merle Miller, *Ike the Soldier: As They Knew Him* (New York: Putnam, 1987);

Forrest C. Pogue, *The Supreme Command* (Washington, D.C.: Office of the Chief of Military History, Department of the Army, 1954);

Russell F. Weigley, *Eisenhower's Lieutenants: The Campaign of France and Germany, 1944–1945* (Bloomington: Indiana University Press, 1981).

EISENHOWER

FALL OF FRANCE

Was the fall of France in 1940 inevitable?

Viewpoint: Yes, the speedy collapse of France was inevitable because of divisive internal politics and low national morale.

Viewpoint: No, with better political leadership and military organization France could have defeated Germany in 1940.

The significance of France's defeat in the summer of 1940 was less in its completeness than its nature. From the first days of the German breakthrough at Sedan, the army and the government unraveled, victimized as much—perhaps more—by their own shortcomings than by German fighting power. Explanations for the catastrophe have been corresponding exercises in value judgments. The soldiers, supported by a right wing that had expressed preferences for Adolf Hitler over the Jewish socialist Leon Blum, insisted that the moral rot and the parliamentary infighting endemic to the Third Republic had deprived France of the crucial components of an effective military. Leftists and liberals countered by charging the armed forces with preparing to fight in the style of the last war, ignoring the revolutionary technological and political developments across the Rhine.

With the advantages of a half-century's scholastic achievements and hindsight, it is clear that the French high command was in fact well aware of post-1918 developments in communications technology and mechanization. They were also aware of political developments in Germany. If France remained committed to a firepower model of battle and an attritional model of war, it was because these models reflected both the general internal circumstances of the Third Republic and the organizational realities of the French armed forces. In France, as in every other state, military preparations are constrained by what the policy will support. The resulting doctrines and force structures were considered good enough to check, then mate, anything Hitler's Germany could offer.

The Third Republic provided its soldiers with armored vehicles as good as any in the German inventory, and with aircraft, particularly fighters, that were not hopelessly inferior to those of the *Luftwaffe* (German Air Force). Far from being an expensive anachronism, the Maginot Line fulfilled its intended function of screening the Rhine frontier and, in principle, freeing up forces for employment in more active sectors. The long hiatus between the outbreak of war and the commencement of active operations offered ample opportunity to address shortcomings already noted in peacetime—inadequate training, for example—and to replace officers clearly not up to their jobs. Yet, wherever one looks, peacetime rust remained. The reasons for what French historian and former soldier Marc Bloch called the "strange defeat" of 1940 are best sought in French headquarters, from French general Maurice-Gustave Gamelin down to the companies and battalions.

Viewpoint:
Yes, the speedy collapse of France was inevitable because of divisive internal politics and low national morale.

By the time Germany launched its assault against the French Army, the French government was already dissolving. French internal dissent bore irresolute policies at the very time France needed steadfast resolve. Communists, Socialists, conservatives, Fascists, and even the Monarchists all fought among themselves while France fell deeper into political chaos. Winning is not always accomplished from the overwhelming strength of one side, but rather is the result of the relative weakness of the other.

Profoundly weakened by their own internal strife, strong antiwar sentiment after the horrifying experience of World War I, flawed doctrine and poor military thinking, and limited American and British support regarding the Germans, France found itself in a winless situation. The signs of confusion and political chaos presented themselves almost immediately after World War I. Railroad worker strikes and other labor disputes occurred on the first Bastille Day celebrations after the Germans signed the armistice. As soon as it stopped shooting at the Germans, France started tearing at itself. Governments came and went in rapid succession with no success concerning the fundamental problems.

Specifically, war debt and severe fiscal problems, poor national security, difficulty in maintaining strong alliances, and a weak armaments policy were all hampered by the revolving door of governments. Aristide Briand, for example, was Premier five different times and he was not the only politician to have a revolving door in and out of government. André Tardieu and Pierre Laval both held office at least three times, and joining the melee were Paul Raynaud and Leon Blum, who served at various times throughout the 1930s. Balancing the fiscal crisis gripping every government, and no single government strong enough to proceed with lasting policies, "a mad game of musical chairs ensued, to be played at a giddier and giddier rate until Hitler's panzers finally stopped the music."

Le Boche payera (the Germans will pay) became the financial slogan of every finance minister. The Germans must be made to pay their reparations in order for France's fiscal house to be made right, and since the Germans lost the war and admitted their guilt, they should pay. After all, France had paid their war reparations when they lost the Franco-Prussian War in 1871. Unfortunately, the French could not force the Germans to pay with money they did not have. The German economy was even more shattered than France's and they did not have the money to settle the overwhelming revenge billed them by the Versailles Treaty (1919). Without a strong army and healthy alliances with the United States and Britain, France found itself unable to force Germany to pay. France bumped its way down the course of low military budgets and faulty military doctrine and forced itself to count on dubious allied support. Giving up its diplomatic freedom to its allies, France found itself unable to affect events as it wished and Germany found itself empowered by France's internal confusion and diplomatic impotence.

World War I caused not only shell-shocked soldiers, but also a shell-shocked nation. France wanted no more Verduns and believed any future war would be the static, high-casualty, low-gain, trench warfare recently experienced. Leaders decided to build a series of fortresses dubbed "The Maginot Line," behind which France would find solid protection against any German onslaught. France appropriated money starting in 1930 and by 1935 France finished the fortresses. However, subsequent French governments and military leaders failed to extend the line along the Belgian border, the avenue of approach for the Franco-Prussian War and World War I, due to Marshal Henri Pétain's firm belief that the French Army must advance into Belgium in the event of war. Despite such a critical gap in the nation's line of defense, the national belief that the Maginot Line would protect them held the imagination of the French people and they dreamed themselves into security.

France believed defending and holding the Germans behind the ramparts was the lesson of World War I. After the dogma of the offensive proved so disastrous during battles such as Ypres, The Nivelle Offensive, The Somme, and Verdun, Pétain and other French military thinkers resorted to the doctrine of defense. However, there were dissenters, and one French colonel in particular lobbied energetically for an elite mobile strike force comprised of tanks, infantry, and artillery that would swiftly move to engage the enemy's weak spots. Colonel Charles de Gaulle published a book to that effect and advocated it in every possible venue. Instead of a rapid development of doctrine and heavy production, the result was no more than ten heavy tanks a month, with little thought on how to train men to employ them effectively. In 1939, France inexplicably allowed tank production to fall to eight per month while on the other side of the border, the German Panzers resolutely invaded Czechoslovakia.

FALL OF FRANCE

Aircraft production fared no better as the French High Command struggled with the idea of how to employ military aviation. With only three of 177 pages in the 1936 High Command's Manual of Instruction devoted to the employment of aircraft, the French Army gave little thought to the details of how it would successfully perform its delineated bombing and reconnaissance missions, not to mention how, if at all, it would coordinate air operations with tanks, infantry, and artillery. Satisfied with the aircraft and tactics that won World War I, and the abiding belief in the Maginot Line, the French neglected their vital air arm. Of course, the Germans did not, and despite the prohibitions against the existence of the *Luftwaffe* (German Air Force) the Germans had a formidable and independent air service by the end of the 1930s. They also knew how to use it. Ironically, the French showed them how in a series of effective attacks at the end of World War I. German General Heinz Guderian personally experienced such attacks and set the German forces on an aggressive path to build better tanks and aircraft and to doctrinally coordinate them.

Why would the victors of World War I be so blinded? How could such experienced military minds be so obtuse? How did their thinking drift into such an ossified view? After the war, the teaching at the military schools preached the defensive and the younger officer students found the academic work feeble and without imagination. The French High Command and the instructors at the war colleges taught their students that the defensive defeated the enemy of the last war and would succeed in the next. Moreover, the culture at the military schools discouraged new ideas and lively debate. De Gaulle's advocation of the elite tank unit caused him to be removed from the promotion list.

Marching into the demilitarized Rhineland in 1936, the Germans took back a great deal of their dignity and national pride. Hitler's daring move demonstrated France's internal consternation as well as its dependence on allies who wished to stay out of Continental affairs. Convinced it did not possess the strength to take on Germany alone, France did nothing and its policy of depending upon allies proved feckless. Despite his Generals' fear of stern French military action, Hitler's risk of going back into the Rhineland paid off. France's last chance to stop its own defeat was in 1936, but despite Germany's vulnerability, France could not muster the confidence, will, and allied support necessary for victory.

Such stymied military thinking and lack of energy gripped the French Army even when the Germans finally invaded in May 1940. One French reconnaissance pilot wrote of the futility of his missions, the loss of men and aircraft for absolutely no gain.

Realizing he and his comrades were risking their lives taking photographs that would be obsolete by the time they reached headquarters, he fought on merely because of his patriotic duty. The French historian and former soldier Marc Bloch admitted with striking candor that the French mind was far too sluggish and that the German triumph was one of intellect. In an even more telling passage, he relates how France's own leaders believed France was an inferior nation and they should be beaten. Admitting his dedication to one of the political factions, Bloch observed the end of France's Third Republic bitterly and blamed all the politicians who fought each other, even when the Nazis were at France's throat. As the incessant attack by one faction after another pressed on, the French people began to believe that France

itself was the failure, not the parade of inept politicians. Slogans such as "Better Hitler than Blum" took their toll on the national morale of France. With a divisive political scene, the military happy to rest on its laurels behind the Maginot Line, and the people despondent and bereft of national spirit, Germany merely needed to push and the self-defeated, fragile French nation would fall.

—DENNIS SHOWALTER,
COLORADO COLLEGE

Viewpoint:
No, with better political leadership and military organization France could have defeated Germany in 1940.

Behind the unanswerable question whether the collapse of France was inevitable in 1940 lie three somewhat more tractable ones. What outcome did reasonable, well-informed people expect of a Franco-German clash in 1940? In hindsight, were there things that France—or Germany—might realistically have done differently so as to produce a different outcome? Was France so weak and divided in 1940 as to be incapable of resistance? In a nutshell, the answers are that a French victory did not seem improbable in 1940, that politically difficult changes to French policies could have made that victory more likely, and that only French leaders, not necessarily the French population, lacked the willpower to resist the Germans after Germany's initial military successes. Of course, victory could have seemed probable and yet proved entirely out of reach, but French confidence was not entirely unwarranted. Major changes in French alliance policy, arms production schedules, military organization, and training would certainly have produced a different outcome. More realistically, even improvement in one single area, the selection and training of French reserve officers, for example, or the provision of adequate training grounds for reserve exercises, might have made the difference between victory and defeat.

On the eve of World War II, French military planners had little reason for alarm. They understood that the next war against Germany would be a long struggle won by the coalition best able to mobilize its military and industrial resources. They believed with Marshal Philippe Pétain that "le fue tue" ("fire kills") and thought France fortunate to be able to adopt a defensive posture. Only after the Germans had exhausted

THE DEAD CITY

Berlin (by cable)—I have passed through many ghost towns in Belgium and northern France since the western offensive began on May 10 but no experience has become more indelibly fixed in my mind than that of entering the French nation's incomparable capital, Paris, on June 14, immediately after the first German vanguard. It seemed inconceivable, even though I stood on the spot, that this teeming, gay, noisy metropolis should be dead. Yet dead it was. It seemed inconceivable that it was in German hands. Yet occupied by German arms it was.

Except for Parisian police standing at street corners there was hardly a soul in this city of over four million. Everybody had fled before Germany's irresistible advance—70% to nearby towns and villages, 30% into the privacy of their homes.

You who have been to Paris, just imagine this picture: at the Place de la Concorde no such merry-go-round of honking autos, screaming news vendors, gesticulating cops, gaily chatting pedestrians as usually characterizes this magnificent square. Instead, depressing silence broken only now and then by the purr of some German officer's motor as it made its way to the Hotel Crillon, headquarters of the hastily set up local German commandery. On the hotel's flagstaff, the swastika fluttered in the breeze where once the Stars and Stripes had been in the days of 1919 when Wilson received the cheers of French crowds from the balcony.

What was true of the Place de la Concorde was true everywhere. Boulevards normally teeming with life, lined with cafes before which sit aperitif-sipping Parisians, were ghost streets. We saw only one cafe on the Champs-Elysées open. Paris' framed galaxy of luxurious hotels had vanished behind the shutters. We saw the swastika instead of the tricolor flying atop the Eiffel Tower, from the Flagstaff of the Quai d'Orsay, from the City Hall and, most grotesque of all, from the Arc de Triomphe. . . .

Source: Louis P. Lochner, "Germans Marched into a Dead Paris," Life, 8 July 1940.

Belgium. There, hoped French planners, French and Belgian troops would deploy together in prepared positions to halt the German onslaught. If the French people had to fight a long war, it would not be on their native soil. To carry out the planned advance into Belgium, the French Army motorized its infantry divisions for rapid movement and established armored divisions, called *Divisions legeres mechanique*. Modeled after the horse calvary they replaced, the DLMs had the mission of reconnoitering German movements and protecting the French infantry divisions during their vulnerable advance into position.

To win the fight in Belgium, French soldiers counted on more than the advantage of the tactical defense. Germany's misguided faith in the offensive effectiveness of tanks would be shattered by inexpensive French anti-tank guns and antitank mines. When it was time to shift over to the attack, the French Army would demonstrate how the job ought to be done with the coordinated artillery, and infantry attacks of the so-called *bataille conduite* (methodical battle). The methodical battle may have appeared to some observers to have been excessively painstaking, but French doctrine was designed for an army of marginally trained reservists commanded by equally inexperienced reserve officers. Such soldiers were poorly suited for immediate offensive adventures, but they could be expected to fight tenaciously in defense of France. After the extended period of defensive combat with which the French Army expected the war to begin, even the greenest French reservist would be ready to attack, especially when supported by copious amounts of high explosive.

Confident in its doctrine, the French Army undertook a major rearmament program in 1936, the year when German rearmament began to threaten a shift in the European military balance. Among the most important elements of that program were a powerful 47mm antitank gun, the production of the excellent SOMUA cavalry tank, and initial studies for the creation of heavy armored divisions (*Divisions cuirassees de la Reserve*) based on the Char B1 tank and designed to counter the new German Panzer units.

Thanks to these developments, Winston Churchill's famous exclamation "Thank God for the French Army!" is hardly surprising. Nor did German soldiers take their French adversary lightly. Even after Germany's stunning results against Poland, General von Leeb, who led Germany's Army Group C in the attack on France, expected a difficult campaign in the west. "The arguments that our mobile and armoured forces succeeded in Poland are fallacious. Not only are armoured forces dependent on the weather, but

themselves in fruitless attacks against the large, strongly entrenched, well-equipped, well-trained Allied army would the Allied forces exploit their matériel supremacy in a carefully orchestrated counterattack.

The first requisite for the success of the French scheme was the construction of fortifications along the Franco-German border. This so-called Maginot Line discouraged a direct attack and tempted the German Army to undertake their westward offensive through the country of the French and the British are both equipped with armoured units and anti-tank weapons, whilst the excellence of the French Army and its commanders must not be underestimated." While a vocal minority of German generals put their faith in independent operations by the new Panzer divisions, most agreed with General Von Sonderstern that armored forces should remain closely tied to the infantry. As the German Army expanded in the wake of the Polish campaign, it relied increasingly on horse-drawn artillery, infantry, and support units. Such forces were not designed for *Blitzkrieg* but for a slower kind of war, the kind that the French Army in 1940, confidently asserted on 28 August 1939 that the French army was "*prete*" ("ready") for war.

France faced the German threat in 1939–1940 with a coherent long-war strategy, an army designed to execute that strategy on the operational level, and a tactical doctrine appropriate to the army's personnel and defensive intentions. In many respects, however, things were worse than they appeared. The most obvious French weaknesses were diplomatic. France refused to negotiate seriously with the Soviet Union, failed to woo Belgium away from her policy of neutrality, and never convinced Great Britain to commit major resources to Continental defense. A strong Franco-Russian alliance might have deterred Hitler altogether while a military alliance with Belgium would have opened the possibility of French peacetime deployment behind prepared positions in Belgium. Preemptive deployment into Belgium may seem irrelevant—or even suicidal—given the actual German axis of attack through Luxembourg, but French commanders waiting composedly in Belgium would have been better able to assess and react to the range of German threats. Focused instead on the futile race for defensible positions in Belgium, they spared no attention to the key Ardennes sector. Moreover, a peacetime deployment in Belgium would have given French general Maurice-Gustave Gamelin reason to rethink the riskiest part of the French campaign plan, the advance along the Channel Coast, not Holland entailed by the "Breda Variant." None of these diplomatic problems was irremediable, given political leaders who recognized the seriousness of the German threat.

Political help would also have been needed to rectify the the worst problem with the French Army, the failure of training to match its excellent armaments. Before the war, poor training resulted largely from the reserve system, lack of training facilities, and the slow production of arms and ammunition, all of which required political effort to mend. Wartime mobilization should have stimulated a keen interest in training, but the cold winter of the "Phony War" saw

little productive activity. Had French officers pursued military training as diligently as their German counterparts, French units would have gained valuable competence and cohesion. That they did not is hardly surprising since the worst deficiency of the French Army was the training of the reserve officers and non-commissioned officers who were responsible in turn for the training of their units.

Even with its admitted deficiencies, it is unlikely that the French Army would have collapsed had the Germans followed their initial war plan and advanced into Belgium in the spring of 1940. Reflecting traditional German operational thinking, such an advance would have been slower and more controlled than Guderian's mad dash through the Ardennes and across the Meuse. Coming in the predicted place and at a slower pace, this assault was a threat with which the French Army and its antitank guns were more or less prepared to deal. With minor improvements in armaments procurement and training, French soldiers indeed could have been ready.

That the German offensive instead took the form of a rapid armored penetration through the allegedly impenetrable Ardennes Forest was a stroke of ill luck for the French Army. The loss of a copy of the German plan in an air crash in Belgium, combined with general German reluctance to adhere so closely to the French vision of the next war, led the German planners to shift the weight of their attack southward to the Ardennes sector. Instead of pushing the French Army south through Belgium into France, the *Sickelschnitt* plan aimed to break the French line at Sedan, drive east for the Channel Coast, and trap the bulk of the French Army in Belgium. Relying on rapid movement from an unexpected direction, this plan aimed directly at the French Army's weaknesses, both geographical and psychological.

Neither the thin Franco-Belgium deployment in the Ardennes sector nor the poor training of French troops to deal with the unexpected was irremediable. Marshal Pétain had pointed out in 1934 that the Ardennes were impenetrable—if certain preparations were made. That the necessary roadblocks and antitank obstacles remained figments of the local commanders' imagination was hardly inevitable. Improved training, too, was possible. As a thorough study of the Sedan campaign has shown, the better-trained French units held their own in the battle. French soldiers fought, but only if properly trained and well led.

Air cover would have helped too, but the French Air Force was neither equipped nor trained for a ground support mission. Neither, strictly speaking, was the *Luftwaffe* (German Air

Force), but it had at least learned some basic concepts in the Spanish Civil War, acquired the terrifying JU-87 *Stuka* dive bomber, and acknowledged that its duties included providing fire support for the German Army. Again, this deficiency was remediable.

The French collapse occurred not only because the spearhead of the German Army struck the weakest sector in the French line but because the Germans energetically exploited their immediate success—more energetically than the German High Command anticipated or desired. Indeed, the German victory would have been less complete had lower-level commanders not challenged their superiors' warnings not to let the mechanized units plunge ahead of horse-drawn supporting units. That certain German commanders fought so aggressively was no more inevitable than was the excessive torpor of some of their French adversaries.

Understanding the reasons for the rapid collapse of the French Army in May and June of 1940 is not the same thing as explaining why the French government so quickly came to terms with the Germans. However disastrous, the defeat of the French forces in the north did not necessarily mean the end of French resistance. The troops remaining could have fought to hold the south of France. If the military situation began too desperate, one option was to surrender the metropolitan armies while carrying on the fight against the Axis with France's considerable colonial resources. Furthermore, the nation that claimed authorship of the concept of the *nation armée* (national army) always retained the option of declaring the *levee en masse* (levy en masse) and subjecting German occupying forces to the inconvenience of guerrilla war.

Given that France had various ways to continue the fight, the haste with which the government sought an armistice provides ammunition for those who claim that France succumbed due to a failure of national will. Detractors find ammunition in the argument of Marc Bloch's eyewitness account *Strange Defeat* (1949) that the French people were too divided politically and socially to continue the struggle. In one sense, however, Bloch's divided France undermines the "failure of will" thesis. Behind General Maxime Weygand's insistence on a rapid armistice was his belief that the centers of anti-German resistance, particularly the French Communist Party and the trade unions, opposed France's traditional economic and political order. Indeed, he announced to French Cabinet on 13 June 1940, the day before the Germans entered Paris, that the city was in the hands of a communist-led

"Soviet." To men such as Weygand, the *nation armée* represented a French popular will more frightening than the prospect of German occupation. Thus, the leaders of France did not so much collapse in the face of the German threat as act decisively to protect their own vision of the true France. Had Prime Minister Edouard Daladier's government not yielded power to men with so little faith in the patriotism of the their own countrymen, France could have held out longer, drained German strength, and avoided the ignominy of collaboration.

—EUGENIA C. KIESLING, U.S. MILITARY
ACADEMY, WEST POINT

References

Martin S. Alexander, *The Republic in Danger: General Maurice Gamelin and the Politics of French Defence, 1933–1940* (Cambridge: Cambridge University Press, 1992);

Marc Bloch, *Strange Defeat: A Statement of Evidence Written in 1940* (London & New York: Oxford University Press, 1949);

Matthew Cooper, *The German Army 1933–1945: Its Political and Military Failure* (London: MacDonald & Jane's, 1978);

Robert A. Doughty, *The Breaking Point: Sedan and the Fall of France, 1940* (Hamden, Conn.: Archon, 1990);

B. H. Liddell Hart, *Strategy* (New York: Praeger, 1954);

Alistair Horne, *To Lose a Battle* (Boston: Little, Brown, 1969);

Euginia C. Kiesling, *Arming Against Hitler: France and the Limits of Military Planning* (Lawrence: University Press of Kansas, 1996);

William Manchester, *The Last Lion: Winston Spencer Churchill Alone, 1932–1940* (Boston: Little, Brown, 1988);

Robert O. Paxton, *Vichy France: Old Guard and New Order 1940–1944* (New York: Columbia University Press, 1972);

Antoine de Saint Exupery, *Flight to Arras,* translated by Lewis Galantiér (New York: Reynal & Hitchcock, 1942);

William Shirer, *The Collapse of the Third Republic: An Inquiry into the Fall of France in 1940* (New York: Simon & Schuster, 1969).

FASCISM

Is fascism fundamentally different from National Socialism?

Viewpoint: No, fascism is a nationalistic political movement that exalted race, promoted economic modernization, and demanded violent suppression of all opposition—like National Socialism.

Viewpoint: Yes, although both fascism and National Socialism came out of the upheaval of World War I and tapped into nationalist sentiments, Nazism was driven by racist doctrine.

Fascism, once described as the great political surprise of the twentieth century, is increasingly recognized as having deep roots in the modern European experience. Once depicted as a movement of losers, attractive only to those who perceived themselves deprived by the Democratic and Industrial Revolutions, Fascism is now understood to have broad-spectrum appeal even in relatively stable societies. Once dismissed as a justification for violence, Fascism is now conceded to possess an intellectual framework that may be refuted, but cannot be ignored.

At the core of that framework is the principle of opposition. Fascism stands against positivism as too restrictive and against liberalism for being too entropic. It rejects conservatism as too rigid and government as arteriosclerotic. In place of these philosophies, Fascism offers not programs but attitudes. "Mass man" and "economic man" will give way to "heroic man," inspired to action and sacrifice by the force of will, in the context of the nation. Fascism depends on synergizing the individual and the collective. It practices the politics of charisma, not balance; it celebrates myth, not reason; and it sees humanity's most distinctive faculty as the capacity to rise above the mundane through the power of belief.

Fascism addresses the complex social structures of the modern West by transcending them. What is important is not a particular social or economic position, but membership in a community that rendered such differences irrelevant. The community may be determined by blood, as was the case in Nazi Germany. It may depend on affirmation, in the fashion of Benito Mussolini's Italy. However defined, it is the focus of both regeneration and progress, channeling the individual wills that cleanse the folk and carry it forward.

The state plays a central role in that process. It implements consensus by indoctrination on the one hand and repression on the other. It provides focal points for the energy it unleashes—usually some form of aggression, preferably against a clearly vulnerable enemy. "Struggle," as defined in Fascism, is essentially agonistic, involving testing individual and community mettle as opposed to engaging in all-out conflict. In that sense Germany was the exception rather than the rule, best demonstrated by Francisco Franco's Spain and Mussolini's Italy—which chose their respective targets far more carefully than did Adolf Hitler.

Viewpoint:
No, fascism is a nationalistic political movement that exalted race, promoted economic modernization, and demanded violent suppression of all opposition—like National Socialism.

The postulate that Fascism, in its general sense and its specifically Italian version, is essentially different from National Socialism has been supported from two positions. One, on a combination of academic and moral grounds, considers the Third Reich as sui generis and is suspicious of the consequences of any attempt to provide a comparative or contextual dimension to its history and ideology. Its scholarly strongholds are in Germany and the English-speaking countries. The other perspective is primarily associated with Italian scholars, such as Renzo de Felice, and their southern and Eastern European counterparts. Often described by critics as revisionists, without being apologists for the experience of particular states between 1920 and 1945, they nevertheless consider the various forms of right-wing authoritarian collectivism that characterized those years as differing essentially from the racist ideology and apocalyptic behavior of Adolf Hitler's Germany. They also believe it impossible to analyze objectively anything tarred with the Nazi brush. When these internal pressures are added to historians' general preference to leave categorization to the political scientists, it is understandable why Fascism tends to be separated from Nazism after a token acknowledgment of their apparent similarities.

"Fascism" has also been damaged as an analytical concept by a half-century of use as a near-generic term of abuse for views unpopular on the Left. Apart from its 1960s application to everyone rightwards of Senator George S. McGovern (D-South Dakota), "Fascist" has been attached to advocates of immigration restriction and welfare limitation, and to critics of feminism, multiculturalism, and gay rights.

Fascism, however, is something more than a synonym for generally conservative views. It is something more as well than a particular political/ideological system that exercised a particular appeal in a particular region of Europe. Dynamic and protean in its manifestations, fascism challenges classification. It nevertheless was a system of beliefs and behaviors that was broad enough and firm enough to embrace and contain a spectrum of variations—including National Socialism. Its basis was a vitalist optimism that not

merely challenged, but transcended, rational analysis. For the Fascist true believer, nothing was impossible: a problem was only a solution that had not yet been developed.

That mind-set had its most obvious impact in countries with a strong national identity, whose civil societies had been eroded by social, economic, and political change. Traditional systems no longer seemed to work. Contemporary alternatives, democracy and Marxism/Leninism, were unappealing because they were perceived as incomplete, excluding too many people from their respective paradigms. Fascism was different. It appealed to some groups and classes more than to others. Nevertheless, attempts to connect Fascism to the lower-middle classes, to describe it as a movement of those left behind by liberalism and industrialization, or to interpret it as a last stand of patriarchal social values, are themselves increasingly recognized as incomplete. Fascism, indeed, gained support largely because of its claim to ignore interests of party, confession, and class. Fascist calls for unity and order were syncretic rather than exclusionist. While it might be necessary to break heads in the early stages, fascists argued that it was most accurately understood as a process of consciousness-raising. Ethnic or cultural "outsiders" might be excluded permanently. No Italian, no German, no member of any nation-state's primary group who truly understood and truly felt the issues, however, could be anything but a Fascist. Fascism's insistence on the central importance of community involved not ignoring, but transcending, internal barriers. Existing social and economic distinctions were to Fascism instrumental. They became means of lifting the community above and outside itself. The worker remained a worker, the boss a boss, and the student a student. Instead of being primary definitions of status and identity, in Fascism these classifications became secondary characteristics. Critics depict this process as a system of smoke and mirrors designed to preserve or enhance power inequalities. It is more accurate to apply Max Weber's concept of status in contrast to class, and to describe Fascism as a status revolution. Fascism's appeal involved its adding a dimension to identities that were understood as being increasingly circumscribed by existing economic, social, and political factors; then insisting that with this new sense of identity a community could rise to greatness. In the end all would share not equally, but equitably, in the fruits of the common enterprise.

That postulate was a sharp challenge to Fascism's principal ideological opponents.

FASCISM

Christianity and communism alike called for repentance and rebirth. The change of heart, required of communist true believers, was a spiritual and intellectual experience no less intense than a born-again experience or its equivalent for Christians. Fascists by contrast had to repent nothing—only move forward into the light. Small wonder that Fascism is so often described as populist: a mass movement that seemed to make its converts almost magically, incorporating groups and individuals with—by conventional standards at least—nothing significant in common.

Fascism, however, was more than an exercise in the mutual raising of self esteem. It also had a productive enterprise: modernization. Its appeal and success were greatest in states made painfully and objectively aware of their relative inferiority. That appeal applied to Germany, recent loser in a war of attrition fought for mortal stakes. It applied to Italy, where for three years blood had replaced steel on the Isonzo River and in the Alps. It applied to Spain, where a moribund central government seemed able to do nothing except levy taxes on the state's productive elements in order to support a military establishment unable even to conquer Morocco without help.

The development Fascism postulated involved developing will as a multiplier for limited material resources. It involved a bootstrapping approach, as much emotional as material. Development along those lines demanded mobilization: the conscious focusing of national effort by a central authority embodied in charismatic leadership. Hitler, Benito Mussolini, even Francisco Franco, and their principal subordinates, challenged the bureaucratization that seemed to be the essence of the modern industrialized state. They did so less by denying it altogether than by putting it at the service of the public will. If in principle nothing was impossible for Fascism, in practice that meant what must be done could be done in the matrix of the state.

It was a mind-set reinforcing Fascism's brutality. World War I had left to all its participants an active legacy of hardness and a passive counterpart of indifference in the face of suffering. The latter was arguably more important to the acceptability of violent repression of perceived opposition, than to the removal of individuals and groups considered dangerous to the general welfare. In that context, even in Nazi Germany racism in an active sense was less important than the negative exclusion of designated victims from the community's protection. What happened afterwards to those unfortunates was a matter of at best remote concern.

Benito Mussolini and Adolf Hitler in May 1938

Mobilization and brutality combined to generate a final Fascist common denominator: conflict. The choice of that word instead of "war" is deliberate. Fascism emphasized the desirability and necessity of struggle for a common goal. Its preferred opponents were those limited in their ability to fight back. For Fascism, struggle was an agonistic experience, a test of individual and cultural virtue. It had no element of "civilizing missions" or "playing the game." In that context weak opponents—such as Libyans, Ethiopians, Poles, and Jews—could provide just as valid a test as could strong ones, at lower cost and lesser risk. Fascism, after all, was about solipsistic obsession with one's own kind. In none of its variations did it show more than marginal comprehension of anything but its own navel. As much as anything else, that blindness set the stage for Fascism's disappearance from a Europe increasingly interdependent as the twentieth century progressed.

–DENNIS SHOWALTER,
COLORADO COLLEGE

Viewpoint:
Yes, although both fascism and National Socialism came out of the upheaval of World War I and tapped into nationalist sentiments, Nazism was driven by racist doctrine.

Already in the early 1920s, intellectuals, politicians, and journalists sought to explain the uncanny similarities shared by Benito Mussolini's Italian Fascism and Adolf Hitler's German National Socialism. By 1923 the Communist Party International (Comintern) warned against the evolution of an "international" fascism, while the American Kenneth Roberts denounced the demagogic anti-Semitism of Hitler's "Beer-Fascisti." The initial successes of these movements were unexpected and confusing, and their aggression and crimes bordering on the inexplicable. As historians struggled to explain the motive forces behind World War II and the Holocaust, there developed an ongoing debate concerning the essence of German National Socialism and its relationship to Italian Fascism. Scholars such as Stanley G. Payne, Roger Griffin, and George L. Mosse assert that these movements shared a common essence reflected in both ideology and action, and that a theory of generic fascism serves as a useful and perhaps necessary analytical device. Certainly, both movements trumpeted their status as uniquely revolutionary; as distinct alternatives to "decadent" materialism and the "failed" nineteenth century ideologies of liberal capitalism and socialism; and as vitally, violently nationalistic and expansionist. Efforts to explain German National Socialism as a single manifestation of a generic phenomenon, however, are flawed because they fail to sufficiently address the centrality of Nazi racism as distinct from Fascist ultranationalism. In fact, Hitler's virulent and paranoid brand of anti-Semitism, combined with a distinct vision of a racist utopia decisively distance Nazism from Mussolini's more conventional dictatorship.

In the immediate wake of World War I (1914–1918) and the Bolshevik Revolution (1917–1918), Europeans witnessed the development of a bewildering new style of populist politics. Four years of trench warfare and routine battlefield barbarism decimated an entire generation of young men and ultimately brutalized its survivors. Moreover, the unexpected success of Vladimir Lenin's violent communist revolution in Russia inspired radicals throughout Europe—in Berlin, members of the *Freikorps* (volunteer paramilitary units) fought pitched battles against Rosa Luxemburg's Sparticists, while Italy suffered from a ruinous wave of strikes during the

"red biennium" of 1919–1920. Within this context of postwar violence and incessant crisis, Italian Fascism and German National Socialism nurtured their myths, developed their ideologies, and perfected their tactics and techniques.

That Fascism and National Socialism shared a similar set of trappings and a peculiar style of politics should hardly prove surprising. Mussolini's successful "March on Rome" in the autumn of 1922 impressed Hitler immensely. Hitler saw in Italian Fascism a prototype for a particular political aesthetic, one that combined the liturgy of national renewal with the evocation of comradeship among committed "political soldiers." Hitler's appropriation of Mussolini's tactics and rhetoric, albeit significant, was superficial at best: Whereas Mussolini shared power with the Italian state and pursued expansionist policies for the sake of national pride, Hitler quickly assumed a position of absolute political authority and embarked on a deliberately aggressive foreign policy, the ultimate end of which would be the conquest of *Lebensraum* (living space) and the racial purification of a burgeoning Germanic *Volksgemeinschaft* (people's community).

Such distinctions were far from obvious to contemporary observers, however, and so comparisons between Fascism and National Socialism based on extrinsic similarities were bound to develop. The gradual evolution of a generic concept of fascism began almost immediately following the organization of Mussolini's *Fasci di Combattimento* ("Leagues of Veterans"). In the autumn of 1920, squadrons of Fasci stepped up their attacks on socialists as Mussolini sought to suppress "Bolshevik" agitation and attract the Italian middle classes to his standard. Because they remained the primary targets of Fascist violence, Marxists were the first to develop a "generic" theory of fascism—one that accounted for the marked severity of its opposition to socialism. Early Marxist explanations situated Fascism within the teleological framework of revolutionary socialist historicism: Fascism, according to Roger Griffin in *Fascism* (1995) served as a counterrevolutionary "agent" of capitalism in crisis, a "characteristic phenomenon of decay, a reflection of the progressive dissolution of capitalist economy and of the disintegration of the bourgeois State." The power of this interpretation was strengthened by Fascist efforts to appeal to the petite bourgeoisie—Marx himself consistently argued that the lower-middle classes served as the most reactionary element of the bourgeoisie, wedged as they were between the hammer of international capitalism and the anvil of revolutionary socialism. In 1933 doctrinaire Marxists had largely codified their definition of fascism: "Fascism is the open, terrorist dictatorship of the most reactionary, most chauvinist and most imperialist elements of finance capital." By the onset of the civil war in Spain (1936), Marxists would routinely and unapologetically label all right-wing dictatorships as fascist. While later, nonorthodox Marxian theory would eventually present highly sophisticated variants to the Comintern position quoted above, it would nevertheless continue to emphasize the central significance of class and capitalist counterrevolution while playing down the importance of Nazi racism.

Attempts by non-Marxist theoreticians to explain Fascism and National Socialism within the scope of their own political experience were often equally reductionist, though certainly colored by decidedly more subtle shades of discursive prejudice. Western liberals attempted to account for existing similarities shared not only by Fascism and National Socialism, but Stalinist-style communism as well (sometimes called "Red Fascism"). Initially coined by the liberal Giovanni Amendola as a political pejorative, the epithet "totalitarian" was appropriated by the Fascists themselves. Totalitarian theory postulated that modern technology made possible a new genus of ideologically driven dictatorship, one that relied on a combination of a single-party dictatorship, mass mobilization, and the liberal application of police terror in an effort to assert its control over all social, political, economic and cultural institutions. In fact, Italian Fascism never approached anything even resembling an ideal totalitarian system and Hitler's regime; though certainly bordering on totalitarian, it suffered from a tolerance of internal anarchy that rendered it functionally inefficient. Following the defeat of the Axis powers and the onset of the Cold War, liberal totalitarian theory assumed an increasing degree of stridency. Only Joseph Stalin's Soviet Union appeared to manifest the necessary symptoms that might justify its diagnosis as "totalitarian." While totalitarian theory proved eminently useful in framing anticommunist discourses, the transparency of its ideological bias insured its steady attrition, and by the late 1980s one could argue that the entire concept of totalitarianism was heuristically flawed and conceptually empty.

The polemical origins of both fascist and totalitarian theories reflect the role of ideology in the current debate concerning the "nature" of National Socialism and its relationship to Italian Fascism; they remain mired in discursive traditions ill-suited to meaningfully explain the nature of either movement. Regrettably, many historians seeking to develop more subtle theories of generic fascism continue to persist in this vein, regarding Nazism as somehow normative; this is in part a function of an existing historiography and the tradition of scholarship, a tradition born

of Marxist and liberal antifascist agitation. Subsequently, historians suffer from the misplaced conviction that it is necessary and desirable to conflate Nazism and Fascism, despite the massive qualitative difference represented by Nazi racism.

National Socialism and Fascism certainly shared much in common: both presented themselves as viable, necessary alternatives to the great nineteenth-century ideologies of liberalism and socialism. Fascists and Nazis attacked liberalism not only because of its slavish adherence to ineffectual parliamentary compromise, but also because it remained the party of the bourgeoisie, whose vision of society revolved around the maintenance of a mechanistic "cash nexus" wherein material acquisition and contractual obligation regulated the behavior of self-interested individual actors. Marxist "scientific" socialism struck them as equally noxious. Although Fascists and Nazis supported the socialists in their hatred of the bourgeoisie, they asserted that the concept of "class" was flawed; that human behavior was motivated by far more than mere material production. In fact, their stress on the positive importance of human irrationalism, historical myth, and longing for a neoromantic organic community served to best differentiate "fascist" movements from their political and cultural opponents. Unlike liberalism and socialism, Fascism and Nazism were conceived in the wake of Friedrich Nietzsche's exuberant embrace of the irrational as well as George Sorel's affirmation of violence as both necessary and natural. The cultural and intellectual "crisis" at the turn of the century laid the foundation for much of the "fascist" worldview.

Of even greater significance was the impact of World War I. The experience of total war was crucial in shaping the evolution of authoritarian interwar political movements as diverse as Corneliu Codreanu's Romanian Iron Guard (1930) and Józef Piłsudski's regime in Poland (1926–1928, 1930). The war seemed to support the assertions of cultural pessimists that human nature was inherently violent and irrational; it brutalized a generation of Europeans and gradually habituated them to the practice of political violence. Returning veterans such as Mussolini and Hitler applied battlefield solutions and technological innovation to everyday political problems—Mussolini called for the rise of a "trenchocracy" while Hitler evoked the memory of the "war experience" in his articulation of the *Führerprinzip* (leadership principle). The exigencies of mechanized warfare necessitated total mobilization of the population and the development of planned economies; the success of these projects informed Fascist corporatism as well as Hitler's insistence on German economic autarky.

BENITO MUSSOLINI DEFINES FASCISM

Fascism, the more it considers and observes the future and the development of humanity quite apart from political considerations of the moment, believes neither in the possibility nor the utility of perpetual peace. It thus repudiates the doctrine of Pacifism—born of a renunciation of the struggle and an act of cowardice in the face of sacrifice. War alone brings up to its highest tension all human energy and puts the stamp of nobility upon the peoples who have courage to meet it. All other trials are substitutes, which never really put men into the position where they have to make the great decision—the alternative of life or death. . . .

The Fascist accepts life and loves it, knowing nothing of and despising suicide: he rather conceives of life as duty and struggle and conquest, but above all for others—those who are at hand and those who are far distant, contemporaries, and those who will come after. . . .

Fascism [is] the complete opposite of...Marxian Socialism, the materialist conception of history of human civilization can be explained simply through the conflict of interests among the various social groups and by the change and development in the means and instruments of production. . . .

After Socialism, Fascism combats the whole complex system of democratic ideology, and repudiates it, whether in its theoretical premises or in its practical application. Fascism denies that the majority, by the simple fact it is a majority, can direct human society; it denies that numbers alone can govern by means of a periodical consultation, and it affirms the immutable, beneficial, and fruitful inequality of mankind, which can never be permanently leveled through the mere operation of a mechanical process such as universal suffrage. . . .

Fascism denies, in democracy, the absurd conventional untruth of political

equality dressed out in the garb of collective irresponsibility, and the myth of "happiness" and indefinite progress. . . .

The foundation of Fascism is the conception of the State, its character, its duty, and its aim. Fascism conceives of the State as an absolute, in comparison with which all individuals or groups are relative, only to be conceived of in their relation to the State. The conception of the Liberal State is not that of a directing force, guiding the play and development, both material and spiritual, of a collective body, but merely a force limited to the function of recording results: on the other hand, the Fascist State is itself conscious and has itself a will and a personality—thus it may be called the "ethic" State. . . .

The Fascist State organizes the nation, but leaves a sufficient margin of liberty to the individual; the latter is deprived of all useless and possibly harmful freedom, but retains what is essential; the deciding power in this question cannot be the individual, but the State alone. . . .

For Fascism, the growth of empire, that is to say the expansion of the nation, is an essential manifestation of vitality, and its opposite a sign of decadence. . . . Fascism is the doctrine best adapted to represent the tendencies and the aspirations of a people, like the people of Italy, who are rising again after many centuries of abasement and foreign servitude. . . . If every age has its own characteristic doctrine, there are a thousand signs which point to Fascism as the characteristic doctrine of our time. For if a doctrine must be a living thing, this is proved by the fact that Fascism has created a living faith; and that this faith is very powerful in the minds of men is demonstrated by those who have suffered and died for it.

Source: Enciclopedia italiana di Scienze, lettere ed arti *(Roma: Istituto Giovanni Treccani, 1929–1939).*

Finally, World War I demonstrated the incredible power of modern nationalism. Socialists attempted to avert war by appealing to the solidarity of an international working class, but it was nationalism that ultimately succeeded in mobilizing the masses and temporarily mitigating class antagonisms.

While Fascism and Nazism had violently rejected the positivist ideologies of liberalism and socialism, they enthusiastically embraced nationalism. In fact, the central significance of nationalism has formed the basis for recent non-Marxian efforts at constructing a viable theory of fascism. Scholars such as Griffin, Mosse, and Payne focus on fascist irrationalism, vitalism, positive valuation of violence, and extreme nationalism; they attempt to locate fascism's core within the context of ideology and culture. For all three of them, the centrality of nationalism, the myth of national decay, and promise of national rebirth constitute that essence.

Hitler's National Socialism, however, is primarily defined by a permutation of mystical-utopian racism combined with conspiratorial anti-Semitism. This fact, which must remain central to any effort at explaining Nazism, decisively distinguishes it from Italian Fascism. While it is true that National Socialism and Fascism both developed narratives of national decay and renewal, the Fascist vision of history was hardly utopian. Mussolini articulated a future wherein the state would assume total authority, where the national myth would inculcate pride and encourage imperial expansion. In contrast, National Socialist intellectuals imagined, and fully intended to realize, the creation of a racially homogenous *Volksgemeinschaft*, a vision as utopian as the Marxist conception of a classless society.

Nationalism need not necessarily be racist, nor is it by definition exclusionary. Neither are racism and nationalism identical. Hitler's evocation of a Greater German Reich was in fact pan-German—Nazi ideology eagerly embraced racially desirable (Nordic) members of any nationality. Payne, Griffin, and Mosse seek to equate racism and nationalism, and in so doing retain fascism as a useful theoretical device while accounting for National Socialism's peculiarities. Mosse, for example, in *The Fascist Revolution: Toward a General Theory of Fascism* (1999) asserts that racism, while possessing an impressive intellectual pedigree in its own right, remains subordinate to nationalism while serving as a "catalyst which pushed German nationalism over the edge." Payne addresses the issue in a similar manner, asserting in *A History of Fascism, 1914–1945* (1995), that all fascist movements espoused doctrines that were "highly ethnicist" and could thereby serve as a "functional parallel to categorical racism." Griffin simply argues that fascism, by virtue of its ultranationalism, is always racist.

None of these attempts to account for Nazi utopian racism within the conceptual framework of a generic theory of fascism succeed. At best they imply that fascism and nationalism are always potentially genocidal—certainly a useful polemical device but one hardly borne out by historical research. At worst they play down the importance of racism and anti-Semitism in the German case. It was not nationalism that spurred Hitler on to war and genocide; his often-repeated intention to acquire Lebensraum in Poland and the Soviet Union reflected a genuine commitment to the racial restructuring of Europe. Hitler couched his position in apocalyptic, millenarian terms, combining his fascination for eugenics and racial hygiene with a prurient representation of the Jew as capitalist, Marxist, pornographer and race-defiler. Italian Fascism promised national rebirth and the creation of a "new man," but largely ignored the issue of race: the Fascist Party itself included a disproportionately large Jewish contingent, and although racial legislation was passed in 1938, it remained superficial and unaccompanied by any systematic racial policy.

In contrast, the Nazi regime began promulgating racial-hygienic and anti-Semitic legislation within weeks of its seizure of power. The premeditated and deliberate murder of at least six million European Jews demonstrates just how seriously the regime adhered to Hitler's brand of paranoid anti-Semitism. Moreover, the Nazi conception of a racial state not only postulated the "Final Solution of the Jewish Question," but also the purification of the German Volksgemeinschaft. This process ultimately involved the persecution (imprisonment, sterilization, or murder) of other ethnic minorities as well as those members of the German population deemed to possess "lesser racial value:" Sinti and Roma, Afro-Germans, Poles, Russians, homosexuals, the "asocial," and the mentally and physically handicapped.

Certainly the most spectacular manifestation of Nazi racism was the invasion of the Soviet Union in 1941. From the onset, Hitler characterized the war in the East as one of "extermination." Not only did the racial war against "Jewish-Bolshevism" act as a justification for the escalation of the Holocaust; it also resulted in the murder of millions of Russians. National Socialist racial theory relegated Slavs to the status of "Mongoloid sub-humans." In the course of a brutal four-year campaign, approximately 3,300,000 Soviet prisoners of war died at the hands of their captors. While many died of starvation or exposure, Germans murdered others in extermination camps such as Auschwitz. By late 1941 the Reich Main Security Office of the *Schutzstaffel* (SS) was busy drafting a blueprint for the future organization and exploitation of eastern Europe as far as the Urals. The *Generalplan Ost* (General Plan East) envisioned a massive resettlement program that would displace at least fifty-one million Slavs to Siberia over the course of several decades. The remainder would serve as slaves to their Aryan masters.

National Socialism and Italian Fascism shared many superficial similarities: common origins in the aftermath of World War I, as well as similar liturgical technique and paramilitary trappings; both movements rejected liberalism and Marxist-style socialism, embraced violence, and pursued the creation of an organic community through the cultivation of a national or racial myth. Theories of fascism initially struggled to explain these similarities in the context of a highly charged political atmosphere leaden with polemic, while historians' adherence to a peculiar tradition of scholarship hamstring more recent efforts at explication. Comparisons are inevitable but Nazism was not simply another permutation of international fascism. Hitler's National Socialism was the expression of a unique vision of a racially pure community and efforts to realize this racist utopia resulted in unprecedented expressions of brutality and genocidal violence that consumed Europe for over six years.

–BENJAMIN ZARWELL,
MADISON, WISCONSIN

References

Hannah Arendt, *The Origins of Totalitarianism* (New York: Harcourt, Brace, 1951);

Richard Bessel, ed., *Fascist Italy and Nazi Germany: Comparisons and Contrasts* (New York: Cambridge University Press, 1996);

Michael Burleigh, *Ethics and Extermination: Reflections on Nazi Genocide* (New York: Cambridge University Press, 1997);

Burleigh and Wolfgang Wippermann, *The Racial State: Germany, 1933–1945* (New York: Cambridge University Press, 1991);

Roger Griffin, ed., *Fascism* (Oxford & New York: Oxford University Press, 1995);

Griffin, *The Nature of Fascism* (London: Pinter, 1991);

Walter Laqueur, ed., *Fascism: A Reader's Guide: Analyses, Interpretations, Bibliography* (Berkeley: University of California Press, 1976);

George L. Mosse, *The Fascist Revolution: Toward a General Theory of Fascism* (New York: Fertig, 1999);

Stanley G. Payne, *Fascism: Comparison and Definition* (Madison: University of Wisconsin Press, 1980);

Payne, *A History of Fascism, 1914–1945* (Madison: University of Wisconsin Press, 1995);

Zeev Sternhell, with Mario Sznajder, and Maia Asheri, *Naissance de l'idéologie fasciste* (Paris: Fayard, 1989), translated by David Maisel as *The Birth of Fascist Ideology* (Princeton: Princeton University Press, 1994).

GERMAN ARMY AND ATROCITIES

Was the Wehrmacht an active and willing participant in German war atrocities?

Viewpoint: Yes, the Wehrmacht was an active and willing participant in German war atrocities, because Nazi indoctrination and racism encouraged German soldiers to view the enemy as less than human.

Viewpoint: No, German war atrocities were usually carried out by special units, not the Wehrmacht; in addition, antipartisan actions were often viewed by German soldiers as acceptable interpretations of the rules of war.

The relationship of the German army to war atrocities remains controversial. One thread of argument separates the generals from the Führer, the soldiers from the SS (*Schutzstaffel*), and the *Wehrmacht* (German Army) from the Nazi Party. More recent research, however, has demonstrated a clear set of links between military operations and mass murder. To say the Werhmacht was responsible for crimes is not to say that every soldier was a criminal or directly complicit in the Nazi regime's crimes. It is not to deny that many German soldiers fought for their country, and did so as cleanly as modern war permits. Yet, the German Army of World War II was a people's army, an integral part of the Nazi system.

Both Adolf Hitler and his generals, albeit for different reasons, sought to establish a militarized national community. In pursuit of that end, the army accepted its gradual political emasculation before 1939. Its commanders accepted and fostered the instruction of their soldiers in Nazi ideology and their indoctrination by Nazi propaganda. In 1941 Hitler left the implementation of his ideologically based race war against the Soviet Union to the military. The army took the initiative in authorizing massive reprisals, in ordering the execution of political commissars, and in confining prisoners of war under subsurvival conditions. Nazi ideas of "hardness" shaped conduct in the front lines and rear areas alike. Pity was considered a weakness. Nazi concepts of heroic vitalism led generals to use their men's courage and lives to substitute for the equipment the Third Reich could not provide. Willpower was expected to prevail against tanks. War-making became an end in itself, with "home" a remote concept symbolized by a few worn photos in the wallet. Everywhere in Europe, if not always directly complicit in the worst aspects of Hitler's policies, the soldiers facilitated or ignored them—less from malice than indifference. The fate of Jews, Russians, Serbs, and anyone else, simply did not matter. As the German army demodernized, it dehumanized as well.

Viewpoint:
Yes, the Wehrmacht was an active and willing participant in German war atrocities, because Nazi indoctrination and racism encouraged German soldiers to view the enemy as less than human.

Although all sides tried to assume the moral high ground in World War II, all militaries committed horrific atrocities. In the Pacific theater, Japanese and American land forces fought a war that historian John Dower called a "war without mercy." In Russia the *Wehrmacht* (German Army) and the Red Army routinely massacred prisoners of war or mistreated them to such an extent that millions died. Civilians also suffered horribly, from the genocide of Europe's Jews to the Japanese army's rampages through Chinese cities to the new weapons of mass destruction that specifically targeted noncombatants. Even given this appalling record, the Wehrmacht stands out as an agent of war crimes and wanton destruction. It behaved like no other military force in the war and bears the responsibility of having been the major instrument of Adolf Hitler's maniacal worldview.

Three major components distinguished the Wehrmacht from other armed forces: its exposure to, and acceptance of, Nazi ideology; the nature of the Wehrmacht's disciplinary system; and the German view of the war in Russia (where the majority of German action took place) as defensive. Of these, ideology played by far the largest role. Armies cannot be removed from the societies that they serve, and individual soldiers cannot be separated from the environments in which they were raised. Nazi ideology was complex and broad in scope, but three main elements are relevant for understanding how the Wehrmacht became complicit in war atrocities: racism, Social Darwinism, and the "stab in the back" myth.

The racism of Nazi society has been well documented and needs not be reexplored here. The effects of that racism on the Wehrmacht ran deep. Nazi ideology promulgated a view of "life unworthy of life" that Hitler's regime first utilized in euthanasia programs that "disinfected" (murdered) tens of thousands of mentally ill adults and children. Wedding this concept to the idea of *Untermenschen,* or sub-humans, produced a belief that the Reich's enemies (especially Slavs and Jews) were also "unworthy of life." The war in Russia, therefore, was not a conflict fought between equals but a war of annihilation that hit civilians hard. Because the Wehrmacht's enemies were believed to be subhuman, they were not

due any considerations normally extended to human beings.

Such an immoral environment quickly dehumanized and demonized the Wehrmacht's enemies. Atrocities and war crimes became easier to commit when the victim was understood to be something less than human. Dehumanization also facilitated the creation of an "us versus them" mentality that in turn further reinforced a view of the enemy as less than human.

These ideas also fit neatly into Nazi Germany's embrace of Social Darwinism. Social Darwinism stated that human races, like any animal species, had to fight for survival, with only the fittest enduring. Nazi racism placed Aryans at the top of the racial hierarchy, with Slavs and Jews at the bottom. The results are not hard to imagine. If life was a struggle between races and Germans were at the top, then eliminating those at the bottom was merely a way of helping nature attain its goals more efficiently. Given such a worldview, the Germans had to win at all costs in order to prove their anointed place at the top of the racial hierarchy. Social Darwinism also explains why the Wehrmacht committed fewer atrocities in the Low Countries, Scandinavia, and France (where their opponents were closer to the Aryan place on the hierarchy) than they did in eastern Europe.

The Nazi rise to power also built upon the "stab in the back" myth to explain Germany's defeat in World War I and the subsequent humiliating Versailles Treaty (1919). According to this myth, Germany's armies had not been defeated in the field; Germany lost because elements at home (notably Jews and Bolsheviks) brought about the nation's defeat from within. The Wehrmacht embraced this view because it deflected blame away from the army as an institution and provided ready scapegoats for reversals. In World War II the Wehrmacht justified its cruel treatment of partisans, Jews, and anyone deemed politically unreliable by maintaining that it was fighting to prevent a second stab in the back. By extension, all Russians and Jews were past, present, and potential future enemies of the Reich and had to be prevented from doing any further harm to Aryans.

The Wehrmacht and its soldiers readily embraced Nazi ideology. Recent studies of the Wehrmacht, such as Stephen G. Fritz's *Frontsoldaten: The German Soldier in World War II* (1995) and Omer Bartov's *Hitler's Army: Soldiers, Nazis, and War in the Third Reich* (1991), confirm that it was among the most thoroughly Nazified institutions in Germany. As early as 1930 Wehrmacht officers provided arms and support to the SS (*Schutzstaffel*). In 1934 the army completed its surrender to Hitler when it required an oath of personal loyalty to him.

According to German military historian Joachim C. Fest, in *Gesicht des Dritten Reiches: Profile einer totalitateren Herrschaft* (1963), the close connections between the Wehrmacht and Nazi Party represented a "deliberate political decision." The army surrendered its independence in return for the rearmament and enhanced prestige that the Nazis promised.

Younger soldiers were, as a general rule, even more Nazified than older soldiers. An eighteen-year-old soldier in the Wehrmacht in 1941 would have been ten years old when Hitler came to power. As such, he would almost surely have passed through Hitler Youth programs or attended schools dominated by the Nazi Party. The Hitler Youth taught German children absolute obedience, reverential worship of Hitler, and contempt for all those outside the *Volk*. These young men formed the backbone of the Wehrmacht that fought in Russia. It is noteworthy that the Hitler Youth and Wehrmacht were the only two institutions in Germany that required a sworn personal oath to Hitler. Youth graduated from the former ideologically prepared to serve in the latter.

As evidence of the deep hold of Nazi ideology, few Wehrmacht officers and enlisted men supported the assassination attempt on Hitler on 20 July 1944. Rather, they read the attempt's failure as further proof of Providence's choice of Hitler as the leader of the German people. As a result the Wehrmacht's support for Hitler proba-

bly grew stronger; the treasonous generals who planned the assassination (another stab in the back) could thereafter be blamed for everything that went wrong.

Nazi ideology might not have led to war atrocities on its own, but that ideology interacted with the Wehrmacht's system of discipline to create a dangerous mix. The Wehrmacht's officer corps (at the senior and junior levels) did little to prevent atrocities. Quite to the contrary, several senior leaders encouraged such atrocities. To cite one example, Field Marshal Erich von Manstein issued orders in late 1941 that read, in part:

> The Jewish-Bolshevik system must be eradicated once and for all. Never again may it interfere in our European living space.
>
> The German soldier is therefore not only charged with the task of destroying the power instrument of this system. He marches forth also as a carrier of a racial conception and as an avenger of all the atrocities which have been committed against him and the German people.

In these orders one can identify the racist world view, the stab-in-the-back myth and the official acceptance, at senior levels, of war crimes.

An important feature of Nazi ideology was that it allowed German soldiers to commit atrocities and still retain the moral high ground as defenders of their race against inferior beings. As

Polish civilians before their execution by German troops in Bochnia, Poland, on 18 December 1939

(Main Crimes Commission for the Investigation of Nazi War Crimes in Poland, Warsaw)

such, no legal, moral, or ideological system acted to prevent war crimes. Neither did the famously harsh discipline of the German army serve as a check. Much more often than not, officers either encouraged atrocities (for racial reasons or to allow the troops to blow off steam) or turned an obvious blind eye. Hitler himself had decreed that the laws of warfare would not be enforced in wars against Poland or the Soviet Union. On rare occasions when commanders did issue orders against atrocities, they found their men reluctant to obey.

The final ingredient in this mix relates to the previous two. Bartov has described a "distortion of reality" that developed inside the Wehrmacht. The Germans justified their invasion of the Soviet Union on the false premise that the Russians were preparing to invade Germany. Hitler and senior officers of the Wehrmacht knew that no such invasion was imminent; in fact, they counted on Soviet lack of preparation to assist their victory march to Moscow. Nevertheless, the idea of a defensive invasion, paradoxical as it might seem, was popular among German soldiers and civilians alike.

If the war was defensive, then the German army was merely giving the Russians what they would have given the Germans had they had the chance. Convoluted though this argument was, it appealed to a nation that had already accepted and internalized an image of Slavs as Untermenschen. A further distortion connected Judaism and Russian Bolshevism, despite a long and deep history of Russian anti-Semitism. As the war worsened for the Germans, soldiers blamed the Russians and Jews for starting a conflict that now promised to end badly. Atrocities piled up on both sides: from the Russians who were motivated by revenge and the Germans who were motivated by fear.

Condemning the Wehrmacht for war crimes does not, of course, mean that every German soldier committed atrocities. Furthermore, it does not mean that only the German army was guilty of war crimes; all of the combatants of World War II degraded previous notions of morality and legality to various degrees. Nevertheless, the German army stands alone in having a volatile combination of racist ideology that preached and practiced genocide, a senior and junior officer corps that encouraged a war of utmost brutality, and a worldview that allowed those who committed atrocities to nevertheless retain the moral high ground. The Wehrmacht was an army of its people and an instrument of its regime. As such, it stands alone in its commitment to the murderous agenda of Nazi Germany.

–MICHAEL S. NEIBERG, U. S. AIR FORCE
ACADEMY, COLORADO

Viewpoint:
No, German war atrocities were usually carried out by special units, not the Wehrmacht; in addition, antipartisan actions were often viewed by German soldiers as acceptable interpretations of the rules of war.

According to the famous dictum of Carl von Clausewitz, war is simply a continuation of politics by other means. Less well known, however, is his belief that implicit in war is a tendency to limitlessness, to an inevitable escalation of violence, and to a steady movement toward moral extremities as a consequence of both sides' actions and reactions. The decision to go to war reflects political motives, but so does the attempt to control or channel the inevitable process of increasing violence once a war has begun. Military leadership, therefore, is not only a question of strategy and tactics, but also one of the rules of war, especially as set down in the various Geneva and The Hague conventions.

This problem of escalating violence and the rules of war strikes at the heart of the controversy over the role of the *Wehrmacht* (German Army) in World War II: whether it acted more or less like other armies, or willingly and actively participated in atrocities. Specifically exonerated of being a criminal organization by the judges at the Nuremberg Trial of Major War Criminals (1945–1946), in contrast to the SS (*Schutzstaffel*), Gestapo, or Nazi Party, for years the Wehrmacht was viewed as having remained immune to the virus of Nazism. The army had fought tenaciously and rigorously, so the argument went, but out of a high-minded sense of duty, all the while maintaining its autonomy from the Nazi state. The 20 July 1944 attempt to assassinate Adolf Hitler seemed only to confirm this notion, as did the fact that virtually all active anti-Nazi resistance within Germany resided in army circles.

In recent years, however, several historians have challenged this view, arguing that army and SS units, among them the notorious *Einsatzgruppen* (killing units), often worked closely together in the killing of civilians, and especially of Jews; that political support for Nazism permeated army leadership; that far from distancing itself from Hitler, top army leaders embraced his racist ideology and conception of the war in the east as a *Vernichtungskrieg* (war of annihilation); and that even the *Landsers,* the ordinary soldiers, participated willingly in these atrocities. Without a doubt, Hitler desired a political army. The point of contention in the present intense debate over the role of the Wehrmacht is the extent to which he actually managed to create one. The problem lies in the fact that the historical reality was much more complex than some of these critical studies suggest (or would admit) and that they often blur cause-and-effect relationships, as well as the distinction between Wehrmacht and SS orders and actual actions.

The personal actions and reactions of men in war, as Gerald F. Linderman has pointed out in *The World Within War: America's Combat Experience in World War II* (1997), reflect both their cultural assumptions and expectations that the other side will agree to the establishment of certain unspoken rules that act to regulate and moderate the level of violence on the battlefield. Cultural propinquity and the ability to create a set of rough rules that restrained behavior on both sides helps explain why the war in the west was so vastly different from that fought in eastern Europe, and also why so many American soldiers fought the Germans, at least until the closing days of the war, with so little hatred or moral indignation. Still, every war results in necessities in which soldiers commit atrocities not out of premeditation but out of the fury of the moment or anger at a temporary violation of the rules by the other side. In western Europe both German and Allied soldiers proved guilty of such actions, including, among other things, killing prisoners of war or the wounded, shooting at medics, and sniping. A persistent problem lay in deciphering the motivation of the other side, in determining whether certain actions represented deliberately unacceptable behavior designed to antagonize the enemy or simply a cultural idiosyncrasy. Thus, while rules violations in the West were common, Linderman concluded that combat soldiers on both sides realized that they had to learn something of the other side's quirks and to accommodate them within the set of informal battlefield rules.

In Russia and eastern Europe, however, cultural patterns and personal expectations proved too dissimilar, while political, ideological, and racial factors interjected new elements, making an explosive mix. Certainly, Hitler's injunctions to Wehrmacht leaders to conduct a war of extermination, and the actions of the SS-controlled Einsatzgruppen in shooting both political commissars and Jews, raised the level of combustibility. Even in the ranks, however, attitudes toward the Soviet Union differed from those toward western European nations. Anticommunist beliefs, notions of cultural and racial superiority, and National Socialist convictions, reinforced by the seeming backwardness and primitiveness of life in the U.S.S.R., undermined the ability, or willingness, of German troops to form the same set of informal rules that moderated combat behavior in the west.

Facing a desperate military situation, Soviet leaders resorted almost immediately to irregular, partisan warfare. The use of soldiers cut off from their units, civilians, and even women as saboteurs, spies, and snipers had enormous consequences. Already inclined to see the Russians as Asiatic barbarians, the Germans felt impelled by this irregular form of war both to respond with increasing ruthlessness and to expand greatly their definition of the enemy. The partisan war proved of crucial importance as the Germans, stung by guerrilla activity, resorted to draconian countermeasures, which resulted in a cycle of escalating violence, of reprisal and counter-reprisal, until soldiers on both sides thought they were fighting "animals" or "beasts." In contrast with western Europe, then, combatants on the Eastern Front formed few rules to moderate behavior, nor did they seek an accommodation with the other side.

Most of the debate over the allegedly criminal nature of the Wehrmacht, then, centers on actions in Russia and eastern Europe, where the army leadership supposedly embraced Hitler's notion of a Vernichtungskrieg, then embarked on systematic, comprehensive, and premeditated atrocities designed to implement this racist New Order. The key to this critical interpretation of the Wehrmacht is the series of orders and instructions issued by Hitler in the months preceding Operation Barbarossa, the invasion of the Soviet Union. Beginning with his pronouncement on 30 March 1941 to his assembled commanders that the war against the Soviet Union would not be fought along traditional lines, but would be a war of extermination between two conflicting ideologies, army leaders allegedly welcomed the opportunity to eliminate the so-called Jewish-Bolshevik enemy. There followed, to little apparent resistance, a flood of criminal orders: on 28 April the regulations concerning the introduction of special units of the Einsatzgruppen into rear areas of the army, their tasks, and the support required of the army; on 13 May the blanket waiver Hitler issued to German forces releasing them from restraints of military law in carrying out certain measures against the civilian population of the Soviet Union; on 19 May the guidelines for conduct of troops, which gave the individual Landser great latitude in the determination and disposition of suspected guerrillas; and on 6 June the infamous "Commissar Order," which called for the immediate shooting of political commissars in the Red Army, as well as others classified as dangerous elements, among them Jewish males.

Much of the top army leadership certainly held strongly anticommunist views, and some were racist, but despite this extensive paper trail of orders and instructions, the evidence suggests a more complex process than the mere dutiful implementation of criminal orders. Even critics of the Wehrmacht disagree as to the repercussion of these orders: some argue that their uncritical acceptance reveals only an anti-Jewish tendency in the army leadership; others state that army involvement in the process of destruction evolved over a period of time; a few contend that the army acted primarily out of hatred of the communist system; and still others assert that a distinction must be made between the anti-Jewish atrocities of the Einsatzgruppen and army measures, which were primarily antipartisan in nature and designed only to secure rear areas.

A more nuanced view of the Wehrmacht, one between total condemnation and complete exculpation, is thus necessary in order to arrive at some understanding and assessment of its actions. Although it certainly formed an integral component of a criminal regime, in this century of totalitarian violence it is not uncommon for an army to follow the instructions of a state leadership that pursues a criminal policy, witness the actions of Joseph Stalin and the Red Army. Moreover, the army leadership was far less autonomous than its critics contend. The criminal orders listed above, for example, are as much about restricting Wehrmacht authority in the administration of occupied areas of the U.S.S.R. as they are indicative of willing collaboration. Hitler's orders not only gave the SS "special tasks," they also sharply limited the extent of army jurisdiction in the occupied territories, while providing the SS with sweeping powers. The time was long past when military objections to the use of Einsatzgruppen, as in Poland, could prevent their employment in France. By the time of the Russian campaign, Hitler had already subjugated the army leadership to his political will. Presented with a fait accompli, their options were limited: obedience; refusal to obey and likely dismissal; circumventing or moderating the criminal orders; or, in an extreme case, a coup d'etat.

An initial point of differentiation, then, would be between frontline troops and rear area security forces. Indeed, the most vociferous critics of the Wehrmacht tend to concentrate almost exclusively on actions in the rear areas, and especially that of Army Group Center, and for good reason, since the available evidence indicates that German combat troops rarely committed atrocities against the civilian population of the U.S.S.R. Even in the matter of implementation of the "Commissar Order," contradictions abound. While top army commanders limited their objections to entries in their personal diaries, an occasional memorandum, or instructions

that little emphasis be placed on implementing this order, field commanders seem to have had more leeway in terms of actually carrying through the order. Some followed the reading of this particular directive with a pointed reminder of the requirements of The Hague Convention regarding treatment of prisoners of war, while others emphasized that pragmatic reasons of self-interest dictated how prisoners should be treated. In some outfits, officers disposed of the problem by separating political commissars and turning them over to *Sichevheitsdienst* (Security Department, SD) units or SS police battalions, while in others they evaded rigorous enforcement of the decree by filing few or ambiguous reports concerning their actions. This latter action seems to have been an especially popular method for skirting the letter of the order, for higher military headquarters complained constantly that field units either failed to submit relevant reports or that they were so unclear as to be useless. Finally, in the relative handful of combat units that did shoot political commissars, the reports indicate surprisingly low numbers of those executed.

If critics fail to distinguish between the attitudes of those at the top of the army leadership and actual actions taken at the local level, as well as attitudes of local commanders, they also discount various efforts at all levels to moderate policy. Again, motivations varied: some commanders worried about maintaining troop discipline; others were concerned about the impact of German actions on stiffening Red Army resistance; and still others hoped to gain cooperation from non-Russian peoples. Taken together, however, they undermine the notion of a monolithic organization engaged in systematic, deliberate, comprehensive, and premeditated atrocities. In addition, many critics interpret the evidence rather freely by failing to differentiate between actions taken by army troops and those of SS, SD, and police units. The agreement between the army and SS concerning the Einsatzgruppen, for example, required the army to provide logistical support to these SS killing squads and, if need be, some personnel for transportation or guard purposes, but frontline troops rarely participated in mass shootings. Certainly, some combat units on occasion did execute Jews, while individual Landsers, often on leave and as a spontaneous response, joined in a killing spree. Army field commanders reacted to such incidents, though, by prohibiting the participation of frontline soldiers in these actions. The tendency, then, seemed to be for SS, SD, and police units to seek to involve army troops in the atrocities against the civilian population in the U.S.S.R., with local Wehrmacht commanders trying to resist this trend.

SS EXECUTIONS

The following is an account by Hermann Graebe, a construction engineer, of the mass executions of Ukrainian Jews from the town of Dubno on 5 October 1942.

"My foreman and I went directly to the pits. Nobody bothered us. Now I heard rifle shots in quick succession from behind one of the earth mounds. The people who had got off the trucks—men, women and children of all ages—had to undress upon the order of an SS man who carried a riding or dog whip. They had to put down their clothes in fixed places, sorted according to shoes, top clothing and undergarments. I saw heaps of shoes of about 800 to 1000 pairs, great piles of under-linen and clothing. Without screaming or weeping these people undressed, stood around in family groups, kissed each other, said farewells, and waited for a sign from another SS man, who stood near the pit, also with a whip in his hand. During the fifteen minutes I stood near, I heard no complaint or plea for mercy. I watched a family of about eight persons, a man and a woman both of about fifty, with their children of about twenty to twenty-four, and two grown-up daughters about twenty-eight or twenty-nine. An old woman with snow white hair was holding a one year old child in her arms and singing to it and tickling it. The child was cooing with delight. The parents were looking on with tears in their eyes. The father was holding the hand of a boy about ten years old and speaking to him softly; the boy was fighting his tears. The father pointed to the sky, stroked his head and seemed to explain something to him. At that moment the SS man at the pit started shouting something to his comrade. The latter counted off about twenty persons and instructed them to go behind the earth mound. Among them was the family I have just mentioned. I well remember a girl, slim with black hair, who, as she passed me, pointed to herself and said, "twenty-three years old." I walked around the mound and found myself confronted by a tremendous grave. People were closely wedged together and lying on top of each other so that only their heads were visible. Nearly all had blood running over their shoulders from their heads. Some of the people shot were still moving. Some were lifting their arms and turning their heads to show that they were still alive. The pit was nearly two-thirds full. I estimated that it already contained about a thousand people. I looked for the man who did the shooting. He was an SS man, who sat at the edge of the narrow end of the pit, his feet dangling into the pit. He had a tommy-gun on his knees and was smoking a cigarette. The people, completely naked, went down some steps which were cut in the clay wall of the pit and clambered over the heads of the people lying there to the place to which the SS man directed them. They lay down in front of the dead or wounded people; some caressed those who were still alive and spoke to them in a low voice. Then I heard a series of shots. I looked into the pit and saw that the bodies were twitching or the heads lying already motionless on top of the bodies that lay beneath them. Blood was running from their necks. The next batch was approaching already. They went down into the pit, lined themselves up against the previous victims and were shot."

"Eyewitness Account of Einsatz Executions," The History Place: World War Two in Europe, *on-line site, www.historyplace.com.*

Another point of differentiation, and one that strikes at the heart of the problem, relates to the fact that even in rear areas, where the great bulk of the alleged atrocities committed by the army took place, disparities existed between different areas of occupation. For example, fewer offenses occurred in the rear area of Army Group South, where cooperation and support from the local non-Russian population was greater and the partisan war was correspondingly less intense, than in Army Group Center, where a savage guerrilla conflict ensued. A factor, perhaps the key factor, in accounting for Wehrmacht atrocities, then, seems to be the existence of active partisan groups and the nature and intensity of the resulting guerrilla warfare in occupied areas of the Soviet Union.

In the rear areas of Army Group South, the research of historians such as Theo Schulte, Truman Anderson, Klaus Hammel, and others, though far from exonerating German occupation (or security) divisions of wrongdoing, does illustrate the complexity of the situation. Although initially charged with the specific tasks of securing the vital railroad and highway links between front and rear, controlling important logistics and supply centers, and protecting areas of strategic significance, the anticipated quick victory, after which administrative duties would be turned over to Party and SS authorities, did not materialize. Few in number to control vast areas with a hostile climate and insufficient infrastructure, inadequately trained for their new responsibilities, poorly equipped, isolated, fearful, and aware of their vulnerability, the beleaguered occupation troops felt a constant sense of danger. From the start, rear area commanders, realizing the difficulty of controlling these immense spaces, aimed to stamp out any potential opposition as quickly as possible. In the rear areas of Army Group South, however, commanders also recognized the generally favorable reception accorded German forces and adopted a nuanced, if still cruel, policy. Reprisal shootings, for example, were to be directed at Jews and communists, with the local Ukrainian population exempted. Indeed, the studies of Army Group South indicate that German commanders pursued a policy of initial restraint, followed by increasingly harsh measures in response to partisan actions—but even then they attempted to moderate or restrict their actions lest German harshness prompt an increase in civilian support for the partisans.

The crucial factor from the German perspective appeared to be the nature and intensity of partisan warfare itself. Historically, German military leaders attached enormous importance to the maintenance of proper combatant status, while viewing irregular or guerrilla wars with particular abhorrence. In both 1871 and 1914, for example, German military authorities had acted ruthlessly to stamp out resistance in occupied areas of France and Belgium on the grounds that initial harshness would intimidate the local population into passivity, and thus in the long run both German and civilian lives would be spared. German commanders generally emphasized four criteria for recognition of an enemy force as a proper combatant, subject to the rules of war: the enemy force had to be subject to clear leadership; they had to wear recognizable markings; they had to carry their weapons openly; and they had to uphold the laws and customs of war. Above all, it was the violation of this last point by the partisans in the U.S.S.R. that especially rankled German military leaders, since according to Articles 42 and 43 of the Hague Convention (1907) the legal use of force in occupied areas rested with the occupying authority, while the civilian population had no inherent right of resistance. Indeed, the same convention provided for a "right of repression" in order to compel irregular forces and the occupied civilian population to abide by the rules of war. To this dubious "right" belonged hostage-taking and reprisal executions that, although they were supposed to be connected with specific atrocities

committed by the enemy and governed by principles of proportionality, gave German commanders a sense of leeway and legitimacy in their actions.

Implicit in the German attitude, as Mark Mazower has pointed out in *Inside Hitler's Greece: The Experience of Occupation, 1941–44* (1993), is a curious sense of honor. German leaders viewed guerrillas as unworthy opponents since they defied the rules of proper combatant status, failed to fight "honestly" in the open, and relied on stealth, deception, surprise, and treachery. In contrast, German commanders believed themselves to be upholding the soldier's code against the forces of barbarism. Furthermore, the Germans saw themselves as the beleaguered party, with the initiative lying with the partisans, who determined the nature and timing of their own actions. Army commanders in rear areas, charged with pacifying vast regions with inadequate forces, thus believed themselves caught in a spiral of action and reaction. Given the inherently inhumane nature of both totalitarian systems and the pervasive German preconception of the communist system as insidious, it was a short step to believing that overwhelming violence and retribution were the only means to deal with these alleged asocials, criminals, and delinquents. The Germans certainly acted harshly, but as Mazower noted, their harshness seemed to stem less from hatred than from a cold and mechanical implementation of a given procedure.

The particular virulence of the partisan war in the U.S.S.R. stemmed from the facts that, from the Wehrmacht's perspective, the Soviet regime had unleashed an "illegal" war against German occupying authorities, that the partisans fought in a manner that violated the rules of war, and that their disregard for the laws and customs of war meant the partisans had no claim on any rights under the rules of war. In general, then, in their response to the escalating violence behind the front lines, the Germans fought the partisans with a shocking harshness, but not with the same rationale as the extermination commandos of the SS. Wehrmacht security divisions sought to stop certain actions of the enemy; the Einsatzgruppen aimed to eliminate whole categories of people arbitrarily deemed the enemy, regardless of their actions. In addition, the partisan war followed a markedly different trajectory, as initial restraint was succeeded by increasing cruelty in response to partisan actions, followed by an attempt by army leaders on the spot to moderate the harshest measures, if only for pragmatic reasons of reducing partisan support among the local population.

In summary, then, the army security divisions in the rear areas did not fight an ideological war of extermination, nor did they give unconditional support to the special commandos of the SS engaged in such actions. The military leadership by and large responded to a partisan war that they saw as illegal with harsh but legally correct measures grounded in the "right of repression." In addition, partisan actions largely began the cycle of escalating violence and ultimately determined the savage nature of German reprisals. In the occupied areas of the U.S.S.R., a domain of conflicting interests between military authorities, SS efforts to extend its power and influence, population and resettlement policies of the Nazi Party, economic objectives, and a racial war of extermination, army leaders had precious little influence on Hitler. Indeed, implicit in the assumption of an identity of interests between Nazi and Wehrmacht leaders in conducting a Vernichtungskrieg is the notion of the interplay of two equal partners. Hitler, however, had long since brought the Wehrmacht under his dominance, making this premise at best contrived and at worst a willful misreading of the true relationship between the two. Given the limited nature of its options, the army leadership chose to focus narrowly on front-line operations and securing the immediate rear areas of occupation.

As Americans later learned in Vietnam, however, once begun, a guerrilla war tends to whirl out of control in an upward spiral of violence. German commanders certainly responded to the partisan challenge with astounding harshness, but this response is different from the systematic, comprehensive, and premeditated atrocities with which they are charged by their critics. The key agents of radicalization in eastern Europe were and remained Hitler, Nazi Party administrators, the SS leadership, and the SS, SD, and police battalions operating just behind the front, which at times took advantage of the partisan war to draw the Wehrmacht into the murder of the local Jewish population. As many a former Landser could testify, the civilian population in the rear areas far preferred Germans with the symbol of the imperial eagle above their right shirt pocket (soldiers) to those who wore it on their left sleeve (SS, SD, and police battalions). Critics have erected a picture of the Wehrmacht that is one-sided and undifferentiated. As unpalatable as it might be, those killed in the partisan war were not necessarily victims of war crimes, since the combating of partisans in an occupied area, and the use of retaliatory measures, was a legitimate act accepted under the rules of war. If the average German soldier was not a passive bystander, neither was he an active war criminal.

—STEPHEN G. FRITZ, EAST TENNESSEE STATE UNIVERSITY

References

Truman O. Anderson, "Die 62: Infanterie-Division," in *Vernichtungskrieg: Verbrechen der Wehrmacht 1941 bis 1944,* edited by Hannes Heer and Klaus Naumann (Hamburg: Hamburger Edition, 1995), pp. 297–322;

Omer Bartov, *The Eastern Front, 1941–45: German Troops and the Barbarisation of Warfare* (Basingstoke, U.K.: Macmillan in association with St. Antony's College, Oxford, 1985);

Bartov, *Hitler's Army: Soldiers, Nazis, and War in the Third Reich* (New York: Oxford University Press, 1991);

Horst Boog and others, *Angriff auf die Sowjetunion* (Stuttgart: Deutsche Verlags-Anstalt, 1983); translated by Dean S. McMurrey, Ewald Osers, and Louise Wilmot as *The Attack on the Soviet Union* (Oxford: Clarendon Press; New York: Oxford University Press, 1998);

Christopher R. Browning, *Ordinary Men: Reserve Police Battalion 101 and the Final Solution in Poland* (New York: HarperCollins, 1992);

Browning, "Wehrmacht Reprisal Policy and the Murder of the Male Jews in Serbia," in *Fateful Months: Essays on the Emergence of the Final Solution,* edited by Browning (New York: Holmes & Meier, 1985), pp. 39–56;

Alexander Dallin, *German Rule in Russia, 1941–1945: A Study of Occupation Policies* (London: Macmillan, 1957; New York: St. Martin's Press, 1957);

Alfred M. de Zayas, *Die Wehrmacht-Untersuchungsstelle: deutsche Ermittlungen uber alliierte Völkerrechtsverletzungen im Zweiten Weltkrieg* (Munich: Universitas-Verlag, Langen Muller, 1980); translated as *The Wehrmacht War Crimes Bureau, 1939–1945* (Lincoln: University of Nebraska Press, 1989);

de Zayas, "The Wehrmacht War Crimes Bureau," *Historical Journal,* 35, no. 2 (1992): 383–399;

Joachim C. Fest, *Gesicht des Dritten Reiches: Profile einer totalitateren Herrschaft* (München: R. Piper, 1963); translated by Michael Bullock as *The Face of the Third Reich: Portraits of the Nazi Leadership* (London: Weidenfeld & Nicolson, 1970);

Stephen G. Fritz, *Frontsoldaten: The German Soldier in World War II* (Lexington: University Press of Kentucky, 1995);

David M. Glantz and Jonathan M. House, *When Titans Clashed: How the Red Army Stopped*

Hitler (Lawrence: University Press of Kansas, 1995);

Daniel Jonah Goldhagen, *Hitler's Willing Executioners: Ordinary Germans and the Holocaust* (New York: Knopf, 1996);

Klaus Hammel, "Kompetenzen und Verhalten der Truppe im rückwärtigen Heeresgebiet," in *Die Soldaten der Wehrmacht,* edited by Hans Poeppel and others (Munich: Herbig, 1998), pp. 178–229;

Wolfgang Hasch and Gustav Friedrich, "Der Partisanenkrieg der Sowjetunion und die deutschen Gegenmaßnahmen im Zweiten Weltkrieg," in *Die Soldaten der Wehrmacht,* edited by Poeppel and others (Munich: Herbig, 1998), pp. 230–255;

Hannes Heer and Klaus Naumann, eds., *Vernichtungskrieg: Verbrechen der Wehrmacht 1941 bis 1944* (Hamburg: Hamburger Edition, 1995);

Helmut Krausnick and Hans-Heinrich Wilhelm, *Die Truppe des Weltanschauungskrieges: die Einsatzgruppen der Sicherheitspolizei und des SD 1938-1942* (Stuttgart: Deutsche Verlags-Anstalt, 1981);

Gerald F. Linderman, *The World Within War: America's Combat Experience in World War II* (New York: Free Press, 1997);

Walter Manoschek, ed., *Die Wehrmacht im Rassenkrieg: der Vernichtungskrieg hinter der Front* (Vienna: Picus, 1996);

Mark Mazower, *Inside Hitler's Greece: The Experience of Occupation, 1941-44* (New Haven: Yale University Press, 1993);

Mazower, "Military Violence and National Socialist Values: The Wehrmacht in Greece 1941-1944," *Past and Present,* 134 (1992): 129–158;

Rolf-Dieter Müller and Gerd R. Ueberschär, *Hitler's War in the East, 1941-1945: A Critical Reassessment,* translation of texts by Bruce D. Little (Providence, R.I.: Berghahn Books, 1997);

Timothy Patrick Mulligan, *The Politics of Illusion and Empire: German Occupation Policy in the Soviet Union, 1942-1943* (New York: Praeger, 1988);

Jeremy Noakes and Geoffrey Pridham, eds., *Nazism, 1919-1945: A History in Documents and Eyewitness Accounts* (New York: Schocken Books, 1990);

Horst Rohde, "Politische Indoktrination in höheren Stäben und in der Truppe—untersucht am Beispiel des Kommissarbefehls," in *Die Soldaten der Wehrmacht,* edited by Poeppel and others (Munich: Herbig, 1998), pp. 124–158;

Theo J. Schulte, *The German Army and Nazi Policies in Occupied Russia* (Oxford & New York: Berg, 1989);

Franz W. Seidler, *Die Wehrmacht im Partisanenkrieg: Militärische und völkerrechtliche Darlegungen zur Kriegführung im Osten* (Selent: Verlag für Militärgeschichte, 1998);

Alfred Streim, *Die Behandlung sowjetischer Kriegsgefangener im "Fall Barbarossa": eine Dokumentation unter Berücksichtigung der Unterlagen deutscher Strafverfolgungsbehörden und der Materialien der Zentralen Stelle der Landesjustizverwaltungen zur Aufklärung von NS-Verbrechen* (Heidelberg: Müller, Juristischer Verlag, 1981);

Christian Streit, *Keine Kameraden: die Wehrmacht und der sowjetischer Kriegsgefangenen 1941-1945* (Stuttgart: Deutsche Verlags-Anstalt, 1978).

GERMAN ARMY
AND ATROCITIES

GERMAN CONQUESTS

Did the Germans finance their war effort by military conquest?

Viewpoint: Yes, military conquest was an effective method of using the land and labor of occupied territories for the German war effort.

Viewpoint: No, the territories occupied by Germany yielded only poor industrial and agricultural products, as well as inefficient troops.

The question of whether conquest paid for the Third Reich is moot. National Socialist ideology was based on exploiting other states and peoples; narrow calculations of profit and loss had no place in Adolf Hitler's worldview. In practical terms, the poorly coordinated, highly competitive rearmament programs begun after the Nazi seizure of power had by 1938 so badly overstrained the German economy that conquest was the only feasible alternative to a downward spiral that neither Hitler nor his generals were willing to contemplate.

Nazi Germany skimmed its conquests rather than exploited them. The *Wehrmacht* (German Army) battened off captured equipment. The Reich took advantage of the Chech Skoda and the French Renault factories, the grain fields of the Ukraine, the labor resources of all Europe—even the volunteers willing for whatever reason to stand in the ranks of the army or the *Schutzstaffeln* (SS). There was no pattern of systematic plundering, to say nothing of cultivated collaboration. The Reich's occupation policies were wasteful—of resources, matériel, people, and goodwill.

This waste was in part, a function of Hitler's practice of placing potential cornucopias, such as the Ukraine in the hands of party officials who were incompetent even by Nazi standards. Waste was also a function of everyday behavior. Given a choice between the closed fist or the open hand, occupation authorities, whether military, bureaucratic, or party, chose the former almost automatically. In 1941 men and women from occupied regions volunteered for work in Germany; by 1944 the Reich was suffering from an acute shortage of slave labor. That was only one aspect of a policy that generated most of its own administrative and policing burdens. Running a servile imperium over any length of time is complicated—far more complicated than it seemed to Hitler, his henchmen, and the many ordinary Germans who preferred the transient pleasures of oppression to the permanent consolidation of power.

Viewpoint:
Yes, military conquest was an effective method of using the land and labor of occupied territories for the German war effort.

Studies by Allied economic experts at the end of World War II revealed a seeming paradox. Confounding expectations, it appeared that Germany, despite its rearmament efforts of the 1930s, never fully mobilized its economy in the early stages of the conflict and belatedly geared up for total war only in 1942, and then not as effectively as its rivals. Two ready explanations lay immediately at hand. The first pointed to the institutional and jurisdictional chaos of the Nazi administrative system, which caused the German economy to perform inefficiently; the second stressed the economic dimension of the *Blitzkrieg* (lightning war) strategy. Although the notion of an inefficient German economy had merit, most attention focused on the Blitzkrieg strategy, whose proponents argued that the partially mobilized German economy resulted not from inefficiency but from premeditation. Because he wanted to fight only limited "lightning wars," so the argument went, Adolf Hitler intended from the outset to put the German economy on a minimal war footing so as to have both "guns and butter." Intending to avoid the burden of a long war of attrition, which he held responsible for the disintegration of the home-front and thus Germany's defeat in World War I, Hitler aimed to wage war against one opponent at a time and without seriously lowering civilian consumption. Thus, Germany deliberately rearmed in "breadth" rather than in "depth," planning for a war in short bursts rather than total war. Following the military reverses in Russia in 1941–1942, it then proved too late for Germany to switch effectively to a total-war economy.

Although accepted by virtually all historians since the war, at least three things are wrong with this thesis: it neglects the serious inefficiency of the German economy; it ignores evidence that points to Hitler's preparations for a long war; and it overlooks the considerable decline in German civilian consumption at the beginning of the war. Certainly, Germany's geographic position made a short war a necessary strategic concept, but Hitler actually anticipated a larger war that would commence in the mid 1940s, a war both to secure Germany's *Lebensraum* (living space) and a life-and-death struggle for its racial existence. The war that began in September 1939 resulted from miscalculation, not intention. With a bit of logic on his side, Hitler had convinced himself by early 1939, and certainly after the conclusion of the Nazi-Soviet Pact in August, that the Western Allies would not risk war over Poland. Hitler thus expected a local war with Poland and not a European war for which Germany remained unprepared.

Both Hitler's ambitions and Germany's rearmament to 1939 reinforce this contention. Through clever diplomacy, Hitler had always intended, either in the absence of war or by a local conflict, to establish a central European base from which Germany could then wage war against its major enemies, above all the Soviet Union. The remilitarization of the Rhineland,

annexation of Austria and the Sudetenland, and absorption of the remaining Czech lands (Bohemia and Moravia) without war illustrated this scheme nicely. Hitler initially believed he could bring Poland into an alliance with Germany, as a junior partner on the lines of Hungary or Romania, on the basis of a shared hostility toward the U.S.S.R. Even when that prospect faded, the likelihood of any genuine western assistance to Poland, given their previous inaction, appeared remote to Hitler, an assessment that seemed to gain validity with the signing of the Nazi-Soviet Pact. That he miscalculated certainly irritated Hitler, but given the reality of what was still a local war with Poland, and the relative German military advantage over France and Great Britain, Hitler believed he still had the upper hand. The subsequent quick German victories in the west, moreover, obscured Hitler's principal long-term goals, which lay in the east.

With the announcement of the Four Year Plan in 1936, in fact, Hitler began to prepare the German economy for this larger racial and economic struggle. Haunted by the British blockade in World War I, Hitler meant to make Germany "blockade-proof" through a restructuring and reorientation of the economy, a process that was to be overseen by Hermann Goering. This reorientation of the economy for war, however, proved slow and cumbersome. Hitler himself did not understand economic processes well, reducing most to a question of will; while Goering proved a poor choice for the task, although admittedly he expected to receive more time for preparation, which is one reason he argued against risking war in 1939. Moreover, with civilian consumption and profits just beginning to rise after the devastating depression of the early 1930s, German industrialists and private businessmen largely ignored or circumvented Goering's instructions for preparing for a long-term war. Indeed, the expansion of the state sector as embodied by the Four Year Plan was itself an admission of the reluctance of the private sector to cooperate. In addition, the inevitable jurisdictional disputes in a system aptly characterized as "institutional Darwinism" hampered efficient economic restructuring. Finally, despite prevailing belief, Germany began full-scale rearmament relatively late and then, because of the cumulative impact of the Treaty of Versailles, had to rebuild from a position of deep inferiority. By the time war began, then, Germany had received relatively little return on its extensive effort at economic reorientation.

Along the same lines, once the war began, conversion to a total-war economy commenced immediately, but was bungled. Far from desiring both guns and butter, Hitler from the first sought to reduce civilian levels of consumption

GERMAN CONQUESTS

drastically, while using incessant propaganda to prepare the German public for the necessity of sacrifice. As R. J. Overy has noted in *War and Economy in the Third Reich* (1994), in the first two years of the war civilian-consumer standards dropped considerably more than in Great Britain, labor was diverted to war-related tasks on a large scale, and throughout the war the proportion of women in the workforce remained higher than in either Great Britain or the United States. In fact, the bulk of the fall in German consumer spending came before 1942. Far from being the easiest years of the war, the period from 1939 to 1942 witnessed the most rapid reduction in the civilian economy. Rationing was introduced on a wide range of goods as early as September 1939, with some items being restricted even earlier. As a result, by 1942 real per-capita consumption in Germany had declined to 68 percent of the 1938 level, versus 86 percent in Great Britain. In addition to the constant exactions on resources made by the escalating demands for weapons, civilian consumption was even less in practice since much putative civilian-goods production actually went to the armed forces. In reality, Hitler's goal was not unlimited consumption but equal distribution—to ensure that all civilians had a guaranteed minimum existence, below which living standards would not be permitted to fall.

In labor mobilization the picture appears much the same. From 1936 on efforts had been made to retrain the German labor force for vital war-production tasks, while once the war began Nazi authorities immediately began closing down unessential production and shifting labor to war projects. On the eve of the invasion of the Soviet Union, according to Overy, roughly 60 percent of the industrial workforce in Germany was engaged directly in war production, a figure higher than the level of labor mobilization in Great Britain at the same time. Once again, because ostensibly civilian industries engaged in high levels of war production, the actual figure was likely greater than estimated. Because of a quirk in the German labor-registration system, many of the infamous "domestic servants," used as proof that Nazi Germany had not mobilized female labor, in fact worked as helpers on farms or in small businesses and thus were not servants in the conventional sense at all. Not only did Germany have a relatively high level of female employment in the late 1930s (37 percent of the labor force to 26 percent in Great Britain), but by the summer of 1944 women comprised 51 percent of the German workforce, compared with 38 percent in Great Britain and 36 percent in the United States. Not only were labor participation rates high for women in Germany, but an exceptionally large number worked either in war production or in vital agricultural tasks, with women comprising fully two-thirds of the native

agricultural workforce in 1944. German labor productivity proved undeniably low between 1939 and 1941, and labor might have been utilized more efficiently, but Nazi authorities certainly made an effort to mobilize labor as extensively as possible.

Germany's surprisingly low output of military production before 1942, therefore, resulted not from a failure to shift resources from civilian to military purposes but an ineffective use of those resources once they were shifted. Albert Speer's considerable success as Minister of Armaments in raising German war production from 1942 thus lay not in mobilizing new resources but in utilizing existing resources more efficiently through rationalization of production, simplification of product design, increased use of special-purpose machine tools, and more effective centralized administration.

Making more effective use of existing resources, also meant ruthlessly exploiting the conquered lands under German control. In truth Germany could not have waged total war without the substantial and continuing contribution of occupied Europe. Although not every conquered territory proved profitable, as a whole they certainly were, with France the most profitable. Particularly in France, as Alan S. Milward has noted in *The New Order and the French Economy* (1970), German calculations of "occupation costs" and exchange rate manipulations provided it with an enormous open-ended purchasing power, while direct taxation added even more to German coffers. By 1944 occupation costs accounted for 38 percent of total German treasury income, with almost half coming from France alone. Indeed, the U.S. Strategic Bombing Survey estimated that France furnished 42 percent of the total foreign contribution to the German wartime economy. On that basis, the French share of Germany's Gross National Product (GNP) would have been 8 percent in 1942 and 1943 and more than 7 percent in 1944; estimates by the Bombing Survey, furthermore, did not include the value of goods and services consumed by the *Wehrmacht* (German Army) without payment outside of Germany, the value of goods seized from Jews, or the contribution of French workers in Germany. In addition, the value of manufactured goods obtained from France constituted at least 5.5 percent of the German GNP in 1943, while agricultural goods furnished 3.9 percent and raw materials 3.1 percent, figures that are certainly understated because of the manipulated wartime exchange rate.

Clearly then, Germany profited enormously from exploitation of the French economy and continued to receive increasingly high returns on its conquest until French liberation in August 1944. Much the same pattern of economic gains from high taxation, inflated occupation costs, diversion of industrial production, and exploitation of raw materials held true in the rest of western and central Europe. The Germans extracted from Belgium and the Netherlands an estimated two-thirds of their national income. In eastern Europe, German economic plunder proved less orderly and more brutal, and thus the gains for the German economy are harder to calculate. Still, a few examples will suffice to illustrate the importance of the occupied eastern territories for the Wehrmacht and German war economy. In 1941, for example, an astounding 100 percent of the potatoes consumed by the Wehrmacht in Russia were supplied from occupied Soviet areas; the corresponding figures for flour were 86 percent and for meat 68 percent. In 1942 Poland and the Soviet Union together provided 92 percent of German imports of rye, 98 percent of barley, 74 percent of oats, 31 percent of butter, 51 percent of wood, and 78 percent of manganese ore. These examples are the most dramatic, but by 1942 the Wehrmacht would not have been able to continue the war in the east without the forced deliveries of clothing, food, raw materials, industrial production, and equipment. In addition, Nazi authorities maintained the desired minimum level of existence domestically by ruthlessly stripping the occupied areas of the east of basic foodstuffs, thus consigning millions of so-called *Untermenschen* (subhumans) to starvation.

An absolutely vital contribution of the occupied territories to the German war effort, and likely the one least quantifiable in monetary terms, was forced labor. The peak figure of seven million officially registered foreign workers, some 20 percent of the German labor force, was reached in May 1944, with Poles and Soviet citizens constituting the largest proportion, augmented by large numbers of French and Italian workers. In the last year of the war, however, Ulrich Herbert, in *A History of Foreign Labor in Germany, 1880–1980: Seasonal Workers, Forced Laborers, Guest Workers* (1990) estimates that fully one-fourth of those employed in the German economy were foreigners. In addition, an estimated seven million more workers who remained in their native countries produced munitions or other goods for the German war effort.

Although large numbers of the foreign workers in Germany were employed in agriculture or mining, the demands of total war forced Nazi authorities to shift an increasing percentage into war production. While in May 1944 foreign workers made up 22 percent of the labor force in agriculture, they constituted over 29 percent of the industrial workforce and over 30 percent of those working in armaments manufacture. By

August 1944, according to Herbert, every second worker in agriculture was foreign, while in mining, construction, and the metals industry the corresponding figure was roughly every third worker. Foreign conscripts also totaled a third of those employed in armaments-related industries, most notably in the aircraft industry, and more than a quarter in machine-building and the chemical industry. In addition, by the last year of the war the *Schutzstaffeln* (SS) ruthlessly exploited concentration-camp prisoners as slave labor on construction projects, such as building aircraft factories inside mountains, that, given the harsh conditions and poor diets, amounted to a virtual death sentence for thousands of people. Despite the deteriorating work conditions and increasing brutality to which foreign workers were subjected, and the fact that they performed at only an estimated 50 to 80 percent of the productivity level of German workers, the German war economy nonetheless sustained high gains in war production though 1944. Thus the deployment of millions of foreign workers and prisoners of war allowed Germany to continue the war long after its own labor resources were exhausted; without them, Germany likely could not have persisted in the war past 1943.

Instead, because of Speer's rationalization program and the increasing ruthlessness of the regime toward its foreign workers, the German war economy pulled off a remarkable achievement after 1942. In some cases, as Overy observes, output increased with almost the same resource base; between 1941 and 1943 a modest 11-percent expansion in the armaments workforce (and an actual decline in the quantity of available steel) resulted in a 130-percent increase in the production of all weapons, while aircraft production expanded almost 200 percent and tank output went up more than 250 percent. By the end of the war, moreover, German industry produced four times as many munitions from the same quantity of steel, while production time for all weapons was greatly reduced. Only strategic bombing finally interrupted this production achievement; Nazi officials themselves estimated in January 1945 that German industry in 1944 produced 35 percent fewer tanks, 31 percent fewer aircraft, and 42 percent fewer trucks than otherwise possible.

As an unfortunate consequence of the strategic-bombing campaign, German authorities subjected the foreign workforce to even harsher discipline and poorer diet, with the Gestapo and SS intensifying their terror and intimidation. For some of these supposedly inferior people this resulted in annihilation from atrocious work conditions, malnourishment, or mistreatment, while the concentration-camp workers trapped in the SS economic empire suffered their own form of hell. While presiding over an impressive productive achievement, therefore, both German industry and Speer's Armaments Ministry were interested in foreign workers only to the extent that they enhanced production. To achieve this enhanced production, as Herbert emphasizes, the death of tens of thousands of foreign laborers, prisoners of war, and concentration-camp workers as a result of the toil necessary to attain this goal was seen as simply a cost of production. Hitler's ideology and military strategy, based as they were on notions of ruthless racial struggle and Lebensraum, which allowed land and labor to be plundered as effectively as possible, thus influenced German economic mobilization—not in the creation of a "Blitzkrieg economy" as some allege but rather in the savage exploitation of those peoples and areas deemed vital for the total war economy.

—STEPHEN G. FRITZ, EAST TENNESSEE STATE UNIVERSITY

Viewpoint:
No, the territories occupied by Germany yielded only poor industrial and agricultural products, as well as inefficient troops.

The German occupation of Europe during World War II was a failure. As it conquered the nations of Europe, Germany looked to increase its agricultural and industrial production capabilities. In those areas where some autonomy was left in place, there were some successes; in regions the Germans chose to directly occupy, however, they found failure. Oppressive administrations led to resistance, and even open warfare, which then required German troops to keep control of the area, utilizing manpower that could have been better used elsewhere. Additionally, harsh production techniques and poor economic planning led Germany to invest in occupied areas, yet they received little return in industrial goods and agricultural products. Poor planning also meant that the few goods produced in the conquered territories provided little to the German war effort.

Germany administered conquered areas in three different ways. First, areas close to Germany were often incorporated into the Greater German Reich. Areas such as Alsace-Lorraine were simply added to Germany and administered in the same manner as the rest of the Reich. Second, some states, including Vichy France, until November 1942, and Romania, were allowed to administrate themselves as satellites of Germany. They were largely left to their own business, as long as they contributed to the German war effort. Third, regions such as the Netherlands and central Poland were directly administered by German civilian or military officials. These states were no longer autonomous and were under the complete influence of the conquering Germans. It was in cases of direct occupation that the Germans demonstrated the failure of Nazi Europe.

Policing the occupied territories constantly caused problems for the Germans. The overbearing techniques of German occupation forces often led to acts of resistance by the people. In response the Nazis retaliated in cruel ways that further alienated the people, leading to more acts of resistance, which in turn called for more policing by the Germans. Nazi attempts to police their conquered territories only led to increased resentment and resistance to their administration. It was a cycle that the Germans could not control.

Acts of aggression toward the Nazis occurred throughout the occupation. In 1942 the Nazis massacred the citizens and destroyed the Czech village of Lidice in retaliation for the murder by resistance agents of Reinhard Heydrich, German Deputy Reich Protector in Bohemia and Moravia. During August of 1943 the Germans limited the autonomy of the Danish government because of ongoing acts of sabotage against German forces. The Danes were forced to continue working their jobs only by threats of violent force. Portions of the Danish navy were scuttled or sailed to Sweden when the Germans attempted to take control of the ships. In France during 1944, the *Schutzstaffel* (SS) soldiers murdered over six hundred citizens of the French town of Oradour-sur-Glane, out of the belief that they had helped to hijack several trucks carrying gold. Acts such as these only helped to sour the relationship between the occupiers and the people. The only result of Germany's harsh policies toward their conquered areas was further resistance.

In many areas, Germany's harsh policies helped to inspire organized resistance groups against the occupation. Some groups were sponsored by the British, but many were established spontaneously. All over conquered Europe individuals attempted to renew their resistance through anti-German literature, sabotage, and clandestine operations. After the June 1941 German invasion of the Soviet Union, organized Communist groups joined the resistance movement, strengthening resistance throughout all of Europe. Agents under French general Charles De Gaulle gathered the separate French resistance groups together under the National Resistance Council, which organized clandestine actions against the Germans in France. The resistance in Norway obtained a major Allied victory by disrupting the German supply of heavy water, a product essential to Germany's atomic program, by raids on the Norsk Hydro plant. Resistance groups in Czechoslovakia committed individual acts of sabotage and assassination. These acts of disobedience hindered the effectiveness of German rule and forced the Germans to put stronger efforts into fighting the resistance.

Even more harmful than the occasional act of sabotage in conquered areas was guerrilla warfare. In Yugoslavia, Josip Broz Tito organized a partisan army to fight the victorious Germans. Originally, Tito's army was communist, but as he became more successful he attracted noncommunists to his ranks. His guerrilla army actually received aid from Great Britain months before they received any assistance from the Soviet Union. As Tito became more daring and active, the Germans had to assign more resources to Yugoslavia to deal with him. Eventually, Tito held fifteen German divisions in Yugoslavia, keeping them fighting an opponent in a defeated area and out of the eastern and western fronts. In occupied areas of the Soviet Union, guerrilla forces worked to assist the Soviet army in defeating the Germans. The Soviet government appealed to all citizens to help defeat the invaders. Small bands of partisans were organized behind enemy lines with many groups, including Soviet soldiers who were caught behind the fast-moving German army. The Soviet government developed training schools for partisans and parachuted instructors to those who could not attend training sessions. Soviet guerrillas tied down their equal strength of German troops and caused thirty-five thousand German casualties. Not only was the occupation a policing burden to the Germans, it was also a military liability. Having to assign large military units to fight irregular forces only hindered German war aims.

The Germans did control large numbers of workers in occupied Europe. Many of the goods they produced, however, were not essential to the German war effort. In the conquered areas, it was the SS who managed these workers and factories. Instead of producing arms or war materials, SS-controlled factories were largely concerned with the production of consumer goods, such as furniture and pottery. The Ministry of Armaments, which desperately needed workers of the conquered areas to make war goods, was given only a limited say as to how workmen outside of Germany proper could be used. Many foreign workers that were assigned to consumer-goods production were skilled and could have benefited Germany more efficiently had they been left in their original industries. Thanks to the

THE UNIVERSITY OF NAPLES

On 7 October 1943 the Allied Fifth Army entered the Italian city of Naples. What they found was mass devastation. The retreating Germans had destroyed the harbor facilities, contaminated the water supply, and booby-trapped many of the buildings. However, the most wanton destruction was reserved for the University of Naples. Veteran war correspondent Herbert L. Matthews described the scene as follows:

On Sunday the Germans broke into the university after having carefully organized their procedure—squads of men, trucks with dozens and dozens of five-gallon gasoline tins and supplies of hand-grenades. Their objective was deliberate and their work was as methodical and thorough as German work always is. The university was founded in 1224 by Emperor Frederick II. The soldiers went from room to room, thoroughly soaking floors, walls and furniture, including archives that went back for centuries. . . .

When everything was ready, the second stage began. The soldiers went from room to room, throwing in hand-grenades. At the same time, in an adjoining building a few hundred yards up the street, an even greater act of vandalism was being perpetrated. There was something apt about it, something symbolic of the whole German attitude. It did not matter to the Germans that they were destroying the accumulated wealth of centuries of scientific and philosophical thinking.

The rooms of the Royal Society contained some 200,000 books and manuscripts, from not only Italy but every country in the world. These books were stacked neatly and soberly on shelves along the walls: in the middle of the rooms were plain wooden tables with chairs. In several rooms there were paintings—some of them by Francesco Solimene of Nocera, the great baroque architect of the seventeenth century. These had been lent by the National Museum, but they will never be returned. . . .

Every one knows how difficult it is to burn one solid unopened book thoroughly until nothing remains but a heap of fine ashes. The Germans burned some 200,000 books in that way. Of course, the fire had to rage a long time and—also of course—the German thoroughness was going to see to it that nothing interfered with the fire.

They set it at 6 P.M. Sunday. At 9 P.M. Italian firefighting squads came up to extinguish the flames. German guards prevented them from entering the Via Mezzocannone. For three days those fires continued burning and for three days German guards kept Italians away.

Source: *Masterpieces of War Reporting: The Great Moments of World War II,* edited by Louis L. Snyder (New York: Messner, 1962), pp. 287–288.

efforts of the SS, consumer goods in Germany continued to flow freely, while at times essential war matériel was scarce.

As the war progressed, labor became a continual problem for the Germans. One solution was to force foreign workers in the conquered territories into war industries. This policy, however, only helped to strengthen the hand of the SS in economics because they were charged with recruiting, training, housing, policing, and often executing skilled workers outside of Germany. When foreign workers did participate in vital industries they only produced low yields. Russian miners, for example, working in appalling conditions, produced less than one-half the amount of coal that German miners laboring in much better conditions could. In order to get skilled foreign workers to contribute to vital war industries in a positive manner, they had to be moved into Germany itself. Forced migration is never a recipe for providing productive workers. Perhaps if production in the occupied areas had been placed under the control of Germany's economic chief Albert Speer, they would have contributed more significantly to the German war machine.

Germany constantly invested money in the conquered areas in hopes of a profitable return. In many ways, however, this stream of money only went one way. The oppressive techniques used to force products out of occupied Europe were doomed to fail. German smash-and-grab policies, of taking what they wanted in a malicious manner, only alienated workers and slowed production. Large sums of money that were sent out into conquered areas could have been better spent building industry in Germany.

Along with acquiring industrial goods, the Germans looked to obtain agricultural products from the conquered territories to feed people at home and soldiers in the field. Though some areas, such as Poland, contributed to the overall German food supply, there were many examples of failure that revealed the mistakes of German occupation policy. They were forced to import agricultural goods into Holland to keep the people there fed. Production of pork and egg products significantly dropped under the occupation. The Germans were also forced to import hundreds of tons of foodstuffs into Croatia in order to keep the people and occupation soldiers from starving, a problem they never really solved. In return they received only a few tons of oilseeds—far from a stunning success.

The failure of direct occupation in agriculture is easy to determine by looking at statistics from France, which was somewhat autonomous, and German-controlled areas of the Soviet Union, where oppression was the rule. Russian territories provided the Germans with its largest producer of agricultural goods; conquered areas in the Soviet Union provided nine million tons of grain for German use. Almost all of these agricultural goods were consumed by the German forces occupying eastern Europe. The much smaller geographical area of France produced five million tons of grain and further produced other items of extreme importance to Germany. It has been calculated that the conquered areas of the Soviet Union only produced one-seventh of the goods produced in semi-autonomous France. Unwise occupation policies had greatly limited the resources that could have been available to the Germans. Perhaps had they attempted to cooperate with the conquered peoples of Europe instead of oppressing them, they would have increased their power and fortune.

The Germans looked to use their occupation of Europe to strengthen their war effort. Instead, they were forced to commit soldiers to the occupation zones as police and to fight guerrilla armies. They invested money and time in occupied Europe with only minimal returns. The occupation did little to help the war effort. The Germans could have helped themselves by giving conquered areas some measure of autonomy and building partnerships with collaboration governments, as they had with Vichy France. Occupied Europe became a liability and did little to bolster their war aims. Occupation was a German mistake.

–DANIEL LEE BUTCHER,
KANSAS STATE UNIVERSITY

References

Earl R. Beck, *Under the Bombs: The German Home Front 1942–1945* (Lexington: University Press of Kentucky, 1986);

Karl Brandt, *Management of Agriculture and Food in the German-Occupied and Other Areas of Fortress Europe: A Study in Military Government* (Stanford, Cal.: Stanford University Press, 1953);

Berenice A. Carroll, *Design for Total War: Arms and Economics in the Third Reich* (The Hague & Paris: Mouton, 1968);

Alexander Dallin, *German Rule in Russia, 1941–1945: A Study of Occupation Policies* (London: Macmillan, 1957; New York: St. Martin's Press, 1957);

Wilhelm Deist, *The Wehrmacht and German Rearmament* (Toronto & Buffalo: University of Toronto Press, 1981);

Ulrich Herbert, "Labor as Spoils of Conquest, 1933–1945," in *Nazism and German Society,*

GERMAN CONQUESTS

1933–1945, edited by David F. Crew (London & New York: Routledge, 1994), pp. 219–273;

Herbert, *Geschichte der Ausländerbeschäftigung in Deutschland, 1880 bis 1980* (Berlin: Dietz, 1986); translated by William Templer as *A History of Foreign Labor in Germany, 1880–1980: Seasonal Workers, Forced Laborers, Guest Workers* (Ann Arbor: University of Michigan Press, 1990);

Edward L. Homze, *Foreign Labor in Nazi Germany* (Princeton: Princeton University Press, 1967);

Burton H. Klein, *Germany's Economic Preparations for War* (Cambridge, Mass.: Harvard University Press, 1959);

Raphael Lemkin, *Axis Rule in Occupied Europe: Laws of Occupation, Analysis of Government, Proposals for Redress* (Washington, D.C.: Carnegie Endowment for International Peace, Division of International Law, 1944);

D. McIsaac, ed., *The United States Strategic Bombing Survey,* 10 volumes (New York: Garland, 1976);

Alfred C. Mierzejewski, *The Collapse of the German War Economy 1944–1945: Allied Air Power and the German National Railway* (Chapel Hill: University of North Carolina Press, 1988);

Alan S. Milward, *The German Economy at War* (London: Athlone Press, 1965);

Milward, *The New Order and the French Economy* (Oxford: Clarendon Press, 1970);

Milward, *War, Economy, and Society, 1939–1945* (Berkeley: University of California Press, 1977);

Rolf-Dieter Müller, "The Occupation," in *Hitler's War in the East, 1941–1945: A Critical Assessment,* edited by Müller and Gerd R. Ueberschär, translated by Bruce D. Little (Providence, R.I.: Berghahn Books, 1997), pp. 283–341;

Jeremy Noakes and Geoffrey Pridham, eds., *Nazism: A History in Documents and Eyewitness Accounts, 1919–1945* (New York: Schocken Books, 1983);

R. J. Overy, *Goering: The "Iron Man"* (London & Boston: Routledge & Kegan Paul, 1984);

Overy, *War and Economy in the Third Reich* (Oxford: Clarendon Press, 1994; New York: Oxford University Press, 1994);

Overy, *Why the Allies Won* (London: Cape, 1995);

Theo J. Schulte, *The German Army and Nazi Policies in Occupied Russia* (Oxford & New York: Berg, 1989);

Albert Speer, *Erinnerungen* (Berlin: Propylaen-Verlag, 1969); translated as *Inside the Third Reich,* by Richard and Clara Winston (New York: Macmillan, 1970);

Alan F. Wilt, *Nazi Germany* (Arlington Heights, Ill.: Harlan Davidson, 1994);

Gordon Wright, *The Ordeal of Total War 1939–1945* (New York: Harper & Row, 1968).

GERMAN CONQUESTS

HITLER AS WAR LEADER

Was Adolf Hitler a competent war leader?

Viewpoint: Yes, although Hitler made many mistakes, he must be credited as a good strategist, especially at the beginning of the war.

Viewpoint: No, Hitler proved less than competent in managing the war. He made major strategic blunders, and he ignored major responsibilities while he concentrated on minor issues.

Adolf Hitler's familiar image as a war leader is of someone who brought Germany to ruin directly, by meddling in operational details, and indirectly by making enemies Germany had no chance of defeating. Both criticisms have a solid factual base. Both behaviors were as well part of Hitler's perception that war had changed essentially since 1914. To Hitler, war had become an affair not of armies, not even of economies, but of peoples. *Rassenwert* (racial value) was the ultimate arbiter of victory. Material factors were important, as evidenced by Hitler's constant concern for acquiring control of land and natural resources. Brute force, however, must ultimately fail against properly applied will and intelligence.

That postulate ran like a thread through Hitler's preparations for war and his early conduct of it. Psychological factors were at least as important to him as were weapons systems. He preferred to outmaneuver his enemies on every level from policy to tactics. To Hitler, battle was not an end in itself but a means to the end of breaking the will of an opponent to continue fighting. Also significant, and a point often overlooked, was Hitler's willingness to provide the "golden bridge" of negotiated capitulation, as opposed to destroying completely a defeated enemy.

The Battle of Britain highlighted the first flaw in this grand strategic concept. It worked only when sufficient direct force could be applied to initiate disruption. The invasion of the Soviet Union demonstrated a second, far more fundamental, weakness in Hitler's way of war. It depended on capitulation as a viable alternative. From the first days of Operation Barbarossa it was clear that Russia's destiny at Nazi hands left no room for hopes and delusions.

As a war leader, Hitler became the victim of a structural contradiction. His approach depended on deluding his enemies, but his aims made it impossible to sustain the illusions on which his methods depended. That conceptual dichotomy did as much as any combination of particular mistakes to bring Nazi Germany to ruin.

Viewpoint:
Yes, although Hitler made many mistakes, he must be credited as a good strategist, especially at the beginning of the war.

One hesitates before offering a monster such as Adolf Hitler any praise whatsoever, even of the faint kind. Nevertheless, a careful look at the historical record of World War II shows that he was, for much of that conflict, a perfectly adequate war leader, often inspired and sometimes brilliant. Germany's defeat in the war, laid at Hitler's feet in a huge pile of books written by both scholarly and popular authors, was more the result of inadequate resources than any particular failing on Hitler's part. Of course, one could argue that it was a mistake for Hitler to launch his war in the first place, but that is a separate, complex issue worthy of consideration elsewhere.

The indictment against Hitler's leadership appeared soon after the war, based largely on the testimony of his generals. According to a series of interviews they gave with western prosecutors and historians, especially British military analyst Basil Henry Liddell-Hart, Hitler managed to do nothing right in six long years of war. He zigged when he should have zagged, bent when he should have stood firm, and turned rigid when he should have been flexible. Ignoring the advice of his staff officers, the finest professional soldiers in the world in their own humble estimate, Hitler was portrayed as an amateur soldier and mere corporal who took it upon himself to run a modern war in all of its minute details. The predictable result was a series of disastrous blunders that led to Germany's catastrophic defeat. It is a compelling argument, but what is often overlooked is its completely self-serving nature, as the officers who conducted the war tried desperately to shift the blame for their defeat on the universally despised, and conveniently dead, former *Führer* (leader).

The argument of the generals became the consensus among historians. It is usually presented as a long, almost ritualistic, series of discrete moments in the war in which, it is said, some inexplicably foolish decision by Hitler turned the tide in the Allied favor just as Germany stood on the brink of ultimate victory. The list usually includes, but is not limited to: Hitler's stop order to the Panzers in front of Dunkirk, which saved the British Expeditionary Force (BEF) from destruction; his shift in the Battle of Britain from a focus on Royal Air Force (RAF) installations to terror bombing of London; his decision to invade the Soviet Union in 1941; his transfer of General Heinz Guderian's tank forces from the central drive on Moscow to the great encirclement battle around Kiev; his sacking of his generals en masse in late December 1941; the "no-retreat" order to the Sixth Army at Stalingrad; the decision to attack at Kursk; his refusal to deploy on the beaches in June 1944, as General Erwin Rommel had desired; and, in general, his increasingly direct involvement in the tactical minutiae of a multi-front war, giving orders for the deployment of individual antitank batteries and Tiger tanks.

While there is enough truth here to prevent Hitler from ever being confused with Alexander the Great or Napoleon Bonaparte, there is also a great deal of distortion, omission, and even outright falsehood in it. First of all, it neglects Germany's preparations in the immediate prewar years and omits the first year of the war, with its dramatic, even improbable, German victories. If one is going to discuss Hitler's refusal to allow the Sixth Army to retreat from Stalingrad (a blunder by any yardstick), one must discuss the decisions he approved from 1933 to 1939, decisions that essentially created the first modern tank army and the new tactical and operational doctrine known as *Blitzkrieg* (lightning war). Soon after Hitler's assumption of office in January 1933, then-Colonel Guderian hosted a demonstration of recent weapons for the new chancellor. For thirty minutes Hitler sat and watched several units go through their paces: a motorcycle platoon; an antitank platoon of 37mm guns, the German standard at the time; and a platoon of experimental light tanks, ancestors of the *Panzerkampfwagen* (Pzkw) I. Originally intended as a trainer only, it remained in the German arsenal through the early years of the war. It was no King Tiger. Its armament consisted of two machine guns in a small turret on the right-hand side of the vehicle, and its armor (between 8 and 15mm) was enough to stop small-arms fire only. But Hitler, a veteran of the trenches himself, immediately recognized its possibilities, enthusiastically exclaiming, "That's what I need! That's what I want to have," as the tiny machines drove back and forth in front of him.

Events moved quickly after that. In July 1934 a *Kommando der Panzertruppen* (Tank Forces Command) was established, under Lieutenant-General Oswald Lutz, with Guderian as his Chief of Staff. The new command had orders to continue organizational and tactical experiments with armored forces. Design work resulted in another light tank, the Pzkw II, with a 20mm gun, and two medium tanks: the Pzkw III (with a 37mm gun) and the Pzkw IV (with a short-barrel 75mm gun). These tanks formed the

Adolf Hitler examining maps at a Luftwaffe base in 1939

(Suddeutscher Verlag GmbH, Munich: Sudd.)

quartet of tanks with which Germany began the war in 1939.

Organization kept pace with these new machines. In the fall of 1935, Tank Forces Command staged large armored maneuvers at Münsterlager. In October, the first three panzer divisions were formed. Three more would follow, along with four so-called light divisions, by 1939. Hitler did not create the theoretical basis for panzer divisions or Blitzkrieg. Those developments had taken place during the Weimar era. He does deserve credit, however, as the figure who laid the political, economic, and material foundation for modern tank warfare. That was no mean achievement.

Any fair assessment of Hitler as warlord must also include the thirty-day conquest of Poland (Case White); the brilliant air-land-sea operation against the Scandinavian countries,

pulled off under the nose of the *Weserübung* (Royal Navy); and, above all, the greatest victory in the history of twentieth-century warfare, the offensive in the West against France and the Low Countries (Case Yellow). This operation was a rare campaign that played out almost exactly as it had looked on the drawing board of General Erich von Manstein. It was a daring attempt to lure the main Allied force to the north, cut across its rear, and trap it in Belgium. The business end of Case Yellow would be a huge armored and mechanized column some fifty miles long, which would snake its way through the impassable Ardennes Forest, cross the Meuse river, and then race for the sea, closing the ring on the hapless Allies to the north. It engendered a great deal of controversy among German staff officers, and it certainly had its share of risks. What if the panzers got stuck in the Ardennes?

What if they got held up crossing the Meuse? What if uncommitted Allied forces to the north or south launched a counter thrust against the panzer columns as they were strung out during their lunge to the Channel? Hitler, however, immediately sized up this plan as the only one presented to him that was likely to offer total victory. The generals themselves wanted to stage a reprise of the Schlieffen Plan, a production that had, of course, opened to mediocre reviews in 1914. Their resistance was overcome only by a direct order of the Führer in favor of the Manstein Plan. Case Yellow was Hitler's finest hour as supreme commander, a brilliantly conceived and perfectly executed plan that he had to force on an unwilling General Staff.

A second weakness of the anti-Hitler argument is that it attempts, unsuccessfully, to reduce the complexities of this most complex war to a particular "magic moment" (each historian choosing his own) in which the tide allegedly turned against Germany as a result of some "Führer-blunder." The fact that historians have identified so many of these moments is an argument against this sort of reductionist approach. After all, how many turning points can one war stand? The real problem with this argument is that it falls apart in the details. Did the "halt-order" to the panzers at Dunkirk really lose the war? Perhaps, but it was a decision with which many members of the General Staff—nervous at the rapidity of their advance across northern France—concurred. At any rate, the BEF that escaped was a skeleton force that had to abandon virtually all of its supplies and heavy weapons. Churchill himself recognized this condition when he reminded Parliament that "wars are not won by evacuations," although the British would wind up getting a fair amount of practice at this type of operation.

The same might be said of Hitler's handling of the Battle of Britain. His switch from attacks on air installations to terror bombing of cities, coming at a time when the Royal Air Force (RAF) was on its last legs, is often seen as his greatest blunder. When the German air offensive against Britain began on 13 August 1940, with heavy raids on British airfields and installations, Chief of the *Luftwaffe* (German Air Force) Hermann Goering boasted that the RAF would be brought to its knees within two weeks. The Luftwaffe, however, had been given a mission for which it was not designed. It was a tactical-support force, trained to cooperate with ground troops. It was not a strategic weapon, able to defeat Great Britain on its own. The JU-87 dive bomber (the Stuka), for example, had been a success in Poland and France. Yet, its tiny bomb load and short range rendered it unsuitable for such a large mission. It couldn't sink Great Brit-

ain, after all. German fighters such as the ME-109 were operating at the limits of their range; most had fifteen to thirty minutes of flying time, tops, over Britain. Finally, the RAF had a new invention, radar, which helped it direct its squadrons to intercept Luftwaffe sorties. By 18 August the Luftwaffe had lost four hundred planes to just 180 for the RAF—and unlike the British, every German plane shot down meant a total loss of its highly trained crew. Still, the Luftwaffe kept attacking. These were anxious days for the RAF. The Luftwaffe could call on some three thousand fighters/bombers, versus only six hundred to seven hundred RAF fighters. By the end of August, Fighter Command's pilots were exhausted, replacements were not keeping up with casualties, and many airfields (especially in Kent) were inoperable. From 24 August to 6 September, the Luftwaffe lost another 386 planes, but the RAF lost 280. At this point Hitler ordered his change in strategy, supposedly the result of a fit of pique after RAF bombers appeared over Berlin—with the historic result of giving the RAF a reprieve in its darkest hour.

Hitler's choice was wrong; that much is clear in hindsight. But how much did he really know about the British situation? As any air force officer will tell, dropping the bombs is the easy part. Assessing the damage is the trick, even with absolute control of the air. By early September, the contending air forces were staggering like two punch-drunk fighters. Both German and British losses had been catastrophic. Goering's boast certainly had not come to pass. There had been no midnight telegram from Churchill to Hitler detailing British air losses. There were many in the Luftwaffe who felt that British civilian morale would be an easier target. So began "the Blitz," fifty-seven straight nights of bombers appearing over London and other cities. They had no more luck cracking British civilian morale than those much larger flights of heavier Allied bombers had over Germany from 1942–1945. Hitler's decision to go for the cities—wrongheaded and foolish, many would argue—would be repeated a hundredfold by the Allies.

Hitler's alleged blunder on the road to Moscow in August 1941 is similarly considered a sign of his weak military leadership. With Soviet forces mauled and the road to Moscow open, so runs the indictment, Hitler suddenly grew concerned about lack of progress on the flanks. He detached most of the armor from Army Group Center and temporarily reassigned it to the northern and southern sectors. An entire tank army (*Panzergruppe*) under Guderian swooped down in a deep arc behind Kiev, helping Army Group South make the biggest single encirclement of the war, perhaps 665,000 men, nearly all of the Fifth, Twenty-Sixth, and Thirty-Seventh Soviet armies. After the war, the German generals—and many others—would point to Hitler's orders as the turning point in the campaign, throwing away certain victory on the road to Moscow for a sideshow in the Ukraine. Certainly, an argument can be made for Moscow. Can any battle, however, that nets 700,000 prisoners of war ever be labeled a blunder? By the time the Kiev pocket surrendered in September the *Wehrmacht* (German Army) had destroyed about one-third of the Red Army's total strength at the start of the war. Military analysts who never tire of repeating that the enemy's army should be the principal target of any campaign—after which terrain objectives can be taken at the victor's leisure—should be a little gentler in their criticism of this incredible annihilation battle. While on the subject of Barbarossa, it is generally recognized that Hitler's order to "stand fast" in the face of the great Soviet Winter Counteroffensive in front of Moscow—a decision taken, once again, in the face of bitter resistance from his generals—is all that saved the Wehrmacht from sharing the fate of Napolean's Grande Armée in the winter of 1941–1942.

The point of this essay is not to argue away every bad decision taken by the Führer. He certainly made his share of mistakes. So did his Allied counterparts. Was his decision not to retreat at Stalingrad, for example, really more mistaken than the British rush of reinforcements to Norway and Greece, or the Allied decision to slog up the Italian boot from 1943 to 1945, or the Soviet waste of the Red Army's armored strength on foolish and uncoordinated counterattacks in the first month of Barbarossa?

One part of the anti-Hitler argument cannot be denied. As the war dragged on, Hitler became obsessed with details better left to his subordinates. A supreme commander has no business playing squad leader. This change does not apply only to Hitler, however, it was just as characteristic of Churchill and Joseph Stalin, two-thirds of the Allied coalition (three-fourths, if you add Chiang Kai-shek). President Franklin D. Roosevelt, for the most part, had the good sense to assemble a team of advisers, then let them run into their share of walls as they learned how to conduct a modern war. He was not typical, and in fact, only a power sheltered behind the twin moats of the Atlantic and Pacific oceans could afford such a strategy.

In the end, what led to the Allied victory was not any one bad decision by Hitler, but the overwhelming material strength of the Grand Alliance, which had the world's largest land power (the Soviet Union), greatest naval power and overseas empire (Great Britain), and strongest financial, economic, and industrial giant

(the United States). In late 1942, as the Red Army began its counteroffensive at Stalingrad, the United States began to flex its industrial muscles, and the huge forces needed to invade Europe were being assembled in Britain, Hitler personally intervened to send six Tiger tanks to the newly established "Tunisian bridgehead," as if that would somehow turn the tide in favor of the Axis. This was a war that, short of the development of a wonder weapon such as the atomic bomb, the Wehrmacht had no hope of winning.

–ROBERT CITINO, EASTERN MICHIGAN UNIVERSITY

Viewpoint:
No, Hitler proved less than competent in managing the war. He made major strategic blunders, and he ignored major responsibilities while he concentrated on minor issues.

Adolf Hitler was a terrible war leader. While Germany did conquer most of Europe under Hitler's leadership, the end results of his efforts speak more strongly than his fleeting successes. Germany entered a war that it stood almost no chance of winning and then fought on until the country lay in ruins, and Hitler was the one person who was most responsible.

In order to get beyond that simple answer, however, one needs to examine the proper role of a wartime leader. That is, what makes a leader "competent" in wartime? What are his or her responsibilities? One central fact is that no leader of a modern state can truly be responsible for everything. Hitler declared himself Führer of Germany in 1934. Theoretically, according the dictatorial principle by which he ran the state, all authority and decisions flowed downward from him. Even under such a system, however, governmental and military actions naturally depended upon a host of people under the Führer as well as upon his own guidance. Thus, one needs to ask several questions. Did Hitler make decisions within the proper spheres and otherwise delegate authority effectively? How good was he at choosing subordinates? Did his leadership philosophy contribute to sound decision making? Did he create a strong organizational structure to carry out his wishes? Finally, did he make good decisions himself?

Hitler brought a distinct leadership philosophy with him into office: the so-called *Führerprinzip* (Leader Principle). According to this philosophy, all responsibility lay with the superior. Whoever was in charge gave the orders; his subordinates were to carry them out to the letter, without question or delay. This philosophy was at odds with a style of command that the German army had been developing for over a century. Called "command by directive," it entailed pushing responsibility as far down the chain of command as possible. A superior would give his subordinates a mission in the broadest terms possible and let them execute it as they saw fit. The Germans recognized that a senior commander could not understand the situation his subordinates faced as well as they could. Hitler believed otherwise, and his personal style of command highlighted the differences between the two philosophies.

The Führer was extremely jealous of his authority. He insisted on absolute control, especially within the spheres that interested him. The actual conduct of military campaigns was one of those spheres. Hitler wanted to be the *Feldherr,* the commander on the spot who sees all and directs his armies personally. This desire was evident, for example, in the titles that he acquired over the course of his rule. By the end of 1941 he was simultaneously head of state, commander in chief of the armed forces, and commander-in-chief of the army. For a time in 1942 he even took direct command of an army group that was fighting roughly eight hundred miles from his headquarters. If anything, though, the course of his daily briefings reveals how much he believed he could control the war. Hitler demanded detailed briefings, to include unit strengths, equipment status, and information on any special projects in which he was interested. His remarks in these conferences might touch on everything from diplomacy with allies to the number of trucks in a particular unit, but in particular he exerted—or tried to exert—more and more control over the actions of units at the front. He pored over small-scale maps and issued detailed commands. During the Battle of Stalingrad in late 1942 he even had a street map of the city brought in so that he could follow the struggle block by block. By the end of the war he had issued a standing order that no unit could move without his permission.

Such a system could not work effectively. First of all, even with the most advanced communications equipment of the time and the most efficient staffs, there was no way for Hitler to get a complete picture of what was happening at the front. Reports took hours to reach his headquarters, and they often contained inaccuracies, both accidental and deliberate. Second, and even more important, Hitler was simply trying to do more than any one person could possibly do. While he meddled in the minute details of his armies' operations, he could not pay attention to other issues that lay more properly within his sphere. Thus, the overall running of the economy, for example, was something

that he left largely to others. This kind of delegation by default contributed to a lack of organized effort in many areas of government that were crucial to the war.

Hitler's choice of subordinates and command organization reflected and reinforced his personal style of leadership. In the former instance, loyalty counted for everything; professional ability was strictly secondary. Hitler deeply distrusted the career army officers who made up the General Staff, but to the extent that he accepted advice from any of them, it was from those who had proven their devotion to him. Moreover, on those occasions when he wanted additional information from the front, he would often send officers from the air force or the SS (*Schutzstaffel*), whose hostility to the army guaranteed a negative report. That kind of internecine squabbling also found expression in the command organization. As the war went on, fundamental divisions within the high command grew. Rival agencies fought with one another over resources and plans, and no one but Hitler had the authority to resolve the disputes. While the Führer did not create that system by himself, he allowed it to flourish. As a result there was little or no common effort, and the staffs wasted precious time and energy.

These flaws were serious in and of themselves, but the most significant problems came from the decisions that Hitler made. Personally he was unsuited for his position in many ways. He was uninterested in consistent work and left what he saw as bureaucratic details to his staff. On the matters he insisted on controlling, he would often vacillate and delay a crucial decision for days. Then, once he had set his mind on a course of action, he would cling to it stubbornly, even in the face of clear evidence in favor of another alternative. He would often become enraged with anyone who challenged his opinions. All of these personal traits overlay the fact that, although he was a decorated combat veteran, he had never held a command in his life. He was unfamiliar with the requirements of modern military campaigns, although he did exhibit a kind of amateur genius from time to time. As a basis for his decisions, he relied on his skewed view of the world and on the "instincts" that he believed made him a superior military leader.

Hitler played his most important part in the history of World War II by defining Germany's national goals and a grand strategy to achieve them. Long before he came into power in 1933, he advertised his belief that Germany could only survive as a nation if it acquired more *Lebensraum* (living space) in order to feed its growing population. That was his most important national goal. He knew that Germany could only acquire that space through military conquest, since its neighbors could certainly not be expected to hand land over without a

HITLER EXPLAINS HIS WAR STRATEGY

In a letter written on 21 June 1941 to Italian leader Benito Mussolini, Adolf Hitler explained his decision to attack the Soviet Union. This choice is often portrayed by historians as a giant blunder.

The situation: England has lost this war. With the right of the drowning person, she grasps at every straw which, in her imagination, might serve as a sheet anchor. Nevertheless, some of her hopes are naturally not without a certain logic. England has thus far always conducted her wars with help from the Continent. The destruction of France—in fact, the elimination of all west-European positions—directing the glances of the British warmongers continually to the place from which they tried to start the war: to Soviet Russia.

Both countries, Soviet Russia and England, are equally interested in a Europe fallen into ruin, rendered prostrate by a long war. Behind these two countries stands the North American Union goading them on and watchfully waiting. Since the liquidation of Poland, there is evident in Soviet Russia a consistent trend, which, even if cleverly and cautiously, is nevertheless reverting firmly to the old Bolshevist tendency to expansion of the Soviet State. The prolongation of the war necessary for this purpose is to be achieved by tying up German forces in the East, so that—particularly in the air—the German Command can no longer vouch for a large-scale attack in the West. . . . The concentration of Russian forces—I had General Jodl submit the most recent map to your Attaché here, General Maras—is tremendous. Really, all available Russian forces are at our border. Moreover, since the approach of warm weather, work has been proceeding on numerous defenses. If circumstances should give me cause to employ the German air force against England, there is danger that Russia will then begin its strategy of extortion in the South and North, to which I would have to yield in silence, simply from a feeling of air inferiority. It would, above all, not then be possible for me without adequate support from an air force, to attack the Russian fortifications with the divisions stationed in the East. If I do not wish to expose myself to this danger, then perhaps the whole year of 1941 will go by without any change in the general situation. On the contrary.

England will be all the less ready for peace, for it will be able to pin its hopes on the Russian partner. Indeed, this hope must naturally even grow with the progress in preparedness of the Russian armed forces. And behind this is the mass delivery of war material from America which they hope to get in 1942.

Aside from this, Duce, it is not even certain whether they shall have this time, for with so gigantic a concentration of forces on both sides—for I also was compelled to place more and more armored units on the eastern border, also to call Finland's and Rumania's attention to the danger—there is the possibility that the shooting will start spontaneously at any moment. A withdrawal on my part would, however, entail a serious loss of prestige for us. This would be particularly unpleasant in its possible effect on Japan. I have, therefore, after constantly racking my brains, finally reached the decision to cut the noose before it can be drawn tight. . . .

I have decided under these circumstances as I already mentioned, to put an end to the hypocritical performance in the Kremlin. I assume, that is to say, I am convinced, that Finland, and likewise Rumania, will forthwith take part in this conflict, which will ultimately free Europe, for the future also, of a great danger. . . .

As far as the war in the East is concerned, Duce, it will surely be difficult, but I do not entertain a second's doubt as to its great success. I hope, above all, that it will then be possible for us to secure a common food-supply base in the Ukraine for some time to come, which will furnish us such additional supplies as we may need in the future. I may state at this point, however, that, as far as we can tell now, this year's German harvest promises to be a very good one. It is conceivable that Russia will try to destroy the Rumanian oil region. We have built up a defense that will—or so I think—prevent the worst. Moreover, it is the duty of our armies to eliminate this threat as rapidly as possible.

United States, Department of State, Publication No. 3023, Nazi-Soviet Relations 1939–1941: Documents from the Archives of the German Foreign Office *(Government Printing Office, Washington, 1948), pp. 349–353.*

fight. Thus the central element in Germany's national strategy would be to launch a premeditated war to the east against Russia. That course held the added attraction of destroying what Hitler saw as the Jewish-Bolshevik Soviet state, his ideological nemesis. In order to keep France and Great Britain from interfering, and because of his long-standing hostility toward those two countries, Hitler believed he would have to go to war against them first. He made all of his theories quite clear in *Mein Kampf* (1925–1927), the first volume of which he published nearly eight years before he came to power, as well as in literally hundreds of speeches and policy statements.

These were the considerations that led Hitler to accept war with France and Great Britain in September 1939, even though by doing so he committed Germany to a war with two world empires. At that point the situation did not look bad, since the Führer had arranged for a nonaggression pact with the Soviet Union and was drawing raw materials from there. Then in 1940, with France defeated and Great Britain seemingly weak, Hitler decided to turn on the Soviet Union (U.S.S.R.) and fulfill his long-held goal. That war began in June 1941. Less than six months later, he declared war on the United States, following the Japanese attack on Pearl Harbor. To Hitler, conflict with the United States was inevitable, and he believed that the Japanese would provide the naval strength he needed to win. In fact, if Germany had any hope at all of winning the war up to that point, this last decision destroyed it. Germany and the other Axis powers could not hope to match the resources of the U.S.S.R., the British Empire, and the United States together.

Military strategy is the military component of a country's grand strategy. In other words, it is the way in which a country uses its armed forces—as opposed to its economic strength or diplomacy, for example—to achieve its national goals. So, for example, the United States's military strategy in Europe was to combine aerial bombardment with an eventual land invasion of Germany. The Germans, on the other hand, had no coherent strategy at the beginning of the war; there was no master plan. Hitler made strategic decisions as he went along, and at times he simply did not know what to do next. That was the case in the summer of 1940, after France fell. Virtually everyone in the German high command expected that the British would simply give up, but they did not. The Germans had made no plans for such an eventuality, and they did not have the forces for an invasion across the English Channel. Hitler spent weeks casting about for a way to proceed. When the air force failed to subdue Britain with the world's first "strategic" bombing campaign, Hitler gave up and decided to attack the Soviet Union.

In the east the choices seemed simpler. There was no pesky water obstacle to get in the way. A land campaign would suffice, and Hitler—as well as his generals—believed they could eliminate the Soviet Union in a matter of weeks, well before the first snows of winter. Then they figured that Great Britain would finally surrender; if not, they would have all the vast resources of the east to support them in their fight. When the United States came into the picture, Hitler's plan was even more vague. He had no idea how to get at the Americans, aside from some hazy plans about using long-range bombers and a huge navy, both of which lay uncounted years in the future.

After the campaign in Russia failed to win victory in the first year, Hitler's strategic plans gradually became less realistic. He tried to knock the Soviet Union out in 1942, before the United States could fully arm itself, but that idea foundered in the snows around Stalingrad. In 1943 he tried to win time in the east and parry the Allied invasion of Italy, and failed on both counts. In 1944 he hoped to defeat the invasion of France and win time and forces to stop the Soviets. When that failed, he could only hope to make the Allies' efforts so costly that their coalition would split up. That goal proved as unattainable as all his earlier ones.

Part of the problem for Hitler was that he truly did not understand military strategy as it applied to global war. Instead he confused strategy with the concept of "operations," which has to do with the conduct of military campaigns in order to achieve strategic goals. For instance, Hitler's strategic goal in May 1940 was to defeat France. To that end, he and his generals had planned operations that included an armored thrust through the Ardennes forest, supported by air power, to cut off the French and British forces in Belgium and the northeast corner of France. With a country the size of France, which has a land border with Germany, such an approach worked. It failed against Britain, which the Germans could not invade by land, and with the Soviet Union, which proved too large to conquer and too politically stable to collapse. Hitler thought that if he won enough battles he would win the war, but he never could win enough battles to defeat such powerful enemies, and he had no other options.

One should note at this point that although Hitler was not the genius he thought himself to be, he was not an idiot or lunatic either. That fact is not obvious from many postwar accounts of his actions and decisions. After the war, many senior German officers wrote memoirs that made Hitler solely responsible for the war and for Germany's defeat, while they themselves appear as having opposed his every decision. Their accounts were convincing, and many historians initially accepted them with little argument. Only with time did the truth become clear: the German generals shared responsibility for their country's fate. They disagreed with many of Hitler's best decisions and supported most of his worst ones—such as the one to invade the Soviet Union. They also stood behind the Führer, almost without exception, to the bitter end. One cannot ignore that reality and hope to understand Hitler's role fully.

Still, Hitler remains the central figure. He provided the ideology and political direction that led Germany to war. He decided on the objectives and the means to achieve them. Together with his generals, he directed his armies in a series of aggressive wars, some of the most brutal that humankind has ever experienced. When the war turned against him, he drove Germany on to the brink of extinction. Then, before his suicide, he wrote his countrymen off as being unworthy of survival. There can be no question of his not being a "competent" war leader.

–GEOFFREY P. MEGARGEE, U.S. COMMISSION ON NATIONAL SECURTIY

References

Alan Bullock, *Hitler and Stalin: Parallel Lives* (London: HarperCollins, 1991);

Robert M. Citino, *The Path to Blitzkrieg: Doctrine and Training in the German Army, 1920–1939* (Boulder, Colo.: Lynne Rienner Publishers, 1999);

Alan Clark, *Barbarossa: The Russian-German Conflict, 1941–45* (New York: Morrow; London: Hutchinson, 1965);

Joachim C. Fest, *Hitler,* translated by Richard and Clara Winston (New York: Harcourt Brace Jovanovich, 1974);

Jürgen Förster, "The Dynamics of *Volksgemeinschaft:* The Effectiveness of the German Military Establishment in the Second World War," in *Military Effectiveness,* edited by Allan R. Millett and Williamson Murray, (Boston: Unwin Hyman, 1988), pp. 180–220;

Norman J. W. Goda, *Tomorrow the World: Hitler, Northwest Africa, and the Path toward America* (College Station: Texas A&M University Press, 1998);

Heinz Guderian, *Erinnerungen eines Soldaten* (Heidelberg: K. Vowinckel, 1950), translated by Constantine Fitzgibbon as *Panzer Leader* (New York: Dutton, 1952);

Eberhard Jäckel, *Hitler's Weltanschauung: Entwurf einer Herrschaft* (Tubingen: R. Wunderlich, 1969), translated by Herbert Arnold as *Hitler's Weltanschauung: A Blueprint for Power* (Middletown, Conn.: Wesleyan University Press, 1972);

Wilhelm Keitel, *The Memoirs of Field-Marshal Keitel,* edited by Walter Gorlitz, translated by David Irving (London: Kimber, 1965);

Ian Kershaw, *Hitler* (London; New York: Longman, 1991);

Ronald Lewin, *Hitler's Mistakes* (London: Leo Cooper, in association with Secker & Warburg, 1984);

Basil Henry Liddell-Hart, *The Other Side of the Hill: Germany's Generals, Their Rise and Fall, with Their Own Account of Military Events, 1939–1945* (London: Cassell, 1948); republished as *The German Generals Talk* (New York: Morrow, 1948);

Erich von Manstein, *Verlorene Siege* (Frankfurt am Main: Athenäum, 1955); edited and translated by Anthony G. Powell as *Lost Victories* (Chicago: H. Regnery, 1958);

Geoffrey P. Megargee, *Inside Hitler's High Command* (Lawrence: University Press of Kansas, forthcoming);

Research Institute of Military History, ed., *Germany and the Second World War,* 4 volumes (Oxford: Clarendon Press & New York: Oxford University Press, 1990–1998);

Rolf-Dieter Müller and Gerd R. Ueberschär, *Hitler's War in the East, 1941–1945: A Critical Assessment,* translated by Bruce D. Little (Providence, R.I.: Berghahn Books, 1997);

Florian K. Rothbrust, *Guderian's XIXth Panzer Corps and the Battle of France: Breakthrough in the Ardennes, May 1940* (New York: Praeger, 1990);

Walter Warlimont, *Im Hauptquartier der deutschen Wehrmacht, 1939–45* (Frankfurt am Main: Bernard & Graefe, 1962), translated by R. H. Barry as *Inside Hitler's Headquarters 1939–45* (New York: Praeger/London: Weidenfeld & Nicolson, 1964);

Gerhard L. Weinberg, *Germany, Hitler, and World War II: Essays in Modern German and World History* (Chicago: University of Chicago Press, 1980);

Weinberg, *A World at Arms: A Global History of World War II* (Cambridge & New York: Cambridge University Press, 1994);

Alan F. Wilt, *War from the Top: German and British Military Decision-making during World War II* (London: Tauris, 1990);

Marshalls Zhukov, Konev, Malinovsky, Rokossovsky, Rotmistrov, Chuikov, and other commanders, *Battles Hitler Lost: And the Soviet Marshalls Who Won Them* (New York: Richardson & Steirman, 1986).

HITLER'S AGGRESSION

Could Adolf Hitler have been deterred from launching WWII?

Viewpoint: Yes, Great Britain, France, the Soviet Union, and the United States could have successfully contained Adolf Hitler by military and political means.

Viewpoint: No, Adolf Hitler could not have been stopped from initiating World War II because neither France nor Great Britain had the commitment or capability to thwart him.

A strong consensus among scholars is that World War II was Adolf Hitler's war—a conflict he desired for ideological, political, economic, and psychological reasons, all unsusceptible to external persuasion. His demonic, nihilistic urges impelled him toward war even when alternatives seemed available. National Socialism was based on the principle of struggle against internal and external enemies. To gain power for those struggles, expansion was necessary.

Yet, Hitler was more than a visionary with the power of a modern state at his back. His foreign policy after 1933 was based on taking risks and predicated on his sense of his own greatness. He was cautious, however, about introducing rearmament in violation of the Versailles treaty (1919). He withdrew from the League of Nations only after Japan had done so. His reoccupation of the Rhineland was a bluff, to be abandoned at any sign of armed resistance. Hitler's confidence became arrogance, then hubris, only as the Western powers floundered in their own indecision, not merely in regard to Germany, but in dealing with Italy and Japan as well.

Manchuria, Ethiopia, and Spain set the stage for the German absorption of Austria, and for the Hossbach Memorandum detailing the next steps to the mastery of Europe. By the Munich Crisis of 1938, Hitler wanted war so badly that he flew into a rage when France and Britain capitulated to his demands. If Hitler wanted war, however, it was not from a compulsion for *Goetterdaemmerung* (Twilight of the Gods), or a Day of Doom, but because he believed the "miserable little worms" he opposed had no chance of defeating him. In that sense his behavior, as opposed to his principles, followed a rational-actor model of pushing until encountering firm resistance, then pushing a little longer to test the firmness.

Deterrence, in the general sense of establishing boundaries in "if-then" contexts, had corresponding potential for modifying Hitler's behavior, at least in the short run. For deterrence to succeed, however, it requires a high level of coherence and coordination, backed by an objectively credible threat of force. Distracted and disarmed, Hitler's opponents were unable to meet either criterion.

Viewpoint:
Yes, Great Britain, France, the Soviet Union, and the United States could have successfully contained Adolf Hitler by military and political means.

A critical element in the examination of determining guilt for World War II is to understand the global nature of this conflict. Many events and circumstances caused this war. Stereotypes of a hyperaggressive Germany must be set aside in order to comprehend the complexity of this war's consummation. For instance, German aggression may not have been totally uncompromising. In fact, German diplomatic and political leaders remained open to European initiatives, many of which could have stopped, or at the least significantly impeded, Hitler's drive to take over Europe and perhaps the entire world. While this argument admittedly enters the realm of the hypothetical, certain actions and inactions on the part of the anti-Fascist nations appear far more critical to the escalation from peace to war than generally appreciated.

The primary events and activities can be divided into two periods during the interwar years, split by the critical event of the Rhineland reoccupation in 1936. During the first period, from the Versailles treaty (1919) until 1936, either the debate over the maintenance of the global status quo or the competing diplomatic advantages and objectives of various nations took top priority. Following the Rhineland crisis, events took a more serious turn and international diplomacy focused increasingly on preventing or at least postponing war. In both of these periods, nations played the game of great-power politics, committed several incredible blunders, and made important decisions that ultimately led to war. The competing national interests and policy differences resulted in an instability that facilitated Hitler's rise to power and a weakness that allowed him to be aggressive without punishment.

While much conventional wisdom adjudicates the final responsibility of the war solely to Hitler and Nazi Germany, no genuinely clear consensus on whom to place the blame has ever emerged. Even former British prime minister Winston Churchill, in a speech at Fulton, Missouri, in 1946, discussed Allied responsibility for the war, saying that, "There never was a war in all history easier to prevent by timely action than the one which has just desolated such great areas of the globe. It could have been prevented without the firing of a single shot." In the two decades immediately following the war, many historians from all of the former Allied powers suggested a variety of answers addressing the issue of prewar deterrence. The culmination of these early contentions appeared with the publication of A. J. P. Taylor's *The Origins of the Second World War* (1961), a work that lays ultimate responsibility for the war on the Western Allies for mishandling the many real opportunities to rein in Hitler. This was the first significant postwar work that was more critical of the Allies than of the Axis. It argued that Hitler's Germany was not an aberration, but rather represented a normal diplomatic regime. In more recent years, the focus of scholarship has focused on the various Allied national goals that ended up conflicting with the interests of other powers.

When examining great-power politics, the most prominent theme is the importance that the victors of World War I placed on the restructuring of the postwar world. Great Britain and France played the two most important roles. These two nations, however, did not share common political, economic, or military goals in the interwar years, and, indeed, found themselves struggling with each other and with the rest of the world to define the shape of new borders and countries. In their desire to prevent another conflagration similar to that of 1914–1918, these two countries, in R. J. Overy's words in *The Origins of the Second World War* (1987), "became committed . . . to the status quo [in an era when] both powers were faced by a galaxy of states and political forces opposed, for one reason or another, to the status quo." Balance-of-power concerns proved dominant for each of these two powers since both countries needed to maintain and advance their overseas empires. In doing so, they often found themselves directly opposed to the other's interests.

During the 1920s and early 1930s, Britain and France frequently engaged in political activities that gave the impression that they were working at cross-purposes. While treaties at the end of World War I for the most part limited the defeated powers to the European mainland, Britain and France maintained global empires, leading to conflict between the two, especially in places such as the Middle East. Also, during the debates on reparations and the Locarno Conference of 1925, France followed its own agenda in solving the reparations and repayment questions. The French preoccupation with the punishment of Germany conflicted directly with Britain's desire to reintegrate the defeated power back into the community of nations in order to strengthen global economic bonds.

Perhaps no other events capture the essence of the inability of the two countries to put forward a united front than the failures of the League of Nations. First in Asia in the early

1930s, regarding Japanese aggression in Man-churia, and then in 1935, in response to Italian aggression into Ethiopia, the League of Nations, under British and French leadership, demon-strated to the world that the organization was incapable of exerting international pressure in times of crisis. In both cases, naked aggression and the outright snubbing of the international community went completely unpunished and demonstrated to Germany the emptiness of Brit-ish and French power.

The actions of the other two major victors of World War I, the United States and the Soviet Union, added to the problems faced by Britain and France. While some authors, most notably Charles Callan Tansill in his 1952 book *Back Door to War: The Roosevelt Foreign Policy, 1933–1941,* may grasp at straws by placing the bulk of responsibility for the war on the shoulders of Franklin D. Roosevelt for backing extreme isola-tionism, the argument does possess substantial credibility. The United States did not enter into the League of Nations, raising serious doubts about the legitimacy of that body. Most Ameri-cans shared the desire of the other victors to avoid a repetition of World War I and instead of attempting to reshape the twentieth-century world, the United States withdrew from it. Attempts to intervene in global affairs became both problematic and unpopular, as indicated by the unwillingness of Americans to confront Japan within the context of the charged diplo-matic atmosphere of the 1930s. Also, the partic-ular distaste that many Americans felt toward the British and French after their unabashed rush to reclaim the former German colonies after Ver-sailles increased the political distance (both per-ceived and real) between the European Allies and the United States.

Similarly, the Soviet Union exhibited isola-tionist tendencies, as Soviet premier Joseph Sta-lin labored to solidify his control over the country. A successful struggle for consolidation required the avoidance of another war such as the debacle of the previous decade. Deepening this divide was the ideological communist fear and distrust of the capitalist world. Historian Robert C. Tucker has argued that Stalin, as the controller of Soviet foreign policy, was willing to ignite a European war through collaboration with Hitler if this would allow a victory for Soviet communism over the Western nations.

The reoccupation of the Rhineland in 1936 proved to be a watershed event in the interwar years. After this time, anti-Fascist diplomatic methods shifted from policies of talk and media-tion to those of appeasement. Primarily in Brit-ain, but also in the United States and France, leaders advocated the maintenance of a balance of power around the world. By refusing to chal-

lenge Hitler's drive into the Rhineland, Britain and France gave Hitler the upper hand both stra-tegically and diplomatically. While the short-term reaction to appeasement policy remained generally favorable in the Allied coun-tries, enthusiasm increasingly became tempered as it became apparent that Hitler's designs would not stop with the Rhineland. From this point, Hitler began to assume greater and greater confidence in his ability to achieve his own desires, because the lack of Allied response to previous German and other international aggres-sion encouraged him.

The mood of the anti-Fascist states grew more somber with each new act of German bel-ligerence. Faulty Western intelligence exacer-bated this mood many times through the ensuing years, both placing the strength and capabilities of the Germans far higher than it actually was, and concurrently selling Western

Wehrmacht troops marching past the cathedral of Cologne in the demilitarized zone of the Rhineland, 7 March 1936

(Ullstein)

nations short on their own capabilities. All of this led British diplomatic efforts to continue the drive to appease Hitler on what policymakers concluded to be pragmatic grounds. Regardless of their actual levels of military preparedness in 1939, all major world powers appeared to be equally inclined to maintain a rapid pace of rearmament to further their own goals. Conversely, however, none of them, including Germany, wanted to risk major conflict either on the European continent or on a global scale at this time.

The historiography of this period points to new short-term causes for the war beyond the actions of Hitler's Germany during this period. According to Soviet historiography, the United States had begun to spur British and French efforts to turn Nazi attention to the East, particularly in the economic realm, arguing that the United States had no reason to oppose anything that might further isolate communism from the rest of the world. Several historians point to the growing gap in the rearmament race. Taylor points out that Hitler felt threatened by the growing industrialization of Soviet Russia—a 400 percent increase in production as opposed to 27 percent in Germany during the 1930s. The Germans were also concerned that the Allies might demand more suppression of Germany. In response to this perceived threat, Hitler launched German rearmament in 1933. Similarly, German armament, according to Taylor, remained far inferior to that of the Allies. Only a failure of British leadership to assist Poland in 1939 allowed for such an easy and swift victory of German forces.

In the above situations, before the mid 1930s all of the victors of World War I exhibited some form of diplomatic weakness that Germany and its allies could easily perceive as tacit acceptance of, and agreement with, their aggressive actions and motives. By attempting to maintain an unmanageable status quo, Britain and France removed themselves from any possible position of strength in negotiating with Hitler and his allies. By refusing to engage in global power-politics and their refusal to counter any aggressive actions, both the United States and the Soviet Union also allowed Nazi aggrandizement. Underlying this situation was an increasingly apparent ideological distrust and fear of one another that kept these nations from acting in unison. When unity of action and strength was necessary, these nations failed to work out a solution to their problems. The inaction of the League of Nations in cases of naked aggression demonstrated clearly this lack of unity. With the United States refusing to participate and the Soviet Union taking part only on the presumption that participation could counteract any foreign activity against communist interests, the

League of Nations continued to be ineffective. Events in Manchuria and Ethiopia demonstrated this. Perhaps more than any event before the occupation of the Rhineland in 1936, decisive reaction to these two world crises could have proved a deterrent to Hitler's aggression.

The second major change the Allies needed to make involved a shift away from the "old-fashioned balance-of-power politics" that Taylor blames for the causes of the war. Taylor writes that "Great Britain and France dithered between resistance and appeasement, and so helped to make war more likely." By insisting on seeing themselves as the primary leaders of a world in which all powers shared the same general ideals, the major powers viewed problems and confrontations that Hitler deemed critical to a national revival of the German nation as nothing more than words and propaganda. The net result before 1936 was much talk and little action on the part of Britain and France, followed by the parallel policy of appeasement, or "balancing-of-risks" by Neville Chamberlain. These policies and posturing left little doubt in the German mind that the Western world was willing to bend before Hitler's desires.

–MICHAEL A. BODEN, U.S. MILITARY ACADEMY, WEST POINT

Viewpoint:
No, Adolf Hitler could not have been stopped from initiating World War II because neither France nor Great Britain had the commitment or capability to thwart him.

Could Adolf Hitler have been stopped if the Allies had come together during the 1930s to deter him? Given the circumstances of the interwar period—particularly the political and military situation in Great Britain and France—such an argument fails. Nothing could have been done to deter Hitler.

Before proceeding farther, one must ask a crucial question: what does deterrence mean? Deterrence is a complicated theory that has been extensively analyzed, and although definitions differ, there are three central propositions behind it. First, wars are caused by states that seek to upset the status quo by expanding either their political or economic influence. Second, in order to maintain the status quo, the deterrent state must have the capability to do so; must be committed to counter any attack against the status quo; and must effectively communicate its intent to maintain the status quo. And third, the belligerent power is perceptive of the defender's capabilities, commitment, and communicated intentions. Deterrence worked during the Cold War because all three propositions were present. Both the United States and the Soviet Union had the capability and commitment to deter each other, and they clearly communicated their intent to do so. The same cannot be said, however, for the state of foreign relations during the years before World War II, particularly for Britain and France. Neither nation had the capability or the commitment to deter the German military threat.

In relation to Germany, neither Britain nor France had the military capability to deter Hitler. While the British government put more of its military strength into defending the empire, the French were in no position to fight an offensive war against Hitler. Complicating the matter was the fact that both nations' intelligence services overestimated the German threat, and in doing so, further limited both governments' acceptance of an armed response.

German military strength increased exponentially from 1933 to 1939. Although the Versailles treaty (1919) had curtailed the size of the German army to one hundred thousand men, the Weimar Republic secretly evaded that limit, so that when Hitler came to power in 1933, plans were already in place to increase the army to three hundred thousand men. By 1935 the German army's seven original divisions had increased to twenty-one. Hitler's buildup gave the German army 103 divisions—fifty-two on active duty and fifty-one in reserve—and eighty-six infantry and six armored divisions at its disposal by 1939. By mobilizing its conscripts, the 730,000-man army could increase to 3.7 million personnel.

During the 1930s the British military had a twofold problem: first, it remained small and relatively weak in comparison to Germany; and second, its primary duty was to protect the empire. Having no conscription system, the British government used volunteers to fill its army, and as a result, was unable to raise large numbers. In January 1938 the army had 387,000 men, and while this number appears formidable, it was not. Of these men only 107,000 were meant for defense of the British Isles. The remaining 280,000 soldiers were parceled out to the empire: India, Burma, Middle East, Mediterranean, Far East, and West Indies. While these men could be recalled if needed, two circumstances prevented such a recourse: the distances involved and the government's military policy. In an age before jet aircraft, the government could not easily recall its military forces from abroad. Complicating this matter further was the fact that the government placed a greater emphasis on defending the empire than on a continental commitment. In 1938, for instance, troops were deployed to Palestine to put down a revolt, the logic being that a disturbance there constituted a threat to the internal stability of the empire—particularly in Egypt and Iraq—and therefore had greater precedence.

The French military situation was just as dire. Because of public pressure in the 1920s, the years men served in the military was reduced. At the end of World War I, military service stood at three years; in 1921, it was reduced to two years. By 1923 it was down to only eighteen months, and by 1928, had been reduced to twelve months. In the end, these reductions cut the army's size by more than two-thirds. At the same time it was further reduced by low birthrates. In 1928 the annual number of military conscripts stood at 240,000 men; however, because of a lower birthrate, the average number still remained low into the 1930s. In the latter part of the decade, the annual number of conscripts stood between 120,000 and 200,000 men, so that by 1936—when Germany reoccupied the Rhineland—France had military forces of 651,000 men, with about 195,000 available immediately.

The French government thus realized that Germany had the advantage. In order to offset this, the government could mobilize its reserves; however, doing so was politically risky and would not give France the military advantage. Most Frenchmen from eighteen to forty years old were in the reserves, and most also worked in France's major industries. Mobilizing the reserves would remove millions from civilian employment and disrupt France socially and economically—especially during the Great Depression. Even had this step been taken, it would not have improved the French military: only a third of reserve officers and a tenth of noncommissioned officers had taken their training seriously, and as a result, the reserves could not be put into immediate service. Before they could be integrated into the standing army, the reserves had to be retrained.

Because of these deficiencies, French military strategy during the 1930s centered around fighting a defensive, not an offensive, war. The government decided to focus on strengthening its defenses rather than upgrading military strength, and thus chose to build the Maginot Line—a system of fortified forts and blockhouses along the Franco-German border designed to defend France from a German assault through Alsace-Lorraine. Ignoring French military strategy, some have argued that Hitler would have backed down had France sent its military forces into the Rhineland. In light of France's military situation, however, such an argument is ludicrous. To have stopped Germany, France would have been forced to launch an offensive war, a maneuver that ran counter to the defensive logic of the Maginot Line.

Further complicating the military situation was the fact that both French and British intelligence overexaggerated German military superiority. In March 1936 French military intelligence, the *Deuxième Bureau,* analyzed German military forces occupying the Rhineland and compiled an accurate assessment: seven divisions of about sixty thousand troops. When the Army General Staff reported these figures to the French government, however, they included 235,000 extra men from paramilitary groups such as the *Sturmabteilung* (SA), the *Schutzstaffel* (SS), and the Labour Front, even though these groups had no military significance. It is not clear why they did so. They may have believed that Germany had military superiority, or they exaggerated the German threat because they did not want to fight German forces.

British intelligence also overestimated German military strength, particularly the *Luftwaffe* (German Air Force). Starting in 1937, intelligence exaggerated Germany's combat-ready bomber force by twofold. In reality, such interpretations were unwarranted. In August 1938 Germany had 582 combat-ready bombers at its disposal; Britain had 1,019. The Royal Air Force also remained ahead in other areas. Britain had 717 combat-ready fighters and 227 combat-ready dive-bombers in September 1938; Germany had 452 fighters and 159 dive-bombers. While British production was not behind German, British intelligence remained firmly convinced—and convinced the government—that Britain's air strength was vastly behind that of the Luftwaffe. According to historian P. M. H. Bell in *France and Britain, 1900–1940: Entente and Estrangement* (1996), "beliefs were more important than facts."

Neither Britain nor France were militarily capable to deter Hitler. On a similar note, neither nation was committed to do so, given the state of British and French public opinion. To deter Hitler would have required both nations to have gone to war against Germany, an act that neither the British nor French public would have supported. Throughout the interwar period, both the British and French expressed common sentiments about foreign policy. Both feared war with Germany—dreading the devastation such a conflict would entail—and as a result, both nations witnessed a resurgence of pacifist movements that worked to prevent a war.

Believing that new technological developments would make a future war far worse than World War I, neither the British nor the French wanted a recurrence of the circumstances that

had led to that conflict. Technologically speaking, the advent of terror bombing against civilian populations—especially the devastation caused by Germany's incendiary bombing of Guernica in 1937 during the Spanish Civil War—reinforced this attitude. The British, in particular, feared aerial bombardment. In October 1936 the Joint Planning Committee of the Chiefs of Staff published a study that argued that by 1939 Germany could launch air attacks against Britain. The study contended that London alone would suffer twenty thousand casualties within twenty-four hours. By the end of a week 150,000 people were expected to be killed. Such analyses naturally affected people's opinions, strengthening long-standing ideas about war. In a speech before the House of Commons in 1934, Stanley Baldwin emphatically stated that "the bomber will always get through," and this report only seemed to confirm such sentiments.

The French public also feared war with Germany. During World War I, France had borne the brunt of fighting on its own soil, and in doing so, lost approximately 1.3 million people and suffered agricultural and industrial devastation in the northeast. The French thus believed that another conflict would be fought on their soil and that the devastation would be far worse. In 1934, Daniel Halévy investigated the state of French public opinion and reported on its antiwar nature, as reported by Bell:

> The war assuredly counts for much in this somber mood which has gripped the peasants. They speak little of its tortures but they forget nothing, and there lies at the bottom of their embittered hearts a desire for vengeance. This is one of the schools of hatred in which the young have been taught. "They will lead you to the slaughter" the father tells his son. "I let myself be led. I've been through it. Don't you go."

Such sentiments led to strong pacifist movements in Britain and France, movements that worked to promote their agendas. One of the largest British pacifist groups was Canon Dick Sheppard's Peace Pledge Union. Sending out fifty thousand postcards to the British people, the organization emphatically pledged its commitment to peace and its strong dislike of armed aggression. "We renounce war and never again, directly or indirectly," the members asserted, "will we support or sanction another."

Pacifist sentiments were especially strong in France. Led by Paul Faure, pacifists argued that peace with Germany could be kept through disarmament and negotiations. In 1933 socialist-philosopher Félicien Challaye published a book of which the title emphasized a pacifist outlook: *Pour le paix désarmée, même en face d'Hitler* (For Disarmed Peace, Even in Face of

DALADIER ON HITLER

Edouard Daladier, premier of France and a proponent of appeasement of Hitler, reacted to the German invasion of Poland with an address to the Council of Deputies on 2 September 1939, a portion of which is included below.

. . . at dawn on September 1 the Fuhrer gave his troops the order to attack. Never was aggression more unmistakable and less warranted; nor for its justification could more lies and cynicism have been brought into play. Thus was war unleashed at the time when the most noteworthy forces, the authorities who were at the same time the most respected and the most impartial, had ranged themselves in the service of peace; at the time when the whole world had joined together to induce the two sides to come into direct contact so as to settle peacefully the conflict which divides them. The Head of Christianity had given voice to reason and feelings of brotherhood; President Roosevelt had sent moving messages and proposed a general conference to all countries; the neutral countries had been active in offering their impartial good offices. . . . I immediately had a definite proposal put to the Fuhrer, a proposal wholly inspired by the real concern to safeguard without any delay the peace of the world now imperiled. You were able to read, I think in fact that you must have read these texts. You know the answer I was given; I will not dwell on it. But we were not disheartened by the failure of this step, and once more we backed up the effort to which Mr. Chamberlain devoted himself with splendid stubbornness. The documents exchanged between London and Berlin have been published. On the one side impartial and persevering loyalty; on the other side, embarrassment, shifty and shirking behavior. I am also happy at this juncture to pay my tribute to the noble efforts made by the Italian Government. Even yesterday we strove to unite all men of goodwill so as at least to stave off hostilities, to prevent bloodshed and to ensure that the methods of conciliation and arbitration should be substituted for the use of violence. Gentlemen, these efforts towards peace, however powerless they were and still remain, will at least have shown where the responsibility lies. They insure for Poland, the victim, the effective co-operation and moral support of the nations and of free men of all lands. What we did before the beginning of this war, we are ready to do once more. If renewed steps are taken towards conciliation, we are still ready to join in. If the fighting were to stop, if the aggressor were to retreat within his own frontiers, if free negotiations could still be started, you may well believe, Gentlemen, the French Government would spare no effort to ensure,

even today, if it were possible, the success of these negotiations, in the interests of the peace of the world. But the time is pressing; France and England cannot look on when a friendly nation is being destroyed, a foreboding of further onslaughts, eventually aimed at England and France. Indeed, are we only dealing with the German-Polish conflict? We are not, Gentlemen; what we have to deal with is a new stage in the advance of the Hitler dictatorship towards the domination of Europe and the world. . . . Today we are told that, once the German claims against Poland were satisfied, Germany would pledge herself before the whole world for ten, for twenty, for twenty-five years, for all time, to restore or to respect peace. Unfortunately, we have heard such promises before! On May 25, 1935, Chancellor Hitler pledged himself not to interfere in the internal affairs of Austria and not to unite Austria to the Reich; and on March 11, 1938, the German army entered Vienna; Chancellor Shuschnigg was imprisoned for daring to defend his country's independence, and no one to-day can say what is his real fate after so many physical and moral sufferings. Now we are to believe that it was Dr. Schuschnigg's acts of provocation that brought about the invasion and enslavement of his country! On September 12, 1938, Herr Hitler declared that the Sudeten problem was an internal matter which concerned only the German minority in Bohemia and the Czechoslovak Government. A few days later he maintained that he violent persecutions carried on by the Czechs were compelling him to change his policy. On September 26 of the same year he declared that his claim on the Sudeten territory was the last territorial claim he had to make in Europe. On March 14, 1939, Herr Hacha was summoned to Berlin: ordered under the most stringent pressure to accept an ultimatum. A few hours later Prague was being occupied in contempt of the signed pledges given to other countries in Western Europe. In this case also Herr Hitler endeavored to put on the victims the onus which in fact lies on the aggressor. Finally, on January 30, 1939, Herr Hitler spoke in loud praise of the non-aggression pact which he had signed five years previously with Poland. He paid a tribute to this agreement as a common act of liberation, and solemnly confirmed his intention to respect its clauses. But it is Herr Hitler's deeds that count, not his word.

Source: Larry W. Jewell, transcriber, "Address by Edouard Daladier, Premier, in the Chamber of Deputies, September 2, 1939."

Hitler). Challaye's interpretation of pacifism was more extreme than Faure's, however. He believed that given the choice between war and foreign occupation, France must choose the latter because the price of war was too great. More importantly, his ideas were influential because they were adopted by the pacifist wing of the Socialist Party. Led by Jacques Pivet, this wing did not form a majority in the party; however, it remained an active minority that influenced the development of French foreign policy vis-à-vis Germany. In 1936 the *Syndicat National des Instituteurs* (National Union of Teachers)—which represented 100,000 of France's 130,000 primary school teachers—passed a resolution that demanded the removal of the German war-guilt clause in the Versailles treaty, called for unilateral disarmament, and forged active alliances with other French unions for a general strike if the government moved toward mobilization.

Did the leaders of Britain and France know, however, how the public viewed warfare? They most certainly did. They merely opened a newspaper to read pacifist literature or monitor public opinion. Public sentiment was well known, especially in Britain. In 1935 the League of Nations Union conducted a poll known as the Peace Ballot. The results confirmed the government's suspicions—almost 11.5 million people expressed support for the League of Nations: an overwhelming majority wanted peace, wished to continue multilateral disarmament, and put greater trust in collective security over unilateral action on the continent.

Yet, does this mean that these leaders had to listen to public opinion? Knowing that Hitler was a threat, could not the British and French leaders have militarily deterred Germany anyway? They certainly could have done so had their governments been totalitarian. It must be remembered that Britain and France had liberal-democratic governments, and unlike the leaders of a totalitarian state, they were subject to the whim of the electorate. Had they wanted to remain in office, they could not have acted in a manner that ran counter to public opinion; and given the state of British and French public opinion, it would have been political suicide for the leader of either nation—be it British prime minister Neville Chamberlain or French premier Edouard Daladier—to have launched an offensive war against Hitler.

Given Britain and France's lack of capability and commitment, the policy both governments followed—appeasement—was a pragmatic one. In a sense, both Chamberlain and Daladier believed that they had deterred Hitler. Appeasement was designed to preserve the status quo by eliminating friction points between the great powers, provided that these friction points were based on legitimate grievances. Believing that Hitler had legitimate grievances arising from the Versailles treaty and that he acted as a traditional statesman, both Chamberlain and Daladier attempted to eliminate those points angering him; however, because they failed to realize that Hitler was not a traditional statesman, they did not understand that their policy was sending the wrong message. At Munich in 1938, Chamberlain and Daladier thus believed that Hitler's demands for German national self-determination had been met by giving him the Sudetenland. They thought they had kept the status quo, but Hitler took this action as a sign of further weakness on their part and of future acquiescence. Therein lies the difficulty with the third proposition of deterrence: communication. Chamberlain and Daladier believed that they were effectively communicating their beliefs to Hitler and that he understood them, but because they misunderstood the Nazi leader's ambitions, they did not realize that their policy was essentially encouraging Hitler to expand further.

This miscommunication certainly undermined any deterrent effects that appeasement may have had. It was the only logical policy the British and French governments could have followed, however, given the fact that both nations had neither the military capability nor commitment to have deterred Hitler in any other way. Deterrence, especially military, may have worked during the Cold War, but it was not feasible during the years between World Wars I and II.

–REGAN HILDEBRAND, OHIO UNIVERSITY

References

R. J. Q. Adams, ed., *British Appeasement and the Origins of World War II* (Lexington, Mass.: Heath, 1994);

Anthony P. Adamthwaite, *France and the Coming of the Second World War, 1936–1939* (London & Totowa, N.J.: Biblio Distribution Center, 1977);

Adamthwaite, *The Making of the Second World War* (London & Boston: Allen & Unwin, 1977);

P. M. H. Bell, *France and Britain, 1900–1940: Entente and Estrangement* (London & New York: Longman, 1996);

Bell, *The Origins of the Second World War in Europe* (London & New York: Longman, 1986);

Keith Eubank, ed., *World War II: Roots and Causes* (Lexington, Mass.: Heath, 1992);

Patrick Finney, ed., *The Origins of the Second World War* (London & New York: Arnold, 1997);

David E. Kaiser, *Economic Diplomacy and the Origins of the Second World War: Germany, Britain, France, and Eastern Europe, 1930–1939* (Princeton: Princeton University Press, 1980);

Wolfgang J. Mommsen and Lothar Kettenacker, eds., *The Fascist Challenge and the Policy of Appeasement* (London & Boston: Allen & Unwin, 1983);

Joseph S. Nye Jr., *Understanding International Conflicts: An Introduction to Theory and History* (New York: HarperCollins, 1993);

R. J. Overy, *The Origins of the Second World War* (London & New York: Longman, 1987);

R. A. C. Parker, *Chamberlain and Appeasement: British Policy and the Coming of the Second World War* (New York: St. Martin's Press, 1993);

John L. Snell, ed., *The Outbreak of the Second World War: Design or Blunder?* (Boston: Heath, 1962);

Paul C. Stern, and others, eds., *Perspectives on Deterrence* (New York: Oxford University Press, 1989);

Charles Callan Tansill, *Back Door to War: The Roosevelt Foreign Policy, 1933–1941* (Chicago: Regnery, 1952);

A. J. P. Taylor, *The Origins of the Second World War* (London: Hamilton, 1961);

Martin Thomas, *Britain, France and Appeasement: Anglo-French Relations in the Popular Front Era* (Oxford & New York: Berg, 1996);

Gerhard L. Weinberg, *The Foreign Policy of Hitler's Germany,* 2 volumes (Chicago: University of Chicago Press, 1970–1980).

HITLER'S AGGRESSION

HITLER'S FOREIGN POLICY

Was Adolf Hitler a revolutionary German leader in his foreign policy?

Viewpoint: Yes, Adolf Hitler employed a radical approach to foreign policy, eschewing traditional balance-of-power politics for an ideologically based plan to dominate the world and eliminate races he considered inferior.

Viewpoint: No, Adolf Hitler's foreign policy falls within traditional European practice, and World War II was the result of bungled policy on the part of his opponents, which he simply took advantage of.

One approach to Adolf Hitler's foreign policy focuses on its ideological dimensions. According to this interpretation, Hitler proposed to construct a self-sustaining power base from the English Channel to the Ural Mountains; then move into Africa and across the Atlantic; and finally confront the United States in a direct bid for global hegemony. The ultimate purpose of these conquests was the establishment of a racially based imperium, with *Lebensraum* (living space) and economic supremacy for the Germans and other "Aryan" peoples secured at the expense of lesser races and through extermination of the Jews.

The second interpretive approach describes Hitler's foreign policy as an extension of traditional German ambitions, continental as opposed to global, emphasizing mastery of western Europe and eventual control of the Eurasian "heartland," arguably even willing to compromise with Britain on imperial issues. In this model, Hitler is an opportunist, taking advantage of his opponents' weaknesses and confusion to disrupt existing power relationships until, paradoxically, he shattered them beyond repair in the second half of 1941 by invading the Soviet Union and declaring war on the United States.

Hitler was both pragmatist and ideologue, both visionary and compromiser. He knew better what he hoped to achieve than how best to get there. His concept of power never produced a concrete plan. As late as 1940 he told Joseph Goebbels that he could not say what was enough—only that when the current war was over, he proposed to be master of Europe. Was this quest the first step or an endgame? The answer died with Hitler.

**Viewpoint:
Yes, Adolf Hitler employed a radical approach to foreign policy, eschewing traditional balance-of-power politics for an ideologically based plan to dominate the world and eliminate races he considered inferior.**

Right up to, and in some cases after, the German invasion of Poland in September 1939, a significant number of western European diplomats and statesmen believed that a war with Adolf Hitler's Third Reich could be avoided. These men, for the most part reared in an era of traditional balance-of-power politics, felt that Nazi Germany was still operating within the normal parameters of established European relations. This being so, they held that Hitler's Germany could be bargained with following the time-tested rules of diplomacy. They could not have been further from the truth.

Hitler was carrying out a foreign policy that was nothing like Otto von Bismarck's familiar *Realpolitik,* but rather it was revolutionary in both its execution and goals. The Führer aimed at nothing less for Germany than world domination. While this in itself was a clear break from traditional European balance-of-power politics, Hitler's means of achieving this goal were even more radical. Uniquely, Hitler based his foreign-policy calculations not upon the normal ideas of state power, but rather in terms of a life-or-death racial struggle. He intended for Europe to be racially cleansed, a process that would create *Lebensraum* (living space), into which the German people could expand and thrive. All other races were to be subjugated and were to serve to augment German power. Hitler's foreign policy was based on his own ideology, rather than the commonly shared rationality of traditional European politics.

Although there were clear paradoxes, both conceptually and practically, in Hitler's foreign-policy program that indicated he was not following a detailed blueprint or timetable, the German leader's goals remained consistent from beginning to end. Indeed, Hitler outlined his radical foreign-policy program in *Mein Kampf* (My Struggle), written while he was incarcerated in the Landsberg Prison and first published in 1925, and he elaborated these core ideas on several other occasions.

Hitler's book was filled with the prejudices of the German Right of the Weimar Republic, but he placed particular emphasis on what he saw as the racial divisions within Europe. Drawing upon Social Darwinism and racialist theory, Hitler saw Europe divided into competing racial groups of differing qualities engaged in a life-or-death struggle. The German Aryans were considered by Hitler to be the finest race, while the Jews were the lowest race. According to Hitler, however, the German race was hemmed in by enemies and unable to expand its population as it should. Without the proper lebensraum, Germany would never achieve its full potential and the German race would never assume the world leadership role it was due.

Hitler came up with a solution to this problem, and it was to take place in several stages. First, Germany was to abrogate the Treaty of Versailles (1919) by rebuilding her military power and remilitarizing the Rhineland. This act would provide Germany with the necessary strength to move to the next stage of Hitler's plan—reuniting all Germans with the Fatherland, and the destruction of France's alliance system in central Europe.

Hitler demanded that those territories taken from the old German Empire at the end of World War I, such as Silesia, the Polish Corridor, and Danzig, be returned and that Germany bring the Austrio-Germans and areas populated by them (the Sudetenland) into the German state. This policy would have the effect of diminishing or destroying the power of the newly formed central European states and of breaking the French system of alliances in central Europe, the Petite Entente. Ultimately, to ensure a strong base from which they were to engage in an expansionist war in the east, Germany was to be made safe from internal enemies by clearing all foreign racial elements from the rebuilt Greater Germany.

After Germany had been united and rearmed, Hitler intended that Germany seize the lebensraum it needed to grow and from which it would dominate Europe. For this space, he looked primarily toward the east, toward Poland and Russia. These lands, inhabited by the "racially inferior" Slavs, appeared to Hitler to be the ideal territory for German colonization. The area's Slavic inhabitants would either be pushed further east or be enslaved. From this territory, Hitler believed Germany could extract the necessary resources to make her invulnerable to any type of blockade, such as the British sea blockade that had choked off Germany from vital supplies of food and raw materials during World War I. In other words, Hitler believed that through this expansion into the east, Germany would become self-sufficient.

Before this conquest of the east could be accomplished, however, Hitler recognized that Germany would first have to secure its Western Front from an attack by France. The destruction of the Petite Entente would be a step towards reducing France's ability to intervene. Yet, this action might not be enough to ensure that France would not attack while Germany was engaged in a war of conquest in the east. France would either have to be defeated in a war or—Hitler's preferred solution—neutralized through a German alliance with Great Britain.

Great Britain also played a role in the final, and most vaguely defined, stage of Hitler's foreign-policy program. After Germany achieved autarky through its conquests in the East, it would, in Hitler's mind, have proven itself the racially superior nation and would accordingly have the right to dominate not only Europe, but also the world. Hitler hoped to enlist the English, racial cousins to the Germans, as junior partners in the confrontation with the United States that surely would follow.

Hitler outlined a foreign-policy program unlike any other seen in Europe. It was not based on the traditional nation-state politics of

Europe, with its assumption of equally sovereign international bodies, but rather on a particular racial ideology. In Hitler's worldview, the nation-state had no meaning. Instead, the important factor was race. Hitler believed that one race would come to dominate all others, and, as he viewed the German race to be superior, he believed ultimately it would dominate Europe and then the world. He therefore followed an ideologically driven foreign-policy program that had unlimited aims. Any long-term compromises were precluded by

Nazi racial ideology. Hitler's policy could only end in the total destruction of either the German race or its enemies.

Indeed, Hitler demonstrated that his writings were not mere rhetoric. Immediately upon coming to power, the Führer set into motion his program. Although other German leaders before Hitler had allowed rearmament to proceed cautiously, Hitler proceeded aggressively and unilaterally. In October 1933, Hitler withdrew Germany from a disarmament conference and from the League of Nations, setting the scene for

German rearmament. By March 1935 universal conscription had been reintroduced and the existence of the *Luftwaffe* (German Air Force) had been announced. Vast sums of money were poured into the rearmament program, which would be needed in Hitler's forthcoming struggle.

Rearmament allowed Germany greater flexibility in the international arena, and Hitler took advantage of it to carry out the remainder of his plan. First, the final vestiges of the Versailles system were done away with. In 1935 the Saarland was reincorporated into Germany after fifteen years of international administration, and the Rhineland was remilitarized. Then, Hitler commenced reuniting all Germans within the German state. In March 1938, the *Wehrmacht* (German Army) marched into Austria, ostensibly at the behest of the Austrians, and it was incorporated into Germany. Hitler turned next to the Germans of the Sudetenland in Czechoslovakia. Here, as Hitler proposed to carve up a sovereign, non-German state, he came into direct and serious confrontation with the other major powers of Europe.

Throughout the years before the outbreak of war in 1939, Hitler proved himself capable of entering into diplomatic arrangements with other European powers, which seemed to indicate that he was willing to operate within the parameters of traditional European diplomacy. Given his ideological foreign policy, however, these could be only short-term, tactical compromises. Thus, Hitler was willing to sign a nonaggression pact with Poland in 1935, and even with his greatest ideological enemy and target—the Soviet Union—in 1939 because it allowed him greater flexibility to operate elsewhere.

During the Sudetenland crisis (September 1938), Hitler again seemed to demonstrate a willingness to play according to the rules. Although reluctant, he agreed to an international conference to deal with his demands, and, in the end, he achieved his immediate goal, the annexation of the Sudetenland, without resorting to force. Wishing above all to avoid war, western European leaders, particularly British prime minister Neville Chamberlain, followed a policy of appeasement and gave in to Hitler's demands. These statesmen believed that Hitler's appetite for territory would be satisfied with the Sudetenland and that Hitler would henceforth cease to make demands of his neighbors.

For Hitler, however, Czechoslovakia was only one step in his program. In 1939 Hitler turned on Poland, initially demanding the previously German portions of its territory, but in reality seeking to destroy the Polish state. By this point, British and French leaders recognized that Hitler had to be stopped and offered guarantees

to Poland. Their position was seriously undermined by Hitler's most cynical diplomatic maneuver—the Nazi-Soviet Non-Aggression Pact (23 August 1939), in which Germany and its archenemy agreed to partition Poland.

Despite their poor strategic situation, the Western democracies at last realized that war was inevitable and determined to stand together to face the Nazi threat. Thus, when German troops crossed the Polish border on 1 September 1939, France and Great Britain honored their commitment and declared war on Nazi Germany. World War II, part of Hitler's program, had begun and would not end until it reached its logical conclusion with either a total Nazi victory or a total Nazi defeat.

–ROBERT T. FOLEY, INSTITUTE OF TACTICAL
EDUCATION, QUANTICO, VA

Viewpoint:
No, Adolf Hitler's foreign policy falls within traditional European practice, and World War II was the result of bungled policy on the part of his opponents, which he simply took advantage of.

Adolf Hitler was no madman who orchestrated the outbreak of World War II according to some preconceived blueprint. Rather, the war occurred by accident, the result of unwitting blunders by European diplomats and others in their attempt to master events.

Hitler must be seen in the general context of European statesmen, all of whom schemed for advantage as they sought to maintain or extend the power of their states. The interests of state always predominated over ideological concerns. Apart from perhaps temperament and tactics, Hitler was no different from traditional German statesmen who sought a dominant position for Germany in central and eastern Europe. Like them, Hitler favored neither war nor conquest of territory, but merely the restoration of Germany's "natural" position in Europe that had been unnaturally diminished by the Treaty of Versailles (1919). Recovery of German dominance did not necessarily require the direct annexation of Austria, the Sudetenland, or all of Czechoslovakia. It would suffice if these and other central and eastern European states and regions would become satellites of the new Germany. On balance, in his efforts to have the Versailles settlement altered, Hitler took advantage of the objective situation in Europe and responded to events as they occurred. Others

HITLER ON FOREIGN AFFAIRS

On 30 January 1937, Adolf Hitler delivered a speech to the German Reichstag, a portion of which follows, on National Socialism and world affairs.

During recent years Germany has entered into quite a number of political agreements with other States. She has resumed former agreements and improved them. And I may say that she has established close friendly relations with a number of States. Our relations with most of the European States are normal from our standpoint and we are on terms of close friendship with quite a number. Among all those diplomatic connections I would give a special place in the foreground to those excellent relations which we have with those States that were liberated from sufferings similar to those we had to endure and have consequently arrived at similar decisions.

Through a number of treaties which we have made, we have relieved many strained relations and thereby made a substantial contribution towards an improvement in European conditions. I need remind you only of our agreement with Poland, which has turned out advantageous for both countries, our agreement with Austria and the excellent and close relations which we have established with Italy. Further, I may refer to our friendly relations with Hungary, Yugoslavia, Bulgaria, Greece, Portugal, Spain etc. Finally, I may mention our cordial relations with a whole series of nations outside of Europe.

The agreement which Germany has made with Japan for combating the movement directed by the Comintern is a vital proof of how little the German Government thinks of isolating itself and how little we feel ourselves actually isolated. Furthermore, I have on several occasions declared that it is our wish and hope to arrive at good cordial relations with all our neighbors.

Germany has steadily given its assurance, and I solemnly repeat this assurance here, that between ourselves and France, for example, there are no grounds for quarrel that are humanly thinkable. Furthermore, the German Government has assured Belgium and Holland that it is ready to recognize and guarantee these States as neutral regions in perpetuity.

In view of the declarations which we have made in the past and in view of the existing state of affairs, I cannot quite clearly see why Germany should consider herself isolated or why we should pursue a policy of isolation. From the economic standpoint there are no grounds for asserting that Germany is withdrawing from international cooperation. The contrary is the truth. On looking over the speeches which several statesmen have made within the last few months, I find that they might easily give rise to the impression that the whole world is waiting to shower economic favours on Germany but that we, who are represented as obstinately clinging to a policy of isolation, do not wish to partake of those favours.

Source: German Propaganda Archive Web Site, Calvin College.

---

seized the initiative; Hitler exploited opportunities presented. An examination of the actions of Hitler and others in the years immediately preceding the outbreak of World War II reflects a traditional German attempt to dominate Europe and others to prevent it.

Those who blame Hitler for the war often begin by focusing on the so-called Hossbach Conference, a meeting among Hitler and his key military and diplomatic leaders on 5 November 1937, at which he outlined his so-called blueprint for conquest. The proceedings were recorded by Friedrich Hossbach, Hitler's army adjutant, and later used at the Nuremburg Trials (1945–1946) to accuse Hitler and the Germans of planning a war of conquest. At this meeting Hitler described Germany's need to resort to force if faced with one of three possible scenarios: one involved going to war in 1943; another considered taking advantage of a possible civil war in France; and a third envisioned dealing with war between France and Italy. None of these scenarios came true. In fact, the purpose of this gathering was to shore up conservative support for greater rearmament by isolating the military from Hitler's widely respected financial genius, Hjalmar Schacht, who opposed the Four Year Plan's rearmament measures. In the months following the conference, Schacht and other hesitant officials resigned and German rearmament proceeded apace. Rather than feature Hitler revealing his innermost thoughts about conquering Europe, the infamous Hossbach Conference merely reflected petty domestic intrigue and political machinations typical of the Nazi system of government.

Those who accuse Hitler of following a "blueprint for conquest" next point to the *Anschluss* (Union), the takeover of Austria only five months after the Hossbach Conference. To be sure, the annexation of Austria was Hitler's first expansionist operation outside of Germany. He was only responding, however, to opportunities presented by others. The new British prime minister, Neville Chamberlain, for example, sent his emissary, Lord Halifax, to Berchtesgaden on 17 November to initiate talks on modifying the unfair Versailles settlement. Following the new policy of appeasement, Halifax suggested that Britain would not oppose territorial changes to satisfy legitimate German grievances that included Austria, Czechoslovakia, and Danzig. He stipulated only that such alterations be made peacefully. As for the Austrian problem itself, Austrian chancellor Kurt von Schuschnigg, hoping to stir the western European powers into action on Austria's behalf, provoked the crisis by sending police to raid the Austrian Nazi headquarters to secure proof of an armed uprising. These events took Hitler by surprise. Then,

Franz von Papen, dismissed German ambassador to Austria, sought favor with Hitler by suggesting that Schuschnigg personally visit Hitler to clarify the situation. Having already been given the "green light" by British appeasers, Hitler—quite naturally—responded to the prompting of von Papen and Schussnigg. The proof that Hitler planned no invasion came when fully 70 percent of German equipment broke down on the trip from the Austrian frontier to Vienna. In any event, 99 percent of united Germans and Austrians approved the union. Hitler would have preferred an evolutionary solution to the Austrian problem; he simply took advantage of the opportunities presented. Unintentionally, he had taken a step on the road to becoming branded a war criminal.

Following the Anschluss, European officials expected Hitler to act against Czechoslovakia. Hitler, however, waited on the course of events and the nerves of others to crack. Although lauded as a flourishing democratic nation, Czechoslovakia was an unstable state of nationalities. Germany had no need to initiate its destruction. Among the many unhappy second-class citizens in this Czech-dominated country, most aggrieved were the Sudeten Germans, who had been stirred to further action by the Anschluss. Hitler had no interest in sending his army against the well-fortified and defended Czechs. He preferred to intrigue and only threaten the use of force to convince the Czechs to treat their German citizens fairly. Here, again, others seized the initiative. The Sudeten Nazis, led by Konrad Henlein, provoked the tension gradually, without Hitler's knowledge or intervention. Czech president Edvard Beneš, who did not want his country to fight alone or aided by his ally the Soviet Union, ratcheted up the tension by pushing the Sudeten Nazis to demand Czechoslovakia's dissolution. In doing so, he hoped the western powers would react to preserve his country's territorial integrity. Again, unintended consequences occurred. The British, seeking so divert the crisis, actually worsened it by suggesting Hitler make demands on the Czechs while urging the Czechs to make concessions. The Munich Conference in September 1938 resulted from Benito Mussolini's initiative, not Hitler's, and the agreement to partition Czechoslovakia actually had been dictated to the Czechs by the British and French. Hitler, as usual, had waited for events to provide him future success.

In the months following the Munich Conference, Hitler drew the appropriate lesson that threats of war, but not war itself, represented his most potent weapon in the diplomatic game of restoring Germany's dominant position in Europe. He waited on events. Having absorbed the German-populated Sudetenland, he had no intention of annexing the Czech lands. He doubted that the rump state of Czecho-Slovakia, having lost prestige and its natural frontiers, could survive in the face of demands from the independent-minded Slovaks and the aggressive Poles and Hungarians. By the spring of 1939, Hitler's concerns had proven accurate. Faced with Slovak demands for autonomy, weakened president Emil Hácha precipitated the immediate crisis by dissolving the Slovak government. This move created the prospect of conflict involving the Slovaks, Czechs, and Hungarians, which would likely lead to a larger war in central Europe. The German move to annex the remainder of Czecho-Slovakia must be seen as a measure to prevent war. Once more, Hitler did not create the problem; he merely took advantage of it.

As for Poland, the final stage on Hitler's so-called intentional road to war, this crisis also was forced on the German leader by others. Hitler had no intention of destroying Poland. His only concern involved Danzig, the German-populated port city that had been severed from Germany and made accessible by land only across the so-called Polish Corridor of Seized German territory. Britain and other western powers frankly recognized the Danzig situation as intolerable for Germany, but Polish foreign minister Józef Beck, who had illusions that Poland was a great power, absolutely refused to negotiate with Germany on the future of the city. At the same time, following Hitler's absorption of Czecho-Slovakia, the British gave ironclad security guarantees to Poland, Romania, and Greece in case of a German invasion. Not only did fulfilling these obligations for Poland and Romania require the intervention of the Soviet Union, the alliance made Britain the prisoner of Polish actions. Danzig was Hitler's "final demand": he wanted only to solve the Danzig issue to preserve good relations between Germany and Poland. The British guarantee to Poland, however, made compromise impossible. Once again, the British, by seeking to forestall war, actually helped to bring it on.

From April to August 1939, Hitler took little action diplomatically. As previous crises had demonstrated, he preferred to wait for others to remove obstacles to peace in Europe. He sensed that Anglo-Soviet negotiations during the summer had no chance of success, because British officials disliked dealing with Communist Russia more than they did with Hitler's Germany and the British could never convince the Poles or Romanians to permit Russian troops to transit their territory. In this instance Hitler was correct. In August, once it became clear British-Soviet talks had failed, Hitler acted to complete a nonaggression pact with the Soviet Union to prevent war, not to bring it on. His bellicose statements threatening war at the end of the month were made for effect, to prompt the British and their allies to negotiate over Danzig. All parties involved miscalculated. The British failed to convince the Poles to negotiate with the Germans; the Poles refused to accept the German offer of 29 August; and Hitler, unfortunately, made his appeal too late to allow sufficient time for the diplomatic process to prevent the outbreak of war. Moreover, after Germany attacked Poland on 1 September, the British and French hesitated two days before declaring war themselves. Given his previous diplomatic victories, Hitler fully expected the western powers to avoid war and reach another diplomatic settlement that would preserve what he believed was Germany's legitimate, dominant position in Europe. As the condition of German armament in 1939 shows, Hitler knew that Germany was unprepared to conquer Europe. He did not seriously intend that general war in Europe occur. He had been too successful diplomatically to risk such a conflict.

The record of events clearly demonstrates that Hitler had no "blueprint for conquest" of Europe. He was a traditional German statesman who sought a commanding presence for his country in central and eastern Europe. As such, he took advantage of opportunities presented by others. Sadly for all concerned, the miscalculations of European diplomats and Hitler produced unintended consequences—a war favored by no one.

—DAVID SPIRES, BOULDER, COLORADO

References

Jost Dülffer, *Deutsche Geschichte 1933–1945: Fuhrerglaube und Vernichtungskrieg* (Stuttgart: Kohlhammer, 1992), translated by Dean Scott McMurray as *Nazi Germany, 1933–1945: Faith and Annihilation* (London & New York: Edward Arnold, 1996);

Ian Kershaw, *The Nazi Dictatorship: Problems and Perspectives of Interpretation* (London & Baltimore: Edward Arnold, 1985);

Gordon Martel, ed., *The Origins of the Second World War Reconsidered: The A. J. P. Taylor Debate After Twenty-five Years* (Boston: Allen & Unwin, 1986);

Norman Rich, *Hitler's War Aims,* 2 volumes (New York: Norton, 1973, 1974);

Gerhard L. Weinberg, *The Foreign Policy of Hitler's Germany: Diplomatic Revolution in Europe 1933–36* (Chicago: University of Chicago Press, 1970);

Weinberg, *The Foreign Policy of Hitler's Germany: Starting World War II* (Chicago: University of Chicago Press, 1980).

HOLOCAUST: COMPLICITY

Did local populations in Nazi-occupied territories play a significant role in Nazi atrocities?

Viewpoint: Yes, local populations played a significant role in Nazi atrocities for a variety of reasons, ranging from ideological to criminal.

Viewpoint: No, the actions of local populations were insignificant in terms of the instigation and extent of Nazi atrocities.

The complicity of local populations and occupation governments in the Holocaust remains a subject both sensitive and controversial. Almost from the beginning of World War II the Germans relied heavily on local helpers who, whatever their specific motives, served their masters voluntarily. Certainly not every auxiliary policeman or similar minor functionary took German pay with conscious aim of killing Jews. Poles and Balts, Ukrainians and Byelorussians, however, did regularly help deport Jews and sequester their property. In western Europe as well, local officials acting under German authority—or in the case of Vichy France, the orders of their own government—enforced anti-Semitic regulations to the letter and beyond.

In such environments it was relatively easy to recruit collaborators. The surprise, indeed, would have been if none had been forthcoming. To some degree the Nazis' helpers were part of a long-standing anti-Semitic tradition in Europe. Nevertheless, it is a long step from prejudice and discrimination, even from pogroms, to continuous mass murder. Hatred was sharpened, particularly in the Baltic states and parts of Poland, by a process of associating Jews with Communism and the Soviet Union. On a slightly more refined level, Eastern European nationalist movements conditioned to regard Russia as an ethnic and political enemy saw "cooperation" on the Jewish issue as a way of currying favor with an occupier brutally indifferent to anything or anyone not directly useful to the Third Reich.

Perhaps most important in the long run was the general erosion of limits on behaviors fostered, directly and indirectly, by Nazi occupation and Nazi ideology. Where turmoil had become king and randomness a way of life, the question increasingly was not, "Why kill the Jews?," it was "Why not kill them? It doesn't matter anyway."

Viewpoint:
Yes, local populations played a significant role in Nazi atrocities for a variety of reasons, ranging from ideological to criminal.

One of the more interesting aspects of World War II and the Holocaust was the degree of collaboration the Nazis received from local populations that came under German occupation. This assistance applies almost across the board. In the west, the number of active collaborators in France was considerably larger than the number of people in the French resistance. Even as late as 1944, membership in the resistance did not even approach one percent of

Lithuanian militiamen rounding up Jews in the summer of 1941

(Archiv Ernst Klee, Frankfurt, Germany)

the total population. This matter rarely discussed in France, at least until the 1983 trial of Nazi war criminal Klaus Barbie reopened many old wounds. The 5th *Schutzstaffeln* (SS) Panzer Division *Wiking* (Viking Division) contained many Belgian and Dutch volunteers. There was also a Belgian SS unit, the Walloon Brigade, led by one of the leaders of the Belgian Rexist Movement (organized in 1930), Léon Degrelle.

In the east, even in Poland, where three million Poles were killed by the Nazis, Poles did at times take part in atrocities against Jews. In the Ukraine, the local population eagerly collaborated with the Germans when the *Wehrmacht* (German army) overran the area in 1941. Even after the nature of German rule in the Ukraine became all too apparent, the Nazi authorities could still count on the collaboration of some elements of the local population, as demonstrated in the infamous John Demjanjuk case (1981–1988). As the war turned against the Germans, Ukrainian nationalist organizations such as the Organization of Ukrainian Nationalists (OUN) and its military wing, the Ukrainian Insurgent Army (UPA), taking the approach of "the enemy of my enemy is my enemy," fought a quixotic and ultimately losing struggle against both the retreating Germans and the advancing Soviets. In the Baltic States, the Germans again found a welcoming local population, especially in Estonia and Latvia, where some elements

quickly gravitated to the German authorities. It is worth noting that among the ranks of minor Nazi war criminals, there are several Estonians, Latvians, and some Lithuanians. The most notable recent examples are Boleslav Maikovskis and Karl Linnas, both of whom were deported to the Soviet Union from the United States during the 1980s after their true identities and activities, which they had kept from U.S. immigration authorities, were discovered. Given that the differences in the horror of German occupation in these areas could be measured only in degrees, the question remains: how were the Germans able to obtain as much cooperation as they did from the local populations in the areas they conquered?

The answer to this question is complex, but can ultimately be divided into two broad and related categories, ideological and nonideological. On the ideological side, there were many people in Nazi occupied territories who shared aspects of Nazi ideology, most notably anti-Semitism and anti-Bolshevism. In the west some of the more than one hundred thousand Belgian, Dutch, and French who ultimately joined the SS did so to answer the German call for a "crusade against Bolshevism." Others did so out of a sense of adventure, boredom, or the apparent prestige that went with the wearing of the SS uniform. The Germans were able to make use of the fractured nature of French politics, especially the Anglophobia rampant after the 1940s, in influencing the policies of the Vichy government, which was ultimately composed of ideologues (Charles Maurras), unscrupulous opportunists (Pierre Laval), and misguided patriots (Henri Pétain). In the other occupied countries of the west, the Germans had no trouble finding the equivalents of Vidkun Quisling in Norway.

In the east, the Germans clearly did not regard all native populations as mere *Untermenschen* (subhumans). The populations of the Baltic States were long regarded as Germanic, and each of these countries had nationalist movements that were strongly pro-German. The populations in these areas also had the benefit of having some powerful friends at the Nazi court, ranging from the muddled Nazi Party "philosopher" Alfred Rosenberg (who was a native of Estonia) to the powerful head of the SS, *Reichsführer* Heinrich Himmler. When the Germans overran these areas in the summer of 1941, Himmler, who was always on the prowl for new sources of manpower, was persuaded by some of his leading subordinates to look with favor upon the populations in those areas.

Mostly Estonians and Latvians answered the call of the anti-Bolshevik crusade. Some fifteen thousand Estonians and six thousand Latvians signed up to join the SS, though only a total of about five thousand men were equipped by April 1943, owing to material shortages. The SS recruited a sufficient number of men in the Baltic States to raise several units, most of which were police battalions. Later in the war, the SS formed one Estonian and two Latvian divisions. These eventually incorporated a Ukrainian unit, the notorious Kaminski Brigade. All of these units were, to some degree, motivated by ideology. They also demonstrated a penchant for committing atrocities. The police battalions came under the control of the local Higher SS Leader and Police Chief. Occasionally in 1941 they worked with the SS *Einsatzgruppen* (special action commandos) operating in the area. Consequently, the police battalions were involved in many atrocities.

The nonideological cause has several aspects to it. The primary of these, certainly in the east, was revenge, pure and simple. The Ukraine had been subjected to the brutalities of the Russian Revolution from 1917 to 1920. Then followed Soviet premier Joseph Stalin's collectivization drives from 1928 to 1932, with its concomitant deportations and executions, the resulting terror famine in 1932–1933, and finally the massive purges from 1937 to 1939. By 1941 the death toll from Soviet rule, beginning in 1918 and ending in 1941, easily ran more than ten million. Thus it should not have been a surprise that by

the summer of 1941 the Ukraine was filled with people who had more than ample reason to seek some degree of vengeance against the Soviet authorities and the representatives of Soviet power. Eastern Poland and the Baltic States were occupied by the Soviet Union in 1939 and 1940, respectively, as part of the Nazi-Soviet Pact of 23 August 1939. Even in the short period of time the Stalinist authorities were in control of these areas, they managed to compile a catalogue of crimes sufficiently grim enough to earn the searing hatred of the local populations. Consequently, many were happy to wreak more than a little revenge upon the Soviet authorities.

This attitude also played a part in the Holocaust. Anti-Semitism had long been a part of the social fabric in the Baltic States, Poland and especially the Ukraine, the scene of several ugly pogroms in the Czarist era. Poles had also conducted pogroms against Jews as late as the winter of 1939–1940, an activity the Germans did little to curtail. Although Stalin was certainly an anti-Semite, the official announced policy of the Soviet Union was to severely condemn anti-Semitism. Given this fact, and the longstanding poor treatment of Jews in these areas, it was not surprising that the Jewish populations in these areas welcomed the Soviet occupation. This development certainly served to reinforce the already strong anti-Semitic aspects of the local nationalist movements, not to mention the notion, so prominent in Nazi ideology, which held that Bolshevism was a creation of the Jews.

Another interesting aspect of Nazi rule both in and outside of Germany was the ability of the Nazis, from Adolf Hitler on down, to corrupt both people and institutions. Hitler, for example, corrupted many of his generals with rather large cash bribes. Nazi officials took advantage of the gross inequities present in the German university system to find aggrieved academics who were more than willing to take over university chairs from fired Jewish colleagues. In the occupied territories, German authorities quickly found the point at which people could be corrupted. Sometimes, it was a matter of mere survival. Many Ukrainian participants in Nazi war crimes, such as Demjanjuk, were captured Soviet soldiers. Given the alternative to a German promise of somewhat better treatment, not to mention survival, their decisions to work with the Germans was to some degree understandable. In Poland, acquiescence to, if not collaboration with, anti-Jewish actions often meant the literal difference between life and death, by starvation or worse. Others, especially in the west, were seduced by the prospect of positions of authority and all of the perquisites—financial and otherwise—that went with it. Finally, as with all totalitarian movements, a fair number of outright criminals, thugs, and degenerates were drawn to Nazisim, largely as a means for them to practice their own depravities. One can only imagine what was going on during the suppression of the Warsaw uprising in 1944 when the Kaminski Brigade, now officially part of the Waffen SS, was criticized by German authorities, including some high ranking SS officers, for excessive cruelty.

While this is certainly no confirmation of Daniel J. Goldhagen's rather overstated argument in *Hitler's Willing Executioners: Ordinary Germans and the Holocaust* (1996), it is abundantly clear that the Germans did get substantial help, at least early on, from the local populations in areas they overran for a variety of reasons. In this context, it is always a good idea to keep the words of German playwright Bertolt Brecht in mind. "Caesar crossed the Rubicon and took Rome. Did he do it by himself?"

–R. L. DINARDO, UNITED STATES MARINE CORPS COMMAND AND STAFF COLLEGE

Viewpoint:
No, the actions of local populations were insignificant in terms of the instigation and extent of Nazi atrocities.

In every German-occupied or allied territory during World War II, some members of the local population participated in large-scale atrocities perpetrated or inspired by the Nazis. Many more, meanwhile, played the important role of impassive bystanders to Nazi crimes. Still, others actively resisted Nazi atrocities and defended the victims. The role and behavior of local populations varied depending on their circumstances in western and eastern Europe, in occupied and unoccupied collaborationist states, and over time. Yet, while the actions of local populations were in many instances significant in terms of absolute numbers or moral implications, they were virtually always insignificant in terms of the instigation and outcome of Nazi atrocities, because the decisive factors were always German intentions and timing.

While the Nazis perpetrated innumerable atrocities against a multitude of victims, the case primarily relevant to the issue of local participation was the Nazi persecution and extermination of the European Jews. In other Nazi atrocities, for example the "euthanasia" program of murdering the mentally and physically handicapped, the genocide of the Sinti and Roma, the murder of Soviet prisoners of war, and the genocidal treatment of non-Jewish Poles, local populations played virtually no role other than that of victims. The Nazi campaign against the Jews, however, was a different matter. Because this campaign was waged throughout Europe, in occupied as well as collaborationist states, it provides the best example of the variety of roles that local populations could perform in Nazi crimes, and the effect, if any, of this participation on the nature and extent of Nazi atrocities.

Across Europe the degree of German control virtually always proved more important than the degree of collaboration on the part of local governments or populations. Whether and when the Nazis occupied a region, how soon they began to kill and deport the Jews of the region, and how early they were driven out by Allied armies nearly always determined the percentage of Jewish victims, regardless of the attitudes and behavior of the non-Jewish population. In addition to the relative insignificance of native anti-Semitism it is important to recognize that in every part of Europe, some individuals risked their lives to help Jews. While this fact does not outweigh the willing contributions of many local inhabitants to the Nazi "Final Solution," it serves as a reminder of the dangers of generalization. The fact that some citizens participated in Nazi atrocities does not mean that the population as a whole collaborated, particularly in view of the severe persecution that local populations frequently faced. Finally, a broad glance at the balance sheet of the Holocaust indicates that while the Nazis took advantage of preexisting anti-Semitism and the willingness of some local collaborations to participate in Nazi atrocities, their participation was not crucial. The Nazis were themselves all too willing and able to carry out their crimes, whether or not local populations assisted them.

The importance of direct German control is evident from the variation in death rates between occupied and collaborationist countries. In countries with collaborationist regimes, which might have been expected to contribute significantly to Nazi crimes, the percentage of Jews killed in the Holocaust was nearly always considerably less than in Nazi-occupied territories, where the local populations enjoyed far less freedom of action. The degree of direct control established by the Nazis was critical in determining the extent of the Holocaust in most cases: in the countries annexed or occupied longest by the Germans—for example, Czechoslovakia, Austria, Poland, the Baltic States, and Holland—the death rate for Jews ranged from 60 to 90 percent. In countries with collaborationist regimes where the Nazis moved late to deport the Jews, meanwhile—such as France, Italy, Norway, and Denmark—death tolls for Jews did not exceed 50

A UKRAINIAN GUARD RECALLS THE HOLOCAUST

Pavel Vladimirovich Leleko, a Ukrainian guard at the infamous Treblinka prison camp from September 1942 to September 1943, was interrogated on 20 February 1945 by Russian counterintelligence officers.

We started to unload the cars with the help of the so-called "blue crew" consisting of doomed prisoners wearing a blue armband on the sleeve.

Those arriving were told that they must first go to the bath house and will then be sent further to the Ukraine. But the sight of the camp, the enormous flaming pyre burning at one end of the camp, the suffocating stench from decomposing bodies that spread from some 10 km around and was particularly strong within the camp itself, made it clear what the place really was.

The people chased out of the cars with whips guessed immediately where they had been brought; some attempted to climb over the barbed wire of the fencing, got caught in it, and we opened fire on those who were trying to escape and killed them. We tried to quiet down the fear-crazed people with heavy clubs.

After all those who were able to walk had been unloaded, only the ailing, the killed and the wounded remained in the railroad cars. These were carried by the prisoners belonging to the "blue crew" into the so-called "infirmary," the name given to the place where the ailing and the wounded were shot and the dead were burned. This place became particularly crowded when the prisoners marked for death who were brought in the railroad cars attempted to commit suicide.

Thus in March 1943 there arrived a train in which half of the prisoners cut their throats and hands with razors. While unloading was going on, the prisoners cut themselves with knives and razors before the eyes of us, the policemen, saying: "anyhow you will kill us." The majority of those who did not die of self-inflicted wounds were shot. After the unloading, all those who could stand on their feet were chased toward the undressing place. There the women were separated from the men and pushed into a special barrack, while the men were told to undress right there outside another barrack.

During the first years of the existence of the camp, women and men undressed together in the same barrack. But it happened once that the prisoners attacked the "chief of the working crew" in the undressing barrack. Somehow the men managed to escape from there. Several policemen and Germans immediately rushed in. One of the Germans started firing into the crowd from his sub-machine gun. After they had stopped shooting, the Germans and the policemen started to beat with clubs and whips those who survived. After this incident, men were assigned to a special place in the open air in which to undress, by the barrack, across from the women's undressing place.

Pushed by the clubs of the Germans and the policemen, the men threw off their clothing, having first handed their valuables and money to a special "cashier's office." The women were obliged to remove their shoes before entering the undressing place. They were forced to remove all their clothing under the supervision of German policemen and prisoners of the so-called "red crew" [*sic*] Those who resisted were whipped. Very often the Germans and the policemen tore off and cut off the clothing of those who did not want to undress or undressed too slowly. Many women begged to be allowed to keep at least some clothing on their persons, but the German, [*sic*] smiling cynically, ordered them to undress "to the end."

The policemen or the workers threw to the ground and undressed those who refused to do so. The undressed women were told to hand over all their valuables and money to the "cashier's office." After this the women were driven in groups to another part of the barrack, where 50 prisoners–"hairdressers" were working. The women sat on a long bench and the "hairdressers" cut off their hair. The cut hair were [*sic*] packed in large bags and sent by trainloads to Germany. One of the Germans told me that in Germany they are used to fill mattresses, also for soft upholstery. He said that this hair make [*sic*] very good mattresses and the Germans buy them willingly.

After their hair was cut the women were sent in batches to the third section of the camp, to the "bath house," but in reality to the gas chamber to be exterminated there. Before entering the gas chamber building they passed along a long path bordered on both sides with a high fence made of barbed wire and branches. Along the edge of the path stood policemen and Germans. Each one held a whip or a club.

Source: *The Nizkor Project, Web Page.*

percent. In Romania, likewise, despite the lack of German occupation and despite the horrific killing of Jews by Romanians independent of Nazi initiatives, more than half of the Jews survived. Finally, in German-allied countries that the Germans never effectively occupied, Bulgaria and Finland, most Jews survived the war.

The variation in Jewish death rates demonstrates that the key variables were the degree of German commitment, and the amount of time available to the Germans to impose their will. The only major exception to this trend confirms the pattern: in Hungary, a German-allied country that the Germans occupied late in March 1944, 70 percent of Hungarian Jews perished. Yet, most Hungarian Jews were still alive by spring of 1944, constituting the last major group of Jews remaining in German-held territory. This fact, as well as the close proximity of the Auschwitz prison camp, made it possible for the Germans to concentrate their efforts against the Hungarian Jews. The atrocities carried out by the Hungarian Arrow Cross from late 1944 through early 1945, furthermore, were made possible by the German occupation, which deposed the Hungarian government and allowed a fascist Arrow Cross regime to seize power in October 1944.

As the Hungarian example demonstrates, the Germans were certainly not alone in their capacity to commit mass atrocities. Considerable numbers of local collaborators actively participated in the killing of Jews and Gypsies, especially in eastern Europe, where many thousands of local auxiliaries served in roving killing squads and as death-camp guards. In the wake of the German invasion of the Soviet Union, pogroms—instigated by the *Einsatzgruppen* (special action commandos)—also raged in the Baltic States and other parts of the occupied Soviet territories. However, as a percentage of the total population, the number of those who took an active part in atrocities was always low, and their criminality should not be assumed to be representative of the total population. Furthermore, the killing in the former Soviet territories took place in the context of a brutal war and occupation which itself followed on the heels of an extended period of chaos and political violence, including World War I (1914–1918), the Russian Revolution (1917–1920), and the Soviet annexation of Poland and the Baltic States (1939–1940). The susceptibility of many individuals to hatred and violence, while hardly justifiable, must be understood within this history and the immediate context for which the German invasion was largely responsible.

Michael R. Marrus has written, in *The Holocaust in History* (1987), that "murder on such a colossal scale involved the entire organization of society to one degree or another and depended on a measure of support everywhere" in Europe. Much of this support, however, came from collaborationist governments and their bureaucratic and security apparatuses in the deportation process, and not from the general population. While the Nazis recruited camp guards and executioners in eastern Europe, the actual numbers required were relatively small compared to the general population—and, it could be added, to their victims. Several hundred thousand men in the Einsatzgruppen and reserve police units were able to kill as many as two million people. The Treblinka death camp, in which roughly eight hundred thousand Jews perished, reportedly had a staff of about one hundred German and Ukrainian guards. While local auxiliaries indeed played a significant role in these crucial instruments of the Holocaust, the Nazis could have summoned the manpower on their own. The surprising ease with which they recruited killers from local populations in eastern Europe is certainly disturbing, but it was not a prerequisite to the murder campaign that the Nazis initiated.

In addition, it must be emphasized that despite the participation of eastern European collaborators in mass killings, atrocities on this scale would not have taken place without German facilitation. Murderous pogroms had ravaged the eastern European Jewish community in the recent past, but it took the Nazi invasion to transform this experience into a campaign of total annihilation. As documented by Raul Hilberg in *The Destruction of the European Jews* (1961), the commander of Einsatzgruppe A, General Walther Stahlecker, even reported that "to our surprise, it was not easy at first to set in motion an extensive pogrom against the Jews" because of a lack of enthusiasm on the part of non-Jewish Lithuanians; after some prodding, the latter were convinced to launch pogroms in which ten thousand Jews were slaughtered. In western Europe, with no tradition of state-sponsored murder, local populations were normally not directly involved in killing operations, though collaborators participated in the process of selection and deportation. In both western and eastern Europe, however, the key ingredients of mass murder were German initiative and commitment and not the relative involvement of the local population.

More generally, local populations across Europe demonstrated a discouraging indifference to the plight of Jews. This indifference may have simplified the Nazis' task of separating, deporting, and exterminating Jews. The failure of local populations to maintain solidarity with their Jewish fellow citizens was, however, the result not only of anti-Semitism, but also of genuine obstacles and conflicts of interests directly created by the Germans. Non-Jewish populations were also persecuted and were subjected to severe punishment and collective retribution for demonstrating solidarity with Jews. Non-Jewish resistance groups, especially in Poland, are often criticized for failing to offer more support to Jewish partisans. Yet, the desperation of Jewish resistance fighters, whose entire communities were being destroyed, often conflicted with the needs of non-Jewish resistance groups to build their (limited) strength and to wait for an opportune moment before rising up against the German occupiers. Anti-Semitism undoubtedly contributed to the lack of solidarity and the indifference of the people of occupied territories to the fate of their Jewish fellow citizens, but Nazi terror was more responsible for determining the behavior of local populations, as well as for the policies of persecution.

The question of significance has been dealt with here in historical, and not strictly moral, terms. There is no doubt that everywhere in Europe, more could have been done to help Jews, especially in collaborationist states, but also in occupied ones. Perhaps—though it seems unlikely under the circumstances of total German control—substantial opposition to the "Final Solution" could have made a difference. This argument is, however, counterfactual. If there had been such opposition, it might have been possible for local populations to have had a significant impact on the course of the Holocaust. In fact there was not, and therefore the role of local populations was ultimately insignificant to the outcome of the "Final Solution," which the Nazis alone had the means and the determination to carry out.

–DANIEL INKELAS, WASHTENAW
COMMUNITY COLLEGE

References

John Armstrong, "Collaboration in World War II: The Integral Nationalist Variant in Eastern Europe," *Journal of Modern History,* 40 (1968);

Randolph Braham, *The Politics of Genocide: The Holocaust in Hungary,* 2 volumes (New York: Columbia University Press, 1981);

Alexander Dallin, *German Rule in Russia, 1941–1945: A Study of Occupation Policies* (London: Macmillan; New York: St. Martin's Press, 1957);

Helen Fein, *Accounting for Genocide: National Responses and Jewish Victimization During the Holocaust* (New York: Free Press, 1979);

Daniel Jonah Goldhagen, *Hitler's Willing Executioners: Ordinary Germans and the Holocaust* (New York: Knopf, 1996);

Raul Hilberg, *The Destruction of the European Jews* (Chicago: Quadrangle Books, 1961);

Richard C. Lukas, *The Forgotten Holocaust: The Poles Under German Occupation, 1939–1944* (Lexington: University Press of Kentucky, 1986);

Michael R. Marrus, *The Holocaust in History* (Hanover, N.H.: Published for Brandeis University Press by University Press of New England, 1987);

Rolf-Dieter Müller and Gerd R. Ueberschär, *Hitler's War in the East, 1941–1945: A Critical Reassessment,* translated by Bruce D. Little (Providence: Berghahn Books, 1997);

George H. Stein, *The Waffen SS: Hitler's Elite Guard at War, 1939–1945* (Ithaca, N.Y.: Cornell University Press, 1966);

Nechama Tec, *When Light Pierced the Darkness: Christian Rescue of Jews in Nazi Occupied Poland* (New York: Oxford University Press, 1986);

Gerhard L. Weinberg, *A World At Arms: A Global History of World War II* (Cambridge & New York: Cambridge University Press, 1994);

Leni Yahil, *The Holocaust: The Fate of European Jewry, 1932–1945,* translated by Ina Friedman and Haya Galai (New York: Oxford University Press, 1990);

Susan Zuccotti, *The Holocaust, the French and the Jews* (New York: BasicBooks, 1993).

HOLOCAUST: THEORIES

Which of the explanations of the origins of the Holocaust is more compelling—the intentionalist or functionalist interpretation?

Viewpoint: From the beginning of his political career, Adolf Hitler had as his intention the elimination of all Jews from Europe.

Viewpoint: The functionalist interpretation of the origins and events of the Holocaust is most compelling, because Hitler seemed to have considered relocation of Jews rather than extermination as late as 1941.

The principle internal debate on the nature of the Holocaust involved positions known as "intentionalist" and "functionalist." The terms originally referred not to the Holocaust in particular, but to the general nature of the Nazi regime. First used in 1979 by British historian Tim Mason, they were nevertheless quickly adopted to describe two developing alternative perspectives on the Final Solution. The intentionalist position argued that it was Adolf Hitler's fixed purpose from virtually the beginning of his public career to kill as many Jews as possible. That postulate formed the core of his ideology. It was well understood not only by his intimates and lieutenants, but by increasing numbers of the German people at large. To the extent the Nazis employed the rhetoric of exclusion or expulsion prior to World War II they were speaking in what Lucy S. Dawidowicz, borrowing a concept from the nineteenth century Russian revolutionaries, called in *The War Against the Jews, 1933–1945* (1975), "Aesopian language"—transparent camouflage for genocidal intentions. Once the war began, Hitler proceeded to implement his intentions as quickly and comprehensively as possible, and at whatever cost.

From a functionalist perspective the road to Auschwitz was twisted rather than straight. Hitler, argued the functionalists, was neither sufficiently powerful or focused enough to implement a grand design. Indeed, he may well have meant some of his statements in 1940 and 1941 suggesting that Jews would eventually be resettled in a restricted part of Poland or on the island of Madagascar. Nazi anti-Semitic policies and programs were introduced haphazardly and piecemeal. Only as it became apparent that the war would continue longer than he had planned did Hitler allow the Nazi system to implement mass killing as a second-best solution of the "Jewish Question."

The ultimate shift from persecution to annihilation was Hitler's. There is no evidence that any of his subordinates, or any significant number of Germans, took any major initiatives in that direction. Nor, in the long history of anti-Semitism, had anyone invaded foreign countries with a primary avowed purpose of removing or killing Jews in those nations. Earlier genocides had been appetitive, satisfied after enough immediate victims had been exterminated. However deep was the Turkish commitment to exterminating Armenians, it did not extend to pursuing fugitives elsewhere in the Middle East or following them across the Atlantic. In that respect as in others, National Socialism and its leader were sui generis.

Viewpoint:
From the beginning of his political career, Adolf Hitler had as his intention the elimination of all Jews from Europe.

The destruction of the European Jews was a massive operation that required the coordination of every branch of government and the participation of many thousands of individual perpetrators. No single person could have planned or carried out such a project. The root cause of the Holocaust, however, was Adolf Hitler, whose rabid and unwavering anti-Semitism demanded a "final solution" to the Jewish problem. Hitler made the persecution of the Jews a chief goal of the Nazi state, launched the war that made possible the destruction of all the Jews in Europe, and almost certainly issued the direct order to commence mass murder. Without the inspired collaboration of his lieutenants in the Nazi regime, Hitler could not have carried out the Final Solution, but without Hitler's implacable will to destroy and without his absolute authority, the Final Solution would not have been possible.

"Functionalist" historians argue that external factors and the function of competing agencies and individuals within the Nazi regime stimulated the evolution of the Final Solution. While the functionalist interpretation tells us a great deal about how the Final Solution came to be, the best answer to why the Nazis contemplated and carried out this campaign is that Hitler's fanatical anti-Semitism demanded a total solution. Hitler was never satisfied with the attempts of the *Schutzstaffeln* (SS) and others to solve the Jewish problem prior to 1941, because the only solution that would satisfy him is what his ideology implicitly demanded from the outset: the physical destruction of the Jews. Hitler signaled every key development in the "cumulative radicalization" of Jewish policy, culminating in 1941 with the decision to murder all the Jews in Europe. Hitler's political career after 1918 was focused on working out the problem of how to destroy the Jews. Before 1941 this task was impossible; at the moment it became feasible, with the invasion of the Soviet Union, Hitler's men set into motion the process of planning and implementing his Final Solution.

The centrality and severity of anti-Semitism to Hitler's worldview, from at least the beginning of his political career to the bitter end, is beyond question. At the beginning of his political career, Hitler railed against the "Jewish-Marxist poison" that he blamed for Germany's World War I defeat, vowing to pour "hatred, burning hatred . . . into the souls of our millions of fellow

Germans." He demanded "the removal of the Jews from the midst of our people." In 1924 Hitler came to view these earlier statements regarding the Jews as "soft," concluding at this time that "the most severe methods of fighting will have to be used to let us come through successfully." This radicalization is apparent in his psychotic ranting in *Mein Kampf* (1925), in which he repeatedly describes the Jew as a parasite, a bacillus, a plague, the defiler of the German race, and destroyer of civilizations. Hitler remarked ominously at the conclusion of his book that if "twelve or fifteen thousand of these Hebraic corrupters of the nation had been subjected to poison gas [during World War I] . . . then the sacrifice of millions at the front would not have been in vain." Through to his vitriolic last will and testament of April 1945, Hitler remained fixated on the Jews as the source of all evil; their destruction was central to the realization of all of Hitler's ideological goals.

Despite the evidence of Hitler's committed, radical anti-Semitism, functionalist historians argue that Hitler was inattentive to detail generally, and specifically indifferent to anti-Jewish measures during the 1930s. Yet, at every key stage in the intensification of Nazi policy towards the Jews during the Third Reich, Hitler played a critical role. In 1935 a last-minute decision by Hitler at the Nazi Party rally in September precipitated the drafting of the Nuremberg Laws, which established a pseudoracial definition of Jews and stripped Jews of German citizenship. In 1937, Hitler's announcement to military leaders of the accelerated timetable for war provided a signal for Hermann Göring and Heinrich Himmler to intensify their anti-Jewish programs of Aryanization and forced emigration. In November 1938, Hitler's anger over the assassination by a young Jewish man of a German official in Paris provided the opportunity for Reich Minister of Propaganda Joseph Goebbels to instigate the *Kristallnacht* (Night of Broken Glass) pogrom on 9 November. Finally, in 1941, Hitler gave the order to exterminate Soviet Jews and later, almost certainly, for the extermination of all European Jews. Hitler instigated or authorized every major policy shift regarding the Jews, even when he left the details to his subordinates.

Why did Hitler wait so long before revealing his murderous intentions? The answer may well be that he himself was incapable of imagining such an unprecedented undertaking as the extermination of an entire people. Clearly, even if he had developed a concrete plan for mass murder, it would have been impossible to achieve before 1941. In January 1939, Hitler explained that "politics is in effect the art of the possible." Five days later he issued before the *Reichstag*

Heinrich Himmler and Rudolf Hess discussing a model of the Dachua concentration camp, 8 May 1936

(Bundesarchiv Koblenz, Germany)

(German Parliament) the prophetic warning that the imminent war would bring about "the annihilation of the Jewish race in Europe." The coming war that Hitler had, indisputably, planned from his earliest days in the Nazi Party, was to provide him the opportunity to take revenge upon the Jews for Germany's defeat in World War I.

The chief components of Hitler's world view from the start of his political career were the destruction of the Jews, the attainment of *Lebensraum* (Living Space) in eastern Europe, and a victorious war to reverse the Treaty of Versailles (1919) and destroy what he saw as the Jewish-Bolshevist Soviet Union. These ideological goals were inextricably linked in his own mind. On the day World War II began, 1 September 1939, Hitler vowed that "a November 1918 shall never repeat itself in German history." Significantly, he would make frequent references over the next five years to his January 1939 Reichstag speech, remembering its date incorrectly as 1 September. In March 1941, Hitler instructed his followers on the nature of the campaign to be launched against the Soviet Union, a brutal war of annihilation that would include at the outset the killing of Jews and political commissars. In October 1941, as construction on the first death camps began, Hitler asserted that "when we finally stamp out this plague [of Jewry], we shall have accomplished for mankind a deed whose significance our men out there on the battlefield cannot even imagine yet." While the extermination of the Jews would thus serve the war effort, the war provided the "aura of terror" that Hitler himself admitted was an important precondition for the Holocaust.

Whether Hitler had consciously decided to kill the Jews by 1920, by 1941, or at some other date, cannot be precisely determined from existing documentation. The evidence assembled by functionalist historians demonstrates quite clearly that many Nazi officials, including top-ranking ones, pursued policies short of, and in apparent contradiction to, mass murder between 1933 and 1941; no concrete plan for the mass murder of the European Jews had been developed within the Nazi regime, certainly, prior to 1941. When this plan did emerge, however, it emerged because Hitler had established the destruction of the Jewish enemy as the chief goal of the Nazi state, and because he gave an order authorizing this destruction by means of mass murder. The evidence suggests that Hitler decided between the summer and fall of 1941 to solve his self-defined Jewish question by murdering all the Jews in Europe; that he conveyed this order, probably orally, to Himmler and others; and that Hitler, therefore, was primarily responsible for the emergence of the Final Solution that followed.

—DANIEL INKELAS, WASHTENAW COMMUNITY COLLEGE

Viewpoint:
The functionalist interpretation of the origins and events of the Holocaust is most compelling, because Hitler seemed to have considered relocation of Jews rather than extermination as late as 1941.

The role and importance of ideology in the Third Reich remains a central point of contention among contemporary historians. The debate over Adolf Hitler's "absolute" or "proscribed" power within the Third Reich led to conflicting portrayals of the führer as either the "Master in the Third Reich" (Norman Rich) or Germany's "weak dictator" (Hans Mommsen). Beginning in the mid 1960s, the questions concerning Hitler's role and the function of National Socialist ideology in the events of the Holocaust led to the division of academic positions into two competing camps denoted by the terms "intentionalism" (sometimes referred to as Hitler-centrism) and functionalism/structuralism. The former position identified the wellspring of the annihilation of the European Jews in "Hitler's obsessed mind," in which, according to Lucy S. Dawidowicz in *The War Against the Jews, 1933–1945* (1975), "the Jews were the demonic hosts whom he had been given a divine mission to destroy." The functionalist position found expression in the contention that under Hitler "the Nazis stumbled toward something resembling a Final Solution to the Jewish Problem." In truth, the construction of the gas chambers at Auschwitz did not emerge from a master blueprint developed in the mind of a failed artist and amateur architect before his accession to power, but rather, the plans for the destruction of the European Jews were sketched line-by-line over the course of several years.

The debate between "intentionalists" and "functionalists" was at times heated and charged with emotion. On one point, however, most intentionalists and functionalists agreed: both sides recognized the central role played by Hitler's anti-Semitism in the destruction of eleven million European Jews and other racial "undesirables" during World War II. Although Hitler's anti-Semitism provided the motive force for annihilation, the path to genocide was marked by a series of spontaneous and ad hoc measures in the period between 1933 and 1945. Indeed, a chronological review of National Socialist actions against the Jews offers critical insights that help to explain the course of the Holocaust. If, as Daniel Jonah Goldhagen argues in *Hitler's Willing Executioners: Ordinary Germans and the Holo-*caust (1996), the German people as a whole embraced a philosophy of "eliminationist anti-Semitism" already by 1933, then one can hardly explain the nine-year interval between the Nazi "seizure of power" in January 1933 and the official declaration of the "Final Solution to the Jewish problem" presented to senior government officials at the Wannsee Conference in January 1942. In fact, the nine-year interval between these two events resulted because of the lack of a long-range or specific plan for dealing with German Jews. Instead, the diffuse and overlapping governmental structures within the Third Reich led to the emergence of numerous competing power centers including the military, the *Schutzstaffeln* (SS) and Police complex, *Nationalsozialistische Deutsche Arbeiterpartei* (Nazi Party) organizations, and big business. To say that Hitler promoted this type of system involving a bureaucratic "survival of the fittest" is not to say that he could in turn foresee or even dictate the direction of the policies taken by these disparate organizations.

The ad hoc or "polycratic" nature of National Socialist policies in the period between 1933 and 1945 clearly emerges when one views the specific measures taken against German Jews. These policies involved an incremental radicalization that began with discrimination, led to exclusion and persecution, and eventually resulted in annihilation. For example, on 1 April 1933, The Reich Minister of Propaganda Josef Goebbels organized a boycott of businesses owned by German Jews. Members of the *Sturm Abteilung* (SA, Storm Troops) and SS stationed themselves in front of Jewish-owned businesses in an attempt to intimidate shoppers from entering. The measure was aimed at the financial livelihood of the shop owners, but carried out under the restriction that "no harm was to be done to any Jew." A further initiative, the passage of the Law for the Restoration of the Professional Civil Service on 7 April 1933 provided the legal pretext for the National Socialists to summarily dismiss or demote civil servants on political, racial, or ideological grounds. Accordingly, the Nazis used the law to dismiss Jews, Social Democrats, and others from positions of authority. Still, exceptions were made within the ranks of the civil service, as in the case of those who had served in the military during World War I. The aim and extent of these initial steps, although clearly discriminatory, can hardly be construed as the inevitable precursors to annihilation. Indeed, the fact that exceptions were made and opportunities were available to German Jews to emigrate (opportunities that existed until 1941) highlighted the limited objectives of National Socialist policies in 1933.

THE JEWISH QUESTION

On 30 January 1939, Adolf Hitler gave a speech in response to international criticism of his government's treatment of Jews, a portion of which appears here.

When the German nation was, thanks to the inflation instigated and carried through by Jews, deprived of the entire savings which it had accumulated in years of honest work, when the rest of the world took away the German nation's foreign investments, when we were divested of the whole of our colonial possessions, these philanthropic considerations evidently carried little noticeable weight with democratic statesmen. . . .

Above all, German culture, as its name alone shows, is German and not Jewish, and therefore its management and care will be entrusted to members of our own nation. If the rest of the world cries out with a hypocritical mien against this barbaric expulsion from Germany of such an irreplaceable and culturally eminently valuable element, we can only be astonished at the conclusions they draw from this situation. For how thankful they must be that we are releasing these precious apostles of culture, and placing them at the disposal of the rest of the world. In accordance with their own declarations they cannot find a single reason to excuse themselves for refusing to receive this most valuable race in their own countries. Nor can I see a reason why the members of this race should be imposed upon the German nation, while in the States, which are so enthusiastic about these "splendid people," their settlement should suddenly be refused with every imaginable excuse. I think that the sooner this problem is solved the better; for Europe cannot settle down until the Jewish question is cleared up. It may very well be possible that sooner or later an agreement on this problem may be reached in Europe, even between those nations which otherwise do not so easily come together.

The world has sufficient space for settlements, but we must once and for all get rid of the opinion that the Jewish race was only created by God for the purpose of being in a certain percentage a parasite living on the body and the productive work of other nations. The Jewish race will have to adapt itself to sound constructive activity as other nations do, or sooner or later it will succumb to a crisis of an inconceivable magnitude. . . .

Today I will once more be a prophet: If the international Jewish financiers in and outside Europe should succeed in plunging the nations once more into a world war, then the result will not be the Bolshevization of the earth, and thus the victory of Jewry, but the annihilation of the Jewish race in Europe!

Source: *"Hitler & The Jewish Question," in* The Speeches of Adolf Hitler, April 1922–August 1939, *volume 1, edited by Norman H. Baynes (London and New York: Oxford University Press, 1942), pp. 737–741.*

The period between 1933 and 1935 certainly witnessed the social ostracism of many German Jews as well as episodic incidences of violence directed at members within the Jewish community. Still, some Nazi leaders condemned these acts as in the case of the Munich *Gauleiter* (District Leader) Adolph Wagner, who described the unauthorized actions by members of the SA who had destroyed several Jewish-owned shops as "criminal" and "anti-Semitic trespassing." Likewise, Reich Economic Minister Hjalmar Schacht openly appealed for an end to attacks on Jewish economic enterprises. It must be noted, however, that both Wagner and Schacht opposed the actions of the SA not on humanitarian, but simply economic grounds. Still, their protests demonstrated the then still limited scope of Nazi policies with respect to the Jews.

The Nuremberg Party rally in September 1935 set the stage for the de jure exclusion of Jews from German society. Hitler expressed exactly this sentiment with his declaration that "The only way to deal with the problem which remains open is that of legislative action." The Nuremberg Laws essentially stripped German Jews of their civil and political liberties by reclassifying them as *Staatsangehöriger* (subjects of the state) versus *Reichsbürger* (citizens of the Reich). Additional legislation prohibited them from flying the Nazi flag, restricted sexual relations between Jews and non-Jews, and forbade Jews from employing "Aryan" domestic servants below the age of forty-five. Clearly, the Nuremberg Laws provided a "legal" pretext for the exclusion of Jews from German society; however, the formulation of the legislation can in no way be considered the result of a premeditated plan. Indeed, the jurist responsible for preparing the laws, Dr. Bernard Lösener, was hastily summoned to Nuremberg and given less than twenty-four hours to draft the legislation. In the final analysis, the Nuremberg Laws signaled an incremental but additional radicalization of Nazi policies with respect to the Jews.

By 1938 the policy of statutory exclusion gave way to acts of open persecution. In the wake of the assassination of a German diplomatic official by a Polish Jew in Paris on 7 November 1938, Goebbels organized a nationwide pogrom aimed at German Jews, Jewish businesses, and synagogues. Sporadic violence erupted on 8 November and intensified on the night of 9 November as members of the SA and SS viciously attacked and summarily arrested Jews. In addition, the SA and SS destroyed hundreds of Jewish stores, ransacked Jewish homes, and burned synagogues throughout Germany. The *Kristallnacht* (Night of Broken Glass) left not only thousands of shards of smashed store windows in streets throughout Germany, but the attacks also caused the deaths of hundreds of Jews (murders and suicides) and the incarceration of thirty thousand people in concentration camps at Dachau, Sachsenhausen, and Buchenwald. The events of November 1938 signaled a further radicalization of Nazi policies with respect to the Jews—it would not be, however, the last. German Jews had suffered discrimination, exclusion, and persecution. The events associated with World War II and the National Socialist dream of *Lebensraum* (living space) stretching into Russia and eastern Europe provided the impetus for a further radicalization of racial policy, embracing the annihilation not only of German Jews, but all European Jews.

As *Wehrmacht* (German army) units invaded Poland on 1 September 1939, the search for solutions to the "Jewish problem" began to undergo a transformation in which annihilation took the place of persecution. Still, the exact method for achieving the destruction of the European Jews remained an open question. One solution involved the creation of forced labor camps in which the Jews would be literally worked to death. For example, the National Socialist leadership viewed the Lublin Reservation, a region of three hundred to four hundred square miles located in German-occupied Poland, as a potential area where the rigors of forced labor might be used, in the words of the senior Nazi leader Arthur Seyss-Inquart, to "cause a considerable decimation of the Jews." In the summer of 1940, in the wake of the surrender of France, the Reich Leader of the SS and Chief of the German Police Heinrich Himmler displayed renewed interest in a plan aimed at the forced migration of European Jews to the French island of Madagascar. The island would essentially become a giant concentration camp manned by members of the *Sicherheitspolizei* (German Security Police). Barring German control of the seas, however, the Madagascar Plan remained a dead letter.

The German invasion of the Soviet Union on 22 June 1941 proved a fateful moment for the Jews of Europe. Although historians have offered competing explanations concerning the motivation for the Final Solution, as well as different time horizons, the majority point to the attack on Russia or the preparations for it as the critical event that initiated the final radicalization of National Socialist racial policies. For example, the American historian Christopher R. Browning persuasively argued in *The Path to Genocide: Essays on Launching the Final Solution* (1992) that the decision for the Final Solution was made in July 1941 as Hitler, euphoric in the face of an apparent rapid victory over the Soviet Union, approved the murder of the Jews. In *Why did the Heavens not Darken?: The "Final Solution" in History* (1988), Arno J. Mayer offered a competing explanation in which the destruction of the Jews emerged as a byproduct of the National Socialist ideological "crusade" against communism and the apparent failure of the German invasion in the fall of 1941. Mayer viewed the failure of the offensive as the catalyst for genocide—an interpretation in which desperation and not premeditation provided the rationale for annihilation.

Without question, the opening of a *Vernichtungskrieg* (war of annihilation) on the Eastern Front in which quarter was neither asked nor given provided the framework not only for Hitler's vision of an eastern empire, but also the blueprint for genocide. The instruments of annihilation included the *Einsatzgruppen* (special action commandos), the forces of the *Ordnungspolizei* (uniformed police) and the Wehrmacht, as well as the efforts of thousands of mid-level bureaucrats. It is clear that the decision for the "Final Solution to the Jewish Question," however, emerged over a period of time in which the search for an answer to the "Jewish problem" led to ever more radical solutions. The route to the death camps was not run by express trains according to a preordained timetable established in the 1920s by a single man. The journey to the gates of Auschwitz resulted from a series of incremental and increasingly more-radical decisions made at all levels of the Third Reich's bureaucracy. This fact in no way lessens the enormity of the crimes committed under the National Socialist dictatorship; it does, however, demonstrate the danger posed when one takes the first step down the slippery slope along the "twisted road" to annihilation.

—EDWARD B. WESTERMANN, UNIVERSITY OF NORTH CAROLINA, CHAPEL HILL

References

Götz Aly and Susanne Heim, *Vordenker der Vernichtung: Auschwitz und die deutschen Pläne für eine neue europäische Ordnung* (Hamburg: Hoffman & Campe, 1991);

Peter Baldwin, ed., *Reworking the Past: Hitler, the Holocaust, and the Historians' Debate* (Boston: Beacon, 1990);

Richard Breitman, *The Architect of Genocide: Himmler and the Final Solution* (New York: Knopf, 1991);

Martin Broszat, "Hitler und der Genesis der 'Endlösung'," *Vierteljahreshefte für Zeitgeschichte,* 25 (1977): 739–775;

Christopher R. Browning, *The Path to Genocide: Essays on Launching the Final Solution* (Cambridge & New York: Cambridge University Press, 1992);

Philippe Burrin, *Hitler et les juifs: gen'ese d'un genocide* (Paris: Seuil, 1989), translated by Patsy Southgate as *Hitler and the Jews: The Genesis of the Holocaust* (London: Edward Arnold, 1994);

Lucy S. Dawidowicz, *The War Against the Jews, 1933-1945* (New York: Holt, Rinehart & Winston, 1975);

Gerald Fleming, *Hitler und die Endlösung: "Es ist des Fuhrers Wunsch . . ."* (Wiesbaden: Limes, 1982), translated as *Hitler and the Final Solution* (Berkeley: University of California Press, 1984);

Daniel Jonah Goldhagen, *Hitler's Willing Executioners: Ordinary Germans and the Holocaust* (New York: Knopf, 1996);

Adolf Hitler, *The Speeches of Adolf Hitler, April 1922–August 1939,* volume 1, edited by Norman H. Baynes (London & New York: Oxford University Press, 1942);

Eberhard Jäckel, *Hitler's Weltanschauung: Entwurf einer Herrschaft* (Tubingen: R. Wunderlich, 1969), translated by Herbert Arnold as *Hitler's World View: A Blueprint for Power* (Cambridge, Mass.: Harvard University Press, 1981);

Victor Klemperer, *Ich will Zeugnis ablegen bis zum letzten* (Berlin: Aufbau-Verlag, 1995), translated by Martin Chalmers as *I Will Bear Witness: A Diary of the Nazi Years, 1933-1941* (New York: Random House, 1998);

Michael R. Marrus, "The History of the Holocaust: A Survey of Recent Literature," *Journal of Modern History,* 59 (1997): 114–160;

Marrus, *The Holocaust in History* (Hanover, N.H.: Published for Brandeis University Press by University Press of New England, 1987);

Arno J. Mayer, *Why did the Heavens not Darken?: The "Final Solution" in History* (New York: Pantheon, 1988);

Hans Mommsen, "The Realization of the Unthinkable: The 'Final Solution of the Jewish Question' in the Third Reich," in *The Policies of Genocide: Jews and Soviet Prisoners of War in Nazi Germany,* edited by Gerhard Hirschfeld (London: Allen & Unwin, 1986);

Karl A. Schleunes, *The Twisted Road to Auschwitz: Nazi Policy Towards German Jews, 1933-1939* (Urbana: University of Illinois Press, 1970);

Leni Yahil, *The Holocaust: The Fate of European Jewry, 1932-1945,* translated by Ina Friedman and Haya Galai (New York: Oxford University Press, 1990).

ITALIAN CAMPAIGN

How important to Allied strategy was the invasion of Italy?

Viewpoint: Though not without controversy, the decision to invade Italy was useful for the overall strategy to defeat Germany because it forced Adolf Hitler after 1944 to fight on three fronts.

Viewpoint: The invasion of Italy had no strategic value and represented a drain on both men and matériel for the Allies.

The Allied invasion of Italy in 1943 was part diplomacy by other means, part practice for the main event in northwest Europe, and part a consequence of circumstance. In the context of Joseph Stalin's ever more strident demands for a second front, invading Italy at least put the Western allies on the European continent. In the context of the complex demands of amphibious landings against effective opposition, Italy offered a chance to refine techniques and acquire experience. Moreover, in the aftermath of the North African and Sicilian campaigns, Allied forces in the Mediterranean were too large to remain inactive. Winston Churchill's metaphor of Italy as the "soft underbelly" of the Axis is easily mocked in the context of geography, to say nothing of subsequent events. However, in 1943 Italy was an active belligerent with a still-powerful fleet, whose presence in the war gave Germany a strategic glacis difficult for the Allies to ignore.

The real question of the Italian campaign is whether it was pursued beyond profitable limits. Italy's volte-face in the summer of 1943 achieved one of the campaign's major objectives. Yet, the rapid German reaction, and the subsequent decision to fight for the peninsula rather than execute an economy-of-force-withdrawal to the Po Valley or the Alps, confronted the Western allies with a mile-by-mile advance into some of the most formidable terrain in Europe—terrain that in good part neutralized Allied advantages in mobility and firepower, contested by an enemy that proved a master of defensive operations.

In spite of these problems, the Italian campaign generated and sustained its own momentum. The option of closing down this theater was never seriously considered. The assertion that the Italian campaign tied down German troops that might have been employed elsewhere is dubious—particularly in the context of the number of Allied divisions committed to Italy relative to the total number available. The withdrawal of divisions and landing craft for the 1944 invasion of southern France has been described as eliminating the possibility of short amphibious end runs up the peninsula. However, given the experiences of Anzio—or for that matter Normandy—nothing suggests that either Allied troops or Allied generals were particularly well suited to that kind of warfare. Moreover, four of the divisions transferred in 1944 were French, and correspondingly unusable anywhere else once the Normandy invasion was accomplished. The Italian campaign, in short, may best be epitomized by the title of an 1862 Italian opera, Giuseppe Verdi's *La Forza del Destino* (The Force of Destiny).

Viewpoint:
Though not without controversy, the decision to invade Italy was useful for the overall strategy to defeat Germany because it forced Adolf Hitler after 1944 to fight on three fronts.

The Allied drive for the liberation of Italy is one of the great epics of World War II. The savage campaign up the Italian peninsula was a long, exhausting, and depressing military operation. Even today controversy surrounds the strategic decision to engage the Germans in the Mediterranean theater. The discord was marked by several poorly conceived command decisions and coalition politics exhibited by the Allied leaders and their military commanders. To mention a few that are debatable were the landing on the Gulf of Salerno, the Anzio-Rapido Campaign, the obliterating aerial bombing of the world-treasured abbey at Monte Cassino, and the battle for the Eternal City. Nevertheless, the strategic decision to invade Italy contributed to the Allied effort to defeat Germany, especially on the Western Front.

With the defeat of Axis forces in Tunisia in May 1943, the question of how to eliminate Italy and when, or to pursue with the cross-Channel invasion of France, became a debatable strategic issue between the two Allied leaders, President Franklin D. Roosevelt and Prime Minister Winston Churchill and their Combined Chiefs of Staff. Earlier, during the January 1943 Casablanca Conference, Allied leaders plotted their next military operations against Sicily. At the second Washington Conference in May, it was agreed to undertake Churchill's strategic preference for "the soft underbelly of the Axis," the Italian mainland. In a spirit of compromise the cross-Channel invasion was postponed until 1944. The grand strategic aim was to provide the unrestricted use of the Mediterranean region for invaluable sites for air bases, establish control of the Adriatic Sea for potential Balkan operations, provide easy access to Near East oil, and sustain a supply line to the Soviet Union. Most importantly, the plan was to force Italy from the war and draw much needed German troops and resources from other fronts and occupied territories before the cross-Channel invasion of France.

On 10 July 1943, the 15th Army Group, under the command of British ground force commander, General Harold Alexander, launched a surprise landing on Sicily with General Bernard L. Montgomery's Eighth Army and Lieutenant General George S. Patton's Seventh Army. By 17 August all of Sicily was secured in spite of tenacious German resistance. The Italian Army, however, showed little desire to fight and began a mass exodus to the mainland. During the Sicilian campaign, the war-weary Italians deposed their dictator, Benito Mussolini. His successor, the inept Marshall Pietro Badoglio, then sued for peace, which was granted on 3 September. As a result, the German commander in southern Italy, Field Marshal Albert Kesselring, secured Rome and ruthlessly began to disarm the Italians. With the fall of Sicily, the German southern command calculated that the Allies' next move would be an early invasion at Salerno.

On 3 September, the 15th Army Group began the invasion of the mainland with Montgomery's experienced Eighth Army landing on the toe of the Italian boot. Six days later the inexperienced U.S. Fifth Army landed at Salerno with the objective to seize the vital port of Naples, thus preventing Kesselring from establishing a coherent front. The Fifth Army was under the command of Lieutenant General Mark W. Clark, whom Patton disliked.

It was apparent that the Allies underestimated the speed of Kesselring's reaction and the determined resistance of the German Tenth Army commanded by Generaloberst Heinrich von Vietinghoff. Von Vietinghoff's position was strengthened by the mountains ringing Salerno and the ability of the Germans to funnel forces more quickly by land than the Allies could by sea. Clark's Fifth Army was in a precarious position facing reembarkation before Montgomery's army reached Salerno from the south. To avoid defeat, Alexander ordered in reinforcements, a heavy concentration of naval gunfire, and aerial bombing. The crisis ended on 16 September with the junction of Montgomery's and Clark's armies. By 1 October the large airfield complex around Foggia and the vital port of Naples had fallen to the Allies. Now it was Kesselring's plan to retreat slowly northward to link up with Field Marshal Erwin Rommel's Army Group in northern Italy in order to establish a defensive line in the Northern Apennines. In spite of being inferior at sea and in the air, the Germans began a classic defensive campaign of delay and attrition warfare brought about by the skill and initiative of Kesselring and his troops.

Meanwhile, the Allies doggedly battled up the Italian boot with the Fifth Army on the Mediterranean side, and the Eight Army on the Adriatic side. Hitler now ordered a change in Kesselring's plans, ordering him to stop the Allies south of Rome. By December the Allies had reached the formidable German defenses south of Rome known as the Winter or Gustav Line, which was a series of in-depth defensive positions, augmented by natural obstacles of riv-

The monastery at Monte Cassino before and after the Allied bombardment in February 1944

(Polish Institute, Sikorsly Museum)

ers and mountains. The critical strategic position was the summit of Monte Cassino, the gateway to Rome through the Liri Valley, beyond which was more suitable terrain for exploitation by armored forces. It was Kesselring's purpose to checkmate Clark and General Oliver Leese, who had replaced Montgomery, with Vietinghoff's Tenth Army and Generaloberst Eberhard von Mackensen's quickly improvised Fourteenth Army. Some of the toughest fighting of the campaign now occurred in this mountainous terrain combined with severe weather conditions. By mid-January 1944, the Allies had been severely battered by determined German resistance.

Alexander, with Churchill's approval, now set in motion an ambitious plan to deal with the impasse. Alexander proposed to outflank the Gustav Line with a frontal attack along the Rapido-Cassino Front with Clark's Fifth Army, while the British Eighth Army put pressure on the Germans on the Adriatic coast in the east. Concurrently, the U.S. VI Corps, under the command of Major General John Lucas, would effect a sea landing on 22 January at Anzio-Nettuno behind the Gustav Line. On 17 January the frontal assaults began and in a few days reached a disheartening stalemate. One of the frontal assaults during this period demonstrated an example of an unsound tactical operation when Clark and Major General Geoffrey Keyes, U.S. II Corps commander, ordered the 36th "Texas" Division to force one of the strongest sectors of the Gustav Line, the marshy Rapido River. The massed firepower of the 15th Panzer Grenadiers cut the American troops to shreds. The decision to cross the river in spite of the division commander's warning to Clark and Keyes on the unsoundness of the attack prompted a congressional investigation after the war.

Meanwhile, the effort at Anzio to outflank the Gustav Line and make a quick breakout toward the Alban Hills south of Rome with the final objective to liberate the Eternal City had failed. Lucas instead preferred to consolidate his beachhead even though he landed most of his forces in forty-eight hours without opposition. The VI Corps commander's offensive inaction was swayed by Clark's reminder of his Salerno agony, advising Lucas not to take reckless chances. Lucas's hesitation allowed for a continued and frantic German buildup, with reinforcements coming from Germany and their occupied countries. One officer, who, in haste, had just arrived at Anzio from Germany, wrote that early in the landings the Germans did not have much of a chance if the Americans attacked. He noted that many German formations were ad hoc units that lacked initial organizational cohesion and heavy weapons to deal with the landings. He believed an aggressive commander such as Patton could have taken Rome with little effort early in the landings.

The expanded Fourteenth Army now pinned the VI Corps to a narrow beachhead, attempting to push the beleaguered Allied troops into the sea. In spite of heavy German counterattacks in deplorable weather conditions, the Allied forces held due to the tenacity of the troops, timely naval gunfire, and air support. Lucas's faintheartedness, however, was no qualification for command. As a result, he was relieved and replaced by the more forceful U.S. 3rd Infantry Division commander, Major General Lucian K. Truscott Jr. In fairness to Lucas, the Anzio landing was conceived on too small a scale and was restrained by logistics demands for sea transportation required to support the upcoming amphibious landings in France. In addition, Allied air support was overextended because of the two fronts, Anzio and Cassino. As it turned out, none of the primary objectives were achieved.

Alexander, in the meantime, attempted to relieve the pressure at Anzio by mounting a series of costly frontal battles along the Gustav Line around Cassino where the medieval Benedictine abbey was the key toward further progress towards Rome. Though no Germans occupied Monte Cassino proper, (only the ridge below it), Alexander, with Clark's concurrence, authorized its saturation bombing beginning on 15 February. The bombing turned the abbey into rubble. The ruptured enemy defenses, however, were not immediately attacked with ground forces. Thus, the Germans, now with excellent cover among the debris, were again able to repel the attackers.

The tactical stalemate continued until May when Alexander, now with sufficient reinforcements and the benefit of an intense Allied air interdiction campaign, was able to concentrate most of his forces on his left flank for an overwhelming offensive designed to destroy the right wing of the German Tenth Army and the Fourteenth Army. Alexander's full-scale frontal attack between Cassino and the sea surprised the defenders, in part because the Allies continued to gain intelligence derived from deciphered enemy communiqués, and because the Germans did not properly reconnoiter the Allied positions. After many grueling and bloody months, a linkup with the VI Corps at Anzio had finally occurred. This operation opened the advance to Rome and the possible capitulation of German forces, especially the Tenth Army. The Rome campaign, however, led to another operational controversy that entangled coalition leadership.

After the linkup at Anzio, Alexander ordered Clark's Fifth Army to turn with sufficient aggressiveness against the German bridgehead at Valmontone just south of the strategic Alban Hills and block the escape of the German Tenth Army. The Tenth Army now seemed doomed. However, Clark avoided the battle of annihilation for a geographical (as well as political) objective. He shifted his effort, directing his main body toward Rome. This shift allowed most of the German forces to retreat and avoid annihilation. Churchill called Clark's actions unfortunate. Alexander later chastised Clark for not executing his military plan for destroying German forces south of Rome. A German Panzer corps commander at the time was also critical of Clark for not sticking to Alexander's plan. There was nothing at the time, he noted, to prevent defeat of the retreating Germans forces. On 4 June Clark, along with his usual entourage of photographers, entered Rome, two days ahead of the massive cross-Channel Normandy landings, now the more important strategic effort to defeat Germany in the West.

ITALIAN CAMPAIGN

THE ARMISTICE WITH ITALY

Fairfield Camp

Sicily

September 3, 1943

The following conditions of an Armistice are presented by General Dwight D. Eisenhower, Commander-in-Chief of the Allied Forces, acting by authority of the Governments of the United States and Great Britain and in the interest of the United Nations, and are accepted by Marshal Pietro Badoglio, Head of the Italian Government.

1. Immediate cessation of all hostile activity by the Italian armed forces.

2. Italy will use its best endeavors to deny, to the Germans, facilities that might be used against the United Nations.

3. All prisoners or internees of the United Nations to be immediately turned over to the Allied Commander in Chief, and none of these may now or at any time be evacuated to Germany.

4. Immediate transfer of the Italian fleet and Italian aircraft to such points as may be designated by the Allied Commander in Chief, with details of disarmament to be prescribed by him.

5. Italian merchant shipping may be requisitioned by the Allied Commander in Chief to meet the needs of his military-naval program.

6. Immediate surrender of Corsica and of all Italian territory, both islands and mainland, to the Allies, for such use as operational bases and other purposes as the Allies may see fit.

7. Immediate guarantee of the free use by the Allies of all airfields and naval ports in Italian territory, regardless of the rate of evacuation of the Italian territory by the German forces. These ports and fields to be protected by Italian armed forces until this function is taken over by the Allies.

8. Immediate withdrawal to Italy of Italian armed forces from all participation in the current war from whatever areas in which they may be now engaged.

9. Guarantee by the Italian Government that if necessary it will employ all its available armed forces to insure prompt and exact compliance with all the provisions of this armistice.

10. The Commander in Chief of the Allied Forces reserves to himself the right to take any measure which in his opinion may be necessary for the protection of the interests of the Allied Forces for the prosecution of the war, and the Italian Government binds itself to take such administrative or other action as the Commander in Chief may require, and in particular the Commander in Chief will establish Allied Military Government over such parts of Italian territory as he may deem necessary in the military interests of the Allied Nations.

11. The Commander in Chief of the Allied Forces will have a full right to impose measures of disarmament, demobilization, and demilitarization.

12. Other conditions of a political, economic and financial nature with which Italy will be bound to comply will be transmitted at a later date.

The conditions of the present Armistice will not be made public without prior approval of the Allied Commander in Chief. The English will be considered the official text.

Source: The Avalon Project at the Yale Law School (1998), Internet Web Page.

Despite the objections of Alexander, the campaign in southern France began on 15 August. It was designed to protect the Allies' southern flank as they raced through France. For the landings to be successful and prevent Hitler from withdrawing troops to shore up his crumbling Westerns and Eastern fronts, it was necessary to sap German strength by containing as many of their troops and supplies as possible in Italy.

After the landings in France, the Italian campaign was reduced to a major diversion as well as a source of experienced Allied troops for other theaters of operation. Clark wrote in his book *Calculated Risk* (1950) that after the landings in France, Italy became the "forgotten front" even though the Germans thought otherwise, putting up strong resistance by establishing a series of defenses in the Apennines. Nevertheless, the Allied forces in Italy aggressively continued to pursue the Germans. Only later, by the end of the war, would Italy again play a political part in the debate over coalition warfare.

Field Marshal Alexander had no doubt that the plan to invade Italy was a wise strategic decision. It forced Hitler, he noted, to fight on three fronts, thus adding to Germany's logistical problems and absorbing strength needed on other military fronts, in addition to depleting troops essential for security duties in occupied countries. The Italian campaign also preoccupied some of the *Wehrmacht's* (German Army) most gifted combat commanders. When the French invasion was launched, Alexander claimed fifty-five German divisions and their required logistical resources were tied down in the Mediterranean theater, thus costing fewer Allied casualties when Western Europe was assaulted. By the end of April 1945 one million Germans had been captured in Italy. The Italian campaign, however, had little impact on the outcome on the Eastern Front.

–GEORGE F. HOFMANN, UNIVERSITY OF CINCINNATI

Viewpoint:
The invasion of Italy had no strategic value and represented a drain on both men and matériel for the Allies.

In January 1944 the American theater commander in Italy, Major General John Lucas, declared that he was unenthusiastic and pessimistic about the upcoming invasion of Anzio, the supposed coup de grâce of Allied efforts to liberate Italy. Lucas said, "The whole affair has a strong odor of Gallipoli and the same amateur is sitting on the coach's bench." The amateur he had in mind was British prime minister Winston Churchill, the strongest advocate of the Italian campaign. In 1915 Churchill planned and oversaw a similar amphibious operation on the Gallipoli Peninsula in Turkey. That operation became one of World War I's most dismal failures. Given Lucas's lack of faith in the main operation of the Italian campaign, it could not have been other than what it was: a misapplication of men and matériel.

In large part because the United States and Britain could not agree on the goals and meth-

ods for the Italian campaign, it never lived up to its lofty billing. Instead, it became, if not a Gallipoli, a distraction for both the Germans and the Allies. Furthermore, the rugged mountains of central Italy virtually eliminated any possibility of the Allies using the flanking movements that had proved successful elsewhere. The geography meant that the Allies had two unpleasant options: deadly frontal assaults uphill or risky amphibious operations. The Allies used both in Italy; in the process they expended tremendous amounts of human and material resources that could, and should, have been used elsewhere.

The Italian campaign began as a weak and uncomfortable compromise between the members of the Grand Alliance. On the strategic level, the British favored an invasion of the supposed "soft underbelly" of Europe as a support, or perhaps even an alternative, to an invasion of northern France (code named Operation Overlord). The British (using mostly Canadian troops) attempted a raid on the French coast at Dieppe in 1942. They lost 3,500 of the invasion force of 6,000 men. The Germans easily repulsed the raid, losing less than 600 men. The disaster made the British even more reluctant to try another invasion of France. An Italian campaign seemed to Churchill and others a safer alternative. He believed that at the very least it could distract the Germans from France and improve the chances for Operation Overlord's success. At most, it might force a Nazi defeat in the east and perhaps make Overlord unnecessary.

To American (and to an extent, Russian) thinking, the Italian peninsula held no real strategic value. The capture of Sicily had achieved the goal of opening vital Mediterranean shipping lanes and had demonstrated how weak the Italian army had become. The Americans and Russians, therefore, remained fully committed to Overlord and a complimentary invasion of southern France, code-named Operation Anvil. The Americans were unwilling to veto British desires for an Italian campaign, but they were equally unwilling to weaken preparations for Overlord in favor of an invasion of Italy.

Thus, if an Italian campaign were to go forward, it would have to compete with Overlord (and to a lesser extent Anvil) for men and supplies. As a result, the Italian campaign received enough resources to keep it going, but never enough to guarantee its success. The infantry forces included units patched together from American, British, Free French, Polish, Indian, and New Zealand troops. Many of the LSTs (Landing Ship, Tank) and other amphibious vehicles used in the invasion of Italy had to be returned to England before Overlord's set time. The timing of the Italian campaign was thus determined by Overlord's schedule, not the situation in Italy.

The Allies never did agree on the operational aims of the campaign. They did not properly train for the challenging mountainous terrain of central Italy and were equally unprepared for the complex amphibious operations that resulted (the landing at Anzio was then the largest amphibious operation in history). The difficulties of simultaneously preparing several different forces for mountain and amphibious warfare led to "a great deal of muddle and miscalculation." The rough terrain frequently favored the Germans. Driving rains throughout the winter and spring of 1944 greatly complicated the situation, turning roads to mud.

German Field Marshal Albert Kesselring's Army Group C included crack *Luftwaffe* (German Air Force) paratroopers. They constructed a series of defenses in the Italian mountains called the Gustav Line anchored around the monastery of Monte Cassino, which dominated the valleys below. The Gustav Line blocked any Allied attempt to seize Rome, which lay about sixty miles to the north. A first attempt to break the line, characterized by appalling frontal attacks on fortified positions reminiscent of World War I, failed terribly in January 1944. The American Fifth Army suffered sixteen thousand casualties in order to advance just seven miles.

Later that month, Allied landings at Anzio, about thirty-five miles south of Rome, further exemplified the confusion and misunderstanding that pervaded the Italian campaign. The Allies had not yet broken the Gustav Line, an achievement originally understood to be a prerequisite for the Anzio landing. Nevertheless, General Sir Harold Alexander, Commander in Chief of Allied forces in Italy, ordered the attack because he knew that Eisenhower would soon recall the landing craft to England. General Lucas was not impressed with rehearsal exercises held on 19 January, but, despite his opinion that his troops were not ready, Alexander refused to delay the landings and it took place two days later.

The hurried timetable and inexperienced troops produced many problems. Despite all of the errors that the Allies made at Anzio, they did achieve complete surprise; hardly any German soldiers contested the landings. By midnight of the first day the Allies had more than thirty-six thousands men ashore and had suffered only thirteen dead. Usually, surprise is a tremendous advantage. In this case, Allied planners, working with less time than they needed, had only prepared to fight Germans on the beaches. They did not have any plans to move inland and seize the Alban Hills, which commanded the high ground over the beaches, or the highways running between Rome and the Gustav Line. In fact, no one on the beach was quite sure which unit had the responsibility for capturing those objectives.

By the time they had it figured out, Kesselring had moved six German divisions to the Alban Hills, trapping the Allies on the beach. Within a few days, the Allies had an impressive, but imprisoned, bridgehead of one hundred thousand men along with supporting artillery and vehicles. The immobility of the Allied forces meant that Kesselring only had to call for three divisions (one from France, one from the Balkans, and one from Russia) to assist him. The Italian campaign thus did not draw away significant German forces from other theaters.

Instead, one hundred thousand Allied troops were stuck on the beach and thousands more were stuck south of the Gustav Line. By the end of March, Anzio had become the world's fourth largest port, an impressive but unintended feat. Allied frustrations led to the nomination of Major General Lucian Truscott to replace Lucas. The change did not help. The Allies continued to disagree about fundamental philosophies and strategies concerning their forces in Italy. The British saw Anzio as the main thrust and attempts to break the Gustav Line as secondary; the Americans saw exactly the reverse.

Again, the timing of Overlord, not the logic of Italy, settled the question. By May 1944 all landing craft had left Italy. The troops in the bridgehead were now trapped between the sea and the Germans in the Alban Hills. The main breakthrough would have to come at the Gustav Line near Cassino. It took four battles and thousands of casualties before a Polish unit finally broke the Gustav Line on 17 May. German troops on the Gustav Line and in the Alban Hills retreated to a second line of defenses in the Apennine Mountains north of Florence known as the Gothic Line, meaning that the Allies would need to fight experienced German troops once more on the ground of their choosing.

One other controversy haunts the Italian campaign. After Allied troops from the Gustav Line and Anzio linked up, commanding general Mark Clark drove for Rome instead of cutting off the retreating Germans before they could reach the Gothic Line. Clark entered the city on 4 June, but as a result the German Fourteenth Army escaped to fight another day. Allied troops had to fight for three and a half more months until they broke the Gothic Line and even then did not reach Milan and Venice until 29 April 1945, just one week before V-E Day.

Contrary to its original intention, the Italian campaign distracted both German and Allied forces. The constraints of coalition warfare meant that Italy absorbed American and British efforts much more than it absorbed German efforts. American and British disagreements confused the campaign from its beginning to its end. Allied efforts in Italy did not make Overlord unnecessary and they did not cause the collapse of German efforts in the east. Russia's own 2.4 million-man offensive (Operation Bagration) in June 1944 deserves the credit for the change in the east. Nor did Italian operations stop Hitler from launching a 30-division offensive (none of them transferred from German forces in Italy) in the Ardennes later that year. Winston Churchill's "soft underbelly" was, in the words of one veteran, "a tough old gut."

–MICHAEL S. NEIBERG, U.S. AIR
FORCE ACADEMY, COLORADO

References

Harold Alexander, *The Alexander Memoirs 1940–1945* (London: Cassell, 1962);

Martin Blumenson, *Anzio: The Gamble That Failed* (New York: Holt, Rinehart & Winston, 1961);

Blumenson, *Salerno to Cassino* (Washington: Office of the Chief of Military History, 1969);

Winston S. Churchill, *Closing the Ring* (Boston: Houghton Mifflin, 1951);

Mark W. Clark, *Calculated Risk* (New York: Harper, 1950);

Carlo d'Este, *Bitter Victory: The Battle for Sicily, 1943* (New York: Dutton, 1988);

d'Este, *Fatal Decision: Anzio and the Battle for Rome* (New York: HarperCollins, 1991);

Dominick Graham and Shelford Bidwell, *Tug of War: The Battle for Italy, 1943–1945* (New York: St. Martin's Press, 1986);

Michael Howard, *The Mediterranean Strategy in the Second World War* (New York: Praeger, 1968);

W. F. G. Jackson, *The Battle for Italy* (New York: Harper & Row, 1967);

Albert Kesselring, *The Memoirs of Field Marshal Kesselring* (London: Kimber, 1953);

Richard Lamb, *War in Italy, 1939–1945: A Brutal Story* (London: Murray, 1993);

Brian Holden Reid, "Italian Campaign," in *The Oxford Companion to World War II*, edited by I. C. B. Dear and M. R. D. Foot (New York: Oxford University Press, 1995), pp. 572–573, 580;

Raleigh Trevelyan, *Rome '44: The Battle for the Eternal City* (New York: Viking, 1982);

F. von Senger and Etterlin, *Neither Fear nor Hope* (London: Macdonald, 1960);

Robert L. Wagner, *The Texas Army: A History of the 36th Division in the Italian Campaign* (Austin: Wagner, 1972).

JAPANESE WAY OF WAR

Was the Japanese military unnecessarily brutal during World War II?

Viewpoint: Yes, the Japanese exceeded the bounds of acceptable military conduct during World War II, adopting a newly modified soldiers' code that required fanatical aggressiveness.

Viewpoint: No, although the Japanese committed atrocities on and off the battlefield, their code of behavior was a consequence of traditional social and institutional mores.

Well before the Bataan Death March of 1942, well before the Burma-Thailand Railroad cost the lives of 12,000 prisoners of war (POWs) and a still-unknown number of local civilians, Japan had been waging a war in China whose brutality can shock even the students of Nazi occupation policies. Mass killings of Chinese civilians culminated, but scarcely ceased, with the December 1937 "Rape of Nanking." Japanese forces left a trail of violence: casual beatings, casual murder, and casual rape, complemented by an official policy of producing and selling drugs on a large scale. The culmination of Japan's China policy was the "Three Alls" offensive of 1944, the stated purpose of which was "kill all, burn all, destroy all."

By comparison, Japan's treatment of Allied POWs seems almost benign. Abuse, neglect, and, above all, forced labor nevertheless took a heavy toll. Captured airmen were beheaded. Prisoners were shipped from place to place without regard for their security against air or submarine attack. They were used in germ warfare experiments. Countless POWs died before liberation. Countless others had their lives shortened by privation.

This pattern of behavior contradicted previous wars, wherein Japan's armed forces had been punctilious in observing conventions regarding the treatment of prisoners, and on the whole had behaved decently toward civilian populations. One explanation emphasizes the institutional contempt for surrender developed and inculcated in Japan's armed forces during the interwar years. Another emphasizes the comprehensively repressive nature of Japanese society, which encouraged its soldiers to shed all restraints when they had the opportunity. A third line of argument suggests that prisoners of the Japanese were not treated exponentially worse than the Japanese prisoners themselves, but were unable to adapt to the conditions. A fourth stresses Japanese racism, an insular indifference/contempt for other cultures and peoples that facilitated brutality. Linking and shaping these factors, however, was official policy. The Japanese way of war was predicated on will-power as a force multiplier. It had no room in principle for the welfare of defeated enemies and conquered people. In that context atrocities occurred and escalated because no institutional structures and policies existed to prevent them. All the pressure was in the other direction.

Viewpoint:
Yes, the Japanese exceeded the bounds of acceptable military conduct during World War II, adopting a newly modified soldiers' code that required fanatical aggressiveness.

In 1995 Japanese prime minister Tomiichi Murayama expressed "acute remorse" for the damage and suffering inflicted by Japanese forces during World War II. Many of the victims of Japanese aggression, however, replied that Murayama's apology did not go far enough in atoning for the criminal brutality they endured. Relentless beatings, torture, and execution of Allied prisoners of war (POWs); the enslavement of Chinese, Korean, and Filipino women as prostitutes; mass rape and murder of civilians during the Rape of Nanking (1937): these atrocities and others revealed a Japanese way of war that was nearly unprecedented in its harshness and horror.

In their wanton brutality Japanese forces were of course not alone. One need only recall the Holocaust, or Germany's starvation and murder of millions of Soviet POWs. Indeed, the German comparison is apposite, since both German (most notably on the Eastern Front) and Japanese atrocities were motivated in part by racist ideologies that reduced enemies to inferior humans unworthy of humane treatment. Atrocities and blatant expressions of racism were common among U.S. soldiers, sailors, or marines in the Pacific. On the home front, the U.S. government forcibly relocated Japanese Americans to internment camps. What distinguished Japanese atrocities from those committed by their opponents, however, was the sheer scale, the tacit approval, and the open encouragement and commendation of these atrocities at the highest levels of the Japanese military and government.

Why did Japan's leaders commend and not condemn these behaviors? Ultranationalism played a role—the exaltation of Japanese cultural uniqueness and superiority together with the wholesale disparagement of "alien" cultures. So too did racism, reinforced by incessant military indoctrination. Perhaps most influential was state glorification of military values, combined with state encouragement of mass conformity and demands for unquestioning obedience to authority, most notably unconditional loyalty to the emperor. In the words of Saburo Ienaga, the end result

was "a Kafkaesque state dedicated to the abuse of human rights."

Exaltation of military virtues, especially absolute obedience and unwavering courage, tapped deep wellsprings in Japanese culture. Japan's leaders selectively mined the mysticism and mystique of the samurai and Bushido—the code of the warrior—to strengthen the Imperial Japanese Army's (IJA) fighting spirit. In contrast, the same leaders deliberately suppressed notions of chivalry and compassion for one's enemy—explicitly advocated in Bushido—in the *Tokuho,* or Soldiers' Code, of 1872 and the Imperial Rescript of 1882. The result was a modified code of military behavior that inculcated fanatical aggressiveness, total lack of concern for one's individual well-being or survival (let alone the well-being or survival of enemies), and the glorification of fighting and dying for the emperor.

The brutal nature of this modified code of Bushido was clearly evinced in the Japanese treatment of POWs. The Japanese considered surrender to be utterly disgraceful and shameful to oneself and, more importantly, to one's family. Unquestioning faith in their own cultural superiority prevented them from understanding or identifying with the enemy. The Japanese therefore treated enemy POWs as disgraced nonpersons, who in surrendering had dishonored themselves and forfeited their rights to humane treatment. Thus, the Japanese marched POWs to death at Bataan (1942) and at Sandakan (1945) in North Borneo (during the latter atrocity nearly 2,000 Australian and 750 British soldiers died). They used POWs as unwitting and expendable experimental subjects on which to test deadly biological agents (the infamous Unit 731 commanded by Ishii Shiro in Manchuria). And they forced POWs to build bridges, fortifications, and railroads (12,000 POWs died constructing the Burma-Thailand Railroad) or to mine copper (the death rate at the Nippon Mining Company exceeded eighty percent).

Lacking medical care and fed a meager diet, POWs often succumbed to beriberi, cholera, dysentery, malaria, or malnutrition. Others were tortured to death or killed in work-related accidents. If they tried to escape and failed, the Japanese executed them. These factors together accounted for a death rate of nearly 27 percent for Allied POWs held in Japanese camps. By way of contrast the death rate for Allied POWs held in German and Italian camps was 4 percent, or nearly seven times lower.

JAPANESE WAY OF WAR

Indifference was only part of the picture. Japanese of all ranks took positive pleasure in brutally abusing and murdering comparatively helpless POWs. They did so in part because the IJA itself—in its encouragement and toleration of physical abuse within its own ranks—had fatally weakened inhibitions against brutality and torture. With brutal discipline the norm rather than the exception, Japanese soldiers quickly became inured to physical punishment, and had few if any qualms restricting their own violence or respecting human rights. Mistreated within their own ranks, Japanese soldiers showed no mercy in lashing out against weak and vulnerable enemies.

Worse than the brutal mistreatment of POWs by the Japanese was the utter contempt they showed for "inferior" Asian women. While the Japanese extolled the virtues of feminine purity within their own culture, they enslaved perhaps as many as 100,000 Chinese, Korean, and Filipino women to serve as "comfort women" or prostitutes for the army. Referred to as "public

toilets" by their Japanese captors, these women were sometimes forced to have sex fifteen to twenty times a day. Most disturbingly, the enslavement and exploitation of "comfort women" was condoned at the highest levels of the Japanese Army, Navy, and the Ministry of Foreign Affairs.

Also condoned at the highest levels of the Japanese government was the mass brutalization and murder of Chinese civilians, epitomized in what has become known as the Rape of Nanking. At Nanking in 1937, the Japanese murdered at least 260,000 Chinese, primarily civilians, in an orgy of violence inspired by Prince Asaka, uncle of Emperor Hirohito, who ordered the IJA to "Kill all captives." Killing quickly became a sport for the Japanese, as soldiers competed with samurai swords or bayonets to behead or stab as many victims as possible. The killing was as indiscriminate as it was ruthless; its horrific nature has been well documented in Iris Chang's study, *The Rape of Nanking: The Forgotten Holocaust of World War II* (1997).

Further examples of officially sanctioned, large-scale atrocities might be cited,

Japanese soldiers on the Great Wall of China following the occupation of Manchuria in December 1931

(Mainichi Newspaper Company)

JAPANESE WAY OF WAR

such as vivisections of captured POWs, the Rape of Manila, or widespread voluntary cannibalism practiced by Japanese soldiers in New Guinea. Here the reader should refer to Yuki Tanaka's *Hidden Horrors: Japanese War Crimes in World War II* (1996) for a comprehensive and sobering study. Considering this catalogue of proven crimes against humanity, one is tempted to conclude that Japanese character in World War II was fundamentally flawed, perhaps even intrinsically evil.

Were the Japanese people the emperor's willing executioners? A detailed discussion of this issue is beyond the scope of the present essay. In coming to grips with this question, however, one must recognize that the vast majority of Japanese, even noncombatants, were willing to fight to the death or commit suicide rather than to surrender. Thus, 250 student nurses on Okinawa—the *Hineyuri* or "Princess Lily" brigade—committed mass suicide rather than surrender to U.S. forces. On Saipan nearly 1,000 Japanese noncombatants, some holding children in their arms, jumped from cliffs into a watery grave. This contempt for one's own life—the belief in *gyokusai* or glorious self-annihilation—contributed significantly to contempt for the lives of other peoples. In short, there was a fundamental difference in how the Japanese defined the very concept of "the life worth living" that drove them to devalue or to dismiss the right to life, and indeed the very humanity, of those peoples who did not share Japan's culture or conceptual framework.

Of course a few Japanese, soldiers or civilians, thought through the implications of their beliefs or their crimes. Many Japanese war criminals were reminiscent of Adolf Eichmann: nondescript and unreflective bureaucratic functionaries in whom Hannah Arendt's concept of "the banality of evil" seemed perfectly embodied. Unreflective obedience and the nearly complete repression of dissident views within Japan during World War II strengthened wartime's cultural tendencies toward jingoistic oppression of "the other." The combination also served to retard (perhaps fatally) postwar efforts by the Japanese to come fully to terms with and to atone for their crimes.

Japan continues to struggle with the legacy of its war crimes, and its victims continue to seek apologies in which the Japanese give full expression to their guilt and shame. Whether Japan shall ever come fully to grips with its monstrous record of war crimes remains to be seen. What is certain is that more and more survivors of Japanese atrocities are reaching the natural end of their lives

without the solace or satisfaction of honest discussion of, and apology for, these crimes.

–WILLIAM J. ASTORE, U.S. AIR FORCE ACADEMY, COLORADO

Viewpoint:
No, although the Japanese committed atrocities on and off the battlefield, their code of behavior was a consequence of traditional social and institutional mores.

The ferocity with which Japan's armed forces fought, and the brutality they demonstrated both to prisoners of war and to civilians under their control, has been so often demonstrated that it seems almost perverse to suggest that it manifested something other than cultural and individual brutality and fanaticism, first institutionalized and then unleashed without restraints. It is, however, possible to analyze the structural factors and the particular circumstances that created what amounted to a code of behavior that, half a century later, still renders the name of Japan a stench in the nostrils in much of the people of Asia.

The process begins with understanding the military decision that Japan could fight a modern war only by emphasizing its moral elements. The experience of World War I indicated that comprehensive hardness, of the kind best manifested by the German storm troop units, was a prerequisite for survival, to say nothing of victory, in modern high-tech combat. As a consequence, discipline, already harsh by Western standards, was tightened to the limit of everyday endurance. The random physical brutality so often remarked by Western observers was considered to prefigure the even greater and more random brutality of the battlefield. Surrender had not been considered inherently shameful in Japan's earlier wars (nor, in passing, the civil wars that had been such a feature of the island's earlier history). After 1918, however, it was presented as unthinkable—a social as well as a military disgrace, permanently dishonoring both the captive and his family. Training emphasized coming to close quarters—"grabbing by the belt" an enemy whose firepower was likely to be exponentially superior to anything Japanese units could muster. Cold steel was emphasized to the point that light machine guns were given bayonet attachments—not that soldiers were actually expected to use automatic weapons weighing almost thirty pounds in close combat, but to epito-

JAPANESE WAY OF WAR

mize the army's priorities. A cult of the emperor that had begun in the Meiji Restoration (1868) as a means of instilling patriotism along Western lines became the focal point for a comprehensive system of ideological indoctrination–supplemented during the 1930s by significant Nazi influence on the lower ranks of the officer corps.

Bushido, an aristocratic warrior creed with its roots in Japan's middle ages, prescribed standards of correct and honorable behavior toward enemies as well as for oneself. Increasingly it became a synonym for a way of war as opposed to a way of life. Japanese soldiers were expected to strike hard, keep moving, and show concern for nothing but their duty and their mission. This ethos by itself can be a recipe for trouble anywhere outside the front lines. It was exacerbated during the Sino-Japanese War by a sense of being hopelessly outnumbered in a sea of hostile and inscrutable aliens. The only Chinese who could be trusted were those held at bayonet point. The Nanking massacre and its antecedents were in good part sparked by Japanese fear of "plainclothesmen": Chinese soldiers who had discarded their uniforms to act as snipers and saboteurs.

As a general rule, armies seek to restrain their troops less for humanitarian reasons than because license behind the lines weakens discipline at the front. A platoon locked together by pillage, rape, and murder resembles a pack of feral dogs. Command in such units is exercised by consensus, with the officers and sergeants little more than facilitators and figureheads. The Japanese army's regimental officers, as has been mentioned, shared the attitudes of their men. And the Japanese army was unique in institutionalizing the principle, familiar in Japanese society, of superiors responding to imperatives enunciated by their juniors. The consequence was a pattern that began with superior officers looking the other way, then themselves adopting the attitude that "stone dead had no fellow":–particularly in dealing with Chinese.

The armed forces' institutionalization of hardness manifested itself in other ways as well. Logistics were a secondary concern for an army obsessed with increasing its combat power. Japanese troops were expected to supplement their rations by requisition and foraging. From the plains of China to the jungles of the South Pacific, that practice became an entering wedge for small-scale brutality. From using a rifle butt on a recalcitrant peasant, it was a short step to teaching the women who their new masters were, and from there to burning what could not be carried away.

Prolonged war tends to stretch the limits of acceptable behavior in all armies. It was scarcely surprising that by the time the Pacific war began,

the Japanese armed forces—the army in particular—were already well past the point of "hard war" and on their way to norms of conduct that to their western victims seemed nothing other than calculated bestiality. The Japanese, in contrast, had real difficulty understanding what the fuss was about. The familiar notion that the Japanese military regarded POWs as having forfeited honor by surrendering is reasonably accurate. Its direct consequences, however, must not be exaggerated. Japanese troops were expected to make endurance marches on a minimum of food and water. Why should the Filipinos and Americans who surrendered on Bataan expect other treatment. Noncombatant personnel were at the end of the Japanese queue for rations, medicine, clothing, and blankets. Should military prisoners and civilian internees be given a higher priority? Japanese personnel transported by ship in the Pacific after 1943 were also at constant risk from U.S. air and submarine attacks. The Geneva Convention, to which Japan was a party, forbade exposing POWs to attack from their own forces. That clause, however, was primarily intended to avert the use of prisoners as hostages. It is asking a good deal of armed forces operating on shoestrings to take more pains with enemy prisoners than with their own personnel.

As for using POW labor, most obviously in constructing the Siam Railway, here again the Japanese army was acting on its highly developed sense of mission. The railway had to be built; any necessary means were correspondingly legitimate. It is worth noting that the Japanese guards and construction personnel assigned to the railway also suffered significant hardship and high death rates—though neither compared the experience of the POWs.

Some of the most gruesome Japanese atrocities involved the murder, especially by beheading, of downed airmen, escapees, and victims selected seemingly at random. Some light may be cast on this particular phenomenon by considering it as a vulgarization of a complex samurai tradition that under certain conditions allowed the execution of hostages or high-ranking captives as symbolic retaliation for their side's victories. Most of the majors, captains, and lieutenants who imitated that behavior in the Pacific war had been born, as the saying went, "with paddy mud between their toes." The swords they wielded so proudly were also ersatz—cheap copies of genuine samurai blades, made often enough from Western scrap metal. But they saw themselves as part of a tradition of honor—and in not a few cases treated their victims as honored by being selected as proxies for their countries.

To explain the behavior of Japan's armed forces during World War II is not to condone it. But to explain it is also to move away from the reductionist cultural anthropology that dominates discussion of the subject with its talk of

violence as an escape from a comprehensively repressive social structure. What happened between 1931 and 1945 was in good part the unintended consequence of specific institutional mores, developed as means of enhancing military effectiveness, interacting with half-understood scraps and fragments of a martial heritage developed under essentially different conditions.

—DENNIS SHOWALTER, COLORADO COLLEGE

References

Hannah Arendt, *Eichmann in Jerusalem: A Report on the Banality of Evil* (New York: Viking, 1963);

Arnold C. Brackman, *The Other Nuremberg: The Untold Story of the Tokyo War Crimes Trials* (New York: Morrow, 1987);

Ian Buruma, *The Wages of Guilt: Memories of War in Germany and Japan* (New York: Farrar, Straus & Giroux, 1994);

Iris Chang, *The Rape of Nanking: The Forgotten Holocaust of World War II* (New York: Basic-Books, 1997);

John W. Dower, *War Without Mercy: Race and Power in the Pacific War* (New York: Pantheon, 1986);

Edward J. Drea, "In the Army Barracks of Imperial Japan," *Armed Forces and Society* 15 (1989): 329–348;

Robert B. Edgerton, *Warriors of the Rising Sun: A History of the Japanese Military* (New York: Norton, 1997);

Meirion and Susie Harries, *Soldiers of the Sun: The Rise and Fall of the Imperial Japanese Army* (New York: Random House, 1991);

Saburo Ienaga, *The Pacific War, 1931–1945: A Critical Perspective on Japan's Role in World War II* (New York: Pantheon, 1978);

Toshio Iritani, *Group Psychology of the Japanese in Wartime* (London & New York: Kegan Paul International, 1991);

Yuki Tanaka, *Hidden Horrors: Japanese War Crimes in World War II* (Boulder, Colo.: Westview Press, 1996);

Peter Williams and David Wallace, *Unit 731: Japan's Secret Biological Warfare in World War II* (New York: Free Press, 1989).

JAPANESE WAY OF WAR

LEND LEASE

Was Western economic aid essential for the Soviet war effort?

Viewpoint: Yes, Western economic aid to the Soviet Union ultimately shortened World War II by a year or more and helped the Russians turn the momentum of the war in 1943.

Viewpoint: No, Western economic aid was important but not decisive in determining the outcome of the war on the Eastern Front.

Great Britain and the United States first committed aid to the Soviet Union in October 1941. Not until 1942, however, did matériel begin reaching the U.S.S.R. in quantity. Just how much was sent, and what role it played in the Russian war effort, was a point of controversy during the Cold War. Soviet authorities insisted that Lend Lease amounted to no more than 4 percent of Russia's own production. Even that trickle of aid, it was asserted, was doled out grudgingly, so that the U.S.S.R. nearly bled itself white meeting the German onslaught.

In fact, a strong case can be made that the Western Allies were the Red Army's quartermasters. Russia received almost as much aluminum as it made itself, and three-fourths of its domestic production of copper wire. Coal and other raw materials compensated for resources lost to the Nazi German invasion. The Allies shipped 34 million uniforms, nearly 15 million pairs of boots, and millions of tons of food—including U.S. Army rations, far more popular in Russia than among their originally intended consumers.

Western tanks and aircraft were less successful in the conditions of the Eastern Front—to the point where some Soviet spokesmen complained that they were being given second-rate hardware. Yet, if the Sherman tank was not on the level with the Soviet T-34, its mechanical reliability and communications systems made it a useful complement to Soviet vehicles in the hands of commanders who knew how to use these qualities. While the P-39 Airacobra, and its successor the Kingcobra, were no match for German fighters in air-to-air combat, they nevertheless had strong advocates among the ground-attack pilots of the Red Air Force. American trucks and jeeps gave the Red Army the logistical and operational mobility to sustain the great offensives of 1944–1945. Without them, the Soviet road to Berlin would have been longer and far bloodier.

**Viewpoint:
Yes, Western economic aid to the Soviet Union ultimately shortened World War II by a year or more and helped the Russians turn the momentum of the war in 1943.**

The numbers speak for themselves. Through the Lend Lease Act approved by Congress on 11 March 1941, the United States alone gave the Soviet Union more than $10 billion in aid. This assistance included trucks, weapons, food, clothing, raw materials and more. Despite tensions between the Western Allies and the Soviet Union, the United States approved a twenty-nine-page list of Soviet needs in 1941 and continued to supply the Red Army until the end of the war. Lend Lease accomplished several important goals. First and most obviously, it provided the Soviets with much needed matériel to defeat the *Wermacht* (German army). Second, American aid allowed the Soviets to specialize in key industrial areas such as tank production. Third, and no less important, Western (mostly American) aid created a vital moral and symbolic link that tied the Russians to their mistrustful and mistrusted allies in the West.

Anglo-American support for the Soviet Union did not come automatically. The British were especially wary of the Soviets after the signing of the Nazi-Soviet pact in 1939 and subsequent Russian invasions of Poland, Finland, and the Baltic states. Many Western leaders feared that the Soviets and the Nazis were working together; any aid to the Russians, therefore, might help the German cause. Even after the German invasion of the Soviet Union in 1941, many Americans argued against extending Lend-Lease provisions to Russia. The *Chicago Tribune* called aid to Joseph "Bloody Joe" Stalin and the Soviet Union "ridiculous."

Despite American misgivings, President Franklin D. Roosevelt quickly extended aid to the Russians. The first agreement between the United States and Russia came in October 1941, while the United States was still neutral. Roosevelt agreed with British Prime Minister Winston Churchill that Russia had to be supplied and had to remain in the war as a counterweight against Adolf Hitler. Consequently, Roosevelt sent his most trusted advisor, Harry Hopkins, to Moscow to oversee Russian aid. Nevertheless, old suspicions remained; Congress took four months to officially approve the aid program.

Suspicions notwithstanding, American aid eventually provided a critical margin of difference. The Americans provided 34,000,000 sets of uniforms; 15,000,000 pairs of boots; 350,000 tons of explosives; 3,000,000 tons of gasoline; untold tons of food (including that most important of war supplies, Spam); 12,000 railroad cars; 375,000 trucks; and 50,000 jeeps. The Russians frequently complained about the quality of some of these supplies, especially the weapons and the food (one Russian historian claimed that "the allies bought German defeat with Russian blood and paid in Spam"), but the quantity had an important quality of its own.

To be sure, the Russians wanted a second front in France more than the uniforms and jeeps, but the supplies permitted the Red Army to develop their strengths and compensate for their weaknesses. The surprise German invasion devastated Russian industry. Soviet authorities

ordered that entire factories be dismantled and reassembled east of the Ural Mountains and, therefore, out of the Germans' reach. In a tremendous feat of human will, the Soviets moved more than 2,593 factories. That figure represents more than 80 percent of Soviet industry. The forced relocations kept the factories out of German hands, but seriously disrupted industrial production. American aid eased the transition period. For example, British and American aluminum, manganese, and coal replaced most of the Soviet supplies of those materials that the Germans seized early in the war.

On the battlefield, American aid allowed the Red Army to become mobile. The Soviets had few trucks and were significantly backward in motorized transportation. American gasoline and trucks transformed the Red Army from a walking army to a motorized one. By war's end, two-thirds of Soviet trucks were foreign-built. Motorization allowed the Soviets to develop a "deep offensive" doctrine in 1943. Based on the German Blitzkrieg model, the deep offensive allowed Russian units to go as far as 200 kilometers (approximately 120 miles) behind enemy lines without resupply. Motorization provided the speed that made the doctrine work. The Russians used it with great success to reduce the Kursk salient in an important 1943 campaign.

Western aid also allowed the Russians to focus their industry toward the production of a key weapons system. For the most part, the Russians welcomed transport equipment more than weapons systems. American Sherman tanks, for example, had difficulty handling the thick Russian mud. As a result, the Soviets wanted to continue production of their own marvelous tank, the T-34. Because the United States and Britain provided the necessary raw materials, they were able to do so. The Soviet automotive industry could also focus production on tanks because of the steady supply of trucks and jeeps coming from the United States. They could also concentrate industrial production into another Soviet strength, artillery.

As a result, the Soviets were well equipped for their 1943 offensives. By April of that year, the Russians had 6,300 tanks and 20,000 artillery pieces versus the Germans' 1,300 tanks and 6,000 artillery pieces. With this numerical superiority, the Russians were able to seize the offensive outside Kursk and maintain it until the end of the war. Most of the weapons systems were Soviet-built, but American and British aid provided the raw materials and allowed for an important concentration of Soviet energy into weapons production.

The Western nations also provided the Soviets with tanks and airplanes, though, as noted above, the Soviets found British and American

LEND LEASE

weapons lacking in important ways. The British sent the Russians 7,000 tanks and 5,000 airplanes while the United States delivered 7,000 tanks and 15,000 airplanes. In early August 1941, when the Russian situation looked particularly dim, Roosevelt ordered one hundred American fighters sent to the Red Air Force, even if it meant that they had to be taken from the active stocks of the Army Air Corps.

Many Western designs proved unsuited to Russian needs. American aircraft were predominately long-range interceptors and heavy bombers. The Russians wanted close air support aircraft and low-altitude fighters. As a result, not all Western weapons systems worked well in the Russian military, though many did. The American P-39 Airacobra performed especially well in the hands of Russian aces A. I. Pokryshkin and G. A. Rechalov. The "superb" American A-20 light bomber also "performed well in the Soviet inventory" according to David M. Glantz and Jonathan House, two renowned historians of the Russian front. The Russians also received 2,400 P-63 Kingcobras, an updated version of the P-39 built exclusively for the purpose of Lend Lease. These aircraft also fit well into the Red Air Force.

More subtly, but no less importantly, Western aid helped to build a bridge on which the Grand Alliance could be built. According to David Kennedy in *Freedom from Fear: The American People in Depression and War, 1929–1945* (1999), "wary suspicion and cynical calculation" characterized the Grand Alliance throughout the war. Much of the mistrust dated to the Russian Revolution of 1917; mistrust continued throughout the 1930s as Nazi Germany and Stalinist Russia grew closer. The mutual suspicions never went away; only the existence of a powerful common enemy kept the alliance together.

In such an environment, American and British aid helped to underscore the idea that all three nations were fighting the same war. For the Americans, it meant much more. Roosevelt and his closest advisers wanted to use Lend Lease to open the Soviet system to American ideas. They hoped that American production and assistance would convince the Soviet leadership that capitalism and liberal democracy were effective and safe systems.

Of course, Western aid did not achieve that end. Stalin remained wary of his Western allies throughout the war. Western assistance did, however, help to create an alliance within which two diametrically opposed systems could function together, at least until a common enemy had been defeated. American aid therefore had an important impact on Soviet morale as well as on Soviet strategy and doctrine. Millions of

tons of American wheat came in packages stamped with an American eagle, making a symbolic link between the American people who raised the food and the Russian people who consumed it.

Western efforts to supply the Soviet Union also created many tensions. The Russians, for example, once asked for eight tons of uranium oxide, a critical component to a fledgling nuclear weapons program. The United States, of course, rejected the request. Furthermore, the Russians complained that much Allied aid consisted of junk and poor quality leftovers. Most fundamentally, no amount of aid could compensate the Soviet high command for Anglo-American reluctance to invade France in 1942 or 1943. Attempts to sell Lend Lease as an industrial second front fell on deaf Muscovite ears.

Still, Western aid made a visible and critical difference to Russian war efforts. According to Glantz and House in *When Titans Clashed: How the Red Army Stopped Hitler* (1995), Lend Lease shortened the war in Russia by twelve to eighteen months. Without Western aid, "every Soviet offensive would have stalled at an earlier stage, outrunning its logistical trail in a matter of days." Instead, American trucks and gasoline kept the Red Army moving and helped the Russians to turn the momentum of the war during 1943. American grain and canned meats also helped Russian civilians survive the horrific sieges at Stalingrad and elsewhere. To this day, terms such as *jeep, Studebaker,* and *Spam* remain familiar to older Russians. Perhaps that familiarity is the greatest testimony of the importance of Western aid to Russian war efforts.

—MICHAEL S. NEIBERG, U.S. AIR FORCE ACADEMY, COLORADO

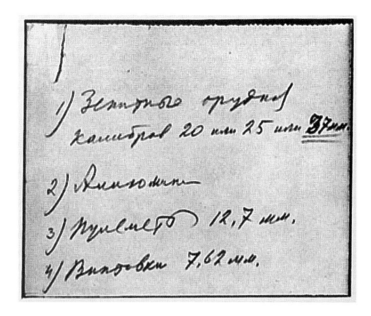

A note from Joseph Stalin to President Franklin D. Roosevelt's personal envoy Harry Hopkins listing the Soviet people's most pressing needs: antiaircraft guns, aluminum, machine guns, and 30-caliber rifles

(Franklin D. Roosevelt Library)

LEND LEASE

Viewpoint:
No, Western economic aid was important but not decisive in determining the outcome of the war on the Eastern Front.

While it is perfectly reasonable to argue that Western economic aid to the Soviet Union during World War II influenced the course of the war on the Eastern Front, it is an exaggeration to judge that contribution to have been essential. To be sure, such an assessment hinges in part on the way in which one employs the word *essential*. Most often, however, in historical discussion of this question, debate focuses on whether or not Western economic aid was indispensable to Soviet survival and victory. In other words, to argue that such contributions were essential is to maintain that the Soviet Union would have been defeated without them.

Few scholars of the war, including even Soviet scholars writing before the close of the Cold War, dismissed American and British economic aid as irrelevant to the outcome. In fact, if we take into consideration Western material aid in all its form:—weapons, raw materials, food, clothing, and equipment—the impact was considerable. In the first place, such contributions were enormously valuable psychologically and politically. They not only bolstered the Soviet strategic position materially but gave vital reassurance that they were not alone. This hope was doubly significant due to the relatively tiny direct commitment of U.S. and British forces to combat against the *Wehrmacht* (German Army) in 1942 and much of 1943. By the same token, Adolf Hitler could take no comfort from this impressive evidence that his enemies were forging a united effort to defeat him. Still, in the end one can only judge the impact of Western support by the course of the war effort itself.

A logical beginning is to examine the extent of Western material aid. American contributions arrived under the auspices of President Franklin D. Roosevelt's Lend Lease program, of which Britain was the largest beneficiary. Although, as the name implies, this program in theory represented contributions that would be returned or for which the United States would be reimbursed, reality was otherwise. Adopted to make U.S. aid more politically palatable to the domestic electorate at a time when many Americans felt that all resources should be pumped into their own war effort, Lend Lease really constituted a program of donations. Lend Lease did not reflect unqualified generosity on the part of the Roosevelt administration. The president well understood that Anglo-American success depended heavily on the ability of the Soviet Union to hold out and defeat Germany in the East.

In any case, the most notable allied donations addressed needs that Stalin believed the Soviets would have the greatest difficulty meeting on their own. Although published figures vary slightly, they are sufficiently similar in magnitude so as to facilitate analysis of their importance. Moreover, the variety alone is impressive. Supplies arriving from the United States Britain during the war included approximately 400,000 trucks and other motor vehicles, and more than 12,000 armored vehicles, 325,000 tons of explosives, 13,000 locomotives and railroad cars, 6,000,000 tons of food, 15,000 aircraft, and 5,000,000 pairs of boots, as well as appreciable quantities of aluminum, zinc, steel, nickel, rubber, tin, high grade petroleum, and lead. In addition, the United States and Britain provided the shipping to deliver these goods over long and perilous sea lanes.

What, then, is the student of history to make of all this? The first consideration should be when, how, and where these resources were applied. In point of fact, precious little of this aid reached the Soviet Union when its survival was in greatest peril. When Soviet armies were holding on grimly in front of Moscow in the fall of 1941, evidence of Allied support in any form was scarce. Thus, in the crucial first phase of the war the Red Army was virtually on its own. Allied aid began to appear in meaningful amounts in the middle of 1942, just in time to support in at least a modest way the Soviet triumph at Stalingrad. The flow increased dramatically, however, in 1943–1944. In sum, the greatest impact of Western economic aid came at that time when the Soviet Union was already winning the war on the Eastern Front. At the same time, Germany was running out of manpower and simply lacked the robust fighting formations to stem Red Army advances.

A second consideration in assessing the impact of Western aid is to establish just what percentage of Soviet equipment and raw materials it actually represented. After the war, the Soviet economist N. Voznesensky calculated that the Anglo-American contribution amounted to about 4 percent of the total production of the Soviet Union from 1941 to 1943. Of course, as Alexander Werth, who spent the war years in the Soviet Union as a British correspondent, wrote in *Russia at War 1941–1945* (1984), that this figure is not a particularly good indicator of the Allied contribution for the war as a whole. Indeed, it is almost certainly deceptive. Such a figure depends first of all on what one counts as war production. Furthermore, even small additions to critically short categories can assume disproportionate meaning. Voznesensky's figure is, however, most important in the context of the discussion at hand. In short, it confirms that Western aid could hardly have been of decisive importance during the first half of the

LEND LEASE

war—the time when the outcome hung in the balance.

To clarify the problem still further, it is also useful to consider the proportions represented by specific types of Western assistance. For example, according to Soviet figures, Allied donations of tanks, combat aircraft, and artillery pieces constituted about 7 percent, 13 percent, and 2 percent of the respective totals available to the Red Army. Trucks began arriving in significant numbers in 1943 when they represented 5.4 percent of the total but rose sharply to 19 percent in 1944. Shipment of grain and flour for the war constituted less than 3 percent of the total consumed. Overall, these supplements were most valuable and welcome. There is no basis, however, to conclude that they were decisive in influencing the outcome of the war.

A third and final measure of the allied contribution must be qualitative. This criterion applies principally to tanks, aircraft, and trucks. The United States and Britain sent the Soviet Union nearly 5,000 tanks through 1942 and about 10,000 tanks in total through April 1944. In this regard, the Soviet Armed Forces Administration complained in 1943 that the preponderance of tanks received were too light for combat against the Germans. For instance, David M. Glantz and Jon House observe in *When Titans Clashed: How the Red Army Stopped Hitler* (1995) that British Valentine and Matilda tanks possessed turrets too small to accommodate a gun exceeding 40 millimeters and were thus significantly inferior to their German counterparts. Meanwhile, the best American tank of the war, the Sherman, was more powerful and durable than British models but unavailable early in the war. In addition, because it was designed to travel on board ships to Europe, its base was narrow. Although this fact was of little consequence on roads or on dry ground, it presented a considerable disadvantage during operations in mud or snow that prevailed for much of the year across Russia's expanses.

Similarly, Soviet satisfaction with aircraft provided by their allies was low. In contrast to their Anglo-American allies, Soviet air power doctrine focused on the role of close support of ground forces. The desired aircraft for such a mission were low-altitude fighters. Because British and American designers had concentrated on the development of long-range, high-altitude strategic bomber fleets, at the start of the war they lacked state of the art aircraft for close support. Consequently, the Soviets had to get along with relatively low performance models such as the P-39 Airacobra and early versions of the British Hurricane. Still, as Luftwaffe strength eroded and Soviet pilots grew more familiar with Lend Lease aircraft, this contribution proved to be of notable worth.

THE LEND LEASE ACT, 11 MARCH 1941

Be it enacted That this Act may be cited as "An Act to Promote the Defense of the United States."

Section 3.

(a) Notwithstanding the provisions of any other law, the President may, from time to time, when he deems it in the interest of national defense, authorize the Secretary of War, the Secretary of the Navy, or the head of any other department or agency of the Government—

(1) To manufacture in arsenals, factories, and shipyards under their jurisdiction, or otherwise procure, to the extent to which funds are made available therefor, or contracts are authorized from time to time by the Congress, or both, any defense article for the government of any country whose defense the President deems vital to the defense of the United States.

(2) To sell, transfer title to, exchange, lease, lend, or otherwise dispose of, to any such government any defense article, but no defense article not manufactured or procured under paragraph (1) shall in any way be disposed of under this paragraph, except after consultation with the Chief of Staff of the Army or the Chief of Naval Operations of the Navy, or both. The value of defense articles disposed of in any way under authority of this paragraph, and procured from funds heretofore appropriated, shall not exceed $1,300,000,000. . . .

(3) To test, inspect, prove, repair, outfit, recondition, or otherwise to place in good working order, to the extent to which funds are made available therefor, or contracts are authorized from time to time by the Congress, or both, any defense article for any such government, or to procure any or all such services by private contract.

(4) To communicate to any such government any defense information, pertaining to any defense article furnished to such government under paragraph (2) of this subsection.

(5) To release for export any defense article disposed of in any way under this subsection to any such government, . . .

Source: *Henry Steele Commager, ed., Documents of American History, 2 vols. (New York: Appleton-Century-Crofts, 1973), II: 449–450.*

Yet, as nearly all observers recognized late in the war, Allied-built trucks and jeeps ultimately constituted the most valuable form of aid. As Werth witnessed firsthand, American trucks were not yet a conspicuous presence at Stalingrad but were widely in evidence by the spring of 1943. By 1944, they played a significant role in the transformation of the Red Army. Late in the war, as a result of the maturation of its commanders and practical refinements in doctrine, the Soviet conduct of combat operations reached a qualitatively new stage. From their victory at Kursk in July 1943, Soviet forces enjoyed the unchallenged initiative on the Eastern Front for the remainder of the war. Employing the concept of deep operations, which placed a premium on rapid deep maneuver in the enemy rear, Soviet forces effected a complete reversal of the fortunes of war. The large-scale infusion of allied trucks played a vital role in lubricating the Soviet transportation net both in the rear area and at the front. The logistical support so necessary to deep operations as well as the speed required to trap German divisions by means of deep encirclements would not have been available in so generous a measure without the bounty provided by the American industrial machine. In a characteristic instance, as noted by John Erickson in *The Road to Berlin* (1983), forces under the command of Marshal I. S. Konev employed 15,000 U.S.-built trucks during the crossing of the Neisse River in 1945. Thus, Glantz and House are not at all unreasonable to suggest that war in the East might have dragged on for an additional twelve to eighteen months had the Soviets been forced to rely exclusively on domestic production.

In the end, it is possible to draw two important conclusions about Western economic aid to the Soviet Union during World War II. First, such aid was important but not decisive in determining the outcome on the Eastern Front. Second, Lend-Lease assistance proved to be an extraordinarily wise investment of resources on the part of Britain and the United States. From 22 June 1941, the date that Germany commenced Operation Barbarossa, to the end of the war, German might have concentrated primarily against the Soviet Union. As Russian historians are quick to point out, at no time in the war did the number of German divisions committed against the U.S.S.R. slip below 55 percent of the total directly engaged in combat. Before July 1943 and the Battle of Kursk, that total never dipped below 66 percent. Viewed another way, when during the combat at Stalingrad in November 1942 Germany maintained 268 active divisions on the Eastern Front, only four and one-half divisions fought Anglo-American forces in North Africa. Only in the aftermath of the Normandy invasion of June 1944 did the Western allies first confront as many as one-half the number of German divisions faced by the Soviet Union at the same time. In sum, it is reasonable to argue that although the Soviet Union would in all probability eventually have won the war against Germany on its own, it is doubtful that Anglo-American forces could have won the war in the absence of Soviet support. As acknowledged by Churchill himself, the Red Army bore by far the greater share of the burden, paying a toll in blood that can scarcely be comprehended in the West. Yet, drawing fully on its deep reserves of human and material strength, the Soviet Union prevailed.

–ROBERT F. BAUMANN, COMBAT STUDIES INSTITUTE, U.S. ARMY COMMAND AND GENERAL STAFF COLLEGE

References

John Erickson, *The Road to Berlin* (Boulder, Colo.: Westview Press, 1983);

David M. Glantz and Jonathon House, *When Titans Clashed: How the Red Army Stopped Hitler* (Lawrence: University of Kansas, 1995);

George C. Herring, *Aid to Russia, 1941–1946: Strategy, Diplomacy, and the Origins of the Cold War* (New York: Columbia University Press, 1973);

John Keegan, *The Second World War* (New York: Viking, 1990);

David Kennedy, *Freedom From Fear: The American People in Depression and War, 1929–1945* (New York: Oxford University Press, 1999);

Nikita Khrushchev, *Khrushchev Remembers: The Last Testament*, translated and edited by Strobe Talbott (Boston: Little, Brown, 1974);

Richard Overy, *Why the Allies Won* (New York: Norton, 1996);

B. V. Sokolov, "The Role of Lend-Lease in Soviet Military Efforts, 1941–1945," *Journal of Soviet Military Studies*, 7 (September 1994): 567–586;

Edward Stettinius, *Lend-Lease, Weapon for Victory* (New York: Macmillan, 1944);

Alexander Werth, *Russia at War 1941–1945* (New York: Carroll & Graf, 1984).

LEND LEASE

LUFTWAFFE

Was the Luftwaffe an effective military instrument?

Viewpoint: Yes, the Luftwaffe was a well-trained, effective air force, especially in the early years of the war, despite poor leadership at the highest levels.

Viewpoint: No, the Luftwaffe was not an effective air force because it was not designed for a war of attrition.

The *Luftwaffe* (German Air Force) began with almost nothing in 1933—at least from a material standpoint. Doctrinally, during the Weimar years, German theorists had developed a broad and integrated concept of air power, one that shaped and defined the Luftwaffe that emerged from Hitler's rearmament program. It was not primarily a ground-support force. Indeed, what is currently defined as "close air support" was only a small element of an air-power doctrine that focused on an independent mission incorporating strategic bombing, joint operations with the army and navy, active and passive defense of German air space, and the creation of airborne and air transport forces able to mount and sustain deep-penetration operations.

Luftwaffe practice involved first securing air superiority, then interdicting both the battlefields and the theater of operations, and finally attacking enemy production capability and morale. At all three stages the number of aircraft was less important than their striking power. Flexibility—supported by a first-rate communications system—was at the core of Luftwaffe successes from 1939 to 1941. Decline set in as Germany found itself in an attritional war, first over England and northern France, then in Russia, and finally over the Reich itself. Operational problems were compounded by shortcomings in aircraft design and procurement, shortages of raw materials, failure to train new generations of pilots, and the comprehensive spectrum of responsibilities that spread thin resources and talent. The incompetence of its commander-in-chief, Hermann Göring, meant that efforts to correct increasingly apparent shortcomings were too few and too late. By mid 1944, despite the introduction of jet aircraft, the Luftwaffe was playing out an end game in its own skies.

Viewpoint:
Yes, the Luftwaffe was a well-trained, effective air force, especially in the early years of the war, despite poor leadership at the highest levels.

History, especially military history, is usually written by the winners. The post–World War II historical analysis of the role and the effectiveness of the *Luftwaffe* (German Air Force) in the war tended to justify the doctrine and operations of the winning air forces—Great Britain's Royal Air Force (RAF) and the U.S. Army Air Force (USAAF). Both the Americans and British had emphasized the role of strategic bombing before, during, and after the war and this agenda tended to color the analysis of military historians for decades. According to this view, the Luftwaffe never realized its potential to be truly effective because it was primarily a "tactical air force," whose primary mission was to support the army and navy. According to the mainstream view of the British and American airmen, tactical aviation, such as the Luftwaffe's, was a subsidiary role of airpower that detracted from the war-winning capability of the strategic bomber. British and American air forces in World War II had emphasized strategic bombing, not tactical operations; since they won the war; therefore, their approach to airpower must have been the correct one.

It is true that the Luftwaffe excelled in tactical operations, especially in the first three years of World War II. The popular view that the Luftwaffe was simply a tactical air force, however, has come in for a good deal of revision in recent years. Having a strong tactical capability does not necessarily detract from developing a strategic bombing force. Indeed, a deeper look at the Luftwaffe shows that it had indeed put a good deal of effort into strategic-bombing doctrine as well as other aspects of air power. While acknowledging that the Allied strategic-bombing campaign contributed a good deal to their victory, one can also acknowledge that the Luftwaffe got a great many things right and played a decisive role in Germany's victories in the first half of the conflict.

When World War II began Germany had, by any reckoning, the most combat-effective air force in the world. Between 1939 and 1942 the Luftwaffe repeatedly defeated large and modern air forces and played a decisive role in Germany's blitzkrieg campaigns. The Luftwaffe's early successes were not simply a result of Germany's massive rearmament in the 1930s or based on superior aircraft. Britain, France, the Soviet Union and the United States also began rearming and produced some first-rate aircraft in the early years of the war. The Luftwaffe's success was largely attributed to sound leadership at the operational and tactical level, combined with a superior comprehensive doctrine of airpower employment.

Germany was forbidden to possess an air force by the Versailles Treaty after World War I. The German army, however, continued to maintain an air staff, train pilots, develop aircraft and secret reserves, and work diligently for the day that Germany could openly assume its role as a major power and field a world-class air force. Some of Germany's most talented air commanders and pilots of World War I remained in the army and formed the nucleus of the German military's (*Reichswehr*'s) secret air force. During the 1920s and early 1930s, before the Nazis came to

power, the secret air staff intensively studied the lessons of World War I and current developments in aviation in order to build a doctrine for a future air force. The secret Luftwaffe staff was able to build on the strengths of the Imperial Air Service (*Luftstreitkraefte*) of World War I, a force that had fought superbly. In World War I the Imperial Air Service had mounted the world's first strategic-bombing campaign, developed highly effective specialized fighter formations and ground-attack units, deployed large flak forces and created an air-defense command for Western Germany that included flak, fighters, and passive air defenses. Based on the experience of four years of war, officers such as Helmuth Wilberg, Helmuth Felmy, and Wilhelm Wimmer laid the foundation of an air force with a comprehensive view of the many roles and missions of airpower. By the time Adolf Hitler assumed power in 1933, the groundwork had been done and Germany possessed a capable cadre of air-force leaders, secretly-developed modern aircraft ready to be put into production, and a comprehensive airpower doctrine the equal of any of the major contemporary air forces. The secret Luftwaffe progressed quickly under the Nazis and by the time that the Luftwaffe was officially revealed in March 1935, it was already a large force with an effective doctrine for modern war.

One of the great strengths of the Luftwaffe was its comprehensive approach to air-force doctrine. Contrary to popular myth, the Luftwaffe's doctrine, like the British and Americans, put considerable emphasis upon a strategic air force and concepts of how to use it. Unlike the British and Americans, who tended to focus on strategic bombing to the exclusion of other aspects of airpower, the Luftwaffe developed a broad vision of airpower and an air force suitable for many different missions. In Germany, all airpower matters became the responsibility of the Luftwaffe, so one of the Luftwaffe's responsibilities was the ground-based air defense force. The Luftwaffe developed a large flak corps of both highly mobile forces to follow the army and provide anti-aircraft support on the battlefront and of heavy flak forces to defend the cities and industries of the homeland. The Luftwaffe was also responsible for the civil-defense training of the population. Germany's weapons factories, built in the 1930s, were carefully sited and designed to reduce vulnerability to air attack. The German population was organized and trained to deal with air attacks during a series of major exercises from 1934–1939—one of the reasons why German morale did not crack under massive Allied air bombardment. The Luftwaffe also developed a large transport fleet, which gave it a tactical and strategic mobility that no other air force of the time possessed. Moreover, the Luftwaffe was open to some radical new ideas of employing air-

German Junkers Ju 87 Stukas during the Polish campaign

power. Starting in the mid 1930s, Germany developed a two-division force of paratroops and glider-borne troops capable of being dropped and supplied behind enemy lines by specialized transport units.

The Luftwaffe emphasized creating bomber units in the 1930s and most of the combat aircraft available at the start of the war were medium bombers of the He 111, Do 17 and Ju 88 types—all excellent aircraft for their day. The Luftwaffe leadership additionally emphasized

the skills necessary for strategic bombing to include long-distance navigation and night flying—basic skills largely neglected in the strategically-oriented RAF. The Luftwaffe built an effective fighter force for homeland defense and bomber escort around the Me 109 and Me 110 fighters. Especially important to the Luftwaffe was its emphasis on close cooperation with the army. The Luftwaffe and army trained together in several exercises throughout the 1930s and the Luftwaffe created a group of liaison officers to

be assigned to army corps and divisions in order to help coordinate close-air support. In addition, the Luftwaffe had a superb close-support aircraft in the Ju 87 dive bomber. Especially important for the maturation of the Luftwaffe was the German assistance to the Nationalists in the Spanish Civil War. The Luftwaffe sent an air group, the Condor Legion, to fight in Spain between 1936 and 1939. Twenty thousand Luftwaffe personnel served combat tours there. In Spain most forms of airpower were practiced, including bombing enemy industries, naval interdiction, and close air support of ground troops. Lessons learned in Spain were quickly incorporated into the Luftwaffe's doctrine. By 1939 the Luftwaffe had more recent combat experience than any other major air force.

In the years from 1939 to 1942, the Luftwaffe showed how an air force could have a decisive effect upon a ground battle. In Poland, the Luftwaffe disrupted Polish troop movements behind the front and assisted the rapid advance of the Panzer divisions by destroying Polish defense positions. In France in 1940 the Luftwaffe quickly gained air superiority by attacking the British and French airfields. Massive Luftwaffe raids broke the French army's morale at Sedan as the Germans initiated their drive across Northern France to the channel. When the Panzer divisions outran their supporting infantry divisions, the Luftwaffe helped the army keep its offensive momentum by protecting the flanks of the German thrust from French counterattacks. German casualties in Poland and France were low, largely a result of the superb air-ground coordination of the Luftwaffe.

In the Norwegian campaign of April 1940, the Germans used paratroops and air-landed troops for the first time to secure vital objectives at the outset of the campaign. When Allied submarines and naval forces interdicted German supply by sea, the Luftwaffe used its formidable transport force to fly reinforcements and supplies to Norway. The Luftwaffe gained air superiority over Norwegian waters and forced the Royal Navy and Allied ground troops to retreat. For the first time airpower proved superior to seapower. Without the Luftwaffe's effective support, the invasion of Norway would have failed miserably in the first hours.

One of the most dramatic lessons about the use of airpower was the use of paratroops and air-landed troops in the Low Countries in May 1940. Luftwaffe glider troops seized the strategic Belgian border fortifications in the first hours of the campaign. German paratroops seized Rotterdam and prevented the retreat of the Dutch army into Western Holland. As a result, the Netherlands fell in only five days. In May 1941 the Luftwaffe again demonstrated the decisive effect of airborne attack by seizing the island of Crete by air assault. While German paratroop losses were heavy, the British lost over twenty thousand men as prisoners and more than twenty warships in the campaign.

In Russia in 1941 and 1942 the Luftwaffe again proved decisive in assisting the army's rapid advance, a campaign that destroyed whole armies and netted millions of prisoners. The Luftwaffe interdicted Russian troop movements in the summer 1941 campaign and provided effective close-air support in other campaigns, such as in the Crimea in 1942. From 1939 to 1942, the Luftwaffe was years ahead of its opponents in the doctrine and techniques of tactical-air support. Indeed, the Allied air forces were so impressed with the Luftwaffe's performance that the British and Americans copied the Luftwaffe in creating paratroop divisions and specialized tactical-air-support forces.

The Luftwaffe's only failure in the first half of the war was in the Battle of Britain. It is often alleged that the Luftwaffe failed to win the campaign because it possessed no heavy bombers or doctrine for strategic air war. It is true that the Luftwaffe had no heavy-bomber force, although not from a lack of doctrine or interest. The Luftwaffe had put a high priority on creating a heavy-bomber force in the 1930s. The problem was the incompetence at the top in the form of Ernst Udet, chief of aircraft production from 1936 to 1941. Udet chose a thoroughly bad heavy-bomber design, the He 177, and poured resources into this hopeless program, thus depriving Germany of a heavy bomber. Poor management by Udet also slowed production of the excellent Ju 88 medium bomber in the first years of the war.

The Battle of Britain was not lost because of any deficiency in German doctrine or in bombing capability. It was lost as a result of an appalling strategic miscalculation at the top and a lack of effective intelligence—problems typical of warmaking in the Third Reich. The Luftwaffe went to war against Britain with poor intelligence about RAF defenses, partly because Hitler had only directed his armed forces to include Britain in war plans in 1938 and there had been little time to collect this needed information. The German intelligence system was also comprised of many competing agencies and was generally incapable of providing an accurate strategic picture of Germany's enemies. In Britain in 1940 the Luftwaffe faced a sophisticated radar-controlled fighter-defense system and knew little about the British defenses and their vulnerabilities. Although the Germans greatly outnumbered the RAF and severely damaged the RAF Fighter Command in airfield attacks, the Luftwaffe was usually fighting blind and had little idea of how to break the British radar system or cripple the small Fighter Command. In addition, the Luftwaffe was flying at long range with short-range escorts versus a capable enemy fighter force with home-field advantages.

What the Battle of Britain showed was not the poor performance of the Luftwaffe, but the tremendous advantage given to the defense in air warfare by radar-controlled fighters and flak. When the RAF tried to gain air superiority over Northern France in 1941–1942 and the tables were turned, a handful of Luftwaffe fighters, with a modern integrated radar system, inflicted prohibitive losses upon the RAF attackers. The Germans built up their own homeland air defenses from 1942–1944 and inflicted enormous losses upon British and American heavy bombers attacking Germany, at times actually stopping the campaign. In the end, the Allied strategic-bombing campaign succeeded, but just barely and at a high price. In 1944–1945 the Luftwaffe was simply bludgeoned to death by Allied numbers.

The greatest weakness of the Luftwaffe was in its pilot training. In 1940–1941 overconfident German leaders failed to expand the pilot-training program to overcome attrition and ensure a greatly expanded force. By 1942 pilot attrition was far heavier than predicted and the Luftwaffe curtailed the training time for pilots. By 1943–1944 the Luftwaffe was sending up pilots with only one hundred hours of total flight time to face British and American pilots with over four hundred and fifty hours of flight time. Although the Germans had fine aircraft, the difference in pilot quality resulted in a massacre of the Luftwaffe's pilots in the last eighteen months of the war.

The Luftwaffe reflected the strengths and the weaknesses of the Third Reich. At the top, the Luftwaffe suffered from some utterly incompetent leadership in the form of Hermann Göring, Commander of the Luftwaffe from 1933 to 1945, and Udet, as chief of aircraft production. General Hans Jeschonnek, the Luftwaffe's chief of staff from 1939 to 1943, was an intelligent officer who, however, proved too trusting and weak-willed to deal with Hitler and Göring. Disastrous decisions by Hitler, Göring, and Jeschonnek—such as the Stalingrad airlift or using up Germany's last bomber reserves in pointless attacks upon London in early 1944—added to the pilot-attrition problem. Nevertheless, in leadership at the tactical and operational level, the Luftwaffe was equal to the best of the British and American air forces. Air-fleet commanders Hugo Sperrle, Albert Kesselring, and Hans-Juergen Stumpf were some of the outstanding air commanders of the war. Field Marshal Wolfram von Richthofen was probably the

best tactical air commander of World War II. In other areas, especially in doctrine, force structure, and tactics, the Luftwaffe proved far superior to the Allies in the first three years of World War II.

—JAMES S. CORUM, US AIR FORCE SCHOOL OF ADVANCED AIRPOWER STUDIES

Viewpoint:
No, the Luftwaffe was not an effective air force because it was not designed for a war of attrition.

On the eve of the German invasion of Poland in September 1939, the *Luftwaffe* (German Air Force) ostensibly appeared a formidable force. Among its more than 4,500 aircraft were the Bf 109 fighter, the Ju 88 multi-role bomber, and the Ju 87 Stuka dive-bomber. Luftwaffe chief, Reichsmarshall Herman Göring, grouped these aircraft into interchangeable units, *Luftflotten* (Air Fleets) and subordinate *Fliegerkorps* (Air Corps). Pilots and ground personnel in these units gained valuable experience from the Luftwaffe's participation in the Spanish Civil War and benefitted from knowledge of the timing and location of the coming attack. As operations in Poland, across Europe to the foothills of Asia, and in North Africa, would demonstrate, these pilots and their technically advanced aircraft were the thin veneer of a fragile organization with numerous vulnerabilities that a multi-theater war was bound to expose.

German chancellor Adolph Hitler tasked the Fliegerkorps to participate in his *Blitzkrieg* (lightning war) strategy, which sought to avoid a repeat of the trench warfare in France during World War I and of the resulting collapse of the government. The Fliegerkorps proved devastatingly effective. In the September invasion of Poland, Luftwaffe warplanes supported the army while simultaneously eliminating the Polish air force. Early in the conflict, the EK VIII Fliegerkorps, under the command of Wolfram von Richthofen, destroyed key bridges and mercilessly attacked army concentrations caught in the open. These attacks cut off lines of retreat and created an anvil upon which the *Wehrmacht* (German Army) struck. The force went on to bomb Warsaw when Polish garrisons there refused to surrender.

The Luftwaffe of the following year established a pattern characterized by the flexible use of air power that combined direct and indirect support of the army with simultaneous air superiority campaigns, which were followed by inde-

LUFTWAFFE

pendent attacks against enemy cities if necessary. Because of Norway's unique geography, Luftwaffe support came most importantly in airlift, landing German paratroopers who captured Oslo and supporting the ground forces under siege from the British at Narvik. It was in France and the low countries in May 1940, however, where the Luftwaffe style of air warfare achieved its apotheosis. Stuka dive-bombers protected the Wehrmacht's flanks as General Rundstedt's Army Group A sliced through the French Army's weak defenses in the Ardennes. On the air superiority side, the Luftwaffe delivered a fatal blow against the French air force and the British task force. The failure of the Luftwaffe to finish off the British Expeditionary Force as it fled the continent at Dunkirk, however, gave the first indication of looming problems when faced with a determined competitor.

Indeed, in the context of a larger, more intense conflict the Luftwaffe failed to replicate its early brand of air warfare. This full-scale conflagration came about initially when the Luftwaffe turned unsuccessfully on Great Britain in July 1940 and then supported the massive invasion of Russia in June 1941. Combat and occupation commitments in the Mediterranean and the Balkans, respectively, further increased the scope of Luftwaffe operations. To achieve Hitler's war aims in these circumstances, the Luftwaffe needed more resources of its own to brawl with the allies or a supreme command of brilliant strategists who could apply Germany's limited resources efficiently and outmaneuver the often clumsy, yet resource abundant, Allies. The Luftwaffe had neither.

The failures of German supreme command came in a variety of forms, although none is perhaps as significant as the failure of the command to find a proper operational balance. This tendency manifested itself in two ways. First, the Luftwaffe leaders failed to find the right balance between dispersal and concentration of their forces, leaning to the former when the inverse promised more satisfactory results. In summer 1942 the Luftwaffe high command (OKL), for example, gave the Fourth Luftflotte two disparate operational objectives. One fliegerkorps supported the push of the First Panzer Division to the oil fields of the Caucuses, while the other, the close air support specialist Fliegerkorps VIII accompanied the Sixth Army and Fourth Panzer Army in their attack into the bends of the River Don, the Volga, and into Stalingrad. When Soviet forces encircled the Sixth Army at Stalingrad, Luftwaffe commanders decided to reconcentrate, which in turn reduced the overall firepower of the forces in the Caucuses and left the army increasingly vulnerable to the Russian air force.

Even when they achieved significant mass through concentration, the Luftwaffe leaders often shifted the focus of these attacks too soon. They tended to do so not only as a result of a natural inclination to take advantage of the mobility of air power, but also because they had wrongly concluded that strikes against certain targets had little, if any, effect on the enemy. The basis for those decisions was either incorrect intelligence reports or a decision by Hitler to change the overall focus of a campaign. In the Battle of Britain, for instance, faulty intelligence reports discouraged Luftwaffe commanders from continuing early attacks against Great Britain's Royal Air Force (RAF) radar sites, leading them instead to shift to more direct strikes against RAF Fighter Command. After the British bombed Berlin in late August, Hitler decided to retaliate with a sustained bombardment of London, despite assessments that noted that RAF Fighter Command was near defeat. A similar situation occurred less than a year later during the invasion of Russia. Despite destroying nearly 5,000 enemy aircraft in the first few days of the invasion, Luftwaffe intelligence failed to identify an additional 5,000 aircraft produced before the war. This information, combined with Hitler's eagerness for more direct Luftwaffe support of the Wehrmacht's encirclement efforts and the general OKL failure to conceive air superiority as a continual, rather than a one-time goal, led to the premature termination of the air superiority campaign. The Soviet air force gained much needed respite, withdrew their sources of production and operations to the Urals, and prepared for future counteroffensives.

The defeat of the Blitzkrieg strategy, symbolized by the Battle of Britain and the stalled invasion against the Soviet Union, made this conflict a war of attrition; the Luftwaffe could remain effective only if it could match or exceed the resources of its opponents. It is doubtful the service could have taken any measures to carry out such an attrition strategy, given the combined industrial might of the United States, Great Britain, and the Soviet Union. In this sense, 1941 marked the end of Luftwaffe effectiveness. The way the high command managed the aircraft industry nonetheless accelerated the oncoming defeat. Among the many factors that hindered aircraft production, perhaps the most significant was the location of the Luftwaffe in a bureaucratic hierarchy. The Luftwaffe was inferior to its army and navy counterparts for reasons both historical and related to Hitler's conception of the character of war. Hitler's strident view that his Blitzkrieg strategy would succeed and that, as a result, the war would be short precluded greater production planning and the actualization of those plans until it was too late. Hitler's decisions to divert resources from bomber and fighter production to the V-1 and V-2 rockets, designed as weapons of terror, undermined production even further.

The failure to wrench significant increases in aircraft production from the German war economy meant that the Luftwaffe would not be able substantially to alter the composition of its air force, despite the clear recognition that the change in the scope and intensity of the war demanded such alterations. Two glaring deficiencies in the capabilities of the force thus remained after 1942. One was limited long-range strategic bombing capability, resulting from an organizational bias toward dive-bombing production and the typical industrial and technical problems inherent in bomber development. While it is pure speculation to assert that a bomber fleet would have decisively changed the overall course of events, it certainly would have contributed positively to operations on the Eastern Front. Strategic bombers would have deprived the remnants of the Soviet air force sanctuary and hindered the withdrawal of Soviet industrial equipment to the Ural Mountains.

Relatively stagnant aircraft production also impinged on the ability of the Luftwaffe to increase its force of air transports. Operations to support the invasion of Russia and reinforce the collapsing Akrica Korps in North Africa exposed this shortfall by the autumn of 1942. The shortfalls in this area became particularly acute by early 1943 after the failed airlift of the beleaguered Sixth Army at Stalingrad. Göring's pusillanimous failure to inform Hitler of the airlift arm's original problem led Hitler to decide to supply the Sixth Army. This operation led to the decimation of the Luftwaffe airlift fleet and, more broadly, contributed to the overall catastrophe that occurred in Stalingrad, a blow from which the Luftwaffe and Germany never recovered.

The collapse of the air defense of Germany exposed a more complex side of the general resource problem. In this area, the Luftwaffe failed to generate the forces to blunt the Allied bombing offensives but not because of a failure in weapons production. Fighter production remained the highest priority within the service since the onset of the allied bombing campaign in 1942 and 1943. Even in late 1943, the rate of production increased. Rather, the organization lacked the oil and skilled pilots to fuel and fly those abundant fighters. This situation resulted from high command decision making and the geographical location of Germany. In 1942 and 1943, the OKL gutted pilot training to compensate immediately for losses in the Mediterranean and the East. An equally pernicious oil scar-

THE LUFTWAFFE OVER BRITAIN

One of the failures of the Luftwaffe was its inability to defeat the British in the Battle of Britain. In this account, Luftwaffe Oberleutnant Gerhard Kadow recounts his experiences being shot down.

At the English coast I counted some twenty dark spots in the distance, somewhat higher than we were. I was certain they were RAF fighters, but couldn't recognise whether they were Hurricanes or Spitfires—but knew that our twin-engined machines were no match for these single-engined fighters. However, it was our duty to protect the Stukas, so they could bomb unhindered. The main strength of [our] Me 110 was the two 20mm cannons and four machine guns in its nose. I pressed the firing buttons and bullets flew like water out of a watering can towards the enemy. The closing speed was high, and at the last minute both I and my attacker had to break away to avoid a head-on collision. Whether I scored any hits or not, I don't know. The next moment, two fighters were on my tail and had opened fire. Almost immediately both of my engines stopped and a return to the Continent was clearly impossible. The enemy saw his success and stopped shooting, but watched me from behind. I flung off my cabin roof for a quick escape, and hoped it would hit him. I ordered Helmut Scholz to do the same. He radioed that the mechanism to ditch his cabin roof would not operate as a result of bullet damage. I couldn't bail out and leave Scholz to his fate, and for the same reason, ditching in the sea seemed unwise. The only alternative was a crash-landing on British soil. After we had landed I found I could not leave the cockpit—a high explosive bullet had hit my seat, causing a big hole. The torn aluminum 'fangs' around the hole had nailed themselves through my parachute pack and tunic and on to my flesh. I pulled myself forward, and suddenly was free. I left the aircraft and smashed the cabin roof of my gunner so he could get out. He was hurt only by shell splinters. The first thing to do was destroy the aircraft. We didn't have a self-destruct charge, so opened the fuel caps and tried to ignite the petrol with the muzzle flash from my pistol. I fired eight shots, but had no success. In hindsight, this was just as well, otherwise the aircraft would have exploded and killed us."

"Speeches and Quotations of the Germans," in The Battle of Britain, *on-line sight, http://www.pnc.com.au/~insight/stories2.htm*

city resulted from the geographical location of Germany, in that it lacked natural reserves, a situation that constant fighting on the peripheries of the Reich only worsened. These trends combined with devastating results on Luftwaffe effectiveness in early 1944. American bomber attacks against Germany's remaining oil reserves forced the OKL to send up their inexperienced pilots to parry the attacks. They proved no match for the better-trained pilots of the P-51 fighters that accompanied the bombers, and the Luftwaffe lost the ability to challenge Allied forces. As the Allies invaded Europe in June 1944 and went on to bomb Germany continuously, few Luftwaffe aircraft met the Allies.

The Luftwaffe showed itself to be an effective force on several occasions after the collapse of Blitzkrieg strategy in late 1941. In May 1942 the Luftwaffe operated closely with the Wehrmacht in the Crimea to destroy Soviet forces on the Kerch peninsula and Sevastopol. During the Battle of Berlin of 1942 and the Schweinfurt raids of autumn 1943, the Luftwaffe fighter command demonstrated that it could, through clever tactics, inflict intolerable losses on allied bombers. However, these victories came only when the conditions of the early years of the war could be replicated, that is, when the allies did not bring the full brunt of their might and technical know-how against the Germans and when isolated operations could be carried out. These circumstances became particularly rare as the war developed. The Luftwaffe, in the final analysis, was not a modern air force with the capability to win a war of attrition over several fronts. When the allies relentlessly attacked on all sides, Luftwaffe deficiencies in strategic bombing, airlift capabilities, and pilot reserves became all too apparent. The Luftwaffe could not compensate for these shortfalls, because they failed to understand that modern war could not be won through knockout blows and that victory did not come cheaply, either in men or matériel.

–DANIEL B. GINSBERG,
ATLANTA, GEORGIA

References

Horst Boog, *Die deutschen Luftwaffenführung 1935–1945: Führungsprobleme, Spitzengliederung, Generalstabsausbildung* (Stuttgart: Deutsche Verlags-Anstalt, 1982);

Donald L. Caldwell, *JG 26 Top Guns of the Luftwaffe* (New York: Orion Books, 1991);

Matthew Cooper, *The German Air Force, 1933–1945: An Anatomy of Failure* (London & New York: Jane's, 1981);

James S. Corum, *The Luftwaffe: Creating the Operational Air War, 1918–1940* (Lawrence: University Press of Kansas, 1997);

Joel S. A. Hayward, *Stopped at Stalingrad: The Luftwaffe and Hitler's Defeat in the East, 1942–1943* (Lawrence: University of Kansas Press, 1998);

Richard Muller, *The German Air War in Russia* (Baltimore: Nautical & Aviation Publishing Company of America, 1992);

Williamson Murray, *Strategy for Defeat: the Luftwaffe, 1933–1945* (Maxwell Air Force Books, Alabama: Air University Press, 1983);

Gerhard L. Weinberg, *A World at Arms: A Global History of World War II* (Cambridge & New York: Cambridge University Press, 1994).

MACARTHUR

Was Douglas MacArthur a great American general of World War II?

Viewpoint: MacArthur was a masterful battlefield tactician who employed maneuver and surprise to defeat the enemy and avoided the wasteful slaughter of his own troops.

Viewpoint: MacArthur was an overrated general who failed to provide an adequate defense of the Philippines and later mismanaged the recapture of the archipelago.

Like that of George S. Patton, Douglas MacArthur's professional reputation has changed with the passing of time. In his case it has declined. The World War II images of the hero of Bataan, the architect of the triumphant return to the Philippines, and the executor of a brilliant campaign of strategic and operational maneuver in the southwest Pacific have been overshadowed by characterizations of an egomaniacal blowhard. This MacArthur singlehandedly forced the dissipation of U.S. resources in an unnecessary two-pronged drive across the Pacific. His insistence on liberating the Philippines was an attempt to wipe out his own shameful abandonment of the islands and their garrison in 1942. Even his New Guinea campaign is described as having traded lives for time in an effort to stay ahead of the Navy's drive across the central Pacific.

To a degree MacArthur's record in the Pacific war has been caught in the riptides of criticism of his post-1945 performances in Japan and Korea. It suffers as well from MacArthur's personality. Imperial and imperious enough that one of his biographers calls him an "American Caesar," MacArthur stands in sharp contrast to the folksy Texan Admiral Chester W. Nimitz to everyman's General Dwight D. Eisenhowser, even to George S. Patton Jr., with his heart on his sleeve and at the tip of his tongue. Nor does MacArthur's outspoken hostility to Franklin D. Roosevelt and the New Deal enhance his acceptability among civilian historians. Institutionally, the U.S. Army regarded the southwest Pacific as a sideshow, and its senior officers considered MacArthur the kind of difficult personality best kept as far as possible from Washington's corridors of power. As a result, the New Guinea/Philippines campaigns have been relegated to an historical backwater, while MacArthur is denied the professional affirmation of his achievements routinely given in the war colleges to his counterparts. Nevertheless, through point and counterpoint, MacArthur's character and performance continue to structure discussion both of his particular effectiveness as a commander and of military-political relations in a democracy.

Viewpoint:
MacArthur was a masterful battlefield tactician who employed maneuver and surprise to defeat the enemy and avoided the wasteful slaughter of his own troops.

Douglas MacArthur was unique among American military commanders, not only during World War II, but in history. This is conceded both by his admirers and detractors—both of whom were, and are, legion. MacArthur was egotistical, proud, vainglorious, grandiloquent, and a poser; he was brave physically and in his convictions; often brilliant in tactics and strategy; and stubborn to the point of single-mindedness. He was learned and never ceased to learn from others and his own experience. All personal qualities aside, MacArthur must be judged like any other general—by his military achievements. The bottom line is he conquered more territory in less time with less material and fewer casualties than any other commander at a comparable level in World War II. From 1941 to 1945, MacArthur lost fewer men than were killed in the Battle of the Bulge (16–25 December 1944).

MacArthur was the last romantic general. To him "fighting men" were real soldiers; staff officers were a necessary evil. Although Chief of Staff of the 42nd "Rainbow" Division during most of World War I, he habitually spent as much time in the front lines, participating unarmed except for a riding crop—joining in trench raids to bring back prisoners and reconnoitering the German wire before an attack. George S. Patton, no mean judge of courage in battle, called MacArthur, "The bravest man I have ever known."

MacArthur also learned to hate frontal assaults against prepared positions, which he considered designed to waste lives needlessly. Before leading his final battle at Cote de Chatillon (15–16 October 1918) against two hundred and thirty fortified machine gun nests, he personally led a reconnaissance patrol of the German wire, discovered a weak spot, and successfully lead a flanking attack that in turn led to a major and final breakthrough for the American armies. He was recommended for the Medal of Honor. In his career he was nominated for that medal, awarded only for supreme gallantry in the face of the enemy, three times. It was finally awarded for his stand at Corregidor (which fell on 6 May 1942)—an ironic coda to a Philippine campaign that was one long string of defeats that generated significant doubts about both MacArthur's capacities as a commander and his personal courage.

Any self-doubts MacArthur may have entertained remained private. His first offensive campaign against the Japanese stronghold of Buna on the northeastern side of New Guinea (January 1943) was nevertheless a sharp series of lessons in modern warfare. MacArthur learned them quickly and well. Foremost he realized he had an unreliable, unimaginative, and, by general consensus, second-rate staff. Its chief, Richard Sutherland, did things by the book. Because he believed artillery of little use in jungle warfare, GIs of the 32nd Division were constrained to assault well-fortified Japanese positions with hand grenades. Sutherland's intelligence reports reiterated that the Japanese held a limited-defense system with no more support than a few machine-gun nests. When Buna was finally taken, the cost of overcoming 2,500 Japanese defenders was 2,343 U.S. combat casualties. The Japanese defense was discovered to be an interlaced network of pillboxes and machine-gun nests. For MacArthur, relieving men such as Sutherland was a waste of time; staff officers were all alike. Instead, declaring "no more Bunas": MacArthur never again admitted Sutherland or any other staff officer into strategic-planning sessions, relying instead on direct information from officers doing the actual fighting. He then gave orders to the staff to do what he believed it did best: work out the logistics and other administrative details. It was "heroic leadership" in a long-standing American tradition.

MacArthur deplored wasteful battles in any theater. When he learned of the battle of Tarawa (November 1943), which cost three thousand lives in the initial landing, MacArthur fired off a letter directly to Secretary of War Henry Lewis Stimson excoriating the Navy for its profligate waste of men against entrenched positions. He did not invent the alternative approach of "island hopping." Envelopment has been part of standard repertoire of war for millennia—Alexander the Great (356–323 B.C.) and Hannibal (247–183 B.C.) used it to devastating effect. Already it had been used in the Aleutian Islands and by Admiral Chester W. Nimitz in the Central Pacific after Tarawa. What was unrivaled about MacArthur was the sweep and speed of his operations. One example will suffice. During the morning of his landing at Hollandia (April 1944), he decided to take the troops not yet disembarked, pick up I Corps, which was bogged down by a swamp, and attack Wadke Island the next morning, four weeks ahead of schedule. He overrode the appalled reaction of his staff and the commander of I Corps that there was no adequate preparation and that it would take at least seventy-two hours to reallocate supplies necessary for invasion. Twenty-four hours later MacArthur controlled both islands.

The Southwest Pacific Area Command (SWPA) was considered by everyone except MacArthur to be the backwater of the war. To be assigned there was considered the equivalent to a demotion. The Army's real war was in Europe. The Central Pacific Area Command under Admiral William F. Halsey Jr. was expected to do all the heavy lifting in the Pacific theater; hence it got most of the ships, aircraft, and men. It did not help that President Franklin D. Roosevelt, Admiral Ernest J. King, Chief of Naval Operations, and Nimitz, Commander of Pacific Operations, MacArthur's three immediate superiors, disliked him to the point of loathing. Curiously MacArthur and Halsey took an immediate liking to each other and generally cooperated together. Roosevelt disliked him for his politics and saw him as the strongest political threat to his reelection in 1944. He never forgot nor forgave MacArthur for harsh words uttered a decade before during budget battles when MacArthur was Army Chief of Staff. King saw him as a poser, a vainglorious, self-serving has-been, and hated the man. Nimitz simply believed the Pacific was the Navy's playground and that Halsey's area of the Central Pacific was the royal road to Japan.

MacArthur, son of a general, knew how to play military politics better than anyone. He was vainglorious and dramatic because he knew it made good copy. He generally received good press to the point of rivaling FDR in popularity on the homefront. As he was to find out, popularity does not translate into votes. As Roosevelt was to say to him, "MacArthur, you are undoubtedly our greatest general and our lousiest politician." He had, however, no hesitation at going over the chain of command: to the Secretary of War, who was, if not a MacArthur enthusiast, at least sympathetic; to his personal clique of mainly Republican devotees in Congress; and incessantly to General George C. Marshall, Chief of Staff—to the point of being ordered by the latter to shut up and stop whining. MacArthur believed the true road to victory lay in the Western Pacific through the Philippines, where his word and heart pledged a return. His focus was concentrated on his area of command. He felt it his duty, right, and obligation to do everything to bring victory. At one point in 1943 he impounded every transport ship that came within reach, regardless of its previous orders, to use in his upcoming operation.

One of the few Army generals to view the ocean as a highway and not an obstacle, MacArthur also quickly became a master in the use of combined forces, especially of air power. Having sat on the court-martial of General Billy Mitchell in 1925, he remained skeptical of strategic bombardment's effectiveness until he accompanied a bombing raid on a Japanese airfield. Afterward his Air Commander, General George C. Kenney, presented him with an airman's insignia and a leather flying jacket. Both became part of his eccentric uniform along with his crushed campaign hat and corncob pipe.

Douglas MacArthur coming ashore in the Philippines, 20 October 1944

(U.S. Army Signal Corps)

MACARTHUR

"BY THE GRACE OF GOD. . ."

In a few passages from a 1998 interview, Jerome Auman, a former Marine who served in the Pacific theater, remembers his participation in the recapture of the Philippine Islands.

I think it was in the Marshall Islands where General MacArthur had his headquarters at that time. And nobody knew where we were going until we left the Marshall Islands. Then they told us we were headed for the Philippines. . . .

To go on with our invasion of the Philippines, why there were so few Marines involved in that I don't know, but there were only 1,500 of us out of over 200,000 Army. See, this was General MacArthur's big thing, "I shall return." There were 1,500 of us, and of course the Marines are part of the Navy. And the Army says, "You belong to the Navy, the Navy is to feed you and deliver your mail." And the Navy says, "No, once we put the Marines ashore, you feed them and deliver their mail." Well, as it turned out we weren't very well fed and we didn't get any mail. Well, there's a saying in the Marines: You can only push a Marine so far till he starts pushing back. And I've got to get this in because I don't know if you noticed what's on the back of my jacket, "By the grace of God and a few Marines, MacArthur returned to the Philippines."

This is one of the greatest stories in Marine Corps history. There are only two things in Marine Corps history I think that are above this, and that's of course the Marine hymn, which will always be first. And then we have the statue of the Iwo Jima flag-raising, which is at Washington, D.C., it's a very beautiful monument, I've been there a couple of times, and to me that's the second. And "By the grace of God and a few Marines, MacArthur returned to the Philippines" is third, because I knew of this almost the day it happened, but I never met the Marines that did it. And I didn't meet one of them until 1995. That's 50 years later, 51 years later, I met the man who penned that phrase. . . .

So they took the lids of these wooden boxes and they made a sign, and they painted on this sign, "By the grace of God and a few Marines, MacArthur returned to the Philippines," and they hung it on their gun.

It hung there probably a few days and the story comes that the Army was sending officers around to inspect the troops, so the officer in charge of the gun ordered it taken down or we'd all be in trouble.

The sign was taken down, and it lay there on the ground, and the three involved lost track of it. Now, Edwin R. Murrow was it? It is said that he knew what happened to this sign, but the records are lost forever because we tried to find it. But the sign was taken to the beach where they thought MacArthur was going to make his highly photographed entrance. And he saw it. And it's said that he fumed and raved, and wanted to have the ones responsible for this sign court-martialed. That never happened, because nobody knew who did it, other than the gun crew. Now, I can't prove it and I don't know for sure, but MacArthur would not admit that there were Marines in that invasion. . . .

It seems that MacArthur, and rightly so, thought a lot of his troops, and if there looked like danger, they'd retreat. Well, I don't think the word "retreat" is in the Marine vocabulary. Besides, how would you pick up a 15-ton gun and move it? So we were at this one place at this one time, and here comes the Army retreating back through our gun positions. We can't move. It took bulldozers to hook up the guns and move, and they're coming back and the Japs are advancing. We were the front line defense at that time. We stopped them. We were shooting 155s point blank range. Now when I say point blank range, we had fuses. If you know anything about artillery or mortars, they had to screw a fuse on. Well, we had fuses that exploded on impact. We had time fuses. We were using time fuses and we were setting them as fast as possible. They were exploding 200 yards out. That's how we held the line. And when the Army saw what was happening, they stopped and fought back with us.

Source: Jerome Auman, interviewed by Aaron Elson, 24 May 1998, Eldred, Pennsylvania, in WWII Oral History, Web Page.

MacArthur thus began his campaign along the coastlines of Northern New Guinea and off-shore islands with a twofold objective of eliminating the Japanese threat and effectiveness on the island itself, and to isolate Rabaul, the largest stronghold in the South Pacific and home of the Japanese fleet. He did this by bypassing strong points and concentrating on lightly held supply bases. This took a combination of good intelligence work, guesswork, intuition, and luck. MacArthur believed in the military value of luck, often inquiring if a new officer was or was not lucky. He possessed the great combination of intuition and fortune. Before one operation intelligence reported that the island of Los Negros, which was invaded on 28 February 1944, was "lousy with Japs." Upon landing the Americans found the island nearly deserted and secured it by noon. On another occasion MacArthur landed his troops on the opposite side of the island from where the enemy commander expected him. They walked ashore virtually unopposed, captured the airfield, and were using it to attack the next island before the Japanese general realized his mistake.

MacArthur understood clearly that war means killing and did not flinch from a fight, or from taking casualties when he deemed it necessary. The 1945 liberation of the Philippines was a long and protracted battle, with heavy losses in the front-line rifle companies. In MacArthur's record, however, there is no Tarawa, no Iwo Jima. Instead, students of war will find masterful use of surprise and maneuver—confounding enemies and critics alike by "hitting them where they ain't."

–JOHN WHEATLEY, BROOKLYN CENTER, MINNESOTA

Viewpoint:
MacArthur was an overrated general who failed to provide an adequate defense of the Philippines and later mismanaged the recapture of the archipelago.

Douglas MacArthur was by all odds the most controversial American senior commander of World War II. His self-centered, self-confident flamboyance was—and is—at odds with a cultural preference for unassuming, "muddy-boots" personae at high military levels. That style is considered more appropriate—and safer—for a democracy whose military history is of citizen armed forces led by professionals. It does not matter that it may itself be a mask, a construction

responding to a social imperative. Those who challenge it do so at a price.

MacArthur's image suffers as well from his being an extreme conservative in an age when history is overwhelmingly written by liberals. His hostility to the New Deal, unconcealed dislike for Franklin D. Roosevelt, and willingness to use nuclear weapons during the Korean War (1950–1953)—such convictions are for many scholars more than enough to render his generalship suspect as well, on the principle of "flawed in one respect, flawed in all."

Yet even when issues of personal style and political beliefs are removed from the equation, MacArthur's performance as a military leader between 1941 and 1945 strongly suggests that his place among America's great captains is vulnerable. The first doubts began with his 1935 appointment as military adviser to a Philippines soon to become independent. MacArthur began by challenging the premise that the islands were indefensible against a serious Japanese attack. That alone is proof of no more than wishful thinking. However, especially as the United States began rearming in 1940, MacArthur sought to justify his position by demanding, with the leverage he possessed as a former chief of staff, more and more of the still-limited supplies of men and equipment, especially B-17 heavy bombers, at whatever cost to national priorities.

That drain might have been justified by temporary success, or even by a holding action that absorbed Japanese resources. Instead, MacArthur not only failed to launch his B-17s in the immediate aftermath of Pearl Harbor—ten hours later a Japanese strike caught his air force completely by surprise. The most credible explanation is that MacArthur went into something like a fugue state. His conduct of the remainder of the Philippine campaign suggests that he might never have quite emerged. His Philippine army, badly trained and under-equipped, fell apart on contact with a numerically inferior Japanese invasion force. The logistical aspect of his withdrawal into the Bataan peninsula as so poorly conceived and executed that hunger did more to defeat the garrison than did the Japanese.

MacArthur left the islands for Australia in March 1942 under direct orders from the president. Yet, while Roosevelt's decision made sense, it required a high level of spin to transform abandoning one's troops into a heroic deed. Certainly MacArthur was determined to erase what he considered the double shame of defeat and flight. He was, however, in an unpromising situation. His new assignment, the southwest Pacific theater, was considered a strategic dead end. It was at the bottom of the list for manpower, supplies, and equipment. Initially all MacArthur was expected to do was secure Australia and New Zealand from invasion—and even that was heavily contingent on the U.S. Navy's victory in the Midway campaign (3–6 June 1942).

As much to the point, MacArthur knew he would stay where he was. Roosevelt had no intention of returning him to the United States, where he might become a rallying point for political and military dissidents. Nor did Army Chief of Staff George C. Marshall wish to have such a contentious personality in Washington. MacArthur, therefore, faced the challenge of redefining the war effort to suit his desires. His initial efforts to challenge the "Germany first" basis of Allied strategy foundered on his lack of leverage. He then shifted his focus to advocacy of a two-pronged offensive in the Pacific—one across the central Pacific, controlled by the Navy, the other up from the south and under his command. The intermediate objective of both would be the Philippines, whose liberation MacArthur insisted was a matter of national as well as personal honor.

MacArthur's initial advocacy foundered on resources and implementation. The Navy, led by the abrasive Admiral Ernest King, was already insisting on increasing U.S. efforts in the Pacific; Marshall was unhappy with a senior general making the same point. Tactically, moreover, MacArthur's initial efforts at a counteroffensive bogged down immediately in the jungle mud of New Guinea. In November 1943 the Joint Chiefs of Staff came down in favor of the Navy's central Pacific drive as the focus of U.S. efforts. They did not, however, designate an overall commander. MacArthur unleashed one of the most successful policy campaigns in American military history to spin the decision in his direction. Ruthlessly using journalistic, political, and military contacts, engaging the Navy with a comprehensive sophistication better employed against the Japanese, by March 1944 he forced the Joint Chiefs to reconsider, and accept the principle of a two-pronged offensive against Japan.

The solution owed more to interservice rivalry, exacerbated to the breaking point by MacArthur, than to operational considerations. It reflected as well Roosevelt's belief that political considerations made both MacArthur's relief and his resignation unacceptably high-risk options. In hindsight the dual approach made military sense. It took advantage of existing force deployments in environments lacking infrastructures. It kept the Japanese off balance, forcing them to keep constantly shifting their limited reserves. The initial aspect of MacArthur's offensive, his New Guinea campaign of 1944, was not quite the triumph of maneuver the general's admirers depict, but it produced quick results at limited cost under unpromising operational conditions. It demonstrated that MacArthur could cooperate successfully with sailors and airmen in subordinate positions. The New Guinea operations, however, also highlighted MacArthur's proclivities for micromanagement and for trusting his intuition at the expense of intelligence information.

Napoleon called the latter tendency "making pictures." It would emerge again during the Philippines campaign of 1945. Begun in a glare of publicity as the culmination of MacArthur's career, it rapidly became an attritional struggle that, from a Japanese perspective, was a classic economy-of-force operation. Until the dropping of the atomic bombs, the Philippines became a vortex, sucking in and pinning down increasing numbers of U.S. divisions in increasingly diffuse landings and attacks whose tactical successes did not obscure the overall lack of an operational concept. Perhaps no general could have maintained a firm grip on the fighting in an archipelago of over seven thousand islands. The fact remains that MacArthur, in the face of mounting civilian as well as military casualties, increasingly let events shape his decisions. It is not coincidental that his admirers focus on New Guinea and draw a curtain over the Philippines. MacArthur's assignment to command the projected invasion of Japan was as much *faute de mieux* as an affirmation of the capacities of a general who might have peaked at army level—or even lower.

—DENNIS SHOWALTER, COLORADO COLLEGE

References

Edwin Palmer Hoyt, *MacArthur's Navy: The Seventh Fleet and the Battle for the Philippines* (New York: Orion, 1989);

D. Clayton James, *The Years of MacArthur,* 3 volumes (Boston: Houghton Mifflin, 1970–1985);

William Manchester, *American Caesar: Douglas MacArthur, 1880–1964* (Boston: Little, Brown, 1978);

Geoffrey Perret, *Old Soldiers Never Die: The Life of Douglas MacArthur* (New York: Random House, 1996);

Carol Morris Petillo, *Douglas MacArthur: The Philippine Years* (Bloomington: Indiana University Press, 1981);

Stephen R. Taaffe, *MacArthur's Jungle War: The 1944 New Guinea Campaign* (Lawrence: University Press of Kansas, 1998).

MACARTHUR

MONTGOMERY

How successful was General Bernard Law Montgomery as a general?

Viewpoint: Bernard Law Montgomery was a great general who understood the need for marshaled strength and the limitations of his troops. He never suffered a serious defeat by the Germans.

Viewpoint: Bernard Law Montgomery's success in World War II was more the result of his personality and position as an "outsider" in the British military establishment than his battlefield prowess.

As controversial as he was successful, Sir Bernard Law Montgomery was one of the defining leaders of Britain at war. Long before 1939 he had established a reputation as an outspoken critic of what he regarded as the gentlemanly amateurism of the British Army. As a division commander in 1940, then as a corps commander in Britain, he demonstrated sufficient skill as a troop trainer and convinced enough superiors of his potential as a combat commander that he was sent to the Middle East in August 1942.

Montgomery proved to be the right man at the right time. He purged the Eighth Army of many tired and overmatched senior officers, demonstrated the potential of managed battle at El Alamein in October, and restored the morale of a polyglot command increasingly uncertain whether its generals had any real idea of what they were doing. Montgomery commanded the Eighth Army in the subsequent advance across North Africa, then in the invasions of Sicily and Italy, with a combination of personal flair and operational caution that maximized its effectiveness. He was the obvious choice to command the British contribution to Operation Overlord and the overall ground operations during the initial stages of the D-Day campaign.

Montgomery's operational performance continued to be effective. His combination of careful planning, close control, and maximum use of firepower recognized Britain's growing inability to replace losses and accepted the war weariness of British front-line formations. His relationship with his American allies—and his American superior Dwight D. Eisenhower—did not incorporate similar realism. By 1944 Montgomery was convinced that he was the only professional soldier in a stable of well-intentioned amateurs. His less-than-veiled contempt for his U.S. counterparts was met with corresponding antagonism from George S. Patton and Omar N. Bradley. His relationship with Eisenhower deteriorated to a point at which he was almost relieved of his command. Nevertheless, Montgomery maintained a British presence in the Atlantic alliance until the end of the war. While he may have lacked imagination, he never suffered a significant defeat in high command. Few who fought the Wehrmacht can show a similar record.

**Viewpoint:
Bernard Law Montgomery was a
great general who understood the
need for marshaled strength and the
limitations of his troops. He never
suffered a serious defeat by the
Germans.**

It is beyond question that Field Marshal
Bernard Law Montgomery was a great military
leader. During and after his career he was criticized for being too abrasive toward others and
being overly cautious in battle. In fact he did
have a personality that was harsh and egocentric.
His personality made him an outsider in the
British Army, but it also enabled him to believe
that he could not lose. He may have been cautious in battle, only fighting when he was ready
and hoarding the slim resources under his command until he could ensure victory. He never suffered a major defeat and did nothing to put
Allied victory in jeopardy. Most of all, Montgomery served as a symbol for the British people, including those not in arms, that boosted
their morale and led them to believe that they
would always be victorious as long as he was
fighting in the field.

Montgomery was a man of extreme ego.
His belief that he was superior to those around
him made him extremely arrogant and hard to
get along with. These traits were present in both
his family life and military career, and often got
him into a great deal of trouble. In defiance of
his mother's wishes that he become a minister,
young Montgomery joined the Army Class at St.
Paul's School in London and showed early his
tendency to be persistent by continuing in his
military studies, but he was not an outstanding
student. He became known as a dedicated soldier who took his job seriously, though most did
not personally like him. Montgomery also
proved himself a gallant warrior in a charge at
the First Battle of Ypres (1914) in World War I,
which left the young captain severely wounded.

Montgomery's experiences in World War I
taught him to use caution. He believed that
attacks had been made without sufficient planning and preparation. For the rest of his life
Montgomery believed that attacks must be carefully planned. In addition, he thought that men
should not be risked without sufficient reason.
He also believed that soldiers should have access
to the supplies and equipment that were needed
to be successful in combat. Montgomery as a
general refused to take risks, including pursuits,
unless he knew that he had the upper hand. This
reluctance did not mean, however, that he supported an entirely defensive posture. As a mem-

ber of the British Expeditionary Force in France
during 1940, Montgomery refused to order his
division to take up posts in coastal defense.
Instead, he went above the heads of his superiors
and received permission from Prime Minister
Winston Churchill to go into a mobile-counterat-
tack mode, that helped stall the victorious Germans and give the British and French extra time
that was used to evacuate troops from the continent. He was one of the last men to escape from
Dunkirk (28 May–4 June 1940).

Montgomery's greatest strength as a general, his attitude, became clear in the desert campaign with his command of the Eighth Army, a
beaten and demoralized entity when he arrived.
Montgomery immediately let it be known to his
new command that the bad times were over. He
visited as much of his command as possible, let-
ting the men know him and his future plans for
beating German general Erwin Rommel and his
famed *Afrika Korps*. Montgomery worked to
supersede Rommel as the dominant personality
in the desert. He wanted his men to get over
their fear of Rommel and instead place their
faith in their commander, and they did. Montgomery ordered both physical and mental training to get the men ready for the coming battle
with the Germans, following his principle of
preparation. He taught them to have confidence
in themselves and their leaders, and instilled it as
no other British general could have. His soldiers
believed in their general.

Even if Montgomery had never achieved
success in Sicily or France, his success in North
Africa would have made him one of the important generals of World War II. It has been
argued that the North African campaign had little to do with deciding the outcome of the war,
but up until 1943 it was the only place where the
British were actively fighting Axis troops. North
Africa was the only major theater that pitted
Great Britain's army against German ground
forces. Many generals had come before him.
Montgomery's immediate predecessor, General
Sir Claude Auchinleck, was viewed as one of the
best minds of the war. Yet, of six commanders of
the Eighth Army prior to Montgomery, none
had been able to achieve success in the desert
against the Germans.

With fortunes at their lowest on 23 October
1942, the British as a nation regained their will
to fight, and they would not lose it again. On
that day the Eighth Army secured its most
important victory at the Second Battle of El
Alamein. After years of going back and forth in
the desert against the Germans, the Allies
would not go on the defensive again against
Rommel. The timing was perfect. The Japanese
had taken control of the Far East from the
Allies. American troops had not yet experienced

a victorious battle in the European theater. Yet, thanks to the leadership of Montgomery, the Allies now had a major victory to build on. Even if the rest of the general's career had been a bust, he would still deserve to be remembered because of El Alamein.

Montgomery bided his time preparing his defenses in the desert. Rommel walked into Montgomery's prepared positions, allowing the Eighth Army to utilize its superior firepower to beat back the Germans, sending the Panzers into retreat at the battle of Alam Halfa Ridge. For two months Montgomery bided his time and prepared to go on the offensive. He gathered superior numbers in men and machinery, achieving a two-to-one ratio over the Axis in manpower and a three-to-one ratio in tanks. The Desert Air Force supported his operation with air superiority. At 6 A.M. on 23 October, the Eighth Army made a diversionary attack to the south of the Germans, then suddenly attacked from the north. The Germans were unprepared for battle on that day and at that spot in their defenses. The Eighth Army, however, could not achieve victory over the hard-fighting Germans, and it took all of Montgomery's will to keep his troops engaged in battle. It was not until 2 November that Montgomery, by force of will and superior capabilities, broke through the Axis forces and sent his opponent on the run. In this battle Montgomery showed why he was a great general. He gathered the resources that he needed to dominate his enemy and carefully planned his attack. He achieved the advantage of surprise over his opponent. Most of all, he displayed his drive to win. He was always watchful of casualties and had lost ten thousand men by 28 October without achieving victory. Lesser men have walked away from battle when victory was almost within their grasp. Montgomery knew that he could not and would not lose, so he willed himself and his men to victory.

Montgomery was appointed the ground commander for Operation Overlord and given charge of the Twenty-First Army Group in 1944. His command was composed not only of British soldiers, but also included Americans and Canadians. Montgomery visited every unit under his command in the build up to the invasion. Wherever he went he impressed the men who would defeat Germany. After seeing him and absorbing some of his self-confidence, ordinary soldiers knew that they too could not be defeated. It was no longer a question of whether they would beat Germany; the common infantryman now believed the only question was *when* they would beat Germany. Montgomery convinced the men through his speech and bearing that he would not allow failure. It would probably be an overstatement to say that the men loved him, but they definitely came to respect him as a leader who would accept nothing less than victory from their efforts.

Montgomery also stood as a symbol of victory for those outside of the military. One of the most important functions that he provided the British people was as a symbol of victory. He spent the months preceding the invasion of Normandy touring Great Britain in his train *Rapier*, stopping at sporting and community events. He made public appearances and spoke to all sorts of organizations and groups. Wherever he went there was cheering and admiration. While soldiers looked upon Montgomery as a competent and successful commander, the British people began a hero cult around him. Montgomery would be the man who would bring victory to the British, and they loved him for it. Though he was small in stature, he appeared crisp and ready to fight. Montgomery seemed a fire-eater who was ready to bite, and any stories of his personal eccentricities or ruthlessness only added to his image. Surprisingly, Montgomery, a man of little humor, was known for making audiences chuckle in glee. The symbol of Monty the fighter raised the hopes and spirits of ordinary people, and like the soldiers, they knew that they could not lose with their hero leading the attack against the Germans. The images conjured up in the mind of the common man by Montgomery's personal appearances remained strong in the memories of British civilians for years after the end of the war. Montgomery adored the admiration of the people and loved to hear the cheers of the crowd.

Even those who experienced Montgomery's ire had to admit that he was a general who won battles. American general Dwight D. Eisenhower, toward whom Montgomery showed contempt at times, wrote in his memoirs that critics of Montgomery's tactics were fighting a losing battle. Montgomery was a patient general, who only committed resources when he knew he could win. He was criticized for not taking risks and not achieving maximum results. Yet, as Eisenhower was quick to point out, if Montgomery had overreached in battle and lost men needlessly, he would have been labeled a butcher. In Eisenhower's view the only way to evaluate a general was by his win-loss record on the battlefield. Montgomery may not have won overwhelming victories, but by Eisenhower's standards he never suffered a major defeat, making him a competent and successful general. Even Montgomery's largest risk, Operation Market Garden, which ended in the failure to take the bridge at Arnhem, did not give the Germans any advantage.

Montgomery may have had faults. He may have had an unattractive personality and may have been overly cautious in battle. He was a great military leader, however, and helped bring about Allied victory. At the nadir of the war his hoarding of men and materials on the battlefield and his force of will brought the British victory at El Alamein. On top of this victory the Allies stacked other successes. In fact, it was a major turning point in the war, putting the Axis on the run for the first time. Other commanders had tried and failed to achieve victory in North Africa. Montgomery's character did not allow

him to fail and brought about victory. After the desert, Montgomery never suffered a major defeat at the hands of the Germans. Years after the war he still served as a symbol of pride for the British.

—DANIEL LEE BUTCHER, KANSAS STATE
UNIVERSITY

Viewpoint:
Bernard Law Montgomery's success in World War II was more the result of his personality and position as an "outsider" in the British military establishment than his battlefield prowess.

In *Montgomery* (1946), his unabashedly favorable biography of Britain's foremost battlefield commander of the Second World War, Alan Moorehead writes "one is hard put to it to think of anyone so peculiarly unfitted for [army] life as Second-Lieutenant Bernard Montgomery when he emerged from Sandhurst at the age of twenty-one." Moorehead explains that Montgomery did not smoke, drink, or date. He was no horseman, nor was he wealthy, handsome, robust, or the progeny of an established military family. He was deeply religious and "nursed a carping discontent with established authority." These character traits hardly endeared Montgomery to his fellow officers. Additionally, unlike most professional officers of the British army of the time who valued "good form" and the intricacies of regimental life over intelligent reflection, Montgomery was wholly dedicated to the study of his profession. As Alistair Horne and David Montgomery (the Field Marshal's son) explain in *Monty: The Lonely Leader, 1944–1945* (1994), such "Cromwellian dedication and intolerance" for those less driven made him unpopular and earned him a reputation as an outsider. Yet, it was this very standing that propelled Montgomery to command of the British Eighth Army in North Africa, a fortuitous posting that became a jumping-off point for a career defined increasingly by personality rather than battlefield prowess.

In July 1942 General Erwin Rommel, *Afrika Korps* (Africa Corps) commander and bane of the British in North Africa, launched an offensive designed to capture the Suez Canal. He was met and stopped at the first Battle of El Alamein by a tired British Eighth Army commanded by General Sir Claude Auchinleck, who held the additional post of Commander-in-Chief Middle East. Spurred by this development, as

MONTGOMERY

well as Ultra intercepts that painted a bleak picture of Rommel's logistics, Prime Minister Winston Churchill urged Auchinleck to mount a counteroffensive with his newly arrived 44th Division in order to complete the destruction of the Afrika Korps. Auchinleck resisted Churchill's pressure, stating that the 44th was untrained for desert warfare and required acclimatization before being thrown against the wily Rommel. Unwilling to countenance such resistance, Churchill replaced Auchinleck as Commander-in-Chief Middle East with General Harold Alexander and appointed General William "Strafer" Gott, formerly Thirteenth Corps commander, to command the Eighth Army. While flying to Cairo to take over his new command, Gott was killed when a lone German fighter shot down his plane. On General Alan Brooke's suggestion, Churchill appointed Montgomery as Gott's replacement.

Just prior to the outbreak of war, Montgomery took command of the Third Division, which he led to France and throughout the subsequent withdrawal to Dunkirk. When his corps commander, Brooke, was recalled to England, Montgomery took temporary command of the corps during the evacuation. Back in England, Montgomery resumed command of the Third Division and then commanded, in order, Fifth Corps, Twelfth Corps, and Southeastern Command, all of which were girding for what seemed an inevitable invasion. During this time, despite pressure to prepare fixed defensive positions, Montgomery stressed training in offensive operations. Fortunately for him, he had a high-placed ally in Brooke who, after relinquishing command of his corps, became Commander-in-Chief Home Forces, and later Chief of the Imperial General Staff.

Brooke had long admired Montgomery and was one of the few officers impressed with his dedication and zeal. He, like Montgomery, also saw the importance of injecting a more aggressive attitude in the British army and had been disheartened when, upon visiting Auchinleck's command in North Africa, he sensed a malaise in Eighth Army. Desirous of turning things around in the desert, Brooke was instrumental in getting Montgomery assigned as Eighth Army commander. Churchill, likewise frustrated by what he felt was an overly cautious attitude permeating the general-officer ranks, welcomed the chance to appoint an outsider to such a post.

Seventeen days after taking command, Montgomery fought the Battle of Alam Halfa, using essentially the same defensive plan that the unfortunate Auchinleck had briefed to Churchill. Urged, as had been his predecessor, to finish off his foe, Montgomery, also like his predecessor, refused to budge before he was ready. Unlike

Auchinleck, though, Montgomery had Brooke's support. Finally, having achieved a greater than two-to-one superiority in guns and tanks (including obtaining newly arrived American M-4 Sherman tanks, an even match for the German Mark IVs), as well as control of the air, Montgomery launched his attack on 24 October 1942, initiating the second Battle of El Alamein. Eventually, Montgomery's superior combat power held sway, and by early November Rommel began a withdrawal that did not end until he reached the Mareth Line in Tunisia, some 1700 kilometers away. Though a turning point of the war, Montgomery's success in North Africa was as much the result of the confluence of fortunate circumstances as it was of his generalship. By late 1942 Rommel's forces were operating on a logistical shoestring since the offensive at Stalingrad was consuming the vast bulk of German supplies and replacements. Furthermore, significant Allied forces landed behind Rommel in Morocco and Algeria during Operation Torch and served to siphon Axis combat power from Montgomery's front. Hence, when Montgomery assumed command of Eighth Army in mid-August 1942, circumstances were ripe for victory. Buffered from Churchill's meddling by his mentor Brooke, resupplied in a manner his predecessors only dreamed of, and faced with a spent foe whose rear was threatened by the first Anglo-American offensive of the war, Montgomery's victory was more expected than miraculous.

As a result of his victory, Montgomery became the darling of Britain. As R. W. Thompson writes in *Montgomery: The Field Marshal* (1969): "The bells pealing out, to proclaim victory in the desert had pealed for Montgomery. He had become Britain's man of destiny, her soldier of good fortune, her 'lucky general.'" When he secretly returned to England in late spring 1943, people soon discovered he was staying at Claridge's Hotel in London, and crowds gathered there every day to get a glimpse of their champion. Moorehead writes "ever since the beginning of the war the people had been hungry for a military hero. . . . Here was a ready-made one and, moreover, a general full of delightful idiosyncrasies, a man who responded to the admiration."

Retaining command of the Eighth Army in the invasion of Sicily and on into Italy, Montgomery continued to bring Britain success. As he had done in North Africa, Montgomery relied on overwhelming firepower to defeat his enemy. Despite being shown up in Sicily by General George S. Patton's Seventh Army in the race to Messina, and getting bogged down in the fight up the Italian peninsula, Montgomery continued to advance. Britains, starved for victory for so long, and enduring daily the Nazi onslaught

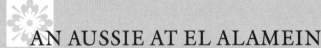

AN AUSSIE AT EL ALAMEIN

The Battle of El Alamein in October 1942 made Bernard Law Montgomery a hero in the eyes of the British. Here an Australian soldier describes the early hours of the battle.

At 2140 hours it was Zero Hour for the artillery. Over the rolling ridges of Miteiriya, pinpoints of light flashed as far south as the Qattara Depression and as quick as summer lightning, these flashes rippled up the long British line. The guns flamed at the Depression, up and around Ruweisat and Himeimat Ridges, across the dusty plain of Alamein, past the station and Qattara Track, on Tel El Eisa and the coastal strip. In a few short seconds, a thousand guns stabbed the air with livid flame and a thousand shells screamed their way to enemy gun positions. I saw the flashes; the next second, earth and air trembled with terrible sound. It was something living and majestic, yet horribly savage with hate. Speech was impossible and the ears tingled with the vibrations. There was never a break in the gunfire, lances of flames stabbed the night all around me. After a minute of firing, a new sound filtered through, it was the dull ugly crump of bursting shells as they exploded in enemy gun positions. Over the horizon and directly in front, a red, angry smudge glowed vividly as our shells found enemy guns and ammunition. For fifteen terrible minutes the guns thundered and then stopped-suddenly. The infantry and tanks moved through our wire and minefields to their start lines.

At 2200 hours, the desert flame into life again. This was Zero Hour for the infantry. The guns splashed light everywhere, and German guns that had escaped our counter-battery fire added their sound and shells. Small arms chattered amid the din. The horizon burned with Very lights; rockets, climbing to the zenith, burst into brilliant coloured lights. Amidst the inferno of sound, I could hear the drone of bombers and the snarl of night-fighters as they passed unseen.

Three miles away, a string of golden brilliant flares hung from the sky as the planes lit the earth below for the advancing infantry. Farther back, more flares hung over gun positions and dull, angry crumps of heavy bombs filtered through to us. The noise drugged our thoughts and we watched vacantly until in one screaming second, we were brought swiftly back to reality. Four shells arrived with shrill screams, exploded, and filled the air with slivers of steel. On the flat, some ninety yards away, ominous black blobs of smoke and dust twisted into fantastic shapes in the moonlight. We dropped and kept our heads well down and after the next salvo detonated, I made a dive for the dug-out and slithered down the steps. The next lot sent jagged lumps whining over the camou-flaged entrance.

Down in the dug-out, where the reports of battle were coming in through by phone and runner, it was fairly quiet. The sound of gunfire was muffled but the walls shook; tiny rivulets of sand ran from the coarse sand-bags. The shells arrived regularly, some rocked the place and filled the air with fine grit. Those who were not on duty played cards, and with each shell the game would be temporarily suspended for that brief moment. An hour passed; the shelling stopped and I went outside for a breath of air, which was cold and bitter with the smell of burnt explosives.

The first phase was over; the guns were silent but small arms rattled viciously. The horizon was hazy with smoke which crawled in long white lanes and hung low to the earth. Coils of white smoke of burnt-out aerial flares spiralled in the still air. The Air Force was very active at this stage; they lit the enemy strong posts with light and the crump of heavy bombs made the earth tremble.

Midnight passed; out in the cold, dry sands men are dying. Australian bayonets are red; men are consolidating for the counter-attacks that will come at dawn. A few hours ago, by the light of the moon, the Commander of the Eighth Army, Lieuten-ant-General B.L. Montgomery, told war correspondents, "During the night there will be a terrific battle. We will know better at dawn to-morrow where we are. There is no doubt on the issue."

The guns have started their final phase of the night's operations and men who know no sleep are moving forward. . . .

Source: *"The Men Who Fought at El Alamein," in* El Alamein, 1942: Sands of Death and Valor, *Web Page.*

from the air, were uninterested in the nuances of tactics and strategy. What enthralled them was their general who, since taking command in August 1942, never suffered a defeat.

In December 1943, after having been pressed by Soviet Premier Joseph Stalin for a firm commitment to a second front in France, U.S. President Franklin D. Roosevelt named General Dwight D. Eisenhower the Supreme Commander for Operation Overlord. Soon thereafter, Eisenhower announced his desire to have a ground commander who would oversee the invasion and who would then move to command the British army group during the campaign in Europe. When asked who he would like in this position, Eisenhower indicated a preference for General Alexander, but deferred the decision to Churchill. General Bernard Paget, Commander-in-Chief Home Forces at the time, had the greatest claim on this position, as he had trained the forces that would conduct the invasion and had also produced the "Skyscraper" plan upon which Overlord had been built. However, as Thompson points out, "to an enormous public, including the rank and file of the Army. . . the choice of Montgomery to command Britain's armies in the last great throw, seemed natural and obvious. His prestige was enormous, his image, his words and deeds, engraved upon the mind of a Nation." On 23 December 1944, Montgomery got the job.

With this appointment Montgomery's personality began to play an increasingly significant role in the conduct of the war. As Horne and Montgomery point out, "Anyone not in England at the time might find it almost impossible to imagine the degree of adulation which Montgomery received in 1944. It was quite unprecedented, far exceeding even that accorded Arthur Wellesley, first Duke of Wellington after Waterloo, even Horatio Nelson at the peak of popularity. It meant he could get his troops, Americans as well as British, to do anything for him." It also meant he could secure resources that had hitherto been denied the Overlord planners. Immediately upon being appointed to his position, Montgomery studied the draft plans and pronounced them inadequate. He demanded more troops in order to expand the lodgment area, more landing craft to carry them there, and the use of strategic bombers to cripple the transportation infrastructure of France prior to the invasion. He got all three and more, using as collateral his immense reputation by threatening to quit if he did not get what he wanted.

He further bolstered his reputation and his ego by traveling throughout England, urging crowds of soldiers and civilians alike to pull together in this last great race. By doing so he alienated much of Britain's upper class, which did not look favorably on such showmanship. Furthermore, the uniformed ranks of the anti-Montgomery camp also increased, and included many who held leading positions in the alliance such as Eisenhower's deputy commander, Air Chief Marshal Arthur W. Tedder and his Chief of Staff General Walter Bedell Smith. Yet, Montgomery remained oblivious. Sequestering himself in the intimate circle of his Tactical Headquarters and secure in the knowledge that the people and his soldiers were behind him, Montgomery's faith in his plan, and his destiny, were unshakeable.

Following the successful landings in Normandy on 6 June 1944, Montgomery's plan seemed to fall apart because of his inability to take the city of Caen. Much controversy surrounds the battle. Montgomery's detractors insist that he had intended to take the city immediately following the landings, while those in his corner counter that it was always his intention to hold the Germans at Caen so the Americans could break out on the right. What is certain is that Montgomery earned increasing enmity from many quarters for his conduct of the battle. As ground-force commander and the man who had been anointed Britain's foremost general, he brooked no criticism and seemed oblivious to the increasingly shrill demands that he get "unstuck" in Normandy. Nor did he take the time to explain to his critics, including Eisenhower and Churchill, what he was attempting to accomplish. Flush with the initial success of the landings, and still aglow from the adulation that he had experienced as he traversed England in the months before D-Day, Montgomery set his own pace. Eventually, as had been the case in all Montgomery's previous battles, overwhelming firepower, this time in the form of strategic bombers used in a close air-support role, proved the key to unlocking the stalemate.

Following the breakout from Normandy, Eisenhower elevated U.S. general Omar N. Bradley to army group command, equal with Montgomery, and took control of the ground war himself. Eisenhower had always maintained that this change would occur and yet, despite the sop of a Field Marshal's baton, Montgomery bridled at the change. From 1 September 1944, when the change became effective, until the end of the war in Europe, Montgomery constantly harangued Eisenhower with his desire to retain control of ground operations, insisting that Eisenhower should remain above the fray at the grand-strategic plane. So heated did these discussions become that at one juncture Eisenhower had to remind Montgomery that he was the boss, and Montgomery could not talk to him in such an insubordinate manner.

Having failed in his bid to retain control of ground operations, Montgomery next railed against Eisenhower's broad-front approach, which he saw as a serious dilution of resources. Instead, Montgomery insisted on the concentration of resources for one full-bodied thrust into Germany that, of course, would be accomplished by his army group and make him de facto ground-force commander. In August 1944 Eisenhower finally acceded to Montgomery's request and diverted scarce resources, most significantly fuel, to his Twenty-First Army Group. The ensuing Operation Market Garden not only failed to achieve a breakthrough into the Ruhr, it also resulted in the destruction of the British First Airborne Division and the stagnation of the entire Allied front. For once, Montgomery's insistent demands failed to bring results, though he himself claimed the operation 90 percent successful, and instead set the stage for the German Ardennes counteroffensive.

Despite the failure of Market Garden, Montgomery remained convinced of his infallibility. This imperiousness, which came to the forefront again during the Battle of the Bulge in December 1944, brought the alliance to a critical point. Certain that he had saved the Americans by his defensive stance during the battle, Montgomery again insisted on the appointment of an overall ground commander and a single thrust into Germany. The easy-going Eisenhower, by that time fed up with Montgomery's carping, composed a letter for the Combined Chiefs of Staff requesting that either he or Montgomery be removed from command. Knowing full well that Eisenhower would not be the one to go Montgomery's Chief of Staff, General Freddie de Guingand, saved the alliance through artful diplomacy and by convincing his commander to withdraw his request. As a result of this clash, uneasy relations existed in the Anglo-American camp for the remainder of the war in Europe. Resources were diverted to the U.S. First and Third Armies respectively, as they spearheaded the crossing of the Rhine, while Eisenhower halted Montgomery in northern Germany.

Montgomery took command of the British Eighth Army as a result of Brooke's backing and his standing as an outsider in the British military establishment. Following his success at El Alamein, he became increasingly convinced of the correctness of his way of war. This indomitable belief in himself, bolstered by the adulation accorded him by his soldiers and the British people, served to make him insistent on getting his way. During the planning for Overlord, such insistence proved valuable in securing needed resources. Once established ashore, however, Montgomery's cries for his retention in com-

mand of the ground forces and for the adoption of his single thrust into Germany resulted in the debacle at Arnhem, the stagnation of the western front, and set the stage for the Battle of the Bulge. Montgomery stated that he never lost a battle. Others would counter that he never fought a "loseable" battle because of his insistence on assembling overwhelming combat power before each fight, and in so doing, prolonged the war.

—GUY LOFARO, U.S. MILITARY ACADEMY, WEST POINT

References

Dwight D. Eisenhower, *Crusade in Europe* (Garden City, N.Y.: Doubleday, 1948);

Nigel Hamilton, *Monty: The Making of a General, 1887–1943* (London: Hamilton, 1981);

Hamilton, *Master of the Battlefield: Monty's War Years, 1942–1944* (New York: McGraw-Hill, 1983);

Alistair Horne and David Montgomery, *Monty: The Lonely Leader, 1944–1945* (London: Macmillan, 1994);

John Keegan, ed., *Churchill's Generals* (London: Weidenfeld & Nicolson, 1991);

Richard Lamb, *Montgomery in Europe, 1943–1945: Success or Failure?* (London: Buchan & Enright, 1983);

Ronald Lewin, *Montgomery as Military Commander* (London: Batsford, 1971);

Lewin, "Field Marshal the Viscount Montgomery," in *The War Lords: Military Commanders of the Twentieth Century,* edited by Michael Carver (Boston: Little, Brown, 1976), pp. 500–508;

Brian Montgomery, *A Field-Marshal in the Family* (London: Constable, 1973);

Bernard Law Montgomery, *The Memoirs of Field-Marshal the Viscount Montgomery of Alamein* (Cleveland: World, 1958);

Alan Moorehead, *Montgomery: A Biography* (London: Hamilton, 1946);

R.W. Thompson, *Churchill and the Montgomery Myth* (New York: M. Evans, 1967);

Thompson, *Montgomery, the Field Marshal: A Critical Study of the Generalship of Field-Marshal, the Viscount Montgomery of Alamein, K.G. and of the Campaign in North-West Europe, 1944/45* (London: Allen & Unwin, 1969).

NAZISM AND RELIGION

Were the churches in Germany in the 1930s quiet accomplices of Adolf Hitler and Nazism?

Viewpoint: Yes, Adolf Hitler's threat to crush the churches frightened church leaders into granting implicit support for his regime.

Viewpoint: No, neither the Protestant nor Catholic Church collaborated with Adolf Hitler and the Nazi regime; in fact, the churches actively opposed and undermined state initiatives relating to religion.

National Socialism achieved its first success in a German Protestant community morally shaken by defeat, economically menaced by inflation and depression, and politically challenged by the ineffectualness of the parties purporting to represent its principles and interests. Divided regionally and confessionally, German Protestantism after 1918 sought to become a "people's church" in the presumed mold of Luther and Calvin, recovering credibility in a population increasingly secularized and socialized. Leaders and communicants alike were correspondingly tempted to see what they wished to see in Adolf Hitler's calls for moral, as well as physical national renewal.

Catholics by contrast were among the last holdouts—less for religious reasons than because of the relative effectiveness of the Center Party in defending Catholic interests and the suspicion with which the Vatican regarded Nazi ideology. Hitler's conclusion of a concordat with the papacy shortly after assuming power alleviated enough of those anxieties to give the New Order ample room to proceed against both forms of Christianity.

The campaign began with the creation in 1933 of an Evangelical Reich Church, designed to absorb the various Protestant congregations. Opponents of this centralization, influenced as well by the overt paganism manifested at this period by some Nazi enthusiasts, responded by organizing the Confessing Church. Increasing persecution of dissenting clergy was accompanied by intensive antichurch campaigns, particularly among young people. Germany's Catholics as well faced an increasing spectrum of challenges to the letter and the spirit of the concordat.

The outbreak of war prevented an open breach between the churches and the Führer. Hitler placed his anti-Christian policies on the back burner. The churches refused to test the loyalty of their communicants and became increasingly involved in wartime welfare work that diverted attention from Nazi atrocities inside and outside Germany. Thus, they preserved a basis for reconstruction after 1945. What they sacrificed in moral and spiritual contexts remains a subject for debate.

Viewpoint:
Yes, Adolf Hitler's threat to crush the churches frightened church leaders into granting implicit support for his regime.

The history of the relationship of the German churches and the Nazi regime is one full of contradictions. On the one hand, they clashed early over religious rights. Subsequently individual church leaders such as Martin Niemöller, Dietrich Bonhoeffer, and Friedrich Weissler played prominent roles in opposing Adolf Hitler's criminal policies. On the other hand, after the early disagreements over church rights, the German churches did not officially oppose the regime, even after the extent of Nazi crimes came to light. In fact, the churches can be said to have generally supported Hitler and his government right up until the very end of the Nazi regime.

Indeed, Hitler had enjoyed the broad support of the churches since his seizure of power in 1933. The conservative pronouncements of the Nazis during their political campaigns had struck a cord among German Protestants and Catholics alike. The German churches had never been comfortable with the Weimar Republic, especially when it was led by a party that was officially atheist—the Social Democrats. They blamed democracy for the weakening of traditional social mores, and for the decline of the role of religion in people's lives that took place in Germany after World War I. By 1933 only one quarter of German Protestants, who made up almost 63 percent of the German population, claimed to be "practising," that is, attending church regularly. Further, under the democratic Weimar system the churches witnessed a steady erosion of their traditional rights, such as parochial education and property ownership. Like many other conservatives in the late Weimar period, the churches looked toward authoritarianism as a means of restoring traditional ideals and their own place in everyday German life. By 1933 Hitler and his Nazi Party seemed to be the means through which a religious renewal would be accomplished in Germany.

Despite the relative decline of the importance of religion during the Weimar Republic, the churches, especially the Catholic Church, still wielded considerable political power. In 1933, 95 percent of the German population belonged to a Christian church, even if a diminishing number were attending church services regularly. Further, the Catholic Church, in addition to playing a prominent role in the Center Party, held sway over the political opinions of many southern German voters. Hitler recognized the central role of religion in the lives of many ordinary Germans and admitted,

if only reluctantly, the continued authority that the church held over many Germans.

Even though Hitler generally viewed traditional churches as inimical to his concept of a "national community" guided by the tenets of National Socialism, this continued political power of the churches caused him to court them consciously in his bid for power. Moreover, this continued authority of the churches set the parameters of Nazi/church relations for the remainder of the regime. As with other political-interest groups, Hitler was adept at identifying and speaking to the churches' main desires. Recognizing that they wanted above all to halt the decline in their influence, the Nazi leader promised to restore their central role in German life. In *Mein Kampf* (1925–1927), the future Führer wrote that he wished the churches to become the "spiritual sword" of the new Germany. The Nazi Party program before 1933 aimed at creating a "positive Christianity," and Hitler publicly promised to respect the place of the churches in education and other spheres. Further, the Nazis stood in stark opposition to the "godless Bolsheviks" feared by the churches. These were all positions calculated to appeal to the church hierarchy and thus gain their political support.

Indeed, the early days of the Nazi regime seemed to live up to the best hopes of ecclesiastics, as Hitler apparently fulfilled his preelection promises. The Protestant churches were most easily "bought off" by Hitler, for several reasons. First, the twenty-eight official Protestant churches in Germany each had a long tradition of respect for the secular political authority, the so-called "throne and altar" tie. Moreover, the Protestant churches had been hardest hit by the secularization of society during the Weimar Republic. They were also highly receptive to Hitler's brand of nationalism. Hitler was able to reward and guarantee their support by addressing one of their longest held goals. In 1933 he created the "Deutscher Evangelischer Kirchenbund," or the "Federation of German Evangelical Churches," which brought the separate Protestant churches together under a single "Reich Bishop."

Hitler's assistance was rewarded by the Protestant churches almost immediately. While the Nazi leader was greeted with cautious optimism, his stance gained him some public support from members of the Protestant hierarchy. For example, at the highly symbolic "Potsdam Day" in March 1933, Bishop Otto Dibelius recalled the words spoken by Court-Chaplain Ernst von Dryander to call the German nation together on the eve of World War I. By doing so, Dibelius linked the new Nazi regime with the old Empire at its height, the period in which all of Germany stood united behind its government.

The Catholic Church proved, at least initially, more resistant to Hitler and National Socialism.

Although they were broadly sympathetic with the Nazis' conservative ideals, the German Catholic Church recognized that Nazism was a threat to its existence. The Catholic Church after World War I had never proven itself to be a friend of democracy and had wholeheartedly supported the Fascist government of Benito Mussolini in Italy. In 1931, however, the Bavarian bishops had denounced National Socialism, condemning its rejection of the Old Testament and its exaltation of race over religion. Indeed, the Catholic Church continued its resistance even after Hitler had taken power. In March 1933, speaking for the church hierarchy, Cardinal Adolf Bertram declared to Franz von Papen that the Catholic Church could never accept the Nazi "revolution." The Catholic hierarchy in Germany, after witnessing the hostility and violence toward Catholics from Nazi Party functionaries, correctly believed that Hitler ultimately wanted to crush the church.

Hitler was nevertheless soon able to win them over in a spectacular fashion. In July 1933, after long negotiation with Cardinal State Secretary Eugenio Pacelli (the future Pope Pius XII), the Nazi leader concluded an agreement with the Vatican. This so-called Reich Concordat guaranteed the rights of the Catholic Church in Germany, including church property and schools. This agreement, Hitler's first with a foreign government, purchased him a great deal of goodwill among German Catholics and with the Vatican, and as a result, Hitler was able to reap great rewards. The most immediate and important of these was the support of the Center Party for the Enabling Act, which allowed Hitler to take almost total control over the German state. At the same time, the leadership of the German Catholic Church publicly dropped its opposition to Hitler's regime and admonished its followers to be loyal to the "lawful authorities." In the long term, the Reich Concordat purchased the goodwill of the German Catholic Church and the Holy See, neither of which ever officially broke with the regime.

The Nazi Party's amicable relations with the German churches did not last long, however. The Catholic hierarchy had been correct in their assumption that Hitler desired to diminish and eventually to destroy the churches, which did not fit into his ideal National Socialist state. Hitler first attempted to undermine the strength of the politically weaker of the two faiths, the Protestant churches. The Führer favored a wing within the Protestant movement, the German Christians, which sought to bring Christianity closer to the

Reich Bishop Ludwig Muller giving the Nazi salute at Nuremberg in 1934

(Presseillustrationen Heinrich H. Hoffman, Zeitgeschichtliches Bildarchiv, Munich, Germany)

NAZISM AND RELIGION

ideals of Nazism. Upon the unification of the Protestant churches, Hitler forced them to accept the German Christian candidate, Ludwig Müller, for the post of Reich Bishop, and hoped that this movement would take over the Protestant churches.

Hitler's German Christians were soon met with sharp opposition from a Protestant countermovement, led by Martin Niemöller. By 1934 over seven thousand of the sixteen thousand Protestant clergy had joined with Niemöller to oppose the ideas of the German Christians. These members of Niemöller's Pastors' Emergency League broke from the main church to form the Confessing Church, creating a schism within the German Protestant movement.

It soon became clear that Hitler's attempt to gain control of the Protestant churches from within had failed. Consequently, he soon dropped his support of the German Christians, and although it lasted until the end of the Third Reich, the movement quickly lost its momentum. By creating a conflict within the Protestant movement, however, Hitler had reduced its ability to cope with external matters. The struggle for control over the Protestant movement made it more difficult for clergymen to respond forcefully and with any unity to the crimes of the Nazi regime.

The strong opposition shown by the seemingly fractious Protestant churches caused Hitler to rethink his approach. The Nazi leader had no desire to repeat the mistakes made by Otto von Bismarck during his long *Kulturkampf* (culture struggle) against the Catholic Church. The *Kirchenkampf* (Church struggle) between the German Christians and the Confessing Church demonstrated to him that, as during Bismarck's time, the churches were too powerful to take on head on. Instead, Hitler pursued a policy of repression against individual clergy, and in some cases against certain denominations, but he never attacked the church hierarchy, be it Protestant or Catholic, directly.

While Hitler feared a modern Kulturkampf, so too did the churches. The Nazi regime had proved adept at destroying completely its political adversaries when it wanted. Although the German churches opposed certain Nazi policies, church leaders did not wish to see the churches completely destroyed. Committed to maintaining their established rights, the churches' official opposition to Nazi crimes was muted at best. The silence of the church hierarchy allowed the Nazis to portray any clergy who spoke out against the regime's excess as rogues from official church policy. Without any statements to the contrary, Hitler could carry out his plan for the reordering of German society and embark on a war of world conquest with the implicit support of the German churches. Indeed, he could count on enough church leaders to speak publicly in support of his goals to make

it seem as if he was backed officially by the German churches. Thus, although Hitler was unable to crush the churches, his threat alone frightened the churches into granting their implicit support for his criminal acts.

–ROBERT T. FOLEY,
KING'S COLLEGE LONDON

Viewpoint:
No, neither the Protestant nor Catholic Church collaborated with Adolf Hitler and the Nazi regime; in fact, the churches actively opposed and undermined state initiatives relating to religion.

The consolidation of all organizations and sociopolitical structures within Germany often has been linked to the seemingly relentless progression of Nazi *Gleichschaltung* (political coordination) in the 1930s. The role of the Christian churches stands out in this debate, particularly in the 1990s with the Vatican's close scrutiny of the persecution of Jews and other minority groups within Nazi Germany. While fully cognizant of their shortcomings, particularly their response to the Final Solution in the 1940s, Protestant and Catholic churches in the 1930s not only failed to support Adolf Hitler's regime openly, but actively opposed certain of its policies. Church leaders, sometimes at great personal risk, frequently voiced complaints against the state and actively resisted Nazi measures to incorporate the churches. Even the state-sponsored German Christian Church, despite all the attention rightfully focused on it, proved relatively weak and unimportant in developing any long-term association between German religiosity and National Socialism.

The development of German religiosity endured great disruption in the 1930s. While the Catholic Church retained its administrative structure and subordinate organizations throughout the 1930s, the Protestant churches suffered through great turbulence. Following the ascension to power of the Nazis in January 1933, a wave of nationalist fervor building in various church circles during the Weimar era caused the creation of a new German Christian Church, one designed to support the "race and nation" policies of Hitler's government. On the other hand, another new church, the Confessing Church, opposed any sort of state intervention into church affairs. Between these two new churches stood the traditional German Evangelical Churches: the Lutheran, the Reformed, and the Prussian United. At the start of 1933, before great rifts became apparent, over 60 percent of Germany's population belonged to one of these three Evangelical congregations.

In *Mein Kampf* (1925), Hitler already had alluded to a "dictatorial" religion, writing that there must be only one religion in the state—one that the public must acknowledge and to which it must adjust. The existence of any other religions could not be tolerated. Hitler expressed a desire to ensure a harmonious relationship between church and state. He also offered assurances that he would place no restriction on the one accepted Church, nor would the Church's relationship with the State change. German nationalist elements, closely associated with the Nazi Party, founded the German Christian Church to fit Hitler's plan; the church only came to prominence in 1930 when leaders of this sect openly began discussions and activities with the National Socialists. Included in the stated aim of the German Christians was "to provide the German churches with a form which will enable them to serve the German people in the specific way the Gospel of Jesus Christ lays upon them for the service of their own people." Religious leaders of the Church should not be chosen democratically by a body of church leaders but appointed by the administrative leader of the church, who, in the mid 1930s, was State Church Commissar August Jäger, a Nazi.

Evangelical pastors strongly disapproved of such actions. In direct response to this threat to the independence of their churches, and in defiance of state policy, Reformed theologian Karl Barth and other religious leaders issued the *Altonaer Bekenntnis* (Altona Confession) on 11 January 1933, stating that "no particular state form is best." Soon after, Otto Dibelius, the General Superintendent of the Land Church of Brandenburg, criticized the views of the German Christians, writing that the gospel should preach "not hate but love, that not folk sentiment but God's kingdom is the substance of its evangelical message." Statements such as this one angered German Christian leadership and strained relations between the state and Evangelical Protestant religious faiths.

In 1933 an outcry led by Berlin minister and decorated World War I U-boat commander Martin Niemöller led to the suspension of a Nazi policy statement calling for the dismissal from their positions of non-Aryan church workers. Although temporary, the suspension reflected the degree to which Protestant disagreement with state policy, here implemented through the German Christian-dominated Prussian Diet, could be overturned. In March 1934 over seven hundred Protestant pastors were arrested for failing to comply with state policy when they violated a state-imposed gag order prohibiting any church officeholder from making written or oral statements against the German Christian Reichsbishop, Ludwig Müller. This event was followed by an attempt on the part of the German Christian-led religious hierarchy to consolidate all of the Evangelical churches into one large German Christian Church. In response to this threat, key Evangelical leaders met at Barmen to establish the new Confessing Church.

The Barmen Declaration (May 1934) rejected the idea that ultimate control over some areas of life belonged to earthly lords rather than Jesus Christ. It also denied that church doctrine could be changed to adhere to "prevailing ideological and political convictions," denying that the state could assume the churches' function in life or that the church can be an "organ of the state." This statement captured the predominant mood of the German people, both spiritually and secularly, and the declaration won widespread grassroots support across Germany, particularly in the Southern *Landeskirchen* (state churches). Although the Confessing Church fragmented somewhat in the latter part of the 1930s, the initial organization and statement of beliefs proved vital in consolidating Christian sentiment in Germany as a separate entity from the state. A second attempt to consolidate the Evangelical churches in October 1934 failed, highlighted by a meeting between the leading bishops and Hitler himself. Hitler apparently satisfied the concerns of the bishops, the Führer personally asserting that he was removing himself from any further conflict with the churches.

Following the failures of 1933–1934, the state began to initiate more subtle actions to bring about religious consolidation. Hans Kerrl, a well known and respected Christian committed to combining Christian beliefs with those of National Socialism, was chosen to head the newly created State Ministry of Church Affairs. For the next two years, however, the state made little headway toward the consolidation of the churches. In church elections of 1937, the Nazi Party adhered to Hitler's policy of remaining aloof from public religious debate and gave no support to the German Christian candidates, resulting in that group's marked failure at the polls. Following the elections in November 1937, Kerrl attempted to limit the ways by which the Confessing Churches could raise money, leading to serious conflict and resulting in the arrest of hundreds of clergymen for violations of state law. Eventually, Confessing pastors dropped their opposition to Kerrl's tactics after they discovered several loopholes and ways around the rule, rendering the law ineffective. Again in 1938 the state declared Niemöller's Confessing association, the Pastors' Emergency League, to be subversive and anti-German. Niemöller was imprisoned for seven months in 1938 and then confined at Dachau in 1941 for the duration of the war. During 1937 alone, over eight hundred Protestant clergymen spent at least two days in jail for noncompliance with state policy.

A GERMAN CLERGYMAN PROTESTS

Martin Niemöller, a German minister and World War I hero, composed the following poem to protest the mistreatment of Jews and other groups by the Nazis. Niemöller spent the majority of World War II at Dachau concentration camp.

They came for the Communists, and I

didn't object—For I wasn't

a Communist;

They came for the Socialists, and I

didn't object—For I wasn't a Socialist;

They came for the labor leaders, and I

didn't object—For I wasn't a labor leader;

They came for the Jews, and I didn't

object—For I wasn't a Jew;

Then they came for me—

And there was no one left to object.

Source: *Cybrary of the Holocaust Web Page.*

The lone state victory during the last years of the 1930s came with the successful enforcement of the new requirements that demanded Confessing Church leaders to take a direct oath to the Führer. Previous efforts to administer the oath in 1934 and 1935 had failed. In 1938, however, the majority of the Evangelical leadership, worn down by the years of conflict and anxious to demonstrate a national solidarity in the face of an increasingly volatile international situation, took the oath. Many others, however, still refused to do so or renounced it soon after taking it. Dibelius had remarked in 1937 that "as soon as the state assumes itself to be the church and wants to take over the control of the souls of individuals and of the sermons of the church, then we, according to the teachings of Martin Luther, are called upon to offer resistance in God's name. And this we will do!" Apparently, many German clergymen felt the same.

In January 1939 the state launched its final prewar attack against the Evangelical churches. Oddly enough, the churches themselves started the trouble, after a vote of more than two-thirds of all German Protestant pastors called for a unified German Evangelical Church separate from state control in the Godesburg Declaration (April 1939). Kerrl and the Church Ministry, while publicly supporting this proposal, inserted assertions into the declaration to try and ensure that this entity would be under German Christian control. While the net result of debate over the Godesburg Declaration further fractured and reduced the political influence of the Evangelical Church, the role of the German pastors also ensured that there would be no unified Protestant Church under German Christian control.

The condition of the German Christian Church demonstrated the Nazi inability to force the churches under its control. As Doris L. Bergen wrote in *Twisted Cross: The German Christian Movement in the Third Reich* (1996), even though the German Christian movement had its successes, "in many ways the movement was a dismal failure. Despite early triumphs and a high profile, it never achieved a membership of more than about six-hundred thousand people—not even two percent of Germany's Protestant population." After winning a two-thirds majority in Protestant Church elections in Germany in 1933, the movement never had official support, either monetarily or verbally, and assistance dwindled in the ensuing years.

While the majority of religious resistance and antagonism against the state occurred in the Protestant camp, the Catholic Church also endured moments of conflict with the Nazis. In any study of the Catholic Church and its relationship with the Third Reich and Hitler, the focal point is the signing of the Concordat with Rome in July 1933. By this arrangement, in return for the Nazi assurance of freedom of faith and public worship to Catholics, and recognition of the protection of priests and church institutions, the Vatican gave up all German Catholicism political organizations and recognized the legitimacy of Hitler's regime. Nonetheless, just as members of the Protestant congregation, Catholics faced many obstructions to worship in the 1930s. Many of the challenges were the same as those faced by other Christians, but many others, particularly the result of the political activity of the Catholic-dominated Center Party in the half-century preceding the Third Reich, were specific to those followers of the Catholic faith. German Cardinal Adolf Bertram wrote to Cardinal Eugenio Pacelli, who in March 1939 became Pope Pius XII, that "Only with the ratification [of the Concordat] will we [the German Catholic Bishops] achieve the possibility of proceeding more definitely against the numerous anti-Catholic measures."

Nevertheless, historians frequently use the Concordat as a sign of capitulation by the Catholic Church to Hitler and the Nazi regime. Among other things, it called for state approval of bishops, an oath of loyalty by all clergymen to the civil government, and a mandatory prayer for *Reich* and *Volk* during services. The German Catholic population of the 1930s, however, saw it also as a restraint on state and party officials and a guarantee to the Catholic Church of certain specific rights. Among the promises guaranteed to Catholics by the Concordat were: rights and terms of marriage laws, maintenance of church subsidies and finances, and, perhaps most importantly, assurance of the maintenance of religious education and church schools. These were the key points that the Church determined to maintain.

Although the Nazi government went back on its word concerning the Concordat on many occasions, for the most part it adhered to the terms of the agreement. This situation does not make the Nazi regime a supporter of the Catholic Church—far from it. With the exception of the forcible integration of all youth organizations, including Catholic Youth Organizations, into the *Hitler-Jugend* (Hitler Youth) and the *Bund Deutscher Mädel* (German Girls' Organization), the state never successfully breached the agreement in any serious way. Hitler wanted to avoid all open conflict with religious leaders, particularly the Pope. After the political bumbling of 1934 with the attempted consolidation of the Evangelical Churches, Hitler remained well aware of the possible problems that might follow if he antagonized the Catholic leadership. This likelihood became clear to him, especially after local government officials poorly handled the reprimanding of a Catholic priest in Würzberg in 1934 and after the Catholic hierarchy had demonstrated its ability to assemble large numbers of people (up to sixty thousand) in support of the Catholic religion in the same period.

The final half of the 1930s witnessed several religious controversies, all of which caused great consternation among the National Socialist leadership. First was the papal statement of March 1937, in which Pope Pius XI published his Encyclical *"Mit brennender Sorge"* (With Deep Anxiety) and expressed concern over German repression of the Catholic churches. The genesis for this letter came about through the aforementioned Nazi initiatives to consolidate all youth organizations and a new initiative to remove all crucifixes from religious schools. While the state was successful in the former endeavor, completed in 1939, the latter caused widespread social unrest and never was completely successful. Additionally, the *Anschluss* (political union, 1938) with Austria saw many newly incorporated bishops speak out against the excesses of the new regime. Moreover, as all these events were going on, the Church took the initiative and actively tried to infiltrate the government with Catholic administrative officials who were also Nazis. All of these events clearly demonstrate that, far from actively supporting the Nazi regime, the Catholic Church remained in near-constant conflict with it.

In 1938, Hermann Göring confessed to Charles A. Lindbergh that he had "told Hitler he would be willing to take on any problem in Germany except the religious problem, but that he did not know how to solve the religious problem." Neither did Hitler. The vast majority of the Führer's initiatives to incorporate into the German state all denominations failed miserably. The victories in the religious realm were usually fairly small, although they could be significant. The churches, for the most part, remained active in their resistance against new doctrinal tenets forced upon them by the state and were among the few groups in Germany that achieved a modicum of success in their endeavors. As historian Ernst Christian Helmreich wrote in *The German Churches Under Hitler: Background, Struggle, and Epilogue* (1979), "Political parties, trade unions, business organizations, professional groups, and even to a great extent the army, succumbed to these *Gleichschaltung* procedures—but not the churches. . . . While the *Kirchenkampf* (Church struggle) as such was primarily concerned with the freedom of the church within the state and did not challenge Nazism directly as a political system, it was nevertheless a broad channel through which criticism of Nazi policy could and did flow."

–MICHAEL A. BODEN, U.S. MILITARY ACADEMY, WEST POINT

References

Doris L. Bergen, *Twisted Cross: The German Christian Movement in the Third Reich* (Chapel Hill: University of North Carolina Press, 1996);

Michael A. Boden, "'Imposed Supervision:' The Struggle of Germany's Confessing *Landeskirche* in 1934," thesis, Vanderbilt University, 1997;

John S. Conway, *The Nazi Persecution of the Churches, 1933–1945* (London: Weidenfeld & Nicolson, 1968);

Ernst Christian Helmreich, *The German Churches Under Hitler: Background, Struggle, and Epilogue* (Detroit: Wayne State University Press, 1979);

Peter Matheson, ed. *The Third Reich and the Christian Churches* (Edinburgh: T. & T. Clark; Grand Rapids, Mich.: Eerdmans, 1981);

Klaus Scholder, *Kirchen und das Dritte Reich* (Frankfurt & Berlin: Ullstein, 1977), translated by John Bowden as *The Churches and the Third Reich*, 2 volumes (London: SCM Press; Philadelphia: Fortress, 1987);

Gordon C. Zahn, *German Catholics and Hitler's Wars: A Study in Social Control* (New York: Sheed & Ward, 1962).

PATTON

Is the reputation of General George S. Patton Jr. as a master of military strategy deserved?

Viewpoint: Yes, Patton was a military leader of the first rank, distinguished by his charismatic leadership, his vision, and his mastery of armored warfare.

Viewpoint: No, though Patton became a master tactician of mobile warfare and a practitioner of the operational level of war, he was not as effective as a military strategist, the highest responsibility of a general in wartime.

Generals resemble athletes in that the reputations of some increase in proportion to the time lapsed after their careers end. George S. Patton Jr. falls into that category. In the immediate postwar years he was one among several U.S. generals with high reputations as army-level commanders. A half-century later he has eclipsed his counterparts to emerge, particularly among aficionados and popular writers, as the only U.S. senior officer who understood and practiced the concept of mobile warfare based on shock and finesse, as opposed to attrition based on superior force.

To some degree Patton's reputation was fostered by his German opponents, who consistently described him as the closest thing to a Panzer general the Western allies produced. To some degree it reflects the growing acceptance in the United States of professionalized models of military effectiveness, as opposed to the "GI-general" and "everyman at war" images projected by such wartime icons as Omar Bradley and Dwight D. Eisenhower. In an age when leaders' feet of clay are regularly sought and exposed, Patton's indiscretions, culminating in the slapping of a combat-shocked soldier, appear less idiosyncratic than they did in 1943—and Patton at least was no hypocrite. His behavior reflected his beliefs: a welcome congruence in an age of spin.

As a field commander, Patton was a risk-taker who believed in forcing the Germans to react, then doing something else unexpected. He based his conduct of operations, however, on a solid grasp of the instruments at his disposal. He was a particular master of integrating air and ground forces, and recognized that mobile war demanded the coordination of armored forces with artillery and infantry at all levels. His flamboyance, unlike Napoleon Bonaparte's, was not aimed at his soldiers. Patton believed Americans were most effective when they knew what they were doing, as opposed to whom they believed in. He expected formations under his command to perform well because he commanded them well. By and large his approach was justified.

Denied command above army level because of his personal behavior, Patton never demonstrated talents beyond those of a battle captain. At that level he was consistently successful. Whether his qualities would have stood transition to higher planes is one of the more interesting might-have-beens of World War II.

Viewpoint:
Yes, Patton was a military leader of the first rank, distinguished by his charismatic leadership, his vision, and his mastery of armored warfare.

The public image General George S. Patton Jr. so carefully crafted has, to an extent, blinded historians to the real essence of the man. This image was further distorted in 1970 with the release of the award-winning movie, *Patton,* starring George C. Scott in the title role. Scott's portrayal, though generally accurate, focused but on one part of the man, the part Patton wanted the world to see. However, behind the resplendent, gun-toting, glory-seeking general who pushed his forces hell-bent-for-leather across North Africa, Sicily, and Europe, was another man, a man who dedicated his adult life to the study and practice of war and who, when presented with the opportunity to put his thoughts into action, did so with stunning results. A closer look at Patton reveals a superb leader, trainer, and motivator of men who understood all aspects of his profession and, in the final analysis, brought the operational use of armor to its highest expression.

Born to affluence in San Gabriel, California, on 11 November 1885, Patton was reared on the martial exploits of ancestors who fought with the British in the French and Indian War (1754–1763), with the Continental Army in the American Revolutionary War (1775–1783), and for the Confederacy in the American Civil War (1861–1865). In 1903 he enrolled at the Virginia Military Institute where he spent a year before entering West Point in June 1904. Forced to repeat his plebe year at West Point for failing mathematics, Patton graduated in 1909 as a second lieutenant in the cavalry. In 1916 he accompanied General John J. Pershing as unofficial aide-de-camp during the expedition to Mexico, where he led a raiding party in automobiles against the camp of one of Pancho Villa's lieutenants (the first such motorized raid in American military history). In 1917 he accompanied Pershing to France where he joined the fledgling U.S. Army tank corps and organized the first American tank training center at Langres. He later led a tank brigade in action during the St. Mihiel and Meuse-Argonne offensives. In the latter action, Patton was seriously wounded, but for his heroism and achievements he earned the Distinguished Service Cross, Distinguished Service Medal, Silver Star, and Purple Heart.

During the interwar years Patton served in a variety of cavalry postings, but with the outbreak of war in Europe he returned to the tank corps and commanded in succession a brigade of the 2nd Armored Division; the 2nd Armored Division itself; I Armored Corps; and the armored training center at Indio, California. Once the United States entered World War II, Patton commanded the Western Task Force during Operation Torch; II Corps in Tunisia after the Kasserine Pass debacle; the U.S. Seventh Army during the invasion of Sicily; the U.S. Third Army during the campaigns in northwest Europe; and finally the Fifteenth Army headquarters. Patton died on 21 December 1945 as a result of injuries sustained in an automobile accident.

Throughout his career Patton was a stickler for discipline, which he was convinced formed the bedrock of combat effectiveness. He stressed neatness of dress, military courtesy, care of equipment, and the ruthless adherence to standards. Nevertheless, Patton was no mere martinet. He preached that in combat, especially given the fast-paced tempo of armored warfare, men's lives depended on split-second decisions, and only well-trained and disciplined troops would emerge victorious.

Patton also had the unique ability to develop an immediate and strong rapport with his soldiers. Though he was the foremost proponent of the most technologically advanced arm of ground combat, he never let technology overshadow personal and dynamic leadership. During training and in combat, Patton was constantly in the field, impressing on his soldiers his own brand of aggressiveness. Whenever possible, he would visit his troops and explain to them what he wanted done, and though this was often accompanied with a liberal dose of profanity, Patton got his point across. In his book *Patton: The Man Behind the Legend, 1885–1945* (1985) Martin Blumenson quotes from a soldier's letter home following one such Patton speech: "'He talked on to us for half an hour, literally hypnotizing us with his incomparable, if profane eloquence. When he had finished, you felt as if you had been given a supercharge from some divine source. Here was the man for whom you would go to hell and back.'" Carlo D'Este, in *Patton: A Genius for War* (1995) quotes a navy lieutenant as saying "'when you see George Patton . . . you get the same feeling as when you saw Babe Ruth. . . . Here's the big guy who's going to kick hell out of something.'" Probably the most spectacular display of the impact of his personal leadership occurred after he took command of II Corps in Tunisia following its defeat at Kasserine Pass. After assuming command, Patton visited every battalion, ensured his troops were resupplied, properly clothed and well-fed, dispelled their fears, and ten days later led that some corps to victory at El Guettar.

PATTON

Lieutenant General George S. Patton with Brigadier General Theodore Roosevelt Jr., during the Sicilian campaign

(Courtesy of the United States Army)

However, Patton was much more than a brash, glittering commander constantly haranguing his soldiers to greater and greater efforts. He truly understood the dynamic of modern armored warfare, and was its foremost practitioner in the Allied camp. This characteristic was perhaps best demonstrated during the campaign in northwest Europe when, after being activated on 1 August 1944, his Third Army outraced friend and foe alike following the breakout from the Normandy beaches. Once given its head, Patton's army raced in three directions at once—west into the Brittany Peninsula, south to the Loire, and east to Paris and the Seine. Though some may argue that the forces facing Patton were not of the same caliber as those facing the British and Canadians, the fact is that during the month of August 1944 alone, Patton's army advanced some 400 miles; inflicted more than 100,000 German casualties; captured or destroyed over

500 German tanks and about 700 guns; and all at a cost of less than 16,000 friendly casualties. Patton out-blitzkrieged the Germans, insisting on an operational tempo he knew the Germans could not match. His forces consistently sought weak points in the enemy defense and then attacked through those areas. By March 1945 Patton's Third Army had captured more than 300,000 Germans, more than any other army in Europe. This figure alone is testament to Patton's ability to disrupt his enemy's command and control, leaving bypassed forces little recourse but surrender. As Russell F. Weigley points out in *Eisenhower's Lieutenants: The Campaign of France and Germany, 1944–1945* (1981), "The American army's historic dedication to mobility failed to develop in most American commanders a corresponding penchant for strategic maneuver. Patton was an exception. He was one American general who

believed that mobility must be exploited into the strategic maneuver of the indirect approach."

In *A Time for Trumpets: The Untold Story of the Battle of the Bulge* (1984), Charles B. MacDonald writes of the 19 December 1944 meeting at Lieutenant General Omar Bradley's 12th Army Group Headquarters at Verdun, France. The Supreme Allied Commander, General Dwight D. Eisenhower, had assembled his senior commanders and key staff officers to discuss what measures to take to counter the German offensive that had engulfed the Allied lines three days before. This situation was but a prelude to another classic Patton exploit. When Eisenhower asked Patton when he could mount a counterattack toward Bastogne to relieve the beleaguered U.S. 101st Airborne Division, Patton replied that he could attack with three divisions in little more than thirty-six hours, an operational and logistical feat that would involve shifting his axis of advance ninety degrees while still in contact with the enemy to his front; once again Patton would be fighting in more than one direction. What Eisenhower did not know is that Patton had initiated preparations for such an eventuality as early as 9 December, five days before the German attack. Having been forewarned about the German buildup by his G-2 (Intelligence) Colonel Oscar Koch, Patton had his staff prepare outline plans to attack into the enemy's flank, and arrived at the historic meeting prepared to execute any one of three counterattack plans. As Bradley wrote in *A Soldier's Story* (1951), "Patton's brilliant shift of Third Army from its bridgehead in the Saar to the snow-covered Ardennes front became one of the most astonishing feats of generalship of our campaign in the West."

There were occasions during which Patton's brand of slashing attack was notably absent, such as his attack toward the Moselle in Lorraine. After crossing the Meuse at the end of August 1944, a gasoline shortage halted Patton's armored spearheads, thereby allowing the Germans to organize a strong defense with first-class troops centered on the strong ring of forts around Metz. Once resupplied, Patton launched a series of bloody attacks on the Metz fortifications that he later admitted were mistakes and for which he has been roundly criticized. By October, still not having taken the fortress complex, Patton broke off the attack and laid siege to the area. There is no doubt that Patton was stymied by the German defenses and the terrible weather and terrain he encountered. Yet, he would have achieved a breakthrough had not critical gasoline reserves been directed to Field Marshal Bernard Law Montgomery's 21st Army Group. Having been stopped short before reaching Metz and Lorraine, Patton was forced to slog through terrain that favored the defense. Such a situation would have stymied any general.

In the final analysis, Patton emerges as a master of the operational art of mobile warfare. Given his head, he forced an operational tempo that his enemy could not match, and in doing so his forces moved faster and farther than any in the war, including the Germans in 1939–1941. Often criticized for avoiding enemy contact, the essence of Patton's style of maneuver warfare was exactly that, to force the enemy to either fight at a disadvantage or surrender. He also had the unique ability to think ahead, to anticipate enemy moves, and therefore take measures to counter them beforehand. In his book, D'Este quotes a captured German officer who revealed "'General Patton was always the main topic of military discussion. Where is he? When will he attack? Where? . . . How? With what? . . . [He was] the most feared general on all fronts. . . . The tactics of General Patton are daring and unpredictable. . . . He is the most modern general and the best commander of armored and infantry troops combined.'" Field Marshal Gerd von Rundstedt told his interrogators "Patton, he is your best." During the Anzio debacle, General Sir Harold Alexander, Supreme Allied Commander, Mediterranean, called London to request Patton's services. He wanted "a thruster like Patton" to get the Allied force off the beach before it got pushed back into the sea. In *Patton: The Man Behind the Legend*, Blumenson observes "Patton had, in truth, raised his Third Army to the level of the greatest fighting armies in history, comparable to Hannibal's, Cromwell's, Napoleon's and Lee's."

The irony is that the persona Patton deliberately manufactured has also served to obscure his true essence. Patton's flamboyance was not that of a man concerned solely with personal gain, but the contrived image he felt was needed to excite his soldiers. In *The Patton Mind: The Professional Development of an Extraordinary Leader* (1993), Roger H. Nye relates some marginalia Patton made while reading Gustave Le Bon's *The Crowd: A Study of the Popular Mind* (1895). One such note reads "'the individual [leader] may dream greatly or otherwise, but he must infect the crowd with the idea [in order] to carry it out.'" A second note by Patton reveals "'given to exaggeration in its feelings, a crowd is only impressed by excessive sentiments.'" That Patton took these words to heart there is no doubt. Yet, Patton was more than caricature. He cared deeply for the men whose spirits he wished to arouse with his fiery oratory and colorful image. Though he sometimes made mistakes, such as at Metz and earlier in Sicily, he sought diligently to minimize friendly casualties while seeking the destruction of his enemy. Testament to his emotional regard for the lives of his soldiers is his countless visits to hospitals where he knelt before his dead and wounded. He had witnessed too much needless bloodshed in the trenches of World War I; he did everything in his power to avoid both the trenches and the bloodshed in World War II. In the final analysis, Patton emerges as a true professional who understood the dynamics of charismatic leadership, discipline, forward thinking, and the phenomenon of armored warfare.

–GUY LOFARO, U.S. MILITARY ACADEMY,
WEST POINT

Viewpoint:
No, though Patton became a master tactician of mobile warfare and a practitioner of the operational level of war, he was not as effective as a military strategist, the highest responsibility of a general in wartime.

To avoid strict definitions of the divisions of war, it would be more appropriate to state each of its goals. In brief, military strategy wins the war, the operational level of war or operational art aims at winning the campaigns, and tactics win the battles in the campaigns. Among the extensive literature on Patton's combat exploits there is debate on his historical significance as a military strategist, tactician, and a practitioner of the operational level of war that link tactics and military strategy and tactics.

Before examining Patton's role in the three divisions of war, it is fitting to note that he was a complex and paradoxical figure. For example, when Patton was commanding the 3rd Cavalry at Fort Meyer, Virginia, early in 1940, he wrote a presumptuous letter to his mentor, Major General Kenyon A. Joyce, encouraging the success of the horse cavalry in upcoming maneuvers. Patton suggested the horsemen engage in radio interference to blunt the movement of the mechanized brigade commanded by Colonel Adna A. Chaffee Jr., who became known as the Father of American Armor. It would be a great joke, Patton wrote, if our friendly foes on wheels and tracks could be totally deafened. Months later Chaffee would support Patton's return to tanks.

In just over a year there appeared on the cover of *Life* magazine's 7 July 1941 defense issue a flamboyant Major General Patton wearing a tanker's helmet and displaying a determined war face, an aspect of his personality designed to motivate his men to action. During the final days of the war in Europe, *Time* featured Patton on its cover as a decisive warrior astride a mailed fist, representing armored warfare. The exalted article described the visible Third Army commander, who already was legendary, as "the star halfback," engaging in his favorite roles of speed and daring. Comparing him to the cautious British Field Marshal Bernard Law Montgomery, the article recorded that Patton's aggressive spirit and swift movement were inherited from his horse cavalry days. He was referred to as an instinctive "colorful swashbuckler, the wild-riding charger, the hell-for-leather Man of Action."

Patton's untimely death in December 1945 added to his mystique. To keep her husband's memory alive, Beatrice Patton prompted the publication of *War As I Knew It* (1947). It was originally dictated by Patton shortly after the war and completed with the assistance of his former deputy chief of staff, Colonel Paul D. Harkins, and noted historian, Douglas Southall Freeman. The book was greeted as a fascinating self-portrait of an American general of exceptional ability. The memoir reflected Patton's military activities and thoughts during the war, especially his art of command and opinions on leadership. Of interest were his concepts on battle tactics. The famous phrase "hold the enemy by the nose and kick him in the ass" was reworded. Patton claimed this tactical policy about winning battles originated in his early years. Eventually he meant holding the enemy at the point of contact with a third of the command and then moving with the rest in a wide envelopment, attacking the enemy's rear. Patton believed the envelopment should be just behind the enemy's artillery, supply, and signal communications. He also differentiated between armored and infantry divisions. In the latter the purpose of tanks was to facilitate the movement of the infantry. Whereas in armored divisions, the infantry was to break the tanks loose for deep exploitation. Though Patton effectively used tactical aviation, he believed air-ground cooperation was still in its infancy.

One of his most controversial biographies was Ladislas Farago's *Patton: Ordeal and Triumph* (1964). The book was hailed as a definitive biography. In spite of the accolade, Farago was accused of plagiarism by Patton's former chief of combat intelligence in Europe, Colonel Robert S. Allen, who wrote a history of the Third Army, *Lucky Forward,* in 1947. Farago, nevertheless, provided a lucid picture of Patton's operational techniques and inspired operational war plans. He concluded, nonetheless, that Patton was mercurial and not quite as good as the legend portrayed him.

GENERAL PATTON'S ADDRESS TO THE TROOPS BEFORE D-DAY

Men, this stuff that some sources sling around about America wanting out of this war, not wanting to fight, is a crock of bullshit. Americans love to fight, traditionally. All real Americans love the sting and clash of battle. You are here today for three reasons. First, because you are here to defend your homes and your loved ones. Second, you are here for your own self respect, because you would not want to be anywhere else. Third, you are here because you are real men and all real men like to fight. When you, here, everyone of you, were kids, you all admired the champion marble player, the fastest runner, the toughest boxer, the big league ball players, and the All-American football players. Americans love a winner. Americans will not tolerate a loser. Americans despise cowards. Americans play to win all of the time. I wouldn't give a hoot in hell for a man who lost and laughed. That's why Americans have never lost nor will ever lose a war; for the very idea of losing is hateful to an American. . . .

We have the finest food, the finest equipment, the best spirit, and the best men in the world. Why, by God, I actually pity those poor sons-of-bitches we're going up against. By God, I do. . . .

Sure, we want to go home. We want this war over with. The quickest way to get it over with is to go get the bastards who started it. The quicker they are whipped, the quicker we can go home. The shortest way home is through Berlin and Tokyo. And when we get to Berlin, I am personally going to shoot that paper hanging son-of-a-bitch Hitler. Just like I'd shoot a snake.

When a man is lying in a shell hole, if he just stays there all day, a German will get to him eventually. The hell with that idea. The hell with taking it. My men don't dig foxholes. I don't want them to. Foxholes only slow up an offensive. Keep moving. And don't give the enemy time to dig one either. We'll win this war, but we'll win it only by fighting and by showing the Germans that we've got more guts than they have; or ever will have. We're not going to just shoot the sons-of-bitches, we're going to rip out their living Goddamned guts and use them to grease the treads of our tanks. . . . War is a bloody, killing business. You've got to spill their blood, or they will spill yours. Rip them up the belly. Shoot them in the guts. When shells are hitting all around you and you wipe the dirt off your face and realize that instead of dirt it's the blood and guts of what once was your best friend beside you, you'll know what to do!

I don't want to get any messages saying, "I am holding my position." We are not holding a Goddamned thing. Let the Germans do that. We are advancing constantly and we are not interested in holding onto anything, ... We are going to go through him like crap through a goose. . . .

There is one great thing that you men will all be able to say after this war is over and you are home once again. You may be thankful that twenty years from now when you are sitting by the fireplace with your grandson on your knee and he asks you what you did in the great World War II, you WON'T have to cough, shift him to the other knee and say, "Well, your Granddaddy shoveled shit in Louisiana." No, Sir, you can look him straight in the eye and say, "Son, your Granddaddy rode with the Great Third Army and a Son-of-a-Goddamned-Bitch named Georgie Patton!

Source: *Martin Blumenson,* The Patton Papers *1940–1945 (Boston: Houghton Mifflin, 1974).*

PATTON

The award-winning movie *Patton* (1970) starring George C. Scott, was based on Farago's book and General Omar Bradley's *A Soldier's Story* (1951). The movie was a popular portrait of a war-lover staged in the imagery of Hollywood. One film reviewer called it "a magnificent anachronism" with Patton being portrayed as a near-schizophrenic. Although, he noted, Patton was one of the most brilliant and outrageous American military figures in the last hundred years, as a tactical genius he could not be excused for his vanities, ignorance, and mental instability. Another film reviewer saw the movie as a dichotomy between glory-seeking generals and the shrieking terror of mechanized warfare.

Meanwhile, noted military historian and commentator S. L. A. Marshall wrote that Patton became a formidable opponent of Dwight D. Eisenhower's broad-front military strategy. Commenting on Farago's biography, Marshall found fault with the argument that Patton's fast-moving armor's lethal blow at the Seine River and beyond the West Wall could have ended the war sooner. The Third Army, argued Marshall, was already overextended by the end of August 1944; it was drained of supplies and human energy. He also questioned Farago's assertion that Patton had inspired operational war plans. According to Marshall, Patton had vague and general ideas with no definable consequences behind them.

In spite of the controversy, credit needs to be given to Marshall, and even Farago, for touching on Patton's conflict between military strategy and the operational level of war. This dichotomy occurred soon after the Third Army was committed to combat in July 1944. The issue, as envisioned by generals Bradley and Eisenhower, was the Allied armies' orderly, linear advance by units forming a compact or broad-front strategy. This strategic approach was challenged by Patton, and at times, circumvented. Patton's use of the free-wheeling 4th and 6th Armored Divisions—commanded by Major Generals John Shirley Wood and Robert W. Grow, respectively—in a nonlinear, single-thrust maneuver of exploitation and pursuit was in defiance of accomplishing a broad-front military strategy. Of interest was the German Chief of General Staff, Army Group G West, Major General F. W. von Mellenthin's comment on the prospects of developing the operational level of war by a combined armored force capable of deep operations. Von Mellenthin believed the Third Army would have been successful in reaching a decisive breakthrough and winning the campaign in the fall of 1944 had Patton grouped the 4th and 6th Armored Divisions with the French 2nd Armored Division in a counterpart of the German Panzer Corps.

In 1972 Martin Blumenson's long awaited *The Patton Papers 1885–1940* appeared, the first of two volumes. What emerged from Blumenson's book was Patton's ambition and deep commitment to his profession that he approached in an individualistic and romantic way. Patton was portrayed as an intense proponent of tanks during World War I and then returning to his beloved horse cavalry. Though a knowledgeable analyst of the rise of mechanization, Patton during the interwar period remained a horse cavalry loyalist because of army politics. In volume 2 Patton's attribute as a master of mobile warfare was evident by his ruthless ability to challenge his tactical commanders. The *Patton Papers,* nonetheless, revealed a more complex person than the heroic warrior articles that appeared earlier in *Life* in July 1941 and *Time* in April 1945.

By far the most critical assessment of Patton, especially as an anti-intellectual, appeared in 1989 in Paul Fussell's *Wartime: Understanding and Behavior in the Second World War*. He considered Patton's dress codes as a quasi-fascistic institution. As a result, his description of Patton as a psychogenic warmonger or a deranged adventurer gained notoriety.

Fussell's assessment of Patton as psychogenic warmonger was challenged by two military historians, Steve E. Dietrich and Roger H. Nye. They demonstrated that Patton was a serious student of history, studying with an utmost perseverance to master his profession of arms. Their appraisal was based on an examination of Patton's extensive book collection located in the West Point Library. Both historians were able to demonstrate how these books influenced Patton's thinking on tactics, strategy, and his contribution to the operational level of war. They set to rest the argument that Patton was an anti-intellectual by verifying he meticulously prepared himself by learning from everything he read.

Yet, Patton continued to have his detractors. Andy Rooney, a nationally syndicated columnist and commentator on *60 Minutes,* related his experience as a front-line war reporter in his *My War* (1995). He claimed he met Patton twice and closely followed his actions during the war. As a result, he had nothing but contempt for the general. He called Patton a jackass general and a dangerous charlatan who was bombastic and self-serving. Rooney believed Patton was a loud-mouthed boor who got too many American soldiers killed. However, the U.S. Army's medical history of the war in Europe noted that Third Army armored divisions always had a lower total casualty rate, but a higher neuropsychiatric rate, than did other divisions. One reason for this situation was the mobility of armored divisions, which involved them in rapidly changing tactical situations. Unfortunately, Patton did not understand the human stresses associated with mechanized warfare.

The most recent full-fledged biography of Patton was Carlo D'Este's *Patton: A Genius for War* (1995). This well-researched book was criticized by John Keegan, a noted British military historian. In his review, Keegan summed up Patton's exploits as heroically mad. He claimed D'Este did not produce a counterbalance to earlier popular portrayals of Patton. He wrote instead that D'Este's meticulous documentation produced an uncanny Patton, who was nearly mad and more unsettling than the 1970 movie character. When a star came his way, Keegan wrote, Patton, the opportunist, would exalt in his superordination. In a more matter-of-fact observation, Sir Michael Howard commented that Patton, in exercising high command, required the creation of a lifelong artificial persona.

Since the 1980s American army officials and military historians have been looking at the operational level of war as a separate field of study. This focus was a departure from the long entrenched habit of examining military conflicts within strategy and tactics. Rather than raking a methodical, linear approach to campaigns, Patton's operational management of the Third Army, with the combined arms of armored force and tactical air power, embodied a flexible, nonlinear paradigm. The lightning drive toward Lorraine, the remarkable maneuver by turning the Third Army from an eastward to a northward adjustment to blunt the Germans at the Ardennes, the rapid thrust to the Rhine River, and the deep penetration into Germany towards Czechoslovakia and Austria—these were the hallmarks of Patton's way of war.

From 1942 until the end of the war U.S. Army tank doctrine called for a highly mobile force for pursuit, exploitation, and destruction of enemy artillery, infantry, and soft-skinned vehicles. Patton supported this concept because it expanded the traditional role of his branch, the cavalry, with the combined arms force known as armored divisions. This tactical doctrine suited Patton, who was a firm believer in the cavalry motto *Mobilitate Vigemus* (in mobility lies our strength). This motto was inherent in horse cavalry tactics of breakthrough, exploitation, and pursuit. Patton was able to visualize a fresh tactical approach to win battles. He was able to think upward to the operational level, focusing on campaigns. He was able to synchronize an operational level of war with the Third Army based on speed, maneuver, and deep operations with the combined arms of armored force supported by air power. Rather than develop a theory of armored warfare, Patton was the first American military leader in the twentieth century to execute and refine armored warfare's practice at the operational

level. However, this level of warfare came in conflict with the broad-front strategy. Patton's disagreement with Bradley and Eisenhower regarding the military strategy and the political goals of coalition warfare suggested he could not reach the highest levels of command in modern war.

–GEORGE F. HOFMANN, UNIVERSITY OF CINCINNATI

References

Martin Blumenson, "The Many Faces of George S. Patton, Jr.," *The Harmon Memorial Lectures in Military History,* U.S. Air Force Academy, Colorado, 16 March 1972;

Blumenson, *The Patton Papers 1885–1940* (Boston: Houghton Mifflin, 1972);

Blumenson, *The Patton Papers 1940–1945* (Boston: Houghton Mifflin, 1974);

Blumenson, *Patton: The Man Behind the Legend, 1885–1945* (New York: Morrow, 1985);

Omar Bradley, *A Soldier's Story* (New York: Holt, 1951);

Charles R. Codman, *Drive* (Boston: Little, Brown, 1957);

Carlo D'Este, *Patton: A Genius for War* (New York: HarperCollins, 1995);

Steve E. Dietrich, "The Professional Reading of George S. Patton, Jr.," Paper presented at the American Military Institute Annual Meeting, Lexington, Virginia, 14–15 April 1989;

Hubert Essame, *Patton: A Study in Command* (New York: Scribners, 1974);

Ladislas Farago, *Patton: Ordeal and Triumph* (New York: Ivan Obolensky, 1964);

Charles B. MacDonald, *A Time for Trumpets: The Untold Story of the Battle of the Bulge* (New York: Morrow, 1984);

Clayton R. Newell and Michael D. Krause, eds., *On Operational Art* (Washington, D.C.: U.S. Army Center of Military History, 1994);

Roger H. Nye, *The Patton Mind: The Professional Development of an Extraordinary Leader* (New York: Avery, 1993);

George S. Patton Jr. *War As I Knew It* (Boston: Houghton Mifflin, 1947).

Russell F. Weigley, *Eisenhower's Lieutenants: The Campaign of France and Germany, 1944– 1945* (Bloomington: Indiana University Press, 1981).

PATTON

ROMMEL

Was Field Marshal Erwin Rommel overrated as a general?

Viewpoint: Yes, Rommel has been vastly overrated as a general and as an opponent of National Socialism. He owed his rise to fame in large part to his close association with Hitler, and his exaggerated reputation as a military leader was a rationalization to explain embarrassing defeats by the British in Africa.

Viewpoint: No, though Rommel was not a brilliant strategist, he was a superb tactician and battle commander at the operational level.

Erwin Rommel's professional reputation is far higher among his former enemies than in his own country, where he tends to be regarded as an excellent division commander, adequate at corps level, yet challenged beyond his capacity when given higher appointments. Rommel owes much of his status to his British opponents in North Africa from 1940 to 1942. "Doing a Rommel" became in some circles of the Eighth Army shorthand for competent performance. Winston Churchill himself paid public tribute to the Desert Fox "across the havoc of war." The future Field Marshal Bernard Law Montgomery, on assuming command in the desert, saw among his primary tasks ending what seemed a sportsman's approach to the commander of the *Afrika Korps* (Africa Corps).

A somewhat more cynical assessment of Rommel's image among the British suggests that exaggerating his genius was a convenient way of explaining the long series of embarrassing thrashings at the hands of the Afrika Korps, without having to examine one's own system for fundamental weaknesses. After 1945, however, Rommel's military image grew brighter as military analysts praised his grasp of the initiative, his mastery of improvisation, and his ability to make maximum use of inferior numbers. It was scarcely coincidental that these were precisely the military qualities considered necessary to counter the conventional military power of the Soviet Union. Finally, Rommel's growing antagonism to National Socialism; his involvement, however peripheral, with the 20 July conspiracy; and his subsequent forced suicide made him the kind of "bridge figure" whose name could safely be given to a major warship of the postwar Federal Republic of Germany.

When the mythic trappings are stripped away, Rommel stands out as a master of battlefield maneuver and charismatic leadership. His tactical focus reflected his conviction that wars are won at the sharp end, that policy and strategy must be implemented in battle. Rommel was a risk taker, quick to make decisions, and even quicker to implement them. He made his share of mistakes—the first attack on Tobruk (13 April 1941), the "dash to the wire" in 1942, and the haphazard attack at Alam el Halfa (31 August–7 September 1942) that set the stage for his defeat at El Alamein (23 October–4 November 1942). Yet, Rommel also reflected on his experiences. His ability to develop theory from practice in the middle of a war, best expressed in the posthumous *The Rommel Papers* (1953), is unusual among senior officers of 1939 to 1945. Rommel stands out, for good or ill, as an artist of war in a conflict fought largely by craftsmen and technocrats.

Viewpoint:
Yes, Rommel has been vastly overrated as a general and an opponent of National Socialism. He owed his rise to fame in large part to his close association with Hitler, and his exaggerated reputation as a military leader was a rationalization to explain the embarrassing defeats by the British in Africa.

"Rommel! Rommel! Rommel! What else matters but beating him!"—In retrospect, British prime minister Winston Churchill's insistence on the importance of the North African campaign to the overall war effort in January 1943 seems a trifle exaggerated, but the magic name of General (later Field Marshal) Erwin Rommel has long lent itself to hyperbole. That Rommel's reputation does his career more than justice is hardly surprising, given the number of people who profited from advertising—and inflating—his virtues.

Adolf Hitler and the National Socialists made full use of this courageous, charismatic, and photogenic professional soldier. They adopted him because he genuinely approved of the Führer and of the new Germany. Moreover, as a mere colonel, a teacher's son, and an infantry man lacking the red trouser stripes of the general staff and the prestige of being a *Kriegsakademie* (war academy) graduate, Rommel stood apart from the army's politically conservative leadership. His frequent and spectacular victories against heavy odds made Rommel an invaluable asset to Propaganda Minister Joseph Goebbels's propaganda machine, and it suited the Nazi Party to see its favorite soldier showered with promotions and decorations.

Although his military superiors generally disliked Rommel for his Nationalist Socialist connections, meteoric advancement, abrasive personality, and ambitious self-promotion, they did their part in creating his postwar legend. Aware of the field marshal's popularity among the Germans and of his respect in the enemy camp, those involved in the 20 July 1944 plot to assassinate the Führer were eager to co-opt him, living or dead, to their cause. In the hope that his demonstrated German patriotism would render the coup palatable to German citizens, he was the conspirators' unwitting choice to replace Hitler as president of Germany. Although Rommel had played no part in the assassination attempt—and rejected the notion of murdering his commander in chief—his forced suicide on 13 October 1944 reinforced the legend of Rommel the resister.

It was a misconception that the genuine plotters had reason to foster and Allied commanders a proclivity to believe. If the honorable Rommel were a conspirator, then all conspirators were honorable men, and German generals were patriotic soldiers rather than war criminals. Rommel was a latecomer to the plots against Hitler, however, and came to favor the Führer's arrest only because his military policies guaranteed Germany's defeat by the Communists. For Rommel, Hitler was not a criminal but a blunderer. Significantly, after the war was over, when Hitler's regime was gone, and participation in the 20 July plot was a source of honor, Rommel's wife continued to deny his complicity with the resistance.

German armies have long attracted an international following disproportionate to their strategic accomplishments. After the war the many foreign admirers of the *Wehrmacht* (German army) combined Rommel the anti-Hitler conspirator with Rommel the apolitical soldier to defend the German Army against charges of collaboration with Hitler's gangster state. Even Rommel's erstwhile enemies participated in the glorification of the man they called "The Desert Fox." Where Germans used the verb "to Rommel" to describe a notable action, the British preferred the noun form "a Rommel." Typical is British general Claude Auchinleck's praise of a Rommel biography, found in Desmond Young's *Rommel* (1950), because "it does justice to a stout-hearted adversary and may help to show to a new generation of Germans that it is not their soldierly qualities which we dislike but only the repeated misuse of them by their rulers."

Historians, of course, have done much to foster Rommel's reputation as a charismatic commander fighting a two-front war against the Allied armies and Hitler's *Ober-Kommando der Wehrmacht* (OKW or High Command) lackeys. While all acknowledge that his forward leadership had its disadvantages and most admit that his overambitious operations tended to fail for lack of resources, major tactical blunders such as his precipitate attack on the British fortress at Tobruk on 14 April 1941 get little attention. Like the foreign officers who admired Rommel, his biographers have shrugged off his attachment to Hitler and to the National Regime as reflecting his naiveté. In *Knight's Cross: A Life of Field Marshal Erwin Rommel* (1993), David Fraser points out that, for example, Rommel exemplified Chief of Staff Hans von Seeckt's principle of military abstention from politics. Fraser never looks at the real political machinations behind the army's protestations of *überparteilichkeit* (beyond partisanship). Apparently, Rommel must have been ignorant of Hitler's crimes because he was too heroic a soldier to have con-

doned them. To his admirers, Rommel advertises a certain notion of military professionalism by demonstrating that the truly professional soldier can honorably serve any government.

Finally, Rommel was never shy to advertise himself. Charismatic leadership has to be seen to be effective, and Rommel's staff of reporters and photographers made certain that no Rommel success went unreported. His display often occurred at the expense of other commanders. Notorious in the French campaign for impeding other units in order to press his own advance, he took personal credit, for example, for General Johannes Streich's initiative in advancing without orders against Agedabia on 1 April 1941.

Efforts to enhance Rommel's reputation have profited from his good fortune in fighting in World War II's cleaner theaters. North Africa, in particular, lent itself to such romanticism as David Irving's epitaph to Rommel, in *The Trail of the Fox: The Search for the True Field Marshal Rommel* (1977):

And when the hot storm blows, and the skies cloud

over with red lying sand, and the *ghibi* begins to howl,

perhaps they hear once more a Swabian voice rasping

in their ears: "*Angreifen!*"

The desert made for a motorized war of movement, tactically interesting and devoid of the ugliness of mud and frostbite. Fluid operations on flat terrain produced large numbers of prisoners of war, who were generally treated decently on both sides. In the absence of enemy civilians, North Africa lacked manifestations of "total war." Fraser writes that: "In Africa . . . there were no SS units. There appeared to be few Jews. There were no commissars, no Communists, no Communists, no Russians. There were not even very many Nazis." Rommel did not receive the criminal orders promulgated elsewhere, and of what Wehrmacht and *Schutzstaffeln* (SS) generals in other theaters of the war did to Jews, commissars, communists, and Russians, he knew little. Innocence, of course, could not last. As commander of Army Group B in Northern Italy, Rommel complained about the looting by SS units. More seriously, after he took command in France, Rommel remonstrated with Hitler, albeit unsuccessfully, about the barbarous behavior of the Das Reich Division at Oradour-sur-Glade. Rommel was known for acts of chivalry toward prisoners. On the other hand, he killed a captured French lieutenant colonel in 1940 for refusing an order to ride on one of his command tanks. Such is Rommel's privileged status that

biographers mention this apparent violation of the laws of war only as an example of Rommel's willingness to do his painful duty.

Rommel was a superb battlefield commander but neither a great general nor an apolitical island of soldierly virtue. In the French campaign of May–June 1940, Rommel demonstrated the weaknesses that undermined his undeniable military talents. When his Seventh Panzer division led the German Army across the Meuse on 14 May 1940, Rommel himself was in the vanguard. Five days later, Rommel remained at the head of his troops as they pushed deeply, and unsupported, into French territory. In 1940, Rommel's personal courage, his insistence on pushing his men forward without respite, and his refusal to acknowledge logistical constraints paid off stunningly. Rommel would justify abandoning his divisional headquarters for a place in the lead tank as necessary to maintain the pace of the advance. Had the Allied forces managed to mount a major counterattack, however, the overextended, poorly supplied, and erratically commanded Seventh Panzer Division would have been embarrassed. As it was, Lord Gort's improvised two-division counterattack at Arras on 21 May 1940 inflicted four hundred casualties on the division. While many of his fellow soldiers looked askance at Rommel's flamboyant style, it—combined with his impeccable Nazi politics—earned him the decorations suitable for advertising the martial successes of the Third Reich.

Rommel defended his dangerous style of leadership with the argument, quoted by Irving, that tank units were modern cavalry "and that means issuing orders from a moving tank just as generals once used to from the saddle," but the fact remained that his habit of riding in the lead tank kept him out of touch with his headquarters and, therefore, with the rest of his force. Problematic for a mere division commander, this habit of being anywhere on the battlefield proved a nightmare for the staff officers who tried to manage the entire *Afrika Korps* (Africa Corps).

Like his dash through France, Rommel's "brilliant" North African successes occurred because he ignored more cautious instructions sent to him from Berlin and lied to the Italian commanders to whom he reported. The resulting victories were ephemeral, the losses in men and material crippling. Field Marshal Hans Günther von Kluge's opening comment to Rommel upon taking Field Marshal Karl Rudolf Gerd von Rundstedt's place were: "The first thing is, you just get accustomed to obeying orders like the rest of us."

Intoxicated by victories over poorly led Commonwealth forces, Rommel "naturally and persistently" dreamed of an ambitious and triumphant German campaign—"'Plan Orient,' the 'Great Plan'—which would take the Wehrmacht through Europe, across the Syrian desert and into Persia, threatening the Soviet Caucasus from the South and in the process denying Middle East oil to Britain." That such operations were logistically insupportable did little to check Rommel's fevered imagination.

Rommel did not, of course, ignore logistics altogether; here too, however, he let his imagination run freely—recalculating requirements according to his own premises whenever he thought his quartermasters' assessments too conservative. Never conceding the existence of logistical barriers to his dreams, he always blamed supply problems in North Africa on the high command's failure to send the necessary matériel rather than acknowledging the impossibility of moving adequate supplies, especially petroleum, along his extended North African supply lines.

Even Rommel's much praised style of personal leadership had ample faults. His courage, toughness, and personal decency are unquestionable, but he was also mercurial, prone both to peaks of irrational enthusiasm and to fits of excessive depression. His treatment of the unlucky Streich, the scapegoat for Rommel's futile assault on Tobruk in April 1941, was not atypical. As one corps commander described the atmosphere at Rommel's headquarters, as reported by Irving, "Rommel is cantankerous and frequently blows his top—he scares the daylights out of his commanders. The first one that reports to him each morning gets eaten for breakfast." According to Matthew Cooper in *The German Army 1933–1945: Its Political and Military Failure* (1978), General Franz Halder, admittedly no friend of Rommel's, complained that "He rushed about all day between the widely scattered units, stages reconnaissance raids, and fritters away his forces. No one has any idea of their disposition and battle strength. The only certainty is that the troops are widely dispersed and their battle strength dispersed."

Far from representing the *Reichwehr's* (pre-WWII German Army) alleged tradition of überparteilichkeit, Rommel felt the appeal of Hitler's policies and personal charm alike. He approved of National Socialist promises to maintain civil order, stimulate the depressed German economy, and revive the German military establishment. Though never a party member, Rommel took his stand as early as June 1934, when he praised Hitler's use of the SS to suppress the unruly *Sturm Abteilung* (SA) during the so-called Night of the Long Knives (30 June 1934). Never did he express any qualms about SS murders, not only of rival SA leaders but also of prominent German politicians, soldiers, and their wives. Rommel's sympathies made him a suitable adviser to

the *Hitler Jugend* (Hitler Youth) movement, which he treated as an instrument for militarizing the youth of Germany. By 1938, Rommel was signing his personal correspondence with the unnecessarily political "Heil Hitler!" Although he was unaware of the lengths to which Hitler's regime would go to "solve" the "Jewish problem," Rommel did acknowledge that, by virtue of the Jews' naturally divided loyalties, some kind of "solution" was in order.

This political reliability brought Rommel command of Hitler's personal headquarters during the *Anschluss* (political union with Austria) of 1938 and, as a major general, again during the Polish Campaign. Such close contact with the Führer furthered his suit for command of a new armored division in the attack on France, led to his selection for the North African command, brought him the benefits of Goebbels's propaganda machine, and shielded him from the consequences of disobedience and insubordination. Far from the brilliant but apolitical general of myth, Rommel was an inspirational but erratic field commander of limited strategic vision who owed his opportunities and much of his reputation to his Nazi loyalties.

—EUGENIA C. KIESLING, U.S. MILITARY ACADEMY, WEST POINT

Viewpoint: No, though Rommel was not a brilliant strategist, he was a superb tactician and battle commander at the operational level.

In January 1942 Prime Minister Winston Churchill stood before the House of Commons and stated that the *Afrika Korps* (Africa Corps) commander, General Erwin Rommel, was a daring and skillful opponent and a great general. The British viewed Rommel as a master tactician in handling mobile formations and a gambler who deserved respect. Six years after the war, the movie *The Desert Fox: The Story of Rommel* (1951), which was based on Desmond Young's book, *Rommel* (1950), humanized Rommel as a brilliant, brave, and decent field commander. In the early 1970s, after months of examining the *Wehrmacht* (German Army) archive, a group of West German military historians concluded that Rommel was more a "prairie chicken" than Desert Fox. They inferred that the field marshal was deficient in working with higher echelons that required more expertise in understanding cooperation with other arms in executing the overall war effort. More so, these historians argued that Rommel had difficulty dealing with his superiors over military strategy and concluded that he was only a superb tactician and battle commander.

There is no doubt Rommel was a skilled battle leader who was also noted for his charisma and chivalry. In less than a year on the Western Front in World War I, Rommel had received the Iron Cross and was wounded twice for his aggressive actions against the French. He was subsequently transferred to a newly formed mountain battalion, the *Württembergische Gebirgsbataillon,* the units of which were organized according to a specifically defined mission. Rommel thus avoided for the rest of the war the stagnation of trench warfare that plagued the Western Front for four years. The move helped Rommel to grasp the nature of combat mobility. After spending time with the mountain battalion, Rommel found himself facing the Italians.

During the Italian campaign Rommel again displayed his tactical expertise, especially in the capture of Monte Matajur in late October 1917. In this action Rommel led his *Abteilung* (combat detachment) in a difficult maneuver in cold, rugged mountain country, capturing 150 officers, 9,000 soldiers, and 81 guns. This spirited tactical move contributed to the Italian Army's rout and disaster known as the Battle of Caporetto (24 October–26 December 1917). For his relentless leadership in this action, Rommel received Germany's highest decoration, the *Pour le Mérite.* When the war ended, Rommel was accepted into the small *Reichswehr* officer corps where he commanded an infantry company during most of the 1920s. During this period he immersed himself thoroughly in learning training and military administration. In 1935 he was posted as a tactical instructor at the War College in Potsdam. One attendee, who later became a General Staff officer and the operations officer of the 56th Panzer korps tasked to defend Adolf Hitler's bunker in Berlin at the end of the war, recalled that Rommel had a most profound impact on the students, especially in his ability to articulate his personal experiences during World War I. These accounts were published and used as tactical text. *Infanterie greift an* (1937) so impressed Hitler that Rommel was posted to command his *Fuhrerbegleitbataillon* (personal guard). At Hitler's headquarters Rommel witnessed a new method of warfare, the *Blitzkrieg* (lightning war) against Poland. Eager to add this new method of warfare to his concept of mobile warfare, he persuaded Hitler for a combat command.

Subsequently, Rommel was posted to the 7th Panzer Division in General Herman Hoth's Panzer Korps for the invasion of France and the ensuing battle of Flanders. Advancing from the German-Belgian border on 10 May 1940, his division reached the Meuse in just two days. This action was indicative of Rommel's ability to handle an all-arms Panzer division in deep operations. Bloodied and blunted briefly on 21 May at Arras by a poorly coordinated British mixed force of infantry and tanks, the 7th Panzer Division rapidly moved to the northeast to Lille; however, not before causing some serious alarm in the Wehrmacht chain of command. On 5 June the 7th Panzer Division crossed the Somme River and raced to the Seine River crossing near Rouen, then swung northeast towards the English Channel. Returning to the Seine, the 7th Panzer Division advanced to the south and west towards Cherbourg, which surrendered to Rommel on 19 June. Ending at the Spanish border, Rommel and his division—now known as the "Ghost Division"—had gained considerable fame for its rapid and daring deep operations in a combined air-ground mechanized force.

In February 1941 Rommel was posted to North Africa to bolster the defeated Italians and defend the Libyan capital. In the ensuing months, Rommel's Afrika Korps instead fought and outmaneuvered some of Britain's best ground forces back and forth over North African. As a result, land communications contracted and expanded as the Desert Fox went dashing off into the inhospitable terain. Rommel made his own decisions, and more than anything, he insisted on complete freedom of action without consulting his superiors. At this point in his career, the sharp-tempered Rommel's brilliance as a tactician was not matched by his strategic ability.

The harsh North African environment was not France, and as a result, different military considerations of terrain, air support, and sea power required a new framework that Churchill called a "triphibian." The formidable logistic obstacles over abrasive terrain forced Rommel to collaborate with the *Comando Supremo,* the Italian high command, whom he blamed for the frequent breakdowns in the German supply system. Rommel, however, was not proactive in dealing with potential logistical problems that required air and sea control of the Mediterranean in order to support the Afrika Korps as it moved in the rugged North African terrain. Rommel was too ambitious in his objective of reaching the Nile River without first controlling the strategic island of Malta, from where British air and naval power exacted a severe toll on critical Italian and German supply tonnage. Rommel's impetuosity and a lack of strategic foresight were further impacted by his relationship with the intelligent and genial "smiling Albert," Field Marshal Albert Kesselring, commander of *Luftflotte II* and the *Oberbefehlshaber Süd* (designated unified commander) of the Axis forces in the central

THE LAST DAYS OF THE AFRIKA KORPS

Montgomery's offensive at El Alamein began on the night of October 23.

The secret of this massed, planned assault had been extraordinarily well kept. It came as a complete surprise, even though indications of an almost immediate offensive had been gathered and assessed by the German Staff during the twenty-four hours before the initial barrage opened. . . .

The 15th Panzer Division in the north and the 21st in the south lay a short way behind the turmoil of the forward line. They had been split into battle groups in accordance with defensive plans that Rommel had drawn up before he left Africa for medical attention in Germany. . . .

Hitler telephoned Rommel in a hospital in Germany at noon on the second day of the battle and asked him at once to fly back to Africa. The situation was desperate. Rommel had been under treatment for only three weeks and was still ill, but he did not think of saying No. He was airborne before daybreak the following morning, only stopping in Italy to find out what was going on, and particularly to learn whether his forces were getting enough petrol . . . He was at Panzer Gruppe Headquarters again a couple of hours after sunset that same night.

I think he knew then that El Alamein was lost: he found out how short of petrol the Afrika Korps was. . . .

Rommel decided to withdraw on the night of November 2–3.

He wirelessed his decision and his reasons to Hitler's headquarters that night. The report was passed to Hitler only the following day: the officer who was on duty when it came through had failed to wake him. (He was reduced in rank.) Hitler raved, and reviled Rommel.

Rommel's retreat was in progress when a wireless signal came from Hitler's H.Q.: "The situation demands that the positions at El Alamein be held to the last man. A retreat is out of the question. Victory or death! Heil Hitler!" The message bore Hitler's personal signature. For some reason or other, although we were already withdrawing, the signal was circulated to Afrika Korps units. . . .

Source: Heinz Werner Schmidt, With Rommel in the Desert (London: Harrap, 1951), pp. 138–141.

Mediterranean theater. In Kesselring's memoirs, published as *The Memoirs of Field Marshal Kesselring,* translated by Lynton Hudson (1953), Rommel was the only general he reproached, in part because of their difference in breeding and temperament. Kesselring, the aristocratic Bavarian, was a staff-trained German General Staff officer; whereas, Rommel, the son of a Württemberg schoolmaster, never had that great honor.

As the supreme commander, Kesselring had control over all Axis forces, including Rommel's Afrika Korps, which was under the command of the Italian High Command. In this position Kesselring was required to manage the military situation with a good deal of tact and persuasion, characteristics evoked more by Rommel and Hitler than the Italians. In addition, Kesselring had to deal with Hitler's opinion of the theater as a wasteful diversion. Yet, Kesselring was given the difficult task to control the air and ensure sea communications by neutralizing Malta, to cooperate with Italian and German forces in North Africa, and interdict enemy supply movements in the Mediterranean. For a time Kesselring was able to readdress the balance in the theater. He had a better overall conception of the operational level of warfare with a combined arms and coalition force than the independent Rommel. His command structure, however, was circumvented and thus compromised by the autonomous-minded Rommel, who had a tendency to use a private channel of communication direct to the Wehrmacht high command. As a result, Rommel, with Hitler's backing, was able to frustrate Kesselring's strategy of interdicting the long and complex supply lines of the British. The most telling controversy was when Kesselring disagreed with Rommel's notion to capture Cairo in August 1942. The *Luftwaffe* and the Axis ground forces were at a critical point on their lines of communications, while at the same time the British—now closer to their major base in Egypt—were being reinforced both on the ground and in the air. Rommel knew that Malta was on Kesselring's strategic plan; however, he decided to chase the British 8th Army toward Egypt. Rommel did not understand that the capture of Malta would have removed a major threat to his supply lines from Europe that were necessary to keep his systematic practice of using a highly flexible formation of all arms. When the Axis forces finally surrendered in the Tunisian perimeter, Rommel had already departed for Germany.

The experience with Rommel was not lost on Kesselring when the Allies invaded the Italian mainland, resulting in a long, grueling defensive action that severely drained the Allied forces. Kesselring proposed to defend Italy south of Rome because it offered excellent terrain features for a defensive war of attrition. Rommel—now Commander of Army Group B in Northern Italy—proposed instead to defend Italy in the northern Apennines. He was concerned about internal communications and being outflanked by an Allied amphibious assault. Kesselring, an excellent diplomat, this time had his proposal accepted by Hitler. Kesselring was more optimistic than the pessimistic Rommel, who more and more found it difficult to deal with his superiors. Subsequently, Rommel was posted to France to make plans for upgrading the coastal defenses in anticipation of the Allied cross-Channel invasion.

Rommel's next display of his growing pessimism over Hitler's strategy in Europe came about over the defense of *Festung Europa* (Fortress Europe). In January 1944 he became commander of German forces in the Low Countries and northern France. His mission was to oversee the reinforcement of the "Atlantic Wall." Rommel's personality and style came in conflict with a holdover from the traditional Prussian officer corps, Field Marshall Gerd von Rundstedt, the commander in chief, west (OB West). They initially disagreed on how to employ the vast mobile-reserve force in France against an anticipated Allied invasion. Rommel proposed a policy of a forward defense capable of defeating the Allies on the beach. He argued that it would be difficult moving armor formations during the daylight because of Allied air superiority, an experience he learned in Africa. Von Rundstedt took the contrary view, proposing to defeat the Allies with a large reserve of Panzer divisions after they landed and then engaging them in a decisive battle, providing the reserves could be deployed. Both plans had advantages and disadvantages. As it turned out, both von Rundstedt and Rommel were replaced. Hitler and the Wehrmacht eventually lost France to overwhelming Allied air superiority and logistic capabilities.

Rommel was a skilled tactician. He was also painted as a noble warrior and an anti-Nazi, because he eventually turned against Hitler over military strategy that was leading Germany to defeat. Yet, he had difficulty in operating at the strategic level because he did not have the expertise to view the overall relationship of political, economic, psychological, and military forces necessary to increase the prospect of victory and lessen the chances of defeat as displayed in North Africa. In addition, Rommel was anathema to Kesselring, whose modest memoirs are a contrast to the Württemberger's *erlebris und erfahrung Infanterie greift an,* which takes every opportunity to publicize Rommel's World War I heroic deeds. Furthermore, he had serious doubts in reconciling military issues at a strategic level, as was the case with his relationship with Hitler and the German High Command over the direction of national strategy.

–GEORGE F. HOFMANN, UNIVERSITY OF CINCINNATI

References

Correlli Barnett, ed., *Hitler's Generals* (London: Weidenfeld & Nicolson, 1989);

Günther Blumentritt, *Von Rundstedt: The Soldier and the Man,* translated by Cuthbert Reavely (London: Odhams, 1952);

Matthew Cooper, *The German Army 1933–1945: Its Political and Military Failure* (London: Macdonald & Jane's, 1978);

David Fraser, *Knight's Cross: A Life of Field Marshal Erwin Rommel* (London: HarperCollins, 1993);

David Irving, *The Trail of the Fox: The Search for the True Field Marshal Rommel* (London: Weidenfeld & Nicolson, 1977);

Albert Kesselring, translated by Lynton Hudson as *Kesselring, The Memoirs of Field Marshal* (London: Kimber, 1953);

Ronald Lewin, *Rommel as Military Commander* (London: Batsford; Princeton: Van Nostrand, 1968)

Kenneth Macksey, *Kesselring: The Making of the Luftwaffe* (London: Batsford, 1978);

Erwin Rommel, *Infanterie greift an, erlebnis und erfahrung* (Potsdam: Voggenreiter, 1937), translated as *Attacks* (Vienna, Va.: Athena, 1979);

Rommel, *The Rommel Papers,* edited by B. H. Liddell-Hart and others, translated by Paul Findlay (London: Collins, 1953);

Martin Van Creveld, *Supplying War: Logistics from Wallenstein to Patton* (Cambridge & New York: Cambridge University Press, 1977);

Desmond Young, *Rommel* (London & Glasgow: Fontana, 1950).

ROMMEL

SECOND FRONT

Should the Second Front have been opened earlier than June 1944?

Viewpoint: Yes, the Second Front should have been opened earlier than June 1944 in order to satisfy the promise made by the Western allies to the Soviets and to promote trust among the Americans, British, and Soviets.

Viewpoint: No, although the Allies wanted to open a second front, the Americans were inexperienced and unprepared for a cross-Channel invasion, while the British favored attacks on the periphery of German occupied territory.

As early as July 1941 a mortally threatened Soviet Union was calling for a "second front"—an Anglo-American invasion of Europe across the English Channel. The appeal was sufficiently compelling that Winston Churchill and Franklin D. Roosevelt made successive attempts to present the invasions of North Africa in 1942 and Italy in 1943 as meeting Soviet criteria. Joseph Stalin was unimpressed, and since then Soviet and post-Soviet historiography has stated or implied that the Western allies delayed invading the European continent unnecessarily, if not hoping to weaken the U.S.S.R. then to spare the lives of their own men at the expense of Russia's.

The most common rejoinder is that Russia had no comprehension of the difficulties involved in preparing and mounting a cross-Channel invasion against an alert and competent defense. It has been suggested that the invasion could have been mounted in the summer of 1943 with good chances of success given the weakness of German forces and defenses compared to 1944. This hypothesis, however, depending heavily on statistical comparisons, has found little support beyond its originators. D-Day remains best understood as a one-time operation, absorbing such a high percentage of U.S. and British material and psychological resources that it could not be undertaken without near-absolute chances of success.

Viewpoint:
Yes, the Second Front should have been opened earlier than June 1944 in order to satisfy the promise made by the Western allies to the Soviets and to promote trust among the Americans, British, and Soviets.

Diplomatic relations among countries can be difficult under nor-mal circumstances. Different cultures, philosophies, and goals provide challenges to negotiations, agreements, treaties, and alliances. Complex relationships frequently become strained and change in wartime, even between closely tied countries. The World War II Anglo-American alliance offers the best example of the intricacies of wartime foreign relations, especially when a third partner, the Soviet Union, entered the picture. One of the issues which perhaps taxed the Allied alliance the most was the establishment

of a second front in Europe by the British and Americans in order to relieve pressure being placed on the Soviet Union by German forces. While the three Allied powers agreed about the necessity of a second front, each one had its own ideas regarding the scope, location, and timing of the campaign.

In general, each of the Allies supported a second front that met its political requirements and military capabilities. By a second front, Soviet premier Joseph Stalin and American president Franklin D. Roosevelt meant a major campaign in France that would force German führer Adolf Hitler to shift troops from the Russian front to combat the new threat. Although he acknowledged that Allied forces would ultimately have to cross the English Channel into France, British prime minister Winston Churchill suggested that a second front could be established anywhere, even North Africa or Italy. The goal was to engage Axis forces in battle in an area that the Germans would have to reinforce, hopefully with troops from the Russian front, and to prevent them from being used against the strained Soviet forces. Heated discussions about the second front increasingly created tension within the alliance, and the issue had ramifications for postwar relations between the Soviet Union and its Western allies.

The second-front issue was introduced early in the war. The Germans invaded the Soviet Union in June 1941. By the end of the next month the Soviets made two major requests of the British and Americans, who were not yet official participants in the conflict. The Soviets asked the United States for aid and an American army to fight on the Russian front. The Soviets also requested the establishment of a second front, without which they would be unable to continue the fight against the Germans. Although both Churchill and Roosevelt denied the Soviet request temporarily, the idea had been planted and would recur in negotiations concerning strategy between the United States and Great Britain.

The British in 1941 rejected Stalin's request for a second front, for example an invasion of France, because they did not have the means to implement such an operation. The United States, although providing Great Britain with supplies, had not yet entered the war. Stalin blamed German successes in Russia and the Ukraine on Britain's failure to invade France. By December 1941 the British had designed a plan for a cross-Channel assault, but they realized that it could not be implemented before 1943. The Japanese attack on Pearl Harbor changed the situation, however, and the British would now have help with the invasion of France.

Shortly after America's entry into the war, Churchill and Roosevelt readdressed the issue of a second front during discussions at the Arcadia Conference in Washington (22 Decem-

Joesph Stalin, Franklin D. Roosevelt, and Winston Churchill at the Teheran Conference in November 1943

SECOND FRONT

ber 1941–11 January 1942). The Soviets wanted the Western allies to attack the Germans from the west as early as possible. While both leaders favored providing relief for the Russians, they recognized that a major cross-Channel assault was probably not feasible in 1942. It would be some time before the American could put an effective force in the field. The British and Americans did, however, pledge to launch an emergency cross-Channel assault in the summer of 1942 if the Russian forces appeared in danger of collapse and to begin plans for a joint invasion of northern France in April 1943. Fear that the Soviet Union would repeat events of World War I and negotiate a separate peace with Germany prompted agreement.

In March 1942, Roosevelt sent a plan for a joint invasion of France to Churchill. The prime minister initially agreed in principle with the cross-Channel invasion plan, but after reconsideration, he expressed his concerns about the possible irreplaceable losses that the British might suffer. Any cross-Channel assault in 1942 would have to be carried out predominantly by British forces. The United States was not yet in a position to contribute much to the operation. Consequently, Churchill renewed a push for an attack against German forces in North Africa, where the British had recently suffered setbacks, or in another location that was not a German stronghold. Roosevelt reiterated the need for a second front to relieve the pressure that the Germans were placing on the Russians. He suggested that a cross-Channel invasion could fulfill an obligation to the Russians even if it was not a military success. With Dunkirk (26 May–4 June 1940) fresh in their minds, the British were reluctant to commit to an amphibious assault that was doomed to failure. The failed assault on Dieppe, France, in August 1942 made the British even more hesitant about the proposed operation.

The debate continued at a second Washington conference in June. Although he verbally supported the American plan, Churchill continued to push for the invasion of North Africa in 1942 instead of a cross-Channel assault called Sledgehammer. Suggesting that Hitler's worst fear was that of fighting a two-front war, Roosevelt's advisers pushed for Sledgehammer. Even if the combined Allied forces were insufficient to launch an offensive in the near future, the buildup of American troops in Great Britain would have a psychological effect on the Germans, which would be almost as important as an actual military offensive. Not convinced that Sledgehammer was possible for 1942, Roosevelt agreed to the

North African campaign, Torch, because he wanted an offensive before the end of the year.

The decision to implement Torch meant the postponement of a cross-Channel invasion, renamed Roundup, until 1943. Fearing Soviet opposition, Churchill went to Moscow. Stalin, who believed that he had received a promise for a second front in 1942, expressed sharp dissatisfaction with the Anglo-American decision. He accused his allies of not treating the second-front issue seriously and suggested that the Soviet Union would not tolerate a postponement of the offensive. By the end of Churchill's visit, however, Stalin accepted Torch with the understanding that the Allies would establish a second front in 1943.

Allied operations culminated in several victories in the fall of 1942: the Russians successfully counterattacked; American and British troops had German forces on the run in North Africa and Egypt. The victories created a paradox for the Allies. The next logical step was the cross-Channel invasion, but success in North Africa indicated the need for further offensives in the Mediterranean—first in Sicily, then in Italy—which would destroy the possibility of Roundup in April 1943. The British argued convincingly in favor of the latter course, claiming the Allies should take steps to force Italy out of the war. Because of German U-boat activity in the Atlantic, the buildup of the invasion force in Britain was proceeding slowly. The supply of troops, shipping, and other material from the United States dictated that only a small-scale offensive in one area would be possible in the spring of 1943. Even if Roundup could be launched in 1943, it could not begin in time to support the Russian summer campaign, and, because of its limited size, it would not result in the shift of German troops from the eastern front to France. Finally, the British argued that Allied forces should take advantage of the situation to maintain the momentum that they had already established. Meanwhile, Stalin pressed for details of the second-front offensive. Victories in the east enabled the Soviets to imply that they were "virtually fighting alone." Some Americans began to fear that if the United States did not become involved in Europe soon, the Soviet Union would claim sole responsibility for victory, not acknowledge American aid or the Mediterranean offensive, and dictate the postwar conditions. Although American military leaders, particularly General George C. Marshall, argued against continued operations in the Mediterranean and in favor of fulfilling the promise of a cross-Channel assault in 1943, the Americans finally agreed to implement the British plan in exchange for a definite date for a second front in Europe.

Because they chose to pursue the Mediterranean campaign, the Allies were forced to delay opening the Second Front until June 1944. Consequently, they failed to attack the Germans from the west as early as they possibly could, which raises several historical issues. The British and Americans failed to establish a second front in Europe as early as they could for many reasons. First, they approached the problem differently, which sparked debate and uncertainty regarding Allied strategy. The Americans believed that the proper course was to concentrate sufficient forces and then assault the enemy directly. The British strategy envisioned engaging the Germans in battle around the periphery of Fortress Europe. After draining away much of Germany's strength, the Allies would then launch the cross-Channel attack. Second, because they had been fighting the Germans for some time, the British "tended to focus on the difficulties of assault, and the tactical and logistical problems involved, while the Americans . . . found it easier to start with the large view of the strategic problem." Finally, the Americans failed to solve certain logistical problems, particularly those surrounding the availability of landing craft, to mount an earlier offensive.

It is highly likely that had a cross-Channel assault been mounted in 1942, it would have failed. The Americans would have been unable to commit a large force to the operation; therefore, the bulk of responsibility would have fallen to the British, who were committed in North Africa, the Middle East, and Asia. To implement a Sledgehammer or Roundup in 1942, the British would have had to withdraw troops from another theater. Reverses suffered in Egypt and North Africa required an increase, not a decrease, in their commitment. As a result, an amphibious landing would have been small and vulnerable. Minimal German response would, in all likelihood, have culminated in another Dunkirk.

Could the cross-Channel operation have been successfully implemented in 1943? Under the right conditions, yes, it could have. Marshall, the leading proponent of launching Roundup in 1943, was right about what course of action the Allies should follow, but failed to convince Roosevelt that the operation was possible. While both the Americans and the British agreed that it would be advantageous to force the Italians out of the war, they did not concur that the best way to accomplish that goal was to mount an offensive on the peninsula. The British prevailed in their strategy and in September 1943 Allied forces landed in Italy. Within a short time the Italians surrendered and the offensive should have been over. The Germans were not willing, however, to allow the Allies to control Italy. Consequently, the Germans increased their commitment in Italy, and the offensive did not progress as the Allies had expected. German resistance was much stiffer than that offered by the Italians. The advance to Rome proved slow and costly, and required another amphibious landing. The landing at Anzio did not proceed as planned and resulted in significant Allied casualties. In fact, Rome did not fall until early June 1944.

It is possible that the war would have ended sooner had Allied troops landed in northwestern France in 1943 instead of 1944. The defeat of German forces in France and Germany, not in Italy, would have resulted in the end of the European conflict. The Allied campaign in Italy had bogged down. The Germans had established several strong lines of defense. A further push up the peninsula would have been costly in terms of lives and material. An attempt to launch an offensive from Italy into southern Germany would have been both impossible and a logistical nightmare. Several historians, particularly Americans, have argued that the offensive in Italy was unnecessary, costly, and delayed the Normandy invasion, as well as the defeat of Germany.

Why should the Second Front have been launched earlier? First, it would have been the fulfillment of the promise made by the Americans and British to their Soviet ally. Both military leaders and historians have accused the British of advocating the Mediterranean offensives in order to prevent the Soviets from determining postwar conditions in the Balkans and Eastern Europe. The Mediterranean campaign delayed the Normandy invasion until 1944, increased the strain on relations between the Western Allies and the Soviets, and helped to demonstrate to Stalin that the Allied leaders could not be trusted to keep their promises. This lack of trust became increasingly apparent in the postwar world and affected postwar agreements and relations. Second, the failure of the British and the Americans to agree upon a strategy, including plans and a date for the cross-Channel invasion, created friction and distrust between the two countries. Had a firm decision to launch the invasion been reached earlier, there would have been no reason for accusations of changing strategy, of lack of commitment, and of being afraid to engage the Germans in battle. Much bitterness on all sides could have been avoided had the Allies stuck to the original plan and not gotten sidetracked in the Mediterranean.

–MARY KATHRYN BARBIER,
LOYOLA UNIVERSITY

INVASION OF NORTH AFRICA

White House news release.

Washington, November 7, 1942

In order to forestall an invasion of Africa by Germany and Italy, which, if successful, would constitute a direct threat to America across the comparatively narrow sea from Western Africa, a powerful American force equipped with adequate weapons of modern warfare and under American Command is today landing on the Mediterranean and Atlantic Coasts of the French Colonies in Africa.

The landing of this American Army is being assisted by the British Navy and air forces and it will, in the immediate future, be reinforced by a considerable number of divisions of the British Army.

This combined allied force, under American Command, in conjunction with the British campaign in Egypt is designed to prevent an occupation by the Axis armies of any part of Northern or Western Africa, and to deny to the aggressor nations a starting point from which to launch an attack against the Atlantic Coast of the Americas.

In addition, it provides an effective second front assistance to our heroic allies in Russia.

The French Government and the French people have been informed of the purpose of this expedition, and have been assured that the allies seek no territory and have no intention of interfering with friendly French Authorities in Africa.

The Government of France and the people of France and the French Possessions have been requested to cooperate with and assist the American expedition in its effort to repel the German and Italian international criminals, and by so doing to liberate France and the French Empire from the Axis yoke.

This expedition will develop into a major effort by the Allied Nations and there is every expectation that it will be successful in repelling the planned German and Italian invasion of Africa and prove the first historic step to the liberation and restoration of France.

Source: *World War II Resources, Web Page.*

Viewpoint:
No, although the Allies wanted to open a second front, the Americans were inexperienced and unprepared for a cross-Channel invasion, while the British favored attacks on the periphery of German occupied territory.

The debate over Anglo-American strategy in World War II started shortly after the war. Nationalism, egos, and the advent of the Cold War greatly influenced the discussion. The issue of the Second Front is part of the larger historical debate on the effectiveness, or ineffectiveness, of American strategic thinking in the final years of the war when the Americans replaced the British as the leaders of the alliance. The historically accepted thesis is that it was not possible in 1942, nor in 1943, to conduct the cross-Channel attack.

At the Arcadia Conference (22 December 1941–11 January 1942), the British outlined a comprehensive strategy, as cited by Michael Howard in *The Mediterranean Strategy in the Second World War* (1968):

(1) The realization of the victory programme of armaments, which first and foremost required the security of the main areas of war industry in the United States and United Kingdom.

(2) The maintenance of essential communications in defeating the German U-boat threat.

(3) Closing and tightening the ring around Germany by sustaining the Russian front, arming and supporting Turkey, building up strength in the Middle East, and gaining possession of the whole North African coast.

(4) Wearing down and undermining German resistance by air bombardment, blockade, subversive activities and propaganda.

(5) The continuous development of offensive against Germany.

(6) Maintaining only such positions in the Eastern theater as will safeguard vital interests and to deny to Japan access to raw materials vital to her continuous war effort while we are concentrating on the defeat of Germany.

Franklin D. Roosevelt and his advisers agreed that Germany was the most dangerous enemy and that the European theater would receive priority for resources rather than the campaign against the Japanese in the Pacific. The British strategy, accepted by the United States, argued that before the Allies could return to the continent and fight the main

German army certain conditions had first to be met. The first condition was the buildup of forces—the mobilization of the vast industrial and manpower resources of the United States, Russia, and the United Kingdom (U.K.). The second condition was the maintenance of sea lanes upon which the UK and Russia depended. The third condition was to contain Germany by keeping the Russians in the war, halting German advances in North Africa, and assisting other governments fighting Germany. The fourth condition was the erosion of German combat power through peripheral operations, strategic bombing, and blockade. These operations were designed to weaken the German army through attrition and dispersion. When all these conditions were met, the British believed the final phase of their strategy could then be carried out—the cross-Channel attack.

Returning to the continent was viewed by the British as part of a much larger grand strategy designed to substantially weaken the German army before the final phase went into effect. To the Americans the final phase was the strategy. Everything that went before it was simply preparation for the main event, the decisive campaign in western Europe against the main German army. The disagreement between the British and Americans was, thus, over the final phase of war.

The U.S. Army Chief of Staff, General George C. Marshall, in keeping with the American preference for a more direct approach to war, advanced a plan for an attack in Europe in 1942, Operation Sledgehammer, or in 1943, Operation Roundup. In May 1942 Roosevelt told Soviet foreign minister Vyacheslav Molotov that he "'hoped" and "expected" Anglo-American forces to open a second front in Europe in 1942. America, however, lacked the wherewithal to conduct such an operation. Japanese successes in the Pacific caused the United States to divert forces and equipment to that region. American forces were still mobilizing and training. New technology such as Landing Ship Tanks (LST), Landing Craft Infantry (LCI), and other amphibious-assault vehicles had to be developed, produced, and deployed. American manpower and technology, as well as operational and tactical doctrines, were untested. Nevertheless, Marshall favored a strategy that took the Anglo-American armies into Europe at the earliest opportunity. He argued for the construction of a large army, and the concentration of forces, for a main effort in Europe. Marshall believed the American people had little tolerance for a long war and expected decisive results. He believed it was correspondingly necessary to focus the nation's efforts and resources on a decisive objective. Peripheral operations were indecisive and dispersed resources in campaigns that could not produce a final victory.

The British believed an invasion in 1942 impossible and one in 1943 improbable. They believed it was first necessary to weaken Germany substantially through peripheral operations. The British were psychologically damaged by the experience of World War I, the Somme (1 July–13 November 1916) and Passchendaele (the Third Battle of Ypres, July–November 1917), and the series of defeats suffered in 1940, culminating with the humiliating retreat at Dunkirk (26 May–2 June 1940). The British needed time and success in a minor theater before they were able to meet again the German Army in Europe. North Africa gave the British the time they needed to recover. The British practice of war emphasized limited, negotiated settlements and indirect attacks on the enemy domain. Churchill believed in the indirect approach to war and took actions to insure that British strategy reflected his thinking. Marshall entered into strategic negotiations with the British unprepared to advance his position, as the U.S. Army's position was not fully developed and the argument could not be made.

The Joint Chiefs of Staff were divided as well. The U.S. Navy, under the leadership of Chief of Naval Operations Admiral Earnest King, and the American people wanted to fight the Japanese who had "treacherously" attacked and destroyed the preeminent symbol of American power—its battleships at Pearl Harbor. Popular support and the urgency of the situation enabled King to advance operations in the Pacific, operations that pulled resources away from the European theater. The British refusal to conduct the cross-Channel attack caused Marshall to move closer to the position of King. Roosevelt, however, interceded to stop the erosion of the Anglo-American alliance. For political and strategic reasons, Roosevelt decided on the North African campaign proposed earlier by the British. Politically, Roosevelt felt it was necessary for the American people to have forces in battle in the European theater in 1942, and strategically he believed it was necessary to maintain the alliance. He therefore overrode Marshall and decided on the British strategic vision. In November 1942 Operation Torch took place. British and American forces were now committed to the British Mediterranean strategy.

The amphibious assault in North Africa highlighted deficiencies in American training and technology, and the battle at Kasserine

Pass, Tunisia (14 February 1943) demonstrated that the Americans were not yet ready to fight quality German units—the U.S. soldiers panicked under fire. The poor showing of the U.S. Army in North Africa was not encouraging to the British. British military leaders were increasingly critical of American leadership, training practices, and manhood.

At the Casablanca Conference in January 1943, Marshall again tried to refocus Anglo-American strategy. He argued for the cross-Channel attack. The British, however, under the leadership of Field-Marshall Lord Alan Brooke, Chief of the Imperial General Staff, argued forcefully and persuasively for the invasions of Sicily, and subsequently, Italy. The agreed-upon strategic objectives for 1943, as recounted by Ed Cray in *General of the Army: George C. Marshall, Soldier and Statesman* (1990), were:

(1) Make the submarine menace a first charge on United Nations' resources;

(2) Concentrate on the defeat of Germany first;

(3) Undertake the conquest of Sicily;

(4) Continue to build troop strength and the number of landing craft in Great Britain;

(5) Launch a series of stepping-stone campaigns in the Solomons, the Marshalls, and at Truk in the Carolines;

(6) Invade Burma in December and open the Burma Road to China;

(7) Bomb Germany around the clock from bases in Great Britain; and

(8) Attempt to get Turkey to cast its lot with the Allies, and provide air bases to bomb the Rumanian oil fields.

British strategy now called for eliminating Italy from the war, securing the Mediterranean for shipping, weakening Germany through an air offensive of bombers flying out of Italy, and winning the "Battle of the Atlantic." It was argued that the U-boat threat had to be defeated before the cross-Channel attack could take place. Brooke sounded the alarm, "a stranglehold on all offensive operations. . . . unless we could effectively combat the U-boat menace, we might not be able to win the war." Roosevelt again accepted the arguments of the British, and the campaign for Sicily was scheduled. Roosevelt also announced the doctrine of "unconditional surrender" to reassure the Russians of continued Anglo-American support. King won approval for offensive operations against the Japanese, and Marshall's fear of dispersing the nation's war effort was realized.

When the Casablanca Conference took place the campaign in North Africa was still in progress. The campaign did not end until May 1943, too late, it is argued, to redeploy forces for a cross-Channel attack in 1943. In July 1943 Anglo-American forces invaded Sicily, and in September, Italy. The Sicilian campaign ended any chance of invading Europe in 1943. Not until June 1944 would the cross-Channel attack take place.

–ADRIAN R. LEWIS, UNIVERSITY OF NORTH TEXAS

References

Arthur Bryant, *The Turn of the Tide: A History of the War Years Based on the Diaries of Field-Marshal Lord Alan Brooke, Chief of the Imperial General Staff* (Garden City, N.Y.: Doubleday, 1957);

Winston Churchill, *The Hinge of Fate*, volume 4 of *The Second World War* (Boston: Houghton Mifflin, 1950);

Ed Cray, *General of the Army: George C. Marshall, Soldier and Statesman* (New York: Norton, 1990);

Carlo D'Este, *Decision in Normandy* (New York: Dutton, 1983);

Walter Scott Dunn Jr., *Second Front Now–1943* (University: University of Alabama Press, 1979);

Michael Howard, *Grand Strategy*, volume 4, *August 1942–September 1943* (London: Her Majesty's Stationery Office, 1970);

Howard, *The Mediterranean Strategy in the Second World War* (London: Weidenfeld & Nicolson; New York: Praeger, 1968);

Henry Kissinger, *Diplomacy* (New York: Simon & Schuster, 1994);

Francis L. Loewenheim, Harold D. Langley, and Manfred Jonas, eds., *Roosevelt and Churchill: Their Secret Wartime Correspondence* (New York: Saturday Review Press, 1975);

Maurice Matloff, "Allied Strategy in Europe, 1939–1945," in *Makers of Modern Strategy: From Machiavelli to the Nuclear Age*, edited by Peter Paret, in collaboration with Gordon A. Craig and Felix Gilbert (Princeton: Princeton University Press, 1986);

Matloff and Edwin M. Snell, *Strategic Planning for Coalition Warfare, 1941–1942* (Washington, D.C. : United States Government Printing Office, 1953);

Leo J. Meyer, "The Decision to Invade North Africa (Torch)," *Command Decisions,* edited by Kent Roberts Greenfield (Washington, D.C.: Office of the Chief of Military History, 1960);

A. W. Purdue, *The Second World War* (New York: St. Martin's Press, 1999);

David Reynolds, Warren F. Kimball, and A. O. Chubarian, *Allies at War: the Soviet, American, and British Experience, 1939–1945* (New York: St. Martin's Press, 1994);

Keith Sainsbury, *The Turning Point: Roosevelt, Stalin, Churchill, and Chiang-Kai-Shek, 1943: The Moscow, Cairo, and Teheran Conferences* (Oxford: Oxford University Press, 1985);

Peter N. Stearns, *World History: Patterns of Change and Continuity* (New York: Harper & Row, 1987);

Mark A. Stoler, *The Politics of the Second Front: American Military Planning and Diplomacy in Coalition Warfare, 1941–1943* (Westport, Conn.: Greenwood Press, 1977);

United States, Department of State, *Foreign Relations of the United States: The Conferences at Washington, 1941–1942, and Casablanca, 1943* (Washington, D.C.: United States Government Printing Office, 1968);

United States, Department of State, *Foreign Relations of the United States: The Conferences at Cairo and Tehran 1943* (Washington, D.C.: United States Government Printing Office, 1961);

Albert C. Wedemeyer, *Wedemeyer Reports!* (New York: Holt, 1958);

Russell F. Weigley, *The American Way of War: A History of United States Military Strategy and Policy* (Bloomington: Indiana University Press, 1973);

Gerhard L. Weinberg, *A World at Arms: A Global History of World War II* (Cambridge & New York: Cambridge University Press, 1994);

Chester Wilmot, *The Struggle for Europe* (New York: Harper, 1952).

SECOND FRONT

SEGREGATION IN THE MILITARY

Can the segregationalist policies of U.S. armed forces during World War II be justifified on the grounds that integration would have impeded the war effort?

Viewpoint: Yes, the U.S. armed forces were justified in concentrating on the destruction of fascism over racism, because fascism was a far more insidious evil that threatened the extermination of a race.

Viewpoint: No, the U.S. armed forces were not justified in their segregationalist policies. Those policies damaged morale and excluded from combat a badly needed fighting corps.

The United States of 1941 was not merely a racially segregated society. African Americans were isolated and marginalized to a point where, outside of a few regions in the agricultural South, their literal disappearance would scarcely have been noticed. National mobilization, however, involved tapping every potential national resource. In particular, it involved accepting blacks into the armed forces.

The U.S. armed forces were more rigidly segregated than at any time in their history. In other cultures and societies, marginal groups have been sought as warriors—Irish and Scots Highlanders in Britain, Cossacks in Russia, and blacks in Latin America. In sharp contrast, pervasive insistence on the inherent inferiority of African Americans had led to a widespread belief in the United States that blacks were even useless as cannon fodder. The air corps and the marines refused to enlist them. In the navy they were restricted to stewards' duties. The army, required by law to maintain four African American regiments, in effect converted them from combat to housekeeping units. It was not a promising beginning.

Stereotypes were reinforced by the poor showing many African American draftees made on aptitude tests designed to reflect levels of education and acculturation. Over three-fourths scored in the two lowest of five categories, the result of decades of segregated and underfunded education. Nor were black prospects improved by a policy of establishing many of the major training centers in isolated sections of the rural South. The resulting tensions led to a general perception that it represented wasted effort for the armed forces to challenge general norms of segregation—especially when those norms seemed borne out by black performance. African American achievement in any aspect of military performance was regarded as exceptional: to be recognized and utilized, but not expected.

Marginalized in the military as in civilian life, organized in segregated units, and commanded largely by white officers, African Americans on the whole met the armed forces' expectations. Despite distinguished performances, in particular by the squadrons of the 332nd Fighter Group and some separate armored and artillery battalions, all-black combat units were considered a liability. All-black service and support units tended to become holding pens for unskilled labor. Given the national policy of maintaining armed forces no larger than were absolutely required, such racial policies were as professionally culpable as they were morally dubious.

Viewpoint:
Yes, the U.S. armed forces were justified in concentrating on the destruction of fascism over racism, because fascism was a far more insidious evil that threatened the extermination of a race.

It is ironic that one of the primary causes of World War II was racism, yet the nation that more than any other represented the cause of equality and freedom could be justly accused of being racist as well. To anyone with a sense of historical perspective, however, and contrary to what some critics might claim, the racism of the United States was a speck in the eye compared to the log in that of Nazi Germany. The United States did not engage in the wholesale massacre of millions, and did not place the elimination of a race at the highest level of priority even beyond that of keeping its armies supplied. Nor did it plan a war strategy in order to fulfill a mad scheme of racial superiority. The same stands true for the American war against Japan, which had trumpeted itself as the champion of Asia over European racism, yet immediately classified Koreans, Chinese, and Filipinos as inferior, then inflicted cruel barbarities against those who suffered under their occupation. To establish the homicidal and genocidal persecution practiced by the Axis powers is not to dismiss the issue of racism in wartime America. Yet, given a choice, no one, regardless of race, would have willingly traded places with those in occupied Europe or Asia.

The top priority in World War II, in America and across the entire world, was the defeat of Nazism and Japanese imperialism. All other issues had to be subordinate to that goal. These twin enemies, along with communism, were the great evils of the twentieth century that threatened the freedom of all mankind, regardless of race.

To place at the highest priority the desegregation of American society during World War II would have been the equivalent of fighting a fire in a smouldering ashtray while a firestorm was burning down the city. To attempt to apply current social values, doctrines, and beliefs to the crisis of the 1930s and 1940s is not true historical study. It is, instead, an exercise in propaganda, as is all revisionism when it seeks to condemn those of the past outside the context of their times.

This is not a dismissal of the problem. Marginalization of over 10 percent of the nation's population based solely on race has been, and always will be, anathema to the ideal of what America represents. It should be remembered that the issue of race and how it was applied to rights and freedoms in a republic had divided the United States in a bloody civil war. The Civil War (1861–1865) was more than seventy years in the past as World War II began. Millions of American citizens still alive had direct memories of that conflict and of the difficult years of Reconstruction afterward.

A forgotten chapter of U.S. history is the fact that the Democratic Party, up until the great tidal shift of political alignment under Franklin D. Roosevelt, had openly billed itself as the party of the "white man." The Ku Klux Klan, feeding not just on racial hatred but also intense anti-immigrant and anti-Catholic sentiments, had reached the peak of its strength less than twenty years before the start of World War II. The racial question was far more volatile in 1941 than it was in 1961.

It was still an intense topic of social struggle even as the Americans went forth to fight World War II. The key point is that the United States was attempting to confront the issue, unlike Germany or the alleged socialist brotherhood nation of the Soviet Union, where entire racial groups were simply annihilated rather than debated with. Such racism did leave the American national cause vulnerable to criticism. It was mistaken not to use black troops, if for no other reason than the fact that it was an underutilization of force, both in the labor front at home and at the front lines of combat around the world. One could argue, however, that though U.S. leaders, and for that matter the entire American population, placed internal racial issues at a lower priority level, they did have a priority nevertheless. In the long run that priority became a stimulus for dramatic social change.

The true nadir of race relations in this country, and particularly in the U.S. Army, was during World War I and immediately afterward. African American regiments had fought in the Civil War, Indian wars, and the Spanish-American War (1898) with valor and distinction. Commanders did not hesitate to commit them in difficult combat situations. Medals of Honor were openly given to African American soldiers, and white officers who served with them expressed pride in their units and fought for equal treatment. Pension records for black veterans were remarkably free of racial taint, and often speak of the obligation our nation had to its "gallant soldiers."

During the Woodrow Wilson years (1913–1921), however, this policy fell apart. Black troops were all but barred from frontline combat with the argument that "colored" troops lacked the mental ability and self discipline to withstand the strain of modern warfare. The few

Lieutenant F. N. Paterson receiving the Bronze Star for actions above and beyond the call of duty in the Battle of the Bulge

(National Archives #111-SC-197376-5)

units that did make it to the front were under-supplied, poorly led, and openly denied the distinction and decorations they truly deserved. It is ironic that the French, no champions of racial equality when it came to their own colonies, actually asked for some of these black units to be assigned to their command because of positive experience fighting alongside blacks from their African colonies.

As the United States entered World War II this mentality was still firmly in place within the army. In the navy black sailors were assigned "non-combat" duties aboard ships. The overwhelming pressures created by full mobilization had to, and eventually did, force change. Manpower demands were such that by the last eighteen months of the war African American units, in some cases led by black officers, were being sent into combat and drawing praise, even from those who had been openly critical of them earlier in the war. Celebrated units such as the 332nd Fighter Group, part of the famous Tuskegee program, or the 761st Tank Battalion, drew

significant press coverage. Even if for no other reason than public relations it still had an effect. More than one "racist" aboard a crippled B-17, or pinned down and cut off from his unit, had to give a salute of acknowledgment and thanks as a black pilot or tanker came to his rescue. Frederick Douglass had declared during the Civil War that once you give the black man a rifle and a cartridge box with U.S. stamped on its side, there was no power on earth that would then be able to deny that man his right of citizenship in a free nation.

On the home front, industries that had been strictly segregated were forced to integrate in order to meet production demands. Roosevelt's executive order 8802 in 1941, prohibiting discrimination and calling for the hiring of blacks in the war industries and establishing the Fair Employment Practices Committee, helped open wartime jobs for many African Americans. Men and women, black and white, who would never have dreamed of mixing in schools, parks, or even churches, now worked side by side on

AFRICAN AMERICANS IN COMBAT

Ollie Stewart, a war correspondent for the Afro-American, *a Baltimore newspaper, described the activities of black soldiers in World War II.*

We were about three miles from the German lines. Heavy gunfire was continuous and German ack-ack was spattering mushroom bursts of flak as our planes dived over their lines and our observation grasshopper planes sailed placidly along, spotting the Germans guns and radioing back their positions.

When a white colonel saw colored troops in the midst of all this, he said: "This is the first time that I have ever seen quartermasters up so close to the front line."

Sgt. Eugene W. Jones, of 1611 W. Butler Street, Philadelphia, replied: "Sir, we are not quartermasters, we are field artillery and we have just been given a firing mission. Want to watch us lay one on the target?"

That was my introduction to the first colored 155-mm. howitzer outfit in France, one of the best groups of artillerymen in the army, white or colored. Two battalions have been in action for weeks and had a big part in the taking of La Saye du Puits. Another unit operating 155-mm. Long Toms has just arrived.

These hard-working gunners will tell you frankly that they know they are good. Their officers told me that they are good. White infantrymen who won't budge unless these guys are laying down a barrage say that they are good, and German prisoners ask to see our automated artillery that comes so fast and so accurate. . . .

The Germans call our artillery whispering death because the shells don't whine and they all sit at the guns day and night, ready for the phone to ring. Before arrival of the Long Tom the group had two colored battalions, but now it has three colored and one white battalion, with white officers except two chaplains, Capt. H.C. Terel, Birmingham, and Lt. Carranza Holliday, Longview, Texas.

On the roads nearby and all around the gun crews are signs of bitter fighting. Our boys entered the area before the mine detector crews and found dead Germans and Yanks and many cattle. I saw dead swollen live stock all around that perfumed the neighborhood; also much discarded equipment, German and American. I saw one American helmet, still full of clotted blood, where a sniper has scored a direct hit on the helmet.

Snipers were still around, and I approached hedgerows cautiously. That first night, I wrapped a blanket around me and slept in a foxhole without undressing. The gun crews had their shoes on for five days. There was no laughter or loud talk as every man realized that this is serious business, with death stalking all day and hovering in the air at night.

As I crawled through the brush to a camouflaged position, a message came over the field phone that enemy planes were approaching the area. I was already nervous and dived into a foxhole dug by the Germans, but these men stayed at their posts, some manning machineguns, others cursing Jerry as they calmly scanned the sky overhead.

Elements of at least three colored combat outfits last week took part in General Bradley's assault north of Coutances which unhinged Nazi lines around Lessay and Periers and resulted in the capture of over six thousand prisoners within the week.

The push began with gigantic air pounding by three thousand bombers. I watched fortresses and marauders pass overhead for more than an hour; the sight made all of us feel better.

Over the rough train, littered with carcasses, blasted tanks, guns, cattle and horses, I trotted with a guide who led me to some hidden gun positions where our boys were sounding off.

As they fired, lines of dazed, dirty German prisoners trudged back to the stockade. The bombing and shelling was so terrific that the Nazis mumbled incoherently and had guns still filled with dirt.

At Cherbourg, the greatest gathering of colored war correspondents in history could be seen. There were Randy Diaxon, Courier; Edward Toles, Defender; Roi Ottley, PM; Rudolph Dunbar, ANP; Allen Morrison, Stars and Stripes, and Ollie Stewart, AFRO.

In the Cherbourgh area there are actually more colored troops than white. No one hesitates to give full credit to our lads for the prominent part they have played in France. . . .

Source: *Ollie Stewart, "Invasion of France," in* This is Our War: Selected Stories of Six War Correspondents *(Baltimore: The Afro-American Company, 1945).*

assembly lines, even in the heart of the old "Jim Crow" South.

World War II reminded many Americans that equal rights were earned on the battlefield. It was the fertile ground out of which the modern Civil Rights Movement would emerge. Tens of thousands of returning black veterans, who never would have dreamed of having the opportunity to pursue an education, now went to college on the G.I. Bill. Black soldiers, after risking their lives to end racism overseas, returned as well, to a nation where again they had to stand at the back of the bus, giving up their seats to many a white man who had avoided serving in the war. The outrageous irony of this would be remembered. One noted civil-rights leader openly declared that his moment of awareness came when he, as a returning soldier, was forced to move to a "colored" railroad car, while German POWs rode up front in luxury.

The death of fascism had to be the highest priority of World War II, regardless of the social injustices at home. The alternative would have been a world where all who were different would have been fed into the furnaces of the Holocaust or returned to slavery. The victory over fascism did bear fruit, for it began the process of self awareness and eventual change. How could a nation that had so valiantly gone forth to save the world from racism, ignore for much longer the racism in its own back yard? Though not directly intended, World War II did have as one of its legacies the end of racism in the United States as well.

–WILLIAM R. FORSTCHEN,
MONTREAT COLLEGE

Viewpoint:
No, the U.S. armed forces were not justified in their segregationalist policies. Those policies damaged morale and excluded from combat a badly needed fighting corps.

In World War II the U.S. armed forces sought to justify their position regarding segregation and assignment policies for blacks by claiming that wartime exigencies precluded using the services as a social laboratory. Their reasons for not wanting to include African Americans in the war effort in a more meaningful way can be summarized as follows. Blacks in World War I had proven that they were not as brave or reliable in combat as whites and thus could not be counted on in battle. Blacks were uniformly less qualified than whites for duty in units requiring

specialized skills, such as aviation and armor, because they lacked the inherent mental ability to handle complex machinery. Finally, bringing an end to segregation or otherwise attempting to alter the status quo with regard to racial policies then in effect would run contrary to the desires of a majority of Americans and would adversely affect the morale of both white and black service members.

Looking back, it is easy to suggest that such arguments were specious because subsequent events demonstrated that these assumptions were clearly off the mark. That involves, however, a certain degree of present-mindedness. A more cogent argument is that, based on the information then available to military planners, their course of action regarding black-white relations was based on biased input and actually worked at cross-purposes with their stated goal.

There are several reasons why many Americans, especially military officers, felt as they did toward African Americans during the first half of the twentieth century. The nation's growing acceptance of social Darwinism, eugenicists' claims of scientific proof that the white race was superior to other races, the migration of blacks to northern industrial centers and the concurrent spread of "Jim Crow" laws to regions not previously affected by them, and the rise of Southern born and bred officers into the senior ranks of the army, navy, and Marine Corps after the turn of the century all helped shape policymakers' thinking.

Despite a solid record of combat service in the Civil War (1861–1865), on the Western frontier, in the war with Spain (1898), and during the Philippines insurrection (1899–1901), the belief that black soldiers made poor fighters became endemic in the army by World War I. Many of the officers who commanded black troops in the 92nd and 93rd Divisions in France in 1918 were sharply critical of their men's battlefield performance. Their observations were used to justify efforts to limit the number of black combat troops in World War II.

The assessments of white officers who thought highly of their men—like Captain Hamilton Fish of the 369th Infantry Regiment, a black New York National Guard unit that earned distinction while serving with the French army on the western front after the 93rd Division was broken up—were largely ignored. Fish, who later became a New York congressman and the author of antidiscrimination legislation, challenged Secretary of War Henry Lewis Stimson's claim that blacks were "unable to master efficiently the techniques of modern weapons." Fish told fellow House members that he emphatically disagreed with Stimson's assessment of African American abilities. He pointed out that education standards had improved among blacks since World War I, when the 93rd Division's four separate regiments had proven their mettle in combat in France. He also wondered how it was that French Senegalese, British Indian, Russian, and Japanese soldiers with less education than African Americans were able to master the complexities of modern warfare and weaponry, and serve with bravery and efficiency, while the U.S. War Department complained that American blacks could not. Clearly, in Fish's view—based on his own experience with black troops and what he observed in the contemporary world—the problem was in the Pentagon. He was not alone in that assessment.

From a practical standpoint, faced with the prospects of fighting the Japanese in the Pacific and the Germans in Europe and the Mediterranean, the War and Navy Departments' decisions to oppose the use of blacks as combat troops seem counterproductive. The armed forces were, after all, cutting themselves off from a substantial manpower source. One way they justified the decision was with the argument that using blacks as laborers would free up more whites for combat duty. That might have been true had America fully mobilized. However, the decision to limit the army to ninety combat divisions ultimately put severe stress on frontline troops—especially in Europe in early 1945, when the number of available combat troops dropped so low that black volunteers were sought to fill out the ranks of white infantry companies. More than forty-five hundred African American support troops leaped at the opportunity to get into the fight. About half of them completed a short training program and served successfully in some thirty-seven black rifle platoons in the First Army and with a handful of black rifle companies in the Seventh Army. General George S. Patton, the fiery Third Army commander, refused to accept any of the black platoons on the grounds that white Southerners would object to their presence.

The army gave in to pressure to allow African Americans the opportunity to become pilots, tank crewmen, and artillerymen despite its protestations that blacks were incapable of mastering modern machinery. The first to demonstrate the fallaciousness of this argument were the so-called Tuskegee airmen, who earned a solid reputation with first the 99th Fighter Squadron in North Africa and Sicily and later the 332nd Fighter Group in Italy. A bomber group, the 477th, was formed but did not see combat. Several separate black armored, artillery, and anti-aircraft artillery battalions saw action in Europe. The 3rd Platoon of Company C, 614th Tank Destroyer Battalion, became the first black ground-combat unit to receive the Distinguished

Unit Citation in recognition of its heroic stand at Climbach, France, in the Vosges Mountains while in support of the 103rd Infantry Division. The 969th Field Artillery Battalion was awarded the Distinguished Unit Citation for its efforts in support of the 101st Airborne Division's defense of Bastogne during the Battle of the Bulge (16–25 December 1944). The 761st Tank Battalion was awarded the Presidential Unit Citation in 1978 after a thirty-three-year fight to be recognized for its superior combat service.

The hardest position to justify was the services' rigid adherence to segregation policies. Once again, the level of effort expended during the early war years in furtherance of this policy appears counterproductive to the goal of forging a disciplined, war-winning military force. In order to meet the legal criteria of having separate but equal facilities for blacks, military bases had to have redundant buildings to house and serve the needs of both black and white troops.

Only one installation in the United States had the ability to house an entire black division: Fort Huachuca, which was isolated in the Arizona desert. There, blacks and whites had their own barracks, hospitals, civilian housing for dependents, clubs, theaters, post exchanges, athletic facilities, and the like. Initially, the 93rd Infantry Division was formed and based at Fort Huachuca. Later, when the 93rd deployed to the Pacific, the 92nd Infantry Division moved there from posts scattered throughout the South and one in Indiana. Shortly after the 92nd was formed, Major General Edward M. "Ned" Almond had ordered his legal staff to identify all local segregation statutes so that he could have commanders at the various installations ensure they were in compliance. The number and degree of segregation laws varied widely, and when the 92nd arrived at Fort Huachuca morale plummeted because men coming from posts with comparative freedom suddenly found themselves forced to comply with the most onerous policies.

The decision to assign mostly Southern white officers to command black units also adversely affected morale. The rationale for the decision was that Southern officers, because of their supposed greater experience in dealing with African Americans, provided the firm leadership necessary. In response to complaints of undisciplined conduct by black troops in 1942, General George C. Marshall, the army chief of staff, dispatched an inspector who determined that the bulk of the officers assigned to black units were of mediocre caliber. The secretary of war subsequently directed that every effort should be made to send only officers who had clearly demonstrated good judgment and common sense, tact, initiative, and strong leadership skills to black units. Finding such officers in the numbers needed to staff the army's segregated units—or any other unit, for that matter—remained a problem throughout the war.

The armed forces eventually took a pragmatic approach to segregation. Realizing that creating separate officer-candidate schools for blacks and whites was impractical, the army trained its officer candidates in an integrated environment—then promptly sent newly commissioned black officers to segregated units. As the number and intensity of black protests against segregation policies mounted, the army authorized local commanders to selectively determine the degree of segregation they would enforce at their installations. The language used, however, made it clear the directive affected only those commanders willing to alter the status quo.

Given such an environment, it is hardly any wonder that black soldiers, especially those assigned to the two segregated infantry divisions whose combat performance was later called into question in Italy and the Pacific, were plagued by anger and despair. Onerous segregation policies were a constant, bitter reminder of their second-class status. Insensitive leadership compounded this. Historian Ulysses Grant Lee, in *The Employment of Negro Troops* (1966) saw the matter as a simple lack of trust. This situation led to an environment in which neither the officers nor the men they led expected a given task to be accomplished—or that it was even worth attempting in the first place.

Racial policies in the navy and Marine Corps initially lagged behind those in the army. No blacks were given combat assignments in either service throughout the war. The navy instead relegated African Americans to support jobs—primarily as cooks, mess stewards, and stevedores in the navy, and as laborers and ammunition handlers in the Marines. Only a handful of blacks were commissioned in the navy during the war, and none in the Marine Corps.

As the demand for sailors increased late in the war, the navy finally opened up twenty-five auxiliary ships on which African Americans could serve in a variety of capacities. The policy proved so successful that the navy opened up all such ships to blacks by the war's end, and it became the first service to abandon segregation altogether.

In the end, none of the armed forces' arguments in favor of segregating blacks or excluding them from combat service held up. Moreover, instead of helping further the war effort, such policies proved more of a hindrance and gradually were relaxed. The sincerity of those who claimed that their focus was on winning the war demands even closer scrutiny in light of postwar efforts to continue segregation policies, especially in the army, even after President Harry S Truman issued his 1948 executive order directing the armed forces to fully integrate.

—DALE E. WILSON, AMERICAN MILITARY UNIVERSITY

References

Gerald Astor, *The Right to Fight: A History of African Americans in the Military* (Novato, Cal.: Presidio, 1998);

Ulysses Grant Lee, *The Employment of Negro Troops* (Washington, D.C.: Office of the Chief of Military History, 1966);

Morris J. MacGregor Jr., *Integration of the Armed Forces, 1940-1965* (Washington, D.C.: Center of Military History, 1981);

Sherie Mershon and Steven Schlossman, *Foxholes & Color Lines: Desegregating the U.S. Armed Forces* (Baltimore: Johns Hopkins University Press, 1998);

Bernard C. Nalty, *Strength for the Fight: A History of Black Americans in the Military* (New York: Free Press; London: Collier-Macmillan, 1986);

Dale E. Wilson, "Recipe for Failure: Major General Edward M. Almond and Preparation of the U.S. 92d Infantry Division for Combat in World War II," *Journal of Military History* 56 (July 1992): 473-488.

Should the West have intervened on the side of the Republicans in the Spanish Civil War?

Viewpoint: Yes, the Western democracies should have intervened in the Spanish Civil War to protect vital interests, including financial investments and strategic positioning.

Viewpoint: No, Western intervention would have been fruitless because the outcome of the Spanish Civil War was a foregone conclusion.

The Republicans and the Nationalists were closely enough matched in terms of local resources that an alternate outcome of the Spanish Civil War was a clear possibility. German and Italian support for Francisco Franco in the early months of the war, particularly the movement by air of troops from Morocco to the Peninsula, is frequently described as giving the Nationalists just enough of an initial edge that they were able to gain ground against a Republic whose well-wishers in France and Britain confined their official support to words. Similarly, the eventual communization of the Republican government under Soviet auspices is presented as in part the consequence of an absence of democratic counterweights.

Was Spain in fact a missed opportunity to challenge the Axis in its early stages and secure, if not an ally, then a benevolent neutral, in the crucial western Mediterranean? Any answer must take into account the absence of public support in either France or Britain for any significant military intervention in what seemed—and indeed was—a Spanish affair. Appeasement was the order of the day for both governments. If challenging the Axis had been a desirable policy, Spain in 1936–1937 was anything but favorable ground. To increase political support for the Republic—for example by allowing free traffic in arms, or dispatching "advisors" in the German or Soviet mode—was to court armed conflict. Britain had no deployable ground forces of which to speak. The Royal Navy, facing the prospect of three enemies in three widely separate theaters, was straining to maintain its current commitments. A France unable to react to the occupation of the Rhineland was unlikely to attempt projecting its power across the Pyrenees.

Even had the Western powers been willing to take the risks of running what was likely to be seen as an obvious bluff, there remained the issue of Soviet influence. The U.S.S.R. saw from the beginning of the war the chance to extend its influence on the cheap. In reality Joseph Stalin did no more than the minimum to keep the Republic alive. Confronted with direct Franco-British participation, he was likely to increase his commitment beyond the West's willingness or capacity to match. The result would have been an even quicker, and more complete, Communization of the Republic—and probable escalation of Axis participation on the Nationalist side, with corresponding risk of sparking the European war France and Britain wanted to avoid. Beyond that, scenarios become too inferential to be worth pursuing. It nevertheless seems that French and British refusal to ally with the Spanish Republic represented a rational, if not heroic, response to the respective countries' circumstances and interests.

Viewpoint:
Yes, the Western democracies should have intervened in the Spanish Civil War to protect vital interests, including financial investments and strategic positioning.

The Western democracies—chiefly Britain and France—should have intervened on the side of the Republicans in the Spanish Civil War of 1936–1939. Aggressive military assistance from the West might have defeated the 18 July 1936 coup in the opening weeks of the struggle. Instead, on 15 August 1936, the governments in Paris and London adopted a policy of strict non-intervention. The Non-Intervention Agreement, which twenty-seven European states eventually signed, prevented the Republic from buying arms from the West, but did little to hinder Adolf Hitler and Benito Mussolini from aiding the rebels. The British and French decision to deny aid to the democratically elected Madrid government not only doomed the Spanish Republic, but permitted fascism to march unchecked across southwestern Europe. In World War II, the Axis-friendly Spanish dictator, Francisco Franco, proved a major impediment to Allied progress in the Mediterranean, and the survival of the repressive Franco regime until 1975 was a constant reminder that the West had chosen the wrong side in Spain's civil war. A pro-Republican policy by the democracies in 1936 was desirable not only in light of strategic considerations, but for political and economic reasons as well.

The strategic importance of Spain to the security of Western Europe has long been appreciated by foreign powers. The Romans labored for two centuries to incorporate the Iberian peninsula into the empire, and its final subjugation in 26 B.C. completed Rome's dominance of the Mediterranean. In the eighteenth and early nineteenth centuries both France and Britain sought to influence or control Spain through dynastic intervention or military occupation. The reasons for foreign interest in the peninsula are clear. From Spanish soil one can quickly strike at both England and France; through the straits of Gibraltar, one controls sea access between the Atlantic and Mediterranean; and finally, the lifeline from Europe to North Africa runs through southern Spain. In sum, Spain lies at the vortex of the Atlantic, the Mediterranean, Western Europe and Northern Africa.

Spain's domestic politics and foreign alliances in the 1930s had the potential to destabilize the emerging doctrine of collective security: the union of communist Russia and the democratic West as a foil to fascist expansion. Beginning with Hitler's rise to power in 1933, the Versailles treaty (1919) suffered several challenges and setbacks, all of which threatened to unseat democratic forces in Europe. German rearmament of the Rhineland in March 1936 was followed in 1938 by the annexation of Austria and several months later by the partition of Czechoslovakia. Italy, a Western ally in World War I, was the first European state to fall to the extreme right. Mussolini's conquest of Abyssinia in 1935 completed Italy's alienation from the West, and propelled the fascist state towards its eventual alliance with Nazi Germany.

In addition to Italy and Germany, several other key European states instituted undemocratic regimes in the interwar period. Before the *Anschluss* (annexation), the Catholic authoritarian Engelbert Dollfuss had brutally oppressed all democratic and socialist opposition in Austria. The Polish government since 1926 was increasingly dictatorial; after Józef Piłsudski's death in 1935, the country was ruled by a junta of semi-fascist, right-wing military officers. The Baltics, too, saw a turn towards nationalist and authoritarian regimes. Indeed, by the mid 1930s, fascist or undemocratic regimes were dominant throughout southern, central, and eastern Europe. Apart from the stable democracies of France and Britain, only Czechoslovakia and Spain were moving away from, rather than towards, authoritarian forms of government.

The July 1936 uprising in Spanish Morocco was an ominous sign of fascism's steady progress across the continent. The Spanish rebels, led by Franco, appealed to and won substantial military support from Hitler and Mussolini. Within weeks Franco's forces, armed with Italian and German weapons, had reached the Spanish mainland and were advancing on Madrid. The *Luftwaffe* (German Air Force) soon dominated Spanish skies, while Mussolini prepared to send a major expeditionary force to join the rebel infantry. By the end of the summer of 1936, Franco was firmly wedded to his fascist supporters, and the future alignment of a conquered Spain was scarcely a point of controversy.

The prospect of the Republic's overthrow sounded alarms through the halls of government in Paris and London. The imposition of a Madrid regime sympathetic to, if not allied with, Hitler and Mussolini would leave France caught in a vice grip between three hostile forces. France's interwar defensive preparations were concentrated solely on the northeastern border and could not possibly defend itself against additional threats from the southeast and southwest. A hostile Spain also threatened France's supply route to its colonies in north-

ern and western Africa. The implication for Britain was obvious: a France surrounded by antagonistic powers would leave London without a major Continental ally.

The strategic stakes were further raised by the dispatch of Soviet arms and advisors to the Republic. Having appealed to all friendly countries for aid, Madrid discovered that only the U.S.S.R. was prepared to supply the Republic with large quantities of tanks, planes, small arms and military experts. Yet, Soviet arms deliveries had an unforeseen impact on the political landscape in Loyalist Spain. The Spanish Communist Party, hitherto inconsequential in Republican politics, soon came to dominate the government. For observers in the West, a new threat could now be imagined: the victory of a Soviet-backed Spanish state. This issue must be clarified by making two important points. First, Soviet involvement in Spain was consistent with the goals of collective security against fascist expansion, and at no time did Moscow intend to convert Spain into a Soviet satellite. Second, the

Republic accepted large-scale Soviet assistance only when it had exhausted all hope of securing weapons from the West. Thus, though the West pointed to Soviet intervention in Spain as a justification for neutrality, it was the Non-Intervention Agreement itself that forced the Republic into its unlikely union with the Soviet state.

Quite apart from the larger issue of ideological alignment was the question of internal Spanish politics. For the Western powers, the political direction of the Loyalist and rebel governments provided a clear window to the type of regime that would emerge in Spain at the conclusion of the war. Yet the signatories to the Non-Intervention Agreement disregarded the obvious political differences between each side and treated them equally. This agreement was perhaps the West's most shortsighted policy of the war, for the political orientation of the Loyalists and insurgents could not have been more opposed.

The Spanish government at the beginning of the war was one of the most progressive

A Spanish soldier at the moment of being shot, 5 September 1936

(International Center for Photography, New York)

SPANISH CIVIL WAR

democracies in the world. The fall of the dictator Primo de Rivera in January 1930 led to the forced abdication in 1931 of Bourbon King Alfonso XIII. In 1931 a Republic was declared, and the monarchical apparatus in place since the eighteenth century was replaced with democratic institutions. The years of Republican rule from 1931 to 1936 saw the implementation of advanced democratic legislation, including a progressive constitution, the separation of church and state, and far-reaching land, education and military reforms. The Republican reform agenda was only partially successful, and powerful constituencies—most notably the clergy, army and landowners—became sufficiently alienated from the regime that they would later back the July uprising. The February 1936 elections were won by the left-wing "Popular Front," a coalition of republicans, socialists, Catalans and communists. The reform potential of this government was interrupted by the civil war itself.

While the Republic during the civil war could be justifiably condemned for allowing atrocities in the rearguard or permitting excessive influence of pro-Soviet elements, these factors emerged from the ravages of war and the Republic's desperate struggle to survive. More indicative of the nature of the Republic were the institutions upon which it was founded—fair elections, an advanced constitution, and guaranteed rights for all citizens. With the rebels defeated, one could have anticipated a transition back to the original democratic character of the Republic. Of course, this supposition is purely counterfactual. The Republic's inability to secure Western support eliminated any possibility for the elected Madrid government to return to normal constitutional functionality.

Franco's political agenda, on the other hand, was undemocratic from the outset. He assumed the lead role in the rebellion in October 1936 when he appointed himself dictator of Nationalist Spain. During the course of the war, and for many years after, Franco wielded unlimited powers, granted not through popular vote or royal appointment, but simply by right of conquest. In April 1937 he gave his authoritarian state a new party, the Spanish Traditionalist Falange, a conservative conglomerate of neo-traditionalist Catholics, fascists, monarchists and right-wing military elite. This party would be the only one allowed to exist throughout the entirety of the Franco regime. Though not a fascist in any strict sense, Franco borrowed from Mussolini and Hitler many of the trappings of the fascist state, including a distinctive salute, party rallies, a separate youth organization, a ministry of propaganda and, most significantly, the doctrine of *caudillaje* (leader worship), the Spanish equivalent of *ducismo* and *Führerprinzip*.

The internal policies of Franco's early regime placed him squarely in opposition to the parliamentary democracies in France and Britain. It could be assumed that a Franco victory would leave Spain heavily indebted to and oriented towards Mussolini and Hitler. In fact, these assumptions were borne out even before the end of the war. As early as 18 November 1936, both Italy and Germany formally recognized the Franco regime. Ten days later Franco and Mussolini entered into a secret agreement that guaranteed the insurgents military assistance from Italy in exchange for access to Spanish raw materials and future support in the event of war. On 20 March 1937, Franco entered into a similar economic and political agreement with Hitler. Later that year, Franco and Hitler signed yet another pact that provided the Germans access to Spanish mineral resources essential for the Nazi war industry. In the next two years Franco would sign more protocols that drew him closer to the fascist states, most notably the Anti-Comintern Pact and a comprehensive Hispano-German treaty of military and economic cooperation. By the end of the civil war, Franco's Spain was bound by multiple agreements to the two fascist dictators.

The alignment of Nationalist Spain with the fascist powers posed a serious threat to Western economic interests on the Iberian peninsula. Prior to the civil war, Britain was the largest outside investor in Spain, its holdings valued at $194 million—a fifth of all foreign capital in the country. British commercial enterprises in Spain included extensive mining interests, most notably the Río Tinto Company, which extracted copper and pyrites. British investors also controlled important waterworks and cork manufacturing plants. The French possessed $135 million in Spain, including railroads and lead mines. Other Western states were major players in the Spanish market. The Belgians had holdings in timber stands, tramways, and coal mines in Asturias. Canada controlled the distribution of electricity in Catalonia. The United States owned automobile and rubber plants in Spain, and controlled a sizable portion of the cotton stocks. Thus, Western interests on the peninsula were considerable, and the future orientation and alignment of Spain was a key concern to investors in democracies on both sides of the Atlantic.

If the West had strategic, political and economic reasons to intervene on the side of the Republic, it must be acknowledged that the worst-case implications of nonintervention never transpired. Though allied with Hitler and Mussolini at the end of the civil war, Franco was willing to alter relationships and principles as Axis fortunes shifted. From 1939 to 1941 the Spanish dictator supplied key raw materials to the German and Italian war industries, and lent his former benefactors the services of Spain's intelligence agents in the West. In 1942, however, Mussolini's Greek disaster and Hitler's setbacks in the Soviet Union and Britain led Franco to abandon the Axis cause and seek rapprochement with the Allies. Internally, Franco also eliminated the overtly fascist aspects of his reign. By the mid 1950s, Spain's international rehabilitation was nearly complete. Yet, strategic and economic cooperation with the West could not free the Spanish people from Franco's straitjacket of governmental control and censorship. Indeed, Spain's long ordeal under the Franco dictatorship and its protracted isolation from Europe remains the most incriminating legacy of the West's 1936 abandonment of the Republic.

–DANIEL KOWALSKY, UNIVERSITY
OF WISCONSIN-MADISON

Viewpoint:
No, Western intervention would have been fruitless because the outcome of the Spanish Civil War was a foregone conclusion.

There was an air of inevitability about the Spanish Civil War. Throughout the nineteenth and early twentieth centuries Spain languished as one of the poorest and least developed nations in Western Europe. From 1923 to 1930 Spain, nominally a monarchy, was a dictatorship under General Miguel Primo de Rivera. Rivera was dismissed in 1930 amidst the rise of antimonarchical sentiment. In 1931 King Alfonso XIII was forced into exile, a republic proclaimed, and a left-wing majority elected to the Cortes. For the next five years Spain was torn by continuous violence between extremes of left and right.

The Spanish Left wanted a rapid transformation of the semifeudal Spanish society. Agrarian reform laws were passed. Catalonia was granted autonomy. The Leftist majority in the Cortes also pushed to break the hold of the Catholic Church upon the Spanish culture: a new constitution revoked Church privileges; divorce was legalized; and a religious reform bill that envisioned closure of Church schools was passed. Industrial workers turned away from the Socialist Party to support the Anarchist and Marxist parties. Conservative groups, namely the armed forces, monarchists, ardent Catholics, businessmen, and landowners fought to hold on to their ideal of a traditionalist and Catholic Spain. In 1932 a coup by some army generals

was suppressed. In October 1933 lawyer José Antonio Primo de Rivera founded a quasi-fascist political party, the Falange. The rightist reaction to the Republican/Socialist government led to the victory of a rightist coalition in the October 1934 election. The new government's first act was to brutally crush a miners' rebellion in Asturias. Out of power, the Socialist party became increasingly revolutionary.

By the elections of 1936 Spain was rather evenly divided between the extremes of right and left, with not much activity in the middle. The left coalition won the 1936 elections with 4.2 million votes to the rightist National Front's 3.8 million votes. Only 681,000 electors voted for the center parties. Disorder mounted as general strikes and insurrections spread in the first half of 1936. A group of army generals under the leadership of General Emilio Mola Vidal prepared plans to seize power. On 13 July 1936 the Spanish right was given justification for a coup when a government police unit, the Republican Assault Guards, arrested and murdered the leader of the monarchists in the Cortes. Four days later, the military uprising began.

The plan was for the armed forces to seize power in all the major cities simultaneously. The rising went well in some regions. Seville in southern Spain and a large part of northern Spain went over quickly to the insurgents. General Francisco Franco took command of the formidable army in Morocco in the name of the junta. The garrisons in Madrid and Barcelona rose against the government as the confused Republicans vacillated. The government was faced with a dilemma; the only way to defend the republic against the army was to arm the unions and leftist parties and set them to fight the soldiers. However, once the workers—who generally adhered to the anarchist or communist line—were armed, there was no way that the moderate Republican government could hope to control them. The government finally decided to fight for its life and armed the workers' militias that suppressed the military revolt in Madrid, Barcelona, and other cities—then summarily executed hundreds of officers and supporters of the coup. Within a week of the start of the rebellion, Spain was divided into regions opposing or supporting the government. One of the most violent and passionate civil wars of the century had begun.

Both sides immediately appealed to foreign powers for military aid. The Nationalists (the junta supporters) asked Germany and Italy for aircraft in order to transport the Spanish Foreign Legion and the Moroccan forces, the best troops of the Spanish Army, from Morocco to the battlefront in southern Spain. The Germans and Italians quickly complied and the airlift was under way. They also promised air units, military specialists and war material to the Nationalists. At the same time France's left-wing Popular Front government allowed weapons and equipment to be sold to the Spanish Republic. The supplies from France, however, lasted only a week as the French government, under pressure from the British, closed the border with Spain and forbade further arms sales. Urgently needing modern equipment, the Republic turned to Soviet Russia, which soon began shipping large quantities of guns, ammunition, tanks and aircraft to the Republic, accompanied by Soviet advisors, specialists and pilots. From the start, both sides were heavily dependent upon outside sources for arms and supplies.

In the first weeks of the war, Spain witnessed an orgy of violence and revenge. In the territory held by the Republic, there was an outburst of spontaneous anticlerical violence in which thousands of clerics, including twelve bishops and an estimated eight thousand priests, monks, nuns, and novices were murdered. Hundreds of churches were looted and burned. In the countryside there were wholesale lynchings of large landowners, long seen as the oppressors of Spain's miserably poor peasantry. In the cities businessmen, Falange members, and suspected Nationalist supporters were killed by the thousands. Having armed the anarchist militias, the moderate elements of the Republic's government had no hope of controlling the social forces that erupted. In Nationalist Spain the use of violence was somewhat more systematic. Peasant and union leaders, as well as suspected supporters of the leftist parties, were arrested and thousands were summarily executed. As the Nationalists' Moroccan troops advanced through southern Spain towards Madrid, any village that had witnessed atrocities against landowners and Nationalist supporters could expect a terrible and deadly retribution from the merciless North Africa troops.

Many of the first reports that the British, French and U.S. governments received came from warships that had rushed to Spanish ports in order to evacuate foreign nationals. As refugees crowded aboard the British, French, American, and German warships in the ports held by the Republic, they told stories of unchecked violence, massacres of clerics, and seizure of businesses by militias. The Spanish Navy had mostly remained loyal to the Republic. At the start of the uprising most officers supported the rightist junta's coup, so petty officers and enlisted sailors seized control of the ships, executed the senior officers, and raised the red flag. Western naval officers who had to deal with the Republic's navy during the evacuation found it extremely distasteful to negotiate with enlisted men who had murdered their officers.

The ports controlled by the Nationalists offered a different picture. There had been plenty of mass arrests and summary executions in the Nationalist zone, but these had been carried out more discreetly. The Nationalist zone was, on the surface, a region of law and order with no burning churches or revolutionary sailors and militias. It was controlled with tight, military discipline. Businessmen had no complaints about rampaging anarchist militias, or revolutionary tribunals seizing property. Indeed, first impressions are the most important ones. Western governments were told by their naval officers on the scene that Republican Spain resembled the worst excesses of the Russian revolution, while bourgeois law and order and respect for property were the norm in the Nationalist zone.

These early impressions of the Spanish Civil War colored the public opinion about the conflict in all the Western democracies. In America, Catholics overwhelmingly opposed the anticlerical Republic and supported the Nationalists; the large Catholic vote was an essential part of President Franklin D. Roosevelt's electoral coalition. While the labor movements in Britain and France, and leftist political parties, staunchly supported the Republic, the conservative parties saw the civil war as something akin to the Russian revolution. The nationalization of British-owned companies in the Republican zone and the arbitrary arrests of British managers by workers' militias angered British businessmen. The conservative government of Great Britain was hostile to the Spanish Republic from the start. France, where the Popular Front coalition was in power, was the only Western nation where there was strong sentiment for intervention on the side of the Republic. However, even when France approved arms sales to the Republic in 1936, and again in March 1938, the French right, which was strongly pro-Franco, protested furiously. With such divided opinion about Spain in the Western democracies there was no realistic possibility that the Western powers could have gotten public support for any intervention on the side of the Republic.

Indeed, the policies taken by the U.S. and British governments essentially undermined the Republic and aided the Nationalists. Both the British and Americans announced an arms embargo that applied to both sides in the conflict. Thus, the internationally recognized legitimate government of Spain was barred from acquiring arms from the Western powers, while British and American companies opened

SPAIN AWAKENS

In a speech delivered to Detroit automotive workers on 18 November 1937, George O. Pershing, field secretary of the Medical Bureau and North American Committee to Aid Spanish Democracy, gave his impressions of the situation developing on the Iberian Peninsula.

Spain, once the great nation that gave to the new world so generously of its culture: Spain, friend of the American colonies in their struggle for independence; that Spain elected a government with a mandate for liberty, justice and progress. Spain threw off the dusty robes of feudalism and awoke to a new day on February 16, 1936.

Every act of the Spanish government since it was elected has been based upon the Spanish constitution of 1931. These acts, in themselves, are a credit to the new government. . . .

In July, 1936, General Francisco Franco led an invasion of the Spanish mainland, supported by about 90% of the officers of the Spanish Army, Spanish legionnaires from Morocco and by Italian and German planes, tanks and cannon. Germany and Italy supported him for two reasons that they have since stated. They desired to gain control of the rich resources of Spain where there are found many of the minerals essential to the rearming of Germany and Italy, and to advance Fascism.

Charges of Communism were made by Franco, Hitler and Mussolini, in explaining their invasion. . . .

Actually the issue in Spain is one of Democracy against Fascism. The government forces, the loyalists, are mainly volunteer fighters from the mines, factories, and mills, from the offices and farms—men who dropped their tools and took up arms to defend the government they had elected and the laws and reforms they desired. They were the embattled farmers of 1776. They are the ragged, untrained army that Washington quartered at Valley Forge. The same echoes that resounded from Bunker Hill during the American Revolution are now heard in the Spanish Pyrenees. The same results will be achieved. . . .

A leading jurist in Spain recently stated that "a Christian cannot be a Fascist." I can add that no person can support Fascism and be an American. To me Americanism means freedom to worship, and the right to a "government of the people, by the people, and for the people."

As a Christian, one cannot remain passive to the bombing of innocent villagers, the machine-gunning of women and children and the destruction of religious freedom that Franco and his Fascist allies are carrying out in Spain. As an American one cannot be passive in the face of the spread of Fascism which is a definite and conclusive threat to any democratic country. . . .

As a friend of Spain, as a fighter against Fascism I can see the hope of democracy in the hands of the trade unions of the world. If labor loses, democracy falls. No one in America wants war and the wholehearted support of the Trade Union movement for peace is conclusive. Yet to have peace we must work for it, to maintain democracy we must support it, and I look to the trade union movement in America to strengthen the constitutionally elected government of Republican Spain. . . .

Spain awakens after centuries of feudalism to throw off the stranglehold of Fascism. She stretches her arms and halts the fascist robbers, she arises and throws off her oppressors.

Spain is the health officer of democracy. She has hung the yellow sign on the door of Fascism. "Quarantine the oppressor" expresses the desire of American democracy and Spain answers,

"We will not stop until the Fascists vote with their legs and run."

Source: *Spanish Civil War Oral History Project, University of South Florida Tampa Campus Library, Web Page.*

SPANISH CIVIL WAR

up trade with the Nationalists. While American companies could not sell arms, Texas Oil Company and Standard Oil provided 3.5 million tons of oil to the Nationalists; Ford, General Motors, and Studebaker exported twelve thousand trucks to the Nationalist zone—both items playing an important part in the Nationalist victory.

For many years a common historical interpretation was that the Spanish Civil War was the true start of World War II, the opening round in the great battle between democracy and fascism. This interpretation overemphasizes foreign involvement in Spain and ignores the Spanishness of the war. Franco was no fascist in the German or Italian sense of the term and the Republic was by no means a liberal democracy. Franco fought for an authoritarian, Catholic and traditionalist Spain. One of his first acts when he became chief of the Nationalist state in October 1936 was to put the Falange under his personal control, and he quietly suppressed its ideologues who wanted to see a social revolution on the German or Italian model.

The Republic, while headed by liberal prime ministers, found its politics dominated by the radical left. From a small power base in 1936, the Communist Party quickly became a dominant force in the Republic. By May 1937 the Communists were powerful enough to launch an attack upon the anarchists who controlled the Catalonian government. After winning a civil war within a civil war in Barcelona, the Communists began a ruthless purge of the non-Stalinist Marxists, reminiscent of Lenin's destruction of the Russian Social Democrats in 1918. One of the major causes of death in the Spanish Civil War was murder and summary execution. In this aspect of the war, neither side can claim moral superiority. Of the estimated 500,000 people killed in the war, 130,000 died by murder and execution (approximately 75,000 Nationalist, 55,000 Republican).

Even had the Western powers provided military aid to the Republic, the course of the war probably would not have been changed. The Russians provided a considerable amount of modern equipment to the Republic, including approximately 1,000 aircraft, 900 tanks, 1,550 artillery pieces, 15,000 machine guns and 4 million artillery shells. The Republic's problem was less one of material than of leadership. It had valiant soldiers but lacked a trained officer corps. Thus, the Republic's major offensives, such as at Brunete in July 1937 and on the Ebro in July 1938, made significant initial gains but soon failed by not exploiting early successes. With only a few

trained officers the Republicans suffered from an inability to coordinate their tanks, infantry, artillery, and air units. While individual divisions performed well, the Republic had too few competent officers to plan and conduct corps and army operations. The Nationalists, on the other hand, had a corps of trained leaders who were able to plan and carry out large operations. From the offensive in the North in 1937 to the end of the war in March 1939, the Nationalist Army proved far more capable than the Republic in conducting large-scale operations.

The Nationalists also proved far more adept at foreign relations than the Republic's leaders. While the Republic was bent on nationalizing foreign properties, Franco assured the British that their investments and properties in Spain would be protected. Franco and the Nationalists identified themselves strongly with the Catholic Church, while the attacks upon churches and clerics in the Republic brought the condemnation of Pope Pius XI. For its part, the German military carefully limited its involvement in Spain in order to avoid provoking French intervention. The Condor Legion was limited to one hundred aircraft and five thousand personnel. The only German ground-force commitment was one small tank battalion. In order to prevent any incidents with the French, all German aircraft in Spain were forbidden to fly within fifty kilometers of the French border. The Italians proved less cooperative and sent large ground forces to Spain, even though Franco had never requested any such assistance. The Italian behavior proved their undoing in the long run: they were so openly ambitious to play a major role in the war and be rewarded with bases in Spain, that after the war Franco and the Nationalists came to thoroughly distrust them. Italy was granted none of its desired bases or economic concessions for its efforts.

The Nationalist victory in Spain gave Germany some benefits during World War II, but Hitler did not get what he hoped for—Spain to enter the war as a German ally and attack the vital British base at Gibraltar. During World War II Spain shipped large quantities of minerals (iron ore, wolfram, and pyrites) to Germany. Spain maintained pro-German neutrality for much of the war and allowed German U-boats to secretly refuel in Spanish ports. Franco saw the German invasion of Russia as an anticommunist crusade and allowed forty thousand Spanish volunteers to serve in the *Wehrmacht* (German Army) on the Russian Front. Franco always focused on the interests of Spain, however, and Spain's urgent need was to recover from the civil war. Franco was cautious enough not to be drawn into any ruinous German adventures and rebuffed Hitler's entreaties to enter the war. Hitler met Franco only once, in October 1940, and remarked that it was the toughest negotiating session of his life.

When the tide of war turned against Germany, Franco changed directions as well. In late 1943 the Spanish Blue Legion was pulled out of the Russian front and returned to Spain. Allied pilots shot down over German-occupied Europe could make their escape through Spain with little fear of internment by the Spanish government. By 1944, Franco welcomed increased trade with the Allied powers. In short, the Nationalists played the classic game that weak powers normally play when confronted by strong powers. They tried to accommodate both sides. In this case, it worked.

–JAMES S. CORUM, USAF SCHOOL OF
ADVANCED AIRPOWER STUDIES

References

Michael Albert, *A New International History of the Spanish Civil War* (New York: St. Martin's Press, 1994);

Charles B. Burdick, *Germany's Military Strategy and Spain in World War II* (Syracuse, N.Y.: Syracuse University Press, 1968);

Willard C. Frank, "The Spanish Civil War and the Coming of the Second World War," *International History Review,* 9 (1987): 368–409;

Allen Guttmann, *The Wound in the Heart: America and the Spanish Civil War* (New York: Free Press of Glencoe, 1962);

Douglas Little, *Malevolent Neutrality: The United States, Britain and the Origins of the Spanish Civil War* (Ithaca, N.Y.: Cornell University Press, 1985);

Stanley G. Payne, *History of Fascism, 1914–1945* (Madison: University of Wisconsin Press, 1995);

Dante Puzzo, *Spain and the Great Powers, 1936–1941* (New York: Columbia University Press, 1962);

Hugh Thomas, *The Spanish Civil War,* revised edition (London: Eyre & Spottiswoode; New York: Harper, 1991);

William E. Watters, *An International Affair: Non-Intervention in the Spanish Civil War, 1939* (New York: Exposition Press, 1971);

Robert H. Whealey, *Hitler and Spain: The Nazi Role in the Spanish Civil War* (Lexington: University Press of Kentucky, 1989);

Peter Wyden, *The Passionate War: The Narrative History of the Spanish Civil War* (New York: Simon & Schuster, 1983).

STALIN

Was Joseph Stalin a great war leader?

Viewpoint: Yes, Stalin was a great war leader who inspired his people, organized the national economy, and led the Soviet Union to victory over the Germans.

Viewpoint: No, Stalin led his nation to victory over the Germans by imposing an inhumane and indefensible policy of terror.

Arguably, Joseph Stalin's clearest claim to greatness as a war leader was his success at overcoming the crises he himself had generated. Purges that eviscerated the Soviet officer corps, westward expansion that left the Union of Soviet Socialist Republics (U.S.S.R.) off balance, and finally a trust in Adolf Hitler that led to denial or downplaying of intelligence warnings of imminent attack—these policies positioned the Soviet Union for disaster in the first months of Operation Barbarossa. All these mistakes were Stalin's direct responsibility.

The Soviet dictator, however, rallied after the initial shock, asserting an even more rigid control of army, state, and society. Stalin benefitted in that process from the absence of any likely challengers to his authority—the purges had seen to that—and as the war progressed Stalin took pains to play successful generals against each other. Stalin's role, however, was more than that of a manipulator of power. His ruthless indifference to losses and his corresponding intolerance of failure produced, under forced draft, some of the most effective field commanders in the war. His command of society ensured that Soviet resources were focused on the war effort. After a series of more or less disastrous attempts to manage the war at operational levels, he learned to take the counsel of professionals.

Stalin was also an outstanding grand strategist. His intention was to aggrandize the Soviet Union as a world power and develop it as a communist state, with the destruction of Nazi Germany the necessary first step. Economic, military, diplomatic, psychological, and even personal factors were structured around those objectives with a degree of coherence and consistency unmatched among the major belligerents. Between 1941 and 1945, the rigidity that eventually ossified the Soviet system was expressed in a focus that brought victory from the jaws of catastrophe—and convinced many, inside and outside of Russia, that communism was indeed the wave of the future.

Viewpoint:
Yes, Stalin was a great war leader who inspired his people, organized the national economy, and led the Soviet Union to victory over the Germans.

When the Soviet Union emerged victorious from World War II, its people knew exactly who had masterminded their victory—their leader, Joseph Stalin. Huge monuments to his heroism were erected all over the country, newspapers and radio announcers hailed Stalin as the savior of Russia, and people everywhere toasted the brilliant leadership that had led to victory. Since 1945, however, many scholars have questioned this image of Stalin as war hero. They argue that this status was awarded him only by a captive and slavish media that pandered to his desire to be a great warrior. They also point to his disappearance from the public eye during the first weeks of the war, to mistakes that Soviet forces made, and to the upheaval he caused in the officer corps in the mid 1930s. While all of these criticisms have some merit, they do not change the fact that Stalin successfully prepared his country for war and led his people to victory, rallying them to the defense of Russia, exhorting them to focus all of their strength on the war effort, and uniting all of the country's forces into an effective fighting machine.

The Soviet Union was able to fight Germany because of the industrialization drive of the 1930s. While this was in many ways a horrific period of Soviet history, it was also a time of enormous industrial growth. The New Economic Policy of the 1920s enabled the country to get back on its feet after World War I and its civil war, but by 1926 economic, and especially industrial, growth had slowed considerably. By forcing rapid industrialization on the country and funneling most resources into military development, Stalin laid the economic and industrial groundwork for a wartime economy. While other countries spent months retooling their industry for war production, the Soviet Union made the shift in a matter of weeks, and, in fact, already had huge stockpiles of equipment when the war started. In addition, the industrialization and collectivization drive spawned a centralized distribution system that allowed the government to redirect food, clothes, and equipment to virtually any location with the stroke of a pen. The mechanisms for rationing, requisitioning, and distributing goods and services already existed. In addition, much of the population had been mobilized for the industrialization drive in the 1930s, and by 1941 the country had a large

skilled labor force that was ready to produce for the war effort. While other countries scrambled to train the unemployed sectors of their populations to replace workers who were sent to the front, the Soviet Union mobilized millions of men quickly without sacrificing industrial and military output. Without the industrialization drive it is doubtful that the Soviet Union could have supported the war with Germany. Stalin's insistence on rapid, forced industrialization prepared the Soviet Union for World War II.

This assertion is not meant to suggest that Stalin foresaw or desired war. In fact, he did all he could to delay open conflict with Germany. Despite his efforts the Germans invaded Russia in June 1941 and during that year pushed their forces to the gates of Moscow and Leningrad. The Soviets did not respond quickly or effectively to the German offensive. One school of thought lays blame for this failure squarely on Stalin. As the feared and ruthless leader of an inexperienced and frightened officer corps, his leadership was essential to mobilize Soviet forces. No one else could or would take the responsibility on themselves for fear that they would be executed for their pains. Stalin's failure to respond quickly to the German attack resulted in the phenomenal success of German forces during 1941–1942.

This argument is compelling, but it suggests that Stalin's leadership was pivotal to Soviet success as well as Soviet failure. If the armed forces were unable to respond to Hitler's armies without Stalin's leadership, then, given that no political changes took place, it follows that they achieved their ultimate victory under Stalin's leadership. Within days of the attack, Stalin overcame his shock of Hitler's betrayal and took an active part in planning the Soviet defense and eventual offense. He oversaw military operations on all fronts, making strategic decisions and maintaining contact with all army leaders. The same army that could not keep the Germans from trampling through western Russia to the capitals was able, a few months later, to begin pushing the Germans back to Berlin—before the second front opened. Stalin's insistence on "not one step back" and encouragement of the scorched-earth policy forced the Germans to pay dearly for every mile of Soviet territory. His ruthless treatment of any officer or soldier who gave way before the German army forced his soldiers to fight hard even in retreat. This policy was brutal and cost the Soviet Union millions of lives, but it also slowed the Germans' advance enough that they got caught in the Russian winter and prevented them from taking the capitals. If Soviet commanders and soldiers had not been more afraid of Stalin than they were of fighting, Hitler's armies would almost certainly have

taken Moscow, giving them not only a huge psychological victory, but also warm quarters and provisions for the winter. Instead, the German armies suffered terrible losses as they waited out the harshest part of the Russian winter in camps.

Stalin's refusal to leave Moscow despite the German advance provided a much-needed boost to Soviet morale. The despair felt by residents of Moscow as the Germans slowly advanced, and most of the government leaders moved to Kuibyshev, can only be imagined, but Stalin's demonstration of confidence in the Red Army as he continued to work from the Kremlin inspired his countrymen to hope as well. During the winter of 1941–1942, as German troops camped within sight of Moscow, Stalin was determined to save the capital as the center of government and as the psychological stronghold of the country. His confidence revived popular support for the war during its darkest and most desperate months.

Stalin understood the importance of symbols in other ways too, and engineered a huge propaganda campaign to mobilize the Soviet people for war. The entire nation turned its attention solely to the war effort—not only industry, but poetry, music, novels, magazines, newspapers, radio, clubs, schools, and churches concentrated almost exclusively on Soviet victory over Germany. While part of the public support stemmed from a spontaneous reaction to the German invasion, it was sustained and reinforced by Stalin's campaign to saturate all aspects of life with the war effort. One has only to contrast the Soviet response to the German invasion of 1941 with the Russian response to the German invasion of 1914. While in 1914 the state steadfastly refused to make use of public sentiment against the Germans to prosecute the war—and thereby lost public support in a few months—the state in 1941 not only encouraged such feelings, but used every tool at its disposal to inflame the public with patriotism and righteous wrath against the invaders and directed this energy into a united and extremely powerful war machine. The symbol for the war was Mother Russia, but the leader to whom everyone looked for direction, inspiration, and strength was Stalin. For his part, Stalin recognized the enormous potential of

STALIN

COMRADES!

On 3 July 1941, after the Germans had attacked Russia, Soviet leader Joseph Stalin broadcast a message of resistence to his nation, portions of which are cited below.

How could it have happened that our glorious Red Army surrendered a number of our cities and districts to fascist armies? Is it really true that German fascist troops are invincible, as is ceaselessly trumpeted by the boastful fascist propagandists? Of course not!

History shows that there are no invincible armies and never have been. Napoleon's army was considered invincible but it was beaten successively by Russian, English and German armies. Kaiser Wilhelm's German Army in the period of the first imperialist war was also considered invincible, but it was beaten several times by the Russian and Anglo-French forces and was finally smashed by the Anglo-French forces.

The same must be said of Hitler's German fascist army today. This army had not yet met with serious resistance on the continent of Europe. Only on our territory has it met serious resistance. And if, as a result of this resistance, the finest divisions of Hitler's German fascist army have been defeated by our Red Army, it means that this army too can be smashed and will be smashed as were the armies of Napoleon and Wilhelm.

As to part of our territory having nevertheless been seized by German fascist troops, this is chiefly due to the fact that the war of fascist Germany on the USSR began under conditions favorable for the German forces and unfavorable for Soviet forces. The fact of the matter is that the troops of Germany, as a country at war, were already fully mobilized, and the 170 divisions hurled by Germany against the USSR and brought up to the Soviet frontiers, were in a state of complete readiness, only awaiting the signal to move into action, whereas Soviet troops had still to effect mobilization and move up to the frontier.

Of no little importance in this respect is the fact that fascist Germany suddenly and treacherously violated the Non-Aggression Pact she concluded in 1939 with the USSR, disregarding the fact that she would be regarded as the aggressor by the whole world.

Naturally, our peace-loving country, not wishing to take the initiative of breaking the pact, could not resort to perfidy. . . .

By virtue of this war which has been forced upon us, our country has come to death-grips with its most malicious and most perfidious enemy—German fascism. Our troops are fighting heroically against an enemy armed to the teeth with tanks and aircraft.

Overcoming innumerable difficulties, the Red Army and Red Navy are self-sacrificingly disputing every inch of Soviet soil. The main forces of the Red Army are coming into action armed with thousands of tanks and airplanes. The men of the Red Army are displaying unexampled valor. Our resistance to the enemy is growing in strength and power.

Side by side with the Red Army, the entire Soviet people are rising in defense of our native land.

What is required to put an end to the danger hovering over our country, and what measures must be taken to smash the enemy?

Above all, it is essential that our people, the Soviet people, should understand the full immensity of the danger that threatens our country and should abandon all complacency, all heedlessness, all those moods of peaceful constructive work which were so natural before the war, but which are fatal today when war has fundamentally changed everything.

The enemy is cruel and implacable. He is out to seize our lands, watered with our sweat, to seize our grain and oil secured by our labor. He is out to restore the rule of landlords, to restore Tsarism, to destroy national culture and the national state existence of the Russians, Ukrainians, Byelo-Russians, Lithuanians, Letts, Esthonians, Uzbeks, Tatars, Moldavians, Georgians, Armenians, Azerbaidzhanians and the other free people of the Soviet Union, to Germanize them, to convert them into the slaves of German princes and barons.

Thus the issue is one of life or death for the Soviet State, for the peoples of the USSR; the issue is whether the peoples of the Soviet Union shall remain free or fall into slavery. . . .

Source: *World War II Resources Web Page*

STALIN

such a phenomenon and endeavored to use all possible means to inspire his people—even going so far as to rehabilitate the Russian Orthodox Church as a possible rallying point for many Russians. Gone were the exhortations to fight for the revolution and in their place stood symbols that were calculated to touch every Russian's soul—their motherland, their history, and their church.

Like the other allied powers, the Soviet government used all manner of propaganda to turn the Germans into beasts in the eyes of the Soviet people. The Nazi belief that Slavs were subhuman and fit only for slave labor lent itself well to dehumanizing the German attacker, and the Soviets made the most of it. Under Stalin's direction, however, the Soviet press also invoked historical images of Russian national heroes to inspire the citizens as well as enrage them. Alexander Nevsky (defender of Pskov against the Teutonic knights in 1242), Ivan Mikhailovich Dolgoruky (founder of Moscow), Dmitry Donskoy (legendary victor over the Mongols [Tartars] in 1380), and Mikhail Kutuzov (hero of the Napoleonic wars, 1803–1815), among others, all served to remind the Russian people of their glorious victories in the past and spur them on to victory in the present. Stalin's decision to abandon the socialist rhetoric of the 1920s and 1930s, and his use of traditional images kept the fighting spirit alive in his people even during the darkest periods of the war.

The people of the Soviet Union certainly believed that Stalin was the hero who had led them to victory. This was due, to a certain extent, to the cult of personality that had emerged in the 1930s around him—people were simply used to thinking of Stalin as the leader. During and after the war, however, Stalin was less in evidence in the public arena. Newspapers and magazines hailed the Soviet people's victory over Germany, not Stalin's victory. The press referred to Stalin as "our leader" but did not dwell on his wartime achievements, and instead concentrated on portraying the heroism of ordinary citizens at the front or on the assembly line. People viewed Stalin as a hero not because the press told them to, but because he had led them to victory. The press did not need to underline Stalin's achievements because people simply believed that Stalin's leadership had enabled them to prepare for war, as well as to unite their talents and courage to defeat Germany.

Heroes are defined not only by what they accomplish, but also by how they are perceived. Stalin is a war hero on both counts. Under his leadership, the Soviet Union won World War II. The Soviet people understood

his importance in their victory and hailed him as savior of their country.

—GRETA BUCHER, U.S. MILITARY ACADEMY, WEST POINT

Viewpoint: No, Stalin led his nation to victory over the Germans by imposing an inhumane and indefensible policy of terror.

By what criteria does one judge a war leader great? Is victory the sole standard? If so, Joseph Stalin was a great war leader. If one calculates intangible factors such as inspiring hope, delegation of responsibility, and general leadership qualities, however, he slips rather badly toward a rather crowded end of the leadership list. What is there of greatness in a war leader who murders 45 percent of his military officer corps just before the battle begins? What is there of greatness in a war leader who judges performance by body count, not in the notorious manner of the U.S. generals in Vietnam of supposedly dead enemies, but of his own dead?

For Stalin, if the number of Red Army casualties in an operation were not high enough, the responsible general had not shown sufficient aggressiveness. Stalin's style of realpolitik, domestic and foreign, is best called opportunism. He was happy to sign in 1939 the Nonaggression treaty with Adolf Hitler and Germany. He believed the Western powers would batter themselves to exhaustion in the coming war, after which he would be able to choose the side most advantageous for the interlocked causes of world revolution and Soviet aggrandizement. Meanwhile, through trade with Germany of raw materials for military machinery and technology, Stalin made a tidy profit from the invasion of France. The Nonaggression treaty also carved up eastern Europe into spheres of influence that allowed Stalin to operate with impunity. Finally, but not least, it allowed him to proceed with his murder program.

By the mid 1930s the Soviet army was fast becoming a modern military force, upgrading organization, material, tactics, and strategy. In 1938, however, the party purges that had populated Siberia with those who avoided a bullet in the basement of *Lubyanka*, the NKVD (Soviet secret police) headquarters, reached a climax with the Moscow trials. Now it was the turn of the military.

By the end of 1938, 45 percent of the senior military and political officers of the army and navy had been relieved of duty or killed, including 720 out of 837 officers holding the rank of colonel or higher. Seventy-one of eighty-five members of the Military Council were dead. It is estimated that 43,300 officers were killed.

The deleterious effects of this purge were not as direct as one might expect; few of those killed had combat experience, and military academies were turning out over twenty thousand new officers a year. Rather, it paralyzed incentive from company level to generals' ranks. The most significant consequence was generalized, random fear. Stalin compounded that fear by appointing a political officer to every military unit above division size. Their effect was twofold. It placed within the heart of every officer the icy knowledge that any word or action deemed varying from the party line—any hint of bourgeois military elitism—would mean arrest and interrogation, as well as execution or gulag exile not only for the officer but also for his wife and children. The second effect was that most political officers were military dunces who considered themselves masters of war while fearing for their own skins. Strategic and tactical battle plans often amounted to headlong rushes against enemy positions and orders to hold one's own ground to the last man. To flank was dubious; to retreat for any reason treasonous; and to break off, or even succeed with too few casualties, was a sign of lack of will.

All of the war leaders, such as Winston Churchill and Franklin D. Roosevelt, meddled in planning and operations. Stalin took that pattern to new levels. Every major military decision in the course of the war was made by Stalin. If increasingly he permitted his commanders to plan operations, they did not take place without his approval. During the Moscow winter offensive in 1941, perhaps the single most important battle of the war, Stalin ordered Marshal Georgy Zhukov, the overall commander of the Russian armies, to personally retake a small, unimportant village. Earlier, during the German siege of Kiev, with his ground commanders pleading for permission to withdraw to a more defensible position, Stalin refused, and 700,000 men and officers were encircled and lost. Orders frequently emanated from the Kremlin that had no relationship to what was happening on the front. Stalin's total control of the army and bureaucracy through fear and terror enabled him to marshal the resources of the U.S.S.R. in an effective, but not economical manner. Mistakes he made at the beginning of the war are counted not by thousands, but millions, of lives. Strategic and tactical decisions made throughout the war were those of blunt force bluntly applied; though successful, they cost millions more in unnecessary casualties. But he won.

–JOHN WHEATLEY, BROOKLYN CENTER, MINNESOTA

References

Seweryn Bialer, *Stalin and his Generals: Soviet Military Memoirs of World War II* (New York: Pegasus, 1969);

Issac Deutscher, *Stalin: A Political Biography* (New York: Oxford University Press, 1949);

John Erickson, *The Road to Berlin: Continuing the History of Stalin's War with Germany* (Boulder, Colo.: Westview Press, 1983);

Erickson, *The Road to Stalingrad* (London: Weidenfeld & Nicolson, 1975);

David M. Glantz and Jonathan M. House, *When Titans Clashed: How the Red Army Stopped Hitler* (Lawrence: University Press of Kansas, 1995);

Robert H. McNeal, *Stalin: Man and Ruler* (Houndmills, Basingstoke, Hampshire: Macmillan; New York: New York University Press, 1988);

Nina Tumarkin, *The Living & the Dead: The Rise & Fall of the Cult of World War II in Russia* (New York: BasicBooks, 1994).

STALIN

TANKS

Were American tanks inferior to their German and Soviet counterparts?

Viewpoint: Yes, American tanks were inferior to both German and Russian tanks in most particulars, although comparisons of characteristics are meaningless outside of the complete strategic and operational contexts, in which armored fighting vehicles are only part of a complex system.

Viewpoint: No, American tanks were not as inferior as is frequently asserted. They were deficient only in certain performance aspects that were often not vital from a broad perspective.

Viewpoint: No, while Soviet tanks were the best overall vehicles in World War II, the American M-4, produced in large numbers, was not designed to engage the larger German tanks. The M-4 was used by the Allies properly, and it helped to win the war.

Viewpoint: No, U.S. tanks were generally superior to most German models and only slightly inferior to Soviet ones.

The inferiority of U.S. tanks to their German opponents is a feature of most narrative accounts of World War II. Particularly in northwest Europe, the M-4 Shermans that were the backbone of the U.S.—and increasingly the British—armored force are depicted as possessing neither the gun power nor the protection to face the German Panthers and Tigers on equal terms. The 75mm gun that was the Sherman's original armament had neither the range nor muzzle velocity to risk tackling even the older German tanks at even odds. The 76mm that replaced it was not much of an improvement. As for maneuverability, the Sherman's cross-country mobility over soft ground was less than that of the heavier Panzers with their wider treads—and much of northwest Europe for most of the war was soft ground. The Sherman's only clear advantage was its mechanical reliability—which, Allied tankers sourly observed—was best used to stay out of the way of their German opposite numbers.

The Sherman tank and its lighter stablemates were products of a doctrine that regarded tanks not as support or antitank weapons but as instruments of exploitation. Developed largely in response to U.S. tankers' understanding of the German mobile victories of 1939–1940, the Sherman was not intended to engage other tanks directly. That mission was for an entirely separate arm, the tank destroyers. Nor were American tanks expected to be parceled out by battalions among infantry formations. However, neither the terrain nor the enemy the United States faced in Europe in 1944 was congenial to sweeping mobile operations.

Logistics was as important as doctrine in the lack of an American tank with the armor and gun power to face the *Wehrmacht* (German Army) heavies on even terms. Two Shermans could be shipped across the Atlantic for every one of the heavy designs considered during the war. Finally, the sheer pace of events kept stateside policymakers consistently about six months behind the curve of operational experience. The result was a tank whose effectiveness in the war's later stages depended heavily on the fighting power of its crews and the tactical skill of its officers—just the qualities purportedly in short supply among America's civilian soldiers. Yet, the Americans won almost all of the D-Day campaign's armored engagements, from company to division levels. Perhaps they were better than their image.

Viewpoint:
Yes, American tanks were inferior to both German and Russian tanks in most particulars, although comparisons of characteristics are meaningless outside of the complete strategic and operational contexts, in which armored fighting vehicles are only part of a complex system.

Some American tanks were inferior to some German and Russian tanks at specific points in time. By 1944, Russian T-34 tanks had better flotation—the ability to travel cross-country—and a better main gun than the American M-4 Sherman. The German Mk V Panther tank had a better main gun, and superior optics than Russian or American tanks. Both the T-34 and Mk V had better armor than the M-4. However, the M-4 was reliable, easy to operate and repair, and had good optics and radios. None of these three armored fighting vehicles were available at the outbreak of war, and each represented evolutionary changes over the course of the conflict. Every major weapons system is a compromise of strategic requirements, operational concepts, and competing technology requirements.

The slaughter of infantry from the combined effects of artillery, machine guns, and barbed-wire barriers during World War I trench warfare launched a desperate search for some effective way to cross the deadly zone. At first, the tank was only a mobile, accompanying gun platform. "Accompanying gun" meant artillery that could move with the attacking infantry. This basic idea yielded the original concept that the tank was simply a device to overcome enemy machine guns. This concept was retained with special vigor after the war by the Americans and the French, with advocates in the British, Russian, and German armies. The German and Russian militaries, however, also developed strong advocates for more imaginative use of armor; the Americans less so. British Major General J. F. C. Fuller wrote a treatise, *Armored Warfare* (1943), advocating the employment of armor as a fleet of land battleships. The Russians followed suit: Marshall Mikhail Tuchachevsky developed the concept of armor as a form of heavy cavalry. There were advocates for both forms in the American Army, but developments were arrested by factors including an overabundance of left-

over tanks from World War I and such dramatic postwar reductions in forces and funds that experimentation was sharply curtailed. It remained for the Germans first to work through the operational concepts and technical requirements to produce an effective armored force.

Losses during World War I had been so horrific that they drove a demand for vehicles with significant protective armor. This protection was accommodated at the sacrifice of main-gun size. This situation was both a strategic and technical issue. All the main guns operate with recoil systems that must be contained within the limited space of a tank turret and are therefore very heavy. Big main guns and heavy protective armor demand a heavy chassis. At first, automotive technology could not accommodate the competing demands and smaller guns were installed. Here was the first trade-off consideration.

The question of vehicle weight in American tank design revolved around the ability of American highway and military pontoon bridges to carry the contemplated loads. There also was another strategic consideration. As American involvement in World War II seemed increasingly probable, whatever force raised would have to be transported to some foreign shore and landed. The development of the Landing Ship Tank (LST) solved the latter problem, but did so by imposing size constraints. The Russians and Germans, being European land powers, did not have to contend with amphibious considerations. As Russia was a vast country without a solid road infrastructure, the Russians needed vehicles that could travel cross-country. Because they adopted the cavalry concept, they wanted tanks that moved fast. The distances at which engagements were likely to take place in Russia demanded a powerful main gun that had sufficient range.

The combination of these factors with the simple fact that Russian soldiers lacked mechanical sophistication meant that Russian tanks would develop along different lines. At first they developed fast, light tanks that proved eminently suitable for the cavalry-like warfare of the Russian Revolution. The Russian tank-building industry—relatively unsophisticated at first—matured quickly. One of its most formidable products was the KV-1, a heavy tank with a heavy gun, a manifestation that some Russians were still wedded to the accompanying gun concept. The KV-1 moved at the speed of attacking infantry, and its motive system was relatively weak. When the Germans encountered these

A Pz Kpfw III tank rolling past a burning lorry in North Africa, 1941

(Bundesarchive)

weapons they often were able to stop them, but then found themselves confronted with an iron pillbox that required the services of a multipurpose anti-aircraft gun, the high velocity, 88mm *Flugzeugabwehrkannon* (FLAK).

The Americans experimented with a variety of tank concepts and designs. When Dwight D. Eisenhower wrote an article for the *Infantry Journal* suggesting that tanks might have better uses than as accompanying guns for the infantry, he was told by the Office of the Chief of Infantry not to repeat such observations. "Ike" obeyed. The American armor community, however, had other issues to deal with. One was a design for a fast tank invented by Walter J. Christie. His tanks incorporated a high-speed, loose-track design. Because it was at odds with the prevailing climate in the infantry—the proponent for tanks in the American Army—Christie went looking for other buyers. His designs appeared in the Soviet T-34 and earlier series tanks. Christie's design fitted exactly with Soviet concepts demanding speed and high flotation.

German designs went through several important evolutions, shaped first by the strategic fact that Germany too, was a land power. As a consequence, weight was not a serious initial consideration, but an immature German tank industry could produce only light tanks at first. Moreover, German experiments in Russia during the Weimar Republic period identified the need for control that resulted in a higher density of

radios per unit than their Russian hosts appreciated for several more years. Because German youth were more technically proficient than the Russians, more sophisticated mechanical performance became possible. Yet, one must view German armor with care. The first German tanks were little more than armored cars with tracks. They were pitifully small, miserably armed, and vulnerable, but they gave an impression of speed. German armored operational concepts were wedded to the same concept that nearly brought the Allies to their knees during the 1918 spring offensives. Shattering speed was the mode of operation—push forward to the limit of endurance! This element of operational philosophy, plus better battle communications, brought victory to these inferior armored vehicles over the French in 1940. Actually, the French Souma and Char B tanks were superior to most of the hodgepodge collection of experimental and first-run production of second-generation tanks the Germans fielded for that campaign. Early German tanks were equally inferior to the British Matilda Infantry tanks as well, but the manner in which they were employed was the factor that turned the tide to overwhelming victory.

When German general Erwin Rommel arrived in Africa, further developments had occurred and German tanks were nearly up to par with their British counterparts. Rommel was spectacularly successful on more than one occasion because he avoided direct tank-to-tank confrontations and lured British armor into the killing zones of his 88mm FLAK guns, whose efficacy as antitank weapons was first demonstrated in the French Campaign.

By the time the Americans landed in North Africa in Operation Torch (1942), American design had progressed to the point that they possessed a fast cavalry tank, the Stuart. It relied on speed for protection, as its armor was light and its 37mm gun weak; the Germans had discarded that caliber in favor of 50mm and 75mm versions. The American M-3 Grant tanks were an ungainly development with an unusually high silhouette, a side-mounted 75mm gun (reminiscent of the British Mark V of World War I) and a cupola-mounted 37mm gun. Many of these tanks were shipped to the British 8th Army in North Africa. They looked ugly but performed well enough against Rommel's older tanks. After the opening disasters against the Afrika Korps, American operational concepts settled into a balanced, combined-arms approach.

Prior to the American arrival in force, the Afrika Korps had received many tanks mounting the high-velocity, long-barrelled 75mm gun. These weapons, in combination with superior optics, made German tanks formidable opponents. In the meantime, German tank design had moved on and the first large tanks mounting the 75mm high-velocity guns were beginning to enter service. Further variations of tanks emerged, with the Mark V Panther being the most formidable. The Tiger tanks, the first to be armed with the 88mm cannon, were most dangerous opponents but were so mechanically sophisticated that they could not stand field service as well as some of the earlier models. Some of this design proliferation was the product of internal politics in the German armaments industry and particularly the result of intrigues in the house of Krupp. Even at their worst though, later German tanks were mechanically reliable, heavily armored, and armed with weapons equal to any tanks fielded during the war. Further, under competent commanders who adhered to German operational concepts, they were, unit for unit, better than any armored forces fielded during the war.

In contrast, the Russian T-34 and its several variants were superior to early German tanks. They were produced in enormous numbers by a centralized tank-production organization that understood that many thousands of "good enough" tanks were what Russia needed. They were simple and fast. Their 76mm, and later 85mm, guns were more than sufficient. Their tactics were those of the Red Army—masses moving at high speed with tight internal control. Few Russian tanks had radios at first, and platoon fire directed by the platoon leader was the solu-

tion to problems of accuracy and individual control. The Battle of Prokhorovka, a subset of the Kursk offensive in July 1943, was the largest tank battle of the war. In it Russian and German tanks clashed in unprecedented numbers and the Russians came out on top.

When the Allies landed at Normandy in June 1944, many German tanks in the invasion zone were the heavy, Mark V Panthers. American M-4 Shermans were simply not equivalent fighting vehicles. They had less armor and their short 75mm cannon could penetrate Panther armor only at close range. The exchange ratio seemed to be five Shermans for each Panther. The Americans, however, had found a design that was easy to mass-produce, rugged and reliable, reasonably fast, and could be transported across oceans to any shore where an LST could be beached. This logistical capability was a critical design consideration in both the Pacific and Mediterranean theaters of operation, as well as in Europe. Later larger-gunned versions were much more effective.

German tanks fell victim to internal Nazi politics that limited steady production runs of "adequate" designs. They also fell victim to the numbers of their opponents' "adequate" tanks, and to both the Russian and American Air Forces, who hunted them mercilessly. In short, tank developments are only part of a larger equation and straight-line comparisons are often not truly meaningful outside of a larger context. Perhaps the question should be, "How does the armored component of a war-winning army complement the combined arms force?"

—DOUGLAS V. JOHNSON II,
CARLISLE, PENNSYLVANIA

Viewpoint:
No, American tanks were not as inferior as is frequently asserted. They were deficient only in certain performance aspects that were often not vital from a broad perspective.

The viewpoint that American tanks were hopelessly inferior to German tanks is based almost entirely on their relative capabilities during tank-versus-tank engagements against the heavier German tanks—for example, the Panther, Tiger I, and Tiger II. When the standard American medium tank, the M-4 (which, during WWII, was dubbed "Sherman" only in the British Army), faced the heavier German tanks, it was at a grave disadvantage. Simply put, the M-4's

75mm gun could not penetrate the frontal armor of the German tanks at any range, while the German tank's ability to pierce M-4s was limited only by their ability to hit them, given the performance of the telescopic sights of the period. The 76mm gun in later M-4s was only a marginal improvement. As a tactical result, Americans took heavy losses when encountering heavy German tanks while being unable to inflict commensurate damage on the Germans. American accounts of tank-against-tank actions are replete with the disheartening refrain that their rounds bounced off the thick German armor. American soldiers did their best to cope with this disadvantage by attacking with superior numbers, using their maneuverability to get shots at the flanks of the German tanks, and a superior turret-traverse mechanism that was a distinct advantage in close terrain. More desperate measures included ricocheting rounds off the Panther's curved frontal turret armor and through the roof of the hull, or bouncing shots from the ground into the belly armor. German superiority was underlined by the fact that American antitank weapons were just as ineffective as were American tanks against the Panthers and Tigers. At the end of the war the complaints of American tankers reached the media and became the general assessment of the quality of U.S. tanks in history books.

The assessment of complete American inferiority is both inaccurate and unfair. Most importantly, killing enemy tanks was not the main task of the M-4, in theory or practice. In theory, American tanks were intended to perform the dual roles of equipping armored divisions for decisive exploitation and supporting infantry offensives. Doctrinally, the M-4 was not intended to engage other tanks—such actions being the responsibility of tank destroyers that were more heavily armed. Many, at the time and since, disagreed with formation of the tank destroyer units as the primary antitank force of the U.S. army in World War II. Be that as it may, before entering the war the Army determined that it needed battalions of tank destroyers that could be grouped together to defeat major armor attacks. By D-Day, the army had a mixture of towed and self-propelled tank-destroyer battalions. In general, towed battalions were attached to infantry divisions, while self-propelled units accompanied armored divisions. Towed units were armed with 3-inch guns. Self-propelled units had either the M-10 with the same 3-inch gun or the fast M-18 with the lighter 76mm gun. The 3-inch and 76mm guns were different but fired the same projectile with exactly the same performance. By late fall 1944 the M-36s, with the powerful 90mm gun capable of engaging Panthers frontally, were replacing some of the M-10s. The exigencies of combat, however, often resulted in tank destroyers not being readily available when German tanks appeared. Most important, the tank destroyers were defensive organizations in an army with an overwhelmingly offensive philosophy, and the U.S. Army disbanded them at the end of the war.

More germane than doctrinal limitations, tank-versus-tank engagements were not what M-4s did in practice. Only a secondary part of the service that the M-4 contributed to allied victory included defeating enemy tanks. Most students of World War II viscerally believe that tank engagements were large and commonplace during the campaign in northwest Europe in 1944–1945. That assumption is not the case. Those willing to devote the time necessary to study the army's excellent official histories of this campaign will find remarkably few armor engagements. To illustrate this point, at Puffendorf, Germany, in November 1944 the American armored division with the longest experience in the European theater, having seen service in North Africa, Sicily, and France, became engaged, according to Lida Mayo in *The Ordnance Department: On Beachhead and Battlefront* (1968), in the "biggest tank battle in 2nd Armored Division experience." The encounter involved only twenty-five German tanks. As a further illustration of the paucity of tank battles, the Sixth Army recorded that its three-inch guns, intended only for antitank use, fired only 29,210 rounds of armor piercing (AP) ammunition during the northwest European campaign, while expending 337,367 rounds of high explosive (HE). Clearly, engaging German tanks was not a commonplace event or an overwhelming concern after D-Day.

In fact, the most important tasks of the M-4 were the doctrinal ones of supporting soldiers in the infantry divisions with HE and machine-gun fire and participating as the spearhead of U.S. armored divisions—either in attack or exploitation roles. For these missions, the M-4 was an effective tank. Its 75mm gun was an efficient HE weapon, more so than the later 76mm. Just as important operationally, the M-4 was more mobile than its German counterparts—an advantage that was reinforced by its superior reliability. The forty-five to sixty-five-ton German tanks had difficulty with many bridges and were cumbersome in confined areas such as woods or villages. These lumbering tanks were not vitally hampered for the defensive roles they were called upon to perform. The M-4, however, was far superior for fast, offensive operations through all types of terrain. In addition, the M-4 could use tactical pontoon bridges needed for offensive operations. The reliability of the M-4 surpassed the German tanks. This reliability also was demonstrated in the challenging conditions of the

Pacific campaigns that the German tanks of course never had to face. Moreover, the M-4 proved available and adaptable for a wide variety of capabilities never demonstrated by German tanks, such as mine clearing, flame throwing, rocket launching, and amphibian maneuvering.

While denigrated by many as a poor substitute for technological capability, the superior numbers of the M-4 were important. They were vital to the overall Allied war effort because the United States made enough M-4 tanks available to fully equip the U.S. Army and Marines worldwide, while also equipping some 60 percent of British units in Europe and contributing to the Soviet tank force. Numbers were also an important operational counterbalance to the technological superiority of the Germans, even though this fact sometimes reflected itself to American tankers as heavier losses. The small numbers of the expensive and difficult-to-manufacture Panthers and Tigers was a serious weakness. After two years of production for each type, there were only some 1400 Tiger Is and 5500 Panthers. These few technologically superior tanks could not cope with production rates in the United States and the Soviet Union, which put out tanks in the tens of thousands. As a result, until mid 1944 the most numerically important German tank was the 25-ton Mark IV that had no marked superiority over American or Russian tanks. Indeed, contemporary American accounts such as George F. Howe's *The Battle History of the 1st Armored Division, "Old Ironside"* (1954), credit the M-4 with the ability to kill Mark IVs frontally at a range of about one thousand yards.

In sum, while the M-4 was at a disadvantage when engaging Panthers and Tigers, its attributes were a major contribution to ultimate victory over the Germans. Mobility, reliability, numbers, and adequate firepower and armor for what in actuality were its most important combat missions made the M-4 an effective weapon. There was, however, an unfortunate cost in blood for its technological limitations when engaging German heavy tanks.

While complaints of American soldiers were a clear source of the view that U.S. tanks were inferior to German armor, there is no such evident basis for the notion that Soviet tanks were also superior. Obviously, American and Soviet tanks did not face each other in battle during World War II. Encounters between American and Soviet tanks during the Korean War were few and inconclusive. The idea of Russian superiority seems to stem from the Germans who were far more laudatory in their postwar writing about Soviet tanks than American ones. The source of this opinion stems largely from the Soviet T-34 that was the most popular and numerous Russian tank during the war. The T-34 was indeed an excellent tank. When the Germans first encountered them in 1941, they were an unpleasant shock.

At the time of Adolf Hitler's invasion of Russia in 1941, the most important German tanks were the Mark III, armed with a short-barreled 50mm gun, and the Mark IV, then armed with a very low velocity 75mm gun. Neither of the tank's guns nor the standard German antitank gun, also 50mm, could penetrate the T-34's 45mm of frontal armor plate, sharply angled at 60 degrees (doubling its effective thickness). Meanwhile, the T-34's 76mm gun was effective against German tanks, while possessing an effective HE capability. Also, the Russian tank had a powerful diesel engine that resulted in greater mobility, while its broad tracks made it more maneuverable on soft or muddy ground.

The reaction of German tankers was to copy the T-34, but from an industrial perspective this would not have been effective. Instead, the Germans rearmed the Mark IV with a higher velocity gun, spurred the completion of the Tiger I, and began development of the Panther. The rearmed Mark IVs were available for the 1942 campaign, while the Tiger and Panther followed in late 1942 and mid 1943, respectively.

While the T-34 earned a well-deserved reputation for effectiveness during the war on the Eastern Front, it had no marked superiority over the American M-4. The T-34's 76mm gun had performance similar to the U.S. 75mm, and at about the time the Russians began equipping their tanks with the 85mm gun the United States changed to the superior 76mm. Similar armament resulted in similar tactics to counter the heavier German tanks. Russian units took their losses while closing as quickly as possible with the Germans to ranges where the 76mm was effective. Sharply angled armor provided somewhat better protection than the M-4, but by 1943 this offered no comparative advantage since newer German tank and antitank guns were equally effective against Russian or American tanks. Russia's tanks offered superior cross-country performance to the M-4, but even Russians using Lend-Lease M-4s noted good performance in this area. On the other hand, the two-man turret of the 76mm T-34 was a distinct disadvantage from the three-man turret of the M-4 and German tanks. The two-man turret meant that the tank commander, who was also the platoon leader or company commander, had to double as loader for the gun. This duty fully occupied the commander and kept his attention inside the turret. As a result, while the commander was loading the gun, he lost awareness of the tactical situation at the expense of unit effectiveness. The Russians realized that this defect was serious and remedied it in the 85-mm gunned version. Other

TANKS

problems of the T-34 included mechanical imperfections such as a difficult transmission that required drivers to keep a hammer to beat it into gear. In sum, while the T-34 was a good tank, it had no marked superiority over the M-4. Finally, Lend-Lease M-4s used by Russian soldiers did not suffer by comparison with T-34s.

In addition to the T-34, the Soviet Army fielded heavy tanks such as the Klim-Voroshilov (KV-1) and later Stalin tanks. However, these tanks were not nearly as numerous or popular as the T-34. Like the heavy German tanks, these would have outclassed the M-4 in tank-versus-tank engagements but offered less mobility for offensive operations.

In sum, the American M-4 medium tank proved to be an effective combat vehicle for most of the roles it was called upon to perform. As American commanders recalled later, "we won the war with the M-4s." Despite this assertion, it is unfortunate that the U.S. Army did not equip American tankers with a vehicle able to cope with the German Panthers and Tigers and reduce casualties when the big tanks had to be confronted.

—CHARLES M. BAILY, SPRINGFIELD, VIRGINIA

Viewpoint:
No, while Soviet tanks were the best overall vehicles in World War II, the American M-4, produced in large numbers, was not designed to engage the larger German tanks. The M-4 was used by the Allies properly, and it helped to win the war.

At first glance, American tanks of World War II seem to have been markedly inferior to their German and Soviet counterparts. In terms of armor and firepower, the United States never did field a tank that, vehicle for vehicle, was equal to the German Panther or Tiger. No U.S. tank of the war could have stood toe to toe with the Soviet T-34 medium tank or the Josef Stalin (JS) series of heavy tanks (and thankfully, none ever had to). Nevertheless, the U.S. tank arsenal, consisting largely of medium tanks of the M-4 "Sherman" series, did prove capable of getting the job done. The M-4, hailed in the immediate postwar years as the weapon that had won the war singlehandedly (as anyone who grew up in those years can testify), has for the past several decades been unjustly maligned—its defects magnified and its considerable virtues ignored.

The Germans started the war with a quartet of tanks. There were two light models: the *Panzerkampfwagen* (Pzkw) I, a two-man vehicle armed with two 7.92mm machine guns in a small turret; and the Pzkw II, crewed by three men and armed with a 20mm cannon. There were also two medium tanks: the Pzkw III, armed with a 37mm gun; and the Pzkw IV, carrying a short-barreled (and thus low-velocity) 75mm gun. None of these tanks was a wonder weapon; most were inferior to the armor they faced in the French campaign. The triumph in France was not one of superior machines but of superior doctrine for using them. Unchained from the pace of their own infantry, working in close cooperation with the German *Luftwaffe* (air force), German tanks drove through, over, and around the Allied defenses they faced in 1939 and 1940—the years that gave us the word *Blitzkrieg* (lightning war). The incredible successes in the opening year of Operation Barbarossa, in which the Wehrmacht overran most of European Russia and the Ukraine, were also the work of these four tanks, again facing decidedly better tanks in the form of the Soviet T-34—with its 76mm gun, its distinctive sloped armor, and its rugged design—and the heavy Klim-Voroshilov (KV) series.

As the war went on, German and Soviet tanks tended to get bigger, more heavily armored, and more powerfully armed—a reflection of the death struggle in which their two nations were locked. In Germany in 1943, the Pzkw V (Panther) was introduced. In its fully developed model, it had a high-velocity 75mm L/70 gun, the same sort of sloping armor as the T-34, 80mm of frontal armor and 50mm on the sides, and weighed nearly forty-five tons. Yet, with its Maybach V-12 engine capable of achieving some 680 horsepower, it had an impressive top speed of thirty-four miles per hour. Its inauspicious debut at the battle of Kursk (July 1943), the result mainly of being rushed into service, is a well-known story. Still, German designers eventually solved its teething problems, and it remained more than a match for any Allied tank up to the end of the war—a mighty combination of speed and power.

With the Panther as their "medium" tank, and such a designation for a forty-five-ton tank shows how much this term had altered since 1939, the Germans also produced a heavy model, the Pzkw VI (Tiger), later upgraded further into a King Tiger. The Tiger weighed fifty-five tons, mainly because of its incredible armor: 100mm on the front, 60–80mm on the sides, and 110mm on the turret. Its main armament consisted of the powerful 88mm gun, the finest antitank gun of the war. Yet, all this weight and armament came with a price: a speed of just twenty-three miles per hour and sluggish maneuverability. Not for nothing did German crews dub it "the furniture van."

The King Tiger was the heaviest and most powerfully armed tank to see combat in significant numbers in the war, with a weight of sixty-nine tons, 150mm of armor on the glacis, and 185mm on the front of the turret. Its sloped armor was a great improvement over the standard Tiger, but its speed was slightly lower, and power/weight ratio, maneuverability, and ground pressure were all significantly worse. Hauling all that weight also resulted in reliability problems for the overtaxed engine and transmission. Making its debut on the Eastern Front in May 1944, it arrived in the west in August. Here it saw several celebrated episodes of combat, although the small size of its production run (only about 500 produced in all) limited its impact. It does figure prominently in the memoir literature of Allied soldiers, though, proving that it had an impact on morale wherever it appeared.

On the Soviet side, the flexible and sturdy T-34 remained the main battle tank, especially in the upgraded version with a long-barreled 85mm gun, the T-34/85. It too was joined by a heavier design, the JS-1. Based on the old KV chassis, it had 110mm of armor and carried a huge 122mm gun, an adaptation of a field artillery piece. Its accuracy was not great, but it more than made up for it in sheer weight of projectile. Despite its size, the JS-1 weighed just forty-six tons, an achievement that came at the expense of crew comfort and ammunition storage. Later wartime models, the JS-2 and JS-3, had even heavier armor, 160mm and 200mm, respectively, though they paid for it with reduced mobility.

Six months after the start of Operation Barbarossa, by which time the Wehrmacht had fought its way to the gates of Moscow, and the U.S.S.R. had already suffered some four million casualties, the U.S. Army suddenly found itself thrust into a war for which it had only begun to prepare. Its main task was to build an armored force, from scratch, as rapidly as possible. Back in 1940, when news first arrived of the incredible German victory in France, there had been precisely eighteen medium tanks in the U.S. arsenal. These were M-2s, built at the newly opened Detroit Tank Arsenal, armed with a 37mm gun and six machine guns. The army now decided that it needed to have a tank that could match the Pzkw IV in firepower; that meant a 75mm gun. Taking the M-2 chassis, engineers placed a 75mm gun in a sponson on the right side of the hull, to go along with a 37mm gun in a high, small turret on the left. The result was the M-3 "Lee." Although it proved to be a reliable, sturdy tank, it was a clumsy and inelegant design with a high target profile, and the army recognized that it was only a stopgap. The limited traverse of its 75mm gun was the main problem. Still, in its modified "Grant" version (with a lower turret), great numbers served with the armor-starved British in their 1942 campaigns in the Western Desert. At a time when no British tank was able to stand up to its German counterparts, the Grant played a key role in halting the advance of the Afrika Korps at Alam Halfa (2 September 1942) and in punching through the German lines at El Alamein (1 November 1942). Again, just as with the King Tiger, the memoir literature—this time written by German soldiers—testifies to the virtues of the Grant.

While the Lee/Grant held the Allied fort, work began in March 1941 on the M-4 "Sherman," a medium tank mounting a 75mm gun in the turret. The original M-4 had an easily produced welded hull, but there was also a more complicated model with a one-piece cast hull (designated M-4A1). The latter reached the production stage first, in February 1942. For the rest of the war, with the exception of the production of the heavy M-26 "Pershing" tank in the last months (armed with a 90mm gun), U.S. tank design and production consisted of an incredibly diverse series of Sherman variations, a testament to the soundness and flexibility of the original design. Banking everything on the Sherman proved to be a wise choice, allowing for mass production and limiting the amount of time that had to be spent on redesign and retooling. Altogether, 6,748 M-4s and 6,281 M-4A1s were produced through January 1944. Another variant, the M-4A2, entered production in April 1942. It had a welded hull and twin General Motors diesel engines. Since the Army decided that only gasoline-powered tanks would be used overseas, it never entered the American arsenal in any appreciable numbers. The design did not go to waste, however, seeing action as a stateside training tank, and most of the 8,053 produced went to the U.S.S.R. and Great Britain under Lend-Lease. The M-4A3 had a welded hull and was equipped with a 500 HP Ford GAA V-8 engine, the model most favored by the Army. Later refinements of this version included a vision cupola for the commander, a loader's hatch, and "wet stowage" of ammunition, with the ammunition racks encased in water and glycerine to prevent fires. A total of 3,071 were produced. By the end of 1942 there were no less than five Sherman variations in production simultaneously. Later improvements upgraded the armament to a 76mm M1/M1A1 high-velocity gun, mounted in a turret developed for the T-23 series medium tank that had never entered production. Later versions of this effective model introduced a modified 76mm M1A1C gun with muzzle-brake. The 76mm was an effec-

TANKS

tive antitank weapon, though its greater penetration was offset by a lack of effective high-explosive ammunition.

The decision to go with the M-4 has not been without controversy. As many analysts have noted, a Sherman tank confronting a Panther one-on-one, on a flat surface, in the open, was probably moments away from destruction. According to U.S. tank doctrine in World War II, however, that scenario was highly unlikely. U.S. planners saw the medium tank as an infantry-support vehicle. It would help the infantry achieve the breakthrough, then exploit into the enemy's rear and pursue the beaten foe—like the cavalry of old. It was not intended to take on German tanks in a one-on-one gunnery duels.

Foremost among those holding this curious view of armored warfare was Lieutenant General Lesley James McNair, Chief of the U.S. Army Ground Forces (AGF) until his death in 1944. Books written since the end of the war have variously portrayed him as a progressive, innovative military thinker or as a reactionary who opposed the march of progress in the armored sphere. What is clear from the historical record is that McNair, more than any other individual, was responsible for the "tank destroyer" concept. While U.S. medium tanks broke through the enemy's line and exploited into his rear, the job of taking on enemy tanks was left to tank destroyers, "armored gun carriages" mounting antitank guns. In their final stage of development, reached with the M-10 or M-18, tank destroyers evolved into lightly armored, turreted vehicles, whose sole mission was to ambush and destroy attacking enemy tanks.

The conception of a tank-versus-tank duel, McNair wrote in 1943, was both "unsound and unnecessary." Combat had proven that "the anti-tank gun in suitable numbers and disposed of properly is the master of the tank. Any attempt to armor and gun tanks so as to outmatch anti-tank guns is foredoomed to failure." The tank's primary mission, he believed, was "the destruction of those hostile elements which are vulnerable to them—not antitank guns." Predictably, he opposed the production of the T-26 prototype (later the M-26 Pershing tank). McNair therefore stands at the forefront of those whose motto was "We'll win the war with the M-4," the mass-produced Sherman.

The tank destroyer concept was purely American, and for good reason—it simply did not work. The M-10, for instance, lacked any overhead armor at all and was only thinly armored on the sides. It was little more than a "hybrid tank," a neither-fish-nor-fowl creature that often had to carry out missions for which it was completely unsuited (for example, close support of attacking infantry). Whatever the Sherman's

inadequacies, it is indisputable that the U.S. Army would have been better off with more of them—and fewer tank destroyers.

Given McNair's emphasis on the tank destroyer, the new 76mm Sherman (designated M-4A3E6) was obviously something of a departure. By the time it arrived in Europe, however, it was already considerably less than state of the art. Its 76mm gun was inadequate to penetrate the frontal armor of the Panthers or Tigers it was sent to face. In fact, it was barely capable of matching the older Pzkw IV, large numbers of which were still in the German inventory. Against the newer tanks, a Sherman had to maneuver for a shot against the flank or a vulnerable tread.

Compared to the Panther, a Sherman had about the same speed, was drastically underarmored, and decisively outranged. Still, it had its advantages. These included better mechanical reliability in the engine and in the rubber-block track (though these meant little in the heat of actual combat); superior maneuverability, at least when on solid ground; a much higher rate of fire, due above all to its powered traverse and gyrostabilizer, which allowed the gun to maintain its aim and elevation even when the tank was moving; and above all, its greater numbers. A large group of Shermans could surround a Panther or Tiger in order to get the required flank shot. The Panther, of course, could only kill one Sherman at a time.

Another testament to the basic soundness of the M-4 was a fine Sherman variant designed by the British. In a truly bizarre development, the nation that had invented the tank and had arguably spent more time than any other in the interwar period thinking about how to use it most effectively actually had to resort to purchases from abroad to equip its "armoured forces." Unable to sift through their own bewildering array of design ideas and conflicting opinions regarding tank doctrine, the British finally settled on the "Firefly," a Sherman with a powerful 17lb (76.2mm) long-barreled gun. This high-velocity weapon was effective against any German tank up to the Tiger.

In analyzing wartime tank development it is possible to rate the major powers that fought the war in Europe. Obviously, the British came in last. Their own vehicles were so poorly designed that it was necessary to buy tanks from the United States. German armored forces rate higher, but despite their glittering reputation, they suffered from some serious defects. At Adolf Hitler's orders, German industry spent far too much time, energy, and treasure in developing an incredible series of experimental vehicles, the vast majority of which never saw action. More than any other warring nation, Germany seemed wedded to the notion of the "miracle tank." Translated into reality, it usually meant one thing: bigger. The result was the monstrous Tiger tank, with unparalleled armor and armament. No one ever called it the best tank of the war, however. It was quite slow and prone to breakdown, the result of overtaxing its inadequate engine. The defeat at Kursk should have shown Germany the bankruptcy of this policy of "miracle tanks"—but it did not. Despite the German reputation for technical and design expertise, virtually all their tanks had higher breakdown rates than those of their enemies and were more difficult to repair.

The best tank force of World War II belonged to the Soviet Union. Even at the start of the war in Russia, the Germans were surprised by the T-34, with its sloped armor, powerful gun, and impressive cross-country ability, not to mention the heavy KV-1, which sailed through German antitank screens with impunity. Despite the arrival of heavier tanks such as the KV-85 or JS series, the T-34 was the best tank of the war. It proved versatile enough for several roles, and with an upgraded gun (the T-34/85) was capable of taking on any German tank. Soviet doctrine, like American, saw the breakthrough as the province of the infantry, supported by all arms. Soviet infantry, despite its courage and steadfastness, needed all the support it could find to get through the skillfully laid-out German defenses. Once the breakthrough had been made, however, the T-34s were able to engage German armor on something like equal terms. Their crews were no match for the Germans, but the Red Army's combination of great tanks and adequate crews was the recipe for success from Stalingrad to Berlin.

It is more difficult to rank the United States. While certainly not producing the war's finest tank, U.S. planners followed a more sensible strategy than Germany. They designed a solid tank, the M-4 Sherman, stuck with it through a variety of upgrades and alterations, and produced it in staggering mass. Designed to concentrate on the roles of infantry support and exploitation, the Sherman nevertheless found itself face-to-face with Panthers or Tigers more often than any sensible U.S. commander would have liked. Therefore, U.S. armored units sustained heavy casualties against their German adversaries, but superior numbers usually gave them victory anyway.

The Sherman was a versatile, sturdy, and reliable design, capable of mass production and almost infinite variation. The "arsenal of democracy" churned out nearly sixty thousand of them during the war, equipping not only the U.S. Army but America's allies as well. That it was never a "supertank" like the Panther should not

blind anyone to the fact that it did, after all, win the war.

–ROBERT M. CITINO, EASTERN
MICHIGAN UNIVERSITY

Viewpoint: No, U.S. tanks were generally superior to most German models and only slightly inferior to Soviet ones.

In deciding whether American tanks were inferior to German or Soviet models, one must specify when, how, and under what tactical conditions U.S. tanks failed to prove their mettle. American tanks did fall short in armor protection and especially firepower during fighting in Europe after D-Day in 1944—weaknesses that the better armed and armored German Tigers and Panthers did not hesitate to exploit. However, American tanks performed well in 1942–1943 and also during the race across France in 1944, when their superior numbers, adaptability, and reliability perfectly complemented U.S. Army doctrine that stressed maneuver and rapid exploitation. On balance, American tanks proved superior to German tanks and slightly inferior to Soviet models—no mean feat, considering that the Soviets produced the most effective tanks of the war.

Early American tanks included light models such as M-3 Stuarts, but their thin armor and small-caliber guns restricted them primarily to reconnaissance duties. In short order the United States developed the M-3 Grant/Lee series of medium tanks which made their debut in British hands against Erwin Rommel's Afrika Korps in 1942. The Grant/Lee medium tanks combined a turret-mounted 37mm gun with a hull-mounted 75mm gun (U.S. industry initially lacked castings and components needed to mount 75mm guns in turrets) and good armor protection. While M-3s had high profiles and their 75mm guns had restricted arcs of fire, they nevertheless proved effective in combat. In particular, their 75mm guns could fire high explosive (HE) rounds at sufficient range to neutralize German fixed antitank guns (the famed 88s) that had accounted for the loss of so many British tanks earlier in the war.

When one thinks of American tanks during World War II, the M-4 Sherman immediately comes to mind, and rightly so. A medium tank weighing 34 tons armed initially with a 75mm gun in the turret, Shermans formed the backbone of America's armored forces from late 1942

TANKS

until war's end. "We'll win the war with the M-4" ran a popular saying. Rugged, reliable, and simple in design, the U.S. produced 14,000 Shermans in 1942 and 21,000 in 1943; total production reached nearly 50,000 by 1945. Comparing this astonishing figure to German tank production in 1945 (approximately 5,500 Panthers, 1,400 Tiger Is, and 500 Tiger IIs), one immediately recalls the Soviet maxim that "quantity has a quality all its own."

First used in combat by the British Eighth Army at El Alamein in October 1942, the M-4 Sherman at this time was arguably the best tank in service on any front. The Soviet T-34/76 had a lower profile, superior cross-country capability, and was comparably armed, but early models had a cramped two-man turret, a design that overtaxed tank commanders. The closest German competitor, the *Panzerkampfwagen* (Pzkw) IVG with a 75mm gun of 43 calibers, was also comparably armed but possessed thinner armor that was poorly sloped.

Admittedly, the Sherman's superiority was short-lived. By 1943 the Soviets were producing an improved T-34, designated the T-34/85, in large numbers. Perhaps the best tank of the war, the T-34/85 mounted a high-velocity 85mm gun of 51.5 calibers in an enlarged, three-man turret that greatly reduced commanders' workloads. The Germans countered with the Tiger I—a 56-ton behemoth mounting an 88mm cannon protected by four-inch-thick armor—and the more sensible and effective Panther. Whereas the Tiger I was underpowered and difficult to maneuver (its German crews called it "the furniture van"), the Panther was a medium tank of great power (it had a 75mm cannon of 70 calibers with a muzzle velocity of nearly 3,100 feet per second [fps]) superbly protected by up to five inches of well-sloped armor. The Germans, however, rushed both models into battle prematurely. Panthers in particular experienced frightful teething pains during their baptism of fire at Kursk in July 1943. By 1944, however, the Germans had worked out most of the bugs, and Panthers became formidable adversaries.

The M-4 Sherman was criticized, and U.S. Army ordnance officers were condemned, for failing to keep pace with German improvements in 1943–1944 in tank firepower and protection. Such criticisms and condemnations had merit. The Sherman's short 75mm gun of 40 calibers, firing armor-piercing ammunition at 2,030 fps, failed to penetrate the frontal armor of Tigers and Panthers, forcing American crews to maneuver for flank shots. Flanking maneuvers were inherently risky and at times impractical. When they were practical, several Shermans were often tasked to distract German tanks, while others moved stealthily to an exposed flank or rear.

Such tactics often resulted in high losses to tanks assigned to create distractions. As General Omar N. Bradley famously noted, "this willingness to expend Shermans [to defeat German tanks] offered little comfort to the crews who were forced to expend themselves as well."

Besides being outgunned, Shermans lacked adequate armor protection, a weakness exacerbated by their high profile. Tracks were too narrow, leading to high ground pressure and a tendency to bog down in mud and soft sand. Despite being fifteen to twenty-five tons heavier, Panthers and Tigers had wider tracks and thus lower ground pressure. They often traversed ground where Shermans sank and bogged down. Early Shermans also had an unfortunate tendency to catch fire when hit (their crews nicknamed them "Ronson Lighters" because they were guaranteed to light the first time).

American tanks had fallen behind for two reasons: doctrinal and logistical. Of the two, doctrinal reasons were more important, since tactical doctrine drove design. Because the U.S. Army failed to reach consensus on the role of tanks in battle, tank designers lacked clear guidance. The most influential American general, Lieutenant General Lesley James McNair, Commander of Army Ground Forces (AGF), believed American tanks should not engage in tank-to-tank battles. Instead, he believed they should support infantry in breaking through the enemy's lines, then employ their speed and weapons to exploit this breakthrough. In McNair's view, enemy tanks could be defeated more efficiently by antitank guns or by a special class of vehicles—self-propelled antitank guns or "tank destroyers"—deployed in elite battalions.

Logical on paper, McNair's doctrine proved dangerously flawed in battle. Its main flaw was that American tanks could not always avoid confronting German tanks head on. Tank destroyers, moreover, had thin armor and open-topped turrets, making their crews vulnerable to artillery, mortar fire, or even small arms fire. McNair had assumed that German tanks would always attack en masse without infantry or artillery support and that tank destroyer battalions could be deployed quickly to defeat these attacks. In practice, German tanks rarely attacked en masse in France in 1944 due to the Allies' overwhelming air superiority. When they did attack, panzer grenadiers and mortar or artillery fire typically supported them.

McNair's flawed doctrine, therefore, effectively dismissed the Sherman's antitank capability (or lack thereof) as being irrelevant, a conclusion that drove decisions to delay production of more powerfully armed (and also heavier) successors to the Sherman. Yet, the logistical advantage of sticking with Shermans was perhaps more central to the army's decision. Every tank the United States produced had to be shipped overseas; the lighter the tank, the more that could be shipped, together with other essential vehicles and supplies. New tank models, moreover, would require additional crew and maintenance training, spare parts, and ammunition. The U.S. logistical train was not only supporting its own armored units but also those of Britain, France, and Poland as well, all of which also used Shermans. Ultimately, the Army decided to win the war with a standardized and proven design. This decision was not without repercussions for Sherman crews who found themselves staring down the longer barrels of the enemy, but it nevertheless won the war.

That Shermans had become outclassed in firepower and armor was also not clearly grasped before D-Day. As McNair concluded in November 1943, "There have been no factual developments overseas, so far as I know, to challenge the superiority of the M-4." His conclusion reflected the army's lack of experience in fighting the latest German models. As Charles Baily has noted, "There was no great demand from overseas for a better tank than the Sherman until the last months of the war in Europe."

What was not obvious early in 1944—that Shermans were dangerously outgunned—became painfully obvious by July. Even at Normandy in June, Shermans held their own but only because they faced mainly Pzkw IVs and various assault guns. The Germans, moreover, committed few tanks to the fighting in the *bocage* (hedgerow country) precisely because it was poor tank country. As the Allies broke out of the bocage, however, they began regularly to confront Tigers and Panthers. These German tanks exacted a heavy toll, particularly on British Shermans during the Goodwood campaign in July 1944. In tank battles on the Roer Plain in November and during the Battle of the Bulge in December, American units similarly suffered high losses of Shermans to the larger guns of German tanks. The firepower of Shermans may have been adequate for McNair's doctrine of fighting enemy infantry and artillery in the exploitation phase, but it proved inadequate in tank-to-tank duels with Tigers and Panthers.

Given its inadequacies, readers might be excused for concluding that Shermans were in fact inferior tanks. That this was not the case was due to the Sherman's inherent advantages. Ruggedness and reliability were the Sherman's hallmarks. Tigers and Panthers, in contrast, were notoriously unreliable. That the mechanical reliability of Shermans was up to five times greater than its German rivals was a major advantage that made possible the Allies' rapid advance across France in 1944. A power-assisted turret

for speedy gun traverse was another important advantage Shermans had. While German crews were frantically hand-cranking their turrets around, Sherman crews could often fire three or four rounds.

Perhaps the key advantage Shermans had was their adaptability, which made possible significant improvements in combat effectiveness. By D-Day the latest Sherman model mounted a 76mm gun with a muzzle velocity 600 fps higher than earlier models (although earlier models fired a more effective HE round). While these upgunned models still could not penetrate the Panther's frontal armor consistently (unless they fired special high-velocity armor-piercing [HVAP] ammunition that remained scarce until March 1945), they did much to restore crew confidence. Later models of the Sherman, such as the M4A3E8 (known as "Easy Eights"), incorporated wider tracks for greater mobility, wet stowage of ammunition to inhibit onboard fires, improved suspensions, and more sharply angled frontal armor. A special assault version of the Sherman, the M4A3E2 "Jumbo," had a much thicker hull and turret armor and proved highly successful. Sherman crews also found ways to augment the M-4's armor by attaching tracks and sandbags to vulnerable areas of the hull. Ironically, the British produced the best armed Sherman of the war, the "Firefly," by incorporating 17-pound (76.2mm) guns that fired solid shot at 2900 fps, making them equal in firepower to Panthers.

Crew skill and tactics also went some way toward neutralizing Germany's edge in firepower and armor. In fighting German tanks, Dmitriy Loza, a hero of the Soviet Union, found that rapid attacks from the flank or at night often resulted in a winning edge. The Germans had learned similar lessons during their invasion of France in 1940. Like American Shermans, German tanks of 1940 generally had thinner armor and less powerful guns than their British and French counterparts. Using combined arms, including close air support, German tank divisions nevertheless outmaneuvered and defeated French and British forces that had them outnumbered and outgunned.

German victories in 1940–1941 showed that big guns and thick armor were not everything. Under certain conditions, however, German weaknesses could be exposed and exploited; the same is true of American tank weaknesses in 1944. Experienced German armored units, and later their American counterparts, stayed alive and won battles by avoiding conditions where enemies could expose and exploit these weaknesses.

How, then, did U.S. armored units compensate for weaknesses? Close air support, artillery,

"GOD, THIS IS GONNA HURT"

Robert Hagerty, a sergeant in A Company of the 712th Tank Battalion, remembers a particular encounter with a German Tiger tank late in the war.

We were in . . . a crossroads with some farm buildings and a few little homes. We needed an outpost, and I went up on a side road and pulled off to the right. There was a little culvert where the farmer had cut a path through to move the wagons and horses.

We could see up ahead. There were some buildings on fire. Sometimes things like that are set on fire by the infantry, maybe they create a kind of a super searchlight, and then the Germans aren't going to come through and expose themselves while they're high-lighted like that.

The fires were up the road, the road was kind of a gentle rise, and an infantry guy came running toward us. He said there's a halftrack coming. So we thought, "Halftrack, boy oh boy, where is she?" Big Andy was my driver. He eased the tank back off of the road.

A fellow named Ted Duskin was my gun-ner. He swings the gun out, and lays it up the road. And through this smoky haze that the fire is making, here comes this German, but it ain't no halftrack. It's one of the big tanks. And I just remember thinking, "God, this is gonna hurt." Because he saw us I'm sure as soon as we saw him. Ted shot right away, as soon as that bulk came through the haze, and he must have hit the turret, there was a big shower of sparks. They were heavily armored in the front, and they were only really vulnerable in the rear.

About a second after we fired, he fired, and a big lick of flame came out of the muzzle of the gun, and it hit our tank. It seemed to hit it down low in the carriage, it made a hell of a sound, and suddenly, the German began to move backward into the smoke. How lucky can you be? We quickly took a look at our tank, and one of the bogey wheels appeared to be almost severed. He hit us down low. It glanced off, fortunately for us, and with the track still being intact, Andy could ease her

back, and we eased her back down that slope, and this German didn't come after us. But talk about being scared, before he made that first shot. . . . They had the firepower. They could penetrate us; we couldn't pene-trate them until we got a larger gun.

After we backed down, around a little curve in the road there was a little rock wall, and there was enough room for us to get in there. Ahead of us, against the same rock wall, was a tank destroyer. They had light armor, but they had a bigger gun than we had, so they could knock out a German tank, which we couldn't. So as soon as we got behind the destroyer, I ran out and told the destroyer's tank commander what was prob-ably going to be coming down the road, so he could get a good shot at it. The German doesn't know the tank destroyer is here.

First thing you know, we could hear little click-clicks. That's about all the noise their tracks made, click-click, they were real quiet. We would make lots of noise, and we'd give ourselves away. He's coming down here, and he had a dismounted soldier leading him. Imagine having that as your job, because this guy's dead the first time he's seen. But he's gonna take the fire and spare the tank. So this foot soldier comes down here with a rifle, and as the tank creeps up behind him, the guy in the tank destroyer fired too soon. It went right across the front of him, missed him, and with that, the Germans threw it in reverse, and went back up the hill. And of course the tank destroyer didn't go after him because he couldn't afford to take a hit, he would lose. But I think Andy and I were genu-inely scared, when we saw that halftrack turn into a big German tank.

Source: Tanks for the Memories: An Oral History of the 712th Tank Battalion in World War II, *edited by Aaron C. Elson (1994), World War II Oral History Web Site.*

TANKS

and tank destroyers often tipped the scales in their favor. Enjoying air superiority, American P-47 Thunderbolts and British Hawker Typhoons often accompanied Allied armored units, firing cannons and rockets and dropping bombs to destroy or damage German tanks. American heavy artillery proved particularly effective at disrupting German armored attacks and killing or wounding accompanying infantry. Despite their thin armor, tank destroyers also did useful work. Especially effective was the M-18 "Hellcat," whose top speed of 55 mph and 76mm gun made it both difficult to hit and effective in flank attacks. Also effective were older M-10s armed with the same 76mm gun mounted on Shermans. By September 1944, M-36 tank destroyers armed with 90mm high-velocity guns began to arrive at the front-line. Along with the Sherman Firefly, the M-36 was the weapon of choice against thick-skinned Tigers and Panthers.

In 1945, however, complaints by Sherman crews that the army had failed to keep pace with German improvements, thereby forcing them to fight at a disadvantage, were aired publicly in *The New York Times*. Such concerns highlight a uniquely American attitude toward technology and war. Soviet leaders showed few qualms in sacrificing men and matériel in prodigious quantities to overwhelm Germany. Overwhelming the enemy with numbers, however, was a less than respectable way of winning for Americans. "Second best but good enough" was not a motto in which Americans took pride. In weaponry American soldiers expected the best, and their government usually proved willing and able to spend treasure to avoid spilt blood. Told in 1944 that their Shermans remained the best tanks in the world, soldiers were at first shocked and then outraged to see their shots ricochet off Tigers and Panthers. The shock of being "second best but good enough" (good enough when aided by artillery, close air support, or tank destroyers) led to postwar recriminations and an exaggerated sense that U.S. tanks were inferior to the enemy's.

Such was not the case. If anything, M-4 Shermans reinforced American strengths and traits. Shermans were reliable, rugged, effective tanks that could be mass-produced in quantity. Their robust design and high-quality components mirrored the very attributes of ruggedness, endurance, and adaptability possessed by their crews. Indeed, one might commend the army for conserving resources by resisting the temptation to build monster tanks or a needless multiplicity of models, a temptation to which Germany fully succumbed. By concentrating on producing Shermans, the army had sufficient resources left-over to produce large numbers of jeeps, trucks, and half-tracks. With these the army mechanized complete divisions, fulfilling the dreams of armor advocates such as Germany's Heinz Guderian. By combining fully mechanized infantry divisions with large numbers of reliable, redoubtable, and resilient Shermans, the U.S. Army hit on the right formula to win the war.

–WILLIAM J. ASTORE, U. S.
AIR FORCE ACADEMY, COLORADO

References

Charles M. Baily, *Faint Praise: American Tanks and Tank Destroyers during World War II* (Hamden, Conn.: Archon Books, 1983);

Omar N. Bradley, *A Soldier's Story* (New York: Holt, 1951);

Robert M. Citino, *Armored Forces: History and Sourcebook* (Westport, Conn.: Greenwood Press, 1994);

Belton Y. Cooper, *Death Traps: The Survival of an American Armored Division in World War II* (Novato, Cal.: Presidio Press, 1998);

Duncan Crow and Robert J. Icks, *Encyclopedia of Tanks* (London: Barrie & Jenkins, 1975);

F. J. Deygas, *Les Chars D'Assaut: Leur passe, leur avenir* (Paris: Charles-Lavauzelle, 1937);

George Forty, *M-4 Sherman* (Poole: Blandford Press, 1987);

Forty, *Tank Warfare in the Second World War: An Oral History* (London: Constable, 1998);

Christopher F. Foss, ed., *Illustrated Guide to World War II Tanks and Fighting Vehicles: A Technical Directory of Major Combat Vehicles from World War I to the Present Day* (London: Salamander, 1977);

John F.C. Fuller, *Armored Warfare Military Classics IV, An Annotated Edition of Lectures on F.S.R. III (Operations Between Mechanized Forces)* (Harrisburg, Pa.: Military Service Publishing, 1943);

Christopher R. Gabel, *Seek, Strike, and Destroy: U.S. Army Tank Destroyer Doctrine in World War II* (Fort Leavenworth, Kan.: Combat Studies Institute, U.S. Army Command and General Staff College, 1986);

Constance M. Green, Harry C. Thomson, and Peter C. Roots, *The Ordnance Department: Planning Munitions for War* (Washington, D.C.: Office of the Chief of Military History, 1955);

Heinz Guderian, *Erinnerungen eines Soldaten* (Heidelberg: Vowinckel, 1950), translated by Constantine Fitzgibbon as *Panzer Leader* (New York: Dutton, 1952);

TANKS

J. P. Harris and F. H. Toase, eds., *Armoured Warfare* (London: Batsford; New York: St. Martin's Press, 1990);

George F. Howe, *The Battle History of the 1st Armored Division, "Old Ironsides"* (Washington, D.C.: Combat Forces Press, 1954);

R. P. Hunnicutt, *Sherman: A History of the American Medium Tank* (San Rafael, Cal.: Taurus Enterprises, 1978);

B. H. Liddell-Hart, *The Red Army: The Red Army, 1918 to 1945* (New York: Harcourt, Brace, 1956);

Dmitriy Loza, *Commanding the Red Army's Sherman Tanks: The World War II Memoirs of Hero of the Soviet Union, Dmitriy Loza,* translated and edited by James F. Gebhardt (Lincoln: University of Nebraska Press, 1996);

K. J. Mackesy, *Afrika Korps* (New York: Ballentine, 1968);

Macksey, *Panzer Division: The Mailed Fist* (New York: Ballentine, 1968);

Macksey and John H. Batchelor, *Tank: A History of the Armoured Fighting Vehicle* (London: Macdonald; New York: Scribners, 1970);

Lida Mayo, *The Ordnance Department: On Beachhead and Battlefront* (Washington, D.C.: Office of the Chief of Military History, 1968);

F. W. Von Mellenthin, *Panzer Battles: A Study of the Employment of Armor in the Second World War,* translated by H. Betzler and edited by L. C. F. Turner (Norman: University of Oklahoma Press, 1956);

Richard M. Ogorkiewicz, *Armor: A History of Mechanized Forces* (London: Stevens, 1960);

Douglas Orgill, *Armoured Onslaught: 8th August 1918* (New York: Ballentine, 1972);

Orgill, *T-34: Russian Armor* (New York: Ballentine, 1971);

Bryan Perrett, *Fighting Vehicles of the Red Army* (New York: Arco, 1969);

Walter J. Spielberger and Uwe Feist, *Panzerkampfwagen VI, Tiger I and II Koenigstiger* (Berkeley: Feist Publications, 1968);

Steven J. Zaloga, *The Sherman Tank in U.S. and Allied Service* (London: Osprey, 1982).

TANKS

U.S. ASIA POLICY

Did U.S. boycotts and economic sanctions push Japan to World War II ?

Viewpoint: Yes, U.S. economic sanctions against Japan were viewed as a threat to economic and territorial expansion by the Japanese military, who then felt compelled to adopt a plan to acquire needed resources and fight the United States if necessary.

Viewpoint: No, the economic embargo imposed on Japan by the United States was more of a pretext than a real factor in the coming of World War II, as the Japanese had a long-standing plan to expand their empire in the Pacific.

For most of the 1930s the United States's Asian policy was cautious. While regularly protesting Japanese treaty violations and challenges to U.S. rights and interests, the government also sought to avoid provoking Japan— at least unilaterally and publicly. President Franklin D. Roosevelt, however, strengthened the navy, sought to improve the self-defense capabilities of the soon-to-be independent Phillippine Islands, and negotiated with the British for joint action in case of war. When in 1938 Japan denounced the naval treaties and challenged traditional U.S. policy of an "Open Door" to China, Roosevelt responded by providing trade credits to Chiang Kai-shek's hard-pressed government. In July 1939 the United States took a much stronger step. It gave notice of intent to terminate its commercial treaty with Japan.

The American challenge was not to Japan's security but to its aggression: modify the unacceptable behavior and the economic status quo would be sustained. The nationalists and militarists controlling Japan's policy making, however, saw the end of the trade treaty as both a deadly threat and a mortal insult. A resource-poor island country, Japan depended heavily on imports to sustain a war machine already suffering overstretch from its enmeshment in China. The Japanese navy in particular was able to calculate almost to the day when it would be unable to refuel its ships should the United States take matters a step further and establish a trade embargo.

The collapse of France in 1940 offered an apparent alternative to direct confrontation. The Japanese military moved south, occupying French Indonesia and putting pressure on the now-isolated and oil-rich Dutch East Indies. At the same time Japan placed large orders in the United States for steel, scrap metal, and aviation gasoline. Roosevelt first restricted, then banned, the exporting of scrap and of an increasing number of other raw materials. He held back from embargoing oil, fearing that move would provoke a Japanese attack at a time when the United States was primarily concerned with its Atlantic frontiers and its European diplomatic relations.

That concern inspired a massive naval program. Though not aimed at Japan, when completed, Japanese naval strategists believed that it nevertheless would reduce Japan's fleet to strategic impotence. At the same time, recent German victories seemed to offer a window of opportunity to seize an empire at minimal cost. Japan's leaders increasingly accepted the inevitability of war with the United States as the price of expansion. They ignored repeated U.S. overtures for negotiation and accommodation. By June 1941 the decision to go to war with the West had been made. The freezing of Japanese assets by the United States in July, which amounted to a de facto oil embargo, only confirmed Japan's course.

Viewpoint:
Yes, U.S. economic sanctions against Japan were viewed as a threat to economic and territorial expansion by the Japanese military, who then felt compelled to adapt a plan to acquire needed resources and fight the United States if necessary.

The image of Japan backed into a corner during the 1930s by American boycotts and sanctions, finally lashing out in desperation to begin a war that it had few chances of winning, was a staple of anti-Roosevelt politics and revisionist historiography for a quarter-century after 1945. In recent years a more sophisticated understanding of Japan's internal dynamics has diminished the intellectual appeal of what is at bottom a fairly crude economic-determinist interpretation of the island empire's behavior in the decade preceding Pearl Harbor. Nonetheless, a core of credibility remains that cannot be denied. America's use of its economic power to create diplomatic leverage may not by itself have impelled Japan to war. It was, however, part of what Colin S. Gray calls, in *The Leverage of Sea Power: The Strategic Advantage of Navies in War* (1992), a "malign synergistic effect" that transformed an ordinarily ambitious, acceptably authoritarian maritime power into an ideologically centered would-be Pacific hegemon.

Japan began its modern existence by modeling itself on Great Britain, another island empire that had used judicious blends of manufacture, trade, and force to achieve power well beyond what its natural resources, human and material, could support. The naval alliance of 1902 was paradigmatic for a focus that, however, encountered increasing resistance from Western powers unwilling to accept a new associate and rival. Japan's industrialization, rapid and comprehensive though it was, could not secure a comprehensive footing in a tightening global market. Heavy industry in particular remained domestically focused. The export products—inexpensive textiles at one end of the spectrum, limited-production luxury items at the other—that defined the Japanese economy were correspondingly vulnerable to external shocks and disturbances.

Even before World War I an alternative school of thought advocated Japan's transformation into a land power—specifically at the expense of China. Initial ambitions of that kind were focused more on commercial expansion and acquiring land for settlement than with developing China's natural resources for Japan's benefit. Perspectives began to change with the emergence of a Soviet Union perceived as both a physical and ideological threat.

In the aftermath of World War I the Japanese Diet, strongly influenced by the business community, successfully sought to curb military and naval budgets criticized for falling between two stools: financing armed forces strong enough to inspire fear among Japan's neighbors, yet insufficient to win a general war. There was enough truth in the analysis that both the army and the navy sought to increase not only their strength, but also the resource base supporting that strength. The naval limitation treaties of the interwar period combined with the Great Depression to limit expansion in material terms. Frustration, however, only increased appetites in both armed services.

That frustration was made clear in 1931, during the first, abortive effort to "coordinate" China. By 1937, for all the hostility that existed between the army and navy, they were agreed in principle that Japan confronted a bleak choice between enhancing the resources under its direct control or resigning itself to second-rank status. The mechanization of land warfare; the increasing displacement of the oil-fueled ships that were a modern navy's heart; the emergence of aviation as a third military element, even more high-tech than its fellows—all combined to demand either expanded political influence or wider access to global markets.

Unfortunately for Japan's purposes, China proved both refractory and retrograde. Within eighteen months of Japan's invasion of China in July 1937 it was clear that far from finding China a springboard to modernization, Japan—at least the army and its air arm, were demodernizing to meet the demands of even minimal control of the parts of China it occupied. Any doubts on that score were eliminated in a series of border clashes with the U.S.S.R. (11 July–10 August 1938), in which Japanese bayonets proved no match for Soviet medium tanks.

At that point the United States took a hand—and by Japanese standards took sides as well. A generalized public sympathy for China in no way carried over into willingness to risk war. Nevertheless, the increasingly internationally minded administration of Franklin D. Roosevelt had no intention of seeing Asia slide into chaos as a consequence of Japan's imperial overstretch. U.S. criticism of Japanese policies, publicly and through diplomatic channels, rekindled a hostil-

Curtiss P-40s of the Flying Tigers squadron in South China

(U.S. Air Force)

ity dating to the turn of the century, when the United States had been widely perceived as committed to frustrating Japan's ambitions—not from its own greed, which would be understandable, but from a sense of moral and racial superiority.

In practical terms at least, the antagonism was one-sided. American public opinion, racist though it might have been, considered the Japanese more a joke than a foe. The two navies had long been each others' principal adversaries in terms of planning and construction, but American senior officers drank no toasts to an inevitable confrontation. There was still room for accommodation when war broke out in Europe in September 1939. Nor did Japan take immediate direct advantage of the discomfiture of its European rivals eight months later. Instead, it used the new situation to increase China's international isolation—a policy that drew the United States correspondingly closer to Chiang's increasingly ramshackle government.

The next stage in the progress of hostility to war was taken by the United States. The naval construction program of July 1940, while not aimed at Japan, would when completed create such an imbalance of forces that the Japanese navy had no chance of waging even a defensive campaign in its own waters. Any attempts to minimize that fact seemed refuted in September,

when an administration still seeking to avoid war—at least in the Pacific and at least temporarily—began imposing restrictions on its trade with Japan. Intended to send a message, the sanctions were initially minimal, involving scrap metal more than essential raw materials such as oil. The questions in Tokyo were whether they would remain so benign and what right the United States had to impose them in the first place.

In the first months of 1941 Japan increased its pressure on the Dutch East Indies and French Indochina, left exposed by the collapse of their European governments. Roosevelt's government protested, then on 25 July announced the limitation of oil exports to Japan and the freezing of Japanese assets in the United States. It should be emphasized that the new policy was intended neither to drive Japan into collapse nor to force it over the brink. In a very real sense, however, the United States had no idea how fine-tuned Japan's economy really was. After 25 July the Japanese navy in particular could calculate almost to the barrel and the date the point when their ships would be unable to operate.

Apart from the fact that with its funds blocked Japan could not even buy on the international market—which by 1941 in any case meant the United States—no sovereign state was likely to accept passively the kind of demeaning insult offered by the sanctions. After the July embargoes the question whether to go to war gave way in Japanese planning circles to three lesser ones: when, where, and how. And the United States, increasingly focused on the threat from Germany, was still unaware of what it had done in the Pacific, charted its own unreflective course towards Pearl Harbor.

–DENNIS SHOWALTER, COLORADO COLLEGE

Viewpoint:
No, The economic embargo imposed on Japan by the United States was more of a pretext than a real factor in the coming of World War II, as the Japanese had a long-standing plan to expand their empire in the Pacific.

Following the defeat of Japan in World War II, many authorities and historians began the process of assigning blame for the outbreak of the Pacific war. While Japan clearly struck the first military blow, some argued that the United States had actually precipitated the conflict by conducting economic warfare against Japan. According to this argument, once the United States cut off the flow of oil, a critical resource both for Japan's military and its civilian economy, Japan had no choice but to go to war to prevent economic collapse. In reality, Japan had many years previously decided to risk war to secure its complete freedom of action. The economic policies of the United States had no impact on Japan's decision to go to war.

Japan made the conscious decision to turn itself into a modern world power following the American "opening" of Japan by Commodore Matthew Perry in the mid-nineteenth century. By the beginning of the next century, Japan had achieved great-power status, complete with a modern army and navy. Japan's defeat of Russia in the Russo-Japanese War (1904–1905) confirmed this status. A decade later, Japan confirmed its great-power status by joining the Allies in defeating the Central Powers. While Japan's role was minor, seizing Germany's Far Eastern possessions, it proved that Japan had become the only Asian state that could rival Europe's Great Powers.

At this moment of triumph Japan saw its status as a great power threatened and even disappearing. While Japan fought on the victorious side in World War I, Japanese analysis of the military lessons of that conflict indicated it

might be Japan's last victory. World War I represented a fundamental change in warfare. European wars since the days of Napoleon had been won or lost in relatively short periods of time with generally light casualties. Most Europeans and Japanese ignored the counter-example of the American Civil War (1861–1865), and the foreshadowing of modern, industrial war that it provided. Japan's most recent experience with war, the Russo-Japanese War, followed the expected pattern. Japanese victory was secured with two brilliant naval battles, Port Arthur (2 January 1905) and Tsushima Straits (27–29 May 1905), exploited with limited-scale land assaults.

World War I, which Japan entered with such optimism, proved that technology had ended the days of quick victories. On virtually all the major fronts the war became a bloody battle of attrition, where the path to victory lay through a graveyard. The winning side kept pouring men and matériel onto the battlefield until their enemies could no longer stand the strain. While the German armies on the Western Front were in retreat at the time of the armistice, Japanese analysts traced the defeat of Imperial Germany not to battlefield reverses but to her inability to obtain vital war materials to supply forces at the front and keep the civilian economy producing. By the end of the war, Germany was short of every critical material, including food, despite having claimed a large piece of Russian territory under the terms of the Treaty of Brest-Litovsk (3 March 1918). Germany simply could not make up for the loss of materials from its prewar overseas trade, which the British blockade ended. The verdict seemed clear—a modern war of attrition would result in defeat for any state that did not have guaranteed access to critical war materials.

This conclusion did not bode well for Japan's future as a great power. The home islands are largely devoid of natural resources, forcing Japan to rely on overseas trade to supply raw materials for an industrial base. Japan was not self-sufficient in any critical material, including food. Even those resources under Japan's direct control, such as its fishing fleet, were vulnerable to outside attack.

Japanese leadership saw before it two choices in the wake of the revelations of World War I. First, Japan could abandon great-power status and ambitions, and hope that foreign goodwill would suffice to provide the materials Japan needed to prevent economic collapse. They could almost dismiss this option out of hand. To achieve great-power status and maintain its independence from imperial powers, Japan believed it had relied only on its own

HIDEKI TOJO EXPLAINS THE WAR

On 27 July 1942, Japanese premier Hideki Tojo broadcast a message to the Japanese people, explaining his country's actions in the Pacific war. The following is a portion of that radio speech.

On this occasion I should like to pay my respects to the people in whose hearts were instilled the destiny of the nation brought about by the memorable date of December 8, 1941. Here then the nation became strongly united, burning in the hearts of every subject the disposal of the objective of the Greater East Asia war. . . . As for the Imperial Government it has complete confidence in the people, and whatever task is undertaken the government approaches with a feeling of sacrifice of Japan. . . .

The government is carrying out policies only necessary under the war-time situation. The world situation today is undergoing changes with bewildering rapidity, and in coping with the rapid and radical changes and in meeting the needs of the armed forces the question of peace and order internally must be dealt with most adequately and must be settled most speedily. The government after giving every consideration to the domestic and external conditions is taking steps to cope with the situation at an appropriate time by means of simplifying the functions of government offices and by arriving at a closer cooperation among the offices. This has been exemplified by the supply of needed men sent throughout the Greater East Asia sphere with government duties to perform. . . .

In order to fight through the war to victory, it is exceedingly important to expand the strength of the armed forces and to establish security in the living conditions on a minimum basis, while carrying out a policy to protect the home front through the efforts of the people at home. As a policy the government is expending every effort in the increase of production of foodstuffs, fuel, materials, and other fields, as well as in the firm establishment of a war time national structure. It is of primary importance that the living conditions of the people be made completely secure and undoubtedly there will be some inconvenience imposed on the people. Among the belligerent nations today there is no other country where living conditions are more blessed than the present conditions existing in Japan. At this time I should like to mention the cooperation of (sea transportation) which concerns the security of the people's living conditions. Sea transportation is utilizing every possible opportunity and is extending a priceless cooperation toward establishing security of the people's living conditions by making sacrifices which are not few. While fighting is in progress, sea transportation is exerting itself in bringing gasoline, sugar, and other goods to the Japan mainland. Such in the spirit of service under the present war situation, and for this rendering of outstanding service we must feel grateful. On this occasion, I wish to express with you our sincere appreciation to the sea transportation service . . . .

At this time, when the nation is confronted with an unprecedented crisis, national structures applicable in the southern regions must be established with some enthusiasm on the part of the people. . . . It is of great importance that the people throughout the nation unite into a ball and go forward in order to spread the Imperial Way throughout the world. Before the August Virtue of His Imperial Majesty, the people must strive toward the establishment of a new world order and at the same time must establish peace. We must by all means complete our sacred mission of this war. . . .

Today I am proud to stand before you with a thought that I am exerting my efforts in a lifelong mission. Because I have passed the last 40 years in the military, fortunately as you see I am robust and healthy. I am determined to give further service for my country by keeping myself physically fit, training my body and mind. Total effort must be collected in the form of total strength and I believe the objective of the Greater East Asia war will be realized with certainty. At the conclusion I wish to thank you again for the cooperation you have extended thus far and I beg of you to extend your continued efforts. I pray for your health. I wish to conclude my talk.

efforts. While Japan had relied on Prussian advice and assistance to create a modern army, and the British had provided the same for the navy, Japan tended to downplay this assistance and developed an ideology that emphasized self-reliance. Failure to maintain economic independence from western powers could lead only to either complete subjugation as a colony of some foreign power, or a tenuous existence in the balance between powers, such as that which China maintained to its detriment.

Japan's other option was vigorously advanced by a rising group of economic thinkers. This path was of autarky or economic self-sufficiency. In choosing this path, Japan would seek to achieve absolute, unbreakable control over any and all vital resources. Thus, no outside power could use economic pressure to bring Japan in line with its own plans, and, in the event of war, Japan could fight a modern war from a position of equality with any great power. Japan's model for autarky was the United States, which had within its boundaries sufficient stocks of virtually every major material needed to wage and win a modern war, and those it lacked were, for the most part, readily available in other Western Hemisphere nations, close at hand and subject to American pressure.

The Japanese decision to pursue autarky was influenced by its leaders' view of their position in the world. Japanese leaders perceived, correctly, that Europeans and Americans did not consider the Japanese their equals. Japanese citizens were subject to immigration restrictions in many countries, including the United States. Japan had built a niche for itself in the world economy by producing inexpensive goods for export, resulting in the perception of Japanese goods as inferior to European or American goods, a perception that carried over into Japanese industry and technology in general. If Japan would not be treated as an equal partner, despite its military successes, then Japan could not trust others to provide needed raw materials.

The final, deciding factor that placed the Japanese on the path to autarky and war was the Great Depression. With the advent of the Depression, many countries began increasing existing tariffs and raising new trade barriers in an effort to protect domestic industry from foreign competition. Such efforts only worsened the Depression for all by encouraging retaliatory measures, but such trade barriers placed Japan in a critical situation. The European empires closed off foreign trade with their colonial possessions, including their Asian dominions, to ensure all the benefits of the colonial trade accrued to the home coun-

try. Japan only survived by making drastic cuts in its domestic economy. It now appeared that Japan was not only in danger of economic ruin in case of war; indeed, ruin was at the door now. To the Japanese leadership, autarky seemed the only possible course to pursue.

In pursuit of this objective, Japan developed a vision it called the Greater East Asia Co-Prosperity Sphere. This concept combined anticolonialism, antiracism (or perhaps reverse-racism), and Japanese autarky. Under Japanese leadership the Asian peoples would unite and eject European and American colonial powers, leaving "Asia for the Asians." Japanese treatment of Koreans, Filipinos, Chinese, and other Asian peoples who fell under Japanese control during World War II showed this vision to be more a tool to achieve Japanese hegemony than any sort of "Asia for the Asians," but the rhetoric was powerful.

With the decision to pursue autarky made, Japan now became impervious to any sort of economic threats or sanctions. Any attempts made to influence the course of Japanese policy through economic pressure would be ignored, as they would only confirm the Japanese leadership's belief that Japan must become economically self-sufficient or become a puppet of foreign states. At the same time, the failure to use such tools would not be seen in Japan as a gesture of restraint or good intentions. Japan felt that the only possibility other than collapse and subjugation was autarky, and any goodwill gestures designed to change that course would be ignored.

The Japanese decision to pursue autarky led to the Pacific War. In order for Japan to achieve self-sufficiency, it must have absolute control of sources of all vital war materials. All such supplies within Japan's reach, however, were already under the control of other nations—the Soviet Union, China, France, Great Britain, the Netherlands, or the United States. Japan would have to use intimidation or force to secure these resources. Mere treaties or guarantees would not suffice, for they could be broken at the most disadvantageous moment for Japan. Indeed, worldwide, many such agreements were broken during the Great Depression. The use of force to secure the resources of East Asia placed Japan in direct conflict with vital interests of the United States.

The United States had long been committed to an "Open Door" policy in China, meaning all powers would be free to trade in China. Both the United States and Japan were signatories to the Nine-Power Treaty (1922), which guaranteed equality of economic opportunity in China, as well as guaranteeing China's territorial integrity and sovereignty. Much of the rest of Southeast Asia was under the control of European colonial powers. While the United States was in general opposed to imperialism and favored the eventual independence of Asian colonies on the pattern proposed for the Philippines, the United States also felt an Axis victory in Europe would be devastating to American security. The United States began providing war materials to the enemies of Germany and Italy, and, though it was inconsistent with anticolonialism, sought to ensure the resources of the Asian colonies continued to flow into Europe to aid the Allied cause. The United States could tolerate neither the subjugation of China nor the diversion of colonial resources away from the war in Europe. Once Germany brought the Soviet Union into the war by invading in 1941, American policy took on an added dimension. For the Soviets to stave off defeat they needed to transfer troops and equipment from the Soviet Far East, where they guarded the border with Japanese-controlled Manchuria, renamed Manchuokuo. Thus, the United States, to continue its policy of preventing an Axis victory in Europe needed to ensure the Japanese did not expand into the Soviet Far East and divide the Soviet Union with their German and Italian allies. American and Japanese policies were on a direct collision course.

Japan could not be persuaded to give up its ambitions of autarky by any measure short of military defeat. The Japanese leadership would not trust any other nation to provide its critical economic resources. Thus, any American efforts to influence Japanese policy were doomed to failure. Neither the presence nor absence of sanctions, nor their severity or leniency, could influence the Japanese drive to autarky. The United States would no more abandon its vital interests in Asia than Japan would. War was inevitable. All that could be influenced was the timing. Japan would go to war with the United States at the point where it seemed further peace efforts would no longer yield economic contributions to Japan's drive for self-sufficiency.

—GRANT T. WELLER, U.S. AIR FORCE ACADEMY, COLORADO

References

Michael A. Barnhart, *Japan Prepares for Total War: The Search for Economic Security, 1919–1941* (Ithaca, N.Y.: Cornell University Press, 1987);

Dorothy Borg and Shumpei Okamoto, with the assistance of Dale K. A. Finlayson, eds., *Pearl Harbor as History: Japanese-American Relations, 1931–1941* (New York: Columbia University Press, 1973);

Robert J. C. Butow, *Tojo and the Coming of the War* (Princeton: Princeton University Press, 1961);

Gordon Daniels, "Japan – 2. Domestic life, economy, and war effort," in *The Oxford Companion to World War II,* edited by I. C. B. Dear and M. R. D. Foot (Oxford: Oxford University Press, 1995): pp. 607–611;

Herbert Feis, *The Road to Pearl Harbor: The Coming of the War Between the United States and Japan* (Princeton: Princeton University Press, 1950);

Colin S. Gray, *The Leverage of Sea Power: The Strategic Advantage of Navies in War* (New York: Free Press; Toronto & New York: Macmillan, 1992);

James William Morley, ed., *The Fateful Choice: Japan's Advance into Southeast Asia, 1931–1941: Selected Translations from Taiheiyo Senso e no michi, kaisen gaiko shi* (New York: Columbia University Press, 1980).

ULTRA

Was the role of Ultra decisive in the outcome of the war in Europe?

Viewpoint: Yes, Ultra was decisive because it gave the Allies crucial information about enemy strategic plans, troop dispositions, and logistics.

Viewpoint: No, although Ultra had significance it was only one aspect of Allied intelligence efforts.

The Allied effort to break Axis codes during World War II was known as Ultra and the key to its success in Europe was German overconfidence. The German Enigma machine was developed between the wars and its code was regarded as unbreakable, to the point where German communicators often failed to take normal security precautions in its use. The first steps in breaking it were made by Polish intelligence. The British continued the effort, periodically assisted by matériel captured from German ships and submarines. The initial research was done at Bletchley Park, a top-secret facility staffed with eccentric intellectuals. After the attack on Pearl Harbor (1941) the United States established a counterpart at Arlington Hall.

The problem was taking advantage of the information. For the first two years of the war, the British often lacked the resources to exploit their knowledge. Ultra, however, was significant in assisting fighter control during the Battle of Britain (1940), and came fully into its own during the Battle of the Atlantic (1941–1945), both in enabling convoys to avoid U-boat wolf packs and, as Allied resources grew, directing hunter-killer teams against the submarines themselves.

Beginning with the Battle of El Alamein (1942), Ultra also consistently influenced land operations. The invasion of the European continent posed some problems because of the German use of alternate means of communications. Controlling modern battle, however, was impossible without radio. First in Italy, then in Normandy, the Allies were able to keep well abreast of German intentions. Intercepted German communications were also a major source of information on the Eastern Front.

Electronic intelligence had drawbacks as well. One involved processing the information collected—sorting the useful from the useless. Another was lead time. Whenever the Germans recalibrated their machines as part of normal security procedures, the flow of data ended until the new settings were solved. This problem in turn highlighted the risks of becoming militarily addicted to Ultra. The Ardennes offensive (1944) achieved much of its surprise because the German preliminary planning was done by telephone lines rather than radio. Special intelligence could become a touchstone, the absence of which was taken to mean that nothing important was happening.

Viewpoint:
Yes, Ultra was decisive because it gave the Allies crucial information about enemy strategic plans, troop dispositions, and logistics.

The best-kept secret of a tell-all age has certainly been the Allied success in decrypting German high-level radio intelligence throughout World War II. Never even hinted at in thirty years of increasingly polarized discussions of who did what between 1939 and 1945, the first revelations of the Ultra secret and its ramifications in the early 1970s inspired a wave of revisionist books and articles claiming that Ultra had won the war in Europe. In its extreme form this thesis virtually ignored such factors as technology, command, and numbers. It was quickly modified to make special intelligence no more than one among many factors, moral and matériel, that had contributed to Allied victory. A case can be made, however, that the Ultra pendulum has swung too far towards the middle. If an enduring ability to read Axis mail did not by itself decide the European war, radio intelligence arguably played, at crucial times and in crucial circumstances, the kind of pivotal role that makes the word *decisive* legitimate in discussing its significance.

Ultra's initial impact was operational. When the Poles turned over the fruits of years of research and espionage to the French and British in August 1939, initial responses were unenthusiastic. That Poland had finally broken Enigma, the electronic coding machine that was the basis for the Reich's top military ciphers, was not deemed an important development: electronic intelligence was not considered vital to the conduct of the kind of total war projected by the military staffs of the Western Allies. Winston Churchill, here as in so many other areas, took the initiative, establishing and sustaining a major decoding center at Bletchley Park, then virtually forcing its material on the service chiefs. Ultra decrypts convinced Field Marshal Lord Gort to prepare the Dunkirk evacuation in May 1940 that rescued the British Expeditionary Force from German encirclement. During the Battle of Britain (1940) special intelligence kept an outnumbered Royal Air Force (RAF) aware of both the general intentions and the specific directions of the German air campaign. Before the United States threw its shipbuilding capacities into the Battle of the Atlantic (1941–1945), Ultra held a ring around U-boats that were commanded and coordinated electronically.

In each of these cases Britain stood on a knife's edge, with no military resources to spare

for a major defeat and with a political commitment to the war that was by no means as absolute as it has been depicted in subsequent mythmaking. Remove Ultra from the equation and negotiated peace—or at least a crippled war effort—becomes a credible possibility. At least as much to the point, Ultra gave Britain something to trade the United States in the dark months of 1941, when foreign exchange was exhausted and American goodwill ephemeral. It represents no denigration of the Churchill-Roosevelt connection to assert that the special relationship was founded on special intelligence particularly welcome to a U.S. Navy considering how to fight an undersea war on a scale exceeding any previous plans. Ultra information was also a crucial element of the intelligence data exchanged with the Soviet Union from 1941 to 1945—an exchange that involved a good deal less reticence on the part of the Western Allies than subsequent revisionist accounts suggest.

As the Battle of the Atlantic developed after the attack on Pearl Harbor, Ultra's monitoring determined when Allied naval and maritime codes were compromised, continually leaving the U-boats and their high command flailing about the North Atlantic in search of convoys to strike. As Allied escort forces grew in size and sophistication, Ultra kept track of U-boat positions and of the operational orders issued by Admiral Karl Dönitz's headquarters. The process was not continuous. Periodically German revisions of their cyphers left Bletchley Park and its newly created U.S. counterpart blinded. The darkness, however, was always temporary. How many merchant ships that supported D-Day in 1944 and went on to sustain the Pacific War would have been sunk without Ultra? The question is rhetorical because the tonnage is incalculable.

Ultra's initial contributions to the Allied war effort were negative; they kept worse things from happening. In the North African campaign (1942–1943) they became positive. The theater's remoteness led the Axis to rely almost entirely on radio communications. British field commanders used intercepted signals to cripple the Italian fleet at Cape Matapan (1941) and to intercept and destroy an increasing number of the supply ships on which General Erwin Rommel's Afrika Korps depended. Bernard Montgomery, convinced of Ultra's value by his experiences with Home Forces, used it in Africa to structure the decisive battles of Alam el Halfa (1942) and El Alamein (1942). By that time Ultra's moral impact was as significant as its operational contributions. The British, and eventually the Americans, were well aware that defeating the European Axis meant defeating the German army. Ultra became a hole card—not by itself a guarantor of victory, but a generalized

A 3-wheel German Army Enigma machine

Ultra's major contribution to the cross-channel attack was its interception of Berlin's communications with its intelligence network in Britain. Every single agent was arrested, neutralized, or doubled; the Germans were completely and consistently deceived about virtually every aspect of invasion planning. Once the Allies were ashore, Ultra provided news of the movement of Hitler's Panzer reserves—notably into the abortive counterattack at Mortain. Between the breakout from Normandy and the advance to the Rhine, Ultra continued to keep Allied commanders up-to-date on German positions and intentions. British and U.S. generals were legitimately reluctant to become militarily addicted to a source of information the Germans could choke off at any time by modifying Enigma. The root of the intelligence problem, however, lay in the growing tendency of senior Allied commanders from Eisenhower downwards to believe that their generalship would flourish independently of electronic eavesdropping. The first serious consequence came at Arnhem (1944), when Ultra provided information of a heavy concentration of German armor in the sector and it was ignored by Montgomery and downplayed by Eisenhower. The subsequent Ardennes counterattack (1944) owed much of its surprise effect to the German use of landlines. Nevertheless, Hitler's order to suspend the use of Enigma as part of the security measures for the offensive should have attracted more intention than it did. In an electronic intelligence campaign, negatives can be as important as positives—and failures of omission can have serious consequences. Ultra's absence was as important as its presence in determining the outcome of the European war.

—DENNIS SHOWALTER, COLORADO COLLEGE

confidence-booster, of vital importance as U.S. and British ground forces sought their footing against a formidable opponent.

This mindset prevailed even when, during the landings on Sicily (1943) and the Italian campaign (1943–1944), the Germans inadvertently improved their communications security by making increased use of landlines. At strategic levels, Ultra kept the Allies informed of Adolf Hitler's policies. Operationally it provided precise, detailed German orders of battle, facilitating the maneuvers that led to the breakthrough at Monte Cassino (1944). Ultra furnished just enough tactical-level information on troop movements and orders to enable the thwarting of the February 1944 attack on the Anzio beachhead that came close to throwing the Allies into the sea. Ultra, in short, fully earned its place at the center of the plans for Operation Overlord, the invasion of Northeast Europe in the summer of 1944.

Viewpoint:
No, although Ultra had significance it was only one aspect of Allied intelligence efforts.

Ultra, the code name given to the intelligence derived from the intercepting, decoding, and interpreting of the German military signals of the Enigma encyphering machine, was not decisive to the outcome of the war in Europe. However, it was a crucial part of an overall intelligence operation against Nazi Germany by Great Britain during the war that included espionage operations, subterfuge, imagery, signals intelligence, and, in one case, the planting of a dead body with false documents

OPERATION MINCEMEAT

In order to deceive the Axis powers about Allied intentions to invade Sicily, British intelligence came up with a plan called Operation Mincemeat. The body of a staff officer with important documents detailing Allied invasion plans of Sardinia and Greece would be allowed to float ashore in Spain where German spies were known to be active. Ostensibly, the fictitious Major William Martin, Royal Marines, was a victim of drowning following an airplane crash. (He had actually died of pneumonia a few days earlier.) On 19 April 1943, the submarine HMS Seraph surfaced one mile off the coast of Spain near the mouth of Huelva River. The body of Major Martin was taken out of a dry-ice canister, put in a Mae West life jacket, and set adrift. British authorities soon received word that a Spanish fisherman had recovered the body. When the major was returned to the British for proper burial, it was found that his briefcase had been carefully opened and the contents photographed.

The false document that caused the Germans so much concern is reproduced in part below. It is a letter to General Sir Harold Alexander of the 18th Army Group. To further the deception, Operation Husky (the real code name for the invasion of Sicily) is used in reference to operations in Greece while Operation Brimstone is used for the planned invasion of Sardinia. Within a few weeks, the Allies knew that the deceit had worked because Adolf Hitler ordered that "measures regarding Sardinia and the Peloponnese take precedence over everything else."

Personal and Most Secret

My Dear Alex,

I am taking advantage of sending you a personal letter by hand of one of Mountbatten's officers, to give you the inside history of our recent exchange of cables about Mediterranean operations and their attendant cover plans. . . .

We have had recent information that the Boche have been reinforcing and strengthening their defences in Greece and Crete and C.I.G.S. felt that our forces for the assault were insufficient. It was agreed by the Chiefs of Staff that the 5th Division should be reinforced by one Brigade Group for the assault on the beach south of CAPE ARAXOS and that a similar reinforcement should be made for the 56th Division at KALAMATA. We are earmarking the necessary forces and shipping.

Jumbo Wilson had proposed to select SICILY as cover target for "HUSKY"; but we have already chosen it as cover for operation "BRIMSTONE". The C.O.S. Committee went into the whole question exhaustively again and came to the conclusion that in view of the preparations in Algeria, the amphibious training which will be taking place on the Tunisian coast and the heavy air bombardment which will be put down to neutralise the Sicilian airfields, we should stick to our plan of making it cover for "BRIMSTONE"—indeed, we stand a very good chance of making him think we will go for Sicily—it is an obvious objective and one about which he must be nervous. On the other hand, they felt there wasn't much hope of persuading the Boche that the extensive preparations in the eastern Mediterranean were also directed at SICILY. For this reason they have told Wilson his cover plan should be something nearer the spot, e.g. the Dodecanese. Since our relations with Turkey are now so obviously closer the Italians must be pretty apprehensive about these islands.

I imagine you will agree with these arguments. I know you will have your hands more than full at the moment and you haven't much chance of discussing future operations with Eisenhower. But if by any chance you do want to support Wilson's proposal, I hope you will let us know soon, because we can't delay much longer. . . .

Best of luck.

Yours ever,

Archie Nye.

Source: *Ewen Montagu,* The Man Who Never Was *(Philadelphia: Lippincott, 1953), pp. 38–41.*

to fool the Germans into moving troops from Sicily prior to the invasion there.

British intelligence processing, evaluation, and exploitation during World War II took place exclusively in a converted manor house at Bletchley Park. This site was where some of the finest analytical minds (mathematicians, chess champions, and musicians) in Britain fought their part of the war: "reading the Germans' mail" or breaking the enemy communications codes, allowing them to know what the Germans were planning. By itself, this information did not win the war, but used properly, it did help dramatically—making its first real appearance in the Battle of the Atlantic (1941–1945) and then assisting greatly in North Africa.

The British encountered the German codes throughout the war. They intercepted the German transmissions frequently, but not until the Polish resistance sent a captured Enigma machine to the British were they actually capable of reading the messages in their entirety. After this coup, it was a matter of time to break the codes and some luck that showed up in 1940 in the form of captured code books.

In intelligence operations there is a peculiar struggle between safeguarding the existence of a source of information and being able to use the information for one's purpose. The British understood this well and instituted strict controls on using Ultra. They limited the number of people with access to Ultra; they ensured that no one with access to Ultra was placed in a position where they might be captured; and they ensured plausible deniability or the ability to have another source of information.

With the advent of unrestricted submarine warfare in mid 1940, German U-boats entered a time in which they were sinking ships with virtually no resistance. The U-boats, hunting in wolf packs, devastated the transatlantic shipping so vital to the British war effort. In just one four-month period of 1940, the British lifeline suffered a loss of 217 ships and just over 1 million tons of matériel.

While the British lost the beginning of the Battle of the Atlantic, it also gave the Royal Navy its first real victories with Ultra decoding. Bletchley Park was intercepting and decoding Ultra from the *Luftwaffe* (German air force), but the *Kriegsmarine* (German navy) used different codes; therefore, they needed to capture or acquire its code books, which is exactly what happened in early 1940. Ultra did not win the Battle of the Atlantic—the crews of the convoys and the improved escort ships actually did—but it did assist in antisubmarine operations, and the lessons learned along with the naval code books were used in the coming fight in the Mediterranean, which was crucial to the end of the war itself.

Even though British commanders were informed of General Erwin Rommel's plans in North Africa, through Ultra he ran circles around their forces while he had sufficient fuel. Cracking Ultra allowed the allies to defeat Rommel's Afrika Korps, but this defeat was due more to the fact that it had insufficient matériel. General Bernard Montgomery did not really beat the German general or outmaneuver him through his own genius, but rather Rommel ran out of fuel and supplies because of Ultra.

The British began by intercepting German radio traffic from North Africa and establishing their plans and intentions. Since they could not seem to defeat Rommel head

on, and realizing that he had difficulty supplying his army so far from friendly support systems, the British decided to attack his lines of communications where they were most vulnerable and where the British were more powerful: at sea.

The British, using Ultra gleaned from captured naval codebooks, specifically targeted German convoys headed to North Africa in order to cripple Rommel's army. They were so successful that they actually decided to allow some shipping through to maintain plausible deniability. Their usual method was to determine, through Ultra, what the convoy route would be, send up a spotter aircraft and ensure it was seen by the German ships who would make a report to their headquarters, then send in the Royal Navy to attack. This process worked so well that in one instance, British authorities were forced to send a "well done" message to a fictional agent in Italy in a code they knew the Germans could read so that they would not know the code was broken.

The Allies won in North Africa, due in no small part to Ultra, and this was absolutely critical to the outcome of the war in Europe for several reasons. The Germans needed the oil for their military campaigns, but more importantly, the British and Allied victory in North Africa gave them will to continue the fight. Africa also provided vital staging areas to jump off into Sicily, Italy, and southern Europe, without which invasions of those areas would have been impossible.

The effects of a German victory in North Africa would have been absolutely devastating, especially after the debacle in France in 1940, the "near miss" of the Battle of Britain (1940), and the pounding the Royal Navy and merchantmen were taking in the North Atlantic. Churchill would probably have been ousted, which could have even meant negotiations with the Axis powers. Clearly, the war in Europe could have been won without total victory in North Africa, but the cost would have been astronomical.

In the long run, reading German mail was vital, even decisive, in North Africa. Beyond this fact, it was not absolutely critical to the outcome of the conflict as few, if any factors, can truly be decisive in a total war. It is always an advantage to learn enemy plans and intentions in war—a great deal of victory comes down to how much you know. Yet, Ultra did not warn of the counterattack in late 1944—the Battle of the Bulge. While Ultra did not win the war, it was one of many important intelligence factors that assisted in the overall victory, saving lives in the process.

—WILLIAM KAUTT, SAN ANTONIO, TEXAS

ULTRA

References

William Casey, *The Secret War Against Hitler* (Washington, D.C.: Regnery Gateway, 1988);

F. H. Hinsley, *British Intelligence in the Second World War* (Cambridge & New York: Cambridge University Press, 1993);

Hinsley and Alan Stripp, eds. *Codebreakers: The Inside Story of Bletchley Park* (Oxford & New York: Oxford University Press, 1993);

David Kahn, *Seizing the Enigma: The Race to Break the German U-Boat Codes, 1939–1943* (Boston: Houghton Mifflin, 1991);

Thomas D. Parrish, *The American Codebreakers: The U.S. Role in Ultra* (Chelsea, Mich.: Scarborough House, 1991);

Bradley F. Smith, *The Ultra-Magic Deals and the Most Secret Special Relationship 1940–1946* (Novato, Cal.: Presidio Press, 1993);

Gordon Welchman, *The Hut Six Story: Breaking the Enigma Codes* (New York: McGraw-Hill, 1982);

Frederick William Winterbotham, *The Nazi Connection* (New York: Harper & Row, 1978);

Winterbotham, *The Ultra Secret* (New York: Harper & Row, 1974);

John Winton, *Ultra at Sea: How Breaking the Nazi Code Affected Allied Naval Strategy during World War II* (New York: Morrow, 1988);

Richard A. Woytak, *On the Border of War and Peace: Polish Intelligence and Diplomacy in 1937–1939 and the Origins of the Ultra Secret* (New York: Columbia University Press, 1979).

ULTRA

VERSAILLES TREATY

Was the Treaty of Versailles responsible for the rise of Hitler and Nazism in Germany?

Viewpoint: The terms of the Versailles agreement were too harsh on Germany, contributing to the economic depression and revival of nationalism that occurred during the Weimar Republic.

Viewpoint: The rise of Hitler and Nazism in Germany was more the result of structural weaknesses inherent within the Weimar political system than of the humiliating terms of the Versailles treaty.

The treaty concluded at Versailles to end the Great War of 1914–1918 has been widely blamed for fostering the subsequent emergence of National Socialism. The treaty's indemnity and reparations clauses are cited for causing the successive financial crises that destabilized the Weimar Republic. Its requirement that Germany assume sole responsibility for the conflict, the "War Guilt clause," is seen as an insult to national pride permanently discrediting the Republic that accepted it. Yet, at the same time, Versailles left the essential elements of German power intact and maintained Germany's existence as an independent state. The result was a peace that fell between two stools. Neither conciliatory nor punitive, it fostered the confusion and destabilization on which the Nazis thrived.

An alternative approach to developments in Germany after 1918 sees the source of the country's economic crisis not in the Versailles treaty but in the economic policies adopted to fight World War I. This view interprets Germany's rejection of the Republic in antidemocratic attitudes and ideas deeply rooted in German society, exacerbated by a comprehensive, officially encouraged effort to present Germany as a victim of Allied vengefulness. The amount of reparations was less significant than Germany's determination to do no more to fulfill its obligations than it was compelled to do.

Scholarly reassessments of the Versailles treaty increasingly depict it as the best possible compromise given the existing circumstances. Its framers regarded it as a work in progress, with the simultaneous tasks of solving the immediate problems arising from the war and establishing the framework of an enduring international system. The treaty was subject to revision and modification in both principle and practice. It gave Europe over a decade of stability and provided a workable basis for negotiations between Germany and its former enemies. Had the Great Depression not struck Europe when it did, the process of peaceful adjustment under the mantle of Versailles might have gone even further.

**Viewpoint:
The terms of the Versailles agreement were too harsh on Germany, contributing to the economic depression and revival of nationalism that occurred during the Weimar Republic.**

"A fearful and gloomy existence awaits us in the best of circumstances!" So wrote historian Friedrich Meinecke in October 1918 as he and his countrymen looked with great anxiety to the end of World War I. His statement summed up the collective sense of the entire German nation quite well. The conclusion of the conflict failed to bring about the establishment of a long-term peace. Of the treaties that comprised the Peace of Paris, the Treaty of Versailles in June 1919 brought with it several elements that antagonized and disconcerted Germany. By failing to conclude a peace in which all participating parties could agree, the victorious Allies ensured that the future of Europe would be filled with dissension about the harsh terms of the agreement.

The Treaty of Versailles, which the Allies concluded without any German representation, gave German lands outright to France, Belgium, Poland, and to the League of Nations to administer. The treaty removed all German colonies from Berlin's control, and did the same to much of Germany proper, including the Saarland and the Rhineland. The German Army was capped at one hundred thousand men, with severe constraints on research, development, and training. Finally, Article 231 of the treaty forced Germany to accept responsibility for causing the war and for all of the damage and destruction that occurred in Europe from its aggression. These incredibly harsh terms greatly alienated Germany from the new world order that the victors envisioned and indeed laid the foundation for the rise of radical political elements in Germany, of which Adolf Hitler's National Socialist German Workers' Party (Nazi Party) proved to be the most successful. As Thomas Mann, the great German novelist, wrote, "having been robbed, the Germans became a nation of robbers." German people greeted the conclusion of the Versailles treaty with shock and indignation. This immediate and antagonistic reaction had two important results: the rise of German nationalism and the beginning of an economic crisis that led to disenchantment. In the end, the harsh terms of Versailles led the German people to support the radical policies of Hitler and the Nazis.

The one element of the Treaty of Versailles that perhaps inspired these feelings of betrayal and angst was Article 231, the War Guilt Clause. That article forced Germany to accept not only the responsibility for the war, but also for the prewar posturing and diplomatic aggression that culminated in the world conflict. This notion particularly galled most Germans, who felt that they had suffered as much as any other people during the four years of fighting; certainly Germany bore no more guilt for the war than any other European power. They simply could not accept the argument that they had started the war. Upon hearing the terms of the treaty, Philipp Scheidemann, a Social Democratic leader not known for radical nationalism, exclaimed, "What hand will not wither that delivers us into such chains?" With this attitude prevailing among the moderate German statesmen, what could the reaction possibly be among the more conservative and bellicose?

German nationalism was a delicate topic from the end of the war and was closely tied with the problems that arose within Germany regarding the questions of whose fault it was that Germany lost the war. With members of the conservative parties and military supporters blaming socialists and liberals for stabbing the German nation in the back, the Weimar Republic was established on rocky footing. The publication of the terms of Versailles hardly helped this unsettled genesis. Within Germany people tended to view the deliberations with at least a modicum of good faith, notwithstanding the fact that no German representative had been invited to the treaty conference. When the harsh nature of the terms was disclosed, it unleashed a flurry of anger in Germany, particularly against American president Woodrow Wilson.

Germans took Wilson's call for self-determination for all peoples to include Germany, too. Many Germans believed that the Allies had betrayed them. Self-determination apparently applied only to those countries who had been opposed to Germany. Worse still, large amounts of territory were taken away from Germany, and even regions that remained part of Germany proper were placed under foreign administration, including Austria, the Saarland, and the Danzig Corridor. The formulation of a League of Nations, led by Great Britain and France and excluding Germany, further solidified this sense of betrayal. It did not help matters that the two European leaders of this new organization soon engaged in a diplomatic race to exert their own authority over Germany's former colonies. In German eyes, the League became nothing more than a

Allied delegates leaving the railroad car in which they signed the Versailles Treaty; Hitler later used the same car to negotiate the surrender terms of France in 1940

(Associated Press)

tool of anti-German territorial enforcement. The German population began to feel that they now stood alone against an antagonistic world in the face of grave, and possibly fatal, threats to their national existence. Similar thought processes helped lead the country toward a policy of passive resistance in the Ruhr in 1923.

The Versailles treaty further stoked the embers of German nationalism by imparting an intense antagonism toward France and anything French. The hostility and enmity between Germany and France became particularly bitter, standing out among the former combatants of World War I. French leaders made no secret of the fact that they desired, first, a permanent peace and, second, a German nation that never again could dominate the Continent. The French did not appear to want a lull in hostilities or a resumption of a world with a balance of power; they wanted full power on the Continent. Subsequent events bore this fear out to Germany. Even some French leaders seemed to foresee the problems, as French marshal Ferdinand Foch remarked despondently and with disturbing foresight: "This is not peace, it is an armistice for twenty years."

The Versailles treaty also drove Germany into the arms of Hitler and the Nazi Party through the stringent application of monetary reparation payments, as well as the arbitrary and high-handed way the Allies forced them upon Germany. The publishing of British economist John Maynard Keynes's *Economic Consequences of the Peace* (1919) publicly served notice that reparations would be a problematic issue from the outset. In this pamphlet, Keynes stated emphatically that Germany could not pay back the initial demands and that this would lead to global financial turmoil. While the accuracy of this argument can be debated, its impact on the people of Germany cannot. Keynes's thesis was emblematic of the German peoples' cry of unfair treatment. The monumental difficulties of making the payments provided a mental justification and legitimization of their belief that the victorious Allies punished them unfairly. As if it were a harbinger of things to come, the debate over reparations did not die down, as many on the Allied side had hoped it would following an ever-lengthening period of peace. On the contrary, all sides continued to debate the issue hotly for the next thirteen years until payments were discontinued in 1932 as a result of the Great Depression.

While German representatives at least were invited to most of the deliberations on the reparation schedules, Allied leaders seldom paid much heed to their input. Unchanging factors in the Allied camp continued to alienate Germany in the diplomatic realm and also made clear to them that they would continue to be required to pay unconscionably high amounts in reparation. First, the French continued to insist that Germany pay for the physical damages of the war. In the French view, western-front warfare had been conducted chiefly on French soil. Flanders and Northeast France had been devastated by the war, and the victors did not believe it their own responsibility to pay for rebuilding. Second, while Great Britain and the United States were antagonistic toward French demands concerning payments, British leaders were unsuccessful in their efforts to persuade France to reduce their demands. Great Britain saw itself as one of the leaders in the postwar world and desired to reincorporate Germany into the community of nations. Only through such a reincorporation could a healthy global-economic system and structure be reestablished. The United States, for its part, had lapsed into a strong isolationist stance, where the actual damages paid by Germany to the European powers was of distant importance to American policy objectives. These objectives comprise the third constant: the United States insisted on repayment of its war debts owed by its allies, particularly France. American demands inspired European powers to pass on the burden to Germany through high reparation payments, deepening the German feeling of helplessness and resentment.

All of this early rancor reached a crucial point in 1923 with the Ruhr occupation and the German policy of passive resistance. The economy in Germany steadily grew worse, eventually devaluing to an exchange rate of 4.2 trillion marks to one U.S. dollar. When the *Rentenmark* (stablized mark based on land values) stabilized the economy during the final months of 1923, many Germans realized they had been wiped out or deeply affected by the repercussions of hyperinflation and the gradually eroding economic situation since the war years. Those Germans who had worked hard all of their lives and had earned enough money to invest or save found their efforts nullified in a single blow. Labor unions found it difficult to protect the jobs of their members and the movement lost much of its power and influence built up in the previous fifty years. Many of the disillusioned would become attracted to new, more radical political parties. In the words of Gordon Craig, in *Germany, 1866–1945* (1978), "Among those groups who had been actually or psychologically expropriated, the resentment was lasting and was reflected in political attitudes hostile to democracy." The Nazi Party benefited greatly from these feelings.

The reparation debate did not go away. Ongoing debates led first to the Dawes Plan in August of 1924, then to the Young Plan in 1929, then, after the stock-market crash of 1929, to the temporary moratorium on payments in 1931. Finally, the Allies completely terminated all payments in 1932 at the Lausanne Conference (16 June–9 July). The debate continued to fuel acrimonious feelings in Germany, as Germans maintained that they had been swindled even as the French insisted that somehow they had failed to receive their due. The German-French enmity deepened over the reparation debates, as the two countries constantly contended throughout the 1920s over the amount and schedule of German reparation payments, figures the French always seemed to want to increase. The almost gleeful French and Belgian "invasion" of the Ruhr in January 1923 and imposition of foreign troops on Germany that followed surprised few, and it led to the German policy of passive resistance, an important outlet for the expression of German spirit. That tactic also caused two significant events that greatly facilitated the rise of Hitler: the climax of hyperinflation and the fall of Gustav Stresemann as chancellor.

There was no easy solution or smooth transition to a post-reparation world, and the debate left lasting scars on the German psyche. The coming of the Great Depression and the ending of reparation payments ended the direct impact of the Versailles treaty on the future of Germany. Its indirect and long-term effects, however, had serious consequences. The feeling of hopelessness and the singular stance against the rest of the free world that Germans felt led to a surge in German nationalism. The failure and unwillingness of the victors to consider a modification of the treaty over the ensuing decade and a half turned this nationalism into the driving force behind new German conceptions of nation and purpose. Economic hardships continually and disdainfully imposed by the Allies on a defeated power had effects far beyond its negative impact on the financial stability of Germany, for the instability it bred helped to ignite the radical party politics, in many cases precisely in those social groups most likely to be antiradical. The Treaty of Versailles, and the many ill feelings it fostered, turned many German citizens to the radical politics of Hitler and the Nazi Party.

–MICHAEL A. BODEN, U.S. MILITARY ACADEMY, WEST POINT

Viewpoint:
The rise of Hitler and Nazism in Germany was more the result of structural weaknesses inherent within the Weimar political system than of the humiliating terms of the Versailles treaty.

On 30 January 1933, Hitler, the Führer of the Nazi Party, was invited by President Paul von Hindenburg to become Reich Chancellor. In only ten years Hitler's party had come from being merely one of many on the right-wing fringe of Weimar politics, with its leader jailed for treason, to the strongest party in the Reichstag and the leader of German government. Within several years of his appointment, Hitler had dismantled the Weimar system completely and set up a dictatorship that would control Germany absolutely until 1945. Hitler's nomination in 1933 marked, if not the beginning of the end of the Weimar Republic, then at least the end of the beginning of its fall.

The Weimar Republic, Germany's first attempt at democracy, emerged in 1918 from the ruins of the German Empire after Kaiser Wilhelm II was forced to abdicate on 9 November by the nearly victorious Allied powers and revolution at home. From its beginning it faced several severe challenges, which the new republic would not be able to master completely and would eventually result in its collapse. First, although the abdication of Wilhelm had paved the way for an armistice with Germany's enemies, a peace treaty had to be negotiated that would bring an end to the war once and for all. Second, and perhaps most crucially, the new government faced enduring hostility from a wide range of political opponents from both the right and the left—opponents committed to bringing the democratic system to an end. Third, the structure of the government of the Weimar Republic contained weaknesses that allowed it to be challenged from within. The Republic had inherited, and indeed depended upon, the organs of state and political elites from the old Empire that were hostile to the democratic system, most notably the civil service and army. The cumulative effect of these challenges, rather than any one single cause, undermined the Weimar Republic to such an extent that, when faced by severe economic and social crises in the late 1920s and early 1930s, it would be unable to master the final assault of Germany's right-wing forces, ultimately led by Hitler and his Nazi Party.

Wilhelm's abdication allowed the signing of an armistice between Germany and her western enemies. These agreements had to be followed by a formal peace treaty, which was drawn up at a conference held in Versailles, France. The terms of the Treaty of Versailles, designed to punish Germany for World War I and prevent a future German offensive war, were exceptionally harsh and extremely humiliating. First, under the guise of "self-determination," Germany was forced to give up territory, some of which had been German for hundreds of years. In the west, Alsace-Lorraine, seized from France during the Franco-Prussian War of 1870–1871, was returned to France. Additionally, the Rhineland and the Saarland on Germany's western border were occupied and demilitarized, and parts of Schleswig-Holstein were given to Denmark. In the east, parts of Silesia, a province seized by Frederick the Great in the 1740s, was transferred to the newly founded state of Poland, as was the city of Danzig. Further, a "Polish Corridor" was created, cutting off the province of East Prussia from the rest of Germany.

The military terms of the Versailles treaty were equally harsh. Germany's army was reduced to one hundred thousand men, her navy to fifteen thousand, and she was allowed no air force. In order to prevent the buildup of reserves, both services were to be professionalized, with men serving twelve years and officers twenty-five years. All heavy artillery was to be handed over to the Allies or destroyed, as was the bulk of the German navy. Allied observers stationed in Germany would oversee the destruction of war material and ensure that new weapons were not made. Under the terms of the treaty not only was Germany unable to wage an offensive war, she would almost certainly not be able to defend herself against Poland, let alone France and Britain.

The treaty also called for Germany to accept legally the responsibility for the outbreak of the war and to pay large amounts of reparations. Ultimately, the issue of reparations proved to be a curse for the fledgling republic in several ways. First, they were a severe burden to the economy of Weimar Germany, and economic hardship fueled political unrest. Second, Germany's failure to meet her payments provided a convenient excuse for France to intervene in the internal affairs of Germany, which helped to undermine German confidence in their new republic.

The harsh terms of the treaty came as a shock both to the German government, which had been excluded from the treaty's negotiation, and to the German people, and the treaty became popularly known as the Versailles *Diktat* (dictated peace). The hatred of the treaty would be an important tool in uniting Ger-

mans of almost all classes and political persuasions, and all governments of the Weimar period, regardless of political party, worked to overthrow the treaty. The right wing, particularly Hitler and the Nazis, best used this political tool. The Right successfully convinced many Germans that Wilhelm's army had not actually been defeated in the field, but instead had been "stabbed in the back" by socialist and democratic elements on the home front. The fact that a Social Democratic government had ultimately signed the treaty made this right-wing fabrication all the more believable to many Germans.

Far more damaging to the fledgling republic than the hatred of the Versailles treaty were the threats it faced from internal enemies and the compromises made to overcome them. Already in the first days following the abdication of the Kaiser, the provisional, Social Democratic–led government was faced with political unrest generated by the revolutionary Left and the reactionary Right. Under the direction of the Independent Socialist Party (USPD) and the so-called Spartacists, German workers, sailors, and soldiers formed revolutionary councils on the Soviet model throughout November and December 1918, and Bavaria even proclaimed its independence from the rest of the country. Not to be outdone by the Left, the forces of the Right also assailed the Republic, the most serious of which was the so-called Kapp Putsch of March 1920. Here, right-wing Freikorps (groups of veterans and unemployed) under the direction of Wolfgang Kapp and General von Lüttwitz, the commander of the armed forces in eastern and central Germany, attempted to overthrow the new government. To make matters all the more difficult for the fledgling democracy, Germany's eastern neighbor, Poland, attempted to seize portions of Germany. The Republic was thus not only faced with revolution at home but also with assault from abroad.

Given these threats, from its inception the Weimar Republic was forced to rely upon the army for support. In order to win political support of the largely conservative/monarchical professional officer corps, the army was allowed to exist almost independently of the republic—in effect, to function as a "state within a state." The army attempted to maintain its allegiance to the higher ideal of the German "state" and saw the republic as merely a transitory phase. As the army was committed to preventing revolution and disorder, however, it protected the democratic government until a preferable form came along. Thus, from the early days of the republic, a precarious rela-

THE VERSAILLES TREATY

The Versailles treaty was signed on 28 June 1919 at the Hall of Mirrors in the Palace of Versailles, France. The following selection contains some of its more important articles.

ARTICLE 231.

The Allied and Associated Governments affirm and Germany accepts the responsibility of Germany and her allies for causing all the loss and damage to which the Allied and Associated Governments and their nationals have been subjected as a consequence of the war imposed upon them by the aggression of Germany and her allies.

ARTICLE 232.

The Allied and Associated Governments recognise that the resources of Germany are not adequate, after taking into account permanent diminutions of such resources which will result from other provisions of the present Treaty, to make complete reparation for all such loss and damage.

The Allied and Associated Governments, however, require, and Germany undertakes, that she will make compensation for all damage done to the civilian population of the Allied and Associated Powers and to their property during the period of the belligerency of each as an Allied or Associated Power against Germany by such aggression by land, by sea and from the air, and in general all damage as defined in Annex I hereto.

ARTICLE 233.

The amount of the above damage for which compensation is to be made by Germany shall be determined by an Inter-Allied Commission, to be called the Reparation Commission and constituted in the form and with the powers set forth hereunder and in Annexes II to VII inclusive hereto.

This Commission shall consider the claims and give to the German Government a just opportunity to be heard.

The findings of the Commission as to the amount of damage defined as above shall be concluded and notified to the German Government on or before May 1, 1921, as representing the extent of that Government's obligations.

The Commission shall concurrently draw up a schedule of payments prescribing the time and manner for securing and discharging the entire obligation within a period of thirty years from May 1, 1921. If, however, within the period mentioned, Germany fails to discharge her obligations, any balance remaining unpaid may, within the discretion of the Commission, be postponed for settlement in subsequent years, or may be handled otherwise in such manner as the Allied and Associated Governments, acting in accordance with the procedure laid down in this Part of the present Treaty, shall determine.

ARTICLE 234.

The Reparation Commission shall after May 1, 1921, from time to time, consider the resources and capacity of Germany, and, after giving her representatives a just opportunity to be heard, shall have discretion to extend the date, and to modify the form of payments, such as are to be provided for in accordance with Article 233; but not to cancel any part, except with the specific authority of the several Governments represented upon the Commission.

ARTICLE 235.

In order to enable the Allied and Associated Powers to proceed at once to the restoration of their industrial and economic life, pending the full determination of their claims, Germany shall pay in such installments and in such manner (whether in gold, commodities, ships, securities or otherwise) as the Reparation Commission may fix, during 1919, 1920 and the first four months of 1921, the equivalent of 20,000,000,000 gold marks. Out of this sum the expenses of the armies of occupation subsequent to the Armistice of November 11, 1918, shall first be met, and such supplies of food and raw materials as may be judged by the Governments of the Principal Allied and Associated Powers to be essential to enable Germany to meet her obligations for reparation may also, with the approval of the said Governments, be paid for out of the above sum. The balance shall be reckoned towards liquidation of the amounts due for reparation. Germany shall further deposit bonds as prescribed in paragraph 12 (c) of Annex II hereto.

Source: *Versailles Treaty, History Department of the University of San Diego Web Page.*

tionship of convenience grew up between the conservative army and the republican government, which would be abandoned by the army when it became clear a new, more preferable form of government was coming.

Indeed, the ideas of the army, and its hostility toward any form of democratic government, were shared by many in Weimar Germany, especially by those of the *Mittelstand* (middle classes). This class, which had been the bulwark of the Wilhelmine state, included such professions as low-level civil servants, craftsmen, and shopkeepers. Generally conservative in nature, they saw democracy as fractious dispute in which political parties representing narrow special interests vied with one another to the detriment of the state. Desiring above all order, stability, and the opportunity to earn a good living, many of the Mittelstand increasingly wished for a return to a strong government not riven by politics.

The Weimar system tended to reinforce these conservative ideas. Throughout the short life of the Weimar Republic, the Reichstag was made up of many small political parties representing narrow interests. Although there were several large parties, most notably the Social Democrats and the Center Party, no one party ever possessed an absolute majority, and thus coalition governments, often short-lived, were the rule. While interests of the parties of the political center coincided, these coalitions were sufficiently strong to ward off threats from either the Right or the Left. With the coming of the economic crisis in the late 1920s the precarious balance of political forces in the Weimar Republic was overthrown, which eventually resulted in the death of the Republic and the rise of Hitler and Nazism.

In 1929, Germany was hit with a severe economic crisis caused by the collapse in world markets, which subsequently developed into a social and political crisis. Unemployment and inflation in Germany skyrocketed, and many believed that the Republic was incapable of mastering this latest challenge. Consequently, there was a sharp shift toward the Right among German voters. The Nazi Party, committed to ending the Weimar system, gained the most from this shift in voting. Through the use of effective political campaigning, as well as scare tactics and political intimidation, the Nazis were able to steal voters from the fractious right-wing parties and even from liberal parties. By 1932 the Nazis had emerged as the first mass party of the Right and, indeed, had become the largest party in the Reichstag.

Even before the Nazis' electoral successes in 1932, the Weimar system had begun to collapse from within. By 1930 the political situa-tion had already deteriorated to such an extent that it was impossible to establish a working coalition in the Reichstag. Using Article 48 of the Constitution, the Reich President, since 1925 the arch-conservative Paul van Hindenburg, called together a cabinet that was empowered to issue decrees under the president's name and without Reichstag approval. Although the opinions of the group around Hindenburg varied, in the end, they clearly intended to do away with the Weimar system and to create some form of authoritarian state. Before this could be accomplished, however, they still needed to gain a broad measure of public support. For this, they hoped to make use of Hitler and his Nazi Party, who by 1932 had captured 37.4 percent of the national vote.

The group around Hindenburg, most notably Franz von Papen and Kurt von Schleicher, sought to enlist Hitler into their cabinet and thus win over the Nazi Party followers. These men of the traditional conservative Right believed that Hitler could be "tamed" and used as a junior partner toward their own political ends. To this end, when Hitler was offered the chancellorship on 30 January 1933, he was brought into a cabinet consisting mainly of old-style conservatives. Only one other cabinet position was given to a fellow Nazi. Far from being tamed, however, once in power Hitler soon wrested control for himself and sidelined his conservative partners. Within several years, Hitler had centralized all political power in himself, including uniting the office of president with the chancellorship upon the death of Hindenburg in 1934, and was free to shape an authoritarian state along his lines rather than those of traditional German conservatives.

In the end, Hitler and his Nazi Party were brought to power not by one factor, such as the harsh conditions of the Treaty of Versailles, but rather by the structural weaknesses inherent within the Weimar political system. Faced with severe challenges to its existence from its founding, the Republic was forced to compromise with conservative elements, most particularly the army, to ensure its survival. The conservative army was never reshaped to bring it in line with democratic ideals. Instead, it was allowed to exist as a "state within a state," content to support the Republic as long as it was in the army's own best interest. The Republic's lack of success at winning over Germans to the ideas of democracy was further demonstrated by the large portion of the population who did not have confidence in its ability to master complex social and economic challenges. This lack of support was first manifested in the election of Hindenburg as president. The lack of support for democracy was further shown by the electoral success of Hitler and his Nazi Party, an organization publicly committed to the destruction of the Weimar system. In the end, the Weimar government was brought down from within. By 1933 both the president and the largest party in the Reichstag were committed to the creation of an authoritarian state. Although the conservatives around the president hoped that they could use the popular support of the Nazis to construct their own version, Hitler in fact used the conservatives to help build his version of an authoritarian state.

–ROBERT T. FOLEY, KING'S
COLLEGE LONDON

References

Anthony P. Adamthwaite, *The Making of the Second World War* (London & Boston: Allen & Unwin, 1977);

William Sheridan Allen, *The Nazi Seizure of Power: The Experience of a Single German Town, 1930–1935* (Chicago: Quadrangle, 1965);

Manfred F. Boemeke, Gerald D. Feldman, and Elizabeth Glaser, eds., *The Treaty of Versailles: A Reassessment after 75 Years* (Washington, D.C.: German Historical Institute; Cambridge & New York: Cambridge University Press, 1998);

Martin Broszat, *Der Staat Hitlers: Grundlegung und Entwicklung seiner inneren Verfassung* (Munich: Deutscher Taschenbuch Verlag, 1969), translated by John W. Hiden as *The Hitler State: The Foundation and Development of the Internal Structure of the Third Reich* (London & New York: Longman, 1981);

Gordon A. Craig, *Germany, 1866–1945* (New York: Oxford, 1978);

R. J. Overy, *The Origins of the Second World War* (London & New York: Longman, 1987);

Detlev J. K. Peukert, *Die Weimarer Republik: Krisenjahre der Klassischen Moderne* (Frankfurt: Suhrkamp, 1987), translated by Richard Deveson as *The Weimar Republic: The Crisis of Classical Modernity* (London: Allen Lane, 1991);

A. J. P. Taylor, *The Origins of the Second World War* (London: Hamilton, 1961).

VICHY FRANCE

Did the Vichy government in France willingly collaborate with the Germans?

Viewpoint: Yes, the Vichy government provided help to the German war effort and the German campaign to eliminate French Jews and resistance fighters. The Vichy regime viewed the German invasion as an opportunity to establish an authoritarian government in France.

Viewpoint: No, the policies and actions of Vichy France were pragmatic attempts to maintain French sovereignty despite German domination.

The French government—known as the Vichy government, from the name of the capital city of unoccupied France—that concluded peace with Adolf Hitler in 1940 faced a spectrum of undesirable choices. France had no practical possibility of continuing the war from its own soil. Following the governments of Norway and the Netherlands into exile in London was unthinkable. Evacuation to North Africa was a possibility—but that meant fighting on as a virtual client of a Britain that had shown no particular aptitude for meeting the Third Reich in a continental war.

On the other side of the ledger, Hitler was willing to allow at least the framework of a sovereign French state with its own government and armed forces. He had not claimed either the fleet or the empire of the defunct Third Republic. As much to the point, no feasible alternatives to German hegemony existed. The U.S.S.R. was Hitler's ally. The United States was an avowed neutral, unmoved even when bombs began falling on London. To the men who formed the new order at Vichy, accommodation seemed a more promising path than confrontation. That was best left to expatriate quasi traitors such as Charles de Gaulle.

Accommodation also offered time to reconstruct a French society many of Vichy's supporters believed had lost its way in the chaos of the republic's final years. The direct affinities between Vichy France and Nazi Germany must not be overstated. Nevertheless, a government based on the principles of "fatherland, family, work" could credibly declare common ground with Hitler's new German order—not least because of Vichy's anti-Semitism.

Underlying Vichy policy was a hope of being accepted as a client— perhaps even an eventual replacement for Italy as the anchor—of Greater Germany's Mediterranean sector. That hope was exposed as a delusion within six months, as Hitler's pressure for concessions in North Africa demonstrated his ideological inability to leave anything on the table for anyone else. For the remainder of Vichy's ephemeral existence, its policy depended on whether Nazi Germany or the western Allies seemed more of a threat at a particular time. Because it stood for less and less, Vichy was mourned by few when Hitler finally swept its remnants into exile or prison after D-Day.

Viewpoint:
Yes, the Vichy government provided help to the German war effort and the German campaign to eliminate French Jews and resistance fighters. The Vichy regime viewed the German invasion as an opportunity to establish an authoritarian government in France.

Amidst the cries of jubilation greeting the Allied liberation of France in the summer of 1944 were protestations of innocence by those Frenchmen who had participated in the government of Unoccupied (or Vichy) France. Taking their cue from Vichy's president, Marshal Philippe Pétain, those who had apparently aided the Germans argued that the entire Vichy enterprise had been a means to protect French citizens from the worst consequences of German occupation. Pétain justified Vichy as the "shield" that had protected France until the "sword" of General Charles de Gaulle's Free French Forces was ready for action. Far from apologizing for their actions, Vichy leaders emphasized the risks involved in guiding France through such perilous times. They even stressed their own moral courage in making the decisions that sacrificed some French citizens to protect the polity as a whole. Self-proclaimed patriots, they were outraged at the accusation that they ever willingly put German interests ahead of French ones.

These, however, were the desperate and disingenuous claims of men whose efforts to collaborate with Adolf Hitler had brought no advantage to France. Only on the last point, that they had never put Germany ahead of France, was there any merit in the self-serving defenses offered by Vichy leaders against the charge of collaboration. While a few extreme Germanophiles such as Gaston Bergery and Marcel Déat hoped to emulate German fascism, most Vichy leaders had little love for Germany per se. Rather, they saw in Germany's triumph a painful opportunity to purge their own ailing country of the evils of social decay and ineffective liberal parliamentary government. For France's sake, not Germany's, they worked to restore conservative political, social, and religious values. In foreign policy, for example, Pétain attempted to remain independent of Germany by retaining close diplomatic ties with the United States. Only in the sense that they did not work in Germany's interest can Pétain's men be spared the collaborationist label.

Nor, however, were they acting in the interests of the French people or of the Allied coalition. Claims to have sacrificed in order to shield France from a harsher German occupation are disingenuous. Rather than taking the minimal measures nec-

essary to preserve France and her people, Vichy seized the opportunity to reshape the country along authoritarian lines. The Vichy "National Renewal" or "National Revolution" aimed to centralize the economy, strengthen the family, revitalize Catholicism, employ schools for moral education, and restore France's agricultural heritage. True Frenchmen, Vichy spokesmen proclaimed, would rally behind this return to France's agrarian, corporatist, hierarchical, and Catholic traditions. Alien influences, communists above all, but also trade unions, liberals, freemasons, and Jews had no place in the new "integral" France.

Although Vichy's spokesmen claimed to reflect a true French spirit suppressed by the artificial constitution of the Third Republic, they relied on their government's relationship with Germany to bring about their "National Revolution." Without the shock of defeat and occupation, and without the continuing threat of German force, few Frenchmen would have been willing to replace the republican creed of *Liberté, Egalité, Fraternité* (liberty, equality, and brotherhood) with the Vichy's *Travail, Familie, Patrie* (work, family, country). For Vichy's leaders, friendship with Germany demonstrated that defeat did not exclude a new authoritarian France from returning to the first rank of European states.

Obviously, some degree of accommodation with the victor was inevitable, especially while the final details of the armistice remained to be worked out and two million French soldiers waited in prisoner-of-war camps. French proposals, however, went far beyond the effort to negotiate better terms and instead sought an active partnership with Germany. In August 1940 Prime Minister Pierre Laval offered the Germans military assistance against Britain and, especially, against de Gaulle's forces in the French colonial empire. Rather than treating de Gaulle himself as the "sword of France," Pétain's army condemned him to death (in absentia) for treason. Although Germany never admitted France into the desired military partnership, it did allow France to increase its military forces in North Africa in exchange for permission to supply Erwin Rommel's troops in North Africa through Bizerte, Tunisia, and to base German submarines at Dakar. Thus, in order to strengthen its position against de Gaulle, the Vichy regime openly aided the German Army against the Allies.

Vichy cooperated with Germany against internal enemies as well. French police worked with the Germans to identify and eliminate members of resistance organizations, and the Vichy government supplied the Germans with the hostages demanded after certain resistance actions. These active efforts to crush the resistance, justified as necessary to maintain order and prevent German reprisals, undermine Pétain's sword and shield metaphor.

VICHY FRANCE

Vichy's collaboration also took economic form, with French industry producing war matériel for the *Wehrmacht* (German Army). Defenders of the policy insisted that it was in the interest of France to build armaments for its erstwhile enemies. Without German orders, the French arms industry would disappear; collaboration, according to Herrick Chapman in *State Capitalism and Working-Class Radicalism in the French Aircraft Industry* (1991), "Preserved the country's extensive network of laboratories and factories as well as its sizable pool of skilled employees, especially designers, production engineers, test pilots, draughtsmen, and skilled metalworkers." That France's postwar military-production facilities survived the war in fairly good shape was, however, anything but a wartime benefit to the Allies.

The most striking example of the extent of Vichy collaboration—and the most damnable element of Vichy policy—was the treatment of France's Jewish population. Just as previously marginal political leaders seized upon the military collapse to rewrite the French constitution, the anti-semitic and anti-immigrant elements never absent from French politics saw the opportunity to

achieve their dream of "France of all the French." Vichy made its anti-Semitism clear on 27 August 1940 by repealing the law preventing newspapers from publishing attacks based on religion or race. Shortly thereafter, the *Statut des juifs* (Statute on the Jews) effectively separated Jews from the rest of French society. Defining Jewishness in even broader terms than similar German legislation, it banned Jews from important positions in public service, the army, and from the professions. On the following day Vichy promulgated a second law authorizing the internment of foreign Jews in camps. Many lost their citizenship through another law mandating the reevaluation of recent naturalizations, while all Algerian Jews were stripped of their citizenship as of 7 October 1940.

Strictly speaking, Vichy anti-Semitic policy was not collaborationist. The Germans did not require or even desire French action against the Jews. Having used Vichy France as a place to "dump" thousands of Jews from the Occupied Zone, Germany found Vichy's "competitive or rival anti-Semitism" inconvenient and saw France as undeserving of an Aryan *judenfrei* (Jewish-free) condition. If it was not literally collaborationist, Vichy

Marshal Philippe Pétain shaking hands with Adolf Hitler at Montoire, France, in October 1940

VICHY FRANCE

legislation against the Jews played neatly into German hands. After the "Final Solution" became policy and, eventually, began to be implemented in France, German agents had little difficulty rounding up their victims. Having performed the necessary census in pursuit of "France for all the French," Vichy police were able to provide the Germans with useful lists of Jewish residents. Moreover, in accordance with Vichy's antisemitic legislation, all foreign or "stateless" Jews had already been interned in camps within France and were readily available for shipment eastward. Vichy apologists later argued that the shipment of 75,000 mostly foreign Jews to the death camps, from which only about 2,500 returned, saved the lives of hundreds of thousands of native French Jews. Leaving aside the moral issues of buying French Jews' lives with those of "stateless" ones, some of whom were "stateless" only after having been stripped of their French citizenship, Vichy could have done much more to protect both groups, if only by granting exit visas to Jews wishing to leave France and avoiding actions, registration, and internment that identified Jews for German collection. Vichy actions from the *Statut des juifs* to the use of French police to guard the deportation trains demonstrated official zeal in carrying out what became the "Final Solution." If this was not collaboration, the crimes resulting from Vichy's competition with Germany were as serious.

Collaboration is not a strictly accurate label for Vichy's actions from June 1940 until November 1942, only because Germany proved unreceptive. As Robert O. Paxton puts it in *Vichy France: Old Guard and New Order 1940–1944* (1972), "collaboration was a French proposal that Hitler ultimately rejected." No adequately harsh word exists, however, to describe the policy by which French leaders took advantage of military defeat to attempt a political revolution that was based in their own cultural fantasies—a revolution incompatible with French values, murderous in its execution, and risible to the bully it was intended to impress.

—EUGENIA C. KIESLING, U.S. MILITARY ACADEMY, WEST POINT

Viewpoint:
No, the policies and actions of Vichy France were pragmatic attempts to maintain French sovereignty despite German domination.

On one level the government that took power in France in July 1940 represented the half of France that regarded the Revolution of 1789 as a

mistake. It represented as well a France unfamiliar, and usually uncongenial, to English-speaking Francophiles. The France of Vichy was the France of the *pays rurale* (rural country) and *pays reelle* (real country): nationalistic to the point of xenophobia, inward-looking to the point of solipsism, and an embodiment of a realism that French novelist Georges Bernanos dubbed "the good sense of bastards." Vichy's supporters and adherents were impatient of the insouciant rationalism and easy cosmopolitanism foreigners liked to associate with Paris. They regarded the French political establishment and French intelligentsia, Left and Right alike, as too clever by half for the country's good. To this mentality the "second debacle" of 1940 was a predictable consequence of listening to the chattering classes and their abstract definitions of liberty, equality, and fraternity. For Vichy, at least in principle, the brotherhood of humanity was a chimera alongside the reality of the French fatherland. The equality of mankind meant nothing compared to the solidity of the family, the basis of all social organization. Liberty, too often defined as the freedom to denigrate the virtues of everyday life through windy rhetoric, must give way to work—the kind of disciplined endeavor that had raised the swastika over the public buildings of half of France. "Fatherland, Family, Work," that was to be the new trinity enabling France to recover its pride, and at least some of its power, in the New European Order of Adolf Hitler.

It was not a particularly heroic ideology. Nevertheless it had wide appeal at a time when heroism seemed at a heavy discount from the Pyrenees to the Rhine. Vichy's genesis, after all, lay in the Third Republic's failure. Despite right-wing rhetoric of "Better Hitler than Blum" (Jewish premier Léon Blum, who served from 1936 to 1938), France had mobilized together in 1939 and stood together against the Nazi onslaught of May 1940. It was not Vichy's supporters who had failed to strengthen discipline and improve training during the months of the "phony war." In 1939 popular entertainer Maurice Chevalier sang of the spectrum of attitudes and opinions in the ranks of an army that nevertheless was made up of "good Frenchmen, good soldiers." By the summer of 1940 that army's image had become that of an unshaven, middle-aged reservist vainly seeking to button an ill-fitting uniform coat over a bourgeois *embonpoint* (paunch).

The obvious contrast was with the youngsters of the German Panzer divisions, warriors as hard and capable as their tanks. Since the mid 1930s increasing numbers of Frenchmen had begun looking across the Rhine, not out of any admiration for Nazi ideology or practices, but to admire what they perceived as the achievements of a strong man.

In 1940, Premier Paul Reynaud might have proposed to continue the fight—perhaps even from

THE FUTURE OF FRANCE

On 10 June 1941 the new vice premier of France, Jean-Louis-Xavier-François Darlan, spoke to the French people on his predecessor and the plight of France.

We owe our present misery to a regime that led us to defeat, to that regime and not the government of the Marshal, which fell heir to the disastrous situation and is trying to remedy the ills from which you are suffering and to shorten their duration.

To succeed needs courage, tenacity, abnegation and the support of the nation. If the nation does not understand this, it will perish. There are many who are trying to darken the nation's understanding. You are nervous and anxious because unhappily many of you believe anything that is said and whispered even without taking time to reflect—many believe that what you hear every day over the clandestine or dissident radio, paid for by a foreign power, is the absolute truth. They do not take the trouble to compare the disturbing similarity between the de Gaullist and Communist propaganda, which aim at the same goal—to create disorder in the country, to increase the misery of the population, to prevent the rebirth of the nation.

And this leads us to believe that the orders which the Communist leaders obey and the money they receive may come from west of our frontiers.

Frenchmen, beware and help the government in its heavy, very heavy task. This task of the government is triple: to ameliorate the French people's situation, to prepare for peace in that measure a conquered nation can, and to prepare France's future in a new Europe. . . .

You ask yourselves why the Germans agree to negotiate since they are the conquerors. Because Germany, which intends to reconstruct Europe, knows that this cannot be done feasibly unless the different European nations participate in this reconstruction of their own free will, Germany does not let victory run away with her to enable us to keep our heads above defeat. Let us know how to reduce the effects of defeat and think of the France of tomorrow.

Do you think that the armies of occupation will consent to reduce their requisitions if they have the feeling that our hostility persists? Do you think that they will permit our farmers to return to their farms if they feel France is still the hereditary enemy? Do you think our prisoners will be liberated if it appears that they will only increase Germany's enemy? Do you believe our farmers who were obliged to leave their farms could return if the Germans have the impression that France remains her hereditary enemy? . . . .

The second task of the government is to prepare for peace. The present situation is unprecedented in history. One of the powers with which we must negotiate is at war with another power and its troops are engaged in operations occupying part of our soil. The signature of a definite peace remains difficult as long as the major problems that are the basis for the present conflict are unsolved.

But now, without waiting for the end of hostilities, the government's duty is to act so as to create an atmosphere favorable to the establishment of an honorable peace. That atmosphere cannot be created unless we dominate our defeat. That means we must regulate our acts reasonably. Face realities courageously. Do not give way to sentimental reactions that have no other result than to widen further to our disadvantage the gap which so many wars have created between two neighboring peoples and which in the interests of European peace we must both start filling.

If that atmosphere cannot be created, I fear a disastrous peace for France. That fear is not founded on impression; it is founded on certainty.

The third task of the government is to prepare for France's future in a new Europe. That task cannot be usefully undertaken unless the second is successful.

If we do not get an honorable peace, if France is cut up into many departments and deprived of important overseas territories and enters diminished and bruised into the new Europe, she will not recover, and we and our children will live in the misery and hatred that breed war.

The new Europe will not live without a France placed in the rank that her history, civilization and culture give her the right to occupy in the European hierarchy. Frenchmen, have courage to dominate your defeat. Be assured that the future of the country is bound closely with that of Europe.

Source: The New York Times, 11 June 1941.

VICHY FRANCE

North Africa. However, a majority of his cabinet was of another opinion. Reynaud's alternate proposal to allow the army to be interned in Switzerland and British prime minister Winston Churchill's twelfth-hour offer of political union with Britain, seemed acts of desperation verging on madness to an increasing number of soldiers and politicians. The cabinet rejected Churchill's proposal, insisting instead on opening negotiations for an armistice. With Pétain representing France there need be no dishonor in negotiating with Hitler while some negotiating room remained.

A British government desperately afraid that Germany would gain control of the French fleet responded by turning the Royal Navy's guns against its ally of yesterday. At Mers el-Kébir on 3 July 1940, more than two thousand French sailors were killed in a surprise attack that eviscerated the French Mediterranean squadron. Other ships were seized, disarmed, and their crews interned. Bitterness ran deep in a France where the navy was its most tangible remaining symbol of independence. There was little opposition when on 9 July the National Assembly met in the resort town of Vichy and by an overwhelming majority voted full power to Pétain.

Under its new premier, Pierre Laval, the "Vichy administration" initially sought close relations with Germany, even entertaining hopes of replacing Italy as Hitler's "faithful second" in the Mediterranean. That hope had at least something to do with the harsh antisemitic campaign directed against both Jewish citizens and refugees from Nazi persecution. Vichy's antisemitism, however, was essentially indigenous. Flourishing even after Laval's dismissal on December 1940 for being too Germanophilic for Pétain to stomach, it epitomized a rejection of the cosmopolitanism Vichy supporters believed had leached away France's vitality under the Third Republic. Not only Jews but other aliens, Spanish refugees, and Polish miners, were excluded from a new order meant to be French above all.

Laval's successor, Admiral Jean-Louis-Xavier-François Darlan, took a more pragmatic line, but nevertheless continued to act on the premise that Germany would be the hegemon of Europe for the foreseeable future. Any degree of autonomy the Vichy government could sustain was just that much protection for a French people that otherwise would stand exposed to the whimsical ferocity of a Nazi regime whose erratic character was becoming more apparent by the month. For Darlan, limited military cooperation, focused in the Mediterranean, was a reasonable primary tradeoff for the appearance, and some of the substance, of sovereignty. Continuing, even increasing, the deportation of Jews was secondary—a gesture of goodwill costing Vichy nothing it could not well spare.

This kind of reasoning was admirably Cartesian in its logical rigor. It also was applicable only so long as it suited Hitler. In the spring of 1942 he began tightening the screws. Laval was restored to the premiership and immediately resumed his plans to extend the scope of Vichy involvement with Germany. When the Allies invaded French North Africa in November, Hitler responded by ordering the military occupation of Vichy. An "Armistice army," little more than a token force, capitulated without even token resistance. What remained of the once powerful navy scuttled itself at anchor. Henceforth, Vichy would have no more than a shadow existence as one of the least of Hitler's client states, useful primarily to impress its own citizens for labor service in the Reich and to keep the boxcars full of Jews while any remained within its amorphous frontiers.

Vichy has found few mourners and fewer defenders as the twentieth century wanes. Nevertheless, for two years it retained some semblance of autonomy. Its principles, moreover, did not vanish in 1945. France remains divided along lines drawn in 1940—suggesting that Vichy's moral legitimacy was far greater than its political viability.

—DENNIS SHOWALTER, COLORADO COLLEGE

References

Herrick Chapman, *State Capitalism and Working-Class Radicalism in the French Aircraft Industry* (Berkeley: University of California Press, 1991);

Stanley Hoffman, "Collaborationism in France during World War II," *Journal of Modern History,* 40 (September 1968): 375–395;

Bertram M. Gordon, *Collaborationism in France during the Second World War* (Ithaca, N.Y.: Cornell University Press, 1980);

H. R. Kedward, *Occupied France: Collaboration and Resistance 1940–1944* (Oxford & New York: Blackwell, 1985);

Michael Maurrus and Robert O. Paxton, *Vichy et les juifs,* translated as *Vichy and the Jews* (New York: BasicBooks, 1981);

Rolf-Dieter Müller and Gerd R. Ueberschär, *Hitler's War in the East, 1941–1945: A Critical Reassessment,* translated by Bruce D. Little (Providence, R.I.: Berghahn Books, 1997);

Paxton, *Vichy France: Old Guard and New Order 1940–1944* (New York: Knopf, 1972).

WEHRMACHT

Was the reputation of the Wehrmacht for military superiority deserved?

Viewpoint: Yes, in mechanized warfare, especially the use of advanced tanks and combined arms strategy, the Germans were superior to their Allied opponents.

Viewpoint: No, a myth of German superiority was promoted to make the Wehrmacht look better and to excuse its defeats.

During its years of triumph from 1939 to 1942, the *Wehrmacht* (German Army) made offensives look easy, consistently embarrassing its adversaries by slashing, wide-open mobile operations. After their defeats at Stalingrad (2 February 1943) and in North Africa (1943) the Germans equally showed themselves as masters of defense, time and again frustrating what seemed to be overwhelming material superiority by tactical skill and sheer determination. It is unusual for an army to play two ways equally. Much of the Wehrmacht's reputation, moreover, is based on the acclamation of its enemies—who should be in the best position to know.

German military effectiveness is usually ascribed to some combination of four factors. First comes professionalism. The German army studied the craft of war, took pains with its details, and rewarded competence in its performance. German small arms and armored vehicles were tailored to the war Germany was fighting. German officers were skilled in combined-arms operations—and in making do with what they had instead of calling for more of everything. Second on the list of the army's qualities is focus. The "German way of war" concentrated on tactical and operational levels to the relative neglect of strategy and policy. That neglect made them vulnerable in the long run of World War II, but it also gave them a specialist's advantages at the sharp end. Third comes training—broadly defined. The Wehrmacht of World War II knew how to prepare soldiers for a modern battlefield. Its emphasis on toughness, its synergies of teamwork and self-reliance, and its encouraging of initiative at all levels created matrices that endured even through the devastating casualties of the Russian Front. Ideology added to the training mix as well. If the German army never fully became a National Socialist force, Nazi emphasis on will power and on German racial superiority nevertheless arguably proved powerful reinforcements to morale in both victory and defeat.

Russian and American soldier-scholars make increasingly strong cases that by 1944 at the latest, their respective armies had caught, and in many ways passed, the Germans in operational effectiveness. Yet, the comparisons are made to a force whose peak was long past, eroded materially by four years of attrition and morally by a decade of complicity with National Socialism. The debate is similar to the hypothetical exchange between two baseball fans: "What would Ty Cobb hit if he were playing now?" "About .240—but remember, Ty'd be eighty years old!"

Viewpoint:
Yes, in mechanized warfare, especially the use of advanced tanks and combined arms strategy, the Germans were superior to their Allied opponents.

On 1 September 1939, lead units of the invading *Wehrmacht* (German Army) crashed over the border into Poland. The operation, code-named Case White, was the world's first look at a devastating new type of mechanized warfare. Highly mobile German formations, spearheaded by massed columns of tanks and working in close cooperation with the *Luftwaffe* (German Air Force), attacked on a narrow front, making deep penetrations of the Polish defenses within hours. The speed and violence of the attack paralyzed enemy response. German tanks scattered enemy reserves as they were coming up, overrunning headquarters, supply dumps, and railheads, preventing the Poles from reforming their line or bringing up their reserves. The climax of these armored drives came far behind the front lines, as the spearheads linked up, trapping the bewildered Polish formations in a series of isolated pockets. Despite the speed of their advance, the mobile columns stayed in communication with their own headquarters and with each other through the use of a recent invention, radio. Air power also played a crucial role, helping the tanks blast through the line, with the *Stuka,* the German dive bomber, serving as mobile artillery on call to the armor. Finally, once the tanks had cleared a path, mechanized infantry and artillery followed, occupying the terrain the tanks had seized and defending it against enemy counterattack, thereby tightening the ring around the trapped enemy forces. Despite their bravery, the infantry and cavalry of the Polish army were outmatched. Cut off from supplies and communications with the rear, they had no choice but to surrender. The main fighting was over in two weeks, although Warsaw held out for another two weeks. In those initial two weeks, the first mechanized campaign in military history, the Germans essentially destroyed the Polish army, inflicting about two hundred thousand casualties and taking almost six hundred thousand prisoners. German losses were negligible.

The events in Poland began a two-year period that would rewrite the book on modern warfare. While many western observers were ready to chalk up the German success in Case White to Polish incompetence or backwardness, the events of the following spring should have changed their minds. In May 1940 the German army launched its great offensive in the west (Case Yellow). With a rapidity that shocked both the military experts and the world at large, Germany's tank and mechanized formations shredded the French, British, Belgian, and Dutch armies. The British managed to retreat from the Continent at Dunkirk (26 May–4 June 1940), although their equipment losses were nearly total. In Case Yellow the mechanized German army showed what it could do when wedded to expert staff work and commanded by generals in the field who truly understood the strategic possibilities offered by its mobility. It was as impressive and complete a victory as the annals of military history have to offer, and still stands as proof of the genius of German generals Fritz Erich von Manstein and Heinz Wilhelm Guderian.

The results were in many ways even more impressive in the Soviet Union in 1941. When Adolf Hitler unleashed Operation Barbarossa in June, it seemed that the tanks had reached their full maturity, breaking through and encircling huge concentrations of enemy troops, with some nine hundred thousand Soviet prisoners of war taken in the pockets around Uman and Kiev alone. As the armored spearheads of *Panzergruppe Guderian* (Armored Group Guderian) approached Moscow in November, it seemed that the war was over. Even more importantly, it seemed that the age of the long, drawn-out war, the sort of bloody stalemate that had characterized World War I, was gone forever. The age of *Blitzkrieg* (lightning war) was upon the world.

The Wehrmacht was the finest army in the field throughout World War II. Its combat effectiveness was equally high in both the attack and the defense. It conquered western Europe in a month; the Allies took five years to reconquer it, including almost a full year of ground campaigning after the Normandy landing. It conquered the western Soviet Union in six months; it took three years for the Red Army to retake it. It managed to hold Italy for three years with a handful of divisions (admittedly aided by good terrain). It consistently inflicted heavier casualties than it suffered. From 1941 to 1945 it held off a literal world of enemies, a Grand Alliance capable of mustering enormous, even overwhelming material strength. It took the world's largest land power (the U.S.S.R.), the world's greatest naval power and overseas empire (Great Britain), and the world's financial, economic, and industrial giant (the United States) to bring down the Wehrmacht in a grinding war of attrition that saw Germany outproduced, but never outfought.

The roots of German military superiority go back to the interwar period. Defeat in World War I had forced the German army into a profound, even painful, reassessment of its methods of waging war. Under a series of progressive commanders, the *Reichswehr* (interwar German Army) became a virtual proving ground for new techniques, tactics, and technologies, while always remaining grounded in the traditions of the Prussian-German army. Leading the way was the Chief of the Army Command after 1921, General Hans von Seeckt. Based on his wartime service on the Eastern Front, as well as an extraordinary flexibility of mind, Seeckt was never impressed with the so-called "lessons of the First World War"—the dominance of fire over movement, the invulnerability of entrenched defenders, and the necessity of fortification. Instead, he continued to see the future in terms of the war of movement. The mass army had to be replaced, he thought, since it was incapable of maneuver—and, therefore, of victory. A small, highly mobile army was the ideal. Consisting of well-conditioned infantry, a large contingent of cavalry, and a full complement of motorized and mechanized vehicles, light machine guns and mobile artillery, it would have the mobility to wage offensive warfare and seek the battle of annihilation with the enemy.

These new ideas found expression in the new manuals and tactical regulations issued during Seeckt's tenure, especially the new field service regulations, *Führung und Gefecht der verbundenen Waffen* (*Combined Arms Leadership and Battle*, known as F.u.G.) issued in September 1921. Others soon followed, dealing with infantry training, artillery, field fortifications, the signal service, training of the rifle squad, and the light machine gun. In their totality they rewrote the book on German doctrine, taking what was new (tanks, radio, and light machine guns) and wedding it to what was tried and true (infantry, cavalry, and artillery). Always, the stress was on combined arms, the inability of any one arm to win the decision on its own, and the necessity for cooperation down to the lowest level.

The emphasis on mobility and combined arms continued after Seeckt's departure from office in 1926. In 1931–1932, for example, Colonel Oswald Lutz, the Inspector of Motor Troops, directed a comprehensive series of exercises involving dummy-tank battalions at the Jüterbog and Grafenwöhr training grounds. In September 1932 he summed up the lessons learned in a report intended to help with the intended revision of Führung und Gefecht.

Lutz began with the basic principles. First, tank units should receive independent battle missions, taking into account their special attributes. Tying them down to support the infantry was a mistake, since it would rob the armor of its principal advantages: speed and range. There could be exceptions, an attack with limited objectives, for instance. Even this type of use, however, con-

A German soldier getting ready to throw a potato masher hand grenade

(Burnback Publishing Service, Ullstein)

tradicted the basic point made above: tanks were for the *Schwerpunkt* (main attack) only, too valuable to waste on a sideshow.

If independence was the first principle, mass was the second. Using tanks in anything under battalion strength was a blunder. Even given the rather primitive state of antitank weapons and training at the time of Lutz's report, an attack by a tank company would not achieve a decisive result. The use of such small units represented a dispersion of the new queen of battle, thus violating the principle of concentration of force.

Lutz's third principle was surprise. An attack at dawn was best, he felt. The assault should be "surprising, sudden, and on a broad front," in order to splinter the defense. It was also necessary to echelon that attack in enough depth to make it possible to switch the Schwerpunkt itself during the pursuit, as well as to crush any newly arriving targets or obstructions.

It is no exaggeration to say that the exercises of 1931–1932, carried out by a disarmed power with dummy tanks, marked the true birth of Blitzkrieg. The unchaining of tanks from the speed of the infantry, the reliance on mass and surprise to tear a hole in the bewildered defense, and the exploitation by mobile reserves of all arms—it was this vision that would revolutionize the face of warfare from 1939 to 1941.

The question was much more profound than simply, "What is the proper employment of the tank?" The exercises had not used armor alone. True to the traditional German emphasis on combined arms, they had included infantry,

MEMORIES OF A GERMAN SOLDIER

Rudolph Salvermoser, a tanker with the Wehrmacht, reflected in the following passage on his army's abilities in contrast to that of the Russians.

We never considered our role as soldiers as "just another job"; it was our duty and honor to be soldiers. We felt we had no other option than be members of the Armed Forces. After all, there was a war, I was just the right age, and I felt like most other young people felt: that the only way to live was to fight for my Fatherland, win the war, and then return in peace to rebuild my country. In the sense that we were dedicated and well-trained, we were professionals. Our capabilities were far superior to those of the Russians. Our Kampfgruppe (task force) alone was able to destroy five Russian tanks for every one we lost, and I believe that this ratio prevailed throughout the whole Russian Front. Unfortunately for us, however, they probably had ten times as many tanks as we had. It was the quickness of our aim and response and the exactness of our hitting that made us superior. We were undoubtedly better trained and our aiming optics excelled theirs. But our tanks were inferior as far as the thickness of the protective armor, engines too small for the tank's weight, and narrow tracks (which could not traverse muddy or swampy terrain) were concerned. Otherwise, because of our quickness, good training and (at least we thought so at the time) our mentality, we always seemed to be superior to the enemy we faced. When I say "we," I am referring to the members of an elite division; this did not necessarily hold true for all other units along the Eastern Front or the other units within the Wehrmacht as a whole.

Source: *Rudolph Salvermoser, "A Großdeutschland Veteran," edited by Robert Witter, German Armed Forces in WWII, Web Page.*

---

artillery, and antitank units. A large part of the report dealt with cooperation of all the arms, which the Germans clearly regarded as the fundamental question of armor, unlike the British stress on the tanks alone. Tanks were crucial, of course. Because of their mobility, firepower, and shock value, whenever they went into action, they temporarily became the principal arm. The main battlefield problem, as Lutz saw it, was how to get the other arms—infantry, artillery, pioneers, and air—to recognize that fact and lend better support to the armor.

In fall 1935, Lutz and his brilliant chief of staff, Guderian, recommended the formation of three Panzer Divisions. They came into existence in October. Each consisted of a tank brigade backed by a motorized infantry brigade. This organization was the same as the Light Mechanized Division formed in France the previous year and also reflective of contemporary British thinking. The Panzer Division had enough tanks to satisfy even the purist: two tank regiments of two battalions each, with a strength of 128 light tanks per battalion. Counting command tanks, the division contained some 561 in all. What was different was the German emphasis on combined arms. The division had a strong infantry component, consisting of a two-battalion motorized infantry regiment, plus a motorcycle battalion. In addition, the true mark of the Panzer Division, there was a complete cast of supporting arms: a motorized artillery regiment, a motorized antitank battalion, and a motorized pioneer company, later expanded into a battalion. There was also a motorized reconnaissance battalion made up of armored cars and motorcycles. The Panzer Division, then, was not just tanks. It was, in the well-chosen words of armor historian Richard M. Ogorkiewicz, "a self-contained combined arms team in which tanks were backed by other arms brought up, as far as possible, to the tanks' standards of mobility."

The outbreak of war, therefore, found the Germans well ahead of their adversaries in doctrinal terms. Insofar as they had thought about it at all, the other powers had a great deal of difficulty with the central question: incorporation of the tank into modern battle. In Great Britain, the land that had invented the tank, the tendency was to emphasize its power at the expense of the other arms. The sometimes brilliant but always obnoxious armor prophet, Colonel J. F. C. Fuller, was a perfect example; so was the fire-breathing commander of the 7th Armoured Division, General Percy Hobart. Both believed that tanks could achieve victory on their own, without adequate infantry or artillery support. They rarely discussed tanks as part of a combined arms force.

Other countries fared little better in developing combined arms warfare. In France, Colonel Charles de Gaulle was the proverbial voice crying in the wilderness, without any real influ-

WEHRMACHT

ence. In the Soviet Union, there was a promising start under Marshal Mikhail N. Tukhachevsky, whose conception of "deep battle," based on powerful and highly mobile mechanized corps, presaged much of the German Blitzkrieg. He was purged and executed in 1938. The mechanized corps were disbanded and replaced by smaller tank brigades. These smaller formations were unsuited for the sort of strategic penetration envisioned by Tukhachevsky and were designed above all for close infantry support. Germany's victories in the west in 1940 caused the Soviets to rethink their move, and the invasion of 1941 would catch them in the midst of yet another reorganization, this time back to mechanized corps.

In the United States, the outbreak of war found the U.S. Army frantically trying to build an armored force. With the development of the M-4 Sherman, the U.S. did find a serviceable—if not spectacular—tank. The attempt to enunciate a warfighting doctrine, however, proved beyond the ability of U.S. staff officers. Essentially, U.S. tanks were infantry-support vehicles. Like the cavalry of old, they would help infantry achieve the breakthrough, then exploit into the enemy's rear and pursue the beaten foe. They were not intended to take on German tanks in a gunnery duel. That was the mission of something called the "tank destroyer," an armored gun carriage mounting an antitank gun. Its mission was to ambush and destroy enemy tanks. In their final stage of development the M-10 and M-18 tank destroyers evolved into lightly armored, turret vehicles. They tended to be grossly underarmored for the increasingly heavy German tanks they were supposed to stalk. In fact, they became little more than "hybrid tanks," often called upon to carry out missions for which they were completely unsuited. The U.S. Army would have been better off with more Shermans.

One example of German battlefield superiority is worth recounting, a tank action that took place on 13 June 1944, early in the Normandy campaign. *Waffen-SS Obersturmführer* Michael Wittman was commanding a section of Tiger tanks, part of the 501st SS Heavy Panzer Battalion. As corps troops of the 1st SS Panzer Corps barring the way to Caen, Wittman received orders to deploy near Villers-Bocage, protecting the left of the Panzer Lehr Division against a flanking attack by the British 7th Armoured Division (the "Desert Rats"), a unit that had acquired an elite reputation of its own in North Africa. Leading the attack was the 22nd Armoured Brigade, equipped mostly with Cromwells, a thoroughly mediocre tank armed with a 75mm gun. Outside of the town, Wittman took

his Tiger into a small patch of woodland beside the road and waited. He let the head of the column, the 4th County of London Yeomanry, approach to within eighty yards, then took out the lead tank with a single shot from his 88mm gun. Trapped on the narrow road by the flaming wreck, the better part of the brigade (containing some fifty-eight Cromwells) was helpless. Realizing that their Tigers had little to fear, Wittman and the rest of his section now broke cover, driving up and down the length of the column, destroying the trailing tank, then turning the rest of the battalion into a blazing inferno. In a matter of five minutes, they destroyed some twenty-five Cromwells, four Fireflies (British-modified Shermans), six armored cars, and a large number of infantry halftracks. Finally, the rest of the column managed to remove the wreck from the rear of the column and make its escape.

Ironically, but fittingly, Wittman died a short time after the action at Villers-Bocage, when his Tiger was surrounded and destroyed by no less than five Sherman tanks of the Canadian 1st Army. His passing was a microcosm of what happened to the entire German Panzer force and, by extension, of what happened to the entire Wehrmacht.

World War II, then, is the story of the finest army in modern times, steeped in a revolutionary new doctrine that blazed new paths while remaining true to the time-honored principles of combined arms warfare—the entire package held together by a staff system that encouraged a level of professionalism largely unknown to other armies. In the course of the war, the Wehrmacht faced a huge coalition, controlling the vast majority of the world's resources, that eventually ground it into powder.

–ROBERT M. CITINO, EASTERN
MICHIGAN UNIVERSITY

Viewpoint:
No, a myth of German superiority was promoted to make the Wehrmacht look better and to excuse its defeats.

Among the most widespread and persistent myths of World War II is that the *Wehrmacht* (German Army), man for man and unit for unit, was significantly superior to its enemies, on all fronts and at all times, in "fighting power"—that ephemeral ability not only to win against odds, but to look good while losing. Wehrmacht superiority has been expressed statistically by studies claiming to establish percentage differences

WEHRMACHT

between German and British or American divisions. It has been expressed anecdotally, by stories of virtuoso performances by formations and even individuals–the case of *Schutzstaffeln* (SS) tanker Michael Wittman in Normandy springs to mind. Challenges have usually been defensive, involving efforts to demonstrate that Germany's rivals (the United States in particular) had good fighting divisions of its own, who were superior to their opposition on some particular occasion "when the odds were even."

On the whole, these approaches tend to strengthen rather than diminish the Wehrmacht mystique. It is easy to make a case that odds in battle are never even, and indeed never should be. The Americans, for example, were in fact significantly superior to their German opponents in the Vosges Mountain campaign (1944). A recent alternative excludes the Wehrmacht from the "fighting power" debate on the grounds that it served a criminal regime, and was itself essentially a criminal organization. There is a certain elegance–and a certain plausibility–to the concept. It can, however, be too easily extended to include such forces as Napoleon's *Grande Armée* and Robert E. Lee's Army of Northern Virginia, since one arguably fought for imperialism and the other to maintain slavery.

A case may be made from an alternative paradigm, namely that general comparisons of operational effectiveness are a war-gamer's shibboleth, whose testing requires the kind of abstractly level playing field that can only be generated by computer-based rules. The point is, however, as irrelevant as it is defensible. Armies, divisions, and regiments have been matched against each other in "what if" contingencies since the Trojan War's debates on the prowess of individual champions, as recorded in Homer's *Iliad*. The sources of any myth are more important in cultural and historical terms than the myth's objective validity. Citing evidence, general or specific, that the Wehrmacht was less effective than its reputation is correspondingly about as intellectually promising as arguing the respective merits of the 1927 and 1998 New York Yankees, or comparing the Boston Celtics of the Bill Russell era to Michael Jordan's Chicago Bulls. It is more appropriate to examine the reasons why the Wehrmacht has the reputation it enjoys among its former opponents.

Some aspects of the Wehrmacht myth are obvious enough to require little elaboration. The first is plausibility. No myth can endure in the face of overwhelming common-sense contrary evidence; and Germany was a formidable opponent, in all sectors and under all conditions of World War II. Related to that is glory–which is best won against worthy opponents. Some version of "the valor of your enemies does you honor" is a proverb in many languages and cultures–including those of Nazi Germany's principal opponents. Third comes

shame, which is usually generated by perceptions of error and failure. War, the province of friction, is a focal point for error and failure. It is, however, less shaming to make mistakes, less shaming to fail, individually and institutionally, the better one's adversary may be. Finally comes professionalism: respect for superior performance of a common activity. Often misdefined as sportsmanship, professionalism rejects the former's agonistic aspects. Instead, professionalism accepts the sovereign importance of the activity in question. In consequence the professional ultimately seeks neither to praise nor denigrate adversaries, but to surpass them.

The development of a Wehrmacht myth in such general contexts is hardly surprising. The surprise, indeed, would be if one had not emerged from World War II. Specific factors, however, have also contributed to the process. First comes a countermyth: that war is unnatural to democracies–including purported social democracies such as Joseph Stalin's U.S.S.R. Such states and their peoples can and do become formidable when challenged, but have to learn the details of war making as they go along. Effective performance in the initial stages of a war is somehow suspect, embodying almost a betrayal of principle. Dunkirk (26 May–4 June 1940), Pearl Harbor (7 December 1941), and Operation Barbarossa (June 1941) in a sense become necessary beginnings. A case can be made that part of America's difficulty in processing the Vietnam War (1961–1973) involved the absence of an early catastrophe. It is even possible to argue that relatively high casualty lists, however unacceptable they may be in other contexts, stand as a kind of ultimate proof of democracies' good intentions in waging war. The blood of sons becomes the price of innocence. There is a good book to be written as well on the almost visceral tendency in the English-speaking world to identify fighting power with high casualty lists.

The dichotomy was enhanced during World War II by Nazi Germany's overt glorification of military preparation and effectiveness–especially accompanied as it was by a strongly implied promise of low losses. Adolf Hitler's fundamental distrust of the German people combined with his generals' commitment to avoiding the bloodbath of 1914–1918 generated at least an image, and perhaps a myth, of future conflict where technology, technique, and moral force would minimize casualties. The newsreels from Poland, Norway, and France reinforced that premise–at least to Hitler's enemies–to a point where even the blindfolded slaughterhouses of the Russian Front did not shake the sense that the Germans had somehow taken war at the sharp end to a higher level–a level that, paradoxically, democracies could not risk seeking lest they sacrifice their essence.

After 1945 the German generals contributed mightily to the extension of the Wehrmacht myth–

at least in the West. The United States in particular was sufficiently aware of its own shortcomings to be interested in learning from its former opponents—particularly as the very real possibility developed of having to fight the Soviet Army in the Fulda Gap. The dark side of the Wehrmacht had been primarily manifested in the East, so there were relatively few memories of war combat atrocities to hinder the exchange of stories. In addition, a German officer corps anxious to distance itself as far as possible from every aspect of the Nazi experience found ready listeners when it emphasized German fighting power and contrasted it with Allied material superiority. Some of the postwar narratives came close to suggesting that the Germans, like the *federales* in the Willie Nelson song, "Only let us win the war/ Out of kindness I suppose."

A final factor in the Wehrmacht mystique involves taboo-breaking. In the final years of the twentieth century, few ways to shock remain. Nothing is beyond discussion—except the Third Reich. There has been, indeed, something of a reverse trend since 1945, with Nazi Germany becoming one of the few remaining accepted metaphors for evil. The attraction of the forbidden has contributed significantly to thriving cottage industries dealing with the artifacts and institutions of the Nazi system. It has arguably contributed as well to the development of the myth of the Wehrmacht as a brotherhood, of the forbidden, embodying skills good people should not seek and deeds good people should not perform—or at least not perform well, and certainly should not enjoy performing at all.

—DENNIS SHOWALTER, COLORADO COLLEGE

References

Larry H. Addington, *The Patterns of War Since the Eighteenth Century* (Bloomington: Indiana University Press, 1984);

Charles M. Baily, *Faint Praise: American Tanks and Tank Destroyers During World War II* (Hamden, Conn.: Archon, 1983);

Keith E. Bonn, *When the Odds Were Even: The Vosges Mountain Campaign, October 1944–January 1945* (Novato, Cal.: Presidio, 1994);

Robert M. Citino, *The Path to Blitzkrieg: Doctrine and Training in the German Army, 1920–1939* (Boulder, Colo.: Rienner, 1999);

James S. Corum, *The Roots of Blitzkrieg: Hans von Seeckt and German Military Reform* (Lawrence: University Press of Kansas, 1992);

David M. Glantz and Jonathan M. House, *When Titans Clashed: How the Red Army Stopped Hitler* (Lawrence: University Press of Kansas, 1995);

Heinz Guderian, *Erinnerungen eines Soldaten* (Heidelberg: K. Vowinckel, 1950), translated by Constantine Fitzgibbon as *Panzer Leader* (New York: Dutton, 1952);

J. P. Harris, *Men, Ideas, and Tanks: British Military Thought and Armoured Forces, 1903–1939* (Manchester & New York: Manchester University Press, 1995);

Hans von Luck, *Panzer Commander: the Memoirs of Colonel Hans von Luck* (New York: Praeger, 1989);

Erich von Manstein, *Verlorene Siege* (Bonn: Athenäum Verlag, 1955), translated by Anthony G. Powell as *Lost Victories* (London: Methuen, 1958);

Richard E. Simpkin, *Deep Battle: The Brainchild of Marshal Tukhachevskii* (London & Washington, D.C.: Brassey's Defense, 1987);

Martin Van Creveld, *Fighting Power: German and US Army Performance, 1939–1945* (Westport, Conn.: Greenwood Press, 1982).

WEHRMACHT

REFERENCES

1. AFRICAN AMERICANS

Astor, Gerald. *The Right to Fight: A History of African Americans in the Military.* Novato, Cal.: Presidio, 1998.

Lee, Ulysses Grant. *The Employment of Negro Troops.* Washington, D.C.: Office of the Chief of Military History, 1966.

MacGregor, Morris J. Jr. *Integration of the Armed Forces, 1940–1965.* Washington, D.C.: Center of Military History, 1981.

Mershon, Sherie, and Steven Schlossman. *Foxholes & Color Lines: Desegregating the U.S. Armed Forces.* Baltimore: Johns Hopkins University Press, 1998.

Nalty, Bernard C. *Strength for the Fight: A History of Black Americans in the Military.* New York: Free Press, 1986; London: Collier Macmillan, 1986.

2. AIR WAR

Caldwell, Donald L. *JG 26, Top Guns of the Luftwaffe.* New York: Orion Books, 1991.

Cooper, Matthew. *The German Air Force, 1933–1945: An Anatomy of Failure.* London & New York: Jane's, 1981.

Corum, James S. *The Luftwaffe: Creating the Operational Air War, 1918–1940.* Lawrence: University Press of Kansas, 1997.

Crane, Conrad C. *Bombs, Cities, and Civilians: American Airpower Strategy in World War II.* Lawrence: University Press of Kansas, 1993.

Craven, Wesley Frank, and James Lea Cate, eds. *The Army Air Forces in World War II,* 7 volumes. Chicago: University of Chicago Press, 1948–1958.

Garrett, Stephen A. *Ethics and Airpower in World War II: The British Bombing of German Cities.* New York: St. Martin's Press, 1993.

Hastings, Max. *Bomber Command.* New York: Dial/J. Wade, 1979.

Hayward, Joel S. A. *Stopped at Stalingrad: The Luftwaffe and Hitler's Defeat in the East, 1942–1943.* Lawrence: University of Kansas Press, 1998.

Kennett, Lee. *A History of Strategic Bombing.* New York: Scribners, 1982.

Levine, Alan J. *The Strategic Bombing of Germany, 1940–1945.* New York: Praeger, 1992.

Macksey, Kenneth. *Kesselring: The Making of the Luftwaffe.* London: Batsford, 1978.

McIsaac, D., ed. *The United States Strategic Bombing Survey,* 10 volumes. New York: Garland, 1976.

Meilinger, Phillip S., ed. *The Paths of Heaven: The Evolution of Airpower Theory.* Maxwell AFB, Ala.: Air University Press, 1997.

Mierzejewski, Alfred C. *The Collapse of the German War Economy 1944–1945: Allied Air Power and the German National Railway.* Chapel Hill: University of North Carolina Press, 1988.

Muller, Richard. *The German Air War in Russia.* Baltimore: Nautical & Aviation Pub. Co. of America, 1992.

Murray, Williamson. *Strategy for Defeat: the Luftwaffe, 1933–1945.* Maxwell AFB, Ala.: Air University Press, 1983.

Overy, R. J. *The Air War, 1939–1945.* London: Europa, 1980.

Quester, George H. *Deterrence Before Hiroshima: The Airpower Background of Modern Strategy.* New York: Wiley, 1966.

Sherry, Michael S. *The Rise of American Airpower: The Creation of Armageddon.* New Haven: Yale University Press, 1987.

3. ARMORED WARFARE

Baily, Charles M. *Faint Praise: American Tanks and Tank Destroyers during World War II.* Hamden, Conn.: Archon Books, 1983.

Citino, Robert M. *Armored Forces: History and Sourcebook.* Westport, Conn.: Greenwood Press, 1994.

Cooper, Belton Y. *Death Traps: The Survival of an American Armored Division in World War II.* Novato, Cal.: Presidio Press, 1998.

Crow, Duncan, and Robert J. Icks. *Encyclopedia of Tanks.* London: Barrie & Jenkins, 1975.

Forty, George. *M-4 Sherman.* Poole: Blandford Press, 1987.

Forty. *Tank Warfare in the Second World War: An Oral History.* London: Constable, 1998.

Foss, Christopher F., ed. *Illustrated Guide to World War II Tanks and Fighting Vehicles: A Technical Directory of Major Combat Vehicles from World War I to the Present Day.* London: Salamander, 1977.

Fuller, John F. C. *Armored Warfare: An Annotated Edition of Lectures on F.S.R. III (Operations Between Mechanized Forces).* Harrisburg, Pa.: Military Service Publishing Company, 1943.

Gabel, Christopher R. *Seek, Strike, and Destroy: U.S. Army Tank Destroyer Doctrine in World War II.* Fort Leavenworth, Kans.: Combat Studies Institute, U.S. Army Command and General Staff College, 1986.

Guderian, Heinz. *Achtung-Panzer!: Die Entwicklung der Panzerwaffe, ihre Kampfstaktik und ihre operativen Moglichkeiten*. Stuttgart: Union Deutsche Verlagsgesellschaft, 1937. Translated by Christopher Duffy as *Achtung-Panzer!: The Development of Armoured Forces, Their Tactics and Operational Potential*. London: Arms & Armor, 1992.

Guderian. *Erinnerungen eines Soldaten*. Heidelberg: K. Vowinckel, 1950. Translated by Constantine Fitzgibbon as *Panzer Leader*. New York: Dutton, 1952.

Harris, J. P. *Men, Ideas, and Tanks: British Military Thought and Armoured Forces, 1903-1939*. Manchester & New York: Manchester University Press, 1995.

Harris, and F. H. Toase, eds. *Armoured Warfare*. London: Batsford, 1990; New York: St. Martin's Press, 1990.

Howe, George F. *The Battle History of the 1st Armored Division, "Old Ironsides."* Washington, D.C.: Combat Forces Press, 1954.

Hunnicutt, R. P. *Sherman: A History of the American Medium Tank*. San Rafael, Cal.: Taurus Enterprises, 1978.

Macksey, K. J. *Panzer Division: The Mailed Fist*. New York: Ballentine, 1968.

Macksey, and John H. Batchelor. *Tank: A History of the Armoured Fighting Vehicle*. London: MacDonald, 1970; New York: Scribners, 1970.

Mellenthin, F. W. Von. *Panzer Battles: A Study of the Employment of Armor in the Second World War*. Translated by H. Betzler, edited by L. C. F. Turner. Norman: University of Oklahoma Press, 1956.

Ogorkiewicz, Richard M. *Armor: A History of Mechanized Forces*. London: Stevens & Sons, 1960.

Orgill, Douglas. *Armoured Onslaught: 8th August 1918*. New York: Ballentine, 1972.

Orgill, *T-34: Russian Armor*. New York: Ballentine, 1971.

Perrett, Bryan. *Fighting Vehicles of the Red Army*. New York: Arco, 1969.

Rothbrust, Florian K. *Guderian's XIXth Panzer Corps and the Battle of France: Breakthrough in the Ardennes, May 1940*. New York: Praeger, 1990.

Spielberger, Walter J., and Uwe Feist. *Panzerkampfwagen VI, Tiger I and II Koenigstiger*. Berkeley, Cal.: Feist Publications, 1968.

Stolfi, R. H. S. *Hitler's Panzers East*. Norman: University of Oklahoma Press, 1991.

Zaloga, Steven J. *The Sherman Tank in U.S. and Allied Service*. London: Osprey, 1982.

4. BIOGRAPHIES

Ambrose, Stephen E. *Eisenhower*, 2 volumes. New York: Simon & Schuster, 1983.

Ambrose. *The Supreme Commander: The War Years of General Dwight D. Eisenhower*. Garden City, N.Y.: Doubleday, 1970.

Barnett, Correlli, ed. *Hitler's Generals*. London: Weidenfeld & Nicolson, 1989.

Blumenson, Martin. *Patton: The Man Behind the Legend, 1885-1945*. New York: Morrow, 1985.

Blumenson, and James L. Stokesbury. *Masters of the Art of Command*. Boston: Houghton Mifflin, 1975.

Blumentritt, Günther. *Von Rundstedt: The Soldier and the Man*. Translated by Cuthbert Reavely. London: Odhams Press, 1952.

Bradley, Omar N., and Clay Blair, *A General's Life: An Autobiography*. New York: Simon & Schuster, 1983.

Bullock, Alan. *Hitler and Stalin: Parallel Lives*. London: HarperCollins, 1991.

Carver, Michael, ed. *The War Lords: Military Commanders of the Twentieth Century*. Boston: Little, Brown, 1976.

Charmely, John. *Churchill, The End of Glory: A Political Biography*. London: Hodder & Stoughton, 1995.

Codman, Charles R. *Drive*. Boston: Little, Brown, 1957.

Cray, Ed. *General of the Army: George C. Marshall, Soldier and Statesman*. New York: Norton, 1990.

D'Este, Carlo. *Patton: A Genius for War*. New York: HarperCollins, 1995.

Deutscher, Isaac. *Stalin: A Political Biography*. New York: Oxford University Press, 1949.

Eisenhower, David. *Eisenhower at War, 1943-1945*. New York: Random House, 1986.

Essame, Hubert. *Patton: A Study in Command*. New York: Scribners, 1974.

Farago, Ladislas. *Patton: Ordeal and Triumph*. New York: Ivan Obolensky, 1964.

Fest, Joachim C. *Hitler*. Translated by Richard and Clara Winston. New York: Harcourt Brace Jovanovich, 1974.

Fraser, David. *Knight's Cross: A Life of Field Marshal Erwin Rommel*. London: HarperCollins, 1993.

Gelb, Norman. *Ike and Monty: Generals at War*. New York: Morrow, 1994.

Gilbert, Martin. *Road to Victory: Winston S. Churchill, 1941-1945*. London: Heinemann, 1986.

Hamilton, Nigel. *Master of the Battlefield: Monty's War Years, 1942-1944*. New York: McGraw-Hill, 1983.

Hamilton. *Monty: The Making of a General, 1887-1943*. London: Hamilton, 1981.

Horne, Alistair, and David Montgomery. *Monty: The Lonely Leader, 1944-1945*. London: Macmillan, 1994.

Irving, David. *The Trail of the Fox: The Life of Field Marshal Rommel*. London: Weidenfeld & Nicolson, 1977.

James, D. Clayton. *The Years of MacArthur*, 3 volumes. Boston: Houghton Mifflin, 1970-1985.

Keegan, John, ed. *Churchill's Generals*. London: Weidenfeld & Nicolson, 1991.

Kershaw, Ian. *Hitler*. London & New York: Longman, 1991.

Lamb, Richard. *Montgomery in Europe, 1943-1945: Success or Failure?* London: Buchan & Enright, 1983.

Larrabee, Eric. *Commander in Chief: Franklin Delano Roosevelt, His Lieutenants, and Their War*. New York: Harper & Row, 1987.

Lewin, Ronald. *Churchill as Warlord*. London: Batsford, 1972.

Lewin. *Hitler's Mistakes*. London: Leo Cooper, in association with Secker & Warburg, 1984.

Lewin. *Montgomery as Military Commander*. London: Batsford, 1971.

Lewin. *Rommel as Military Commander*. London: Batsford, 1968; Princeton, N.J.: Van Nostrand, 1968.

Manchester, William. *American Caesar: Douglas MacArthur, 1880-1964*. Boston: Little, Brown, 1978.

McNeal, Robert H. *Stalin: Man and Ruler*. Houndmills, Basingstoke, Hampshire, U.K.: Macmillan, 1968; New York: New York University Press, 1988.

Mets, David R. *Master of Airpower: General Carl A. Spaatz*. Novato, Cal.: Presidio Press, 1988.

Montgomery, Brian. *A Field-Marshal in the Family*. London: Constable, 1973.

Moorehead, Alan. *Montgomery: A Biography*. London: Hamilton, 1946.

REFERENCES

Nye, Roger N. *The Patton Mind: The Professional Development of an Extraordinary Leader.* New York: Avery, 1993.

Overy, R. J. *Goering: The "Iron Man."* London & Boston: Routledge & Kegan Paul, 1984.

Perret, Geoffrey. *Old Soldiers Never Die: The Life of Douglas MacArthur.* New York: Random House, 1996.

Petillo, Carol Morris. *Douglas MacArthur: The Philippine Years.* Bloomington: Indiana University Press, 1981.

Reynolds, David, Warren F. Kimball, and A. O. Chubarian. *Allies at War: the Soviet, American, and British Experience, 1939-1945.* New York: St. Martin's Press, 1994.

Thompson, R. W. *Churchill and the Montgomery Myth.* New York: Evans, 1967.

Thompson, *Montgomery, the Field Marshall: A Critical Study of the Generalship of Field-Marshal, the Viscount Montgomery of Alamein, K.G. and of the Campaign in North-West Europe, 1944/45.* London: Allen & Unwin, 1969.

Young, Desmond. *Rommel.* London & Glasgow: Fontana, 1950.

5. DIPLOMACY

Adams, R. J. Q. *British Politics and Foreign Policy in the Age of Appeasement, 1935-39.* Basingstoke: Macmillan, 1992.

Bell, Peter. *Chamberlain, Germany and Japan, 1933-4.* Houndmills, Basingstoke, Hampshire, U.K.: Macmillan, 1996; New York: St. Martin's Press, 1996.

Charmley, John. *Chamberlain and the Lost Peace.* London: Hodder & Stoughton, 1989.

Dallek, Robert. *Franklin D. Roosevelt and American Foreign Policy, 1932-1945.* New York: Oxford University Press, 1979.

Divine, Robert A. *The Illusion of Neutrality.* Chicago: University of Chicago Press, 1962.

Freidel, Frank. *Franklin D. Roosevelt: A Rendezvous With Destiny.* Boston: Little, Brown, 1990.

Haigh, R. H., and P. W. Turner. *British Politics and Society 1918-1938: The Effect on Appeasement.* Sheffield: Sheffield City Polytechnic, Department of Political Studies, 1979.

Heinrichs, Waldo. *Threshold of War: Franklin D. Roosevelt and American Entry into World War II.* New York: Oxford University Press, 1988.

Herring, George C. *Aid to Russia, 1941-1946: Strategy, Diplomacy, and the Origins of the Cold War.* New York: Columbia University Press, 1973.

Jonas, Manfred. *Isolationism in America, 1935-1941.* Ithaca, N.Y.: Cornell University Press, 1966.

Kissinger, Henry. *Diplomacy.* New York: Simon & Schuster, 1994.

Lammers, Donald N. *Explaining Munich: The Search for Motive in British Policy.* Stanford, Cal.: The Hoover Institute on War, Revolution and Peace, Stanford University, 1966.

Middlemas, Keith. *The Strategy of Appeasement: The British Government and Germany, 1937-39.* Chicago: Quadrangle Books, 1972.

Parker, R. A. C. *Chamberlain and Appeasement: British Policy and the Coming of the Second World War.* Houndmills, Basingstoke, Hampshire, U.K.: Macmillan, 1993; New York: St. Martin's Press, 1993.

Reynolds, David, Warren F. Kimball, and A. O. Chubarian. *Allies at War: the Soviet, American, and British Experience, 1939-1945.* New York: St. Martin's Press, 1994.

Reynolds, P. A. *British Foreign Policy in the Inter-War Years.* London & New York: Longmans, Green, 1954.

Rock, William R. *Appeasement on Trial: British Foreign Policy and its Crisis, 1938-1939.* Hamden, Conn.: Archon Books, 1966.

Rock. *Chamberlain and Roosevelt: British Foreign Policy and the United States, 1937-1940.* Columbus: Ohio State University Press, 1988.

Sainsbury, Keith. *The Turning Point: Roosevelt, Stalin, Churchill, and Chiang-Kai-Shek, 1943: The Moscow, Cairo, and Teheran Conferences.* Oxford: Oxford University Press, 1985.

Seton-Watson, R. W. *Britain and the Dictators: A Survey of Post-War British Policy.* Cambridge: Cambridge University Press, 1938; New York: Macmillan, 1938.

Stettinius, Edward. *Lend-Lease, Weapon for Victory.* New York: Macmillan, 1944.

Stoler, Mark A. *The Politics of the Second Front: American Military Planning and Diplomacy in Coalition Warfare, 1941-1943.* Westport, Conn.: Greenwood Press, 1977.

Thompson, Neville. *The Anti-Appeasers: Conservative Opposition to Appeasement in the 30s.* Oxford: Clarendon Press, 1971.

United States, Department of State. *Foreign Relations of the United States: The Conferences at Washington, 1941-1942, and Casablanca, 1943.* Washington, D.C.: U.S. Government Printing Office, 1968.

United States, Department of State. *Foreign Relations of the United States: The Conferences at Cairo and Tehran 1943.* Washington, D.C.: U.S. Government Printing Office, 1961.

Weinberg, Gerhard L. *The Foreign Policy of Hitler's Germany,* 2 volumes. Chicago: University of Chicago Press, 1970-1980.

6. EUROPEAN THEATER: EASTERN FRONT

Bartov, Omer. *The Eastern Front, 1941-45: German Troops and the Barbarisation of Warfare.* Basingstoke, Hastings, U.K.: Macmillan in association with St. Anthony's College, Oxford, 1985.

Beevor, Antony. *Stalingrad.* London: Viking, 1998.

Blau, George E. *The German Campaign in Russia: Planning and Operations, 1940-1942.* Washington, D.C.: Department of the Army, 1955.

Boog, Horst, and others, *Angriff auf die Sowjetunion* Stuttgart: Deutsche Verlags-Anstalt, 1983. Translated by Dean S. MacMurray and others as *The Attack on the Soviet Union,* volume 4 of *Germany and the Second World War.* Oxford: Clarendon Press, 1998; New York: Oxford University Press, 1998.

Clark, Alan. *Barbarossa: The Russian-German Conflict, 1941-45.* New York: Morrow, 1998; London: Hutchinson, 1965.

Dallin, Alexander. *German Rule in Russia, 1941-1945: A Study of Occupation Policies.* London: Macmillan; New York: St. Martin's Press, 1957.

Erickson, John. *The Road to Berlin.* Boulder, Colo.: Westview Press, 1983.

Erickson. *The Road to Stalingrad.* London: Weidenfeld & Nicolson, 1975.

Fugate, Bryan I. *Operation Barbarossa, Strategy and Tactics on the Eastern Front, 1941.* Novato, Cal.: Presidio Press, 1984.

Glantz, David M., and Jonathan M. House. *When Titans Clashed: How the Red Army Stopped Hitler.* Lawrence: University Press of Kansas, 1995.

REFERENCES

Hart, B. H. Liddell. *The Red Army: the Red Army, 1918 to 1945*. New York: Harcourt, Brace, 1956.

Müller, Rolf-Dieter, and Gerd R. Ueberschär. *Hitler's War in the East, 1941–1945: A Critical Reassessment*. Translation of texts by Bruce D. Little. Providence, R.I.: Berghahn Books, 1997.

Mulligan, Timothy Patrick. *The Politics of Illusion and Empire: German Occupation Policy in the Soviet Union, 1942–1943*. New York: Praeger, 1988.

Schulte, Theo J. *The German Army and Nazi Policies in Occupied Russia*. Oxford & New York: Berg, 1989.

Werth, Alexander. *Russia at War 1941–1945*. New York: Carroll & Graf, 1984.

Marshalls Zhukov, Konev, Malinovsky, Rokossovsky, Rotmistrov, Chuikov, and other commanders. *Battles Hitler Lost: And the Soviet Marshalls Who Won Them*. New York : Richardson & Steirman, 1986.

7. EUROPEAN THEATER: FRANCE AND GERMANY

Ambrose, Stephen E. *D-Day: June 6, 1944: The Climatic Battle of World War II*. New York: Simon & Schuster, 1994.

Bonn, Keith E. *When the Odds Were Even: The Vosges Mountain Campaign, October 1944–January 1945*. Novato, Cal.: Presidio, 1994.

MacDonald, Charles B. *A Time for Trumpets: The Untold Story of the Battle of the Bulge*. New York: Morrow, 1984.

Mansoor, Peter R. *The GI Offensive in Europe: The Triumph of American Infantry Divisions, 1941–1945*. Lawrence: University Press of Kansas, 1999.

Weigley, Russell F. *Eisenhower's Lieutenants: The Campaign of France and Germany, 1944–1945*. Bloomington: Indiana University Press, 1981.

8. EUROPEAN THEATER: ITALY

Blumenson, Martin. *Anzio: The Gamble That Failed*. New York: Holt, Rinehart, & Winston, 1961.

Blumenson. *Salerno to Cassino*. Washington, D.C.: Office of the Chief of Military History, 1969.

Clark, Mark W. *Calculated Risk*. New York: Harper, 1950.

D'Este, Carlo. *Bitter Victory: The Battle for Sicily, 1943*. New York: E.P. Dutton, 1988.

D'Este. *Fatal Decision: Anzio and the Battle for Rome*. New York: HarperCollins, 1991.

Etterlin, F. von Senger und. *Neither Fear nor Hope*. London: Macdonald, 1960.

Graham, Dominick, and Shelford Bidwell. *Tug of War: The Battle for Italy, 1943–1945*. New York: St. Martin's Press, 1986.

Howard, Michael. *The Mediterranean Strategy in the Second World War*. New York: Praeger, 1968.

Jackson, W. F. G. *The Battle for Italy*. New York: Harper & Row, 1967.

Lamb, Richard. *War in Italy, 1939–1945: A Brutal Story*. London: Murray, 1993.

Trevelyan, Raleigh. *Rome '44: The Battle for the Eternal City*. New York: Viking, 1982.

Wagner, Robert L. *The Texas Army: A History of the 36th Division in the Italian Campaign*. Austin, Tex: Robert L. Wagner, 1972.

9. FASCISM AND NATIONAL SOCIALISM

Arendt, Hannah. *The Origins of Totalitarianism*. New York: Harcourt Brace, 1951.

Bessel, Richard, ed. *Fascist Italy and Nazi Germany: Comparisons and Contrasts*. New York: Cambridge University Press, 1996.

Burleigh, Michael, and Wolfgang Wippermann. *The Racial State: Germany, 1933–1945*. New York: Cambridge University Press, 1991.

Childers, Thomas. *The Nazi Voter: The Social Foundations of Fascism in Germany, 1919–1933*. Chapel Hill: University of North Carolina Press, 1983.

Childers, and Jane Caplan, eds. *Reevaluating the Third Reich*. New York: Holmes & Meier, 1993.

Griffin, Roger. *The Nature of Fascism*. London: Pinter, 1991.

Griffin, ed. *Fascism*. Oxford & New York: Oxford University Press, 1995.

Kershaw, Ian. *Der Hitler-Mythos: Volksmeinung und Propaganda im Dritten Reich*. Stuttgart: Deutsche Verlags-Anstalt, 1980. Translated as *The "Hitler Myth": Image and Reality in the Third Reich*. Oxford: Clarendon Press, 1987; New York: Oxford University Press, 1987.

Laqueur, Walter, ed. *Fascism: A Reader's Guide: Analyses, Interpretations, Bibliography*. Berkeley: University of California Press, 1976.

Mosse, George L. *The Fascist Revolution: Toward a General Theory of Fascism*. New York: Fertig, 1999.

Noakes, Jeremy, and Geoffrey Pridham, eds. *Nazism, 1919–1945: A History in Documents and Eyewitness Accounts*. New York: Schocken Books, 1990.

Payne, Stanley G. *Fascism: Comparison and Definition*. Madison: University of Wisconsin Press, 1980.

Payne. *A History of Fascism, 1914–1945*. Madison: University of Wisconsin Press, 1995.

Sternhell, Zeev, with Mario Sznajder, and Maia Asheri. *Naissance de l'idéologie fasciste*. Paris: Fayard, 1989. Translated by David Maisel as *The Birth of Fascist Ideology*. Princeton: Princeton University Press, 1994.

10. GENERAL HISTORIES

Addington, Larry H. *The Patterns of War Since the Eighteenth Century*. Bloomington: Indiana University Press, 1984.

Buruma, Ian. *The Wages of Guilt: Memories of War in Germany and Japan*. New York: Farrar, Straus & Giroux, 1994.

Churchill, Winston. *The Second World War*, 6 volumes. Boston: Houghton Mifflin, 1948-1953.

Craig, Gordon A. *Germany, 1866–1945*. New York: Oxford University Press, 1978.

Dear, I. C. B, and M. R. D. Foot, eds. *The Oxford Companion to World War II*. Oxford: Oxford University Press, 1995.

Deutsche Reich und der Zweite Weltkrieg. Translated as *Germany and the Second World War*, by P. S. Falla, Dean S. McMurrey, Ewald Osers, and Louise Willmot, 4 volumes to date. Oxford: Clarendon Press; New York: Oxford University Press, 1990-1999.

Dülffer, Jost. *Deutsche Geschichte 1933–1945: Fuhrerglaube und Vernichtungskrieg*. Stuttgart: Kohlhammer, 1992. Translated by Dean Scott McMurray as *Nazi Germany, 1933–1945: Faith and Annihilation*. London & New York: Edward Arnold, 1996.

Keegan, John. *The Second World War*. New York: Viking, 1990.

Kennedy, David. *Freedom From Fear: The American People in Depression and War, 1929–1945*. New York: Oxford University Press, 1999.

Milward, Alan S. *War, Economy, and Society, 1939–1945*. Berkeley: University of California Press, 1977.

Overy, R. J. *Why the Allies Won*. London: Cape, 1995.

Purdue, A. W. *The Second World War.* New York: St. Martin's Press, 1999.

Sallagar, Frederick M. *The Road to Total War: Escalation in World War II.* Santa Monica, Cal.: Rand, 1969.

Van Creveld, Martin. *Fighting Power: German and US Army Performance, 1939–1945.* Westport, Conn.: Greenwood Press, 1982.

Weinberg, Gerhard L. *Germany, Hitler, and World War II: Essays in Modern German and World History.* Chicago: University of Chicago Press, 1980.

Weinberg. *A World At Arms: A Global History of World War II.* Cambridge & New York: Cambridge University Press, 1994.

Wilmot, Chester. *The Struggle for Europe.* New York: Harper, 1952.

Wright, Gordon. *The Ordeal of Total War 1939–1945.* New York: Harper & Row, 1968.

11. GERMANY AND THE CHURCHES

Barnett, Victoria. *For the Soul of the People: Protestant Protest Against Hitler.* New York: Oxford University Press, 1992.

Bergen, Doris L. *Twisted Cross: The German Christian Movement in the Third Reich.* Chapel Hill: University of North Carolina Press, 1996.

Conway, John S. *The Nazi Persecution of the Churches, 1933–1945.* London: Weidenfeld & Nicolson, 1968.

Dietrich, Donald J. *Catholic Citizens in the Third Reich: Psycho-Social Principles and Moral Reasoning.* New Brunswick, N.J.: Transaction Books, 1988.

Helmreich, Ernst Christian. *The German Churches Under Hitler: Background, Struggle, and Epilogue.* Detroit: Wayne State University Press, 1979.

Lewy, Guenter. *The Catholic Church and Nazi Germany.* New York: McGraw-Hill, 1964.

Littell, Franklin H., and Hubert G. Locke, eds. *The German Church Struggle and the Holocaust.* Detroit: Wayne State University Press, 1974.

Matheson, Peter, ed. *The Third Reich and the Christian Churches.* Edinburgh, Scotland: T. & T. Clark; Grand Rapids, Mich.: Eerdmans, 1981.

Scholder, Klaus. *Kirchen und das Dritte Reich.* Frankfurt & Berlin: Ullstein, 1977. Translated by John Bowden as *The Churches and the Third Reich,* 2 volumes. London: SCM Press, 1987; Philadelphia: Fortress, 1987.

Stoltzfus, Nathan. *Resistance of the Heart: Intermarriage and the Rosenstrasse Protest in Nazi Germany.* New York: Norton, 1996.

Zahn, Gordon C. *German Catholics and Hitler's Wars: A Study in Social Control.* New York: Sheed & Ward, 1962.

12. GERMANY: HOMEFRONT

Beck, Earl R. *Under the Bombs: The German Home Front, 1942–1945.* Lexington: University Press of Kentucky, 1986.

Carroll, Berenice A. *Design for Total War: Arms and Economics in the Third Reich.* The Hague & Paris: Mouton, 1968.

Crew, David F. *Nazism and German Society, 1933–1945.* London & New York: Routledge, 1994.

Fest, Joachim C. *Gesicht des Dritten Reiches: Profile einer totalitateren Herrschaft.* Munich: R. Piper, 1963. Translated by Michael Bullock as *The Face of the Third Reich: Portraits of the Nazi Leadership.* London: Weidenfeld & Nicolson, 1970.

Herbert, Ulrich. *Geschichte der Ausländerbeschäftigung in Deutschland, 1880 bis 1980.* Berlin: Dietz, 1986. Translated by William Templer as *A History of Foreign Labor in Germany, 1880–1980: Seasonal Workers, Forced Laborers, Guest Workers,* Ann Arbor: University of Michigan Press, 1990.

Homze, Edward L. *Foreign Labor in Nazi Germany.* Princeton: Princeton University Press, 1967.

Jäckel, Eberhard. *Hitler's Weltanschauung: Entwurf einer Herrschaft.* Tubingen: R. Wunderlich, 1969. Translated by Herbert Arnold as *Hitler's Weltanschauung: A Blueprint for Power.* Middletown, Conn.: Wesleyan University Press, 1972.

Kershaw, Ian. *The Nazi Dictatorship: Problems and Perspectives of Interpretation.* London & Baltimore: Edward Arnold, 1985.

Kershaw. *Popular Opinion and Political Dissent in the Third Reich: Bavaria 1933–1945.* Oxford: Clarendon Press, 1983; New York: Oxford University Press, 1983.

Milward, Alan S. *The German Economy at War.* London: Athlone Press, 1965.

Overy, R. J. *War and Economy in the Third Reich.* Oxford: Clarendon Press, 1994; New York: Oxford University Press, 1994.

Peukert, Detlev J. K. *Volksgenossen und Gemeinschaftsfremde: Anpassung, Ausmerze und Aufbegehren unter dem Nationalsozialismus.* Cologne: Bund-Verlag, 1982. Translated by Richard Deveson as *Inside Nazi Germany: Conformity, Opposition, and Racism in Everyday Life.* New Haven: Yale University Press, 1987.

Speer, Albert. *Erinnerungen.* Berlin: Propylaen-Verlag, 1969. Translated as *Inside the Third Reich* by Richard and Clara Winston. New York: Macmillan, 1970.

Wilt, Alan F. *Nazi Germany.* Arlington Heights, Ill.: Harlan Davidson, 1994.

13. GERMAN OCCUPATION

Brandt, Karl. *Management of Agriculture and Food in the German-Occupied and Other Areas of Fortress Europe: A Study in Military Government.* Stanford, Cal.: Stanford University Press, 1953.

Gordon, Bertram M. *Collaborationism in France during the Second World War.* Ithaca, N.Y.: Cornell University Press, 1980.

Kedward, H. R. *Occupied France: Collaboration and Resistance 1940–1944.* Oxford & New York: Blackwell, 1985.

Lemkin, Raphael. *Axis Rule in Occupied Europe: Laws of Occupation, Analysis of Government, Proposals for Redress.* Washington, D.C.: Carnegie Endowment for International Peace, Division of International Law, 1944.

Maurrus, Michael, and Robert O. Paxton. *Vichy et les juifs,* translated as *Vichy and the Jews* (New York: BasicBooks, 1981);

Mazower, Mark. *Inside Hitler's Greece: The Experience of Occupation, 1941–44.* New Haven: Yale University Press, 1993.

Milward, Alan S. *The New Order and the French Economy.* Oxford: Clarendon Press, 1970.

Paxton, Robert O. *Vichy France: Old Guard and New Order 1940–1944.* New York: Knopf, 1972.

14. THE HOLOCAUST

Baldwin, Peter, ed. *Reworking the Past: Hitler, the Holocaust, and the Historians' Debate.* Boston: Beacon, 1990.

Bartov, Omer. *Murder in Our Midst: The Holocaust, Industrial Killing, and Representation.* New York: Oxford University Press, 1996.

Bauer, Yehuda, with the assistance of Nili Keren. *A History of the Holocaust*. New York: F. Watts, 1982.

Benz, Wolfgang. *The Holocaust. A German Historian Examines the Genocide*. Translated by Jane Sydenham-Kwiet. New York: Columbia University Press, 1999.

Braham, Randolph. *The Politics of Genocide: The Holocaust in Hungary*, 2 volumes. New York: Columbia University Press, 1981.

Breitman, Richard. *The Architect of Genocide: Himmler and the Final Solution*. New York: Knopf, 1991.

Browning, Christopher R., *Ordinary Men: Reserve Police Battalion 101 and the Final Solution in Poland*. New York: HarperCollins, 1992.

Browning. *The Path to Genocide: Essays on Launching the Final Solution*. Cambridge & New York: Cambridge University Press, 1992.

Browning, ed. *Fateful Months: Essays on the Emergence of the Final Solution*. New York: Holmes & Meier, 1985.

Burleigh, Michael. *Ethics and Extermination: Reflections on Nazi Genocide*. New York: Cambridge University Press, 1997.

Burrin, Philippe. *Hitler et les juifs: gen'ese d'un genocide*. Paris: Seuil, 1989. Translated by Patsy Southgate as *Hitler and the Jews: The Genesis of the Holocaust*. London: Edward Arnold, 1994.

Dawidowicz, Lucy S. *The War Against the Jews, 1933–1945*. New York: Holt, Rinehart & Winston, 1975.

Eckardt, A. Roy, with Alice L. Echardt. *Long Night's Journey Into Day: Life and Faith After the Holocaust*. Detroit: Wayne State University Press, 1982.

Fein, Helen. *Accounting for Genocide: National Responses and Jewish Victimization During the Holocaust*. New York: Free Press, 1979.

Fleming, Gerald. *Hitler und die Endlösung: "Es ist des Fuhrers Wunsch . . ."* Wiesbaden: Limes, 1982. Translated as *Hitler and the Final Solution*. Berkeley: University of California Press, 1984.

Gellately, Robert. *The Gestapo and German Society: Enforcing Racial Policy, 1933-1945*. Oxford: Clarendon Press, 1900; New York: Oxford University Press, 1990.

Goldhagen, Daniel Jonah. *Hitler's Willing Executioners: Ordinary Germans and the Holocaust*. New York: Knopf, 1996.

Hayes, Peter, ed. *Lessons and Legacies: The Meaning of the Holocaust in a Changing World*. Evanston, Ill.: Northwestern University Press, 1991.

Hilberg, Raul. *The Destruction of the European Jews*. Chicago: Quadrangle Books, 1961.

Hilberg. *Perpetrators, Victims, Bystanders: The Jewish Catastrophe, 1933-1945*. New York: Aaron Asher Books, 1992.

Hirschfeld, Gerhard, ed. *The Policies of Genocide: Jews and Soviet Prisoners of War in Nazi Germany*. London: Allen & Unwin, 1986.

Horkheimer, Max, and Theodor W. Adorno. *Dialektik der Aufklarung: Philosophische Fragments*. Amsterdam: Querido, 1944. Translated by John Cumming as *Dialectic of the Enlightenment*. New York: Herder & Herder, 1972.

Jäckel, Eberhard. *Hitler's Weltanschauung: Entwurf einer Herrschaft*. Tubingen: R. Wunderlich, 1969. Translated by Herbert Arnold as *Hitler's World View: A Blueprint for Power*. Cambridge, Mass.: Harvard University Press, 1981.

Katz, Steven T. *The Holocaust in Historical Context*, volume 1: *The Holocaust and Mass Death before the Modern Age*. New York: Oxford University Press, 1994.

Lukas, Richard C. *The Forgotten Holocaust: The Poles Under German Occupation, 1939–1944*. Lexington: University Press of Kentucky, 1986.

Marrus, Michael R. *The Holocaust in History*. Hanover, N. H.: Published for Brandeis University Press by University Press of New England, 1987.

Mayer, Arno J. *Why did the Heavens not Darken?: The "final solution" in History*. New York: Pantheon, 1988.

Mendehlson, John, ed. *The Holocaust: Selected Documents in Eighteen Volumes*. New York: Garland, 1982.

Rosenbaum, Alan S., ed. *Is the Holocaust Unique?: Perspectives on Comparative Genocide*. Boulder, Colo.: Westview Press, 1996.

Rummel, R. J. *Democide: Nazi Genocide and Mass Murder*. New Brunswick, N. J.: Transaction Publishers, 1992.

Schleunes, Karl A. *The Twisted Road to Auschwitz: Nazi Policy Towards German Jews, 1933–1939*. Urbana: University of Illinois Press, 1970.

Stein, George H. *The Waffen SS: Hitler's Elite Guard at War, 1939-1945*. Ithaca, N. Y.: Cornell University Press, 1966.

Tec, Nechama. *When Light Pierced the Darkness: Christian Rescue of Jews in Nazi Occupied Poland*. New York: Oxford University Press, 1986.

Yahil, Leni. *The Holocaust: The Fate of European Jewry, 1932-1945*. Translated by Ina Friedman and Haya Galai. New York: Oxford University Press, 1990.

Zuccotti, Susan. *The Holocaust, the French and the Jews*. New York: BasicBooks, 1993.

15. INTELLIGENCE

Casey, William. *The Secret War Against Hitler*. Washington, D.C.: Regnery, 1988.

Hinsley, F. H. *British Intelligence in the Second World War*. Cambridge & New York: Cambridge University Press, 1993.

Hinsley, and Alan Stripp, eds. *Codebreakers: The Inside Story of Bletchley Park*. Oxford & New York: Oxford University Press, 1993.

Kahn, David. *Seizing the Enigma: The Race to Break the German U-Boat Codes, 1939-1943*. Boston: Houghton Mifflin, 1991.

Parrish, Thomas D. *The American Codebreakers: The U.S. Role in Ultra*. Chelsea, Mich.: Scarborough House, 1991.

Smith, Bradley F. *The Ultra-Magic Deals and the Most Secret Special Relationship 1940-1946*. Novato, Cal.: Presidio Press, 1993.

Welchman, Gordon. *The Hut Six Story: Breaking the Enigma Codes*. New York: McGraw-Hill, 1982.

Winterbotham, Frederick William. *The Nazi Connection*. New York: Harper & Row, 1978.

Winterbotham. *The Ultra Secret*. New York: Harper & Row, 1974.

Winton, John. *Ultra at Sea: How Breaking the Nazi Code Affected Allied Naval Strategy during World War II*. New York: Morrow, 1988.

Woytak, Richard A. *On the Border of War and Peace: Polish Intelligence and Diplomacy in 1937-1939 and the Origins of the Ultra Secret*. New York: Columbia University Press, 1979.

16. MEMOIRS

Alexander, Harold. *The Alexander Memoirs 1940-1945*. London: Cassell, 1962.

Bialer, Seweryn. *Stalin and His Generals: Soviet Military Memoirs of World War II*. New York: Pegasus, 1969.

REFERENCES

Bradley, Omar N. *A Soldier's Story*. New York: Holt, 1951.

Doolittle, James H. "Jimmy," with Carroll V. Glines. *I Could Never Be So Lucky Again: An Autobiography*. New York: Bantam, 1991.

Eisenhower, Dwight D. *Crusade in Europe*. Garden City, N.Y.: Doubleday, 1948.

Fraser, George MacDonald. *Quartered Safe Out Here: A Recollection of the War in Burma*. London: Harvill, 1992.

Hansell, Haywood S. Jr. *The Strategic Air War Against Germany and Japan: A Memoir*. Washington, D.C.: Office of Air Force History, 1986.

Hart, B. H. Liddell. *The Other Side of the Hill: Germany's Generals, Their Rise and Fall, With Their Own Account of Military Events, 1939–1945*. London: Cassell, 1948. Published in the United States as *The German Generals Talk*. New York: Morrow, 1948.

Hynes, Samuel Lynn. *Flights of Passage: Reflections of a World War II Aviator*. New York: F. C. Beil, 1988; Annapolis: Naval Institute Press, 1988.

Keitel, Wilhelm. *The Memoirs of Field-Marshal Keitel*. Edited by Walter Görlitz, translated by David Irving. London: Kimber, 1965.

Kesselring, Albert. *The Memoirs of Field Marshal Kesselring*. London: William Kimber, 1953.

Khrushchev, Nikita. *Khrushchev Remembers: The Last Testament*. Translated and edited by Strobe Talbott. Boston: Little, Brown, 1974.

Loza, Dmitriy, *Commanding the Red Army's Sherman Tanks: The World War II Memoirs of Hero of the Soviet Union, Dmitriy Loza*. Translated and edited by James F. Gebhardt. Lincoln: University of Nebraska Press, 1996.

Luck, Hans von. *Panzer Commander: the Memoirs of Colonel Hans von Luck*. Westport, Conn.: Praeger, 1989.

Manchester, William Raymond. *Goodbye, Darkness: A Memoir of the Pacific War*. Boston: Little, Brown, 1980.

Miller, Merle. *Ike the Soldier: As They Knew Him*. New York: Putnam, 1987.

Montgomery of Alamein, Bernard Law Montgomery. *The Memoirs of Field-Marshal the Viscount Montgomery of Alamein*. Cleveland: World, 1958.

Moran, Lord. *The Anatomy of Courage*. London: Constable, 1945.

Murphy, Audie. *To Hell and Back*. New York: Holt, 1949.

Patton, George S. Jr. *War as I Knew It*. Boston: Houghton Mifflin, 1947.

Sajer, Guy. *Soldat oublié: recit*. Paris: Robert Laffont, 1967. Translated as *The Forgotten Soldier: The Classic WWII Autobiography*. Washington, D.C.: Brassey's, 1990.

Sledge, E. B. *With the Old Breed, at Peleliu and Okinawa*. Novato, Cal.: Presidio, 1981.

Standifer, Leon C. *Not in Vain: A Rifleman Remembers World War II*. Baton Rouge: Louisiana State University Press, 1992.

Tobin, James. *Ernie Pyle's War: America's Eyewitness to World War II*. New York: Free Press, 1997.

Wilson, George. *If You Survive*. New York: Ivy Books, 1987.

17. NAVAL OPERATIONS

Belote, James H., and William M. Belote. *Titans of the Seas: The Development and Operations of Japanese and American Carrier Task Forces During World War II*. New York: Harper & Row, 1975.

Boyne, Walter J. *Clash of Titans: World War II at Sea*. New York: Simon & Schuster, 1995.

Brown, David. *Carrier Operations in World War II: The Pacific Navies, Dec. 1941–Feb. 1943*. Annapolis, Md.: Naval Institute Press, 1974.

Dull, Paul S. *A Battle History of the Imperial Japanese Navy 1941-1945*. Annapolis, Md.: Naval Institute Press, 1978.

Hoyt, Edwin P. *Carrier Wars: Naval Aviation from World War II to the Persian Gulf*. New York: McGraw-Hill, 1989.

Hoyt. *How They Won the War in the Pacific: Nimitz and His Admirals*. New York: Weybright & Talley, 1970.

Hoyt. *MacArthur's Navy: The Seventh Fleet and the Battle for the Philippines*. Annapolis, Md.: Naval Institute Press, 1983.

Keegan, John. *The Price of Admiralty: The Evolution of Naval Warfare*. New York: Viking, 1988.

Macintyre, Donald. *Aircraft Carrier: The Majestic Weapon*. New York: Ballantine, 1968.

Miller, Nathan. *War at Sea: A Naval History of World War II*. New York: Scribners, 1995.

Morison, Samuel Eliot. *The Two-Ocean War: A Short History of the United States Navy in the Second World War*. Boston: Little, Brown., 1963.

Parillo, Mark P. *The Japanese Merchant Marine in World War II*. Annapolis, Md.: Naval Institute Press, 1993.

Potter, E. B., and Chester W. Nimitz, eds. *Triumph in the Pacific: The Navy's Struggle against Japan*. Englewood Cliffs, N.J.: Prentice-Hall, 1963.

Reynolds, Clark G. *The Fast Carriers: The Forging of an Air Navy*. Huntingdon, N.Y.: Krieger, 1978.

Y'Blood, William T. *Hunter Killer: U.S. Escort Carriers in the Battle of the Atlantic*. New York: Orion, 1989.

Y'Blood. *The Little Giants: U.S. Escort Carriers Against Japan*. Annapolis, Md.: Naval Institute Press, 1987.

18. NORTH AFRICA

Goda, Norman J. W. *Tomorrow the World: Hitler, Northwest Africa, and the Path Toward America*. College Station: Texas A&M University Press, 1998.

Mackesy, K. J. *Afrika Korps*. New York: Ballantine, 1968.

19. ORIGINS OF WWII

Adams, R. J. Q., ed. *British Appeasement and the Origins of World War II*. Lexington, Mass.: D. C. Heath, 1994.

Adamthwaite, Anthony P. *France and the Coming of the Second World War, 1936–1939*. London: Cass, 1977; Totowa, N.J.: Biblio Distribution Center, 1977.

Adamthwaite. *The Making of the Second World War*. London & Boston: Allen & Unwin, 1977.

Allen, William Sheridan. *The Nazi Seizure of Power: The Experience of a Single German Town 1930–1935*. Chicago: Quadrangle Books, 1965.

Bell, P. M. H. *France and Britain, 1900–1940: Entente and Estrangement* (London & New York: Longman, 1996);

Bell. *The Origins of the Second World War in Europe*. London & New York: Longman, 1986.

Boemeke, Manfred F., Gerald D. Feldman, and Elizabeth Glaser, eds. *The Treaty of Versailles: A Reassessment after 75 Years*. Washington, D.C.: German Historical Institute, 1998; Cambridge & New York: Cambridge University Press, 1998.

Broszat, Martin. *Der Staat Hitlers: Grundlegung und Entwicklung seiner inneren Verfassung*. Munich:

Deutscher Taschenbuch Verlag, 1969. Translated by John W. Hiden as *The Hitler State: The Foundation and Development of the Internal Structure of the Third Reich*. London & New York: Longman, 1981.

Deist, Wilhelm. *The Wehrmacht and German Rearmament*. Toronto & Buffalo: University of Toronto Press, 1981.

Eubank, Keith, ed. *World War II: Roots and Causes*. Lexington, Mass.: D. C. Heath, 1992.

Finney, Patrick, ed. *The Origins of the Second World War*. London & New York: Arnold, 1997.

Horne, Alistair. *To Lose a Battle: France 1940*. Boston: Little, Brown, 1969.

Kaiser, David E. *Economic Diplomacy and the Origins of the Second World War: Germany, Britain, France, and Eastern Europe, 1930–1939*. Princeton: Princeton University Press, 1980.

Klein, Burton H. *Germany's Economic Preparations for War*. Cambridge, Mass.: Harvard University Press, 1959.

Martel, Gordon, ed. *The Origins of the Second World War Reconsidered: The A. J. P. Taylor Debate After Twenty-five Years*. Boston: Allen & Unwin, 1986.

Mommsen, Wolfgang J., and Lothar Kettenacker, eds. *The Fascist Challenge and the Policy of Appeasement*. London & Boston: Allen & Unwin, 1983.

Nye, Joseph S. Jr. *Understanding International Conflicts: An Introduction to Theory and History*. New York: HarperCollins, 1993.

Overy, R. J. *The Origins of the Second World War*. London & New York: Longman, 1987.

Parker, R. A. C. *Chamberlain and Appeasement: British Policy and the Coming of the Second World War*. New York: St. Martin's Press, 1993.

Peukert, Detlev J. K. *Die Weimarer Republik: Krisenjahre der Klassischen Moderne*. Frankfurt: Suhrkamp, 1987. Translated by Richard Deveson as *The Weimar Republic: The Crisis of Classical Modernity*. London: Allen Lane, 1991.

Rich, Norman. *Hitler's War Aims*, 2 volumes. New York: Norton, 1973–1974.

Snell, John L., ed. *The Outbreak of the Second World War: Design or Blunder?* Boston: D.C. Heath, 1962.

Stern, Paul C., and others, eds. *Perspectives on Deterrence*. New York: Oxford University Press, 1989.

Taylor, A. J. P. *The Origins of the Second World War*. London: Hamilton, 1961.

Thomas, Martin. *Britain, France and Appeasement: Anglo-French Relations in the Popular Front Era*. Oxford & New York: Berg, 1996.

Watt, Donald Cameron. *How War Came: The Immediate Origins of the Second World War, 1938–1939*. London: Heinemann, 1989; New York: Pantheon Books, 1989.

Robert J. Young, *France and the Origins of the Second World War*. Basingstoke: Macmillan; New York, 1996: St. Martin's Press, 1996.

20. PACIFIC THEATER

Barnhart, Michael A. *Japan Prepares for Total War: The Search for Economic Security, 1919–1941*. Ithaca, N.Y.: Cornell University Press, 1987.

Borg, Dorothy, and Shumpei Okamoto, with the assistance of Dale K. A. Finlayson, eds. *Pearl Harbor as History: Japanese-American Relations, 1931–1941*. New York: Columbia University Press, 1973.

Brackman, Arnold C. *The Other Nuremberg: The Untold Story of the Tokyo War Crimes Trials*. New York: Morrow, 1987.

Butow, Robert J. C. *Tojo and the Coming of the War*. Princeton: Princeton University Press, 1961.

Chang, Iris. *The Rape of Nanking: The Forgotten Holocaust of World War II*. New York: BasicBooks, 1997.

Dower, John W. *War Without Mercy: Race and Power in the Pacific War*. New York: Pantheon Books, 1986.

Edgerton, Robert B. *Warriors of the Rising Sun: A History of the Japanese Military*. New York: Norton, 1997.

Feifer, George. *Tennozan: The Battle of Okinawa and the Atomic Bomb*. New York: Ticknor & Fields, 1992.

Ienaga, Saburo. *The Pacific War, 1931–1945: A Critical Perspective on Japan's Role in World War II*. New York: Pantheon, 1978.

Iritani, Toshio. *Group Psychology of the Japanese in Wartime*. London & New York: Kegan Paul, 1991.

Isely, Jeter A., and Philip A. Crowl. *The U.S. Marines and Amphibious War; Its Theory, and Its Practice in the Pacific*. Princeton: Princeton University Press, 1951.

Morley, James William, ed. *The Fateful Choice: Japan's Advance into Southeast Asia, 1931–1941: Selected Translations from Taiheiyo Senso e no michi, kaisen gaiko shi*. New York: Columbia University Press, 1980.

Spector, Ronald H. *Eagle Against the Sun: The American War with Japan*. New York: Free Press, 1985.

Taaffe, Stephen R. *MacArthur's Jungle War: The 1944 New Guinea Campaign*. Lawrence: University Press of Kansas, 1998.

Tanaka, Yuki. *Hidden Horrors: Japanese War Crimes in World War II*. Boulder, Colo.: Westview Press, 1996.

Williams, Peter, and David Wallace. *Unit 731: Japan's Secret Biological Warfare in World War II*. New York: Free Press, 1989.

21. PAPERS & DIARIES

Bland, Larry I., and Sharon R. Ritenour, eds. *The Papers of George Catlett Marshall*, 4 volumes. Baltimore: Johns Hopkins University Press, 1981–1996.

Blumenson, Martin. *The Patton Papers*, 2 volumes. Boston: Houghton Mifflin, 1972–1974.

Bryant, Arthur. *Turn of the Tide: A History of the War Years Based on the Diaries of Field-Marshal Lord Alanbrooke, Chief of the Imperial General Staff*. New York: Doubleday, 1957.

Butcher, Harry C. *My Three Years with Eisenhower: The Personal Diary of Captain Harry C. Butcher, USNR, Naval Aide to General Eisenhower, 1942 to 1945*. Garden City, N.Y.: Simon & Schuster, 1946.

Chandler, Alfred D. Jr., and others, eds. *The Papers of Dwight David Eisenhower: The War Years*, 17 volumes. Baltimore: Johns Hopkins University Press, 1970.

Eisenhower, Dwight D. *Dear General: Eisenhower's Wartime Letters to Marshall*, edited by Joseph Patrick Hobbs. Baltimore: Johns Hopkins University Press, 1971.

Eisenhower. *The Eisenhower Diaries*, edited by Robert H. Ferrell. New York: Norton, 1981.

Hitler, Adolf. *The Speeches of Adolf Hitler, April 1922–August 1939*, 2 volumes. Edited by Norman H. Baynes. London & New York: Oxford University Press, 1942.

Klemperer, Victor. *Ich will Zeugnis ablegen bis zum letzten*. Berlin: Aufbau-Verlag, 1995. Translated by Martin Chalmers as *I Will Bear Witness: A Diary of the Nazi Years, 1933–1941*. New York: Random House, 1998.

Loewenheim, Francis L., Harold D. Langley, and Manfred Jonas, eds. *Roosevelt and Churchill: Their Secret*

Wartime Correspondence. New York: Saturday Review Press, 1975.

Rommel, Erwin. *The Rommel Papers*. Edited by B. H. Liddell Hart and others, translated by Paul Findlay. London: Collins, 1953.

22. SERVICEMEN, ALLIED

Ambrose, Stephen E. *Band of Brothers: E Company, 506th Regiment, 101st Airborne Division: From Normandy to Hitler's Eagle's Nest*. New York: Simon & Schuster, 1992.

Ambrose. *Citizen Soldiers: The U.S. Army from the Normandy Beaches to the Bulge to the Surrender of Germany, June 7, 1944–May 7, 1945*. New York: Simon & Schuster, 1997.

Doubler, Michael D. *Closing With the Enemy: How GIs Fought the War in Europe*. Lawrence: University Press of Kansas, 1994.

Ellis, John. *On the Front Lines: The Experience of War Through the Eyes of the Allied Soldiers in World War II*. New York: Wiley, 1990.

Fussell, Paul. *Doing Battle: The Making of a Skeptic*. Boston: Little, Brown, 1996.

Leinbaugh, Harold P. and John D. Campbell. *The Men of Company K: The Autobiography of a World War II Rifle Company*. New York: Morrow, 1985.

Linderman, Gerald F. *The World Within War: America's Combat Experience in World War II*. New York: Free Press, 1997.

Marshall, S. L. A. *Men Against Fire: The Problem of Battle Command in Future War*. New York: Morrow, 1947.

McManus, John C. *The Deadly Brotherhood: The American Combat Soldier in World War II*. Novato, Cal.: Presidio, 1998.

Stouffer, Samuel A., and others. *The American Soldier: Combat and Its Aftermath*. Princeton: Princeton University Press, 1949.

23. SERVICEMEN, AXIS

Bartov, Omer. *Hitler's Army: Soldiers, Nazis, and War in the Third Reich*. New York: Oxford University Press, 1991.

Citino, Robert M. *The Path to Blitzkrieg: Doctrine and Training in the German Army, 1920–1939*. Boulder, Colo.: Lynne Rienner Publishers, 1999.

Cooper, Matthew. *The German Army 1933–1945: Its Political and Military Failure*. London: MacDonald's & Jane's, 1978.

Fritz, Stephen G. *Frontsoldaten: The German Soldier in World War II*. Lexington: University Press of Kentucky, 1995.

Harries, Meirion and Susie Harries. *Soldiers of the Sun: The Rise and Fall of the Imperial Japanese Army*. New York: Random House, 1991.

24. SPANISH CIVIL WAR

Albert, Michael. *A New International History of the Spanish Civil War*. New York: St. Martin's Press, 1994.

Guttmann, Allen. *The Wound in the Heart: America and the Spanish Civil War*. New York: Free Press of Glencoe, 1962.

Little, Douglas. *Malevolent Neutrality: The United States, Britain and the Origins of the Spanish Civil War*. Ithaca, N.Y.: Cornell University Press, 1985.

Puzzo, Dante. *Spain and the Great Powers, 1936–1941*. New York: Columbia University Press, 1962.

Thomas, Hugh. *The Spanish Civil War*, revised edition. London: Eyre & Spottiswoode, 1991; New York: Harper, 1991.

Watters, William E. *An International Affair: Non-Intervention in the Spanish Civil War, 1939*. New York: Exposition Press, 1971.

Wheatley, Robert H. *Hitler and Spain: The Nazi Role in the Spanish Civil War*. Lexington: University Press of Kentucky, 1989.

Wyden, Peter. *The Passionate War: The Narrative History of the Spanish Civil War*. New York: Simon & Schuster, 1983.

25. STRATEGY, LOGISTICS, AND MILITARY PLANNING

Addington, Larry H. *The Blitzkrieg Era and the German General Staff, 1865–1941*. New Brunswick, N.J.: Rutgers University Press. 1971.

Burdick, Charles B. *Germany's Military Strategy and Spain in World War II*. Syracuse, N.Y.: Syracuse University Press, 1968.

Butler, James Ramsay Montagu, ed. *Grand Strategy*, 6 volumes. London: Her Majesty's Stationery Office, 1956-1976.

Citino, Robert M. *The Evolution of Blitzkrieg Tactics: Germany Defends Itself Against Poland, 1918–1933*. New York: Greenwood Press, 1987.

Corum, James S. *The Roots of Blitzkrieg: Hans von Seeckt and German Military Reform*. Lawrence: University Press of Kansas, 1992.

D'Este, Carlo. *Decision in Normandy*. New York: Dutton, 1983.

Doughty, Robert Allan. *The Seeds of Disaster: The Development of French Army Doctrine, 1919–1939*. Hamden, Conn.: Archon Press, 1985.

Dunn, Walter Scott Jr. *Second Front Now—1943*. University: University of Alabama Press, 1979.

Godson, Susan H. *Viking of Assault: Admiral John Lesslie Hall, Jr., and Amphibious Warfare*. Washington, D.C.: University Press of America, 1982.

Gray, Colin S. *The Leverage of Sea Power: The Strategic Advantage of Navies in War*. New York: Free Press, 1992; Toronto: Maxwell Macmillan Canada, 1992; New York: Maxwell Macmillan International, 1992.

Green, Constance M., Harry C. Thomson, and Peter C. Roots. *The Ordnance Department: Planning Munitions for War*. Washington, D.C.: Office of the Chief of Military History, 1955.

Greenfield, Kent Roberts, ed. *Command Decisions*. Washington, D.C.: Office of the Chief of Military History, 1960.

Howard, Michael. *The Mediterranean Strategy in the Second World War*. London: Weidenfeld & Nicolson, 1968; New York: Praeger, 1968.

Kiesling, Eugenia C. *Arming Against Hitler: France and the Limits of Military Planning*. Lawrence: University Press of Kansas, 1996.

Manstein, Erich von. *Verlorene Siege*. Frankfurt am Main: Athenäum, 1955. Edited and translated by Anthony G. Powell as *Lost Victories*. Chicago: Regnery, 1958.

Marshall, S. L. A. *Blitzkrieg: Its History, Strategy, Economics and the Challenge to America*. New York: Morrow, 1940.

Matloff, Maurice, and Edwin M. Snell. *Strategic Planning for Coalition Warfare, 1941–1942*. Washington, D.C.: United States Government Printing Office, 1953.

Mayo, Lida. *The Ordnance Department: On Beachhead and Battlefront*. Washington, D.C.: Office of the Chief of Military History, 1968.

Mikche, Ferdinand O. *Attack, A Study of Blitzkrieg Tactics*. New York: Random House, 1942.

Murray, Williamson, and Allan Millett, eds. *Military Innovation in the Interwar Period* Cambridge & New York: Cambridge University Press, 1996.

Newell, Clayton R. and Michael D. Krause, eds. *On Operational Art.* Washington, D.C.: U.S. Army Center of Military History, 1994.

Paret, Peter, with Gordon A. Craig and Felix Gilbert, eds. *Makers of Modern Strategy: From Machiavelli to the Nuclear Age.* Princeton: Princeton University Press, 1986.

Perrett, Bryan. *A History of Blitzkrieg.* London: Robert Hale, 1983; New York: Stein & Day, 1983.

Pogue, Forrest C. *The Supreme Command.* Washington, D.C.: Office of the Chief of Military History, Department of the Army, 1954.

Rich, Norman. *Hitler's War Aims.* New York: Norton, 1973.

Rommel, Erwin. *Infanterie greift an, erlebnis und erfahrung.* Potsdam: Voggenreiter, 1937. Translated as *Attacks.* Vienna, Va.: Athena, 1979.

Simpkin, Richard E. *Deep Battle: The Brainchild of Marshal Tukhachevskii.* London & Washington: Brassey's Defense, 1987.

Van Creveld, Martin. *Supplying War: Logistics from Wallenstein to Patton.* Cambridge & New York: Cambridge University Press, 1977.

Wallach, Jehuda L. *The Dogma of the Battle of Annihilation: The Theories of Clausewitz and Schlieffen and Their Impact on the German Conduct of Two World Wars.* Westport, Conn.: Greenwood Press, 1986.

Warlimont, Walter. *Im Hauptquartier der deutschen Wehrmacht, 1939–45.* Frankfurt am Main: Bernard & Graefe, 1962. Translated by R.H. Barry as *Inside Hitler's Headquarters 1939–45.* New York: Praeger, 1964; London: Weidenfeld & Nicolson, 1964.

Weigley, Russell F. *The American Way of War: A History of United States Military Strategy and Policy.* Bloomington: Indiana University Press, 1973.

Wilt, Alan F. *War from the Top: German and British Military Decision-making during World War II.* London: Tauris, 1990.

REFERENCES

CONTRIBUTOR NOTES

ASTORE, Major William J.: Assistant professor of history at the U.S. Air Force Academy, Colorado Springs, Colorado; author of *Observing God: Thomas Dick, Evangelicalism and Popular Science* (forthcoming).

BAILY, Charles M.: Independent scholar, Springfield, Virginia; consultant with the National Missile Defense program; author of "The 823d at Mortain: Heroes All," *Armor*, 1 (January–February 1992) and *Faint Praise: Tanks and Tank Destroyers during World War II* (1983).

BARBIER, Mary Kathryn: Adjunct professor in history at Loyola University; author of "The 1940 Louisiana Manuevers," *Southern Studies: An Interdisciplinary Journal of the South*, 5 (Winter 1998).

BATEMAN, Robert L., III: Professor of history at the U.S. Military Academy, West Point.

BAUMANN, Robert F.: Historian at the U.S. Army Command and General Staff College; author of *Russian-Soviet Unconventional Wars in the Caucasus, Central Asia, and Afghanistan* (1993); co-author of *Invasion, Intervention, "Intervasion": A Concise History of the U.S. Army in Operation Uphold Democracy* (1999).

BLUM, George P.: Professor of history emeritus at the University of the Pacific; author of *The Rise of Fascism in Europe* (1998).

BODEN, Major Michael A.: Assistant professor of history at the U.S. Military Academy, West Point; doctoral candidate in history at Vanderbilt University.

BUCHER, Greta: Assistant professor of Russian and Soviet history at the U.S. Military Academy, West Point; author of "Struggling to Survive: Soviet Women in the Postwar Years," *Journal of Women's History* (forthcoming).

BUTCHER, Daniel Lee: Doctoral candidate in history at Kansas State University.

CITINO, Robert M.: Professor of history at Eastern Michigan University; author of *The Evolution of Blitzkrieg Tactics: Germany Defends Itself Against Poland, 1918-1933* (1987) and *The Path to Blitzkrieg: Doctrine and Training in the German Army, 1920-1939* (1999).

CORUM, James S.: Professor of Comparative Military Studies at the USAF School of Advanced Airpower Studies; author of *The Roots of Blitzkrieg: Hans von Seeckt and German Military Reform* (1992), *The Luftwaffe: Creating the Operational Air War, 1918-1940* (1997), and, with Richard Muller, *The Luftwaffe's Way of War* (1998).

DINARDO, Richard L.: Associate professor for National Security Affairs at the U.S. Marine Corps Command and Staff College, Quantico, Virginia; author of *Mechanized Juggernaut or Military Anachronism?: Horses and the German Army of World War II* (1991), *Germany's Panzer Arm* (1997), and "The Dysfunctional Coalition: The Axis Powers and the Eastern Front," *Journal of Military History* (1996).

FOLEY, Robert T.: Completed his doctorate in German strategy during World War I at the Department of War Studies, King's College London; author of *Alfred von Schlieffen's Military Writings* (2000).

FORSTCHEN, William R.: Assistant professor of history at Montreat College; author of *The Lost Regiment* series.

FRITZ, Stephen G.: Professor of history at East Tennessee State University; author of *Frontsoldaten: The German Soldier in World War II* (1995).

GINSBERG, Daniel B.: Independent scholar, Atlanta, Georgia; MA in political science from Johns Hopkins SAIS.

GODA, Norman J. W.: Associate professor of history at Ohio University; author of *Tomorrow the World: Hitler, Northwest Africa, and the Path Towards America* (1998).

HILDEBRAND, Regan: Doctoral student in international studies at Ohio University; author of *Eastern Europe's Search for Security: A Readers' Guide With Annotated Bibliography* (Arlington, Va.: Foreign Service Institute, National Foreign Affairs Training Center, 1998) and "Only George Lucas Needs Star Wars," *Think Piece Series*, 62 (Contemporary History Institute, Ohio University, 1999).

HOFMANN, George F.: Adjunct professor of history at the University of Cincinnati; author of *Cold War Casualty: The Court-Martial of Major General Robert W. Grow* (1993); co-editor, with Donn A. Starry, of *Camp Colt to Desert Storm: The History of U.S. Armored Forces* (1999).

INKELAS, Daniel: Instructor in history at Washtenaw Community College; manager, Summer Institute on the Holocaust and Jewish Civilization (Northwestern University/Holocaust Educational Foundation), 1997, 1998; author of "German Nationalist Jews and the 'Jewish Question' in Weimar Germany: The Verband Nationaldeutscher Juden, 1921–1935," *Cincinnati Judaica Review,* 3 (Spring 1992).

JOHNSON, Lieutenant Colonel (ret.) Douglas V. II: Research Professor at the U.S. Army War College; co-author, with Rolfe L. Hillman, of *Soissons, 1918* (1999).

KAUTT, Captain William: USAF, San Antonio, Texas; former assistant professor of History at U.S. Air Force Academy, Colorado; author of *The Anglo-Irish War, 1916–1921: A People's War* (1999).

KIESLING, Eugenia C.: Associate professor of history at the U.S. Military Academy, West Point; author of *Arming Against Hitler: France and the Limits of Military Planning* (1996).

KING, Major Curtis S.: Currently serving in Bosnia.

KINGSEED, Colonel Cole C.: Chief of Military History at the U.S. Military Academy, West Point; author of *Eisenhower and the Suez Crisis of 1956* (1995) and "Education of a Combat Commander," *Military Review,* 65 (December 1985).

KOWALSKY, Daniel: Doctoral candidate in history at the University of Wisconsin-Madison; George W. Mosse teaching fellow in European History and recipient of Fulbright Fellowship for Spain; author of "Researching Spanish history in the Russian Federation," *Bulletin of the Society for Spanish and Portuguese Historical Studies,* 23 (Autumn 1998).

LEWIS, Adrian R.: Assistant professor of military history at the University of North Texas; author of "The Failure of Allied Planning and Doctrine for Operation Overlord: The Case of Minefield and Obstacle Clearance," *Journal of Military History,* 62 (October 1998) and "The Navy Falls Short at Normandy," *Naval History,* 12 (December 1998).

LOFARO, Lieutenant Colonel G. A.: Assistant professor of history at the U.S. Military Academy, West Point; doctoral candidate in history at the State University of New York at Stony Brook.

McJIMSEY, Robert: Professor of history at Colorado College; author of "A Country Divided?: English Politics and the Nine Years' War," *Albion,* 23 (Spring 1991) and "Crisis Management: Parliament and Political Stability, 1692–1719," *Albion* (forthcoming).

MEGARGEE, Geoffrey P.: Ph.D. in military history from Ohio State University in 1998; researcher, U.S. Commission on National Security/ 21st Century; author of *Inside Hitler's High Command* (forthcoming, April 2000).

NEIBERG, Michael S.: Assistant professor of history at the U.S. Air Force Academy, Colorado Springs, Colorado; author of *Making Citizen Soldiers: ROTC and the Ideology of American Military Service* (2000).

PEGELOW, Thomas: Doctoral student in history at the University of North Carolina at Chapel Hill; author of "'Feminism' and 'Postmodernism': Are There Some Things at Stake in Lyotardian Thought for Feminist Theorizations," *Working Papers of the John F. Kennedy Institute for North American Studies,* 104 (1997).

SHOWALTER, Dennis: Professor of history at Colorado College; president of the Society for Military History; visiting professor at the U.S. Military Academy and U.S. Air Force Academy; author and editor of many books; joint editor of *War in History.*

SPIRES, David: Independent scholar, Boulder, Colorado.

WELLER, Captain Grant T.: U.S. Air Force Academy, Colorado.

WESTERMANN, Edward B.: Doctoral candidate in history at the University of North Carolina, Chapel Hill; author of "'Ordinary Men' or 'Ideological Soldiers'? Police Battalion 310 in Russia, 1942," *German Studies Review,* 21 (February 1998) and "'Friend and Helper': German Uniformed Police Operations in Poland and the General Government, 1939–1941," *Journal of Military History,* 58 (October 1994).

WHEATLEY, John: Independent scholar, Brooklyn Center, Minnesota.

WILLIAMS, Kathleen Broome: Associate professor of history at the Bronx Community College of the City University of New York, Bronx, New York.

WILSON, Major (ret.) Dale E.: Professor of military history at American Military University; author of *Treat 'Em Rough!: The Birth of American Armor, 1917–20* (1989) and "Recipe for Failure: Maj. Gen. Edward M. Almond and Preparation of the 92d Infantry Division for Combat in World War II," *Journal of Military History,* 56 (July 1992).

WINTON, Harold R.: Professor of military history and theory at the School of Advanced Airpower Studies, Air University, Maxwell AFB, Alabama; author of *To Change an Army: General Sir John Burnett-Stuart and British Armored Doctrine, 1927–1938* (1988); co-editor, *The Challenge of Change: Military Institutions and New Realities, 1917–1941* (2000).

YOUNG, Major (ret.) Duane C.: Doctoral student at the Institute for the Study of War and Society, De Montfort University; contributor, *Encyclopedia of the American Civil War,* edited by David S. and Jeanne T. Heidler (forthcoming).

ZARWELL, Benjamin D.: Doctoral candidate in history and lecturer at the University of Wisconsin, Madison.

INDEX

ISBN 1-55862-410-4

90000

9 781558 624108